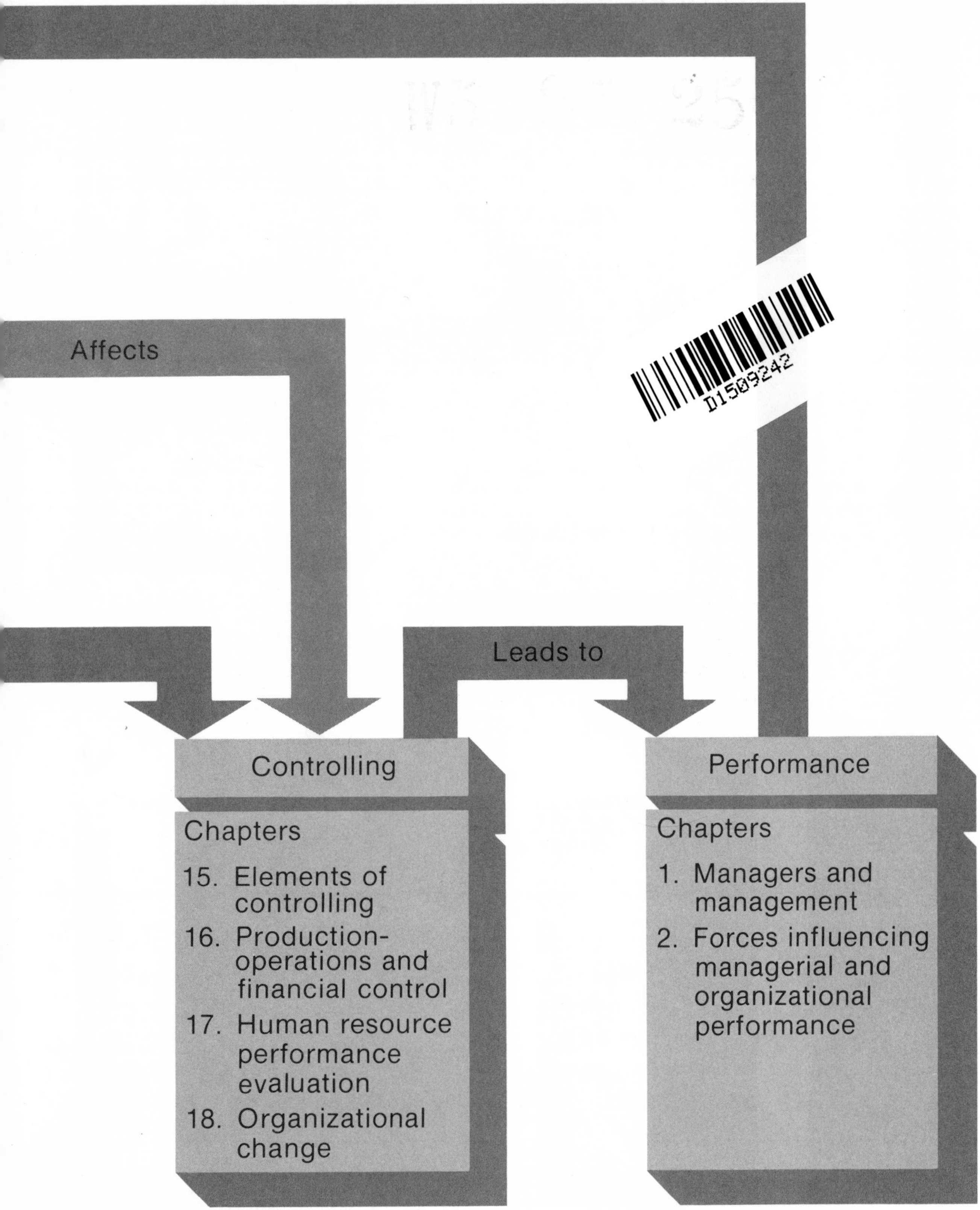
Affects
Leads to
Controlling
Chapters
15. Elements of controlling
16. Production-operations and financial control
17. Human resource performance evaluation
18. Organizational change
Performance
Chapters
1. Managers and management
2. Forces influencing managerial and organizational performance

Managing for Performance

An Introduction to
the Process of Managing

John M. Ivancevich
Hugh Roy and Lillie Cranz Cullen Chair and
Professor of Organizational Behavior
and Management
University of Houston

James H. Donnelly, Jr.
Professor of Business Administration
University of Kentucky

James L. Gibson
Professor of Business Administration
University of Kentucky

1983 · Revised edition

BUSINESS PUBLICATIONS, INC.
Plano, Texas 75075

Managing for Performance

An Introduction to the Process of Managing

ISBN 0-256-02913-X
Library of Congress Catalog Card No. 82–71972

Printed in the United States of America

2 3 4 5 6 7 8 9 0 K 0 9 8 7 6 5 4 3

Preface

This edition of *Managing for Performance* provides students and instructors with a relevant and contemporary *introduction to the process of managing.* The emphasis of the presentation is the attainment of individual, group, and organizational performance through effective managerial performance of *planning, organizing, leading,* and *controlling functions.* These four functions provide the bases for presenting the subject matter included in this book.

Instructors and students responded favorably to several features of the previous edition. The present edition retains and reemphasizes the following:

- Practical applications of management theory and concepts are fully explained and illustrated.
- Writing style and presentation of material emphasize clarity and directness.
- Comments of practicing managers illustrate important management issues.
- Reports of current management practices introduce each chapter and establish the relevance of the material in the chapter.
- Self-assessment exercises enable students to consider their beliefs, opinions, and attitudes about key management issues.
- Study aids such as part introductions, chapter objectives, management summaries, discussion and review questions, and a glossary of terms reinforce understanding of text material.
- Cases and learning exercises extend understanding of text material.

New material in this edition

In this edition, we have tried to respond to the suggestions and criticisms of students and instructors. Accordingly, this edition includes important new subject matter as well as new and additional learning approaches. For example:

Part introductions Each of the major parts of the book has a detailed introduction with an accompanying diagram which explains *why* the part includes the subject matter it does, and *how* the subject matter in the part relates to the central focus of the part.

Chapters Several chapters have been entirely restructured, rewritten, and repositioned in the sequence of presentation. In addition, there are four new chapters in this edition. The two chapters comprising the introductory section "Managers and Management" and "Forces Influencing Managerial and Organizational Performance" are new as well as the chapters on "Managing the Multinational Company" and "Managing Work-Related Stress."

Cases There are 18 additional cases in this edition. Each of these new cases reports a problem in an actual organization as reported in the business periodicals and journals such as *Business Week, Fortune,* and *Management Review.* The cases feature organizations and current issues that are well known to students.

Comprehensive cases At the end of each of the four major parts of the book is a comprehensive case. These cases enable instructors to bring together relevant aspects of the entire section in the context of the case analysis if they choose.

Learning exercises At the end of each of the four major parts of the book are learning exercises. These experiences stimulate individual thinking and group discussion.

Numerous other changes and improvements have also been made which need not be mentioned here. However, taken in total, they make this edition better organized, more relevant for the student, and a better teaching aid for the instructor.

Framework of the edition

As we mentioned at the outset, this book is organized around the management functions of planning, organizing, leading, and controlling. The text has six major parts:

Part 1 consists of two chapters which together introduce the subject matter. Chapter 1 presents the various meanings of the term *management* and a discussion of the evolution of the discipline of managements. The major purpose, however, is to present the framework for the book, *the process of management.* Chapter 2 presents both the internal and external forces which influence managerial and organizational performance, including the increasingly important issues of social responsibility and productivity.

Part 2 contains four chapters which focus on the management function of *planning:* Separate chapters are devoted to the elements of planning, planning as decision making, strategic planning, and management by objectives.

Part 3 focuses on the management function of *organizing.* It contains four chapters: "Elements of Organizing," "Designing the Organization," "Staffing the Organization," and "Developing Careers and Human Resources."

Part 4 focuses on the management function of *leading.* The four chapters in this section focus on the elements of leading, interpersonal and organizational communication, motivation, and group behavior.

Part 5 presents the management function of *controlling.* It contains four chapters: "Elements of Controlling," "Production-Operations and Financial Controls," "Human Resource Performance Evaluations," and "Organizational Change."

Part 6 contains three chapters which focus on important contemporary and emerging challenges for management: "Managing the Multinational Company," "Managing Work-Related Stress," and a summary chapter of future challenges and managerial responses.

Contributors to this edition

The authors wish to acknowledge the contributions of reviewers of the first edition whose ideas and suggestions are reflected throughout this edition. For this edition, we are especially indebted to Eric S. Emory of Sacred Heart University, Vincent T. Luchsinger of Texas Tech University, Ronald Lundstrom of Kearney State College, Arlyn J. Melcher of Kent State University, and James Thomas of the University of Houston.

Finally, A. Benton Cocanougher, dean of the College of Business Administration, University of Houston, and Richard Furst, dean of the College of Business and Economics, University of Kentucky, provided much support for our efforts. Erin Mandolare and Judy Holladay provided immeasurable assistance in preparing the manuscript.

Acknowledgments

Included in this text are actual managerial and organizational practices and experiences of the following firms and institutions. They are the bases for illustrative and case materials which add realism and relevancy to the text discussion.

Alcoa
American Automobile Association
American Management Association
American Telephone & Telegraph
Booz Allen & Hamilton Inc.
Boston Consulting Group

Campbell Soup Company
J. I. Case Co.
Chrysler Corporation
Citizens and Southern National Bank
Coca-Cola
Continental Can Co.
Control Data Corporation
Curtice-Burns, Inc.
Docutel Corporation
Dr Pepper
Du Pont
Emery Air Freight
Equitable Life Assurance Company
ESCO Corporation
Exxon Corporation
Ford Motor Company
General Electric
General Foods Company
General Metropolitan Ltd.
General Motors
B. F. Goodrich Company
Great Atlantic & Pacific Tea Company, Inc.
Gulf Oil Corporation
Heublein, Inc.
Hewlett-Packard Company
Hill Brothers
Intel Corporation
International Business Machines
International Harvester
Johnson & Johnson International
Johnson Products Company
Jordache Enterprises, Inc.
Katharine Gibbs School Inc.
Korn/Ferry International
Lehman Brothers
Arthur D. Little Company
Lockheed Aircraft Corporation
Marakon Associates
Mary Kay Cosmetics
McDonald's Corporation
McKinsey and Co.
Mercedes Benz
Morgan Adhesives Company
Non-Linear Systems
Northrop Corporation Defense Systems Division
Parsons, Brinckerhoff, Quade & Douglas, Inc.
J. C. Penney Company
Philips Industries
Pitney Bowes
PPG Industries
Procter & Gamble
Prudential Insurance Company
Revlon, Inc.
Rockwell International
Saab-Scandia
Sears Roebuck & Co.
Siemens, Inc.
Sony Corporation
Stow/Davis Furniture
Strategic Planning Institute
Sybron Corporation
Syntex Corporation
Tenneco Company
Texas Instruments
3M Company
Trans Telecommunications Corporation
United Rubber Workers, Local 87
U.S. Civil Service Commission
Virginia National Bankshares
Western Electric Corporation
Westinghouse Electric Corporation
Worthington Industries
Xerox

John M. Ivancevich
James H. Donnelly, Jr.
James L. Gibson

Contents

Part I Managers and performance — 3

A management profile: Chester Barnard — 4

1 Managers and management — **5**

- Management influences everyone — 7
- Management is controversial — 8
- Management has different meanings — 8
- Summary and definition — 10
- Purpose of the book — 10
- The process of management — 10
- Learning how to manage — 12
- Management knowledge—the evolving discipline of management — 12
- Attempting to integrate the three approaches to management — 20
- Plan for this book — 22

2 Forces influencing managerial and organizational performance — **27**

- The management system — 29
- The external environment — 37
- Management dilemmas caused by the external environment — 39
- Organizational and managerial performance — 44
- Organizational and managerial performance and the internal and external environments — 45

Part II The planning function — 49

A management profile: Lee Iacocca — 50

3 Elements of planning — **53**

- Understanding the need for planning — 56
- Elements of planning — 59

Cases

- Planning problems at Exxon Enterprises — 74
- Defending the need for planning — 75

4 Planning as decision making **77**

Why study decision making? 79
Types of decisions 80
The decision-making process 82
Influences on individual decision makers 92
Group decision making 96
Cases
Key decisions rescue Docutel Corporation 101
Managers are paid to make decisions 102

5 Planning through strategic analysis **105**

Strategic analysis 107
The strategic planning process 108
Strategic objectives 111
The situation analysis 113
Developing organizational strategies 119
The completed strategic plan 121
Cases
New strategy at General Electric 124
Strategic planning at The Illusion 125

6 Planning through management by objectives **127**

What is MBO 130
The basic principles of management by objectives 131
The MBO process 133
Appraising MBO 141
Cases
Management by objectives at Hewlett-Packard Company 148
HAIR, Inc. 149

Part II Learning exercise
Protecting the organization by planning 152

Comprehensive case
National Lumber Company 153

Part III The organizing function **159**

A management profile: Ralph Cordiner 160

7 Elements of organizing **163**

Organization structure 165
The four primary elements of organization structure 167
Dividing the task: Job specification 170
Combining jobs: Departmentation 172

Span of control 178
Delegation of authority 181
Cases
Decentralization at Curtice-Burns, Inc. 188
Recentralization for the 1980s? 189

8 Designing the organization 191
Alternative organization designs 193
Contingency organization design 197
Hybrid organization designs 201
Cases
Organization design at General Motors 206
What organization design is best? 207

9 Staffing the organization 209
The staffing process 211
Human resource planning 212
Recruitment 213
Selection 218
Orientation 222
Training and development 223
Performance evaluation 227
Compensation 227
Promotion, demotion, and discharge 227
Cases
Executive recruitment as practiced at Korn/Ferry International 231
A heart attack victim fights back 232

10 Developing careers and human resources 235
The concept of career 238
Career development for recent hirees 247
Career development for midcareer managers 250
Career planning and pathing 254
Some difficult career and human resource development issues 258
Cases
Career development practices at AT&T, IBM, and Hewlett-Packard 265
Success has a price 266

Part III Learning exercise
Designing the new venture 268
Comprehensive case
Chandler's Restaurant 269

Part IV The leading function 277

A management profile: George E. Johnson 278

11 Elements of leading 281

Functions of leaders 284
Personal characteristics of effective leaders 285
Behavior of effective leaders 289
Situational leadership 296
Thinking about leadership 302
Cases
Leadership at Revlon, Inc. 306
Changing a leadership style 307

12 Interpersonal and organizational communications 311

A framework for understanding communications 313
Organizational communications 317
Interpersonal communications 320
Why communications break down 326
How communications can be improved 330
Cases
Safety communications at Stowe/Davis Furniture 337
Get the job done 338

13 Motivation and performance 341

Motivation and behavior 343
Nonsatisfaction of needs 347
Personality and motivation 351
The two-factor theory of motivation 352
The expectancy theory of motivation 354
Managerial approaches for improving motivation 356
Cases
A motivational program at General Motors Inland plant 372
Motivating different individuals 373

14 Work groups and performance 375

Classification of groups 377
The formation of work groups 381
The development of work groups 383
Characteristics of work groups 385
End result: Group performance 397
Cases
The work team approach at Texas Instruments 401
The underperforming group 402

Part IV Learning exercises
Ranking motivators 404
Group and conflict resolution 406

Comprehensive case
Work group ownership of an improved tool 408

Part V The controlling function **415**

A management profile: Robert McNamara 416

15 Elements of controlling **419**

Necessary conditions for control 421
Three types of control 423
Management information for control 428
Organization structure and information needs 431
Designing a management information system (MIS) 432
Cases
Managerial control at Intel Corporation 440
Precontrolling purchasing decisions 441

16 Production-operations and financial control **445**

Production-operations control 447
Financial controls 463
Cases
Inventory control at PPG Industries 472
Strategic control 473

17 Human resource performance evaluation **477**

An overview of performance evaluation 479
Purposes of performance evaluation 480
Performance standards 484
Administering performance evaluation 487
Traditional performance evaluation methods 490
Nontraditional performance evaluation methods 496
A review of potential performance evaluation programs 500
Cases
Performance appraisal at Gulf Oil 504
Evaluating managerial performance 505

18 Organizational change **509**

A model for managing change 511
Forces for change 512

Recognizing the need for change 514
Diagnosing the problem 515
Identifying alternative change techniques 517
Recognizing limiting conditions 525
Overcoming resistance to change 526
Implementing and monitoring the change process 528
Cases
Organizational change at Johnson & Johnson International 532
Resisting better working conditions 534

Part V Learning exercises
Paper Plane Corporation 535
Controlling the appearance of employees 536
The need for change 538

Comprehensive case
Supra Oil Company 539

Part VI Managing for performance: Trends and perspectives **547**
A management profile: Mary Kay Ash 548

19 Managing the multinational company **551**
The multinational company 553
Environmental differences in international management 556
The management functions in international management 563
The MNC and the contingency approach to management 569
Case
General Metropolitan Ltd., expands to the United States 572

20 Managing work-related stress **575**
What is stress? 578
General adaptation syndrome 579
Consequences of stress 580
A stress framework 583
Some sources of work-related stress 587
Some personal sources of stress 590
Coping with and managing work stress 594
The Type A scoring system 601
Cases
Control Data Corporation's Stay Well program 602
A widow sues for a job-stress-initiated loss 603

21 Managing future challenges and responses **605**

The manager's world in the 1980s 607

Changes in the manager's world 610

The environmental forces 611

Portrait of a future manager 622

Glossary of terms **627**

Index **637**

Managing for Performance is. . .

Photo Courtesy of Celanese Corporation.

Photo Courtesy of Celanese Corporation.

a process. . .

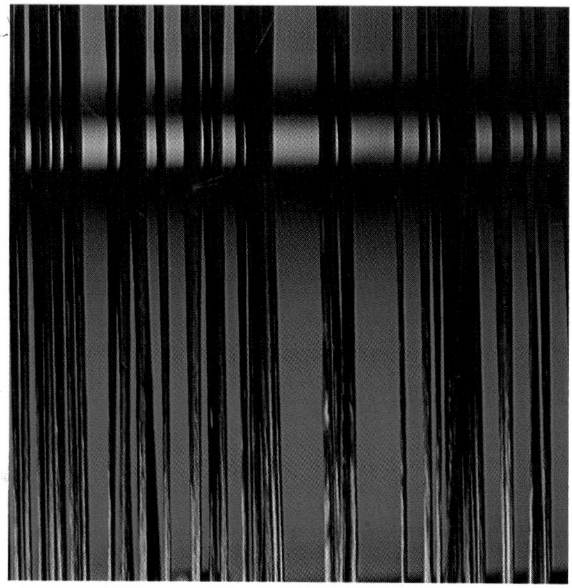

Photo Courtesy of Celanese Corporation.

Photo Courtesy of Image Vendors, Inc.

a discipline. . .

Photo Courtesy of Celanese Corporation.

Photo Courtesy of Celanese Corporation.

Photo Courtesy of Celanese Corporation.

a career. . .

Philip Jon Bailey/Taurus Photos, Inc.

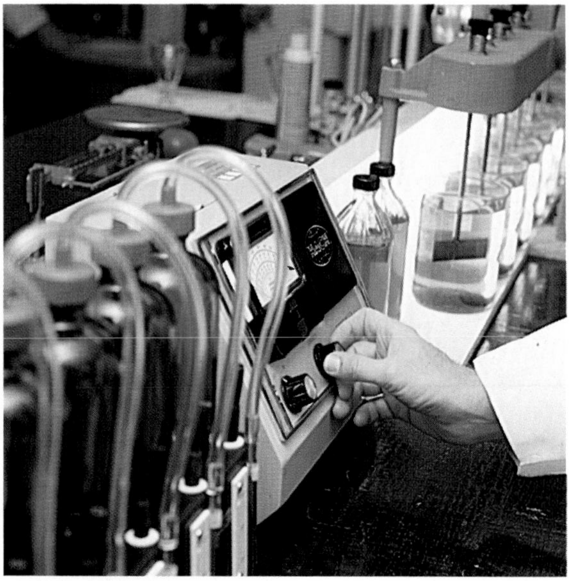

Photo Courtesy of Image Vendors, Inc.

Photo Courtesy of Textron Corporation, Homelite Division.

Photo Courtesy of Celanese Corporation.

decision making. . .

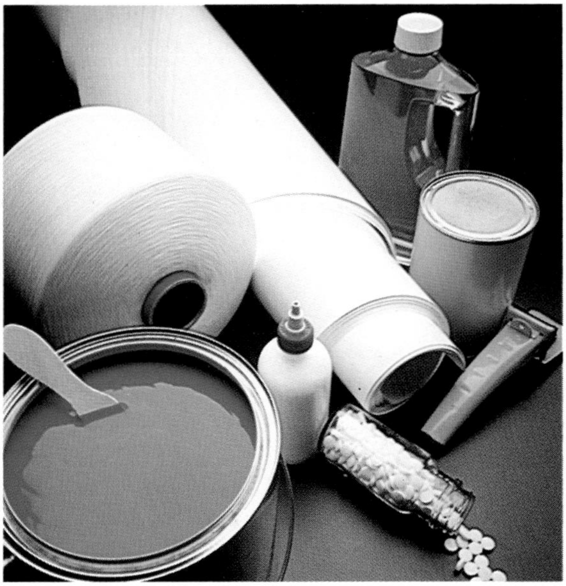

Photo Courtesy of Celanese Corporation.

Omar Marcus/Atoz Images, Inc.

planning. . .

Photo Courtesy of Celanese Corporation.

Courtesy of Bob Hahn/Taurus Photos, Inc.

organizing. . .

Photo Courtesy of Celanese Corporation.

Photo Courtesy of Celanese Corporation.

controlling

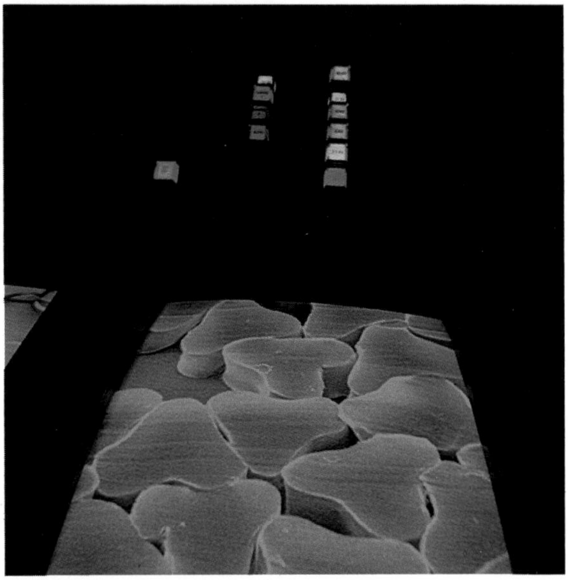

Photo Courtesy of Celanese Corporation.

Marty Heitner/Taurus Photos, Inc.

Managing for Performance

An Introduction to the Process of Managing

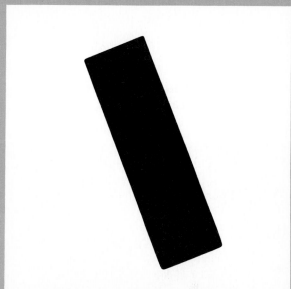

Part I
Managers and performance

1. Managers and management
2. Forces influencing managerial and organizational performance

A management profile
Chester Barnard

A good man is hard to find—and that may explain why Chester Barnard was always in demand. The longtime president of New Jersey Bell donated his administrative talent and boundless energy to public services as diverse as his interests. Among the agencies that received a share of Barnard's time were the National Science Foundation, the Board of Health of New York City, the Rockefeller Foundation (of which he was president), the National Bureau of Education, the New Jersey Relief Administration, the Bach Society of New Jersey, and the Newark Art Theatre. Barnard served as president of the USO during its period of largest development, and under his leadership, the organization quadrupled its facilities.

Though much of Barnard's life was dedicated to public service, as a young man he took help from no one. He worked his way through high school as a janitor and attendance monitor in the school chapel. He attended Harvard on a scholarship, earning spending money as a piano tuner and as a dance-band leader.

Impatient with university rules, Barnard left Harvard without a degree and found work as a translator in a Boston office of American Telephone & Telegraph. He rose rapidly from his $50-a-week job, moving to the New York office the next year to be sent abroad to study European telephone systems. With the knowledge gathered from this trip, Barnard became an expert on telephone rate structures. In 1915, as a commercial engineer for AT&T, he formed the commercial practices of the Bell system. After various vice presidencies and five years of general management at the Bell Telephone Company of Pennsylvania, he became the president of the newly formed New Jersey Bell in 1927.

Barnard has long been ranked as an authority in the field of executive management. His eight lectures delivered at Harvard—the basis of his book *Functions of the Executive* (1948)—are widely regarded as classics in the field of management. Barnard believed that open communication among all levels of a business organization was essential to good management and that the successful executive had to provide clear goals and rewards to his or her assistants.

Barnard the manager was able to explain what managers do on the job in understandable language. He explained each of the functions of management covered in this book. Much of this book's foundation was provided by Barnard's emphasis on the need to examine the objectives, structure, and consequences of organizational systems. Barnard wanted others to pay attention to how organizations survive and are influenced by external forces such as competition and the government, and to how managers do their jobs. His writings and ideas ushered in an era that emphasized the importance of managers in enhancing the performance of organizations. This entire book is about managers and what they do to encourage performance from employees.

Courtesy of New Jersey Bell Telephone

Source: Elizabeth J. Kenny for P. S. Associates, Inc., Sterling, Massachusetts.

1

Chapter one Managers and management

Many of us were awakened this morning by a local radio program on a radio manufactured in Japan. It was followed by an announcement by a candidate for governor who said that if elected he will rid the state government of waste and inefficiency. We showered and dressed using a variety of cosmetic and clothing products. We stopped on the way to campus for a quick breakfast and noted how efficient and well managed the restaurant seemed to be. We were delayed on our way to campus because of road repairs and a malfunctioning traffic signal. Upon arriving on campus, we were told that the course we wished to enroll in is unavailable because someone underestimated the demand for the course.

This fictional account serves the purpose of indicating that managers and organizations influence many aspects of our lives. For example, radio station managers and restaurant managers direct these service businesses. International managers direct exporting and importing activities. Plant managers direct manufacturing operations that produce cosmetics, food, clothing, and automobiles. Marketing managers direct the marketing activities for these products. Personnel managers provide the work force for most organizations. Governors, administrators, and commissioners manage our city and state governments. Presidents and deans manage our colleges.

With this in mind, we would like to introduce our discussion of management by stating that management **influences everyone**, management is **controversial,** and management **has many meanings.** Let us examine each statement.

Management influences everyone

As indicated above, important work in our society is done by individuals who have such titles as restaurant manager, production manager, marketing manager, chairperson, dean, superintendent, mayor, and governor. They may work in different types of organizations with different purposes, but they all have one thing in common: They all practice management. Furthermore, our society depends on the goods and services provided by the organizations these individuals manage.

Each of us is influenced by the actions of managers every day because we come into contact with organizations every day. Our experiences may be as students in a college, patients in a hospital, customers of a business, or citizens of a state. Whether we are satisfied with our experiences depends greatly on the individuals who manage the organization. *All* organizations are guided and directed by the decisions of one or more individuals who are designated *managers.*

Management is controversial

Most people who occupy managerial positions in various kinds of organizations believe that they know how to manage even though many may have trouble describing exactly what management is. Nevertheless, it is through their skill and judgment that our society allocates its scarce resources toward numerous and often competing purposes. Managers have the authority and responsibility to build or destroy cities, to produce safe or unsafe products, to purify or pollute our environment, to wage peace or war. Managers establish the conditions under which we work, for the provision of jobs, incomes, lifestyles, products, education, government services, and health care.

Because it is difficult to find someone who is not subject to the decisions of a manager, a manager's actions are often the subject of controversy. A city government that is facing bankruptcy will, in most cases, trace its plight to poor management. A business organization that consistently is beaten by competitors blames management. A college football team experiences a poor season, and the coach is fired. In fact, any adverse situation in any type of organization is almost always attributed to management.

Management has different meanings

The term **management** can have different meanings. It is important at this point to understand these different meanings. They are so important in fact, that they will be the focus of the remainder of this chapter so we need only discuss them briefly at this point.

Management as a process

Have you ever said "that is a well-managed company" or "that organization has been mismanaged?" Have you ever thought what you mean by such statements? Such statements seem to imply that (1) management is apparently some type of work or activities that must be performed if someone is going to manage something and (2) sometimes the activities are performed well and sometimes not so well. You may not be able to exactly define it, but you are saying that management is a **process** involving certain functions that managers must perform. This is what managers do: engage in the process of management and some do it better than others. What this management process is and what functions managers actually perform as part of the process is the major focus of this book.

Management as a discipline

The statement that one is a student of management, or majoring in management, refers to the discipline of management. Management as a discipline implies an accumulated body of knowledge that can be learned. Thus, management is a subject with principles, concepts, and theories. One major purpose of studying the discipline of management is to learn how to manage, that is, how to engage in the process of management.

Management as people

When someone says "that company has an entirely new management group" or "she is the best manager I've ever worked for," that person is referring to those individuals, the people, who guide, direct, manage organizations. Management as used in this manner refers to the people, **managers,** who engage in the process of management. Managers are the people who are primarily responsible for seeing to it that work gets done in an organization. The majority of this book is devoted to the distinctive set of activities, or functions, these people perform as they manage.

Management as a career

"Mr. Johnson has held several managerial positions since joining the bank upon graduation from college." "Upon graduating from college, Ms. Becker entered the company's management training program." Such statements imply that management is a career. People devote their working lives to the process of management and progress through a sequence of new activities and, often, new challenges. Later in the book, we devote an entire chapter to the career of management.

Summary and definition

As a form of summary, let us try to relate the different meanings of the term *management.* We shall present it as follows: **People** who wish a **career** as a manager must study the **discipline** of management as a means toward practicing the **process** of management. Thus, the emphasis of a book about management must focus on the process. We shall define management as follows:

> Management is the process undertaken by one or more persons to coordinate the activities of other persons to achieve results not achievable by any one person acting alone.

As most commonly used in this text therefore, the term *management* shall refer to the above process.

Purpose of the book

The purpose of this book is to present ideas, opinions, and theories which describe what *managers actually do* and what *managers should do* to be effective. The book will concentrate on the *process* of management. Governors, executives, restaurant managers, office managers, mayors, and deans all share the common problem of having to depend on other people to achieve the results of the organization. Therefore, they all practice management as it is defined here.

The process of management

In our earlier brief discussion of management as a process, we noted that it is a form of work that managers engage in. In performing this work, a manager performs certain activities or functions. In other words, the process of management consists of certain basic **management functions.** The entire process and the individual management functions are presented in Figure 1–1.

Figure 1–1 indicates that the management process is an integrated whole. However, it is often easier to understand something as complex as the management process when it is described as a series of separate activities or functions that make up the entire process. The model of management used throughout this book identifies the management functions as **planning, organizing,** and **controlling,** linked together by **leading.** Planning determines

Figure 1–1

The managerial process

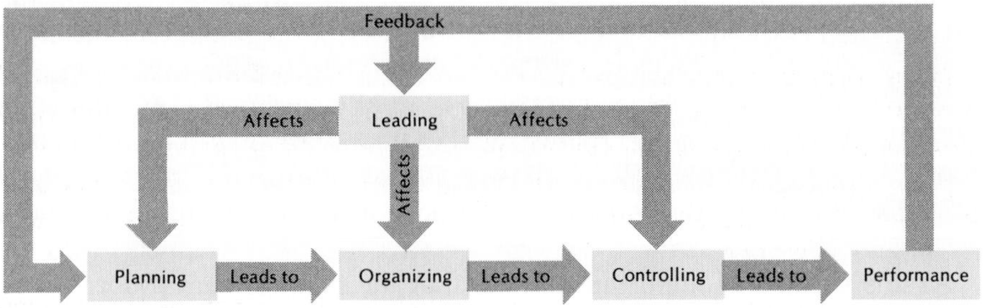

what results the organization will achieve; organizing specifies *how* it will achieve the results; and controlling determines *whether* the results are achieved. Throughout planning, organizing, and controlling, managers exercise leadership.

Planning

The planning function provides the plans that are needed to give the organization its objectives and the appropriate means to achieve the objectives. Managers, through their plans, outline what the organization must do to be successful. Planning is done by managers at all levels in an organization. While plans may differ in focus, they are all concerned with achieving organizational performance in both the short and long run.

Organizing

After managers develop objectives and plans to achieve the objectives, they must design and develop an organization that will be able to achieve the objectives. Thus, the purpose of the organizing function is to design a structure of task and authority relationships. Tasks identified during planning are assigned to individuals and groups within the organization in order to achieve the objectives identified during planning. Organizing then, can be thought of as turning plans into action.

Leading

Once objectives have been developed and the organization structure has been designed and staffed, the next step is to begin to move people and the organization toward the stated objectives. Sometimes the leading function is called *directing,* or *motivating.* Whatever the term, it involves influencing the members of the organization to perform in ways that will bring about the achievement of objectives. The leading function focuses directly on the people in the organization, since its major purpose is to channel human behavior toward organizational objectives.

Controlling

Finally, a manager must make sure that the actual performance of the organization conforms with the performance that was planned for the organization. This is the controlling function of management, and it requires three elements: (1) establishing *standards* of performance, (2) *information* which indicates deviations between actual performance and the established standards, and (3) *action* to correct performance that does not meet the standards. Simply speaking, the purpose of management control is to make sure the organization stays on the path that was planned for it.

At this point, it is important to note that the management process does not involve four separate or unrelated activities but a group of closely related functions. Also, the four functions we have described do not necessarily occur in the sequence we have presented. In fact, the only time they might is when a new organization is being formed. In reality, various combinations of the four activities usually occur simultaneously in organizations.

Learning how to manage

This book is about management written for future managers, but reading a book is not the only way to learn about management. The fact is that it is unlikely that a book alone can make you a manager. What the book seeks to do is to provide future managers the **knowledge, attitudes, and skills to apply to their experience once they become managers.** You would probably learn these attitudes and skills on the job, but the process would certainly take longer and not be as well organized. The important thing to remember is that no one is born with management knowledge so while this book may not make you an effective manager by itself, it will help you accomplish this goal. At this point, then, it seems appropriate that we discuss the major sources of the management knowledge upon which this book is based.

Management knowledge—the evolving discipline of management

Knowledge about management comes from the field of management itself and from many other fields as well. The early writers were mostly practicing executives who described their own experiences from which they developed broad principles. They wanted to share with others the practices that seemed to work for them. A great deal of management knowledge comes from the autobiographies and memoirs of people who practice management.

On the other hand, there are individuals who have contributed knowledge to management whose interest in management was or is strictly for scientific reasons. Many psychologists, sociologists, and anthropologists consider management to be a very important social phenomenon and managers to be an important social resource. Their interest then is strictly scientific; they want to understand and to explain the process of management. Numerous other professions such as mathematics, accounting, economics, law, political science, engineering, and philosophy have also contributed to the discipline of management.

With so many individuals with different purposes, as well as so many diverse fields of study contributing to our knowledge of management, we face a problem: How can we approach the study of the discipline of management in some coherent way? We must organize the knowledge in some way so that it is meaningful to the student of management.

Contemporary management knowledge is the product of three basic approaches: the **classical approach**, the **behavioral approach**, and the **management science approach.** We believe that the ideas of each approach contribute positively to the total body of knowledge of the discipline of management. Through these three approaches, we can see an evolution of what *is* known and what *should be* known about management. Let us examine each one.

The classical approach

Serious attention to management began in the early years of this century. One of the critical problems facing managers at that time was how to increase the efficiency and productivity of the American work force. Since this marked the beginning of the study of modern management, it was eventually labeled the classical approach as is usually the case with the beginning efforts of every field of study.

We believe that the classical approach to management can be better understood by examining it from two perspectives. These two perspectives are based on the problems examined. For example, one perspective concentrated on the problems of lower-level managers dealing with the everyday problems of the work force. This perspective is known as *scientific management.* The other perspective concentrated on the problems of top-level managers dealing with the everyday problems of managing the entire organization. This perspective is known as *classical organization theory.* For the student of management, the contributions of the classical approach are critical. These insights are, in fact, what constitutes the core of the discipline of management and the process of management and are a major part of this book. Let us briefly examine each.

Scientific management At the turn of the 20th century, business was expanding, new products and new markets were being created but labor was in short supply. Two solutions were available: (1) substitute capital for labor or (2) use labor more efficiently. Scientific management concentrated on the second solution.

Probably the greatest contributor to scientific management was Frederick W. Taylor. Taylor joined the American Society of Mechanical Engineers in 1886 and used this organization to develop and test the ideas he developed while working in various steel firms. It was in one of these firms, Midvale Steel Company, that he observed men producing far less than their capacities. Taylor believed this waste was due to ignorance of what constituted a fair day's work. At that time, there were no studies to determine expected daily output per man (work standards) and the relationship between work standards and the wage system. Taylor's personal dislike for waste caused him to rebel at what he interpreted as inefficient labor and management practices that were based solely on hunch, common sense, and ignorance.

Taylor tried to find a way to combine the interests of both management and labor to avoid the necessity for sweatshop management. He believed that the key to harmony was to seek to discover the one best way to do a job, determine the optimum pace, train people to do the job properly, and reward successful performance by using an incentive pay system. Taylor believed that cooperation would replace conflict if workers and managers knew what was expected and the positive benefits of achieving mutual expectations.[1]

To the modern student of management, Taylor's ideas may not appear to be pioneering. Given the times in which he developed his ideas, his ideas were, and continue to be, lasting contributions to the way work is done at the shop floor level. He urged managers to take a more systematic approach in performing their job of coordination. His experiments with stopwatch studies and work methods stimulated many others at that time to undertake similar types of studies.[2]

An interesting fact about scientific management is that if it were evaluated in terms of its impact on management practice at the time of its development, scientific management would receive a low grade. Its impact on modern management is more pronounced and significant. While some firms adopted scientific management, the methods of Taylor and his followers were largely ignored. One cause of the seeming failure is the fact that Taylor and other supporters of scientific management failed to fully understand the psychological and sociological aspects of work. For example,

---

[1] Lyndall Urwick, *The Golden Book of Management* (London: Newman Neame Ltd., 1956), pp. 72–79.

[2] Frederick W. Taylor, *Principles of Scientific Management* (New York: Harper & Row, 1911), pp. 36–37. Also see Claude S. George, Jr., *The History of Management Thought* (Englewood Cliffs, N.J.: Prentice-Hall, 1968).

scientific management made the implicit assumption that people are motivated to work primarily by money. During the time in which it was made, it undoubtedly was a valid assumption. Today, however, the assumption is far too simplistic.

Classical organization theory As noted above, a body of ideas developed at the same time as those of scientific management. These ideas focused on the problems faced by top managers trying to manage large organizations. Since this branch of the classical approach focuses on the management of organizations while scientific management focused on the management of work, this branch is labeled *classical organization theory.* Its two major purposes were (1) develop basic principles that could guide the design, creation, and maintenance of large organizations and (2) identify the basic functions of managing organizations.

While engineers were the prime contributors to scientific management, practicing executives were the major contributors to classical organization theory. As with scientific management, there were many contributors to classical organization theory. We shall select Henri Fayol for discussion here because his ideas reflect classical organization theory.[3]

For 50 years, Henri Fayol practiced management and reflected upon just what it was that he did as managing director of a French coal company. He began writing about his experiences in articles around 1916 and published a book in 1925 which was translated into English in 1929.[4]

Fayol wanted to develop principles of management which would be flexible and adaptable to a wide variety of circumstances. Deciding which principle to use was in Fayol's judgment the art of managing. He believed that a great number of principles might exist and described the ones that he most frequently applied in his own experience. In addition to *principles,* Fayol also presented what he believed were *functions* of managers. We shall discuss them in that order.

Principles of management Fayol proposed 14 principles to guide the thinking of managers in resolving problems. He never suggested total obedience to the principles but suggested that a manager's "experience and sense of proportion" should guide the degree of application of any principle in a particular situation. They are presented in capsule form in Figure 1–2. As with scientific management, the reader should keep in mind the time in which Fayol developed his principles and his intent. His work was probably the first major effort devoted to problems of managing large-scale

[3] Some other very important contributors to classical organization theory were James D. Mooney and Alan C. Reiley, who wrote *Onward Industry* (New York: Harper & Row, 1931), and Lyndall F. Urwick, who wrote *The Elements of Administration* (New York: Harper & Row, 1943).

[4] Henri Fayol, *General and Industrial Management,* trans. J. A. Conbrough (Geneva: International Management Institute, 1929). Another more widely available translation is by Constance Storrs (London: Pitman Publishing Corp., 1949).

Figure 1–2

Fayol's 14 principles of management

1.	Division of labor	8.	Centralization
2.	Authority	9.	Hierarchy of authority
3.	Discipline	10.	Order
4.	Unity of command	11.	Equity
5.	Unity of direction	12.	Stability of staff
6.	Subordination of individual interest to the common good	13.	Initiative
7.	Remuneration of personnel	14.	Esprit de corps

business organizations which at that time in our history were relatively new phenomena.

Functions of management Fayol was perhaps the first individual to discuss management as a process with specific functions that all managers must perform. He proposed four management functions:

1. Planning Fayol believed that managers should make the best possible forecast of future events that affect the organization and draw up an operating plan to guide future decisions.

2. Organizing Fayol believed that managers must determine the appropriate machines, material, and human mix which are necessary to accomplish the task.

3. Commanding In Fayol's scheme, this involved directing the activities of subordinates. He believed that managers should set a good example and have direct two-way communication with subordinates. Finally, they must continually evaluate the organization structure and their subordinates, and they should not hesitate to change the structure if they consider it faulty, or to fire subordinates if they are incompetent.

4. Controlling Those activities which assure that actual activities are consistent with planned activities fall under this function. Fayol did not expand the idea except to state that everything should be "subject to control."

The reader can see that Fayol's description of the management process is very similar to the one presented in Figure 1–1 as the focus of this book. Fayol's *commanding* function is our *leading* function.

Contributions and limitations of the classical approach

Contributions The greatest contribution of the classical approach was that it identified for the first time management as an important element of organized society. This idea has, if anything, increased in importance today. The idea that management skills must be applied in schools, government, and hospitals, as well as business firms is stressed throughout this book. Advocates of the classical approach believed that management, like law, medicine, and other occupations, should be practiced according to principles that managers can learn.

The identification of management functions such as planning, organizing, and controlling provided the basis for training new managers. As we know, they are the focus of this book. The manner in which the management functions are presented often differs depending upon who is presenting them. But any listing of management functions acknowledges that managers are concerned with *what* the organization is doing, *how* it is to be done, and *whether* it was done.

The contributions of the classical approach, however, go beyond the important work of identifying the field of management, and the process and functions of management. Many management techniques used today are direct outgrowths of the classical approach. For example, time and motion analysis, work simplification, incentive wage systems, production scheduling, personnel testing, and budgeting are techniques derived from the classical approach.

Limitations One major criticism of the classical approach is that the majority of its insights are too simplistic for today's complex organizations. The critics argue that scientific management and classical organization theory are more appropriate for the past when the environments of most organizations were very stable and predictable. The changing environment, changing worker expectations, and the changing expectations of society will be discussed in the next chapter.

The behavioral approach

The behavioral approach to management developed partly because practicing managers found that following the ideas of the classical approach did not achieve total efficiency and workplace harmony. Managers still encountered problems because subordinates did not always behave as they were supposed to. Thus, there developed an increased interest in helping managers become more effective in managing people.

The behavioral approach to management has two branches, the first branch, the *human relations approach,* became very popular in the 1940s and 1950s. The second branch, the *behavioral science approach,* became popular in the 1950s and today still receives a great deal of attention.

The human relations approach The term *human relations* refers to the manner in which managers interact with subordinates. In order to develop good human relations, followers of this approach believed that managers must know why their subordinates behave as they do and what psychological and social factors are important to them.

Human relations followers brought to the attention of management the important role played by individuals in determining the success or failure of an organization. They tried to show how the process of management and the functions of management are affected by differences in individual behavior and the influence of groups in the workplace. Thus, while scientific management concentrated on the *physical* environment of the job, human relations concentrated on the *social* environment.

Human relations experts believe that management should recognize the need of employees for recognition and social acceptance. They suggest that since groups provide members with feelings of acceptance and dignity that management look upon the work group as a positive force which could be utilized productively. Therefore, managers should be trained in people skills as well as in technical skills.

The behavioral science approach Other individuals who were university trained in various social sciences such as psychology, sociology, and anthropology began to study people at work. They had advanced training in applying the scientific approach to the study of human behavior. These individuals became known as *behavioral scientists* and are considered to be apart from the human relations approach.

The individuals in the behavioral science branch of the behavioral approach believe that man is much more complex than the "economic man" description of the classical approach and the "social man" description of the human relations approach. The emphasis of the behavioral science approach has concentrated more on the nature of work itself, and the degree to which it can fulfill the human need to use skills and abilities. This is because they believe that an individual is motivated to work for other reasons than solely to make money and/or form social relationships.

Contributions and limitations of the behavioral approach

Contributions For the student of management, the behavioral approach has contributed a wealth of important ideas and research results on the managing people aspect of the discipline of management. The basic rationale is that since management must get work done through others, management is really applied behavioral science because a manager must motivate, lead, and understand interpersonal relations. Therefore, the logic is that managers must be aware of behavioral science contributions to management.

Limitations The basic assumption that managers must know how to deal with people appears valid. However, management is more than applied behavioral science. For the behavioral approach to be useful to managers, it must make them better practitioners of the process of management. It must help them in problem situations. In many cases, this objective has not been achieved because of the tendency of some behavioral scientists to use technical terms when trying to communicate their research findings to practicing managers. Also, in some situations, one behavioral scientist (a psychologist) might have a different suggestion than another (a sociologist) for the same management problem. Human behavior is complex and is studied from a variety of viewpoints. This complicates the problem for a manager trying to use insights from the behavioral sciences.

The management science approach

The management science approach is in one sense a modern version of early emphasis on the "management of work" by those interested in scientific management. Its key feature *is the use of mathematics and statistics to aid in resolving* ***production*** *and* ***operations*** *problems.* Thus, the approach focuses on solving technical rather than human behavior problems. The computer has been of tremendous value to the growing importance of this approach because it has enabled analyses of problems that were previously not possible because of their complexity.

The management science approach has only formally existed for approximately 40 years. It began during the early part of World War II when England was faced with some complex military problems that had never been faced before, such as antisubmarine warfare strategy. To try to solve these kinds of problems, the English formed teams of scientists, mathematicians, and physicists. They named the teams *operations research* teams, and they proved to be extremely valuable. When the war was over, the approach began to be used by American business firms.

Today the operations research approach has been formalized and renamed the management science approach. Basically, it involves mixed teams of specialists from whatever fields the problem being attacked calls for. The team analyzes the problem and often develops a mathematical representation of the problem. Thus, they can change certain factors in the equations to see what would happen if such a change was actually made in the real world. The results of their work, then, often become useful to management in making a final decision. One of their important purposes is to provide management with *quantitative bases* for decisions.

Contributions and limitations of the management science approach

Contributions Today the most important contributions of management science are in the areas of production management and operations management. *Production management* focuses on manufacturing technology and the flow of material in a manufacturing plant. Here management science has contributed techniques that help solve production scheduling problems, budgeting problems, and maintenance of optimal inventory levels, among others.

Operations management is very similar to production management except that it focuses on a wide class of problems and includes organizations such as hospitals, banks, government and military, which have operations problems but do not use technology to manufacture products. For these types of organizations, management science has contributed techniques to solve such problems as budgeting, planning for manpower development programs, and aircraft scheduling.

Limitations We noted in our discussion of the behavioral approach that management is more than applied behavioral science. At this point, we should say that management science *is not* a substitute for management. The techniques of the management science approach are especially useful as aids to the manager performing the management process. However, while it is used in many problem areas, management science does not deal with the people aspect of an organization.

Attempting to integrate the three approaches to management

Recently, there have been some attempts to aid managers in accomplishing some type of integration of the three approaches to management. One of these attempts, the **systems approach,** stresses that organizations must be viewed as total systems with each part linked to every other part. The other, the **contingency approach,** stresses that the correctness of a managerial practice is contingent upon how it fits the particular situation in which it is applied, in other words, "depends on the situation." Let us briefly examine each.

The systems approach

The systems approach to management is really a "way of thinking" about management problems. It views an organization as a group of interrelated parts with a purpose. The action of one part will influence the other parts, and managers cannot deal separately with the individual parts. Thus, it is incorrect to think that if a production problem exists, that the solution to the problem will not have an impact in the marketing area. In solving problems, then, managers must view the organization as a dynamic whole and try to anticipate the intended as well as unintended impacts of their decisions.

Viewing the management process using the systems approach, managers would understand that they do not solve individual problems. Rather, they intervene in a total system of interrelated parts and the management functions of planning, organizing, leading, and controlling are the primary ways in which they intervene.

Systems thinking can be useful to managers in their approaches to solving problems. It encourages them not to think broadly about a problem and not to concentrate only on the results they want because these results will have impacts on other problems and parts of the organization. The age-old confrontation between the production objective of low-production costs and the marketing objective of a broad product line to compete better is a good example. Both objectives cannot be achieved at the same time. For production costs to be their lowest, the firm would produce one color and one style. To achieve the marketing objective, several models and several colors would be required. In this situation, a compromise is necessary for the overall system to achieve its objective. The objectives of the individual parts must be compromised for the objective of the entire firm.

Using the systems approach in the above example, we can see that individual managers must adopt a broad perspective of their jobs. With a systems perspective, managers can more easily achieve coordination between the objectives of the various parts of the organization and the objectives of the organization as a whole.[5]

The contingency approach

The systems approach forces managers to recognize that organizations are systems made up of parts that are interdependent and that a change in one part will affect other parts. This insight is important. Beyond this, however, it would be useful for managers to see how the interdependent parts fit together. The contingency approach can help better understand this interdependence.

The basic idea of the contingency approach is that there is no one best way to manage. Do not interpret this to mean that managers can do what they please or that it doesn't matter what managers do. What it means is that there is no one way to plan, or to organize, or to lead, or to control. Rather, managers must find different ways that fit different situations. A method that is highly effective in one situation may not even work in other situations.

Actually, the idea of contingency or situational thinking is not really new. Recall that Henri Fayol did not expect blind adherence to his principles but permitted managers to make allowances in selecting which principle to apply and how to apply it. Another writer in the classical approach spoke of the "law of the situation" during the 1920s. Mary Parker Follett noted that "different situations require different kinds of knowledge, and the man possessing the knowledge demanded by a certain situation tends in the best managed businesses, other things being equal, to become the leader of the moment."[6]

---

[5] See Fremont E. Kast and James E. Rosenzweig, "General Systems Theory: Applications in Organizations and Management," *Academy of Management Journal,* December 1972, pp. 447–65.

[6] The many contributions of Mary Parker Follett are collected in Henry C. Metcalf and Lyndall Urwick, eds., *Dynamic Administration* (New York: Harper & Row, 1941).

The contingency approach has grown in popularity over the last two decades because some research has shown that given certain characteristics of a job and certain characteristics of the people doing the job, certain management practices work better than others. For example, at times, rigid plans, clearly defined jobs, authoritative leadership, and tight controls have resulted in high productivity and satisfied workers. At other times, just the opposite (general plans, loosely defined jobs, democratic leadership, and loose controls), have produced the same results.[7]

When facing a problem, a manager using the contingency approach does not assume a particular practice will work. For example, if productivity needs to be increased, the manager will not automatically assume a new incentive system is needed (a classical solution) or that a new motivational approach needs to be tried (a behavioral solution). Instead, the manager studies the characteristics of the workers, nature of the job, and his or her own leadership approach before deciding on a solution.

Both the systems approach and the contingency approach have developed valuable insights for students of management. At this point, however, they are in rather early stages of development. Thus, it is too early to know if either or both approaches will achieve the objective of integrating the three approaches to management thought which comprise the discipline of management.

Plan for this book

It is hoped that at this point, the reader can see that writing a management book for future managers is not an easy task. Management is a discipline in continual evolution. Three well-established approaches—classical, behavioral, and management science—have made contributions to our ability to manage different aspects of organizations, namely work and organizations, people, and production and operations.

Thus, it would be virtually impossible to write a management book without including contributions from all approaches. In addition, wherever possible, the book should try to encourage "systems thinking" and a "contingency perspective." The plan for our book is outlined in Figure 1–3, which is an expansion of Figure 1–1.

Figure 1–3 indicates that the *process* of management is the focus of the book. Indeed it should be. This contribution of the classical approach produced the core *functions* of management and has endured throughout

[7] See Fred Luthans, "The Contingency Theory of Management: A Path out of the Jungle," *Business Horizons,* June 1973, pp. 62–72; and Harold Koontz, "The Management Theory Jungle Revisited," *Academy of Management Review,* April 1980, pp. 175–88.

the evolution of the discipline of management. Figure 1–3 indicates that the bulk of the material in the book is organized around the management functions of planning, organizing, leading, and controlling. Throughout our discussions of the management process and each of the management functions, the contributions of the classical approach will be evident. Indeed, it is they who have produced much of the knowledge that is specific to the discipline of management as opposed to being drawn from other disciplines.

Figure 1–3 indicates that the contributions of the behavioral approach should in no way be viewed separately from the classical approach. Examining the topics covered indicates that the behavioral approach has made contributions to the human aspects of the *organizing, leading,* and *controlling* functions. In subsequent chapters on staffing, career development, motivation, leadership, communications, organizational change, and performance evaluation, we will draw upon the contributions of the behavioral approach.

The contributions of the management science approach are seen in various facets of the *planning* and *control* functions. In subsequent chapters on planning, decision making, managerial control and information, and

Figure 1–3

Plan for the book

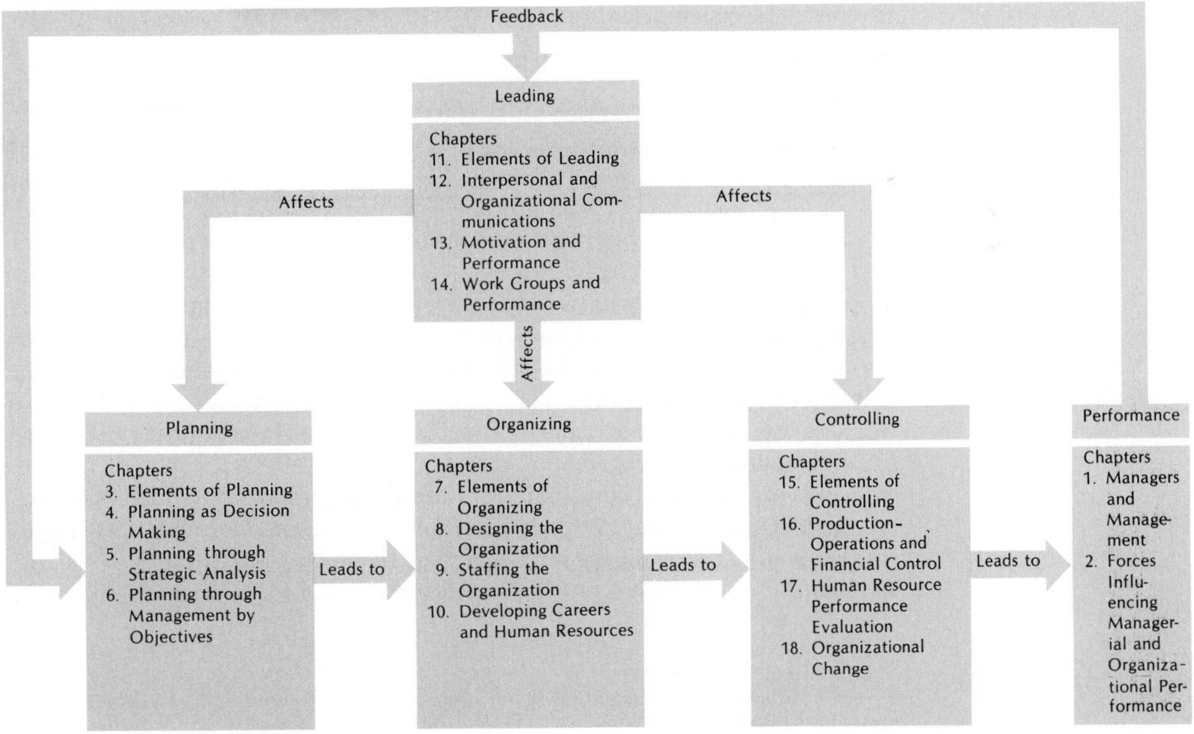

production/operations and financial control, we will draw upon the contributions of the management science approach.

In summary, the management process is the focus of our book. We have selected only that knowledge which we believe will help improve the performance of a management function. Thus, while management draws on relevant aspects of other disciplines, it also has certain identifiable characteristics such as the process and functions of management that are its own.

The reader should know that only learning the many techniques and concepts that other disciplines have contributed to the discipline of management will not necessarily produce an effective manager. It is knowing in which situations to use which techniques in combination with the functions of management that will result in being effective. This view is clearly stated by Peter Drucker:

> Managers practice management. They do not practice economics. They do not practice quantification. They do not practice behavioral science. These are tools for the manager. . . . As a specific discipline, management had its own basic problems . . . specific approaches . . . distinct concerns. . . . A man who only knows the skills and techniques, without understanding the fundamentals of management, is not a manager; he is, at best, only a technician.[8]

When you finish this book, you will be equipped with the knowledge, attitudes, and skills that will enable you to evaluate which management practice fits which situation.

Review and discussion questions

1. As a beginning student of management, what do you expect to learn from this book? Why?
2. Clearly distinguish between the process of management and the functions of management. How are they related?
3. What do you think of the following statement: "Anyone can manage, all it is is common sense."
4. List the organizations that influence your life. In what ways do they influence you?
5. Someone has said that managers are a very important social resource in the United States. Why do you think this person made this statement? Do you agree or disagree? State your reasons.
6. Think of something you have had experience in. It might be a sport,

[8] Peter F. Drucker, *Management: Tasks—Responsibilities—Practices* (New York: Harper & Row, 1973), p. 17.

job, musical skill. If you were asked to teach a group of people what you know, can you see any possible problems? Why?

7. Can you think of any reasons why there are three approaches to management thought comprising the discipline of management?
8. Have you ever been a manager? Can you think of a situation in which you played a managerial role? Outline your planning, organizing, leading, and controlling functions.

Suggested reading

Barnard, C. I. *Organization and Management.* Cambridge: Harvard University Press, 1952.

Cass, E. L., and F. G. Zimmer. *Man and Work in Society.* New York: Van Nostrand Reinhold, 1975.

Drucker, P. *The Practice of Management.* New York: Harper & Row, 1954.

Kantrow, A. M. "Why Read Peter Drucker?" *Harvard Business Review,* January–February 1980, pp. 74–82.

Krajewski, L., and H. Thompson, *Management Science: Quantitative Methods in Context.* New York: John Wiley & Sons, 1980.

Locke, E. A. "The Ideas of Frederick W. Taylor: An Evaluation." *Academy of Management Review,* January, 1982, pp. 14–24.

Merrill, H. F., ed. *Classics in Management.* New York: American Management Association, 1960.

Wrege, C. D., and A. G. Perroni. "Taylor's Pig-Tale: An Historical Analysis of Frederick W. Taylor's Pig Iron Experiments." *Academy of Management Journal,* March 1974, pp. 6–26.

2

Chapter two Forces influencing managerial and organizational performance

This chapter focuses on two environments which are sources of many of the forces which influence managerial and organizational performance, **the management system,** and the **external environment.** These two environments comprise much of the setting in which managers perform their functions.

The management system

As an organization increases in size and complexity, its management must adapt by becoming more specialized. This section addresses some results of the specialization of the management process with discussions of the **types** of managers, managerial **skills,** and managerial **roles.**

Types of managers

The history of most ongoing firms can be understood as a process by which the management has, in successive steps, evolved from one manager with many subordinates to many managers with many subordinates. The development of different types of managers has occurred as a result of this evolution. For example, Figure 2–1 illustrates a one-manager–many-subordinate firm. In this situation, the manager performs all of the management functions. Let us assume that the firm is successful, and the manager decides to add some new products and sell to some new markets. As the manager becomes overworked because of the increased complexity of the job, the manager may decide to specialize **vertically** by assigning the task of supervising subordinates to another person (Figure 2–2) or may decide to specialize **horizontally** by assigning certain tasks, such as producing the product and marketing the product, to another person (Figure 2–3). Whichever one is chosen, the management process is now being shared, specialized, and more complex.

As the management system evolves to an even higher degree of specialization (Figure 2–4), relationships among the managers and nonmanagers become more complex. In Figure 2–4, it is clear that the managers in produc-

Figure 2–1

One manager and many subordinates

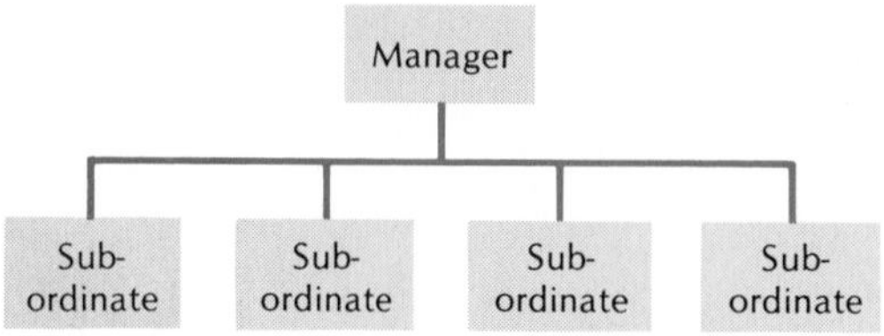

tion, marketing, accounting, and research are concerned not only with managing their own subordinates, but that they are the object of managerial efforts by *their* manager as well. Figure 2–4 illustrates three types of managers.

First-line management These managers coordinate the work of others who are not themselves managers. The subordinates may be blue-collar workers, salespersons, accounting clerks, or scientists, depending upon the particular tasks that the subunit performs, for example, production, marketing, accounting, or research. Whatever the case, first-line managers are responsible for the basic work of the organization according to plans provided by their superiors. First-line managers are in daily or near daily contact with their subordinates, and they are ordinarily assigned the job because of their ability to work with people. They must work with their own subordinates and with other first-line supervisors whose tasks are related to the tasks of their units.

Middle management Unlike first-line managers, middle managers plan, organize, lead, and control the activity of other managers; yet, like first-line managers, they are subject to the managerial efforts of a superior. The middle manager coordinates the activity (for example, marketing) of a subunit.

Top management Top management is responsible for the performance of the entire organization through the middle managers. Unlike other man-

Figure 2–2

Vertical specialization of the management process

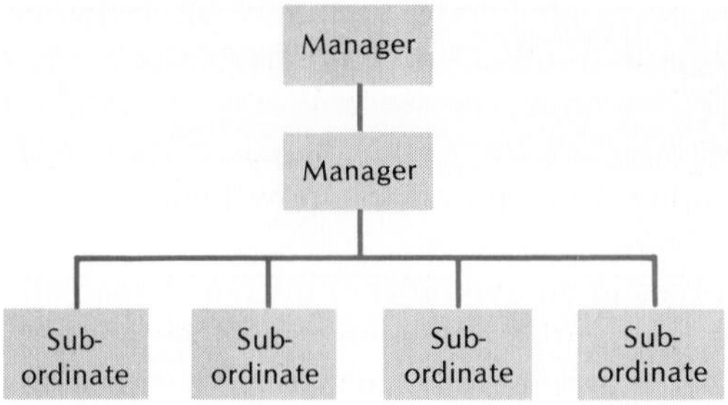

Figure 2–3

Horizontal specialization of the management process

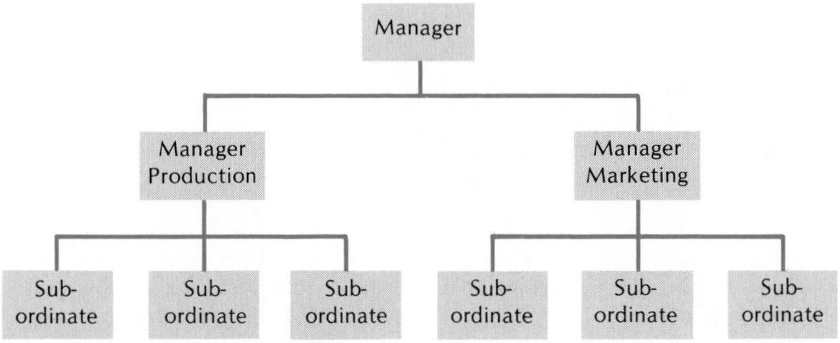

agers, the top manager is accountable to no other manager, but instead to the owners of the resources used by the organizations.

The designation *top, middle, first-line,* classifies managers on their vertical rank in the organization. The completion of a task usually requires the completion of several interrelated activities. As these activities are identified, and as the responsibility for completing each task is assigned to a manager, that manager becomes a functional manager.

Functional management As the management process becomes horizontally specialized, a functional manager is responsible for a particular activity. In Figure 2–4 the management process has been specialized into four functions: production, marketing, accounting, and research.

Thus, a manager can be a first-line manager in production, another may be a middle manager in the marketing function. The function refers to what *activities* the manager actually manages as a result of horizontal specialization of the management process. The level of the manager refers

Figure 2–4

Vertical and horizontal specialization of the management process

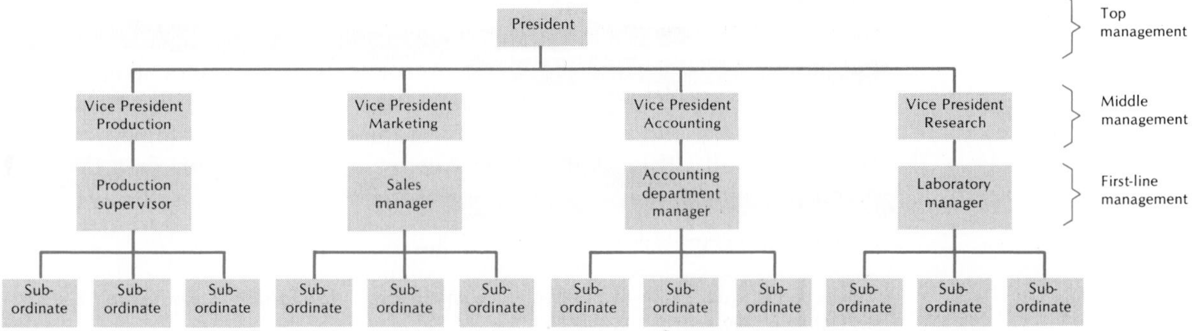

Figure 2–5

Management level and the management functions

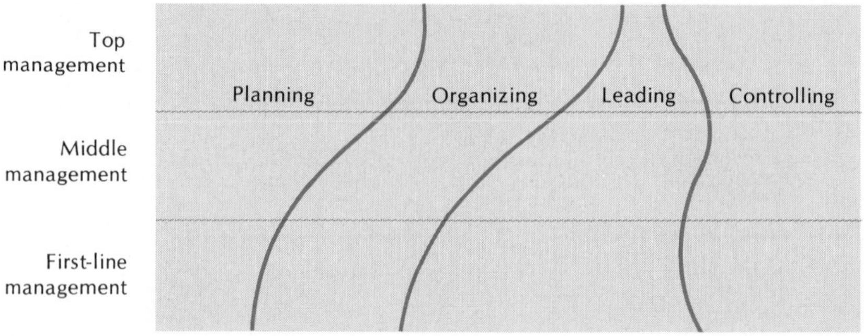

to the *right to act and use resources* within specified limits as a result of vertical specialization of the management process.

Management level and the management functions In the last chapter, we noted that the management functions of planning, organizing, leading, and controlling are performed by all managers. However, the amount of time and effort devoted to each function will depend upon the level of the manager in the organization. Figure 2–5 attempts to illustrate this relationship. For example, first-line managers usually spend less time on planning than top managers. However, they spend much more time and effort performing the leading and controlling functions. Should one move to higher levels in the organization, far more time would be spent on planning and less on leading. The amount of time and effort devoted to the organizing and controlling functions are usually fairly consistent at all levels of management.

Managerial skills

Regardless of the level of management, managers must possess and seek to continually develop numerous critical skills.[1] These are the skills considered to be essential to effectively perform the management functions. Let us briefly examine each one.

Technical skill This is the ability to use *specific* knowledge, techniques, and resources in performing work. *Accounting* supervisors, *engineering* directors, or *nursing* supervisors must have the technical skills of accounting, engineering, and nursing to perform their management jobs.

Analytical skill This skill involves using scientific approaches or techniques to solve management problems. There are many quantitative tech-

[1] See Robert L. Katz, "Skills of an Effective Administrator," *Harvard Business Review*, September–October 1974, pp. 90–102.

niques useful to managers in the planning and controlling functions. A marketing manager may need to forecast sales. A production manager may need to control inventory levels.

Decision-making skill All managers must make decisions. The quality of these decisions determines how effective the manager is. The manager's decision-making skill in selecting a course of action to solve a problem will greatly influence performance.

Human skill Since managers must "get work done through other people," the ability to work with, and understand others is very important. This skill is essential at every level of management in an organization.

Communication skill Effective communication—the transmission of common understanding both written and orally—is critical for effective managerial performance. It is a skill that is probably critical to success in every field, but especially to managers who must achieve results through the efforts of others.

Conceptual skill This is the ability to see the big picture, the complexities of the overall organization, and how the various parts fit together. Recall in our discussions of the systems approach as a way of thinking about organizations, we stressed the importance of knowing how each part of the organization interrelates and contributes to the overall objectives of the organization.

Managerial skills and management level While the above skills are all-important, the relative importance of each will vary according to the level of the manager in the organization. Figure 2–6 illustrates the skills required at each level. For example, note that technical skill and human skill are more important at lower levels of management. These managers have greater contact with the work being done and the people doing the work. Communication skill is equally important at all levels of management and analytical skill slightly more important at higher levels of management where the environment is less stable and problems less predictable. Finally, decision-making skill and conceptual skill are extremely critical to the

Figure 2–6

Managerial skills and management level

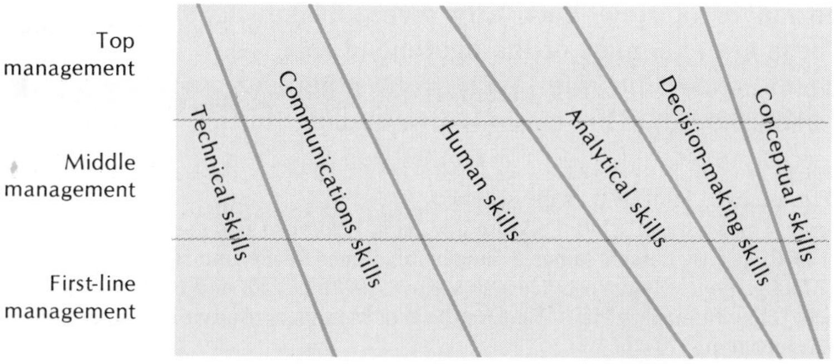

performance of top managers. Top management's primary responsibility is to make the key decisions that are executed or implemented at lower levels. To do this top management must be able to see the big picture in order to identify the opportunities in the environment and develop the strategic plans to capitalize on the opportunities. The many skills required of an effective manager is one of the reasons so many individuals find the field so challenging. A newly promoted middle manager commented on the challenge he faced as a manager:

> *That's why I enjoy my work so much. It forces me to analyze so many different aspects of myself. I know I am strong in certain skills and not so strong in others. To be a good manager therefore, I must develop certain facets of my own self. It is always a challenge but at least when you work on developing yourself you are also improving yourself as a manager.*

Managerial roles

We now know that managers perform at different levels and require different skills. At this point, we want to examine what managers actually do and how they spend their time. Recently it has been determined that managers perform 10 different but closely related roles. These are illustrated in Figure 2–7. The figure indicates that the 10 roles can be separated into three different groupings: interpersonal roles, informational roles, and decisional roles.[2]

Interpersonal roles These roles focus on interpersonal relationships. The three roles of figurehead, leader, and liaison are a result of the manager's formal authority. By assuming these roles, the manager is able to move into the informational roles which, in turn, lead directly to the decisional roles.

All managerial jobs require some duties that are symbolic or ceremonial in nature. This is the *figurehead role.* A college dean will hand out diplomas at graduation, a shop foreman attends the wedding of a subordinate's daughter, the mayor of New York City gives the key to the city to an astronaut. These are examples of the figurehead role.

The manager's *leadership role* involves directing and coordinating the activities of subordinates. This may involve staffing (hiring, training, pro-

[2] Henry Mintzberg, "The Manager's Job: Folklore and Fact," *Harvard Business Review,* July–August 1975, pp. 49–61; Jay W. Lorsch, James P. Baughman, James Reece, and Henry Mintzberg, *Understanding Management* (New York: Harper & Row, 1978), p. 220; and Neil Snyder and William F. Glueck, "How Managers Plan—The Analysis of Managers' Activities," *Long Range Planning,* February 1980, pp. 70–76.

Figure 2–7
Managerial roles

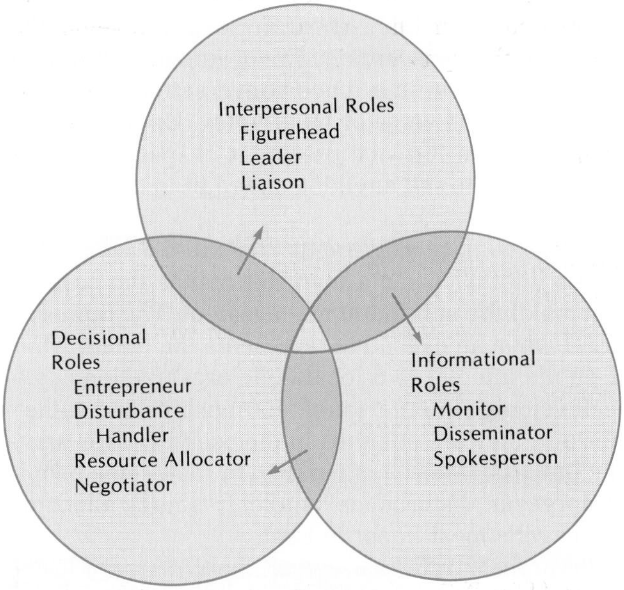

moting, dismissing) and motivating subordinates. The leadership role also involves controlling, making sure that things are going according to plan.

The *liaison role* gets managers involved in interpersonal relationships outside of their area of command. This role may involve contacts both within and outside the organization. Within the organization, managers must interact with numerous other managers and other individuals. They must maintain good relations with the managers who send work to the unit as well as those who receive work from the unit. For example, a college dean must interact with individuals all over the campus, a supervisory nurse in an operating room must interact with supervisors of various other groups of nurses, a production foreman must interact with engineering supervisors and sales managers. Finally, managers often have interactions with important people outside of the organization. It is easy to see that the liaison role can often consume 50 percent of a manager's time.

Informational roles This set of roles establishes the manager as the central focus for receiving and sending nonroutine information. As a result of the three interpersonal roles discussed above, the manager builds a network of interpersonal contacts. The contacts aid the manager in gathering and receiving information in the monitor role and transmitting that information in the disseminator and spokesperson role.

The *monitor role* involves examining the environment in order to gather information, changes, opportunities, and problems which may affect the unit. The formal and informal contacts developed in the liaison role are often useful here. The information gathered may be competitive moves that could influence the entire organization or knowing whom to call if the usual supplier of an important part cannot fill an order.

The *disseminator role* involves providing important or privileged information to subordinates that they might ordinarily not know about or be able to obtain. The president of a firm in a lunch conversation hears that a large customer of the firm is on the verge of bankruptcy. Upon returning to the office, the president contacts the vice president of marketing who in turn instructs the sales force not to sell anything on credit to the troubled company.

In the *spokesperson role,* the manager represents the unit to other people. This representation may be internal when a manager makes the case for salary increases for members of the unit to top management. The representation may also be external when an executive represents the organization on a particular issue of public interest to a local civic organization.

Decisional roles While developing interpersonal relationships and gathering information are important, they are not ends in themselves. They serve as the basic inputs to the process of decision making. In fact, some people believe these roles—entrepreneur, disturbance handler, resource allocator, and negotiator—are a manager's most important set.

The purpose of the *entrepreneur* role is to bring about changes in the unit for the better. The effective first-line supervisor is continually looking for new ideas or new methods to improve the unit's performance. The effective college dean is continually planning change which will result in higher quality education. The effective marketing manager continually seeks new product ideas.

In the *disturbance handler role,* managers make decisions or take corrective action in response to pressure that is beyond their control. Because they are disturbances, the decisions must usually be made quickly, which means that this role will take priority over other roles. The immediate goal is to bring about stability. When an emergency room supervisor responds quickly to a local disaster, a plant supervisor reacts to a strike, or a first-line manager responds to a breakdown in a key piece of equipment, they are dealing with disturbances in their environments. These responses must be quick and must result in a return to stability.

The *resource allocator role* places a manager in the position of deciding who will get what resources. These resources include money, people, time, and equipment. There are never enough resources to go around. The manager must allocate the scarce resources toward numerous possible ends. Resource allocation, therefore, is one of the most critical of the manager's decisional roles. A first-line supervisor must decide whether an overtime schedule should be established or whether part-time workers should be hired. A college dean must decide which courses to offer next semester, based on available faculty. The president of the United States must decide whether to allocate more to defense and less to social programs.

In the *negotiator role,* a manager must bargain with other units and individuals to obtain advantages for his or her unit. The negotiations may be over work, performance, objectives, resources, or anything else influencing the unit. A sales manager may negotiate with the production department over a special order for a large customer. A first-line supervisor may negotiate for new typewriters, while a top manager may negotiate with a labor union representative.

Management level and management roles As you might expect, the level in the organization will influence which managerial roles are emphasized. Obviously, top managers spend much more time in the figurehead role than first-line supervisors. The liaison role of top and middle managers will involve individuals and groups outside the organization, while at the first-line level, the liaison will be outside the unit but inside the organization. Top managers must monitor the environment for changes that can influence the entire organization. Middle managers monitor the environment for changes likely to influence the particular function (for example, marketing) which they manage, while the first-line supervisor is concerned about what will influence his or her unit. However, while the amount of time in the various roles, and the activities performed in each role may differ, all managers perform interpersonal, informational, and decisional roles.

The external environment

Thus far in this chapter, we have examined some important factors—level in the organization, skills, and roles—which influence managerial behavior and performance. We know that the importance of each of these forces will differ from situation to situation and manager to manager. In the remainder of this chapter, we will discuss the external environments in which managers must perform. These are outside forces and as such, less likely to be controlled by the manager. However, they may have a profound impact on how well a manager performs the management functions.

The significance of what goes on out there is magnified as news of energy shortages, double-digit inflation, international economic crises, and social unrest fills the headlines and newscasts. It is not possible for us to discuss every possible environmental influence in these few pages. However, it is necessary to outline the broad impacts of environmental influences on the job of managing.

All organizations exist in some type of general environment. The specific attributes of the environment have a strong impact on the management functions. One way to classify an organization's environment is as being either **turbulent, hostile, diverse,** or **technically complex.**[3]

[3] Pradip N. Kdandwalla, *The Design of Organizations* (New York: Harcourt Brace Jovanovich, 1977), pp. 326–40.

A turbulent environment

An organization in this kind of environment faces rapid changes on a regular basis. These changes may be from technological innovations, changes in government regulations, or economic or competitive shifts. Because of this lack of stability, this is an extremely difficult environment in which to manage.

A hostile environment

When the organization faces intense competition for customers, resources, or both, it is operating in a hostile environment. The American automobile industry faces such an environment not only domestically but from international competitors as well. As the competition for resources (fuel) pushes costs up, domestic airlines must in turn compete more intensely for customers. Many colleges must now compete intensely for students and faculty.

A diverse environment

A business firm which operates all over the world is a good example of an organization that faces a diverse environment of different languages, governments, and cultures. This diversity can influence not only what the organization does but how it does it as well as the conditions under which it does it. For example, because of government restrictions or cultural differences, a manufacturer may have to alter its product and methods of marketing in different parts of the world.

Domestic companies which produce numerous products which are sold to different markets also face a diverse environment. For example, Tenneco Inc., produces food products, automobile parts, aircraft carriers, natural gas, and chemicals. Each is made using different technology, different raw materials, and are sold to different markets.

A technically complex environment

The electronics, computer, and nuclear energy industries operate in technically complex environments. That is, they need sophisticated information and highly technical personnel to survive. New developments can occur quickly, and present products can become obsolete quickly because of technological breakthroughs. In such cases, the environment is not only technically complex, but also turbulent.

These terms—*turbulent, hostile, diverse,* and *technically complex*—are general descriptions of the type of environment an organization can face. This does not mean that an organization cannot face more than one. For example, it is very possible for a firm to be in a technically complex environment while at the same time facing a hostile competitive environment.

Such a situation (for example, in the home computer business) only complicates the management process even further.

Management dilemmas caused by the external environment

In addition to influencing the management process by creating constraints as well as opportunities, the external environment also poses two very important dilemmas that managers often must face. The first dilemma is that which exists between the need of individuals for satisfying jobs and the organization's need for efficiency. A second dilemma involves society's need for socially responsible business behavior and the organization's need for profitability.

The satisfying job—efficiency dilemma

The basic cause of this dilemma is the conflict which may arise between individual needs and organizational needs in the design of jobs. We saw in the opening chapter that what people are expected to accomplish and the conditions under which they work have been analyzed since the earliest efforts of the classical approach. These efforts dealt primarily with issues related to the efficient use of humans in work organizations. Through time and motion studies and other techniques, managers had ways by which efficient and productive jobs could be designed.

Then the behavioral approach advocates criticized these efforts for ignoring the human element. They believe that the design of jobs must include opportunities to satisfy needs such as achievement and esteem. They have developed several techniques such as participative management, job enrichment, and job enlargement designed to improve the quality of worklife (QWL). The techniques will be discussed later in the book, but a major purpose of each is to make jobs more satisfying.

The important element of a QWL program is the opportunity for individuals and groups at any level in the organization to influence what goes on in connection with their work. A high-quality worklife is supposed to exhibit the following characteristics:[4]

1. Jobs are interesting, challenging, and responsible.
2. Workers are rewarded through fair wages and recognition for their contributions.

---

[4] Tom Lupton, "Efficiency and the Quality of Worklife," *Organizational Dynamics*, Autumn 1975, p. 68.

3. Workplaces are clean, lighted, quiet, and safe.
4. Supervision is minimal but available when needed.
5. Workers are involved in decisions which affect them and their jobs.
6. Jobs are secure and promote the development of friendly relationships with co-workers.
7. Organizations provide facilities for personal welfare and medical attention.

These characteristics can be found in many QWL programs being implemented in such organizations as AT&T, General Electric, General Foods, Motorola, Procter & Gamble, and General Motors.

It is very likely that the pressure to improve the quality of worklife will continue in the future. Evidence currently indicates that (1) traditional sources of cheap and submissive labor such as rural out-migration, children, and women are drying up; (2) the mix of jobs is changing from mostly blue collar to white collar; (3) legislation has created greater obligations on work organizations to deal directly with quality of worklife issues such as health and safety; and (4) the level of education and literacy continues to rise for all segments of American society.[5]

The result of these conditions is that future managers will have to deal with increasingly educated and aware individuals. Their attitudes and values will place importance on autonomy, growth, and self-development. And many of their interests will be protected and promoted by law. This view was emphasized by a personnel manager in a large business firm:

> *I believe the work force of the future will be more interested in the quality of work than any other work force in the history of our nation.*

At the same time, however, the future manager will be forced to pay even closer attention to the efficient use of resources. Sources of energy are also drying up. A problem for managers will be to know and recognize the conditions where an improvement in the quality of worklife also improves efficiency. The dilemma and therefore the choice comes down to deciding between efficiency and quality of worklife when the two outcomes are inversely related.

The social responsibility—profitability dilemma

During the last decade, society has been placing increased demands on large business organizations for greater social responsibility—that is,

[5] Stanley E. Seashore, "The Future of Work: How It May Change and What It May Mean," *Industrial and Labor Relations Report,* Fall 1975, pp. 14–16.

business involvement in solving both social and ecological problems. Some managers have replied, "Why us?" while others have agreed. Some firms commit resources to social action programs; others agree they should but, as yet, have not; and still others believe that they meet their social responsibilities by being profitable, providing employment, and paying taxes. The problem is a very real and complex one with which managers and our society will be forced to come to grips during the next decade.

Changing views on management's social responsibility Many people believe that laws, regulations, and attitudes toward businesses' social involvement have gone through at least three phases in the United States: profit-maximizing management, trusteeship management, and quality of life management.[6]

Profit-maximizing management emerged in the 19th century as the Industrial Revolution swept through the United States carrying with it new attitudes toward business. Profit maximization was viewed as a socially responsible action because it created a stronger economy. Meeting the applicable laws of the time was the only requirement management needed to be concerned with through the early years of the 20th century.

During the 1920s and 1930s, a somewhat different view of management's social responsibility began to develop. The idea of *trusteeship management* is that managers are responsible not only for profits but also for balancing the often competing interests of stockholders, employees, customers, suppliers, and the community. Management should behave as a trustee to all of these contributing groups. Thus, for the first time, the idea of social responsibility was broadened beyond its original more narrow definition of profit maximization.

Sometime during the 1950s, beliefs began to be expressed that managers should direct some of their efforts and resources to the solution of broader societal problems. Thus, *quality of life management* expands beyond improving the nation's standard of living by stressing the quality of life rather than only the quantity of life.

In the context of present times, the quality of life view of management would have expectations in such areas as educating the young, policing the streets, cleaning up polluted air and water, teaching disadvantaged citizens how to earn a living, rebuilding ghettos, and providing management expertise for city governments.

As problems such as these continue to mount, managers of the future will be more than ever faced with reconciling their responsibilities to two groups of people: stockholders and society in general. In addition to the idea that power implies responsibility, there are other reasons why the modern corporation will be looked to for help in solving society's problems. For example, more and more citizens are realizing that in addition to having

[6] Robert Hay and Ed Gray, "Social Responsibilities of Business Managers," *Academy of Management Journal,* March 1974, pp. 135–43.

the power, the modern business corporation also has the technical know-how to aid in solving the nation's problems. The federal government itself holds a similar viewpoint and has begun actively soliciting the aid of the large corporation.

Management responses to demands for social responsibility Figure 2–8 presents three possible management responses to demands for social responsibility: social obligation, social responsibility, and social responsiveness.[7] Each of the three possible responses is described in terms of how the organization would respond to social pressures, governmental actions, legislative and political activities, and philanthropy.

Social obligation refers to behavior by the organization that is designed to deal only with legal requirements and competitive market forces. In the *social responsibility* stage, we see corporate behavior that complies with the contemporary values, norms, and expectations of society. The most extreme behavior is *social responsiveness* where management anticipates various societal demands and changes and takes appropriate preventive action.

While there are strong arguments *for* social responsibility by business organizations, there are also some powerful arguments *against* it. For example, there are those who maintain that the large corporation presides over a wealth that it does not own and, therefore, should not be forced to develop a social awareness over the use of assets that are owned by private citizens (stockholders). Others question whether it is proper to place public problems on the shoulders of corporate managers. They point out that persons who are highly skilled in business matters may not be so in matters of politics, the humanities, and the social sciences. They also note that such persons are in no way accountable to the voters for their decisions, and, therefore, should not determine what is good for society.

The dilemma for future managers will come when they attempt to become involved in society's problems and may be faced with a group of angry stockholders who maintain that business organizations have no legal right to retain earnings for such uses and that since it is their money the stockholders should decide how the money should be spent. On the other hand, when managers attempt to maximize profit for the stockholders, they may be faced with angry citizens who claim that managers have no respect for the needs of society as a whole and are failing to safeguard the environmental conditions that provide for the survival and growth of the business organization.

It is inconceivable to imagine that a society can be confronted with critical shortages, insufficient natural resources, and ecological pollution without experiencing a change in values. During the past several decades,

[7] S. Prakash Sethi, "A Conceptual Framework for Environmental Analysis of Social Issues and Evaluation of Business Response Patterns," *Academy of Management Review,* January 1979, pp. 63–74.

managers operated for the most part in an environment characterized by abundance and a societal commitment to growth. If the next decade is characterized by shortages and a societal commitment to conservation, the social responsibility–profitability dilemma will surely intensify.

Figure 2–8

Management responses to demands for social responsibility

Dimensions of behavior	Stage one: Social obligation	Stage two: Social responsibility	Stage three: Social responsiveness
Response to social pressures	Maintains low public profile but, if attacked, uses PR methods to upgarde its public image; denies any deficiencies; blames public dissatisfaction on ignorance of failure to understand corporate functions; discloses information only where legally required.	Accepts responsibility for solving current problems; will admit deficiencies in former practices and attempt to persuade public that its current practices meet social norms; attitude toward critics conciliatory; freer information disclosures than stage one.	Willingly discusses activities with outside groups; makes information freely available to public; accepts formal and informal inputs from outside groups in decision making. Is willing to be publicly evaluated for its various activities.
Activities pertaining to governmental actions	Strongly resists any regulation of its activities except when it needs help to protect its market position; avoids contact; resists any demands for information beyond that legally required.	Preserves management discretion in corporate decisions but cooperates with government in research to improve industrywide standards; participates in political processes and encourages employees to do likewise.	Openly communites with government; assists in enforcing existing laws and developing evaluations of business practices; objects publicly to governmental activities that it feels are detrimental to the public good.
Legislative and political activities	Seeks to maintain status quo; actively opposes laws that would internalize any previously externalized costs; seeks to keep lobbying activities secret.	Willing to work with outside groups for good environmental concedes need for change in some status quo laws; less secrecy in lobbying than stage one.	Avoids meddling in politics and does not pursue special interest laws; assists legislative bodies in developing better laws where relevant; promotes honesty and openness in government and in its own lobbying activities.
Philanthropy	Contributes only when direct benefit to it clearly shown; otherwise, views contributions as responsibility of individual employees.	Contributes to noncontroversial and established causes; matches employee contributions	Activities of stage two, *plus* support and contributions to new, controversial groups whose needs it sees as unfulfilled and increasingly important.

SOURCE: Adapted from S. Prakash Sethi, "A Conceptual Framework for Environmental Analysis of Social Issues and Evaluation of Business Response Patterns," *Academy of Management Review*, January 1979, p. 67.

Organizational and managerial performance

Thus far, this chapter has described some of the more important forces that influence managerial performance. We have seen how managerial jobs are similar but different because of differences in the level, skills, and roles of managers. We have also discussed two important dilemmas managers often face. All of these internal and external forces influence managerial performance. What remains for us to do in this chapter is to understand organizational and managerial performance.

Organizational performance

We regularly make judgments on the performance of various enterprises. For example, most of us would agree that Penn Central Railroad, W. T. Grant, A&P, and Montgomery Ward did not perform well during the 1970s. On the other hand, the performance of IBM and AT&T was outstanding during the same time period.

An obvious criterion of corporate performance is *survival.* W. T. Grant and Penn Central both ceased operating. Beyond survival, however, it is not that easy to identify criteria for successful corporate performance. But we must have some type of criteria to use in judging how an organization is performing.

In this book, we shall use four broad criteria of organizational performance. We present them as the overall objectives they must achieve to insure the ultimate objective of survival. These four criteria are *profitability, competitiveness, efficiency,* and *flexibility.*

Thus, to survive, a firm must be profitable, it must be able to compete, it must use its resources efficiently, and it must be flexible in order to adapt to changes in its internal and external environments. Business firms usually develop specific measures of these criteria. Some popular measures are:

- *Profitability*—return on equity, return on assets.
- *Competitiveness*—percentage growth in sales, market share.
- *Efficiency*—labor cost per unit of output, total cost per unit of output.
- *Flexibility*—employee satisfaction and turnover, investment in employee development, expenditures on research and development for new products.

Since these criteria will be discussed in much detail in the next chapter, it is only necessary at this point that the reader see that these criteria for successful organizational performance are used throughout this book.

We can evaluate organizational performance as good or bad to the degree that measures such as return on investment, market share, and employee turnover improve relative to past performance and/or relative to performance by similar organizations.[8]

Some criteria of organizational performance are objectively measurable, but we must nevertheless use them with caution. There are some important questions associated with the measurement of organizational performance.

1. *How stable is the measure?* A measure used at one point in time may not be as valid at some other point. For example, growth in share of market may be important in a rapidly expanding market but not in a stable or shrinking market.

2. *How precise is the measure?* Not only are many measures difficult to compute but in many instances there is more than one way to arrive at them. For example, employee satisfaction and investment in employee development can be measured in a variety of ways.

3. *How important is time?* It is important to evaluate the measures in the short run and long run. For example, a measure of profitability or competitiveness may appear excellent in the short run but may be jeopardizing employee satisfaction or the condition of plant and equipment in the long run.

Managerial performance

Ideally, managers should strive for consistent results in all four areas of organizational performance. The purpose of managerial performance is to achieve organizational performance. Thus, while there are other influences on performance such as technology and the external environment, we can say that generally speaking, the closer the organization comes to achieving its organizational objectives, the more effective is its managerial performance.

Organizational and managerial performance and the internal and external environments

Figure 2–9 summarizes what we have said in this chapter. It indicates that both the internal and external environments influence the management

[8] *Forbes* magazine, *Fortune* magazine, and *Business Week* magazine evaluate corporate performance in this way. For example, in its January issues, *Forbes* magazine measures managerial performance by combining various financial and marketing indexes and rating every major company both within its own industry and in comparison with industry as a whole. *Business Week* magazine develops similar ratings every quarter, and *Fortune* magazine rates the "Fortune 1000" firms.

Figure 2–9

Managerial and organizational performance and the internal and external environments

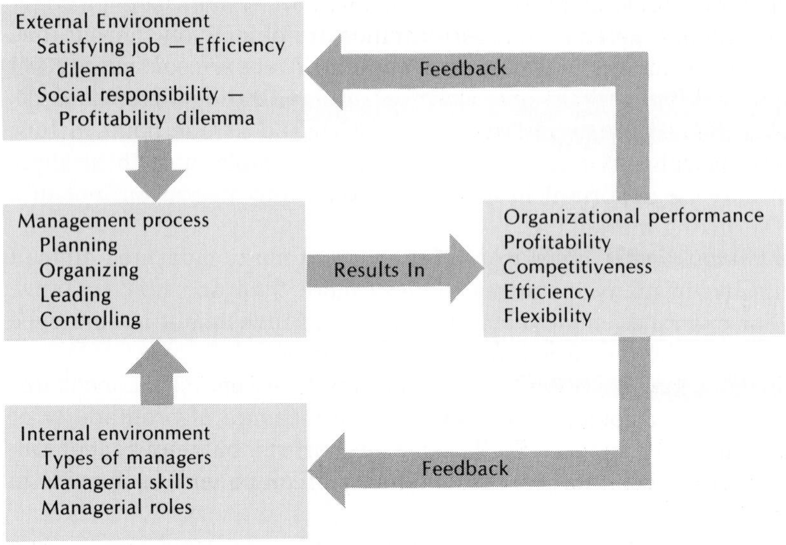

process. The management functions of planning, organizing, leading, and controlling result in organizational performance. The measures of organizational performance used in this book are profitability, competitiveness, efficiency, and flexibility. The results of organizational performance in turn influence the management process through both the internal and external environments.

Review and discussion questions

1. If you were trying to identify top managers at the school you attend, what titles would you look for? Suppose you had to identify them based on what they do, what would you look for?
2. Discuss technical, human, and conceptual skills in relation to a college instructor. What would be a good mix in your opinion, and why?
3. In the previous chapter, we discussed the systems approach and the contingency approach. What managerial skill do you believe would be important to use these approaches? Discuss in detail.
4. Describe an encounter you recently had with a manager. It could be in a business, civic, school, hospital, or government organization. What managerial role or roles do you believe they were performing?

5. Describe the environment your school currently faces. Is it turbulent, hostile, diverse, or technically complex?
6. What do you believe is the primary role of the business corporation in American society? Do you believe this role should change? Why?
7. Discuss briefly the satisfying job-efficiency dilemma and the social responsibility–profitability dilemma faced by managers. Which do you believe will be the most important during the 1980s? Why?
8. Discuss the relationship between managerial performance and organizational performance.

Suggested reading

Allen, F. T. "Corporate Ethics, A View from the Top." *Industry Week,* April 11, 1977, pp. 52–54.

Arlow, P., and M. Gannon. "Social Responsiveness, Corporate Structure, and Economic Performance." *Academy of Management Review,* April 1982, pp. 235–41.

Bucholz, R. A. "Alternative to Social Responsibility." *Business Topics,* Summer 1977, pp. 12–16.

Fry, L. W., G. D. Kein, and R. E. Meiners, "Corporate Contributions: Altruistic or For Profit?" *Academy of Management Journal,* March 1982, pp. 94–106.

Holmes, S. L. "Corporate Social Performance: Past, Present, and Areas of Commitment." *Academy of Management Journal,* September 1977, pp. 433–38.

Ostland, L. E. "Attitudes of Managers toward Corporate Social Responsibility." *California Management Review,* Summer 1977, pp. 35–49.

Saul, G. K. "Business Ethics: Where Are We Going?" *Academy of Management Review,* April 1981, pp. 269–78.

Shorris, E. *The Oppressed Middle: Politics of Middle Management,* New York: Doubleday Inc., 1981.

Part II
The planning function

3. Elements of planning
4. Planning as decision making
5. Planning through strategic analysis
6. Planning through management by objectives

A management profile
Lee Iacocca

He may be president of Chrysler these days, but Lido Anthony "Lee" Iacocca knew from the start that there was a Ford in his future. The man who gave us the Mustang, the Maverick, the Pinto, and the Fiesta grew up in the industrial environs of Allentown, Pennsylvania. After graduating from Lehigh University and Princeton, he immediately joined up with the Ford organization.

He sold cars in Philadelphia and in Washington, D.C., attracting the attention of Ford higher-ups by painting stripes on some models to boost sales during an otherwise sluggish year. When Iacocca left the sales floor for Detroit, he became in quick succession truck marketing manager, car marketing manager, vehicle marketing manager, and vice president and general manager of the Ford division. It was as Ford general manager that he introduced what *Dun's Review* called "possibly the most successful new product in modern industrial history"—the Mustang. The introduction was based on strategic planning and confident decision making. Without sound planning and decision making in a situation involving risk, Iacocca's success story would not have been possible.

Riding the crest of the Mustang's success, at age 40 Iacocca was made vice president of the corporation's car and truck group and elected to the board of directors. He built a reputation as a tough, hard-nosed executive who like to say to his subordinates, "Get with it, you're being observed." He was the first Ford vice president to show an interest in the youth market, and he was instrumental in entering Fords on the racing circuit.

After 25 years with the company, Iacocca was tapped by Henry Ford II to be president of Ford. By the time he reached the company's number two slot, Iacocca had become the auto industry's most outspoken executive. His opinions about labor, materials, government regulation, and multinational business were well known in American industry.

In 1978, he abruptly left the company over a policy dispute with Henry Ford II. Just as abruptly, he was snapped up by the ailing Chrysler Corporation to be its chief executive. Industry analysts aren't sure what will happen at Chrysler, but most agree that if anyone can turn the company around, Iacocca will do it because in his career he has gained the reputation of being an astute planner.

This section of the book is about planning and decision making. The principles presented helped Lee Iacocca become a successful manager. However, it is not the principles themselves that explain his success, but how he used them to accomplish organizational objectives such as profitability, competitiveness, efficiency, and flexibility.

Courtesy of Chrysler Corporation

Source: Elizabeth J. Kenny for P. S. Associates, Inc., Sterling, Massachusetts.

Introduction to Part II

Part II, The planning function, contains four chapters. They are:

Chapter 3—Elements of planning
Chapter 4—Planning as decision making
Chapter 5—Planning through strategic analysis
Chapter 6—Planning through management by objectives

The inclusion of the material contained in the four chapters is based upon the following rationale:

The planning function involves managers in activities which lead to the identification of objectives and the determination of strategies to achieve those objectives. Planning has become increasingly important as organizations and their environments have become more complex. Chapter 3 describes the **five elements that are present in any form of planning.**

Chapter 4 presents **planning in the context of decision making.** The material in this chapter presents several perspectives on decision making, including the relationship between managerial levels and types of decisions made at each level and the relationship between degree of uncertainty and decision criteria. The planning function requires *choices* of objectives and decisions. Decision making is, therefore, an inherent feature of planning.

Chapters 5 and 6 describe two planning approaches—**strategic analysis and management by objectives (MBO).** Although the two approaches are presented separately, managers can combine them into a single integrated system. Strategic analysis focuses on the organization's environment and the appropriate responses (strategies) to changes, constraints, and opportunities in that environment. Thus, strategic analysis is an externally oriented planning approach. MBO focuses on developing objectives for individuals and units and integrating those objectives into a coherent whole. MBO, then, is an internally oriented planning approach.

The figure below depicts the four aspects of the planning function.

The planning function

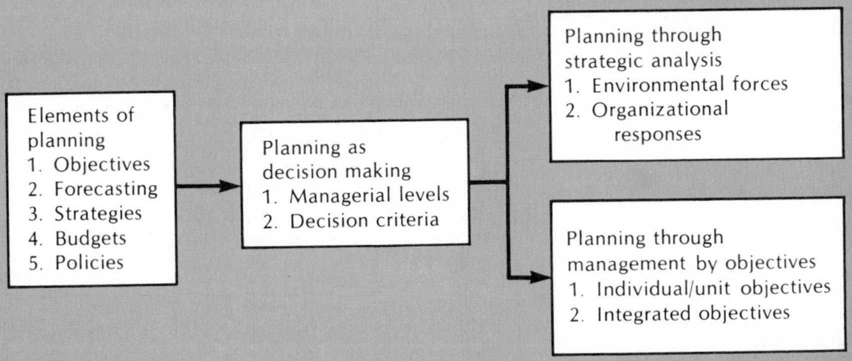

3

Chapter three Elements of planning

Performance objectives

- **Define** each element in the planning process.
- **State** the factors which contribute to the necessity for planning.
- **Describe** the relationship between objectives and strategies.
- **Explain** why forecasting is a key element of the planning process.
- **Discuss** the primary purposes served by policies.

Management update*

Planning involves the commitment of company resources to future courses of action. Managers must make these commitments, and they do so in response to pressures and expectations of various groups which have vested interests in the company's activities. Stockholders constitute a significant group which influences management's strategic planning decisions.

In recent years, American business firms have lost their competitive strength in the world markets. According to Akio Morita, president of the Sony Corporation, managers and stockholders share the blame for this decline. Morita states that "The short-term orientation of U.S. managers and shareholders has discouraged investment in technology and equipment that would have allowed the United States to keep pace with Europe and Japan."

Studies by Arthur D. Little, a prominent management consulting firm, support the idea that the decline of American productivity in relation to other countries is due to differences in investment in technology, plant, and equipment and not to differences in workers' individual productivity. That is to say that the average Japanese worker is more productive than the average American worker because he or she works with better and more up-to-date equipment than does the American. So why do American managers not make the investments in technology that would restore American productivity and competitiveness?

Part of the answer, according to the Little Company, is that contemporary American business incentive systems reward for short-term performance-profit and profitability—rather than long-term competitiveness—productivity. To obtain long-term gains in productivity would require American managers to make strategic investments in research and development which could take years to pay off in profits. But American managers are typically paid according to short-run profits, not long-term competitiveness. Thus, to encourage investment in courses of action which would restore American businesses' competitive edge will require changing the way managers are rewarded.

---

* This Management Update is adapted from Anthony J. Marolda, "Pressure on Managers for Short-Term Results Causing Poor Decisions," *Management Review,* March 1981, pp. 29–30.

Planning is without question the keystone management function. The functions of organizing, leading, and controlling carry out the decisions of planning. The increased emphasis on planning can be readily seen by the great number of executive conferences, workshops, and writings on the subject during the last five years.

Although some organizations operate in more uncertain environments than others, the fact is that *all* organizations operate in uncertain environments. If an organization is to succeed, management must somehow cope with, and adapt to, change and uncertainty. Planning is the *only* tool that management has to help it adapt to change. What this means is that if an organization does no planning, where that organization is in five years will be the result of any momentum built up previously and of luck (hopefully, good). The organization will follow some course during the next five years, and if management wishes to have any control over that course, then it *must* plan. Otherwise, it must rely on defensive reactions rather than on planned actions, responding to current pressures rather than long-run needs. This reality has been well stated by the president of a large manufacturer of business products:

> *Planning is for everyone who wants to survive. Without it, you're open to some rude surprises.*

Contrast this with the observation of a retail fashion buyer:

> *Everyone talks about planning, but who does anything about it?*

During the last decade, many managers have stopped talking about planning and started doing something about it.

In one way or another, every manager plans. However, it is the approach or manner of arriving at plans and the completeness of plans that differ from organization to organization. Formal planning (as distinguished from the informal planning that we do in thinking through proposed actions prior to their execution) is an activity that distinguishes managers from nonmanagers. In addition, it has become clear that it also distinguishes effective managers from ineffective ones. An executive of a plastics manufacturer offered this opinion:

> *I believe in planning. It's part of the whole way you view the job of a manager. There are those of us who make things happen and those who let things happen. I like to think that those of us who believe in planning are in the first group.*

An important requirement for one who aspires to manage effectively the performance of individuals and organizations is to understand the concept of, and the necessity for, planning. When one hears a manager say that planning is an important function of management, nothing is revealed about the nature of the activity; this statement merely tells us who does the planning. Planning is that part of the management process which attempts to define the organization's future. More formally, **planning includes all the activities that lead to the definition of objectives and to the determination of appropriate strategies to achieve those objectives.**

In order to justify the time and resources expended in planning, some distinct benefits must accrue to the planner. The following have been suggested:

- Forces managers to think ahead.
- Leads to the development of performance standards which enable more effective management control.
- Forces management to articulate clear objectives.
- Enables better preparedness for sudden developments.

The above are general benefits. More direct benefits can also result in specific situations. One manager commented:

> *I need the time devoted to planning. It makes me focus my attention away from everyday fire-fighting activities and onto larger, more important issues.*

Understanding the need for planning

Probably the most important prerequisite to developing a sound plan at any level of the organization is understanding and appreciating the necessity for planning. If a manager does not believe in the value of planning (and some managers do not), then there is little likelihood that a useful plan will ever be developed. To appreciate the need for planning, a manager need only consider the four important factors that underscore the necessity for planning.

The increasing time spans between present decisions and future results

The time span that separates the beginning of a project from its completion is increasing in most organizations. Managers must look farther into the future than ever before. For example, it took 10 years to develop the supersonic jet and 10 years for General Foods to develop Maxim (concentrated instant coffee), whereas the Campbell Soup Company spent 20 years in developing its line of dry soup mixes and Hill Brothers spent 22 years in developing its instant coffee.

Obviously, planning is critical in situations in which the results of decisions occur long after the decisions are made. In order to develop plans, managers must attempt to see what could happen that might affect the outcome. With large time and monetary commitments, management must seek every way possible to minimize uncertainty and its consequences. Planning is the only tool that managers have to help them cope with change. An airline executive stated clearly the issue of time spans between decisions and results:

> *We make decisions today which will influence the performance of this airline when I'm dead. You don't commit huge sums of money to new equipment, to seeking new routes, or to planning future routes without some overall plan. If you do, you'll be turning over in your grave.*

Increasing organizational complexity

As organizations become larger and more complex, the managerial job becomes increasingly complex because of the interdependence among the various parts of the organization. It is virtually impossible to find an organization (or even a division of a large organization) in which the decisions of the various functions, such as research and development, production, finance, and marketing, can be made independently of one another. The more products an organization has and the more markets it operates in, the greater is the volume of its decisions. Planning in these situations is necessary for survival. A hospital administrator commented:

> *I'll even make it simple for you. Let's just take four of the groups I deal with every day—anesthesiologists, nurses, technicians, and physicians. I cannot think of a decision I could make with respect to one of these groups that wouldn't also affect the other three.*

Consider the midwestern bank that has over 175 services just for consumers (not business customers). In these and similar firms, planning is vital to enable each unit in the organization to know the job that needs to be done and the way to go about doing it. With such a blueprint of the stated objectives, there is less likelihood of changes in direction, costly improvising, or engaging in the wrong activities.

Increased external change

A principal managerial responsibility has always been that of change initiator, innovator, doer, in continuous search for new markets, businesses, and expanded missions. Rapid rates of change in the external environment will force managers at all levels to focus on larger issues rather than solely on solving internal problems. The faster the pace of change becomes, the greater will be the necessity for organized responses at all levels in the organization. Organized responses are the results of well-thought-out plans. The young president of a bank made the following comment:

> *In the next 10 years, I see three groups of banks emerging—those that innovate, those that imitate the innovators, and those that are left behind. I'm willing to bet that there will be very little planning done by the last group during that time.*

Planning and other management functions

The need for planning is also illustrated by the relationship between planning and the other management functions. We already know that planning is the beginning of the management process. Before a manager can organize, lead, or control, there must be a plan. Otherwise, there is no purpose or direction to any of these activities. It is clearly defined objectives and well-developed strategies that set the other management functions into motion.

The important relationship between planning and the other management functions can be clearly illustrated by using the function of control. Once a plan has been translated from good intentions into actions, its important relationship to control becomes obvious. With the passage of time and as the organization engages in its activities, managers can compare actual results with the planned results. This comparison may lead to corrective action, and this, as we shall see later in the book, is the essence of controlling.

Elements of planning

Planning is advance thinking as the basis for doing. It involves determining what needs to be done, how it will be done, and whether, in fact, it was done. The planning process involves at least five elements as follows:

1. Establish objectives to be achieved by the unit.
2. Analyze the factors in the environment that could help or hinder the unit from achieving its objectives. This involves the activity of *forecasting.*
3. Develop a set of actions (strategies and programs) for achieving the objectives, evaluate these alternative courses of action, and select among them.
4. Develop budgets.
5. Establish policies.

Let us examine each phase.

Objectives

Perhaps the most important element of planning is establishing objectives. Objectives determine the direction that the organization will take and the activities to which it will devote human and financial resources. The Management Update indicates the importance of objectives as factors to explain the decline of America's industrial productivity. In fact, **objectives are quantitative and qualitative commitments to action which contribute to the achievement of the organization's larger social purposes.**

One important purpose of objectives is to translate the organization's broad social purposes into workable terms. **Objectives** serve as guides for action and as starting points for more specific and detailed objectives at lower levels in the organization. Well-managed business organizations have at least four categories of objectives: **profitability, competitiveness, efficiency,** and **flexibility.**

1. Profitability In business organizations, profitability is unquestionably the single most important objective. Profitability is necessary to provide the financial resources for future expansion or innovation. The profitability objective is usually expressed in terms of return on investment—net profit divided by the capital invested in the organization. Every profit-seeking organization should establish a profitability objective. Remember that besides competing for customers for their products, business firms must also compete for resources (particularly capital). An organization's earnings provide the return on investment, and it is for the sake of this return on investment that a shareholder is willing to supply capital. To compete successfully for this resource, it is usually necessary to earn a return equivalent to the risk of doing business.

2. Competitiveness This objective focuses on the prospects for long-term profitability. It measures the competitive strength of the organization. What is the difference between competitive strength and profitability as stated above? Consider this analogy. Assume that your present normal blood pressure indicates that you are healthy (profitable) today. Assume further that your objective is to remain healthy six months from now. To insure your accomplishments of this profitability objective, you must establish objectives in other areas today (exercise, weight control, proper diet, etc.). Measuring how well you are doing in these other areas will provide you with some idea of your "competitive strength." Each of these areas is an indicator of how profitable you are likely to be in the long run.

Thus, well-managed organizations establish objectives which concentrate on specific rates of increase in sales and market share. If the economy is expanding at a certain rate, then sales growth objectives should be considerably greater than this percentage.

It should be clear that measuring performance in competitive strength is different from measuring performance in profitability. It is entirely possible for an organization to have been profitable in the past but, based on performance in the competitiveness measures, to have poor prospects for long-run profitability.

3. Efficiency To bring about the prospect of long-run profitability, an organization must maintain certain types of short-run efficiencies. Measures of efficiency reflect how well the organization's resources are employed. Thus, a ratio such as return on assets (net profit divided by total assets) when compared to that of similar organizations gives management some indication of how efficient the organization is internally.

A final concern relating to efficiency which has a direct influence on performance involves the human and nonhuman resources of the organization. Well-managed organizations, regardless of size, establish objectives with respect to the quality of management, the succession of management, the depth of critical personnel, and employee turnover. Nonhuman resources such as the age and the condition of the plant and the equipment are also important indications of efficiency. Objectives should therefore also be established in these areas. The importance of establishing objectives in these areas is reflected clearly in the following account from an executive with a warehouse equipment manufacturer.

> *The major growth in our organization took place after World War II. It was during the next decade that most of our dealerships were established throughout the*

country. Now, all of a sudden, the majority of our dealers are about to retire or have lost considerable interest in improving performance. Some others are getting older, making substantial incomes, and would rather play golf than worry about doing more business. I can't say I blame them either. However, management never thought about succession with respect to the management of our dealerships. We never planned for it, and now we're facing a real problem: Where are all of the qualified people who will be needed in the next 10 years to come from?

4. Flexibility We noted earlier that managers plan, not to predict the future, but to uncover important factors in the present in order to insure that there is a future. One way in which managers guard against unforeseen problems is to maintain certain types of flexibilities. For example, a manufacturer of consumer products operating in a volatile market has a flexibility objective which states the maximum percentage of sales that can be derived from a single product. If this percentage is reached, the firm attempts to introduce a new product. Thus, if customers suddenly change their minds about any one of the organization's products and stop purchasing it, the impact on profitability will be minimized. Another organization allows only a certain percentage of sales to be derived from government contracts. This practice insures that the organization maintains its flexibility and does not become dependent on government contracts. A manufacturing executive emphasized this point when he stated:

I tell all my people to make sure we don't get dependent on any other organization, whether it be for income or for supplies. When you start depending on a few good customers or a few suppliers, you at that point become vulnerable.

Figure 3–1 provides a few examples of some objectives for a manufacturing organization. Note that the statements specify the end points of the organization's purpose and the results that it seeks. Note that these outcomes include not only the organization's desired results with respect to customers and other external parties but also the results that it hopes to accomplish internally.

The objectives in Figure 3–1 are also *action commitments* on the part of the organization. They are all capable of being converted into specific targets and actions at lower levels in the organization. They also indicate that a well-managed organization must be *profitable, competitive, efficient,* and *flexible.*

Figure 3–1

Examples of organizational objectives for a manufacturing firm

Profitability	To achieve an annual rate of return on investment of at least 15 percent per year.
Competitiveness	To make our brands number one in their field in terms of market share.
	To be a leader in introducing new products by spending no less than 7 percent of sales for research and development.
Efficiency	To manufacture all products efficiently as measured by the productivity of the work force.
	To protect and maintain all resources—equipment, buildings, inventory, and funds.
	To identify critical areas of management depth and succession.
	To maintain timely and appropriate quality responses to customer needs.
Flexibility	To derive a maximum of 40 percent of sales and/or profits from one product or market segment.
	To consistently develop and deliver new products.
	To respond appropriately to environmentally induced changes.

Forecasting

A critical element in planning is forecasting the future. The two basic issues that must be resolved through forecasting are (1) What level of activity can be expected during the planning period and (2) what level of resources will be available to support the projected activity? In a business organization, the critical forecast on which all others depend is the sales forecast.

Sales forecasts The projected sales volume of the firm's product or service provides the basis for all other activities. The sales estimate sets the level of production and determines the level and timing of the financial resources required to meet the sales volume. Because the sales forecast is so fundamental, we will discuss the methods of forecasting in the context of the sales forecast.

Forecasting is the process of using past and current information to predict future events. There are four widely used forecasting methods, each of which requires its own type of data. These methods range in degree of sophistication from the hunches of experienced managers to econometric models.

1. *Hunches* are estimates of future events that are based on past sales data, on comments by salespeople and customers, and on reactions to

the general state of affairs. The hunch approach is relatively cheap, and it is usually effective in firms whose market is stable or at least is changing at a predictable rate.

2. *Market surveys of customer intentions* provided by the customer or by salespeople in the field can improve the accuracy of sales forecasts. At least, through statistical sampling techniques, the forecaster can specify the range of projected sales and the degree of confidence that he or she has in the estimates. Of course, one should be very careful to evaluate the reliability of the information that goes into the market survey.

3. *Time-series analysis,* a third technique of forecasting, is a fairly complex statistical device, yet is no more effective than the good judgment of the analyst. It involves nothing more than analysis of the relationship between sales and time, as shown in Figure 3–2. The chart shows points corresponding to the annual sales for each of the years. A straight line is drawn through the points to show that there has been an upward pattern in the sales of the firm during the period.

The short-run question of sales during the first quarter of 1983 cannot be answered from Figure 3–2 if there is seasonality in the firm's sales pattern. If such were not the case, the quarterly sales would be approximately one fourth of the annual sales, but the sales of most firms are seasonal. If a company markets fishing equipment, demand is highest during the spring and summer months, declining to quite low levels during the fall and winter. The prediction of annual sales can be attempted from the annual data, provided one is willing to make the assumption that condi-

Figure 3–2

Sales-time relationship

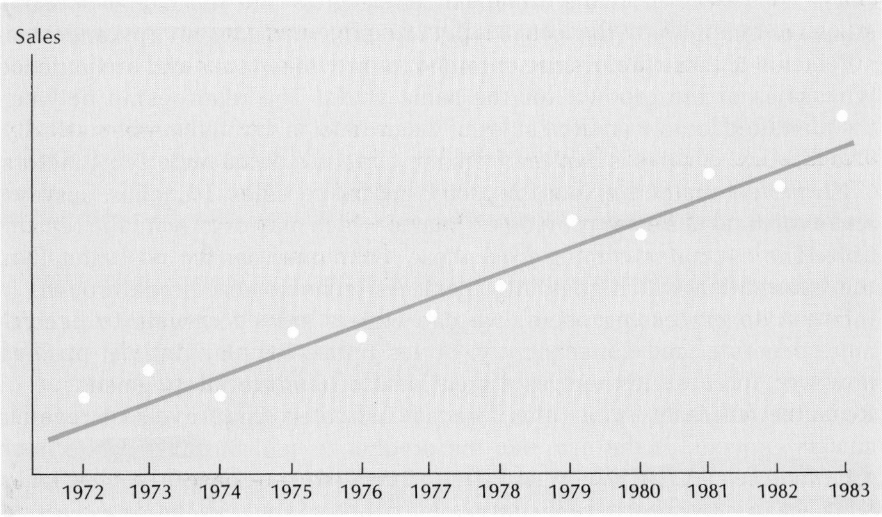

tions which contributed to previous sales levels will prevail in the future. If not, the forecast must include variables other than time in the analysis.

The reader should not be led to believe that time-series analysis is simply the naive projection of the historical trend. In the hands of the unskilled, it may be, but if skilled analysts are supplied with the right information they can confront a whole range of questions. The movement of sales over time is affected by at least three factors: seasonal, cyclical, and trend; that is, the firm's sales may vary in response to seasonal factors, in response to cycles common to business activity generally, and in response to a trend of long duration. The management of a brewery knows that peak sales occur during the summer months, but it is also aware of the cyclical nature of beer consumption, as beer drinkers shift to liquor when their incomes increase and shift back to beer when their incomes decline. For long-term planning, the management must also know something about the trend in beer consumption—consumer tastes change with time and with the introduction of new products. Yet even the availability of these refinements does not undo the fact that time is the only determinant of sales that is included in the time-series analysis. Econometric models are means for more systematically evaluating the impact of a number of variables on sales.

4. *Econometric models* are applications of statistical techniques to economic analysis. They permit the forecaster to discover the historical relationship between sales and a number of other variables. Econometric models are the most sophisticated of the forecasting methods, yet they offer no hope for the elimination of all uncertainty; management judgment is still needed.

The econometric approach begins with identification of the factors and forces which affect the sales of the firm's product. Among the factors are price, competing products, complementary products, the age of existing stocks of the product, the availability of credit, and consumer tastes. Measurements of these factors are obtained for previous years and are matched with sales of the product for the same years. The relationship between the identified factors and the sales of the product is derived mathematically. The *forecast* of sales is derived from the *forecasts* of the underlying factors.

No perfect method exists for projecting future sales. Hunches, surveys, and statistical analyses provide estimates which may or may not be reasonable. The estimates coming from these techniques can be no better than the information which goes into them. As technological breakthroughs in information processing occur, we can expect sales forecasts to become more accurate, and consequently, better guides for planning. At present, however, forecasting requires a great deal of managerial judgment.

Resource forecasts The sales forecast indicates what levels of revenue can be expected if the firm has the product to sell. But in order to have a product to sell, the firm must have the necessary resources. Accordingly, it is necessary to forecast the future availability of such resources as personnel, raw materials, and capital. The techniques for forecasting resources are the same as those employed to forecast sales—that is, hunches, market surveys, time-series analysis, and econometric models. The only difference is that the planner is seeking to know the quantities which can be purchased rather than the quantities which can be sold.

The energy shortage of the 1970s has brought into sharp focus the necessity for resource forecasting. The effects of the shortage were real at every level of the economy, and the early warning signals had apparently gone unheeded. Yet, when it became apparent that energy resources would not be available in the expected quantities, managers could respond only reactively. More astute planning would not necessarily have prevented an energy shortage, but it would have enabled managers to respond in more orderly ways.

Thus, the sales forecast, whether for 1 year or 10 years, is a prediction of the firm's level of activity. At the same time, the prediction is conditioned by the availability of resources, by general economic and social events beyond the control of management, and by the predetermined objectives.

Strategies

The elements of strategy formulation focus on the ways and means to achieve the established objectives, given the sales and resource forecasts. In some areas of the organization, such formulations are referred to as *strategies,* whereas in other areas they are referred to as *programs.* For consistency we shall use the term **strategy.**

It is important to note that every objective must have at least one strategy. All this means is that management should have at least one stated course of action to accomplish every objective. Also, every strategy must be associated with at least one objective. Otherwise, management will be engaging in a course of action for which it does not have a predetermined purpose (objective). A marketing executive described this problem:

> *You would be surprised how many activities you can engage in that look and sound good, but if you don't have any specific objectives, you don't really know why you are engaging in them. In my department, anyone who suggests changing our advertising theme or introducing a new promotion had better relate it to some objective we have established. We do not do anything unless it has a prestated purpose.*

Figure 3–3 illustrates this relationship between objectives and strategies. The figure is not meant to be exhaustive or to illustrate effective strategies. Its purpose is to illustrate the relationship between courses of action (strategies) and hoped-for results (objectives).

Figure 3–3

Objectives and some possible strategies

	Objective	Possible strategies
Production	To produce the most maintenance-free product on the market.	1. Install new stamping machine by January 1. 2. Reevaluate quality control program.
Personnel	To evaluate the managerial potential and the training needs of middle managers by year-end.	1. Conduct a merit review of all middle managers. 2. Evaluate available university executive programs for continuing executive development.
Marketing	To increase the purchase rate by existing buyers of Brand X 10 percent by year-end.	1. Increase the unit of purchase (e.g., larger sizes, 8- and 12-packs). 2. Make product more widely and conveniently available.
Finance	To reduce overdue accounts receivable to five months or less by year-end.	1. Hire part-time college students to analyze all accounts receivable and identify those which are overdue by more than five months.

Budgeting

The next element of managerial planning is the development of budgets for each important element of the organization. Budgets are widely used in business and government. A considerable body of literature deals with budgeting techniques. We should recognize the very close relationship between budgeting as a planning technique and budgeting as a control technique.

In this section, we are concerned only with the preparation of budgets prior to operations. From this perspective, budgeting is a part of planning. However, with the passage of time and as the organization engages in its activities, the actual results are compared with the budgeted (planned) results.

The process of implementing the firm's profitability and efficiency objectives and of integrating the activities of the firm's various subunits is financial budgeting. Budgeting can be viewed as an important method for coordinating the efforts of the organization.

The complexity of the financial budgeting process is simplified in Figure 3–4. The key position of the sales forecast is evident from the placement of the sales budget; all other budgets are directly or indirectly related to the sales budget. For example, the production budget must specify the materials, labor, and other manufacturing expenses that are required to support the projected sales level. Similarly, the marketing budget details the costs associated with the level of sales activity that is projected for each product in each sales region. Administrative expenses must also be related to the predicted sales volume. Finally, the projected sales and expenses are combined in the financial budget, which consists of pro forma financial statements.

The usefulness of financial budgets depends mainly on the degree to which they are adaptable to changes in conditions. The forecast data are based on certain assumptions regarding the future. If these assumptions

Figure 3–4

The financial budgeting process

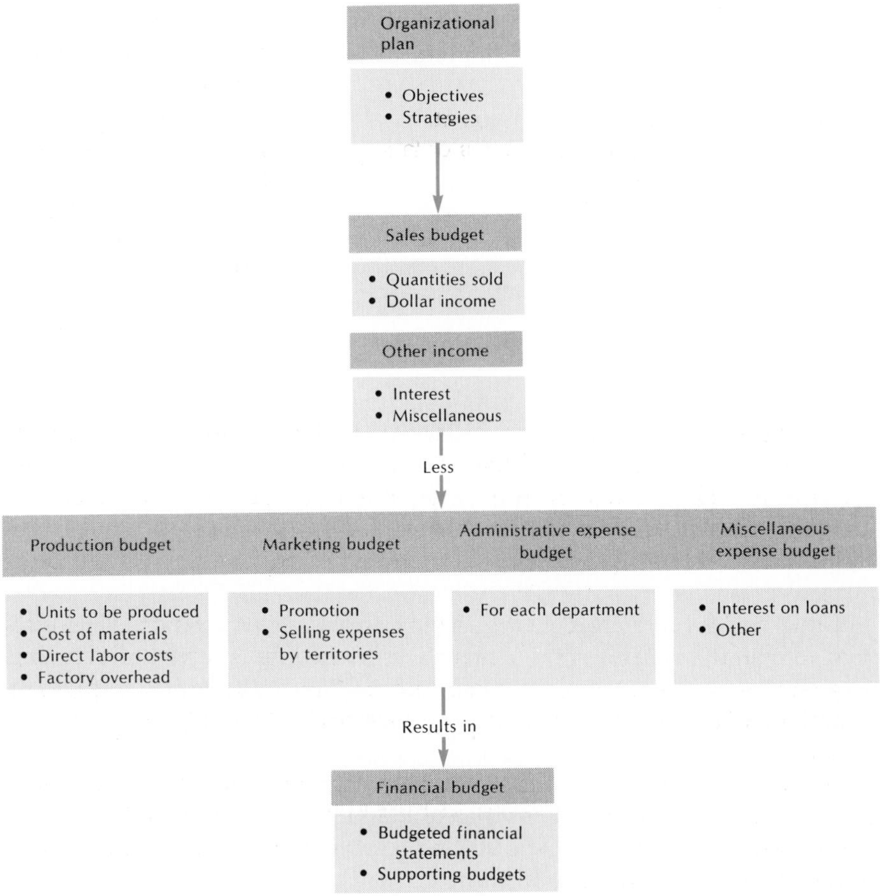

prove wrong, the budgets are inadequate. Two principal means exist to provide budgetary flexibility—variable budgeting and moving budgeting.

1. *Variable budgeting* provides for the possibility that actual output deviates from planned output. It recognizes that certain costs are related to output (variable costs), whereas others are unrelated to output (fixed costs). Thus, if actual output is 20 percent less than planned output, it does not follow that actual profit will be 20 percent less than planned profit. Rather, the actual profit will vary, depending on the relationship between costs and output. Figure 3–5 demonstrates a hypothetical situation.

The relationships shown in Figure 3–5 take the form of the familiar breakeven model. The point to be made here is simply that profit varies with output variations, but not proportionately. Table 3–1 shows a variable budget that allows for output variations and demonstrates the behavior of costs and profits as output varies.

Variable budgeting requires adjustments in all supporting budgets for completeness. The production, marketing, and administrative expense budgets must likewise allow for the impact of output variation.

2. *Moving budgeting* is the preparation of a budget for a fixed period, perhaps one year, with updating at fixed intervals, such as each month. For example, the budget is prepared in December for the next 12 months, January through December. At the end of January, the budget is revised

Figure 3–5

The relationship between profit and output

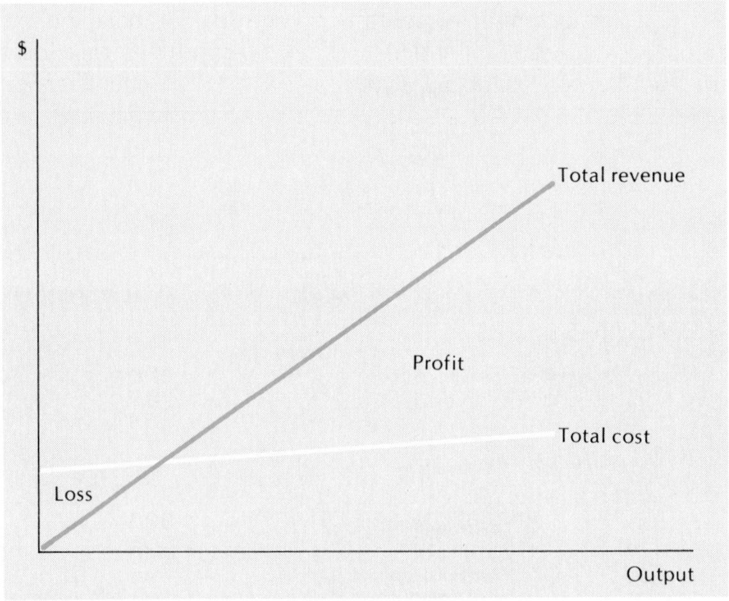

and projected for the next 12 months, February through January. In this manner, the most recent information is included in the budgeting process. Assumptions are constantly being revised as management learns from experience.

Moving budgets have the advantage of systematic reexamination, but the disadvantage of being costly to maintain. Budgets are important instruments for implementing the objectives of the firm. However, the efforts given to them must be kept in perspective and must be viewed as competing with other demands on managerial time.

Policies

Policies are guidelines for managerial action which implement objective-oriented strategies. Policies, like plans, are both specific and general, abstract and concrete, short run and long run.

Policymaking is an important planning element for insuring that action is oriented toward objectives. Policies explain *how* the objectives are to be achieved, and as such, policies direct the behavior of persons in the organization. The interrelations among the managerial functions are reflected in the nature of policies.

Policy statements are developed to achieve *consistency* and *direction* and to *protect the reputation of the organization.* Colleges have policies regarding the grade average and the number of credit hours that are necessary to graduate. These policies insure that advisers and decision makers in all departments obtain direction and that all students, regardless of major, attain a certain level of achievement before being graduated. Thus, it is hoped that consistency of output will be obtained. Similarly, business organizations have product policies relating to quality, financial policies relating to discounts for early payment of bills, and policies relating to returned goods. In all cases, these organizations attempt to achieve consistency, to provide direction for decision makers, and to protect their reputations.

Table 3–1

A hypothetical variable budget

Output (units)		1,000		1,200		1,400		1,600
Sales @ $5.00		$5,000		$6,000		$7,000		$8,000
Variable costs @ $3.00	$3,000		$3,600		$4,200		$4,800	
Fixed costs	1,000		1,000		1,000		1,000	
Total costs		4,000		4,600		5,200		5,800
Planned profit		$1,000		$1,400		$1,800		$2,200

Effective policymaking requires recognition of the many sides and characteristics of policies. The following are some important criteria of effective policies:

1. Flexibility A policy must strike a reasonable balance between stability and flexibility. Conditions change, and policies must change accordingly. On the other hand, some degree of stability must prevail if order and a sense of direction are to be achieved. There are no rigid guidelines for determining the exact degree of flexibility that is required; only the judgment of management can determine the proper balance.

2. Comprehensiveness A policy must be comprehensive enough to cover any contingency if plans are to be followed. The degree of comprehensiveness depends on the scope of the actions that are to be controlled by the policy. A policy that is directed toward very narrow ranges of activity—for example, hiring—need not be as comprehensive as a policy that is concerned with public relations.

3. Coordinative A policy must provide for coordination of the various subunits whose actions are interrelated. Without the coordinative direction that policies provide, each subunit will be tempted to pursue its own objectives. The ultimate test of any subunit's activity should be its relationship to the policy statement.

4. Ethical A policy must conform to the canons of ethical behavior which prevail in society. The manager is ultimately responsible for the resolution of issues which involve ethical principles. The increasingly complex and interdependent nature of contemporary society has resulted in a great number of problems involving ethical dimensions which are only vaguely understood.

5. Clarity A policy must be written clearly and logically. It must specify the intended aim of the actions it governs, define the appropriate methods, and delineate the limits of the actions that are permitted to those whose behavior is to be guided by the policy.

The ultimate test of the effectiveness of a policy is whether the intended objective is attained. If the policy does not lead to the objective, it should be revised. Thus, policies must be subjected to reexamination on a continual basis. Some examples of policies which an organization might adopt and which are consistent with the above criteria are:

1. A grocery chain's giving store managers authority to buy fresh produce locally rather than from a company warehouse whenever they can get a better buy in this way.
2. An oil company's deciding to lease properties and buidings for its service station operations so as to minimize long-term capital requirements.
3. A firm's practice of requiring each of its product divisions to file weekly sales and profit reports with headquarters as a means of monitoring and evaluating progress toward corporate goals.

4. A hospital's requiring all patients to make a $100 cash deposit upon being admitted, as part of its plan for maintaining financial solvency.

The planning function consists of five distinct but interrelated elements: *objective setting, forecasting, strategy development, budgeting,* and *policy-making* as summarized in Figure 3–6. We have not tried to state specific time periods for plans. A bank might consider a long-term loan as one for over five years and a short-term loan as one for under one year. Some individuals apply the same logic to planning. Admittedly, the logic is convenient. However, in actual practice, it does not stand up. A long-run plan in the aircraft or automobile business could extend to more than five years, but in the volatile world of women's fashion a long-run plan might extend to only one or two years. In the children's toy business, a production or marketing plan might cover only one selling season. In other words, the organization's product, technology, and market will dictate what long-term and short-term plans are. Here we see the contingency nature of managerial planning. The point to remember, however, is that regardless of the time spans, all organizations need planning.

Figure 3–6

The elements of the planning process

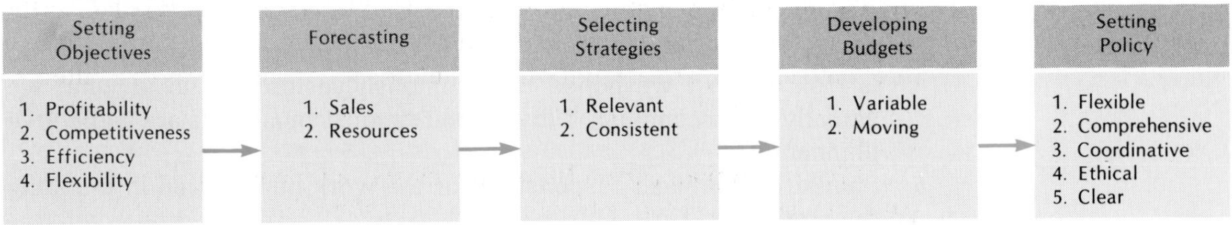

Management summary

1. The necessity for planning has increased because of the increasing time span between present decisions and future results, increased organizational complexity and external change, and the increased importance of the relationship between planning and the other management functions.
2. Effective managers are involved in planning.
3. The planning process consists of five distinct phases: objective setting, forecasting, strategy formulation, budgeting, and policymaking.
4. Objectives are quantitative and qualitative commitments to action which contribute to the achievement of the organization's larger social purposes.

5. Strategies define courses of action, or what will be done.
6. Every objective must have at least one strategy. If not, then the manager has a stated objective without a stated course of action to achieve it.
7. Every strategy must be associated with at least one objective. Otherwise, the manager will be engaging in a course of action for which there is no predetermined purpose (objective).
8. Policies are guidelines for managerial action that must be adhered to at all times. Their purpose is to achieve consistency, to provide direction for decision makers, and to protect the reputation of the organization.
9. An effective policy statement should be flexible, comprehensive, coordinative, ethical, and clear.

Review and discussion questions

1. What is the relationship between the organization's broad purposes and the objectives which are part of its various plans?
2. Why is it desirable that an objective be specific and measurable?
3. Give an example of a "bad" statement of an objective. Point out why the statement is bad and then reword it to eliminate its defects.
4. Most of us are not good planners. To realize this, all we need to do is look at what we hoped to accomplish yesterday and at what we actually did accomplish. Why do you suppose most of us are ineffective planners?
5. Should the manager responsible for the work be involved in planning the work? Explain?
6. What are some of your instructor's policies in your management class? Why do you think they have been established?
7. Consult your school's catalog. Select any school policy statement and evaluate it, based on the criteria for a good policy statement discussed in the chapter. What is your evaluation?
8. What skills do you believe an individual should have to be an effective planner? How do you believe those skills can be acquired?

Suggested reading

Allen, L. A. "Managerial Planning: Back to the Basics." *Management Review,* April 1981, pp. 15–20.

Christopher, W. F. "Is the Annual Planning Cycle Really Necessary?" *Management Review,* August 1981, pp. 38–42.

Luksus, E. J. "Strategic Budgeting: How to Turn Financial Records into a Strategic Asset." *Management Review,* March 1981, pp. 57–61.

Robinson, R. B. "The Importance of 'Outsiders' in Small Firm Strategic Planning." *Academy of Management Journal,* March 1982, pp. 80–93.

Shirley, R. C. "Limiting the Scope of Strategy: A Decision Based Approach." *Academy of Management Review,* April 1982, pp. 262–68.

Tavernier, G. "Using Employee Communications to Support Corporate Objectives." *Management Review,* November 1980, pp. 8–13.

Applying what you have learned about elements of planning

Cases:

Planning problems at Exxon Enterprises
Defending the need for planning

Planning problems at Exxon Enterprises*

About 10 years ago, Exxon Corporation, the oil giant, decided to enter the office automation/information processing business through a subsidiary, Exxon Enterprises. In 1980, it declared its intention to take on the industry leaders, IBM and Xerox, in the rapidly growing market for office systems.

Apparently, the company is now rethinking its plan for becoming a dominant force in office automation. The reason is that it is losing money at a rate that would bankrupt almost any other manufacturer of office systems. For example, in 1980, the Information Systems Group lost $150 million on sales of $270 million. These losses continued in 1981 with none of the 15 companies which comprise Exxon Enterprises operating at a profit.

However, in spite of these losses, many people still believe that Exxon Enterprises can become a dominant force in office systems. They believe that the oil company's vast financial resources will allow it to absorb the losses for as long as it wishes if it so wishes. The $150 million loss in office products does not appear so terrible when compared to Exxon's net income of $5.7 billion in 1980. One Wall Street analyst stated, "It's more of an embarrassment than anything else."

One of the reasons cited for Exxon's problems is its managerial planning. Specifically, this means combining oil industry planning procedures with that which is required in the fast-paced information processing business. A former senior planner for Exxon Enterprises described the

* This case is adapted from "What's Wrong at Exxon Enterprises," *Business Week,* August 24, 1981, pp. 87–90.

atmosphere at the New York headquarters as "total chaos." He stated, "I was shocked and surprised at the immaturity of the planning process. They use no sophisticated tools." Others noted that efforts to carry out the planning process have been stifled by red tape and bureaucracy.

In the end, many industry analysts believe that Exxon Enterprises has missed too many excellent opportunities and do not give the company much chance of being successful. One consultant stated, "I don't think they have the glue that is necessary to bring all their companies together and provide a product for the user."

Questions:

1. What might be some differences between the oil industry and the information processing industry that might influence the planning function?
2. What might the consultant mean when he refers to "the glue"? Why?
3. Should Exxon get out of the information processing business? Why?

Defending the need for planning

Many managers do not plan, others do not plan adequately, and still others would like to do more planning and admit that planning is their most neglected activity. Several explanations for these situations undoubtedly exist.

Following are some sentiments expressed by managers with respect to the function of planning:

1. "We are a relatively young organization, and we are doing very well without a formal plan. As we progress and more time is available, I suspect we will do some planning. Right now, we don't need a formal plan."
2. "The president of our bank grew up in this town, as did his father and his father's father. Believe me, he knows the business without a plan."
3. "We tried planning a few years ago. It was simply too time consuming."
4. "I think a formal plan would be too confining. Our business moves and shakes so fast that we've got to be flexible."
5. "Plans are a waste of time. No one ever reads them."
6. "I've seen a lot of nice planning systems and models. The only trouble with them is that they only look good in the book. They never fit my organization."

Questions:

1. Do statements such as these make you question the usefulness of the material that you've read in this chapter? Why?
2. Logically and specifically, refute each of the statements.

4

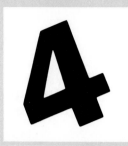

Chapter four Planning as decision making

Performance objectives

- **Define** the major types of managerial decisions.
- **State** why managers at different levels in the organization concentrate on certain types of decisions.
- **Describe** the process of decision making and the various phases of the process.
- **Explain** the importance of the various influences on the decision-making process.
- **Discuss** group decision making and compare it to individual decision making.

Management update*

Decision making involves selecting from among alternative courses of action. The B. F. Goodrich Co. believes that creativity is a key aspect of effective decision making and problem solving. The company's view reflects the idea that creative individuals consider and evaluate numerous and innovative alternatives that other individuals typically ignore. The company believes that individuals can be trained in creative and innovative thinking. Moreover, B. F. Goodrich believes that a corporate climate which is conducive to creativity can be established through a training program.

The training program seeks to get managers and supervisors to overcome and remove personal and organizational obstacles to creativity. Lorna P. Martin, the director of the program, states the importance of having a supportive climate: "After all, good ideas can emerge from anywhere in the organization and at all levels. Sometimes one individual may come up with an idea. But it needs someone else, perhaps in quite a different part of the organization, to develop or improve an idea. That is why we believe it is important to develop an organizational approach to creativity and innovation, rather than to rely on personal development."

The training program devotes considerable time to group-centered creativity in decision making. Of special interest is the idea that every individual in the group contributes to establishing the climate in which creativity occurs. The training encourages individuals to be open and receptive to ideas, no matter how absurd they may seem at the time, and to be willing to take risks. The training staff has prepared course materials and exercises that foster the development of group creativity as well as individual creativity. But the most important purpose of the training is to develop the concept of creative decision making as an integral aspect of B. F. Goodrich.

---

* This Management Update is adapted from "Creative Training: B. F. Goodrich's New Approach," *Management Review,* March 1980, pp. 29–30.

The focus of this chapter is decision making. The chapter is placed at this point in the book because it should be apparent that planning is in many respects decision-making. Obviously, planning involves making decisions. Planning involves deciding which objectives to set, which forecasting method to use, which strategies to associate with each objective, how much and what types of resources should be budgeted, and which policies are appropriate. Evidently, the manager is in a continual state of decision making throughout each element of planning. The quality of plans as means for achieving effective performance is related in large part to the decision-making skills of managers. In this chapter, the process of decision making is presented in the context of planning. Yet, it is possible to view decision making in the context of all other managerial functions, organizing, leading, and controlling.

Why study decision making?

Managers at all levels in the organization make decisions. These decisions may ultimately influence the survival of the organization or the starting salary of a new college trainee. All decisions, however, will have some ultimate influence on performance, whether that influence is large or small. Thus, it is important for managers to develop decision-making skills if for no other reason than that they spend a great deal of time making decisions. The manager of a chain of motels commented.

> *The difference between a manager and a nonmanager is simple—managers make all the decisions.*

There is a more important reason for studying decision making. Like it or not, managers are evaluated and rewarded on the basis of the importance, number, and results of their decisions. The quality of the decisions that managers reach is the yardstick of their effectiveness and of their value to the organization.

Types of decisions

Although managers in large business organizations, government offices, hospitals, and schools may be separated by background, lifestyle, and distance, they all sooner or later must make decisions. They will all face situations involving several alternatives and an evaluation of the outcome. In this section, we will discuss various types of decisions.

Programmed decisions

Programmed decisions are the decisions which managers make in response to repetitive and routine problems. If a particular situation occurs often, managers will develop a routine procedure for solving it. Thus, a decision is programmed if it is repetitive and routine and management has developed a definite procedure for handling it.

Nonprogrammed decisions

When a problem has not arisen in exactly the same manner before, or it is complex or extremely important, it will require a nonprogrammed decision. Thus, decisions are nonprogrammed when they are for novel and unstructured problems. Nonprogrammed decision making benefits from training in creativity, as described in the Management Update. Such decisions deserve special attention from management.

The two classifications are broad, yet they point out the importance of differentiating between programmed and nonprogrammed decisions.[1] The managements of most organizations face great numbers of programmed decisions in their daily operations. Such decisions should be made without expending unnecessary time and effort on them. What is important, however, is that the need for nonprogrammed decisions be properly identified. On the basis of this type of decision making, billions of dollars worth of resources are allocated in our nation every year. Government organizations make decisions that influence the lives of every citizen. Business organizations make decisions to manufacture new products. Hospitals and schools make decisions that influence patients and students years later. Unfortunately, very little is known about this type of human decision making.

Figure 4–1 presents examples of programmed and nonprogrammed decisions in different types of organizations. It indicates that programmed and nonprogrammed decisions require different kinds of procedures and apply to very different types of problems.

[1] Herbert Simon, *The New Science of Management Decision* (New York: Harper & Row, 1960), pp. 5–6.

Figure 4–1

Programmed and nonprogrammed decisions

Type of decision	Type of problem	Examples	Procedures
Programmed	Repetitive, routine	Business: Processing payroll vouchers College: Processing admission applications Hospital: Preparing patient for surgery Government: Using state-owned motor vehicle	Rules Standard operating procedures Policies
Nonprogrammed	Complex, novel	Business: Introducing a new product College: Constructing new classroom facilities Hospital: Reacting to regional disease epidemic Government: Solving spiraling inflation problem	Creative problem solving

In most organizations, programmed decisions are handled through policies. In some organizations and industries, management scientists have developed mathematical models which have greatly facilitated these types of decisions. Nonprogrammed decisions are usually handled by general problem-solving processes, judgment, intuition, and creativity.

Types of decisions and managers

Ideally, the focus of top management should be on nonprogrammed decisions, while first-level management should be concerned with programmed decisions. Middle managers in most organizations concentrate mostly on programmed decisions. The nature of the problem, how frequently it arises, and the degree of certainty surrounding it should dictate at what level of management the decision should be made. Problems that arise infrequently and have a great deal of uncertainty surrounding them are often of a long-run nature and should be the concern of top management. Problems that arise frequently and have fairly certain outcomes should be the concern of lower levels of management.

The decision-making process

There are numerous approaches to decision making. Each approach is undoubtedly appropriate at a certain time. Which approach is "best" will depend on the nature of the problem, the time available, the costs of individual strategies, and the mental skills of the decision maker.

Decisions should be thought of as *means* rather than ends. They are mechanisms through which a manager seeks to achieve some desired state. They are the manager's (and hence the organization's) responses to problems. Every decision is the outcome of a dynamic process which is influenced by a multitude of forces. Thus, **decision making is the process of thought and deliberation that results in a decision.** The point is that a decision is the end result of an involved process. Obviously, we are more interested in the process than in the result. It is the process that influences how good the decision is likely to be. The basic process is presented in Figure 4–2.

Figure 4–2

Decision making in the planning function

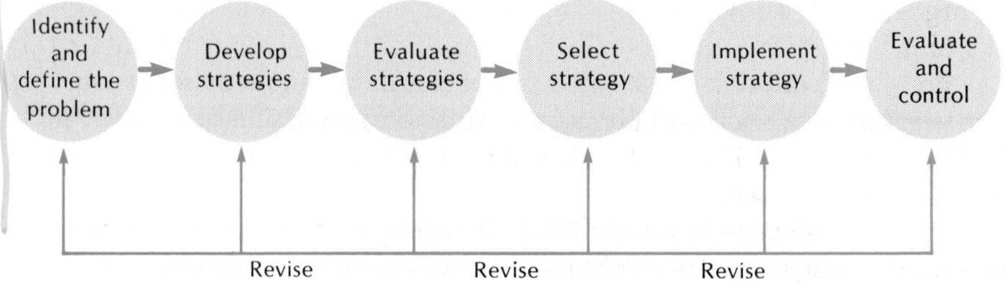

The reader should not interpret Figure 4–2 to mean that decision making is a fixed procedure. Instead, it is presented as a sequential process. In most decision situations, managers go through a number of stages that help them think about the problem and develop alternative strategies. The stages need not be rigidly applied, but their value lies in their ability to force the decision maker to structure the problem in a meaningful way. Figure 4–2 also enables us to examine each stage in the normal progression that leads to a decision. The major point worth learning here is that of a systematic, sequential approach to decision making. You may find it helpful to develop your own list of the stages that you believe should be included in the decision-making process. On this point, the president of a bank stated:

> *While executives may not be aware of it consciously, we all have a process we go through when making a decision. It's probably never written down or thought about, but I suspect that if it were, we would see much similarity among all of us.*

Examination of Figure 4–2 reveals that the process is more applicable to nonprogrammed decisions than to programmed decisions. Problems that occur infrequently with a great deal of uncertainty surrounding the outcome require that the manager utilize the entire process. For problems which occur frequently, it is not necessary to consider the entire process. If a policy is established for such problems, it will not be necessary to develop and evaluate strategies each time the problem arises.

Identifying and defining the problem

A necessary condition for a decision is a problem. If problems did not exist, there would be no need for decisions. In other words, there must be a gap between some desired level of performance and the existing level. The gap will be some sort of performance inadequacy in terms of the organization's objectives. For example, if a college establishes an objective of 5,000 full-time students in five years, and the actual enrollment at the end of the period is 3,000, there is a performance inadequacy (assuming that the objective was realistic). If a business organization has a profitability objective of a 15 percent return on investment, and it is achieving 9 percent, there is a gap.

Here again we see the relationship between planning and decision making and the importance of establishing specific and measurable objectives. How critical a problem is for the organization is measured by the difference (or gap) between the levels of performance specified in the objectives and the levels of performance attained. Of course, if performance does not reach a predetermined objective, the problem may be with the objective. In our chapter on the management function of control, we shall see that in order to be useful, objectives must permit the establishment of meaningful standards for control.

Identifying problems is not as easy as it may seem. There are several methods that managers use to locate problems.

1. Deviation from past performance If some established pattern of performance suddenly varies, this often indicates that a problem has developed. When employee turnover increases, sales decline, student enrollments decline, selling expenses increase, or more defective units are produced, a problem usually exists. Thus, managers look for departures from historical patterns as a signal of a problem.[2] A sales manager described this situation in the following way:

> *I look to the past for symptoms of problems in the present. If my sales are declining, if market share is shrinking, I recognize it as a symptom. Then I go looking for the problem.*

2. Deviation from the plan When results do not meet planned objectives, a problem is likely. For example, a new product fails to meet its market share objective; profit levels are lower than planned; the production department is exceeding its budget; or the construction of a new plant is far off schedule. These occurrences signal that some plan is off course.

3. Criticism Outsiders may identify problems. Customers may be dissatisfied with a new product or with their delivery schedules. A labor union may present grievances. Investment firms may not recommend the organization as a good investment opportunity. Alumni may withdraw their support from an athletic program. These are examples of problems identified by outsiders.

4. Competition The organization's competitors for resources and clients can certainly present problems. A competitor that introduces a superior new product or a college that hires away valued faculty forces problems and therefore decision situations.

Developing strategies

The next phase of decision making is the development of strategies to solve the problem. At this point, the manager begins to address the issue of what can be done about the problem. Feasible strategies are actually potential solutions to the problem, and the manager must consider the potential consequences of each strategy. Here we suggest some approaches that managers can use to decide upon the appropriate strategy.

Developing strategies is a process in which the relevant internal and external environments of the organization are investigated to provide information that relates to possible strategies. For example, suppose that not meeting a profitability objective has been identified as the problem. The specific case may be a profit squeeze, with costs increasing and prices being pressured downward by competition. Assume that management gathers more information and concludes that competitive pressures will remain and that the only avenue is to reduce costs. Management can then begin to examine strategies to reduce selling expense or production costs. Obviously, this search is conducted within certain time and cost constraints,

[2] William F. Pounds, "The Process of Problem Finding," *Industrial Management Review,* Fall 1969, pp. 1–19.

since only so much effort can be devoted to developing alternatives. Therefore, the number of feasible alternatives is limited accordingly. Developing strategies is an extremely difficult and critical process, since the decision will probably involve choosing one of the feasible strategies. This point was clearly made by a production manager:

> *I've found that the most difficult part of making a decision is thinking through all of the possible alternatives. Sometimes I'll think, What if you've left one out?*

Evaluating strategies

In every planning situation, the objective is to select that strategy that will produce the most favorable outcomes and the least unfavorable outcomes. Thus, once strategies have been developed, they must be evaluated and compared on the basis of previously established objectives. Three possible relationships may exist between the strategies and the possible outcomes: certainty, risk, and uncertainty.

Conditions of certainty If a manager has enough information to know what the outcome of each alternative strategy will be, then the manager is operating under conditions of certainty. Assume that you have a certain amount of money to invest. The only two strategies you are considering are government bonds and long-term certificates of deposit from your local bank. Both earn a predictable interest rate. You would base your decision on the outcome you prefer, given the interest rates and the length of the investment. You have sufficient information to act as if a condition of certainty exists.

Conditions of risk Rarely will managers face conditions of certainty in decision making. Unfortunately, they must try to estimate the consequences of their decisions. In some situations, managers may be able to estimate the likelihood that particular outcomes will occur. In other words, a manager might think, "I believe we have a 50 percent chance of capturing the youth market with our new product." Such estimates are really *probabilities* that a particular outcome will occur. When a manager can estimate the likelihood (probability) of a particular outcome, the manager is operating under conditions of risk. An example would be the actuarial tables used by insurance companies. Based on certain information, the companies can estimate the likelihood (probability) that an individual will live to a certain age or that a home in a specified location will be subjected to flood, theft, and other calamities. Based on these estimates, they decide what rates to charge for life insurance or homeowner's insurance. Obviously, the insurance companies have no way of knowing *exactly* how many individuals will die or how many homes will flood, and hence, how many claims will be filed. Thus, their decision involves risk. The insurance companies do know, however, that their probabilities will be reasonably accurate for a great number of cases over the long run.

The use of probabilities can be useful in ther ways to a manager facing a decision under conditions of risk. Probabilities enable the calculation of the expected value of a given alternative. The **expected value** of a particular decision is nothing more than the average return in the long run; in other words, it is an average of the returns that you would obtain if you made the same decision in the same situation over and over again. The expected value is found by taking the value of an outcome if it should occur and multiplying that value by the probability that the outcome will occur. For example, if you flip a coin, the probability is 0.50 that it will turn up heads. If you bet a friend $5 that you will flip a head, then the expected value of your decision can be found by taking the value of the outcome if it should occur ($5) and multiplying that value by the probability that the outcome will occur (0.50). This yields $2.50, which is the average return you could expect over the long run if you made this same bet many times. Let us work through an example to illustrate this very useful idea.

Assume that you are the president of a college and that you are faced with an important decision. You are trying to decide whether to build a new football stadium or to remodel the existing facility. A new stadium would seat more people and result in more revenue for the school. However, you are also aware that fan interest and ticket purchases will rise and fall with the success of the team. If the team is winning, the additional seats in a new stadium would easily be filled. If the team has a string of mediocre or losing seasons, the additional seats would be empty. After much thought and consideration and consultation with the athletic director, you develop the information presented in Table 4–1, which is in the form that is commonly known as a **payoff table.** Table 4–1 is a payoff table because it shows the monetary payoffs for each alternative, given the demand for tickets. A payoff table is also a convenient way to summarize all the relevant data.

For example, if the president decides to construct a new stadium and the demand for tickets is low, the payoff will be $1 million. A decision to remodel the present facility would result in a payoff of $2.3 million if

Table 4–1

Payoff table of conditional values

	Demand for tickets		
Alternatives	Low	Moderate	High
Remodel present stadium	$2,000,000	$2,300,000	$3,000,000
Construct new stadium	1,000,000	2,200,000	4,200,000

the demand for tickets were moderate. All of the payoffs in Table 4–1 are really conditional values because they are conditioned on the demand for tickets. For example, $2 million is the amount that will be made if the present facility is remodeled and the demand for tickets is low. The decision to remodel or build is controlled by the decision maker, but the demand for tickets is less controllable. The alternative selected by the president must be based on what the demand for tickets is likely to be.

As we mentioned earlier, under conditions of risk, the decision maker is able to develop estimates of the likelihood that relevant things will happen; in this case, the demand for tickets. The ability to estimate may result from experience or from incomplete but reliable information. In situations in which estimates are made, there is a *risk* involved, but the knowledge needed to reach a decision is not completely lacking.

Let us assume that the president has reason to believe that there is a 0.30 chance that the demand for tickets will be high because the team will win consistently. Because the team has never lost consistently, the chances of low demand for tickets are estimated at 0.20. More than likely, the team will perform as it has during the last decade, so the chances of moderate demand for tickets are estimated at 0.50.

Using the probability estimates of the demand for tickets, it is now possible to calculate the expected value of each possible outcome. These are presented in Table 4–2. Note that the expected value for each outcome was calculated by multiplying the conditional value from Table 4–1 by the probability estimate of the demand for tickets. For example, the expected value of the outcome of remodeling the present facility accompanied by a low demand for tickets is calculated as follows:

$$\text{Conditional value} \times \text{Probability of low demand} = \text{Expected value}$$
$$\$2{,}000{,}000 \times 0.20 = \$400{,}000$$

All of the expected values in Table 4–2 were calculated in the same manner.

The *total expected value* of each alternative is equal to the sum of the

Table 4–2

Payoff table of expected values

	Demand for tickets			
Alternatives	Low (0.20)	Moderate (0.50)	High (0.30)	Total expected value
Remodel present stadium	$400,000	$1,150,000	$ 900,000	$2,450,000
Construct new stadium	200,000	1,100,000	1,260,000	2,560,000

expected values under each possible level of demand. The total expected value for each alternative is also shown in Table 4–2. This represents the *average payoff* that would be received by the president if he chose that particular alternative on a great number of occasions under the same conditions. That payoff may not result from only one choice, but if the same decision were made over and over again, the average payoff would be $2,450,000 if the president remodeled the present facility.

Table 4–2 indicates that the total expected value is higher ($2,560,000) if a new stadium is constructed than if the present facility is remodeled ($2,450,000).

Using these amounts, the decision would be to construct a new stadium. It is important to point out that the probability estimates may not be accurate. Perhaps the president is not aware of certain economic or social trends that may influence the demand for football tickets. This clearly indicates that the decision to remodel or build is made under conditions of risk.

Conditions of uncertainty When the decision maker has absolutely no idea of the probabilities associated with the various alternatives, a condition of uncertainty exists. In many decision situations, many factors influence the outcome and a manager can in no way predict what the possible outcome might be. In such situations, the intuition, judgment, and personality of the decision maker can play an important role.

For instance, let us assume that in our example the president believes that there is no possible way to assign any probabilities to the different levels of demand for tickets. Any attempt to do so would be sheer guesswork and thus no better than assuming complete uncertainty. Still, a decision must be made.

In such a situation, the decision becomes a much more personal thing. Suppose that the president is a risk avoider or that he dislikes football. What might happen if the president's family enjoys football or if a big contributor to the alumni fund enjoys football? Under conditions of uncertainty, all of these factors might influence the decision. To describe what could happen, depending on what type of decision maker we are dealing with, let us reproduce the payoff table of conditional values as Table 4–3 for easy reference.

Table 4–3

Payoff table of conditional values

	Demand for tickets		
Alternatives	Low	Moderate	High
Remodel present stadium	$2,000,000	$2,300,000	$3,000,000
Construct new stadium	1,000,000	2,200,000	4,200,000

Let us assume that the president is an *optimistic* decision maker who consistently seeks to achieve the maximum possible payoff. This obviously involves thinking optimistically about the occurrence of events influencing the sale of tickets. If this approach were followed, the decision maker would select the alternative under which it is possible to receive the most favorable payoff. It is dangerous to use this criterion because it ignores possible losses and the chances of not making a profit. An optimistic decision maker would examine the conditional value payoff table and seek to maximize the profit gain.

Returning to our example, if the president were such a decision maker, he would list the most favorable payoff for each alternative:

Remodel present stadium	$3,000,000
Construct new stadium	4,200,000

If maximum possible payoff were the objective, the decision would be to construct a new stadium.

On the other hand, there are managers who make decisions believing that only the worst possible outcome can occur. Such *pessimistic* individuals are likely to select the alternative that would maximize the least favorable payoff. In other words, they would select "the best of the worst." If the president in our example were such an individual, he would list the least favorable payoff for each alternative:

Remodel present stadium	$2,000,000
Construct new stadium	1,000,000

The decision in this case would be to remodel the present stadium. The decision maker would have maximized the minimum payoff.

Let us provide one more example of decision making under conditions of uncertainty. Suppose that a decision maker believes it might be useful to try to employ probabilities in a decision situation under conditions of uncertainty. Since there is no previous experience or other basis on which to assign probabilities, how could this be accomplished? The reasoning here is that if managers do not know the probabilities associated with various possible outcomes, they should assume that all outcomes are equally likely to occur. In other words, if there is no reason to believe that one outcome is likelier than another, equal probabilities should be assigned to each.

Applying this reasoning to our example, we would assign equal probabilities to each of the levels of demand and compute the expected value of each alternative as we did under conditions of risk.

$$\text{Remodel present stadium} = 0.33\ (\$2{,}000{,}000 + \$2{,}300{,}000 + \$3{,}000{,}000)$$
$$\text{Total expected value} = \$2{,}433{,}333$$

$$\text{Construct new stadium} = 0.33\ (\$1{,}000{,}000 + \$2{,}200{,}000 + \$4{,}200{,}000)$$
$$\text{Total expected value} = \$2{,}466{,}667$$

In this situation, the president would decide to construct the new stadium.

The discussion points out clearly that depending on the orientation of the manager, different strategies would be selected. This example indicates the difficulty of making decisions under conditions of uncertainty. The difficulty may have been expressed best by the senior bank officer who said:

> *Decision making is a very lonely business. Decisions that I make influence the careers, families, and futures of my subordinates. Many times, this influence is negative. However, I must make the decisions I believe are best for them as well as the organization. I don't have anyone but myself to rely on when I make decisions. Sometimes it's very difficult.*

Our discussion also points out how the manager's past experience, intuition, and personality can influence a decision.

Selecting a strategy

The purpose in selecting a strategy is to solve the problem in order to achieve predetermined objectives. This point is very important. It indicates that a decision is not an end in itself but only a *means* to an end. In other words, the decision itself is not an isolated act. The decision maker should not forget the factors that led up to the decision or the factors that follow the decision, such as implementation and evaluation. One manager reinforced this point clearly when she stated:

> *Decision making is more than just the act of choosing. The entire process should be the center of attention.*

Unfortunately for most managers, situations rarely exist in which the chosen strategy will achieve the objective without at the same time having an impact on some other objective. This point was viewed as critical by a sales manager who stated:

> *Every decision will have impacts apart from the intended impact on the problem, and a manager had best try to anticipate those impacts.*

Often, a situation will exist in which two objectives cannot be fully achieved at the same time. If one objective is achieved to its fullest, the other cannot be. For example, a manufacturing firm might have a competitiveness objective of a high-quality product and an efficiency objective of low-maintenance costs. Obviously, both of these objectives cannot be achieved to their fullest at the same time. In all likelihood, an attempt to keep maintenance costs at their lowest would eventually influence the quality of the product. The multiple objectives of most organizations complicate the real world of the decision maker.

A situation might also occur in which an organization's objective might conflict with a societal objective. Society's objective of clean air conflicts with the profitability objectives of some manufacturing firms. Society's objective of equal rights has conflicted with some bank credit practices, specifically credit policies toward the poor and toward women. In any case, whether one objective conflicts with another objective or with a societal objective, the values of the decision maker will influence the strategy chosen. Such influences on the decision-making process will be discussed later in this chapter.

Thus, *optimal* solutions are often impossible in managerial planning because the manager can in no way be aware of every possible strategy or the possible consequences of each strategy. In reality, most managers are therefore not optimizers but are instead *satisficers.* They select the strategy that they know meets some minimal, yet *satisfactory,* standard of acceptance.

Implementing the strategy

A planning decision is useless unless the strategy is implemented. The choice must be effectively implemented to achieve the objectives for which it was made. Thus, one could argue that implementation may be more important than the activity of selecting a strategy. In fact, a product manager in a large consumer products firm went so far as to say:

> *I really believe it is possible for a good decision to be hurt by poor implementation. And I have also seen situations where a bad decision was improved by good implementation.*

In most situations, implementing decisions involves people. Although a decision may have been well thought through, it can easily be undermined by dissatisfied subordinates. People cannot be manipulated in the same manner as other resources. What this means is that a manager's job is not limited to skill in selecting good solutions. The manager also needs the skill and knowledge necessary to make the decisions become part of the behavior of the people in the organization. This is accomplished by communicating effectively to individuals and groups. Effective communication is necessary for effectively implementing decisions. Communication is the subject of an entire chapter later in the book.

Evaluation and control

As we know, the management function of control involves comparing actual performance with the performance specified in the objectives. If deviations exist, changes or corrections must be made. This is indicated clearly in Figure 4–2. Here again we see the importance of measurable objectives. If they do not exist, then there is no way to judge performance. A manager in a major oil company commented:

> *You just cannot set objectives during coffee breaks. Since they will determine the course you take and the decisions you will make, you'd better pay attention to them.*

If actual results do not match planned results, then changes must be made in the alternative that was selected, how it was implemented, or in the original objective if the manager determines that it was not attainable. Figure 4–2 indicates that if the original objective must be revised, then the entire decision-making process must be reactivated. The important point is that a manager should not assume that once a decision has been implemented, the objective will be reached. Some system of evaluation and control is necessary. The manager of a chain of women's apparel stores noted the necessity for control when she stated:

> *In my business, and I'm sure in most, your solution will not stay put because the problem will change. It is important to consciously update the results of decisions. The more rapidly things change, the more critical this becomes.*

From our discussion of the decision-making process, it is easy to see why some managers believe that *what managers do is make decisions.* There is some truth in this belief because the steps in the decision-making process outlined in this chapter are very much like the functions of managers.

Influences on individual decision makers

There are many important influences on the decision-making process. Some of them affect only certain phases of the process, but others can affect the entire process. Each influence, however, will have some impact and therefore must be understood. Although such influences are numerous, we shall discuss what we believe are the four most important—the importance of the decision, time pressures, the manager's values, and the manager's propensity for risk.

The importance of the decision

The mayor of a city may make two decisions in an afternoon, one extending the school year for children because of missed days caused by bad weather, the other committing $50 million to constructing an expressway around the city. In each case, the steps in the decision-making process were probably covered, but the time and techniques used were certainly different. There are numerous ways to measure the importance of a decision—the amount of resources involved, the number of people influenced by the decision, and the time required to make the decision. The important point is that managers must allot more time and attention to significant problems. In deciding to extend the school year, the mayor may have considered only a small number of possibilities because the amount of time a public school student must spend in class each year is determined by law. Before deciding on constructing an expressway around the city, however, more alternatives were generated, more time and thought were utilized, and more detailed information was required. The importance of the decision in terms of monetary commitments, time commitments, and number of people affected should influence the amount of time and money spent on making the decision.

Time pressures

An important influence on the quality of decisions is how much time the decision maker has in which to make the decisions. Unfortunately, managers must make most of their decisions in time frames established by others. This is strongly stated by a marketing executive?

> *Suppose my competition makes a price change or introduces a new product. How much time do you think I've got? I have to respond, and do so swiftly. I make my decision based on the information available to me or information I can obtain in the time I have available to me. Sure, time may prove my decision to be a poor one, but based on what I know at the moment, the decision must be made. I make the best decision I can. After that, I don't worry about it. I could always second-guess myself when I get additional information two weeks later.*

Obviously, when time pressures are significant, managers may be unable to gather enough information or to consider additional alternatives. However, managers must deal with this reality.

The manager's values

An individual's values serve as guidelines when he or she is confronting a choice. These values are acquired early in life, and they are a basic, often taken-for-granted part of an individual's thoughts. Because our values are basic to us, we are usually unaware of how they influence us. Their influence on the decision-making process is great.

Many experts consider values to be one of the most important influences on human behavior. Values are the likes, dislikes, shoulds, oughts, judgments, and prejudices that determine how we view the world. Once they become a part of an individual, they become (often subconsciously) a standard for guiding his or her actions.

What values do managers espouse? This is a very important question. Figure 4–3 describes what most experts believe are the six major value orientations. Studies clearly indicate that American managers place a higher value on economic, theoretical, and political ends than on religious, aesthetic, and social ones.[3]

The idea that managers as a group tend to be oriented more toward the economic or practical values has commonsense appeal. Psychologists have known for a long time that individuals with such values would be compatible with management, especially business management.

The value orientations of managers underlie much of their behavior. How they approach the management functions of planning, organizing, leading, and controlling reflects their values. The decisions managers make in identifying their objectives and strategies, and how managers interpret society's expectations, also reflect their values. Some specific influences of values on the decision-making process are:

1. Value judgments are necessary in the development of objectives and the assignment of priorities.
2. In developing alternatives, it is necessary to make value judgments about the various possibilities.
3. In selecting an alternative, value judgments will be reflected in the alternative chosen.

It is safe to say that most readers of this book are not managers at present. The purpose for which most of them are reading this book is to acquire a basis for a career in management. Therefore, we should address the issue of the extent to which the values of today's young people are compatible with those of today's managers. The question is simply, "If the values of future managers conflict with those of present managers, will the future managers change their values to conform to the job or will they change the job to conform to their values?"

[3] E. J. Luck and B. L. Oliver, "American Managers' Personal Value Systems—Revisited," *Academy of Management Journal*, September 1974, pp. 549–54.

Figure 4–3

Six major value orientations

1. *Theoretical* persons are primarily interested in discovering truth. They are less interested in the beauty or utility of objects, seeking mainly to observe and to reason. Their interests are critical, rational, and intellectual.
2. *Economic* persons are interested in what is useful. They are interested in the practical affairs of the business world; in the production, marketing, and consumption of goods; and in the accumulation of tangible wealth. They are "practical," and they fit the stereotype of the American businessman.
3. *Aesthetic* persons are primarily interested in the artistic aspects of life. They may not be creative artists, but they view each event in their lives as something to be enjoyed for its own sake.
4. *Social* persons love people as ends, and they tend to be kind, sympathetic, and unselfish. They find individuals with theoretical, economic, and aesthetic orientations to be rather cold. In its extreme form, their orientation is selfless and approaches the religious attitude.
5. *Political* persons are oriented toward power, not necessarily in politics, but in whatever area they function. Most leaders have a power orientation. Many believe that power is a universal motive, but for some it is uppermost, driving them to seek personal authority, influence, and recognition.
6. The dominant value of *religious* persons is unity. Such persons seek to relate themselves to the universe in a meaningful way, and they often have a mystical orientation.

SOURCE: Summarized for W. D. Guth and R. Tagiuri, "Personal Values and Corporate Strategies," *Harvard Business Review*, September–October 1965, pp. 125–26.

There is evidence that today's students, like today's managers, stress practical values. Unlike today's managers, however, they would rather achieve their ends through their own efforts, not the efforts of others. Perhaps these students will be tomorrow's entrepreneurs and will not seek careers in ongoing organizations.

Many students espouse social and humanistic values. They are very concerned with what is good for society rather than with what is good for organizations. They also believe that organizations of all types should take on more socially oriented goals that they have in the past.

There is no doubt that the values of the younger generation will be reflected in their decisions as managers. The basic functions of management will not change, but the ways in which they are performed may. Depending on value orientations, there will be different outcomes from the process of decision making. However, organizations at present seem to be able to accommodate different values among managers. There is really no reason to believe that they will not be able to do so in the future. A corporate treasurer expressed this view when he stated:

We need people who think differently. We must stop trying to recruit everyone who thinks alike. It might be easier for us, and we might get along better, but in the end nothing new is likely to happen.

The manager's propensity for risk

Risk taking is a necessity in most decision situations. From personal experience, the reader is certainly aware that decision makers vary greatly in their propensity to take risks. This aspect of the decision maker's personality has a strong influence on the decision-making process. A manager who is less inclined toward risk taking will establish different objectives, evaluate alternatives differently, and select different alternatives than will a manager who is more inclined toward risk taking. This is important because the propensity for risk does not enter the picture only when the time comes to make a choice. It influences the entire decision-making process. One manager will be inclined toward situations in which the risk or uncertainty is low or in which the certainty of the outcome is high. Another, because of a greater propensity for risk, will choose the opposite kinds of situations. In the next and final section of this chapter, we shall see that very often decision makers are bolder, more innovative, and inclined toward greater risks when they are participating in a group than when they make decisions individually. It appears that many individuals are more willing to accept risk as members of a group.

Group decision making

Throughout this chapter, we have focused on individual decision makers. However, a great number of the decisions reached in most organizations are reached by groups. These groups may be called committees, teams, task forces, project groups, and so on. What is important is not what they are called, but that they make decisions.

Group decision making is utilized because managers frequently confront situations in which they must seek and combine the judgments of many individuals. This is especially true for nonprogrammed decisions. It is rare in most organizations for an individual to consistently make these types of decisions. The problems involved are usually complex, and their solution requires specialized knowledge in numerous fields. Usually no one person possesses all of the kinds of knowledge needed. The use of group decision making has also increased because many units are affected by the decisions reached, and most decisions must eventually be accepted and implemented by many units. In fact, most managers spend most of their time in group meetings of some type.

Are group decisions more effective?

There is a great deal of debate over whether group decisions or individual decisions are more effective. Groups will, in most cases, take more time to reach decisions than will individuals. However, some people argue that the bringing together of specialists and experts will usually result in better decisions. Other people argue that group decisions can be influenced by one individual with a dominant personality or that persons higher in the organization will inhibit group members who are lower in the management system. It is held that the latter will go along, even though they believe that their ideas are superior. B. F. Goodrich's training program in decision making, described in the Management Update, attempts to overcome inhibiting group pressure.

Figure 4–4

Important advantages and disadvantages of group decision making

Advantages	Disadvantages
1. In developing objectives, groups provide a greater amount of available knowledge.	1. The implementation of a decision, whether or not it is made by a group, must be accomplished by individual managers. Since a group cannot be held responsible, group decisions may result in a situation in which no one is responsible, and buck-passing results.
2. In developing alternatives, the individual efforts of group members can enable a broader search in the various functional areas of the organization.	2. Considering how valuable time is as an organizational resource, group decisions are costly.
3. In evaluating alternatives, groups have a wider range of viewpoints.	3. Group decision making is inefficient if a decision must be made promptly.
4. In selecting alternatives, groups are likely to accept more risk than are individual decision makers.	4. Group decisions may in some cases be the result of compromise and indecision on the part of group members.
5. Because of participating in the decision-making process, the individual members of groups are more likely to be motivated to carry out the decision.	5. If superiors are present, or if one member has a dominant personality, the decision of a group may in reality not be a group decision.
6. Greater creativity results from the interaction of individuals with different viewpoints.	

Some decisions appear to be better made by individuals, while other decisions appear to be better suited for group decision making. Nonprogrammed decisions appear to be better suited for group decision making. The problems involved in nonprogrammed decisions require the pooling of talent to reach decisions. Figure 4–4 summarizes the advantages and disadvantages of group decision making. The figure indicates clearly that as with so many of the problems facing managers, the usefulness of an approach is contingent on many other factors. In other words, group decision making may be effective or ineffective, depending on the situation, as the following statement indicates:

> Watergate presents America with the profound puzzle of why. What is it that led such a wide assortment of men, many of them high public officials, possibly including the President himself, either to instigate or to go along with and later try to hide a pattern of behavior that now appears not only reprehensible, but stupid?[4]

Management summary

1. Planning and decision making are two managerial activities that cannot be separated. Every stage of the planning function involves decision making.
2. The quality of management decisions determines to a large extent the effectiveness of plans.
3. Managers are evaluated and rewarded on the basis of the importance, number, and results of their decisions.
4. Decisions may be classified as programmed or nonprogrammed, depending on the type of problem. Each type requires different kinds of procedures and applies to very different types of situations.
5. Decision making is a many-phased process. The actual choice is only one phase.
6. Decisions should be thought of as *means* rather than ends. They are a manager's responses to problems and the results of a process of thought and deliberation.
7. Different managers may select different alternatives in the same situation. This is because of differences in values and in attitudes toward risk.
8. Managers spend a great deal of time in group decision making. This is especially true for nonprogrammed decisions. Much evidence exists that in certain situations, group decisions are superior to individual

[4] *Washington Star and Daily News,* editorial, May 27, 1973.

decisions. However, there are exceptions, and problems do exist in group decision making.

Review and discussion questions

1. What is a decision?
2. We make decisions daily. Describe in detail two programmed decisions that you make each day. Why do you consider them to be programmed? Were they ever nonprogrammed? If so, discuss why.
3. Describe what you believe is a nonprogrammed decision that you recently made. Describe the circumstances surrounding the decision and state why you believe it was nonprogrammed. Did this belief influence your decision-making approach? In what ways?
4. Reexamine the decision you described in question 3 and discuss it in terms of the decision-making process outlined in the chapter.
5. Select a major political decision or a business decision with which you are familiar. Evaluate the decision in terms of how "good" you think it was. Be specific, and state how you determined the quality of the decision.
6. What type of risk taker do you believe you are? Indicate how this has influenced some decisions that you have made recently.
7. Describe a group decision-making situation in which you were involved. Did any problems develop? Describe them in detail. Was the decision reached by the group different from the one you would have made as an individual? Do you think that the group decision was better? Why?
8. Why are the management function of planning and the process of decision making so closely related?
9. Think of a decision that you or someone you know has made recently. Do you believe that any of the various influences on the decision-making process discussed in the chapter could have affected the outcome? Discuss each of those influences and indicate how it may have affected the decision.

Suggested reading

Archer, E. R. "How to Make a Business Decision: An Analysis of Theory and Practice." *Management Review,* February 1980, pp. 54–61.

Hunsaker, P. L., and J. S. Hunsaker. "Decision Styles—In Theory, in Practice." *Organizational Dynamics,* Autumn 1981, pp. 23–36.

Keen, P. G. W. "Decision Support Systems: Translating Analytical Techniques into Useful Tools." *Sloan Management Review,* Spring 1980, pp. 3–16.

King, J. L. "Cost-Benefit Analysis for Decision Making." *Journal of Systems Management,* May 1980, pp. 12–14.

Murnighan, J. K. "Group Decision Making: What Strategies Should You Use?" *Management Review,* February 1981, pp. 55–62.

Ohmae, K. "Foresighted Management Decision Making: See the Options before Planning Strategy." *Management Review,* May 1982, pp. 46–57.

Smith, W. C. "Catastrophe Theory Analysis of Business Activity." *Management Review,* June 1980, pp. 26–28, 37–40.

Applying what you have learned about planning as decision making

Cases:

Key decisions rescue Docutel Corporation
Managers are paid to make decisions

Key decisions rescue Docutel Corporation*

New firms that develop and pioneer new products have often failed to cash in on the large markets that later develop for their inventions. One firm that came close to being an example is Docutel Corporation. Docutel developed and introduced the first automatic teller machine (ATM) in 1971. However, the tiny Dallas firm was slow to incorporate new technological advances into their machines and quickly lost their market to larger more powerful firms like Diebold, Inc. In 1977, when the firm lost $8.5 million dollars, it was near collapse and in the words of the chief executive, "We were written off by everybody."

Today, Docutel is doing very well. Apparently, the cause of the turnaround were three key decisions: (1) investing resources to develop a low-cost component for its aging machines; (2) arranging for TRW, Inc., to perform the maintenance on installed units; and (3) purchasing a profitable knitwear company to take advantage of Docutel's tax-loss situation. According to the company's president, the three decisions were a "perfect strategy."

Regaining its original dominant position in the market will probably be impossible. However, the firm believes that it is in a position to win a large share of what is expected to be a rapidly increasing market for ATMs in the 1980s. Sales of ATMs are being forecasted at around 6,000 units a year for the next five years. This positive outlook is the result of the increasing costs of opening and

---

* This case is adapted from "Docutel: Born Again—and Counting on New Vigor in Automated Tellers," *Business Week,* July 21, 1981, pp. 51–52.

operating bank branches, the likely end to bans on interstate banking, and increasing turnover among bank tellers.

The firm believes that the market will "shake out" to two or three companies, Docutel, Diebold, and either IBM, NCR, or Burroughs. Its present market share is 20 percent. With record sales and earnings in 1980, top management has established a market share objective of 35 percent.

Questions:

1. Why is this case an illustration that in many respects, planning is decision-making?
2. What method(s) of locating problems were most likely used in this case?
3. Were the decisions in this case solutions to a problem? If so, what was the problem?

Managers are paid to make decisions

Bob Wilson was president of Security National Bank (SNB). During the seven years that he had been president, the bank had become one of the three largest banks serving metropolitan Rockford. It had been extremely successful, mostly at the expense of competitive banks.

On his desk, Wilson had a report from Barbara Stark, the bank's director of marketing. The report focused on the bank's entry into the first phase of electronic banking: the purchase and installation of automatic tellers (ATs). Wilson had been very impressed by the report and had asked Stark to come to his office to discuss the proposal. It was a very positive meeting, with both parties agreeing on the necessity for getting the program started. Stark said:

"Mr. Wilson, most experts believe that before very long every bank in the country will be faced with a decision concerning these machines. The decision will be either offensive (to install them in order to be the first in the market) or defensive (to respond to a competitor that has already installed them). I believe that to maintain the growth rate we have achieved during your seven years as president, our move should be an offensive one."

"I don't think anyone would argue with you on that point, Ms. Stark," Wilson said.

President Wilson was extremely impressed by the position of the director of marketing and in general agreement with it. He decided to take up her proposal at the next meeting of the board of directors and to strongly support it before the board. In addition, he sent a copy of the report to Dick Bryan, vice president of branch operations, along with a memo supporting the proposal and asking Bryan for additional ideas that he might have.

Five days later, Bryan asked to see Wilson concerning the report. What he had to say came as a surprise to Wilson.

"Mr. Wilson, I have read carefully the report concerning ATs. Let me say that I am in total agreement with the philosophy of aggressive, consumer-oriented banking that you have instilled into each of us at SNB. Certainly, we have been successful. I also agree that the concept of electronic banking is the wave of the future and support each of the benefits outlined in Ms. Stark's report.

"I see one potential problem, however, in implementing any decision in this direction. It involves the dismissal of several tellers. First, from the standpoint of social responsibility, I do not think that this would be very responsible and it might subject us to much criticism in the community. I can relate to each of the tellers because I remember the late 1950s and what my family went through when my father's plant was being automated. Maybe that experience has biased my thinking in this matter, but I feel it necessary to at least express it.

"Second, this decision could create morale problems for the remaining tellers. Remember, I must work through all of these people, the branch managers, and the people in the branches. They are our contact with customers, and as you have said many times, an unhappy, rude teller is an unhappy, rude bank to the customer. I believe there is a potential problem here that was not addressed in Ms. Stark's report. That is, what will the impact be on our branch managers and our branch personnel when they see their subordinates and peers being replaced by a machine?

"Since branch operations is my area, I feel compelled to let my views be known. I know that the decision is not mine to make and that many other factors must be considered. In fact, I can't say I disagree with the concept, but I do know that if we go with ATs, it will have to be implemented through my area."

That evening, President Wilson thought about what Bryan had said. It was certainly something he had never considered, and it was a good thing that Bryan had brought it to his attention. He tossed around all the benefits, costs, and problems associated with the decision. What position should he take on the matter at the meeting of the board of directors? Oh, well, he thought, I guess this is what I'm paid for, to make decisions like this.

Questions:

1. Analyze this decision situation in terms of what you know about the process of decision making and the influences on it.
2. If you were a consultant to the president, what would your advice be? Why?

5

Chapter five
Planning through strategic analysis

Performance objectives

- **Define** in terms meaningful to you the "what" and "why" of strategic planning.
- **State** why strategic planning has become increasingly important.
- **Describe** the planning system outlined in the chapter.
- **Explain** why organizational objectives are necessary for strategic planning.
- **Discuss** the major considerations in developing an organizational mission.

Management update*

One of the fastest growing industries in the U.S. economy is strategic consulting. In 1979, consultants and consultant firms collected more than $100 million in fees from American business firms. These fees represent the value of expertise in analyzing a firm's competitive strengths and weaknesses and devising strategies to which the firm's resources should be deployed. The general attitude of consultants in the area of strategic analysis is that a very large proportion of American companies (perhaps as high as 90 percent) are incapable of developing and executing meaningful corporate strategies.

The leading firms in strategic consulting include McKinsey and Co., Boston Consulting Group, Strategic Planning Institute (a nonprofit research organization), Marakon Associates, Bain and Co., and Strategic Planning Associates. In addition, many of the more traditional management consulting firms such as Arthur D. Little and Booz, Allen, and Hamilton have begun to develop expertise and clients in the general area of strategic planning. The success of these consultants, at least in terms of demand for their services, would seem to reflect the growing importance of long-range strategic analysis and planning in American industry.

The array of techniques and analytical aids that strategic consultants have devised is impressive. Some of the more popular ones include (1) the concept of strategic business unit, or SBU (devised at General Electric with the aid of McKinsey and Co., and referring to a group of related products serving the same market) and (2) the concepts of experience curve (the idea that unit cost of product declines as a firm produces more of it and gains experience in its production) and the growth-share matrix (the idea that each firm's product or SBU can be described in terms of its market share and rate of growth of the industry in which it competes), both devised by the Boston Consulting Group. As more and more firms become involved in strategic analysis, the list of techniques and concepts will doubtless expand.

---

* This Management Update is adapted from Walter Kiechel III, "Playing by the Rules of the Corporate Strategy Game," *Fortune,* September 24, 1979, pp. 110–12, 114, 118; and Walter Kiechel III, "Oh Where, Oh Where Has My Little Dog Gone? Or My Cash Cow? Or My Star?" *Fortune,* November 2, 1981, pp. 148–50, 152, 154.

Strategic analysis is the focus of this chapter. In recent years, managerial interest in the issues of strategic analysis has become more intense as indicated by the Management Update. But what specifically is meant by strategic analysis?

Strategic analysis

Although the concepts and practices of planning have typically involved consideration of environmental factors in making company and organization plans, in recent years, managers have rediscovered the importance of the environment, as noted in the Management Update. Consequently, managers now pay greater attention than ever before to the impact of relevant environmental factors on the company's *overall strategy.* As stated by an influential writer, "The essence of formulating competitive strategy is relating a company to its environment. Although the relevant environment is very broad, encompassing social as well as economic forces the key aspect of the firm's environment is the industry or industries in which it competes."[1] In a more straightforward statement, strategic decisions involve "the selection of product mix and markets . . . the match between the firm and the environment."[2]

Other definitions could be presented, yet each would emphasize the importance of management determining the firm's response to environmental threats and opportunities. In a business firm, that response is essentially and fundamentally the decision of what products to produce for what markets. All other decisions flow from that decision, thus the designation of it as a *strategic decision.*

Based upon a firm's strategic decision, resources will be allocated to the various divisions and units which comprise the organization. Specific

---

[1] Michael E. Porter, *Competitive Strategy: Techniques for Analyzing Industries and Competitors* (New York: Free Press, 1980), p. 3.

[2] H. Igor Ansoff, *Corporate Strategy* (New York: McGraw-Hill, 1965), p. 5.

decisions with respect to advertising, promotion, pricing, distribution, human resources, and technological investments will be based upon their relationship to the overall strategy of the firm. As will be seen in this chapter, strategic analysis is the key managerial process for determining the basic character and activities of any organization.

The strategic planning process

Strategic planning involves developing the organizational *mission, objectives,* and *strategies.* These three components constitute the strategic plan and are the output of the strategic planning process. Organizations vary in the way they develop their strategic plans. However, it is safe to say that Figure 5–1 accurately presents the general process of strategic planning. Let us examine each stage.

The organization's mission

The mission of an organization is a long-term vision of what the organization is trying to become. The mission is the unique aim that differentiates the organization from similar organizations. The basic questions that must be answered are, "What is our business? What should it be?" Although such questions seem simple, with an obvious answer, they are rarely asked. In fact, many individuals believe that the inability to ask and answer these questions has been the greatest cause of business failure.[3] Defining an organization's mission requires a great deal of thought and study. The techniques for developing a corporate mission have not been clearly established. This may in part explain why many organizations avoid the problem. There are at least three important considerations in formulating a corporate mission:

1. The organization's environment Before articulating a corporate mission, managers should predict the future states of the various components in the firm's environment. What will the future technological, economic, legal, and regulatory environments be like? Are social changes occurring that will probably influence the organization? For example, the expected decline in college-age people during the 1980s should certainly be considered in the long-range missions of institutions of higher learning, manufacturers of school equipment, and textbook publishers.

One point has been clearly stressed throughout this chapter. The arena of strategic management is an arena of change. The effective strategic

[3] See Peter F. Drucker, *Management: Tasks, Responsibilities, Practices* (New York: Harper & Row, 1974).

Figure 5–1

The strategic planning process

planner is necessarily a diligent student of change. This is because whether social, economic, or political change creates or destroys strategic opportunities, the constant monitoring of environmental developments must be an essential ingredient of strategic planning.

2. Distinctive competences **Distinctive competences** are those factors which give the organization an advantage over similar organizations. They are what the organization does well. For example, a distinctive competence of Procter & Gamble is its knowledge of the market for low-priced, repetitively purchased consumer products. In this case, the distinctive competence is a special capability. It may also be human resources, financial resources, location, computer capability, or a distribution network. When Coca-Cola acquired Minute Maid, one of the motivating forces was undoubtedly Coca-Cola's distinctive competence in distribution. Coca-Cola distributes to almost 2 million outlets worldwide. A hospital may be distinctively competent in the treatment of specific types of disease, and a college may be distinctively competent in certain programs of study. In some instances, analyzing the organization's distinctive competences may cause management to avoid certain activities which look promising on the surface. This is apparently why General Electric no longer manufactures vacuum cleaners. Even though General Electric was the largest manufacturer of vacuum cleaners and the market was expanding, it decided to stop manufacturing and selling them. The firm decided that its competences were in selling appliances through its GE dealers. To compete effectively in selling vacuum cleaners required competence in in-home selling. GE did not have such competence, and it decided not to invest the money to acquire it. It decided to leave the vacuum cleaner market to other firms and to concentrate on what it did best.

3. Organization's clients Although the environment and distinctive competences are important, the needs of the organization's clients are the critical factor in formulating a mission. A key feature of a statement of mission should be that its focus is *external* rather than *internal*. The statement of mission should focus on the broad class of needs that the organization is seeking to satisfy (external focus), *not* on the physical product or service that the organization is offering at present (internal focus). Consider the following statement:

> The railroads are in trouble today not because the need was filled by others (cars, trucks, airplanes, even telephones), but because it was *not* filled by the railroads themselves. They let others take customers away from them because they assumed themselves to be in the railroad business rather than in the transportation business. The reason they defined their industry wrong was because they were railroad-oriented instead of transportation-oriented; they were product-oriented instead of customer-oriented.[4]

What this statement indicates is that railroad management defined its business in terms of current physical products (or services) instead of changing markets. In other words, because individuals change in how they satisfy broad classes of needs, organizations should not define their business in terms of what they are doing at present to fill a broad need, but rather in terms of the broad need itself—for example, health care, vocational education, entertainment, personal financial management.

What the organization makes (or does) at present must be seen as only a temporary claimant to a changing market. And as markets change, so must products and services change. If an organization defines its business in terms of current products, the inevitable tendency is to operate without vision, in fact with blinders on. That is, economic, competitive, technological, and political events change the very nature of the organization's markets, yet its products remain the same. Contrast this situation with the following statement by the former president of IBM:

> We want to be in the problem-solving business—this is our mission. Our business is not to make computers. It is to help solve administrative, scientific, and even human problems.[5]

What is implied in this statement is that although computers are now widely used to solve management problems, someday they may not be. If anything should ever replace them, IBM plans to be there.

A market definition of the business rivets management attention to the constantly changing market. A continuing challenge becomes that of serving the changing market by whatever is required and feasible for the organiza-

---

[4] Theodore Levitt, "Marketing Myopia," *Harvard Business Review*, July–August 1960, pp. 45–46.

[5] Jacques Maisonrouge, former president of IBM, as quoted in the *Harvard Business Review*, January–February 1972, p. 45.

tion. Adapting to change might involve altering present products, developing new products, or even entering new businesses. One executive in a packaging firm commented:

> *We had to realize some years ago that our business was not glass packages. That was our current product. Our business is containerization. That is our market, and we had to prepare ourselves to serve the changing needs of that market when plastics became more and more attractive. If we continued to view our business as glass packaging, I wouldn't be talking to you today.*

As you can see, defining the business by product rather than by market contributes to a vulnerably narrow perspective and to shortsightedness. Using a product definition, the organization falls into the same trap as did the railroads and the American Automobile Association. For years, the American Automobile Association had thought of its business as auto-club membership (its product) instead of as "solving the away-from-home problems of travelers" (its market). As a result, in the 1950s and 1960s, the AAA failed to see the possibilities of entering the car rental field, the campsite field, the motel/hotel training field, and the convention planning field. Other missed opportunities included various types of club memberships, such as offering a corporate membership whereby a frequent air traveler could, with one phone call, have AAA make airline, hotel, car rental, meeting room, and entertainment arrangements for a given trip.

All of these examples should point up the importance of clearly defining the organization's market in formulating the organization's mission. Just as important is formulating a clear mission statement in developing a strategic plan. As you can see, this may be the most difficult phase of strategic planning. Perhaps that is why, as we mentioned earlier, the phase is often avoided.

Clear definitions of purpose enable managers to design sharply focused, results-oriented strategic objectives and strategies. It is safe to say that managerial performance tends to begin with a clarity of purpose—with a clear-cut concept of what the organization is trying to become.

Strategic objectives

Strategic objectives are typically statements of long-run achievement. They are long-run because strategic analysis is intended to provide relatively fixed direction to the organization and to its parts such as divisions, departments, and units. Thus, strategic objectives should be well considered, researched, and analyzed. Although strategic objectives represent relatively fixed commitments, they are of course subject to change as the organization's environment, distinctive competences and clients change. The same three factors that affect the organization's mission also affect its strategic objectives.

Purposes served by strategic objectives

The importance of formulating strategic objectives would seem obvious and require no justification. Yet, many organizations do not have formal statements of long-run objectives. General understandings may exist among the managers as to what levels of profitability, competitiveness, efficiency, and flexibility are appropriate. The importance of strategic objectives is, however, such that managers should consider more formal approaches to specifying them.

As noted by one contributor to modern strategic analysis practice, William F. Glueck, strategic objectives serve three important purposes:[6]

1. Strategic objectives define the organization in its environment. Organizations must be able to justify their existence to their customers, to the government, and to the larger society. Organizations that publicize clearly stated and socially responsible objectives are more likely to obtain public support and resources than organizations which operate behind a veil of secrecy.
2. Strategic objectives are the underlying and fundamental standards for assessing performance at all levels of the organization. Our central theme in this text is managing for performance, and the development of strategic objectives is a necessary first step in obtaining high levels of performance.
3. Strategic objectives coordinate objectives throughout the organization. In a sense, strategic objectives are the bases for all objectives in the organization, right down to the individual employee. Thus, it is proper to think of strategic objectives as the first rung in a hierarchy of objectives.

Functional and business objectives

The strategic objectives must permeate the entire organization if they are to serve their three purposes. Exactly how they are made known to lower levels of the organization depends upon whether the organization is a single-business or a multibusiness firm. For example, a single-business

[6] William F. Glueck, *Strategic Management and Business Policy* (New York: McGraw-Hill, 1980), pp. 37–38.

firm such as Wrigley which has specialized in producing chewing gum would need to transmit its strategic objectives to each of the functional units of the organization. Thus, the managers in charge of Wrigley's production, marketing, finance, engineering, and research units would of necessity have to prepare *functional objectives* which contribute to the corporation's *strategic objectives.*

Multibusiness corporations operate in more than one industry. In these organizations, strategic corporate objectives must be translated into *business objectives* and then into functional objectives. Companies such as Rockwell International do business in diverse industries, and a set of business objectives and strategies must be devised which complement corporate objectives. Rockwell, for example, does business in at least six industries: automotive; textile machinery; graphics systems; fiberglass; valves, meters, and power tools; and home entertainment and appliances.[7] In a general sense, corporate strategy (in multibusiness firms) is concerned with *what* set of businesses the firm should be in and business strategy is concerned with *how* to compete in each business.[8] In single-business firms, corporate and business strategies are one and the same, but regardless of whether a firm is in one or several businesses, functional objectives must be established.

The situation analysis

Many forces are beyond the control of managers. In this context, situational analysis refers to those factors in the organization's environments which influence the selection of appropriate strategies. Obviously, some organizations must survive in more uncertain environments than others. In any case, a major task of the planner is to anticipate and adapt to change that is *beyond* the control of the organization in order to initiate change that is *within* its control. Figure 5–2 presents the major components of the organization's environment. It is important to note that the components can influence an organization in two important ways. They may act as *constraints* or as *opportunities.* Many organizations enjoying above-average rates of growth have capitalized on opportunities presented by their environments. Firms such as Sears, McDonald's, and Xerox have benefited substantially through strategic planning which enabled early adaptation to environmental changes. Unfortunately, other firms, such as

[7] Milton Leontiades, *Strategies for Diversification and Change* (Boston: Little, Brown, 1980), pp. 79–82.

[8] Charles W. Hofer and Dan Schendel, *Strategy Formulation: Analytical Concepts* (New York: West Publishing, 1978), pp. 27–29.

A&P, Hershey's, and Montgomery Ward, have lost considerable ground in recent years through late adaptation to environmental changes. These firms did not react to changes, which ultimately influenced their performance. The changes may have been social changes, technological changes, competitive moves, or changes in consumer tastes. Whatever the case, the changes were not properly identified and constructive responses to them were not developed.

Economic conditions

The state of the economy affects the level of demand for the organization's products or services, the cost of its resources, and the opportunities available to it. For example, the economic problems of the 1970s had a negative impact on many educational and business organizations.

Technological changes

Changes in technology can influence the destiny of an organization. Technology may be a constraint when opportunities exist but the necessary technology is not present. However, technological innovations can create entirely new industries or vastly alter existing industries. Consider the

Figure 5–2

The environment of the strategic planner

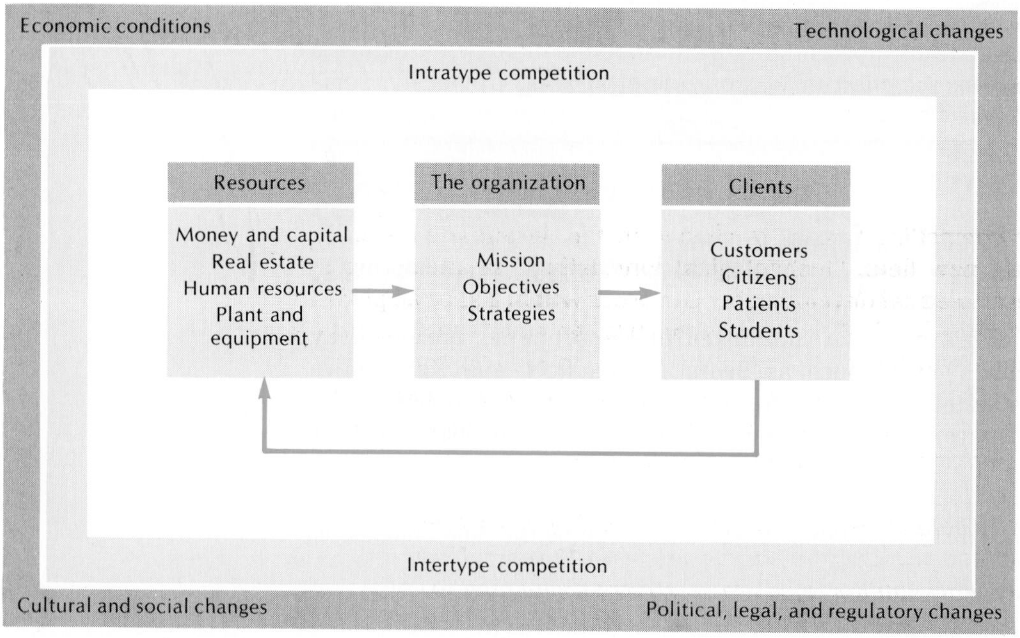

impact of teaching machines on education, of electronic funds transfer and automated teller equipment on banking, and of synthetic fibers on the apparel and carpeting industries. Technological innovations have vastly altered educational instruction in many fields. Because of technological innovations, instructors have had to learn new ways of teaching and students have been exposed to new learning methods. Electronic banking has reduced operating costs for bankers and has made banking services more widely and conveniently available to customers. To appreciate the pace of technological achievement, examine Figure 5–3. Science and technology will be compelling forces for change in the decades to come. In fact, a relatively new field, "technological forecasting," is attempting to predict what technological developments can occur within a specific period of time with a given level of resource allocation. In some organizations, strategic planners will be forced to be alert and to plan to compensate for technological changes, while in other organizations, a prime managerial function will be to instigate such changes. Concerning the impact of new technology on banking, a bank executive commented:

Figure 5–3

Some expected technological advances by the year 2000

1. Undersea farming and mining.
2. Mechanical devices to replace human organs.
3. Automatic language translators.
4. Reliable weather forecasts.
5. Controlled affective relationships and sleep.
6. Extensive use of robots and machine slaves.
7. Centralization of business information and high-speed data processes.
8. Human hibernation for fairly extensive time periods.
9. Increased mastery of energy.
10. New rapid transit systems.

> *I really believe we are not presently selling more than half of the products we will be selling in 10 years. Now if you don't think I've got some strategic planning to do, you're sadly mistaken. We are going to be forced*

to become product developers like consumer product manufacturers. If we face a string of new-product failures in the next decade, it will be because we failed in our strategic planning today. Strategic planning is the weakest managerial skill in our industry at the present time.

Political, legal, and regulatory changes

Numerous laws legislated by a multitude of authorities characterize the political, legal, and regulatory environment that is faced by most organizations. Strategic planning must consider these laws because they may also act as constraints as well as opportunities. For example, government action to combat inflation in the early 1970s constrained the builders of single-unit housing while providing opportunities for apartment builders. In the mid-1970s, the Vocational Education Act provided opportunities for certain types of educational institutions while acting as a constraint on others. Finally, while some groups of organizations, such as insurance companies, viewed Medicare as a constraint, nursing homes capitalized on the opportunities provided by Medicare. An example of how legal and regulatory changes can influence strategic planning was provided by an oil company executive:

In 1972, there was no such thing as unleaded gasoline. Because of environmental protection laws, over one third of the gasoline sold in 1978 was unleaded and was over one half by 1980.

Cultural and social changes

Change appears to be a constant element in our social system. Strategic planners must identify the changing cultural and social conditions that will influence the organization. The fact is that many organizations have not considered the impact of such changes or have underestimated their impact. The importance of cultural and social changes can be readily seen from the impact of the ecology movement on numerous industries, the consumerism impact on the automobile and supermarket industries, and the general societal demand for more social responsibility on the part of both public and private organizations. These changes, coupled with the more specific problems of equal rights for women and minority groups, make cultural and social change an environmental component which cannot be ignored. Societal values must eventually be reflected in strategic plans. A member of the corporate planning staff of a large consumer products firm clearly illustrated the impact of cultural and social changes when he stated:

> *No one will ever convince me that American industry could not have averted the pollution problems. Also, imagine having to be told you must replant trees, build safe cars, and label your packages truthfully. That's hard to believe. We have to realize that people want organizations to be responsive. Strategic planning, in my opinion, can enable organizations to be more responsive to society's expectations. The fact that we must examine the social environment as part of the strategic planning process should enable us to stay abreast of society's expectations.*

Competition

At a more immediate level, the actions of competitors have a significant impact on strategic planning. **Intratype competition** is competition between institutions engaged in the same basic activity and is the form of competition described in economic studies. Kellogg competes with Post for cereal customers. Ford competes with General Motors for automobile customers. The University of Kentucky competes with the University of Tennessee for undergraduate and graduate students, faculty members, and athletes. Your bank competes with the bank across the street for savings and checking account customers. **Intertype competition** occurs between different types of institutions. Kellogg competes with Procter & Gamble for shelf space in supermarkets, hospitals compete with health maintenance organizations for medical practitioners, and recently, some colleges and universities have faced competition from professional teams for high school athletes. The important point here is that all organizations face some type of competition for either resources or clients.

Resources

Our nation's recent problem with oil has underscored the reality that the ability of an organization to compete for and attract resources must be a critical consideration in strategic planning. The availablity of resources determines the organization's capacity to respond to the threats and opportunities presented to it. Depending on the type of organization, some resources will be more critical than others. A publicly supported college, for example, needs alumni backing, faculty, students, and the backing of state legislators who influence budget allocations. A hospital needs funds and qualified staff. A business organization needs capital and managerial talent.

The organization

The organization is, of course, the focal point of the strategic planning process. From a manager's point of view, how well the organization performs depends on how well it integrates and directs the conversion of resources in response to the needs of its clients and on how well it interacts with its environment. The organization's performance is the ultimate purpose of the practice of management, the improvement of which is the aim of this book.

View Figure 5–2 again. Although it may not specify every component of a strategic planner's environment, it does underscore the danger of viewing any organization as an independent entity. Managers can no longer afford the luxury of concentrating solely on the internal functioning of their organizations. Things are changing more rapidly now than ever before. Strategic planning represents management's attempt to anticipate the future and to guard itself against the threat of change. Consider the following comment by a marketing executive in a large consumer products firm:

> *Given how volatile our business is, and the serious impact some of the changes have had, I'm considering ways to incorporate an ongoing threat analysis into our planning process. I don't know exactly how to do it, but I know we should put forth some type of effort to identify, appraise, and propose reactions to threats from outside.*

Clients

Ultimately, how effective any organization is depends on how well it satisfies the needs of its clients. For a business organization, the customer plays the pivotal role in decision making. The main client publics of a college are prospective students, present students, and the organizations which hire its graduates. The important influence of clients on strategic planning is underscored by the fact that ultimately the economic and social justification for the existence of all organizations is to serve some clients.

When the situation analysis is completed, management will have a much better idea of what needs to be done (strategies) in order to achieve the organization's mission and objectives. It will be in a better position to develop sound organizational strategies.

Developing organizational strategies

When management has effectively determined what it would like to do (objectives) and what it is capable of doing (situation analysis), the time has come to develop strategies. The role of strategy in strategic planning is to identify the *general approaches* that the organization will utilize to achieve its continuing objectives. Table 5–1 presents the major component of strategy, the product-market matrix. The table indicates the product and market entries and growth paths that the organization can utilize to achieve its objectives. The table also indicates that an organization can grow in a variety of ways by concentrating on present or new products and on present or new customers.

Table 5–1

Product-market matrix

Markets \ Products	Present products	New products
Present customers	Market penetration	Product development
New customers	Market development	Diversification

Market penetration strategies

These strategies focus on improving the position of the organization's present products with its present customers. Such a strategy may involve devising a marketing plan to encourage present customers to purchase more of the product or a production plan to produce more efficiently what is being produced at present. In other words, it concentrates on improving the efficiency of various functional areas in the organization.

Market development strategies

Following this alternative, the organization would seek to find new customers for its present products. Recently, Johnson & Johnson successfully marketed its baby shampoo to adults. A situation analysis had indicated that the number of baby customers was declining and that an increasing number of adults were washing their hair more often than before. The firm knew that in order to achieve its objectives it would have to follow a strategy other than market penetration. Not so recently, Du Pont found new uses for its industrial product Teflon in kitchen utensils, and cosmetic firms found new customers (males) for hair spray, lotions, and other cosmetics.

Product development strategies

Utilizing these strategies, an organization would become involved in new-product development. The new products developed would, however, be aimed at present customers. Procter & Gamble produces over a dozen laundry detergents, about a half-dozen hand soaps, four heavy-duty household cleaners, and three liquid kitchen cleaners. This company is truly a master at product development. Gillette has also been extremely successful with a constant stream of new razor blades and shavers. Some colleges and universities have developed new programs that are aimed specifically at females and blacks who are already enrolled.

Diversification strategies

An organization diversifies when it seeks new products for customers whom it is not serving at present. It may attempt to manufacture the products itself, or it may acquire or merge with an ongoing organization. Earlier, we mentioned Coca-Cola's acquisition of Minute Maid. The firm is also planning to enter the wine business. Similarly, Pepsi-Cola acquired Frito-Lay.

On what basis does an organization choose one (or all) strategies? Why did Coca-Cola acquire Minute Maid rather than some other firm? Despite the increasing importance of analytical tools for strategic analysis, as noted in the Management Update, the ultimate answer is more subjective than objective. The answer, of course, lies in the organization's mission and its distinctive competences. Management should select those alternatives which take advantage of the organization's distinctive competences and are consistent with its mission. For example, a midwestern organization began as a chain of minisupermarkets emphasizing "convenience" (long hours, etc.). It has diversified into self-service filling stations, fast-food restaurants, and self-service dry cleaning establishments. All of this diversification centered on the broad class of needs for convenience. Had the organization viewed its mission in terms of food, it certainly would not have diversified so far afield from the food business. However, since it viewed itself as being in the convenience business, the diversification strategy made great sense.

The completed strategic plan

Figure 5–4 indicates the relationship between a completed strategic plan and appropriate functional plans for a firm in a single market or industry. Manufacturers with similar product lines or limited product lines will develop a strategic plan similar to the one in Figure 5–4. However, firms such as General Electric with both widely diversified product lines and widely diversified markets will usually develop several strategic plans ei-

Figure 5–4

Relationship between the strategic plan and functional plans

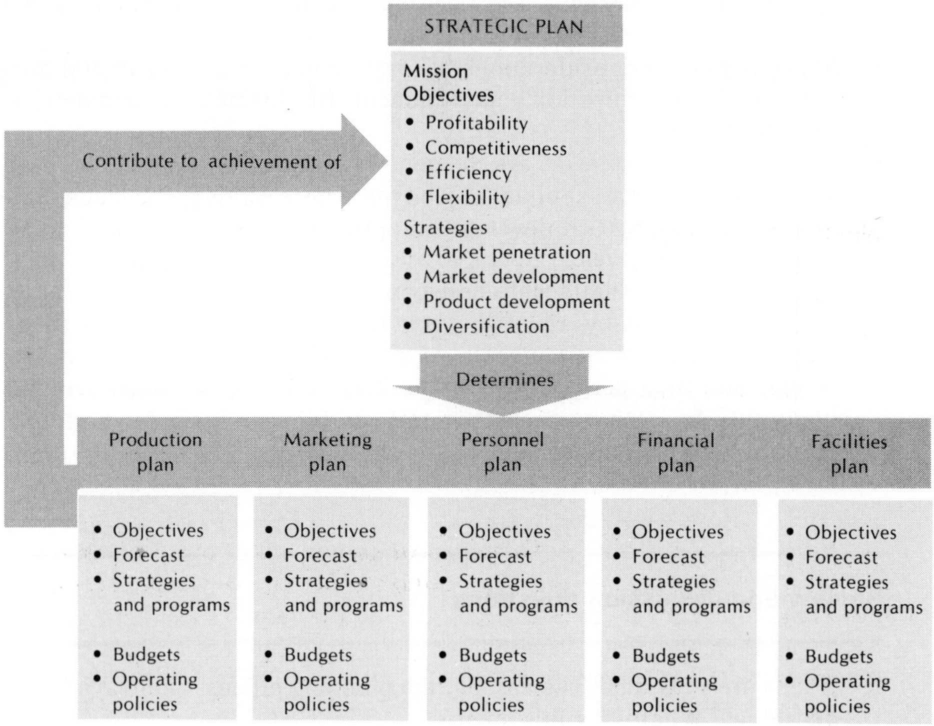

ther by units or by divisions, termed "businesses." These plans are usually combined into a master strategic plan.

Completing the strategic plan facilitates the development of plans in each of the business and functional areas. Given a completed strategic plan, each area knows exactly where the organization wishes to go and can then develop objectives and strategies which are consistent with the strategic plan. All plans, however, will be derived from the strategic plan, and the activities of the entire organization are integrated toward strategic objectives.

Management summary

1. Strategic analysis has increased in importance because of the rapidly changing world that managers face. Strategic analysis represents management's attempt to anticipate the future and to guard the organization against the threat of change.
2. A strategic plan consists of a clearly stated organizational mission, organizational objectives, and organizational strategies.
3. The organizational mission is a long-term vision of what the organization is trying to become. The basic questions that must be answered are "What is our business? What should it be?"
4. Three important considerations in formulating the organizational mission are the organization's environment, its distinctive competences, and its clients.
5. Organizational strategies are the general approaches that will be used to achieve the organizational objectives. These strategies include market penetration, market development, product development, and diversification alternatives.
6. There is a direct relationship between strategic planning and the planning that is done by all of the managers in the organization. If the organization's strategic plan is properly executed, the scope, range, issues, and time perspectives will differ but all of the organization's plans will be derived from the strategic plan and after a time will contribute to its achievement.

Review and discussion questions

1. "Plans are sometimes useless, but the planning process is always indispensable." What does this mean?
2. What is meant by the statement "Every manager plans"?

3. How can components of the environment act as constraints or opportunities?
4. In your opinion, what is the major distinctive competence of:
   a. The New York Yankees?
   b. McDonald's?
   c. *People* magazine?
   d. Sears?
   e. Nader's Raiders?
5. Choose any organization you are familiar with and develop a statement of organizational mission for it.
6. If Hugh Hefner of Playboy Enterprises came to you and asked the questions "What is my business? What should it be?" what would your answers be?
7. Why did you choose to attend your present school? Can your reasons be considered distinctive competences of your school? Can schools have distinctive competences? What do schools compete with, and for what do schools compete?
8. Someone once quoted a well-known cosmetic executive as saying, "In the factory we make cosmetics; in the drugstore we sell hope." What does this statement indicate about the executive?

Suggested reading

Beard, D. W., and G. G. Dess. "Corporate-Level Strategy, Business-Level Strategy, and Firm Performance." *Academy of Management Journal,* December 1981, pp. 663–88.

Fox, H. W. "The Frontiers of Strategic Planning: Intuition or Formal Models?" *Management Review,* April 1981, pp. 8–14.

Kast, F. "Scanning the Future Environment: Social Indicators." *California Management Review,* Fall 1980, pp. 22–31.

Kiechel, W. "Playing the Gobal Game." *Fortune,* November 16, 1981, pp. 111, 114, 118, 122, 126.

Klein, H. E., and W. H. Newman. "How to Integrate New Environmental Forces into Strategic Planning." *Management Review,* July 1980, pp. 40–48.

Kudla, R. J. "The Effects of Strategic Planning on Common Stock Returns." *Academy of Management Journal,* March 1980, pp. 5–20.

Reimann, B. C. "Organizational Competence as a Predictor of Long-Run Survival and Growth." *Academy of Management Journal,* June 1982, pp. 323–34.

Schwartz, H., and S. M. Davis. "Matching Corporate Culture and Business Strategy." *Organizational Dynamics,* Summer 1981, pp. 30–48.

Tolley, L. "Management in the 1980's—Key Issues and Priorities." *Long-Range Planning,* February 1981, pp. 55–59.

Applying what you have learned about planning through strategic analysis

Cases:

New strategy at General Electric
Strategic planning at The Illusion

New strategy at General Electric*

In a recent poll of the top executives of the nation's 500 largest firms by *Fortune* magazine, General Electric ranked as the nation's best-managed industrial company. For 1981, the firm was expected to report earnings of $1.6 billion on revenues of approximately $28 billion. Its 250 individual businesses produce everything from silicon chips to nuclear reactors, from microwave ovens to robots, from Australian coal to computer time-sharing services. This diversification has protected profits in economic downturns; GE has recorded 26 straight quarters of improved earnings, through 2½ recessions.

Unfortunately, however, this outstanding performance has not had the same impact on the price of GE stock. For example, if an investor put $1,000 into GE stock 10 years ago, the stock would today be worth only $454 in constant 1971 dollars. Even including dividends, a shareholder wouldn't have beaten inflation. Analysts believe that the broad business base that protects the firm in bad times prevents the stock price from taking off when times are good. They also believe it makes the company difficult to understand.

In 1981, John F. Welch became the youngest chairman in the 90-year history of the company. One of his first tasks is to work on the slow-growth, stodgy image that GE has among investors. A difficulty will be to bring about changes without damaging the reputation for stability, predictable increases in earnings, and sound management that GE has achieved.

One of his first moves was to begin shifting decision-making power back toward GE's 250

---

* This case is adapted from Ann M. Morrison, "Trying to Bring G.E. to Life," *Fortune,* January 25, 1982, pp. 51–57.

businesses. Previously, operations have been very centralized to a point, Welch believes, that some managers believed their initiative was stifled and risk was avoided. Now Welch wants managers to think and act more like entrepreneurs than bureaucrats, and he is beginning to give them the responsibility, authority, and incentives to do so. However, he demands that they strive toward one overall objective: They must establish their businesses as No. 1 or No. 2 in their industries or achieve a clear marketing advantage as a result of a decided technological edge.

The trouble with some of GE's market leaders, apparently, is that they are not growing. "Being No. 1 or 2 in hula hoops would not do much good," says Welch. One of GE's hula hoops is nuclear power. In keeping with the more entrepreneurial spirit, Welch asked the managers running that business to come up with a plan for the 1980s. At first, they presented a strategy that called for building three nuclear reactors a year. Welch rejected the idea (there hasn't been an order for a nuclear reactor since 1975 that has not been cancelled). The managers then proposed (1) to fulfill existing contracts for building reactors, (2) to concentrate on providing fuel and technology to customers, and (3) to continue research on safer technologies. Welch believes such a plan will result in good profits in the short run. He expects GE to phase out of nuclear power, except for service, fuel, and research in the next decade.

The process by which the solution was arrived at for the nuclear power business is expected to be repeated in other slow-growth businesses, even those where GE has traditionally dominated the field. It will certainly be done in the 30 percent of GE's businesses that are not first or second in their markets, even if they are showing good growth rates. Welch tells his managers, "You've got to come up with a plan. You can't wish things will get better."

Welch believes that the objective of leading and leading-edge businesses is also important internally. "Every person running a business will have a clear-cut understanding that if he can be No. 1 or No. 2, he'll have a great job, an upside opportunity, success, and all the money he needs . . . if it works internally, it will work, in time, externally."

Welch believes that if he can get the investment community to understand his central idea, that GE is not going to move in 90 directions at once, and that the firm is positioning itself to provide growth with safety, then GE shares will get a higher price.

Questions:

1. What is your opinion of the things that Mr. Welch is doing?
2. What do you think Welch means when he says "if it works internally, it will work, in time, externally"?
3. How can an organization do as well as GE has done and not have it reflected in the demand for its stock?

Strategic planning at The Illusion

Johnny Fame is owner of The Illusion, a nightclub in a large Northeastern city. For over 25 years, it has been a top night spot, attracting good crowds with live top-name entertainment. Johnny was proud of the fact that "all the big acts had played The Illusion at one time or another."

During the last five years, however, business has been declining steadily. Johnny has spent a great deal of his time during the last six months trying to identify the causes of the problem and possible solutions to it. He has identified what he believes to be three changing environmental forces that are severely threatening his club.

1. *Social.* Rising crime rates in the inner city are causing people to avoid coming into the city at night and on weekends.
2. *Competition for resources.* One of The Illusion's chief resources is entertainers. Unfortunately, entertainer fees are skyrocketing. This is because television competes for the same resources, and an entertainer can make more for appearing on one TV special than for doing two shows a night for a week at The Illusion.
3. *Competition for clients.* Better TV programming and more successful movies are taking customers away.

Johnny believes that it will be necessary for him to find new ways for attracting people and reducing nightclub costs.

Questions:

1. Is Johnny facing a problem in strategic planning? Why?
2. Are there any other possible environmental changes which Johnny has not considered?
3. What advice would you give Johnny? Why?

6

Chapter six
Planning through management by objectives

Performance objectives

- **Define** management by objectives (MBO).
- **State** the difference between MBO as a management technique and MBO as a way of planning.
- **Describe** the major stages of the MBO process.
- **Explain** the critical nature of participation in objective setting to the success of an MBO program.
- **Discuss** the major benefits and problems associated with MBO.

Management update*

Georgia's Citizens and Southern National Bank (C&S) has recently realized impressive gains in earnings, dividend payouts, stock price, deposits, and other performance measures. In part, these gains are the result of revised operating procedures and policies, but also, in part, due to the installation of a management by objectives (MBO) planning approach. The MBO approach to management reflects the managerial philosophy of Bennett A. Brown, chief executive officer (CEO) of C&S, who in 1978 took on the task of revitalizing a once successful financial institution.

Since assuming the position of CEO, Brown has developed the MBO idea as a method for planning each individual's and each unit's contributions to the overall performance of C&S. The present planning system took several years to develop, and it is still evolving. The MBO system consists of several basic elements and practices. The basic element is a five-year plan which is developed by Brown and the executive committee of the board of directors. The five-year plan sets targets for the principal measures of the bank's overall performance. Brown himself is accountable to the executive committee for the achievement of these results. Brown, in turn, meets with senior managers to set objectives for the five-year period and for shorter, intermediate periods of time. The senior managers meet with lower-level managers to set mutually agreeable objectives. The intent of the MBO planning system at C&S is to integrate the activities of all the bank's units toward common and acceptable objectives.

Another basic element of the system is the quarterly review of progress toward the planned objectives. The review sessions require managers to meet with their subordinates, to gauge progress, and to identify obstacles and opportunities. Managers, in turn, meet with their superiors, and the review process culminates when Brown reviews the quarterly progress with the executive committee.

A key practice which reflects Brown's managerial approach is to give subordinates considerable autonomy in choosing methods for achieving their objectives. As Brown stated: "You put a guy in charge, and if he doesn't do it, you get rid of him." The MBO system, as developed at C&S, provides opportunities for individuals to participate in setting objectives toward which they plan their activities. The system encourages accountability for performance of those objectives throughout the organization, from Brown on down.

---

* This Management Update is adapted from "How One Troubled Bank Turned Itself Around," *Business Week*, August 24, 1981, pp. 117, 122.

Management by objectives (MBO) may be one of the most important developments in the field of management during the last two decades. During this time, it has achieved growing acceptance not only in business organizations but also in health care organizations, governmental organizations, and school systems. The appeal of MBO is undoubtedly a result of its characteristics. MBO is very straightforward. Therefore, it is not difficult for a manager to understand, although it is not always as easy to implement. Most managers believe that MBO agrees with common sense and that it is what good managers should be doing.

MBO has acquired many followers since it was first introduced in the 1950s. Peter Drucker, who introduced the concept, described it as follows:

> The objective of the district manager's job should be defined by the contribution he and his district sales force have made to the sales department, the objectives of the project engineer's job by the contribution he, his engineers and draftsmen make to the engineering department. . . .
>
> This requires each manager to develop and set the objectives of his unit himself. Higher management must, of course, reserve the power to approve or disapprove these objectives. But their development is part of a manager's responsibility; indeed, it is his first responsibility.[1]

It is easy to see why to many managers the above ideas appear to reflect plain common sense. One executive with an insurance company commented:

> *We have always managed that way. We have always had some kind of objectives, and everyone knows what they are.*

What this insurance executive was talking about is not MBO. Many managers who have had several years of experience in trying to apply the formal

[1] Peter Drucker, *The Practice of Management* (New York: Harper & Row, 1954), pp. 128–29.

approach of MBO in their management work tend to admit that they had not really managed this way in the past. What do we mean by the formal approach to MBO? It is perhaps best summarized in this statement from one of the early advocates and developers of the concepts underlying MBO:

> a process whereby the superior and subordinate managers of an organization jointly identify its common goals, define each individual's major areas of responsibility in terms of the results expected of him, and use these measures as guides for operating the unit and assessing the contribution of each of its members.[2]

What is MBO

MBO can be viewed as a motivation technique because the components of objective setting, participation, and feedback are important enhancers of motivation. It can also be viewed as a performance appraisal technique, since evaluations of subordinates are based on how well they achieve mutually agreed-upon objectives. It can also be viewed as a technique for developing and changing an organization. In this respect, managers can evaluate the need for change, establish mutually agreed-upon objectives for changing the organization (or a subunit of the organization), and then evaluate periodically the progress that has been made in accomplishing the changes. Last, but by no means least, MBO is a management planning technique because mutually agreed-upon objectives become the bases for subsequent planning activities. Actual results are compared to the established objectives, and any deviations can be addressed. Thus, MBO can be viewed as a technique with a variety of uses.

In the context of managerial planning, MBO is a process through which each individual and each unit in an organization identifies the basic objectives of their activities, as illustrated in the Management Update. The strength of MBO as a planning process is that it causes individuals to focus on what they are trying to *get done* (objectives), rather than on what they *are doing* (activities). As the objectives of each individual and unit are identified and correlated with those of related individuals and units, a plan for allocating resources can be developed that has as its foundation the explicit statements and commitments to relevant objectives. Thus, the strength of MBO is its focus on accomplishment of legitimate objectives.

[2] George Odiorne, *Management by Objectives* (New York: Pitman, 1965), p. 26.

The basic principles of management by objectives

Throughout the evolution of MBO and the current thinking on the approach, there appear to be four basic underlying principles. These are objectives, time, participation, and motivation.

Objectives

As noted earlier, objectives are specific concise statements of expected accomplishments. They may be *quantitative commitments* to action; for example, "Reduce the number of defective units by 15 percent by the end of the year" or "Increase the sales volume of product A by 10 percent over the next two years."

In many jobs, the objectives are vague. For example, an engineering-oriented organization with many highly educated technical personnel defines objectives in the area of "technical skill improvement." An engineer with the organization outlined it as follows:

> *We discuss any barriers to performance that we feel our subordinates might have. For example, I supervise a group of product development engineers in our office products division. I have found that most of them are deficient with respect to capital budgeting and other financial analysis techniques. This has been defined as an area where improvement is needed for success in the current job. They all agreed, so now once a week a professor from a local university teaches a three-hour seminar on the subject.*

Objectives established in such less tangible areas become *qualitative commitments* to action. Figure 6–1 provides samples of quantitative and qualitative objectives for a sales executive.

Time

The element of *time* is very important in MBO planning approaches. Such approaches include a time schedule for reaching various levels of accomplishment. The time designated may be six months, one year, and in some cases, five years. The purpose of the time schedule is to encourage the individual to accomplish specific objectives within a stipulated period.

Figure 6–1

Sample objectives for a sales executive

Quantitative	Qualitative
1. Increase sales volume of new product line by 7 percent next year.	1. Develop new compensation plan for salespeople.
2. Reduce advertising expenditures by 10 percent next year.	2. Evaluate alternative sales incentive programs and select one by year-end
3. Expand sales to new customers by $250,000 over the next two years.	3. Develop more efficient reporting system to cut down paperwork for salespeople.

Thus, the purpose of timing the completion of objectives is to induce discipline in the achievement of objectives.

Participation

Subordinates must play a significant role in establishing objectives. Although there has been much controversy over the value of subordinates' participation, it has been found that meaningful participation usually brings favorable results. When individuals perceive that they have some control over the way objectives are set and over the means for reaching them, they view participation as meaningful and will respond favorably more often than not. A manager in a public utility underscored the importance of participation as follows:

> *If you ask me what the most important aspect of MBO is, I would have to say jointly establishing objectives. If you didn't have that, you wouldn't have MBO. All you would have is someone telling you what to do. What makes MBO work in this organization is participation by manager and subordinate in establishing objectives for the subordinate. It really makes the difference.*

Motivation

The motivational aspect of MBO is very important because individual commitment to, and achievement of, results can lead to a high level of job performance. The clearer the individual's idea is of what he or she is trying to accomplish and why, the greater are the chances of accomplishing it, especially if the individual has played a role in planning that part of the job.

Thus, MBO focuses on the *results* of work and not on the work itself. As a planning approach, MBO appears to have a number of distinct advantages:

The concrete objectives that MBO develops can direct performance, reduce uncertainty, and serve as an instrument of communication.

MBO can disclose where greater coordination among managers is necessary. For example, one organizational unit may have to lower a budget request when it is pointed out that another unit needs it more.

MBO can result in improved planning because the subordinate knows what the objectives and the superior's expectations are.

MBO can result in more effective management control because a manager who knows what the objectives are can respond immediately to deviations from standards.[3]

The MBO process

The MBO planning system is a process by which the members of an organization jointly establish its objectives. The process comprises three stages:

1. Individuals in an organization and their superiors meet and determine, agree upon, and state very precisely the specific results that are to be accomplished by some designated future date. These agreed-upon objectives may be set for the individuals or for the units they manage.
2. Action plans are developed to accomplish the objectives. This stage involves developing strategies and policies. The end result is an action plan which details precisely how the individuals or the units will accomplish the objectives.
3. At designated times, performance is reviewed. The results achieved by the individuals or the units are measured against the objectives that were set previously.

The basic concepts of MBO cannot bring about improved performance until they are translated into action. It is because of the actual application

[3] Michael J. Etzel and John M. Ivancevich, "Management by Objectives in Marketing: Philosophy, Process, and Problems," *Journal of Marketing,* October 1974, p. 48.

and implementation of the three stages described above that MBO has proven useful in many organizations. The three stages are diagramed in Figure 6–2. Because of their importance, we shall examine each stage in detail.

Developing objectives

Obviously, the core of any MBO effort is the process of determining exactly what it is that an organization, a subunit of an organization, or an individual should seek to accomplish. Controversy exists about the best way to go about establishing objectives. Specifically, much discussion often centers on whether objectives should be established from the top downward or from the bottom upward. There seems to be general agreement that the effort must be two-way. The following comment from an executive in an organization that has used MBO successfully expresses this view clearly:

> *We discovered very early that the objective-setting process cannot be exclusively top-down or bottom-up if it is to be a truly joint effort. The communication and the effort involved in planning must go in both directions.*

The issue of participation in objective setting is a very important one. Participation simply means that the superior and the subordinate get together to produce a set of mutually agreed-upon objectives. Participation

Figure 6–2

The MBO process

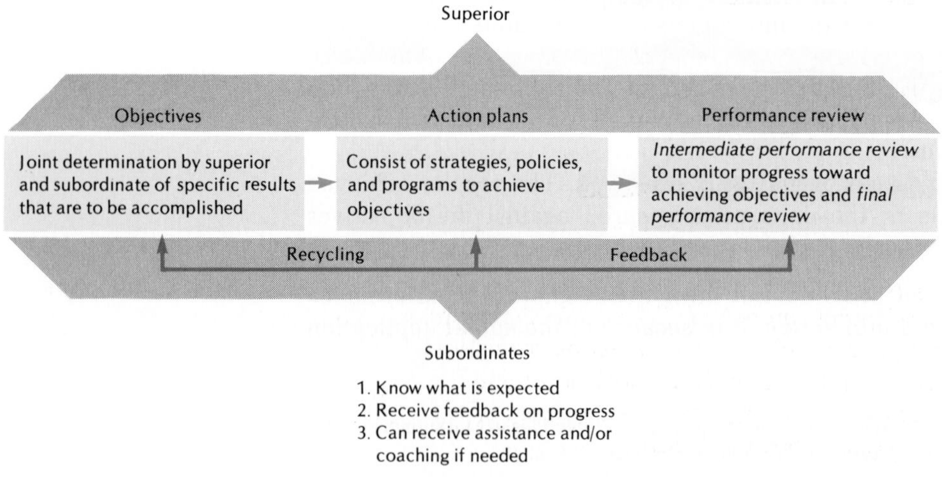

in the objective-setting process is designed to increase the subordinates' understanding of their roles in the organization and to let them know what is expected of them. It is also hoped that it will result in greater commitment to achieving the objectives. However, this aspect of MBO is often misunderstood, as was noted by the above executive in the following statement:

> *There is one aspect of objective setting that you must not misinterpret. Participation in the objective-setting process does not mean that your subordinates can decide to do whatever they please. On the other hand, it also does not mean a contrived meeting where you spend your time convincing your subordinate that your objectives are the ones that you should both agree to. Objective setting must be a truly mutual activity that takes into account both the subordinate's and the organization's needs.*

The development of acceptable specific objectives leads to better performance on the part of subordinates. However, there are potential pitfalls in the process. For example, objectives that an individual perceives as very difficult to achieve may lead to decreased rather than increased performance. In addition, to be truly effective, organizational objectives must take into account the personal objectives of the subordinates. When these considerations are combined with the recognition that objectives differ in their difficulty of achievement and that the time frame for accomplishing objectives varies, the process of objective setting becomes quite complex.

Another difficulty in establishing objectives relates to their measurability. If objectives are measurable, one's success or lack of success in achieving them is readily apparent. However, in attempts to quantify objectives, two problems can arise. First, "proxy" measures that do not adequately measure performance may be used. An example of this problem was provided by a bank training officer.

> *We have a basic sales training course that all of our customer contact personnel must go through. The purpose of the program is to improve the selling skills of tellers, new accounts people, and other branch personnel. When I came here last year, I was surprised to find that everyone assumed that because we had this training program, the objective of improved selling skills was being accomplished. I'm now in the process of developing some indicators of sales performance (e.g., number of new accounts opened, additional services used) which will be included as part of the employees' performance evaluation.*

Second, less measurable objectives such as professional development may be overlooked. The problem of establishing objectives in less tangible areas of performance was noted earlier in the chapter. It is important to mention it again here because in areas of the organization where quantitative performance measures are plentiful (e.g., production and marketing), intangible but very important areas of performance, such as employee development, may not be adequately emphasized by managers.

Each organization must develop its own MBO form to list objectives and target dates, record progress, and plan future activities. These forms are in reality agreements between the superior and the subordinate on expected performance. Each retains a copy of the form, which becomes the focal point of the progress review and evaluation sessions. An example of such a form is presented in Figure 6–3. The objectives, projections, and plans to achieve the objectives are worked out by the superior and the subordinate. At each periodic review (there are three in Figure 6–3), the actual performance is filled in and any changes in the plans are briefly described.

The critical role of the objective-setting phase of an MBO program cannot be overemphasized. It is the core of any MBO effort. Figure 6–4 presents some useful guidelines for establishing objectives.[4]

Developing action plans

Note that the form in Figure 6–3 provides space for a statement of a plan of action to achieve the objectives. This second phase of the MBO process is, in fact, a key step in implementing an MBO planning system. The action plan details the specific behaviors that the subordinate will engage in as time passes. For example, suppose that you establish the objective of losing 15 pounds in the next five months. This measurable objective appears to be achievable but challenging. To lose the weight, you must develop an action plan which involves establishing a series of subobjectives relating to the number of calories consumed per day, certain exercises completed each evening, and weekly weigh-ins. Keeping track of the accomplishment of your progress and of the results of your weekly weigh-ins provides you with feedback on how well your action plan is working.

An action plan may be developed by the manager and the subordinate jointly or by the subordinate alone shortly after the objectives have been mutually agreed upon. Once the action plan has been developed, it should be reviewed by the manager. Certain checkpoints should be identified to enable a periodic review of progress. Note that the form in Figure 6–3 provides for a review every three months. The end result of the action

[4] Developed from W. E. Rief and G. Bassord, "What MBO Really Is," *Business Horizons*, June 1973, p. 26.

Figure 6–3

Sample MBO form

Performance and action plan for ______________________ Job title ______________________

Objective statement	3 months		*Plan*	6 months		*Plan*	9 months		*Plan*	1 year	
	Projected	Actual		Projected	Actual		Projected	Actual		Projected	Actual
1.											
2.											
3.											

Figure 6–4

Some guidelines for establishing objectives

1. Objectives should be related to the needs of the organization and should support organizational objectives.
2. Objectives should be clear, concise, and realistic.
3. Objectives should be measurable and quantified whenever possible.
4. Objectives should be guides to action; they should state what to achieve, not how to achieve it.
5. Objectives should be ambitious enough to offer a challenge, so that subordinates can be proud when they achieve them.
6. Objectives should take into consideration internal and external constraints; that is, factors not subject to control by the individual who is responsible for results.
7. Setting objectives is a joint undertaking, and objectives should be mutually agreed upon by the responsible individual and the superior.

plan is a planning document that enables the manager and the subordinate to monitor progress over time. In fact, the action plan can serve as the core of the subordinate's job description for the period covered by the plan. This is because it outlines clearly and specifically the subordinate's activities and objectives. Action plans were strongly supported by the plant manager of a manufacturing firm:

> *The managers in my unit have told me that the actual doing of the work is easy compared with planning what to do and how to do it. They certainly don't mind working and doing what they set out to do. It sounds corny to say it, but I believe that when they really have a say in establishing their own objectives and developing their own plans, they go to work with a greater commitment. When problems do arise, they are a challenge to overcome.*

Figure 6–5 summarizes some guidelines for developing action plans.[5] An important problem that often arises in MBO programs is the lack of attention that is given to this phase of the process. Apparently, many managers concentrate on developing objectives but forget that MBO is a way of planning. Although objectives are obviously the critical element, it is the action plans to achieve the objectives that give the organization its direction.

[5] Summarized from ibid., p. 27.

Figure 6–5

Some guidelines for developing an action plan

1. Divide all of the necessary activities and tasks into steps. This enables proper attention to be given to each phase of the action plan. Define the purpose of each step, state what is required to perform it, and set forth the expected results.
2. Note the relationships among steps, being careful to identify any sequences. Scheduling can be improved considerably if steps overlap, and the time required to achieve objectives can be reduced if there is no need to delay one action until another has been completed.
3. Decide who is responsible for each step.
4. Determine what resources are needed.
5. Estimate how much time is required to perform each step and set specific dates for the completion of the various steps.

Reviewing performance

Because the operations of most organizations are ongoing, the review of progress toward objectives becomes a continuous, ongoing process. We shall discuss that process in two phases: the intermediate performance reviews and the final performance evaluation.

Intermediate performance reviews When objectives have been established and action plans developed, progress toward achieving the objectives must be monitored. The importance of monitoring progress toward objectives was clearly stated by a sales executive:

> *If you want to focus people's attention on results, you have to keep them informed about things that affect those results. These may be things which they have control over or things which they have no control over, such as a new product by a competitor or a sluggish economy. The important thing is that they know how they are doing and that they also know that we do everything we can to keep them informed about how they are doing and about things that can affect them.*

Managers usually perform two roles in the intermediate review process. First, they listen to and evaluate the subordinate's remarks concerning progress toward attainment of the objectives. If an upward or downward revision in the objectives appears appropriate, the manager must decide whether the subordinate is assessing the situation realistically. An executive with a chain of restaurants stated his organization's approach to this aspect of the intermediate review process as follows:

We emphasize that an objective, once carefully considered and approved, is not changed easily. A manager's task is to reach the objectives, not change them when things get rough. An objective is changed only after an effort is made to develop a new action plan that will enable the achievement of the original objective.

Second, managers provide the subordinate with pertinent information on matters that may affect the achievement of objectives, such as organizational changes or the activity of competitors. A sales exexutive expressed the following opinion regarding this phase:

It seems to me that providing useful feedback on matters influencing the subordinates' objective achievement is important for two reasons. First, it lets the individual know that the MBO process is a two-way street and that management is sincere. If an objective becomes unachievable, for whatever reason, what can be accomplished by holding the subordinate to it except mistrust on the part of the subordinate and a collapse in the entire MBO process? Second, our industry is a volatile one. Keeping our salespeople informed of market or competitive changes that might influence their goal achievement allows them to adjust their action plans based on the feedback. It seems to me that this can only have a beneficial impact on the performance of the salespeople, with a resulting beneficial impact on the performance of the organization. What can you accomplish by forcing people to continue with action plans that won't work?

The intermediate sessions should be supportive and serve as positive reinforcement for subordinates while also acting as a checkup to locate potential problems before they can seriously interfere with progress toward the objectives.

Final evaluation The final step in the MBO process is the evaluation of progress. This final meeting between the manager and the subordinate focuses on performance over the entire period. The final review must accomplish two important purposes: (1) an evaluation of the objectives achieved and the relation of these accomplishments to rewards, such as salary increments or promotions and (2) an evaluation of performance that is intended to aid the subordinate in self-development and to set the stage for the next planning period.

Since the final evaluation follows several intermediate performance reviews, it should not contain any surprises for either of the parties involved. The following comment from an executive with a large manufacturing company summarizes how the process should occur:

> *If an objective is not achieved, the manager and the subordinate should first try to determine why. Perhaps the objective was unrealistic or unattainable for some other reason. If they agree that the objective was achievable, they focus their efforts on what got in the way of achieving it. They should jointly try to uncover the mistakes of the period past so that those mistakes can be avoided in the next period.*
>
> *Of course, a situation often arises where an objective is exceeded. This may be good, but in the evaluation meeting, some consideration should be given to whether this performance resulted in any difficulties for other units. Perhaps other units had not planned for overaccomplishment of the particular objective. If sales volume far exceeds its objective, this could have caused problems in the production or shipping departments. This is a good exercise because it underscores the interdependence of the various organizational units. Obviously, you also try to determine what accounted for overachieving an objective so that, if desired, this can be repeated in the next period. All of this points up what I believe is a very valuable and often overlooked benefit of the MBO process, that is, using both the good and bad experiences of the past to bring about improved performance in the next period.*

Recycling The end of one MBO planning cycle is also the beginning of another. The final performance evaluation session leads directly into establishing objectives for the next period. Divisional or departmental objectives are established; individual objective-setting sessions are conducted; and the MBO process recycles, as outlined in Figure 6–2.

Appraising MBO

Now that the reader is familiar with the funadmentals of MBO, some important points should be clear. At the outset of the chapter, we noted that MBO has a great commonsense appeal and that most managers agree that it is what they should be doing. In fact, many managers believe that they should develop plans of what they hope to accomplish, and then they should utilize the plans as their major tool for controlling progress toward their objectives. MBO is a sound approach for planning, and it has produced positive results from some managers and subordinates. In this section, we shall identify the major benefits associated with MBO and the problems it has encountered.

Benefits of MBO

The usefulness of a planning system such as MBO should be measured by its contribution to improved performance.

Improved managerial performance An important means of improving organizational performance is to improve the performance of the managers in the organization. Supporters of MBO believe that it improves managerial performance because it increases the likelihood that managers will achieve what they set out to achieve. For example, if a sales manager plans to reduce selling expenses by a certain percentage, the expenses will be reduced. If a production manager plans to reduce defective units by a certain percentage, the number of defective units will be reduced. MBO forces individuals to plan what they wish to do and provides direction in planning their work. An executive in an organization with a successful MBO program stated this benefit in the following way:

> *We like it because it produces results—plain and simple results that usually show up on the bottom line.*

Improved planning Planning has always been the key management function. Many managers believe that MBO makes them more effective planners because it provides them with a rigorous approach to developing "complete" plans. Managers know what their objectives are and how they will accomplish them. The director of a state government agency expressed a change in his approach to planning as follows:

> *I actually reversed the way I viewed the task of management. I never thought about it before, but I used to focus on the activities or the work that needed to be done. I just assumed that results would be forthcoming as a result of work. Now I think first of the results I want to achieve. Then I decide what activities we should engage in, what work we should do to accomplish the objectives. I always thought I was a planner, but now I believe I'm an effective planner.*

> *My attention is focused on results, and my activities are derived from the results I expect to achieve.*

Thus, MBO enables better performance of the management function of planning because managers know more clearly than before what they are trying to do. The experience of Georgia's C&S Bank, described in the Management Update, illustrates this benefit.

Improved superior-subordinate relationships One of the often mentioned benefits of MBO is that it decreases the necessity for close supervision. Since subordinates participate in establishing objectives and planning the work, they become less dependent on superiors. The participation of subordinates results in improved relationships among the various levels of management and between superiors and subordinates.

Improved management development MBO has proved to be useful for developing managerial abilities. It gives managers the opportunity to assume responsibility for their performance. The intermediate review sessions and the personal development session of the final performance evaluation provide information and opportunities that enable managers to improve the knowledge and skills they need to perform their jobs. Another management development benefit was mentioned by a manager in a government agency who said:

> *One thing we found is that MBO has enabled managers to get involved with, and take responsibility for, developing subordinates. This is important for managers to do, and MBO builds it directly into the management job.*

Problems with MBO

MBO is not without problems, not the least of which are the major effort and the commitments of both time and money that are necessary. The top management of an organization must be totally committed to MBO and must be ready to invest the time and effort to make it work. When MBO has not worked, the reasons are usually attributed to the following problems:

Establishing clear objectives In many cases, problems arise because of difficulties in developing precise objectives. There are probably several causes of these difficulties. First, managers have to learn how to plan by objectives. Despite the logic and the commonsense appeal of MBO, the process must be learned. Effective training programs must be developed to teach the process to managers. This is an important step, and if it is not done effectively, unsuccessful implementation of MBO can result.

Second, managers will often focus only on those objectives that have been clearly defined. As a result, they ignore other important activities because these are less explicit. This is especially the case where qualitative objectives are necessary. The problems associated with qualitative objectives were discussed earlier in the chapter.

Developing a climate of trust In a situation in which superiors and subordinates participate in objective setting, a climate of trust is essential. This problem was discussed by a bank branch officer:

> *Unfortunately, top management cannot send a memo to every employee declaring that henceforth everyone will trust each other. You cannot gain commitment and cooperation without a climate of trust. Let's face it, some organizations cannot achieve this. Subordinates view MBO as another manipulation technique by management. I'm sure it's related to the history of the organization, but if mistrust exists, you can forget MBO.*

Participation in objective setting only works if people want to participate. This is certainly not always the case, since many individuals prefer to be directed.

Adapting information systems The importance of information feedback to a successful MBO program has been noted. Feedback is especially important for the intermediate performance reviews. Unfortunately, in some cases, the organization's information system may not be capable of supplying truly relevant information. In other cases, it may produce too much irrelevant information.

Procedural problems Some MBO programs have encountered serious procedural problems. The director of a state social agency identified the cause of the failure of MBO in her agency:

> *MBO didn't work here in my opinion because the consultants who implemented it were more concerned about technique than about the program itself. The amount of paperwork was absurd. The need to process, complete, and update MBO forms became so excessive that the directors just didn't complete them. It was a case of the tail wagging the dog.*

Overemphasis on results The focus of MBO is on *results* and not on the activities to accomplish the results. Critics point out that reaching the objective at a prohibitive cost will not improve organizational performance because it may sacrifice efficiency, flexibility, and competitiveness.

Management summary

1. During the last two decades, MBO has achieved growing acceptance as a planning technique in many private and public organizations.
2. There are four underlying principles of MBO; objectives, time, participation, and motivation. These principles are the basic foundation of every successful MBO program.
3. The MBO process involves three major phases. First, individuals in an organization and their superiors meet and determine, agree upon, and state very precisely the specific results that are to be accomplished by some designated date. These objectives may be for individuals or for units. Second, action plans are developed to accomplish the agreed-upon objectives. Third, performance is reviewed at designated times. The results achieved by the individual or the unit are measured against the previously established objectives.
4. The issue of participation in objective setting is a very important one. The participation of subordinates in objective setting has the purpose of increasing their understanding of their role in the organization and of letting them know what is expected of them. It is hoped that this will result in the greater commitment of subordinates to achieving the objectives.
5. Action plans in the MBO process detail exactly how the subordinates will proceed and what specific behaviors they will engage in. An action plan may involve establishing activities that are designed to achieve the overall objective.
6. The review of performance should take place in two phases. The intermediate performance reviews are used to monitor progress toward the achievement of objectives. The final performance evaluation is the meeting between the superior and the subordinate at which the subordinate's performance over the entire period is reviewed.
7. The final performance evaluation is usually conducted in two stages: (1) an evaluation of the objectives achieved and the relating of these accomplishments to such reward systems as salary increments and promotion and (2) an evaluation of performance that is intended to aid the subordinate in self-development and to set the stage for the next period.
8. The end of one MBO cycle is the beginning of another. The final performance evaluation leads directly into the establishing of objectives for the next period.
9. MBO has been shown to provide some distinct benefits when it is implemented successfully. These are improved managerial performance, improved planning, improved control, improved superior-subordinate relationships, and improved management developement.

10. MBO is not without problems and critics. Where it has been unsuccessful, this has often been attributed to problems in establishing clear objectives, in developing a climate of trust, or in adapting information systems; to procedural problems; or to an overemphasis on results.

Review and discussion questions

1. Why, in your opinion, is MBO thought to have a great deal of commonsense appeal?
2. Some managers believe that MBO is what they have always been doing. Do you agree? What differences, if any, do you see?
3. We have presented MBO as "a way of planning." In a paragraph, describe what this means to you.
4. Discuss the four basic principles of MBO; objectives, time, participation, and motivation. Why do we consider them to be the foundation of MBO?
5. Assume that you have decided to establish objectives relating to your performance in your management class. State one quantitative objective and one qualitative objective that you might establish.
6. Outline the three stages of an MBO program. Could this approach be utilized by your management instructor in the classroom? Explain.
7. Select two instructors with whom you take classes at present. Suppose that each of them asked you to participate in an objective-setting session relating to your performance in the class. Describe what your reactions would be. Would they differ for the two instructors? If so, explain why.
8. Why is MBO often referred to as a continuous process?
9. In your opinion, what is the most important factor that will determine whether MBO planning is successful? Support your choice.
10. Some critics believe that MBO places too much emphasis on results. Do you agree?

Suggested reading

Barton, R. F. "An MCDM Approach to Resolving Goal Conflict in MBO." *Academy of Management Review,* April 1981, pp. 231–42.

Dossett, D. L., and C. I. Greenberg. "Goal Setting and Performance Evaluation." *Academy of Management Journal,* December 1981, pp. 767–79.

Kondrasuk, J. N. "Studies in MBO Effectiveness." *Academy of Management Review,* July 1981, pp. 419–30.

Martin, R. A., and J. C. Quick. "The Effect of Job Consensus on MBO Goal Attainment." *MSU Business Topics,* Winter 1981, pp. 43–48.

McConkie, M. L. "Classifying and Reviewing the Empirical Work on MBO: Some Implications." *Group and Organizational Studies,* December 1979, pp. 461–75.

Pringle, C., and J. G. Longenecker. "The Ethics of MBO." *Academy of Management Review,* April 1982, pp. 305–12.

Applying what you have learned about planning through management by objectives

Cases:

Management by objectives at Hewlett-Packard Company
HAIR, Inc.

Management by objectives at Hewlett-Packard Company*

The following is an excerpt from the *Corporate Objectives* of the Hewlett-Packard Company:

> **Management objective** To foster initiative and creativity by allowing the individual freedom of action in attaining well-defined objectives.
>
> In discussing H-P operating policies, we often refer to the concept of "management by objective." By this we mean that insofar as possible each individual at each level in the organization should make his or her own plans to achieve company objectives and goals. After receiving supervisory approval, each individual should be given a wide degree of freedom to work within the limitations imposed by these plans, and by our general corporate policies. Finally, each person's performance should be judged on the basis of how well these individually established goals have been achieved.
>
> The successful practice of "management by objective" is a two-way street. Management must be sure that each individual understands the immediate objective, as well as corporate goals and policies. Thus, a primary H-P management responsibility is communication and mutual understanding. Conversely, employees must take sufficient interest in their work to want to plan it, to propose new solutions to old problems, to stick their necks out when they have something to

* This case is based on *Statement of Objectives*, Hewlett-Packard Company.

contribute. "Management by objective," as opposed to management by directive, offers opportunity for individual freedom and contribution; it also imposes an obligation for everyone to exercise initiative and enthusiasm.

In this atmosphere, it is particularly important that the strength of the whole company is kept in mind and that cooperation between individuals and between operating units is vital to our profitable growth.

It is important for everyone to realize there are some policies which must be established and strictly maintained on a corporate-wide basis. We welcome recommendations on these corporate-wide policies from all levels, but we expect adherence to them at all times.

Questions:

1. Is Hewlett-Packard making use of MBO as a planning technique?
2. What other benefits does Hewlett-Packard see in MBO?
3. What is your opinion of MBO as a motivation technique?

HAIR, Inc.

Janet Hoover and Rob Hundley opened their first hair design shop 10 years ago. With two other haircutters, the two of them began what was to become a very successful organization.

Both Jan and Rob keep up to date on the latest hairstyles and the latest hairstyling techniques. They attend international schools and seminars on hair design, they transmit the knowledge they acquire to their employees through training sessions. Every new employee must be trained by Jan or Rob. HAIR, Inc., promotes quality delivery of the latest in hair-styling. Modern music is played in their shops, and their haircutters are dressed in the latest fashions to promote the image that HAIR, Inc., represents the latest in hair fashions.

HAIR, Inc., appeals equally to men and women and to all age groups. Occasionally, a visiting rock star or other celebrity will patronize HAIR, Inc. Because of this, HAIR, Inc., has become very popular with teenagers who come to its shops to get their hair styled but also hoping to see a current rock star.

HAIR, Inc., has been so successful that there are now HAIR, Inc., shops in five major cities. This expansion has caused Jan and Rob some concern. Their concern centers on maintaining effective performance with a growing number of employees.

After considerable thought, they decided that some type of results-oriented or objective-type planning system might be useful. Both Jan and Rob had been reading a great deal in their trade publications about effective management, and more recently they had been reading about MBO.

Jan and Rob knew that they could not develop a standardized program for the entire organization because different employees specialized in different activities, for example, cutting and styling, coloring, permanents, hair-pieces. In addition, some employees were classified as apprentice cutters and others as master cutters. Jan and Rob therefore concluded that their first step should be to try to identify results that they should expect and to incorporate these results into an MBO form. They would then begin training sessions on the philosophy and process of MBO with groups of employees. This would be followed by participative objective-setting sessions with each employee.

HAIR, Inc. Performance Form			Name ______	
Responsibility Cut and style ______ Coloring ______ Permanents ______ Hairpieces ______ Apprentice ____ Master ______	*Minimum daily performance*	*Average daily performance*	*Maximum possible performance*	*Actual performance*
Expected quantity				

The accompanying performance form is a first draft that was developed by Rob. After examining Rob's form, Jan observed that quantity of work completed should certainly be an expected result and an important objective. Being *quantitative,* this objective was easy to measure. However, in their business, customer satisfaction was absolutely critical. In fact, HAIR, Inc., had a policy that a customer who for any reason was not satisfied with the work could return and have additional work done free of charge. Jan noted that most people's self-image was closely tied to their appearance and that hairstyling, hair coloring, and permanents could be extremely upsetting if they did not make people look as they thought they should look or as they wished to look.

HAIR, Inc. Performance Form			Name ______	
Responsibility Cut and style ______ Coloring ______ Permanents ______ Hairpieces ______ Apprentice ____ Master ______	*Minimum daily performance*	*Average daily performance*	*Maximum possible performance*	*Actual performance*
Results expected (quantity)				
Results expected (quality)				

Thus, Jan suggested a *qualitative* objective that would focus on the result of customer satisfaction. She believed that such an objective could be measured by the percentage of jobs that were acceptable to the customer when completed. For example, a minimum expected level of performance might be to have 90 percent of all cuts and styles acceptable to the customer, an average expected level might be 95 percent, and a maximum expected level might be 98 percent. This, she believed, would enable her and Rob to monitor performance toward achieving their objective of customer satisfaction. "In addition," she said, "a qualitative objective will help the employees focus on how they perform their work and not solely on the quantity of their output." With these ideas in mind, Jan developed the accompanying version of Rob's performance form.

Questions:

1. Do the problems faced by HAIR, Inc., appear to be of a type which MBO might be able to help solve?
2. What is your opinion of Jan and Rob's potential as managers? State your reasons.
3. Are Jan and Rob implementing MBO as a planning system? Explain.

Applying what you have learned about the planning function

Learning exercise:

Protecting the organization by planning

Comprehensive case:

National Lumber Company

Learning exercise Protecting the organization by planning

Purpose: The purpose of this exercise is to emphasize the importance of planning in organizations.

Setting up the exercise:

I. First, every person in the class should be assigned the same organization from the list below and should answer the following questions.

   A. What events in this organization's environment should be considered in developing short- and long-run plans?
   B. How likely are the events to occur? What is the probability of the events (e.g., a gasoline shortage, government regulations, foreign competition, a drastic change in consumer demand)?
   C. How can planning improve the organization's chances of capitalizing on, or adjusting to, the occurrence of the events cited in your answer to question B?

   The organizations for the exercise:

NASA	Bell & Howell
Red Cross	J. C. Penney
R. J. Reynolds	Procter & Gamble
Winnebago	Burger King
Toyota	Crocker National Bank
Shell Oil	Gerber Foods

II. After the members of the class complete the first part of the exercise individually, the instructor will form groups of five to eight students. The groups will each be assigned one of the remaining organizations. Each group will be assigned a different organization. The groups should answer question A, B, and C and report their answers to the class.

A learning note: This exercise will require some out-of-class homework to prepare the answers. It will also show that some organizations need planning more than others because of the forces they must deal with in the environment.

National Lumber Company*

Frank Jensen was general manager of the Fabricated Components Division of the National Lumber Company. Located in Trenton, New Jersey, the Fabricated Components Division manufactured and sold a line of prefabricated components such as walls, floors, and roofing systems to building contractors on the Eastern seaboard. By utilizing the products of the Fabricated Components Division contractors could, under certain circumstances, achieve great economy in construction of their projects.

The Fabricated Components Division was significantly different from the other operations of the National Lumber Company. National Lumber Company manufactured and sold a wide range of lumber products from a series of plants and wholesaling points throughout the United States. The National Lumber Company was a large, successful organization which had been in business for over 75 years. The Fabricated Components Division had been started on an experimental basis, as the management of the National Lumber Company felt that prefabricated components offered real promise in the construction industry, and it wished to be aware of the problems and opportunities in the field. By establishing this division, management felt that valuable experience and insights could be gained and that the National Lumber Company would be in a good position to capitalize on the expected boom in components.

A large modern plant, more than adequate for the expected level of immediate operations, was erected in Trenton. Mr. Jensen, who had a great deal of experience in the fabricated components business as manager of one of the small independent organizations which were engaged in this type of activity, was hired for the purpose of supervising the construction of the plant and for heading the operations of Fabricated Components Division after the plant was completed. He was considered to be a very capable administrator by executives of National Lumber Company.

During the first year of operation many diverse things had to be done: building an organization to both manufacture and sell the products, staffing the office force, working at production and control difficulties, and establishing a market for what was basically a new, relatively untested concept in the building industry. Many problems were encountered, but at the end of the first year the Fabricated Components Division had shown a profit of $24,000 on sales of $800,000 and an investment of $500,000.

The second year was, according to Mr. Jensen, a continuation of the "shakedown period." Changes in both the product and the organization were made, additional capital was invested in the plant, and advertising and selling expenditures were increased. The product line seemed to be gaining the approval of many contractors, although competition with the more traditional methods of construction was severe. At the end of the second year the operating statements showed a net loss of

* Copyright 1976 by Professor Harry R. Knudson, Graduate School of Business, University of Washington. Reprinted by permission from *Organizational Behavior: A Management Approach,* Harry R. Knudson and C. Patrick Fleenor, Winthrop Publishing Co., 1978.

$8,000 on sales of $700,000 and a net investment of $600,000.

The third and fourth years of the life of Fabricated Components Division were, in Mr. Jensen's words, "a madhouse." Several new products were introduced, the plant was again expanded, advertising expenditures were increased still more, and a great number of people were added to the organization to handle the increased volume of business. Sales for the third year totaled almost $2 million. However, a net loss of $126,000 was realized. Mr. Jensen stated:

> It was mass confusion and things just got away from us. We had too many things to do and too many people involved. When we lived through the third year without going under, we expected things to go very well from then on, but we had unexpected problems with some of our people quitting. We also lost a lot of money on a big government order, partly because we didn't have good enough control of our operations. During the fourth year of operations we lost $160,000 on the big job and over-all $254,000. But I felt that we were learning through our mistakes and that we still had great potential in this part of the business. We had pretty well perfected our manufacturing operations in Trenton, had added some new equipment and had our organizational problems pretty well worked out.
>
> I was concerned about the increasing pressure I was subjected to from National Lumber, however. Naturally, I didn't expect top management to be overjoyed by our performance. When we started, both they and I knew that we would have some difficult times, but neither of us expected our financial picture to be quite so bleak. Although we were doing some very good work and were by far the most outstanding outfit in this part of the business, we did not seem to be able to make any money.

Pressures from above increased greatly during the fifth year. At one time or another Mr. Jensen was called on by literally every member of the top management of National Lumber, including the chairman of the board of directors. According to Mr. Jensen, these visits were relatively pleasant, but unproductive and prevented him from attending to what he considered at that time to be the most important part of his job—getting sufficient sales so that the large plant could be operated on a profitable basis. Mr. Jensen stated:

> We were like Grand Central Station! I couldn't get anything done, and the constant stream of top-level visitors was upsetting to our plant and office people. They knew that we hadn't yet proved ourselves financially, and all the top brass made them nervous.
>
> Some of our visitors were quite candid. One man told me he had no faith in the basic ideas of our organization and that he stopped by just "to see the rathole we're pouring all our money down." And when I found out many of our visitors were charging the expenses of their visits to our operations and we were getting billed for them through interdivisional charges, I really got pretty angry.
>
> But the main thing was that we got little realistic advice or help from these people. Several suggested we "do better," but didn't tell us how we might.
>
> There were several things that I felt they could have done—but I got nowhere. Everyone had a gloomy attitude except

> me. I knew what our capabilities were and had great hopes. I didn't feel that many people understood the differences between running an old established business such as National Lumber and a new, struggling business such as the Fabricated Components Division.

During the fifth year Mr. Jensen was under considerable pressure from his immediate superior, Avery Randell, Eastern Regional Manager for the parent company. Mr. Randell sent Mr. Jensen a "confidential memo" about every other week in which he commented upon events that had occurred or decisions that Mr. Jensen had made that did not meet with his approval. Mr. Jensen regularly ignored these memos. He kept them locked in his desk—to which only he had a key—as he did not want their contents known to his subordinates for fear of the effect upon their morale. Mr. Randell also frequently asked Mr. Jensen to have lunch in New York, where Mr. Randell's office was located, so that he could keep in closer touch with the activities at Fabricated Components Division. Often Mr. Jensen would decline these invitations, but he did have lunch with Mr. Randell in New York City about every two weeks. In an effort to satisfy Randell's demands for information, Mr. Jensen started to send him a weekly report on the activities of Fabricated Components Division. The information that went into this report was carefully screened by Mr. Jensen so that nothing that would upset Randell or increase his demands on Jensen's time was included. According to Jensen, "The sole purpose of these reports was to keep him off my back."

Mr. Jensen made the following comments about his relationship with Mr. Randell:

> Avery's O.K., but he's quite nervous about our operations. His division almost runs itself. His people are experienced and well trained, and he really doesn't have too much to do. He plays golf a lot and cruises on his boat for long weekends, while I'm at the plant seven days a week and most evenings. He doesn't know much about what we're trying to do and this makes him uncomfortable. We're a thorn in his side and the only "disreputable" part of his division financially. He inherited us because we're geographically close to him, but he doesn't have much sympathy for or understanding of what we're trying to do and the problems we face. I keep telling him that I'll take all the blame for our operations, but with all the attention we're getting from top management he's very much interested in taking part in many of our decisions—even though he doesn't know what is going on and is technically incompetent to assist in managing Fabricated Components Division. Personally, I like him and enjoy his company. Our meetings are very pleasant and we go to some very nice places for lunch. Avery does give us some kinds of help, too. For example, we've had some minor legal problems which he has gotten off our hands. But, in general, he is more of a hindrance than a help. He doesn't know enough about our operation to really help us, and the things he could do, he doesn't. I've wanted to hire another salesman for a long time, but I can't get Avery to approve it. It would cost us about $3,000 a month, but we need more sales and a good man would pay for himself in no time. But Avery's so upset about our losses that he won't let me hire anyone else without his approval, and he won't give it. I would guess that I spend 30 percent of my time either dealing with Avery or worrying

> about our relationship. I've told him that if I answered all of his memos, I wouldn't have time for anything else. He's been a real problem for me, and it keeps me from doing the really important things. I'd like to hire some kid to do all of that kind of thing so I would have time to run the business.

About two months before the end of the fifth year of operations, a meeting of top management of the National Lumber Company was held in New York to decide the future of Fabricated Components Division. Mr. Jensen was not asked to attend this meeting, which irritated him considerably. He was asked to submit his plans for the next year's operations, as well as several alternative plans and a capital and expense budget for the coming year. He spent a great deal of time preparing this information and submitted alternative plans ranging from considerable expansion of operations to shutting down of the plant completely and going out of business. In the letter submitting this information, he requested that he be permitted to attend the meeting. He received no reply to this request.

Two weeks after the meeting had been held Mr. Jensen had not been informed of what decision, if any, had been made. As he had had no information to the contrary, he assumed that operations for the next year would continue about as they had in the past. About three weeks after the meeting. Mr. Jensen began to hear rumors that the Fabricated Components Division would be shut down at the end of the year. These rumors came from sources both within and outside the company. On hearing these rumors, Mr. Jensen called Mr. Randell who told him that, "Things are still undecided, but don't spend any more money than you have to." Mr. Jensen then called the chairman of the board of directors who informed him that the company had decided to shut down the Fabricated Components Division and go out of that part of the business. Shortly thereafter, Mr. Jensen received a letter from the president of National Lumber Company confirming this information. Mr. Jensen then began making plans for closing down the Fabricated Components Division. He felt that a poor decision had been made, but that it would be useless to attempt to have the decision reversed.

During these last few weeks of operation Mr. Jensen was faced with several unique problems:

He was not sure what, if anything, to tell his employees—or what the timing should be. He was not greatly concerned about the 50 men in the plant, for they were skilled workers who could easily find other employment without suffering financial losses. He was especially concerned about the future of the production manager, the sales manager, and the office manager, all of whom had been with him since the start of Fabricated Components Division. Because none of these people had been with the National Lumber Company for very long, they would get little severance pay and though capable people, could well be faced with a period of unemployment until they found other jobs. He wanted to give these people adequate time to find new positions, yet felt that if the news was out, efficiency would drop considerably and the Fabricated Components Division would have an even greater loss than anticipated for its fifth—and last—year of operation.

Mr. Jensen also faced another kind of problem. He still had great faith in the kind of thing that the Fabricated Components Division was doing and had often considered the advantages of operating his own company in this field. When he had learned that the Fabricated Components Division was to be shut down, he had quietly explored the possibilities of buying the business and had found that he could arrange adequate financing without too much difficulty. Much of the equipment was specialized and not readily saleable. He didn't know of anyone—other than himself—who might want to buy the Fabricated Components Division and felt that he could get everything that he needed to operate with at a reasonable price. Thus, if the Fabricated Components Division showed a great loss for the year, this might discourage any other prospective buyers, as well as increase National Lumber Company's desire to get out of an unprofitable venture for any kind of recovered investment, thus driving down the price he might have to pay.

Along these same lines, Mr. Jensen was undecided about what action, if any, should be taken regarding several large sales that were in the closing stages. It would be quite easy to defer action on these sales until after he had purchased the operations and thus start on his own with a considerable order file. If the sales were closed now, the customers would probably revert to the conventional construction techniques when they learned that Fabricated Components Division was not going to be in business. Or it was possible that these orders would be farmed out to small independents by National Lumber Company before Mr. Jensen could get operating on his own.

In reflecting upon the history of the Fabricated Components Division Mr. Jensen observed that this was an excellent example of a good idea that had been defeated because of lack of support and meddling on the part of top management. "They bought the idea of the Fabricated Components Division in theory but refused, or were literally unable, to recognize the kinds of problems that would arise. When these problems did arise—and almost any new operation faces the same kinds of problems—they wouldn't leave me alone long enough to solve them. Certainly, I must take a great share of the blame for our poor record, but I sincerely believe that if we hadn't had so many visitors and so much attention from top management, we would have had a respectable, if not spectacular, financial success."

Avery Randell made the following comments regarding the Fabricated Components Division:

> Frank Jensen is a very capable man, but we never really got him to operate as part of the company. He ran the Fabricated Components Division as if it were an independent organization and never really accepted or respected our advice. This past year in particular we had the very definite feeling that Frank wanted no part of us, even though several of our top management people went considerably out of their way to help him. Frank has not yet learned how to live in a relatively large organization and, because of his inability to accommodate the organization, creates a lot of problems for himself and detracts considerably from his excellent technical skills. He probably knows more about prefabricated components than anyone in the country, but, because of his inability to adjust to the organization, he has been an unsuccessful manager for us.

Questions:

1. Did the management of National Lumber engage in planning activities when deciding to set up the Fabricated Components Division?
2. Would specific objectives and a strategic analysis have helped in improving the chances of success in the Fabricated Components Division?
3. Why was the new division not successful?

Part III
The organizing function

7. Elements of organizing
8. Designing the organization
9. Staffing the organization
10. Developing careers and human resources

A management profile
Ralph Cordiner

Ralph Cordiner's wheat farmer parents in Walla Walla, Washington, may have had great dreams for their son, but they probably never expected that he would one day become the president of General Electric and one of the most innovative men in the history of American industry.

Cordiner probably had as humble beginnings as any boy growing up in the rural West at the turn of the century. He attended a one-room schoolhouse and helped his father on the farm. One year, to help pay for his college expenses, he took a part-time job as an appliance salesman for the Pacific Power and Light Company.

Right from the start, Cordiner showed an understanding of what consumers wanted. Pacific Power and Light recognized his keen selling ability and offered him a full-time job upon his graduation from college. But before he had completed a year with PP&L, Cordiner went over to Edison General Appliances, where he began his long affiliation with the company that was later known as General Electric.

Cordiner's selling instinct took him to the top at GE. Along the way, he carefully selected positions which would put his talents in easy view of the men in power. Early on, he served at corporate headquarters, and over the years he managed various divisions within GE. Wherever Cordiner went, sales soared. In 1950, he was named president and chief executive officer of GE. During his years with the company, he doubled both sales and profits.

Cordiner may be best remembered for starting what has been called a revolution in management: decentralization. World War II had caused an explosive growth in the electronics industries, and new management techniques were needed to tame the new corporate giants. Cordiner restructured GE so that each of its 120 departments was independently managed. Executives and managers made decisions independently of the central office, leaving top officers free to concentrate on planning.

Cordiner believed that decentralization maintained both the clout of the large company and the flexibility of the small firm. Praised as a brilliant solution to a modern managerial dilemma, decentralization is now the backbone of many successful corporate organizations. Decentralization involves the delegation of authority to the lowest possible level in the management hierarchy. In this part of the book, such elements of organizational design as decentralization are treated. Ralph Cordiner practiced decentralization, and his contribution to the field of management will become more obvious as you read this part of the book.

Courtesy of General Electric Corporation

Source: Elizabeth J. Kenny for P. S. Associates, Inc., Sterling, Massachusetts.

Introduction to Part III

Part III, the organizing function, contains four chapters. They are:

Chapter 7—Elements of organizing
Chapter 8—Designing the organization
Chapter 9—Staffing the organization
Chapter 10—Developing careers and human resources

The inclusion of the material contained in the four chapters is based upon the following rationale:

The organizing function consists of four logically connected sequences of actions. In the first place, managers must design an organization structure. The structure can be understood as a system of interrelated jobs, groups of jobs, and authority. Jobs, departmental bases, spans of control, and delegated authority are the necessary elements of all organization structures. Chapter 7 develops the important ideas concerning the **elements of organization structures.** The design of an organization refers to the specific structure which managers decide is appropriate to achieve optimal performance. The specific design depends on such factors as the organization's strategy, the technology it uses to produce the goods or services it provides, and the environment in which it exists. Chapter 8 develops the managerial considerations relevant to the **design of an organization structure.**

The organization structure exists to facilitate getting the work done. But obviously it is people who do the work. The next step in organizing is to **staff the organization.** Chapter 9 discusses the important managerial considerations that are related to selecting, training, placing, and promoting the right people for the right jobs. Managers must match the demands and responsibilities of jobs with the skills and abilities of people. An optimal design staffed with the right people will certainly contribute to overall performance.

The organizing function is dynamic. A properly designed and staffed organization must be maintained and adapted. The means through which management assures that the right people are performing the appropriate jobs include **career and human resource development.** The human resources of organizations are crucial to performance, and it is more and more apparent that organizations have an important stake in developing their employees to their fullest potential. The practices currently in use in career and human resource development are the subjects of Chapter 10.

The figure below depicts the four aspects of the organizing function. Although the four aspects are presented sequentially, the reader should understand that they actually occur simultaneously and interactively.

The organizing function

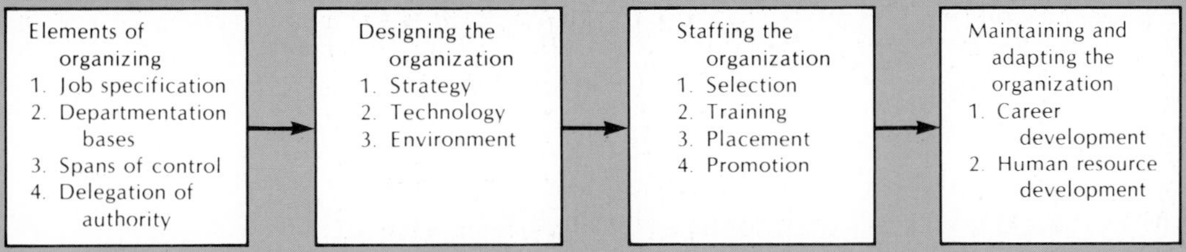

Chapter seven
Elements of organizing

Performance objectives

- **Define** in practical terms what is meant by the organizing function and organization structure.
- **State** the four fundamental elements of organization structure.
- **Describe** any organization structure in terms of the four fundamental elements.
- **Explain** the relationships between delegation of authority and the chain of command.
- **Discuss** the advantages and disadvantages associated with alternative degrees of specialization of labor, departmentation bases, spans of control, and delegation of authority.

Management update*

The three Nakash brothers, Joe, Ralph, and Avi, established Jordache Enterprises, Inc., in 1977. The company's product, tight, yet well-fitting jeans, has attained such market acceptance that the company has grown to a $300 million enterprise. Jordache jeans are produced at the rate of 1.2 million pairs per month and are marketed in 25 countries. The company's success has made millionaires of the three Nakash brothers whose highly personal management styles and entrepreneurial skills led to that success.

The company has now reached a familiar stage in the history of successful firms. It has reached the stage of being too large and complex to be managed by personalized managerial styles. The Nakash brothers must now consider the advantages of more conventional managerial planning and organizing methods. At issue is whether Jordache can make the transition without dampening the entrepreneurial spirit that made it successful.

A senior vice president noted: "We are continuously moving toward structure. We have gone from several people wearing many hats to having controllers, a personnel manager, vice presidents—the division of duties gets clearer every day. We're emphasizing that individuals must operate and control their own departments."

In 1981, Jordache had undergone a number of changes which reflected greater interest in developing an appropriate organization structure for a company with Jordache's characteristics. Presently, the company has six divisions: jeans, children's clothes, menswear, handbags, active wear (sneakers, running suits, and other athletic apparel), and junior-related separates. These six divisions specialized in producing and promoting the products assigned to them. As is evident, Jordache is involved in more than the jeans business, although that division still contributes two thirds of the company's revenue.

To support the more formalized organization structure and the more complex scale of operations, Jordache has increased its staff support. For example, it increased its computer capacity and is automating its inventory data, credit information, cash flow data, and accounts receivable. The growth of a company's product line creates managerial problems that seem to be solvable only through formalized organization structures and enlarged staff assistance. Jordache's experience is consistent with that general rule.

---

* This Management Update is adapted from "Jordache's New Executive Look," *Business Week*, November 2, 1981, pp. 121–22.

The idea of an organization structure is very abstract. An organization structure cannot be seen, heard, smelled, felt, tasted, or sensed in any way. What we sense in business firms, hospitals, universities, and all organizations is *people doing work.* Certainly, some people do work better than others because some people are more skilled and motivated than others. But a major factor in how well work is performed is the way it is organized. A former governor who initiated widespread reorganization of state government stated his views on the importance of organization structure as follows:

> *State government must be efficient; it must be effective. Because of civil service and merit employment regulations, governors have little freedom to hire and fire people, but I did have the power to change the way people do their jobs. Our reorganization efforts were aimed at changing the way jobs should be performed and thereby changing the way people perform.*

Organization structure

One way of thinking about an organization structure is to reflect on your own work experience. More than likely, you have worked for a company, or perhaps a church, governmental agency, summer camp, or some other organization in which numerous other people also worked. (Perhaps you are now employed.) The fact that other people worked in the organization (company, church, etc.) means that someone had previously specified what each person, including yourself, should be doing and how he or she should do it. Early on, your boss told you what your job would involve—what machines you should use, what you should produce, including how many and how often you should produce. For example, if you were employed in a bank as a teller, you were trained to deal with each type of customer transaction—deposits, withdrawals, check cashing, and even loan payments. Each type of transaction required a slightly different method, and you were taught those methods.

You were also taught, or you quickly learned from experience, which other people you had to work with to complete your job satisfactorily. For example, you were perhaps required to secure the approval of another person before you could cash a check for someone who was not a customer of the bank. In this instance, you were acting on orders or directives which defined how much authority you had to complete a transaction. In any setting, an individual's job is specified in terms of basic tasks and authority to complete those tasks.

You also quickly found out another piece of important information—the name of your boss. And that is important for you to learn because your boss is the individual who will be supervising your work to see that you do it properly and within the bounds of *your* authority. But perhaps more important, your boss has authority over you. He or she has the right to tell you what work to do, to assign your work, and to evaluate your work, If the boss is pleased with your performance, then you know that you have a good chance to continue working and even to get pay raises and promotions.

Another piece of information that is important for you to discover is the names of other persons who are also directed by your boss. These other people are the members of your department or unit or group. You may even attend a meeting of your co-workers during which the boss introduces you to them. You find out what they do. The chances are that all your jobs are more or less similar. You are called tellers, and your boss is the head teller. The fact that you all have the same **job title,** teller, indicates that the work you do is much the same. Some of your co-workers may have more tasks than others and more freedom (authority) to do those tasks. As you discern these differences, you probably discover that they are the result of the longer experience and the greater skill of those co-workers in doing the work. You also find out (or suspect) that those co-workers make more money than you do.

If you continue to work in the bank, you discover that people in your department come and go. Some are fired; some are promoted to other jobs. But as quickly as one person leaves a job, another person is hired to fill it. Thus, you begin to realize that the work goes on despite the comings and goings of different people. It may even be that your boss—the head teller—changes. Your original boss may have been promoted, or may have retired, or may have quit to take another job. But shortly thereafter, another person took the job. Perhaps a teller in your department was promoted. These experiences cause you to understand that the bank has created ways to avoid dependence on people. It has devised, in effect, a system of jobs, departments, and authority which enables the work to be done irrespective of the people who are employed at the time.

As you gained experience in your job, and as you became more familiar with what went on in the bank, you began to see that the bank consisted of numerous jobs and departments. You also discovered that your boss had a boss who in turn had a boss. You may have even been curious enough to ask someone about how the bank was run. The chances are that you were given a bank publication, for example its annual report, and that there you saw an **organization chart.** Figure 7–1 is a facsimile of a representative organization chart. Now you see the whole picture. Complicated, isn't it? What does it really show? What concepts enable you to understand it? Why is the bank organized in the way it is and not in some other way? Why were you hired? How could the organization be changed? This chapter and those which follow will present ideas that will enable you to answer your questions.

The four primary elements of organization structure

Managers who are responsible for deciding on a specific structure of tasks and authority must consider four basic issues.

1. Job specification Managers must decide the appropriate way to divide the total task of the entity into smaller tasks. The smaller, specialized tasks must then be combined into jobs. For example, the total task of Ford Motor Company is to develop, manufacture, and sell automobiles,

Figure 7–1

Sometown Bank: Organization chart

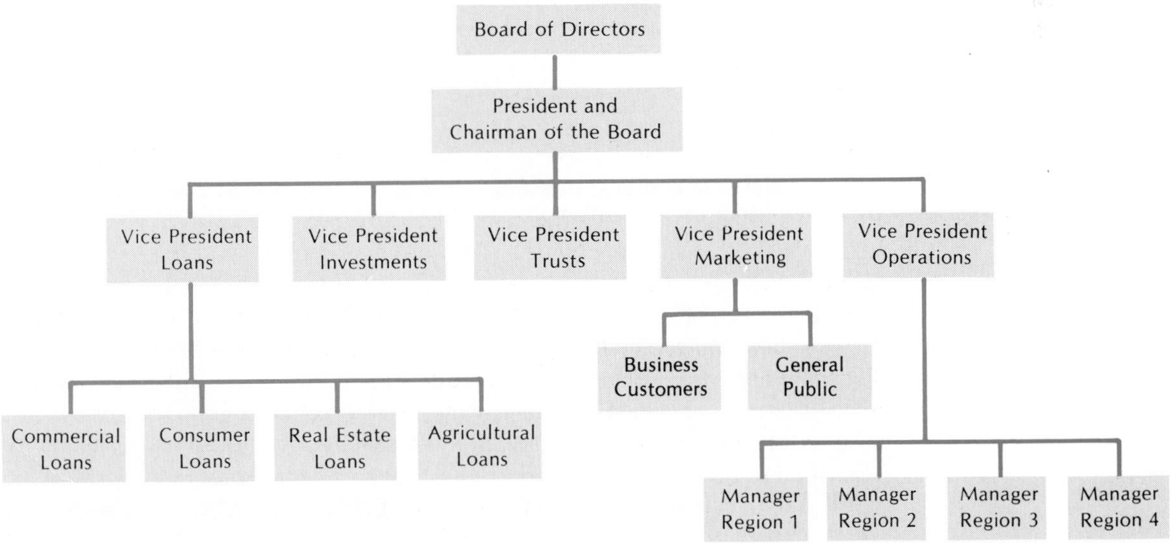

trucks, and tractors. The Sometown Bank could not possibly serve its customers with only one person doing the work. Obviously, 1 person, or even 10, cannot perform that task. It is necessary to divide and subdivide the task. The result of this first issue is **job specifications;** that is, the responsibilities of each job are defined in terms of what the jobholder is expected to do.

2. Departmentation The next step is to decide how to group the jobs. The reason that they must be grouped is in order to achieve coordination of the individual jobs. Once the jobs have been grouped, a manager can be assigned the responsibility of coordinating each group. It is unlikely that one individual could possibly coordinate all the jobs at Sometown Bank. There would simply be too much work for one person to perform effectively. The decisions which managers make about how to group the individual jobs result in *departments,* and the decision-making process which precedes those results is termed **departmentation.**

3. Span of control The third step is to decide how many jobs should be included in each department. This key decision specifies the number of jobs that the department manager will be responsible for coordinating. As we will see, that number will vary from manager to manager, from relatively few to relatively many. The result of this decision is the specification of each manager's **span of control.**

4. Delegation of authority Finally, managers must decide how much authority jobholders should have to do their jobs. In this context, **authority is the right to make decisions without having to obtain approval from a**

Figure 7–2

Wide and narrow spans of control

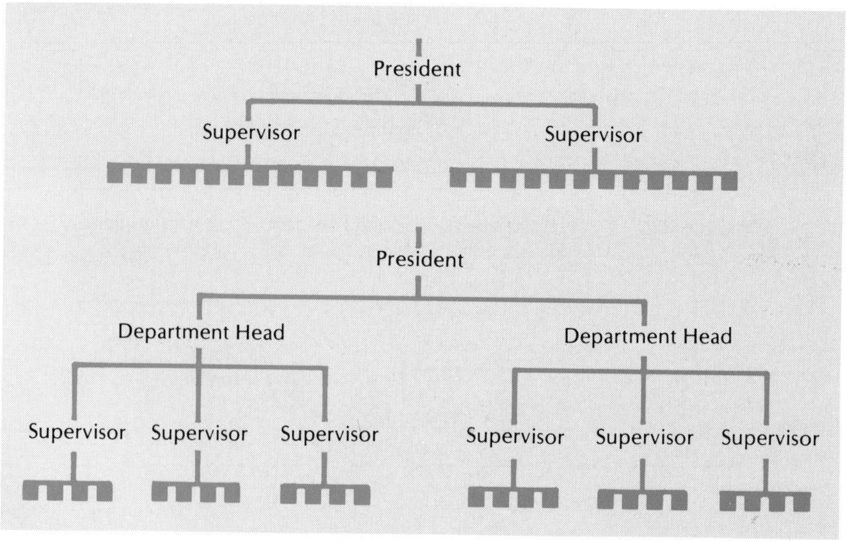

higher-up. Some managers will be granted greater authority than others; few managers are ever satisfied that they have enough authority in light of their responsibilities. In managerial terms, defining the authority of jobs is called **delegation.**

The design of an organization structure varies, depending on the attributes of each of the four elements. Conceptually, each of the four can vary along a continuum as shown here:

Job specification	Specialization	High ⟷	Low
Departmentation	Basis	Homogeneous ⟷	Heterogeneous
Span of control	Number	Few ⟷	Many
Authority	Delegation	Centralized ⟷	Decentralized

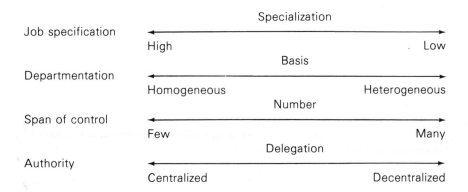

The result of the process by which managers specify these four elements is the structure of the organization.

An organization in which there are low specialization in jobs, heterogeneous departments, wide spans of control, and decentralized authority differs markedly from one in which there are highly specialized jobs, homogeneous departments, narrow spans of control, and centralized authority, Consider, for example, the impact of different spans of control. In Figure 7–2, we have a graphic comparison of two structures, each of which has 24 people to be managed. In the first case, the maximum span of control is 12 and there are two levels of management and three managers (a president and two supervisors); in the second case, the maximum span of control is 4 and there are three levels of management and nine managers (a president, two department heads, and six supervisors). Generally, organization structures will tend toward one extreme or the other along each continuum.

The comments of two managers employed in two insurance companies contrast the differences in organization structures. The first manager stated:

> *Our home office is organized around our clients' needs. Each of our employees is able to handle all the transactions of a particular policyholder, from changing beneficiaries to processing loan applications. Our supervisors must also be broadly trained to be able to deal with a wide range of problems.*

The second manager's comments describe an entirely different organization structure:

> *We believe it is important to treat each policyholder transaction as a separate specialty. We train our people in only one insurance transaction and assign them to a specific department which is managed by an individual who is an expert in that specialty.*

Dividing the task: Job specification

The issues associated with job specification are concerned with the extent to which jobs are specialized. All jobs are specialized to a degree, and the ability to divide work among many jobholders is a key advantage of organizations. For example, rather than have a bookkeeper in a hospital perform emergency room tasks, the work is divided so that the bookkeeper concentrates on preparing bills and the emergency room clerk concentrates on admitting patients.

A major decision in developing an organization structure is determining how much division of labor should exist. Advocates of dividing work into a small number of tasks often cite the advantages of specialization. Two of the major advantages are:

1. If a job contains few tasks, it is then possible to quickly train replacements for personnel who are terminated, transferred, or absent. The minimum training effort results in a lower training cost.
2. When a job entails only a limited number of tasks, the employee can become highly proficient in performing those tasks. This high level of proficiency is reflected in a better quality of output.

These benefits are largely economic and technical, and they usually apply to nonmanagerial jobs. However, similar economic and technical benefits are applicable to specialized managerial positions.

The gains derived from narrow divisions of labor can be calculated in purely economic terms. As the job is divided into ever smaller elements, additional output is obtained. However, more people and capital must be employed to do the smaller jobs. At some point, the costs of specialization (labor and capital) begin to outweigh the increased efficiency of specialization (output) and the cost per unit of output begins to rise.

Specialization, or division, of labor at the job level, varies from high to low. The concept is therefore a relative one. It is possible to say that one job is more or less specialized in comparison to another. In making this comparison, it is useful to identify the aspects that differentiate jobs. The following five aspects are different from job to job.

1. *Work pace*—the more control the individual has over how fast he or she must work, the less specialized the job is.
2. *Job repetitiveness*—the more different tasks there are to perform, the less specialized the job is.
3. *Skill requirements*—the more skilled the jobholder must be, the less specialized the job is.
4. *Methods specification*—the more latitude the jobholder has in using methods and tools, the less specialized the job is.
5. *Required attention*—the more mental attention the job requires, the less specialized it is.

If we now return to the job specification continuum, we can identify the specific characteristics of jobs that are relatively high or low in specialization.

Specialization

High	Low
1. No control over pace	1. Control over pace
2. Repetitive	2. Varied
3. Low skill requirements	3. High skill requirements
4. Specified methods	4. Unspecified methods
5. No required attention	5. Required attention

Based upon the ideas above, it is possible to predict that the jobs in Jordache Enterprises, Inc., will become more routine and repetitive as the company creates more specialized positions to deal with the problems of increased size.

The contrast between jobs in terms of specialization can be seen in this statement of a manager of a national grocery chain store:

> *I remember how happy I was when, as a beginner, I was transferred from the job of stockboy to that of meat market clerk. That was back in the days when we sold meat across the counter to the customers. Now it is all prewrapped, and they just pick it up. But before that, the meat market was a great place to work compared to putting cans on the shelf. All customers would be different in some way—they would want special cuts of meat, or special slicing and trimming. Every day was different because we had to be customer conscious. I learned a lot in that job about people and about me. It sure beat talking to cans and bottles all day long.*

The principle of specialization of labor guides the manager in determining the content of individual jobs. From a different perspective, the principle also guides how jobs should be grouped together.

Combining jobs: Departmentation

The process of combining jobs into groups is termed **departmentation,** and the managerial problem is to select a basis, or rationale, for combining them. The process of specifying individual jobs is analytic: That is, the total task of the organization is broken down into successively smaller tasks and jobs. But then it becomes necessary to combine the jobs into groups. Numerous bases for departmentation exist, as will be demonstrated in the following discussion.

Functional departmentation

Jobs can be grouped according to the functions of the organization. The business firm includes such functions as production, marketing, finance, accounting, and personnel. The hospital consists of such functions as surgery, psychiatry, housekeeping, pharmacy, and personnel. The functions of Sometown Bank are the basis for the departments at the very top of its organization chart, as shown in Figure 7–3. Within each of the five departments are individuals who occupy specialized jobs in the areas of loans, investments, trusts, marketing, and operations. A partial organization chart for a manufacturing firm is shown in Figure 7–4. It reflects the basic functions that are required to manufacture and sell a product.

An important advantage of functional departmentation is that it combines the benefits of specialization. That is, it seems logical to have departments which consist of experts in particular fields such as production or accounting. By having departments of specialists, management creates, theoreti-

Figure 7–3

Sometown Bank: Partial organization chart, functional departmentation

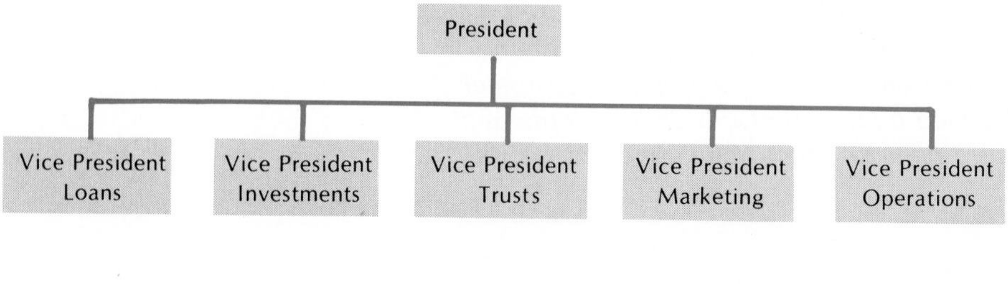

Figure 7–4

Business firm: Partial organization chart, functional departmentation

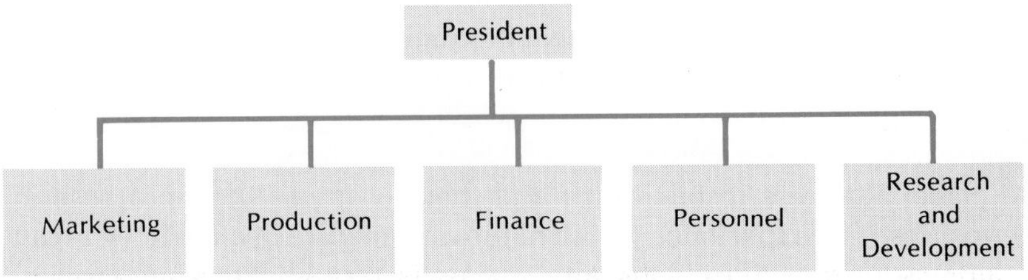

cally, the most efficient unit possible. Functional departments make it possible to realize all the benefits of specialization.

A major disadvantage of the functional arrangement is that because specialists are working with and encouraging one another in their respective areas of expertise and interest, the organizational objectives may be sacrificed to departmental objectives. Accountants may see only their problems, and not those of production or marketing or the total organization. In other words, identification with the department and its objectives is often stronger than identification with the organization and its objectives.

Territorial departmentation

Another commonly adopted departmentation method is to establish groups on the basis of geographic areas. The logic is that all activities in a particular area or region should be assigned to a manager. This individual would be in charge of all operations in that geographic area. The operations department of the Sometown Bank is subdivided into four geographic regions, each served by a branch bank. Perhaps, to return to our earlier discussion, you were a teller in the branch bank in region 1. Figure 7–5

Figure 7–5

Sometown Bank: Partial organization chart, territorial departmentation

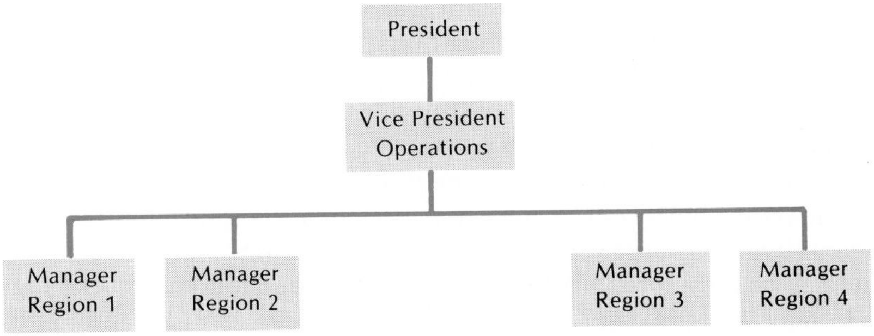

depicts that part of the Sometown Bank which is organized according to territorial bases.

A business firm which is dispersed geographically will often use territory as a departmentation basis. The territorial basis is often used by firms whose operations are similar from region to region. Chain stores, railroads, airlines, bakeries, and dairies are typical users of territorial bases.

An advantage often associated with territorial departmentation is that it provides a training ground for managerial personnel. The company is able to place managers in territories and then to assess their progress in their territories. The experience which managers acquire in a territory away from headquarters provides invaluable insights about how products or services are accepted in the field. The territorial basis also enables the firm to develop local market areas and to adjust more quickly to the needs of local customers. These advantages are reflected in the following statement by a corporate sales manager:

> *The best experience I got was when I managed the California sales office. The Chicago home office had other problems on its mind at the time, so I did pretty much as I pleased. I ran a good office that consistently met quotas and provided good customer service. I was able to manage. Now that I am in Chicago, I try to give my regional managers the same freedom I had.*

The disadvantages of territorial departmentation must also be recognized. They include the difficulties of maintaining consistent adherence to company policy and practices, duplication of effort, and the necessity for a relatively large number of managers. Companies using territory as a primary basis for departmentation often find it necessary to create a large headquarters staff to control the dispersed operations.

Product departmentation

In many large diversified companies, activities and personnel are grouped on the basis of product. As a firm grows, it becomes difficult to coordinate the various functional departments and it becomes advantageous to establish product units. This form of organization allows personnel to develop total expertise in researching, manufacturing, and distributing a product line. Concentrating authority, responsibility, and accountability in a specific product department allows top management to coordinate activities. The need for coordinating production, engineering, sales, and service cannot be overestimated. Figure 7–6 is a partial organization chart that would be representative of a large electrical products company.

Within each of these product groups, we find production and marketing personnel. Since group executives coordinate the sales, manufacture, and distribution of a product, they become overseers of a profit center. This is the manner in which profit responsibility is exacted from product organizational arrangements. Managers establish profit goals at the beginning of a time period and then compare the actual profit with the planned profit. This is the approach used in the Buick, Cadillac, Chevrolet, Pontiac, and Oldsmobile divisions of General Motors.

The disadvantages of product-based organizations result from the need to create relatively independent divisions. Therefore, each division will have all the resources and types of jobs necessary to be in business. Each division will have accountants, lawyers, engineers, market researchers, and scientists assigned to it. Thus, the product-based organization runs the danger of duplication of effort among divisions.

Product-based departmentation is used in the Sometown Bank. The vice president of the loan department is responsible for four units—commercial loans, consumer loans, real estate loans, and agricultural loans. The partial organization chart is shown in Figure 7–7. The reader should at this point, recognize that Jordache Enterprises, Inc., is organized on the basis of prod-

Figure 7–6

Business firm: Partial organization chart, product departmentation

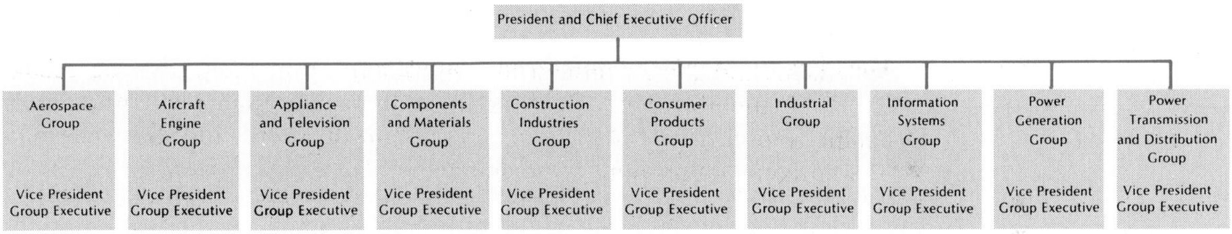

Figure 7–7

Sometown Bank: Partial organization chart, product departmentation

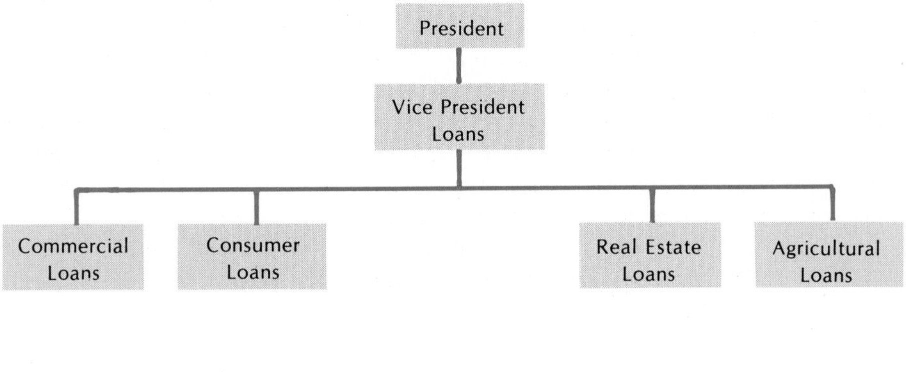

uct—jeans, children's clothes, menswear, handbags, active wear, and junior-related separates are the bases for the company's six divisions.

Customer departmentation

Examples of customer-oriented departments are the organizational structures of educational institutions. Some educational institutions have regular (day and night) courses and extension courses. In some instances, a professor will be affiliated solely with the regular students or the extension students. In fact, the titles of some faculty positions often specifically mention the extension division. Some department stores are departmentalized to some degree on a customer basis. They have such groupings as university shops, menswear, boys' clothing, and bargain floors that carry a lower quality of university, men's, and boys' clothing.

The advantages and disadvantages of customer- or client-based organizations are identical to those of product organizations. Figure 7–8 depicts the manner in which the Sometown Bank uses customers as the basis for organizing the marketing function. The bank management evidently believes that marketing and promotional efforts are sufficiently different for business versus nonbusiness customers to justify specialization along those lines.

Multiple bases for departmentation

The methods cited above for dividing work are not exhaustive; there are many other ways. Furthermore, in most large organizations, a number of different methods of dividing work are used at the same time. For example, at the upper levels of management, the vice presidents reporting to the president may represent different product groups. At the level directly below the vice presidents, the managers may be part of a particular opera-

Figure 7–8

Sometown Bank: Partial organization chart, customer departmentation

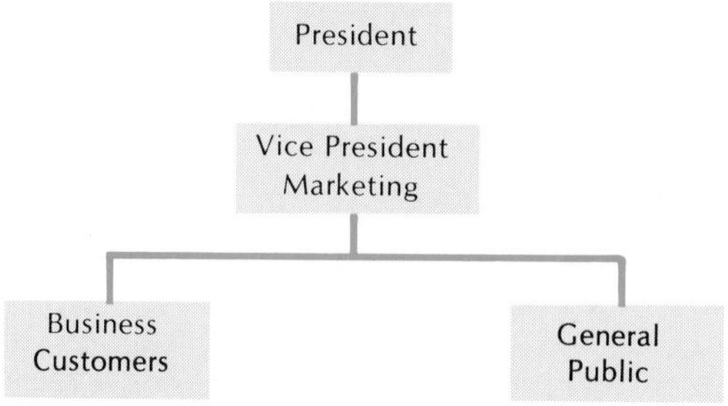

tional function. At the next level in the organization, there may be a number of different technical classifications. This approach of a multiple division of work in organizational design is illustrated in Figure 7–9. This business example can be compared to the banking example in Figure 7–1.

The principle of departmentation specifies the general purpose to be followed in grouping activities, but the basis actually chosen is a matter of balancing advantages against disadvantages. For example, the advantage of departmentalizing on the basis of customers or products is that of bringing together under the control of a single manager all the resources necessary to make the product for the customers. In addition, the specification of objectives is considerably easier when the emphasis is on the final product. At the same time, the ease of objective identification and measurement can encourage the individual departments to pursue their own objectives at the expense of company objectives. A second disadvantage of product and customer departmentation is that the task of coordinating the activities tends to be more complex. Reporting to the unit manager are the managers of the various functions (production, sales, and finance, for example) whose diverse but interdependent activities must be coordinated.

Departmentation based on functional operations has advantages as well as disadvantages. The primary advantage is that such departmentation is based on specific skills and training, and activities assigned to the departments emphasize the skills which individual members bring to the job. Because of the similarity of the subordinates' jobs, the mangerial task of coordinating the activities of functional departments is considerably less complex than that of coordinating the activities of product departments. At the same time, the disadvantages of functional departments must be recognized, the principal difficulty being to provide the managers of such groups with sufficient job depth to make their jobs challenging. Since creat-

Figure 7–9

Business firm: Organization chart

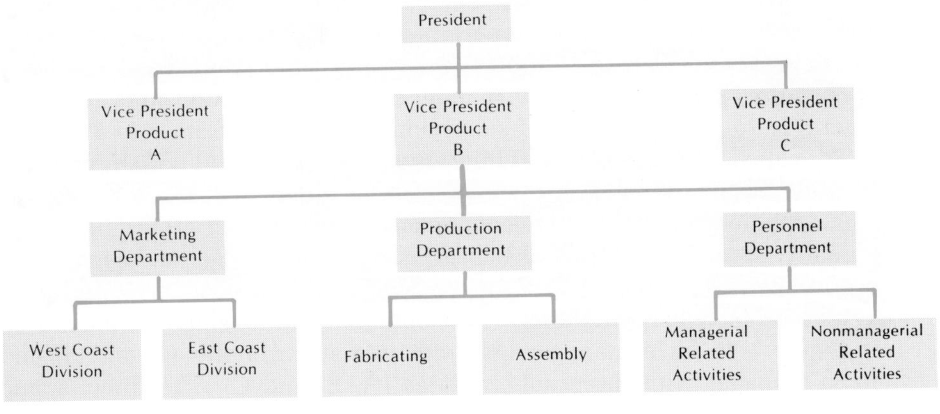

ing functional departments involves breaking up a natural work flow and assigning parts of that flow to each department, each department manager must work extra hard to coordinate the work of his or her department with the work of all the other departments.

Span of control

The determination of appropriate bases for departmentation establishes the *kinds* of jobs that will be grouped together. But it does not establish the *number* of jobs to be included in a specific group. That determination is the issue of *span of control.* Generally, the issue comes down to the decision of *how many people a manager can effectively oversee;* that is, will the organization be more effective if the span of control is relatively larger or smaller? The issue is basically concerned with determining the volume of interpersonal relationships that the department's manager is able to handle. In this context, it is important to distinguish between two types of relationships between a manager and subordinates—**potential** and **required.**

Potential relationships between manager and subordinates

A manager can, potentially, relate to every unique combination of individuals and groups of individuals that comprise his or her department. The number of *potential* relationships between a manager and subordinates can be calculated by the formula:

$$R = N\left(\frac{2^N}{2} + N - 1\right)$$

where R designates the number of relationships and N is the number of subordinates assigned to the manager's group. The number of relationships, R, increases geometrically as the number of subordinates, N, increases arithmetically. For example, the number of potential relationships increases from *6 to 18* as the number of subordinates increases from *2 to 3.*

The calculation assumes that the manager must contend with three types of relationships: (1) direct single, (2) direct group, and (3) cross. Direct single relationships occur between the manager and each subordinate individually. Direct group relations occur between the manager and each possible group of subordinates. Finally, cross relationships occur when subordinates interact with one another. These potential relationships are illustrated in Figure 7–10 for a manager (M) with two subordinates (A and B) and for a manager with three subordinates (A, B, and C). The direct group

Figure 7–10

Potential relationships among a manager and two or three subordinates

Manager (M) and two subordinates (A and B)		Manager (M) and three subordinates (A, B, and C)	
Direct single	1. M → A	Direct single	1. M → A
	2. M → B		2. M → B
			3. M → C
Direct group	3. M → A with B	Direct group	4. M → A with B
	4. M → B with A		5. M → A with C
			6. M → B with A
			7. M → B with C
			8. M → C with A
			9. M → C with B
			10. M → A with B and C
			11. M → B with A and C
			12. M → C with A and B
Cross	5. A → B	Cross	13. A → B
	6. B → A		14. A → C
			15. B → A
			16. B → C
			17. C → A
			18. C → B

relationships differ, depending on which subordinate assumes the leadership role in the interaction with the manager. Depending on the issue to be discussed or the problem to be solved, we would expect different members of the group to emerge as group leaders.

Required relationships between manager and subordinates

At the same time that we note the number of potential relationships between a manager and subordinates, we must recognize that not all relationships will occur, and those that do will vary in importance. At least three factors appear to be important in analyzing the frequency and intensity of relationships which are actually required of the manager.

1. Required contact In research and development, medical, and production work, there is a need for frequent contact and a high degree of coordination between a superior and subordinates. The use of conferences and other forms of consultation often aids in the attainment of goals within a constrained time period. For example, the research and development team leader may have to consult frequently with team members so that a project can be completed early enough to enable the organization to place a product on the market at a given time. Thus, it is in the best interests of the organization for the team leader to have as many in-depth contacts with the team as possible instead of relying on memos and reports. A wide span of control would preclude the team leader from contacting subordinates so frequently, and this could impede the completion of the project.

2. Level of subordinate education and training The training of employees is a critical consideration in establishing required interactions at all levels of management. It is generally accepted that a manager at a lower organizational level can oversee more subordinates because work at the lower level is more specialized and less complicated and requires fewer interactions between managers and subordinates.

3. Ability to communicate Instructions, guidelines, and policies must be communicated verbally to subordinates in most work situations. The need to discuss job-related factors influences required relationships. An individual who can clearly and concisely communicate with subordinates is able to communicate less frequently and with more people at one time than an individual with poor communication skills.

Factors affecting the span of control

The exact number of jobs (and people) reporting to a manager cannot be stated in specific terms for all managers in all organizations. Rather, the only feasible approach is to weigh the relative importance of the factors which are related to the optimal span of control for an individual manager. Those factors take into account both potential and required relationships and include at least the following:

1. *The competence of both the manager and the subordinates.* The more competent they are, the wider the span of control can be.
2. *The degree of interaction that is required between and among the units to be supervised.* The more the required interaction, the narrower the span of control must be.
3. *The extent to which the manager must carry out nonmanagerial tasks.* The more technical and job-related work the manager has to do, the less time is available to supervise others, and thus, the narrower the span of control must be.
4. *The relative similarity or dissimilarity of the jobs being supervised.* The more similar the jobs, the wider the span of control can be; the more dissimilar the jobs, the narrower it must be.
5. *The extent of standardized procedures.* The more routine the jobs of subordinates are, and the greater the degree to which each job is

performed by standardized methods, the wider the span of control can be.

6. *The degree of physical dispersion.* If all the people to be assigned to a manager are located in one area, and within eyesight, the manager can supervise relatively more people than one whose people are dispersed throughout the plant or countryside at different locations.

Managers do not of course always consider these factors when fixing spans of control. The chairperson of a department of business administration stated:

> *The organization of this college makes no sense to me. I chair a department which has 36 faculty representing almost every discipline found in a university. Mathematicians, sociologists, psychologists, lawyers, and statisticians are members of the departmental faculty. How I am supposed to evaluate their performance, particularly their research, is beyond me. It is even more discouraging when I see the chairman of the accounting department with only 12 faculty to manage making a bigger salary than I do.*

Delegation of authority

The final issue which managers must consider when designing an organizational structure is that of delegation of authority. In practical terms, the issue concerns the relative benefits of decentralization, that is, delegation of authority to the lowest possible level in the managerial hierarchy. The concept of decentralization does not refer to geographic dispersion of the organization's operating units; rather, it refers to the delegated right of managers to make decisions without approval by higher management. Let us evaluate some of the arguments for decentralization.

The advantages of decentralized authority

First, some experts assume that decentralization encourages the development of professional managers. The point is that as decision-making authority is pushed down in the organization, managers must adapt and prove themselves if they are to advance. That is, they must become generalists who know something about the numerous job-related factors that they must cope with in the decentralized arrangement.

Because managers in a decentralized structure often have to adapt and to deal with difficult decisions, they are trained for promotion into positions of greater authority and responsibility. In a decentralized structure, managers can be readily compared with their peers on the basis of actual decision-making performance. In effect, the decentralized arrangement can lead to a more equitable performance appraisal program and to a more satisfied group of managers because under this arrangement managers can be evaluated on the basis of results, not personalities. It should be remembered, however, that it is extremely difficult to develop specific performance criteria for most managers.

Second, the decentralized arrangement leads to a competitive climate within the organization. The managers are motivated to contribute in this competitive atmosphere, since they are compared with their peers on various performance measures.

Third, in the decentralized pattern, managers are able to exercise more autonomy and this satisfies the desire to participate in problem solving. This freedom is assumed to lead to managerial creativity and ingenuity, which contribute to the flexibility and profitability of the organization.

These are only three of the advantages associated with decentralization. The advantages are not free of costs, and most advocates of decentralization are aware that certain costs may have to be incurred if an organization shifts from centralized to decentralized authority. Some of the costs are:

1. Managers must be trained to handle decision making, and this may require expensive formal training programs.
2. Since many managers have worked in centralized organizations, it is very uncomfortable for them to delegate authority in a more decentralized arrangement. Their attitudes are difficult to alter and often lead to resistance.
3. Accounting and performance appraisal systems must be made compatible with the decentralized arrangement, and this is costly. Administrative costs are incurred because new or altered accounting and performance systems must be tested, implemented, and evaluated.

These are, of course, only some of the costs of decentralizing. As with most issues, there is definitely no clear-cut answer about whether decentralization is better for an organization. It would appear that a prerequisite for reaching decisions concerning decentralization is the thorough consideration of each organizational factor (for example, work force requirements, size, and control mechanisms).

The conflict between decentralization of authority and the need for control is keenly felt by many managers. One store manager in a national discount chain store stated:

Every year at the annual store managers' meeting, we are told by corporate to run our store just like we owned it. But then I get back home, and on my desk are directives from corporate marketing telling me what ad to run in the Sunday paper, from corporate personnel telling me what I can pay my clerks, and from corporate buyers telling me how much shelf space to set aside for Christmas toys. Apparently, I have a different understanding of what an owner should be able to do because it sure doesn't square with corporate's understanding.

The chain of command and authority

One result of delegated authority is the creation of a **chain of command.** The chain of command is the formal channel which specifies the authority, responsibility, and communication relationships from top to bottom in an organization. Figure 7–11 depicts the chain of command for a hypothetical managerial hierarchy. In theory, the chain should be followed whenever directives are passed downward or whenever communications are passed upward and downward.

At the same time, it is recognized that means must be provided for bypassing the formal chain when conditions warrant it. Consequently, a subordinate is often empowered to communicate directly with a peer outside the chain, provided that the appropriate superiors indicate beforehand the circumstances under which the crossovers will be permitted. Figure 7–12 shows a bridge between F and G (the dashed line) which D and E have approved. Under special circumstances, F and G may communicate directly without going through channels, yet both would be accountable only to their respective superiors—in this case, D and E.

Figure 7–11

Chain of command

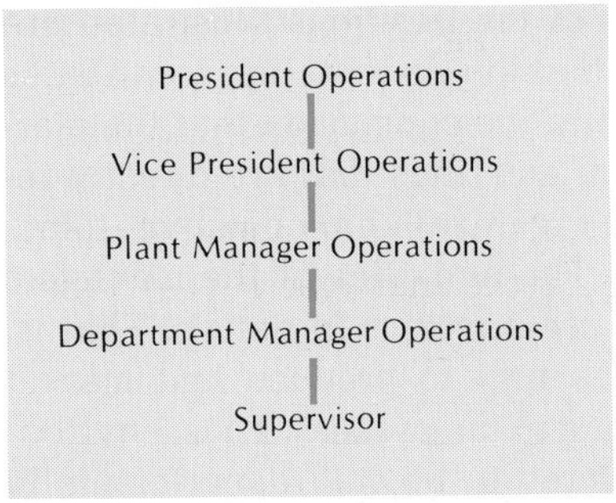

Figure 7–12

Communication bridge

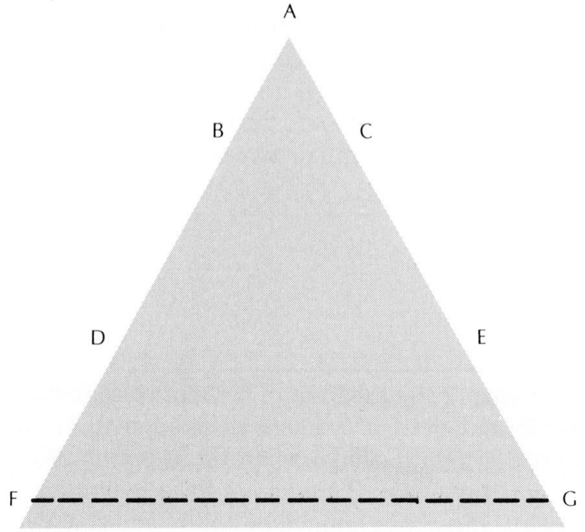

The line-staff distinction

An important point in examining organization structure is to distinguish between line and staff. The definitions for line and staff are endless. Perhaps the most concise and least confusing approach is to view **line** as deriving from operational activities in a direct sense—creating, financing, and distributing a good or service—whereas **staff** is an advisory and facilitative function for the line. The crux of this view of line and staff is the degree to which the function contributes directly to the attainment of organizational objectives. The *line function* contributes directly to the accomplishment of the major objectives of the organization, and the *staff function* contributes to their accomplishment indirectly. Figure 7–13 illustrates a line and staff organizational design of a hypothetical firm.

Assuming that the organization depicted in Figure 7–13 is a manufacturing firm would enable one to conclude which of the positions illustrated are line and which are staff. Using the criterion that the line function contributes directly to the firm's objectives would lead to the conclusion that the marketing and production departments perform activities that are directly related to the attainment of a most important organizational objective—placing an acceptable product on the market. The activities of the managers of environmental control and engineering are advisory in nature. That is, those activities are helpful in enabling the firm to produce and market its product, but they do not directly contribute to the process. Thus, environmental control and engineering are considered to be staff departments in this particular firm.

Figure 7–13

A line and staff design
(partial organization chart)

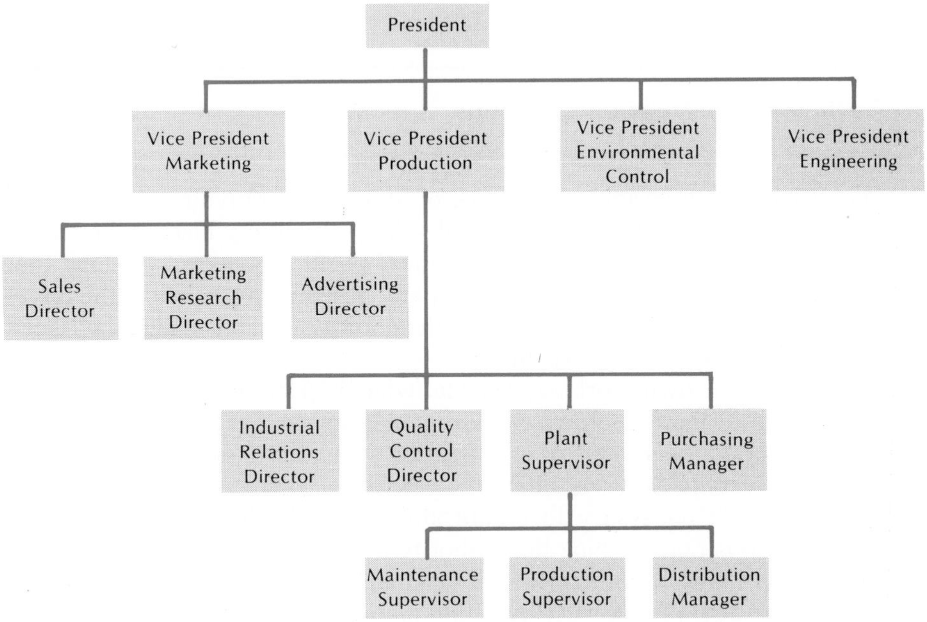

Management summary

1. The organizing process includes action steps which managers take to determine the jobs and the authority relationships that are necessary to implement plans and policies.
2. The four primary elements of an organization structure are job specification, departmentation bases, spans of control, and delegated authority. These elements are conceptually different, but in practice they are highly interrelated.
3. Job specification involves deciding the appropriate tasks and authority to be assigned to each job and jobholder.
4. Departmentation involves deciding the bases to use in grouping jobs that are to be directed by a manager. The typically used bases are function, territory, customer, and product.
5. The number of jobholders who report to a manager is termed the *span of control.* Deciding the appropriate span is a key organizing decision, and although there are no precise rules, managers can follow guidelines to determine optimal spans.
6. The delegation of authority involves providing jobholders with the right,

or the freedom, to make decisions without approval by higher management. The relative advantages of centralization versus decentralization must be weighed.

Review and discussion questions

1. What are the primary purposes of an organization structure?
2. Assume that the management of a large company has completed its review of progress toward its annual profit objectives. Assume that the review indicates that the company is significantly below the target profit. Explain how the causes of the poor performance might be traced to the organization structure.
3. From your own work experience, what important information is not shown in the Sometown Bank organization chart (Figure 7–1)?
4. Use the four elements of organization structure to describe the college or university that you attend.
5. Why is it necessary to create staff positions in organizations? Do these positions reduce the authority of line managers? Explain.
6. Explain why it is important for managers to distinguish carefully the extent of staff authority over line managers.
7. What is your understanding of the term *authority?* Is it different from the term *responsibility?* Explain.
8. Which of the three different types of interactions (direct single, direct group, and cross) are most difficult for managers to deal with? Explain.
9. Explain how a functional-base organization is most effective in obtaining the advantages of specialization of labor?
10. What factors other than structure contribute to organization performance? Explain.

Suggested reading

Blackburn, R. S. "Dimensions of Structure: A Review and Reappraisal." *Academy of Management Review,* January 1982, pp. 59–66.

Chonko, L. B. "The Relationship of Span of Control to Sales Representatives' Experienced Role Conflict and Role Ambiguity." *Academy of Management Journal,* June 1982, pp. 452–56.

Dalton, D. R.; W. D. Todor; M. J. Spendolini; G. J. Fielding; and L. W. Porter. "Organization Structure and Performance: A Critical Review." *Academy of Management Review,* January 1980, pp. 49–64.

Fuller, S. H. "How to Become an Organization of the Future." *Management Review,* February 1980, pp. 50–53.

Handy, C. "The Changing Shape of Work." *Organizational Dynamics,* Autumn 1980, pp. 26–34.

Lutchen, M. D. "Protecting the Company from Bureaucratic Slowdown." *Management Review,* April 1980, pp. 41–45.

Walton, E. J. "The Comparison of Measures of Organization Structure." *Academy of Management Review,* January 1981, pp. 155–60.

Applying what you have learned about elements of organizing

Cases:

Decentralization at Curtice-Burns, Inc.
Recentralization for the 1980s?

Decentralization at Curtice-Burns, Inc.*

Curtice-Burns, Inc., consists of seven food manufacturing divisions with sales in excess of $270 million. The company grew primarily through acquisitions of food companies which then became divisions of the company. The management philosophy at Curtice-Burns, Inc., emphasizes decentralization and autonomy. Each division is completely responsible for its own business with the exception of major capital investments. To underscore the importance of decentralization, the company has a headquarters staff of only 12 people.

President and CEO Hugh Cumming is committed to decentralization and can readily identify the advantages and disadvantages of the approach. The primary advantage is the clearly defined responsibility of each division's CEO for that division's performance. The CEO whose division's performance is below planned performance cannot blame headquarters for meddling in division matters because he or she alone makes all the strategic and functional decisions.

A second advantage is one that derives from the company's incentive plan. Because of the cyclical nature of the food business, Curtice-Burns does not tie its incentive plan to the performance of a single division. Rather, it is based upon overall corporate results and allocated to the divisions on the basis of payroll. The incentive plan creates positive peer pressure because a poorly performing division will reduce the bonus for all divisions.

Decentralization stimulates and sustains the

---

* This case is adapted from "Food Conglomerate Gives Autonomy, Gets Results," *Management Review*, November 1979, pp. 32–33.

entrepreneurial spirit so often found in small business, but often missing in large corporations. All the top-management personnel began their careers in small business, and they tend to continue to manage entrepreneurially. For example, when one division decided it was time to get into the natural potato chip business, it did so in less than a month. By contrast, Pepsico's Frito-Lay division took 15 months to bring out the product.

The decentralized concept is not without difficulties. For example, the emphasis on divisional marketing of regional brands does little to promote the visibility of Curtice-Burns stock. Consequently, the stock sells at prices lower than what the company's board of directors thinks is appropriate. Investors simply are not familiar with Curtice-Burns.

A second disadvantage of decentralization is the inherent duplication of functions such as accounting, sales, and marketing. A corollary problem is that some divisions (acquired companies) are too small to operate independently. Small divisions often cannot support the full range of functional support required to operate as an independent unit.

A third problem is difficult to define. But it relates to the managerial question of knowing when headquarters should assist or even overrule a division decision. Constant interference in division affairs obviously ruins the concept, but total disregard is likewise ruinous. Striking the balance between the two extremes is a problem only because it is a matter of managerial judgment.

Cumming believes the advantages of decentralization outweigh its disadvantages. In fact, he sees the practice as the primary cause for the company's steady growth. In the 10 years ending in 1978, earnings per share went from $.62 to $3.67.

Questions:

1. Evaluate Curtice-Burns, Inc.'s policy of decentralization.
2. What specific company strategies facilitate the use of decentralized authority?
3. At what point should Cumming consider centralizing certain functions? What functions are most likely to be centralized when and if that point is reached?

Recentralization for the 1980s?*

The most dominant organization structure during the 1950s and 1960s featured decentralized authority to product-based department managers. Management consultants and practitioners advocated decentralization as the best structural form for corporations with diversified product lines and national and international markets. Throughout the 1970s, however, many firms shifted from decentralized to centralized authority. These shifts appear to reflect long-term trends that can be projected into the 1980s.

A most pervasive cause of recentralization is the increasing influence of government—state and local as well as federal. Governmental influence has caused organizations to create centralized headquarters units to deal with such issues as foreign contract negotiations, affirmative action programs, energy conservation, and political contributions. Apparently, the more closely regulated an organization is, the more

* Based on Willys H. Monroe, "Changing Patterns in Organizational Planning," *Management Review*, October 1977, pp. 29–30.

likely it is that the organization will centralize authority.

A second cause of recentralization is the shortage of managerial talent. This shortage has resulted from (1) the rapid expansion of organizations through acquisitions and mergers and (2) the drop in the birthrate during the 1930s (the birth dates of managers who typically are ready to assume significant managerial positions during the 1980s). Organizations have discovered that there are simply too few managers to staff decentralized organizations. Centralized structures require less management personnel; sometimes they require up to one-third fewer managers.

Questions:

1. Assuming that organizations continue to recentralize authority during the 1980s, what will the impact be on job definitions, departmentation bases, and spans of control?
2. As more authority is centralized in corporate headquarters, and as the tendency toward conglomerates continues, is it likely that *one person* can assume responsibility for the total corporate entity? Explain your answer.
3. What professional and occupational specialties are likely to become more valued in closely regulated firms?

8

Chapter eight
Designing the organization

Performance objectives

- **Define** in practical terms what is meant by organizational design.
- **State** the main criticisms of the bureaucratic, classical, and behavioral approaches to organizational design.
- **Describe** the main characteristics that are used in developing a contingency approach to organizational design.
- **Explain** how strategy, technology, and environment are interrelated and affect organizational design decisions.
- **Discuss** the advantages and disadvantages of project and matrix organization designs.

Management update*

Large, diversified companies which rely upon advanced technology for process and product development typically use product-based organization structures. Each product, or product group, is a profit center and has all the production, sales, engineering, and support services required to function as an independent business. The advantage of this type of structure is its ability to react quickly to changes in the marketplace.

Unfortunately, in many such companies innovation suffers, and at a time when foreign competition places a high premium on innovative products, the consequent cost is significant. The causes of innovation failures are not easily isolated, but some observers believe that a principal reason is the way these companies are organized. They point out that product-based organizations must provide each product division the resources necessary to compete successfully. Included in necessary resources are scientists and engineers through whose efforts innovation is expected. But the structure tends to discourage the very processes required for successful innovation.

As a consequence of the necessity to assign scientific personnel to each product group, communication barriers are created. The result is that research on similar or same problems can be ongoing on several product groups without any sharing of ideas or information. Since each group is expected to generate profits, there is little incentive to cooperate. Managers have devised numerous methods, including periodic meetings and company seminars, to facilitate the interaction among research personnel in different divisions, but with little success.

One company, Texas Instruments (TI), has been able to compete with foreign competitors. TI's success is due to a number of factors, but its organization design contributes to it. Rather than grouping engineers and scientists by products, TI groups them by technical expertise. Thus, mechanical engineers report to an engineering manager who is an expert in mechanical engineering rather than to a general product division manager. When new product development is required, a program manager is appointed who, in turn, estimates the amount and kind of technical resources required. The appropriate technical staff are then assigned to the program manager to whom they are accountable for progress toward development objectives, but they continue to report to their technical manager. When the product is developed, the staff will be reassigned to a new project. This form of organization, termed **matrix organization,** permits TI to assign resources to projects and problems as they occur but without the necessity of creating permanent organizational units.

---

* This Management Update is based upon Gerald C. Werner, "Does a Product Group Structure Inhibit Technological Developments?" *Management Review,* March 1981, pp. 47–51.

Organization design is the specific structure of task and authority relationships that managers explicitly decide is optimal to achieve performance objectives. As noted in the previous chapter, organization structures vary in terms of four elements: task specialization, departmental bases, spans of control, and delegation of authority. The initial managerial decision is to determine the specific arrangement of these four elements. Thus, the concept of organization design implies *conscious* and *proactive* managerial action to create and maintain the optimal structure of jobs and job relationships. Thus, organization design is both a *process* (designing, selecting, deciding) and a *result* (design, structure, arrangement).[1]

This chapter reviews contemporary theory and practice of organization design. Despite the importance of organization design to the attainment of performance objectives, not a great deal is known about how design and performance are related. It is known that organization designs are different, and it is also known that different designs are appropriate in different situations. But the exact nature of the optimal fit between a design and a situation is but little known, much less understood.

Alternative organization designs

Alternative organization designs tend to reflect differences in the four elements of organization structures. At one extreme are organization designs which have high specialization of labor, homogeneous departments, narrow spans of control, and centralized authority. Designs having these extreme characteristics are referred to as *bureaucratic, classical, formalistic, mechanistic,* and *System 1.* All of these terms describe essentially the same organizational design. Throughout the following discussion, the

[1] Ralph H. Kilmann, Louis R. Pondy, and Dennis P. Slevin "Directions of Research on Organization Design," in *The Management of Organization Design: Research and Methodology,* ed. Ralph H. Kilmann, Louis R. Pondy, and Dennis P. Slevin (New York: Elsevier North-Holland, 1976), p. 1.

term **System 1** will describe this design thus avoiding the value-laden connotations of the other terms.

Organization designs at the opposite extreme have low specialization of labor, heterogeneous departments, wide spans of control, and decentralized authority. Terms which identify this extreme design include *nonbureaucratic, behavioral, informalistic, organic,* and *System 4.* **System 4** will be used in the following discussion to identify this design. Figure 8–1 summarizes the important characteristics of these two extreme types. In reality, organizations will be somewhere between these extremes and contain characteristics of both extremes. In addition, the units within an organization can be different one from the other in the degree to which they reflect characteristics of System 1 and System 4 designs.

System 1 organization design

The earliest writers, those of the classical approach to management, made forceful arguments for the superiority of System 1 organization design in comparison to any alternative design. According to their reasoning, System 1 organizations are natural extensions of specialization of labor to the institutional level. The use of System 1 organization was widespread during the late 1800s when industrialization of Western civilization was at its height. A primary social, and therefore managerial, concern was *efficient* use of resources and *maximum* production. Out of these times two different, yet compatible, sets of ideas emerged. One set of ideas has come to be associated with *bureaucracy* as an "ideal type" of organization. The other set of ideas are those of the *classical approach.*

Figure 8–1

System 1 and System 4 organization designs

	System 1 design	System 4 design
Alternative terms often used to describe the design	*Bureaucratic* *Classical* *Formalistic* *Mechanistic*	*Nonbureaucratic* *Neoclassical* *Informalistic* *Organic*
Defining characteristics	High specialization of labor Homogeneous departments Narrow spans of control Centralized authority	Low specialization of labor Heterogeneous departments Wide spans of control Decentralized authority

Bureaucracy Bureaucracy refers to the form of organization first described in the literature of public administration as government by bureaus, that is, unelected civil servants. However, it is more usually associated with negative consequences of large organizations such as red tape, unexplained delays, and general frustration. But its more important meaning is to describe an organization design which is "superior to any other form in precision, in stability, in the stringency of its discipline, and its reliability. It thus makes possible a high degree of calculability of results for the heads of the organization and for those acting in relation to it."[2]

The characteristics of the ideal-type bureaucracy are as follows: First, it has a clear division of labor, with each job well defined, understood, and routine. Second, each manager has a clearly defined relationship with other managers and subordinates which follows a formal hierarchy. Third, there is a reliance on specific rules, policies, and procedures to guide behaviors. Fourth, favoritism is minimized through the impersonal application of rules, policies, discipline, and rewards. Fifth, rigid and equitable selection criteria are used to screen candidates. The most qualified candidates receive vacant jobs. The effect of the ideal type is to deemphasize the idiosyncracies of human behavior and to emphasize the predictableness of machines and mechanical behavior.

As summarized by Max Weber, the bureaucratic design compares to other designs "as does the machine with nonmechanical modes of production."[3] Weber based this conclusion on extensive analyses of the Prussian civil service and military organizations. He believed that the advantages of bureaucracy were applicable in any context, whether government, military, or business.

Classical organization design The classical approach to organization design refers to ideas that were expressed in the early 1900s. These ideas propose that the design of organization structures, that is, the *process* of design, should be guided by certain *principles of organization.*[4] Thus, managers who are guided by these principles would design a certain type of organization structure, that is, a *classical* design.

The important principles of organization are:

1. Specialization of labor—Work should be divided and subdivided to the highest possible degree consistent with economic efficiency.
2. Unity of direction—Jobs should be grouped according to function or process, that is, like jobs should be grouped.

---

[2] Max Weber, *The Theory of Social and Economic Organization,* trans. A. M. Henderson and Talcott Parsons (New York: Oxford University Press, 1947), p. 334.

[3] Max Weber, *From Max Weber: Essays in Sociology,* trans. H. H. Gerth and C. W. Mills (New York: Oxford University Press, 1946), p. 214.

[4] See Henri Fayol, *General and Industrial Management,* trans. C. Storrs (London: Pitman Publishing, 1949), pp. 19–42, for the original statement of classical principles.

3. Centralization of authority—Accountability for the use of authority is retained at the executive, or top-management, level.
4. Authority and responsibility—A jobholder must have authority commensurate with job responsibility.
5. Unity of command—Each jobholder should report to one and only one superior.

The application of these principles results in organizations in which jobs are highly specialized, departments are based upon function, spans of control are narrow, and authority is centralized. Such organizations tend to be relatively "tall," with several layers of management through which communications and directions must pass. Taken together, bureaucratic and classical design theories describe the essential features of System 1 organizations. System 1 organizations are means for obtaining maximum efficiency and production results.

System 4 organization design

In a historical sense, System 4 organization design is a reaction to System 1. As noted earlier, System 4 is the exact opposite of System 1; in System 4 organizations, jobs are relatively despecialized, departments contain a heterogeneous mix of jobs, spans of control are wide, and authority is decentralized.

The support for the application of the System 4 design derives from two perspectives. One perspective notes the inherent flaws of the System 1 design. A second perspective notes its limitations in particular settings.

The inherent flaws of System 1 organization were first noted in the famous Hawthorne studies, a series of experiments carried out at the Western Electric plant in Hawthorne, Illinois. These studies were the bases for the contention that extensive specialization of labor and centralized authority underestimates the complexity of employees. Rather than being a passive and inert being, dumbly performing assigned tasks, the average employee is a complex, multifaceted person who seeks more than monetary rewards from work. The researchers at the Hawthorne plant found that workers were members of friendship groups which defined the level of output considered fair and equitable. These groups seemed to exert far greater influence on employees than their managers, even though the groups had no authority to back up their influence.

Other writers take the position that System 4 organization is more compatible with the needs of individuals and that System 1 designs create inherent conflict. For example, Chris Argyris believes that System 1 organizations suppress the development and growth of employees.[5] The domina-

[5] Chris Argyris, *Personality and Organization* (New York: Harper & Row, 1975); and Chris Argyris, "Personality and Organization Revisited," *Administrative Science Quarterly* (1973), pp. 141–67.

tion of subordinates through the use of rules and hierarchy has caused subordinates to become passive, dependent, and noncreative. Such conditions are not congruent with the human needs for autonomy, self-expression, accomplishment, and advancement. Consequently, the organization forfeits a considerable portion of its human resources through the use of System 1.

The limitations of System 1 designs in contemporary situations derive from the fact that such designs are no longer compatible with society. As noted earlier, System 1 designs gained in popularity during the early periods of industrialization and economic development, the late 1800s and early 1900s. A period of relative stable and predictable change gave way to one of instability and uncertainty. Advanced technology in communications, transportation, manufacturing processes, and medicine creates the necessity for organizations to be adaptable and flexible so that new ways of doing work can be quickly utilized.

A leading advocate of System 4 design is Rensis Likert.[6] After considerable study, Likert proposed that in contemporary society, System 4 organizations utilize human and technical resources more fully than System 1.

The System 4 design emphasizes the importance of decentralized authority and nondirective, participative management behavior. Relatively wide spans of control and heterogeneous departments facilitate the interaction of multiple and diverse points of view. Consequently, as circumstance and technology change, the organization is able to respond because of the diverse perspectives that can be brought to bear on any issue or problem that it confronts.

Thus, the staunchest advocates of System 4 organization design believe that it is universally applicable. But more important they believe that it is the best way to organize in modern society. System 4 is therefore seen as the superior alternative in comparison to System 1. An alternative point of view, termed **the contingency approach,** is that *either* System 1 *or* System 4 can be the best way to organize depending upon the nature of such underlying factors as the organization's strategy, environment, and technology.

Contingency organization design

The essence of the contingency approach to organization design is the understanding that different organization structures facilitate different purposes. System 1 organizations are relatively *more* efficient and productive,

[6] Rensis Likert, *New Patterns of Management* (New York: McGraw-Hill, 1961); and Rensis Likert, *The Human Organization* (New York: McGraw-Hill, 1967).

but relatively *less* adaptive and flexible, than System 4 organizations. A particular organization, whether a business firm, government agency, hospital or university, or a particular unit within an organization should be structured depending upon whether it must be relatively (1) efficient and productive or (2) adaptive and flexible. A given mix of strategy, technology, and environment determines which is the case.

Strategy

As noted in our discussion of the planning function, strategy involves the selection of missions and objectives and appropriate courses of action to achieve these objectives. Logically, several courses of action could be identified for any given objective, and for each alternative strategy an alternative organization design exists. Thus, the specific organization design should follow from a specified strategy.

The contemporary impetus for the idea that structure follows strategy is the work of Chandler.[7] After a study of the history of 70 of America's largest firms, Chandler concluded that organization structures follow the growth strategies of firms. He also found that growth strategies tended to follow a certain pattern. In their initial stage, firms are typically plants, sales offices, or warehouses in a single industry, in a single location, and they perform a single function such as manufacturing, sales, or warehousing. But they grow if successful, and their growth follows fairly standard paths.

The first stage of growth is through *volume expansion;* firms simply manufacture, sell, or distribute more of their product or service to existing customers. The next stage of growth is *geographic expansion* through which the firm continues to do what it has been doing but in a larger geographic area by means of field units. The third growth strategy is *vertical integration,* as firms either buy or create other functions. For example, manufacturers integrate backward by acquiring or creating sources of supply or forward by acquiring or creating sales and distribution functions. The ultimate growth strategy, *product diversification,* involves the firm in new industries either through merger, acquisition, or creation (product development).

As a firm moves through each stage, it must change its organization structure in successive steps from System 1 to System 4. The initial System 1 structure is appropriate because volume expansion of a single product or service in a single industry stresses low unit cost (efficiency) and maximum resource utilization (production), with relatively low concern for response to change and uncertainty. But the change to geographic expansion and, ultimately, product diversification increases the firm's concern for adaptability and flexibility in the face of diverse and complex environments. Thus, the organization structures of such firms are characterized by product-based divisions and departments, decentralized authority, and

[7] Alfred D. Chandler, *Strategy and Structure* (Cambridge, Mass.: MIT Press, 1962).

relatively wide spans of control. The underlying force, then, is the environment that the firm faces as a consequence of its strategic choice. As noted in the Management Update, Texas Instruments must be able to adapt to rapidly changing environments as a consequence of its corporate strategy of product innovation.

Environment

Every organization must operate within an environment. There are competitors, suppliers, customers, creditors, and the government, each making demands on the organization. Each of these external forces can have an effect on the organization's design.

The environment can be *stable,* that is, one in which there is little unpredictable change. In a stable environment, customer tastes remain pretty much what they have been. New technology is rare, and the need for innovative research to stay ahead of competition is minimal. There has been little change in the environment affecting the manufacturers of accordions, zippers, and book covers.

Turbulent, hostile, diverse, and *technologically complex* environments exist when changes are unexpected and unpredictable. New competitive strategies, new laws, and new technology can create a turbulent condition. Electronic firms such as IBM, Hewlett-Packard, and Honeywell face unexpected environmental forces.

Matching an organizational design to the environment would require accurate managerial assessment of the environmental forces. A group interested in organizational design studied 20 English and Scottish firms. Through analysis of interview responses, it concluded that two types of organizational systems exist—mechanistic and organic.[8] These should be considered the two ends of a continuum of designs that are available to managers.

The *mechanistic* system is characterized by a differentiation of job tasks, a specific authority hierarchy, a reliance on rules and procedures, and objectives set by top-level managers. The mechanistic system has the characteristics of the System 1 design.

The *organic* system is characterized by open communication channels, a professional orientation, and employee commitment to the organization. This design has a behavioral orientation, and it is like a System 4 design.

After completing its study, the group concluded that in a stable environment, a System 1 was more appropriate. However, a System 4 was most suited to a turbulent environment. Organizations in a diverse environment would probably achieve better performance by using a combination of the two systems.

[8] Tom Burns and G. M. Stalker, *The Management of Innovation* (London: Tavistock Publications, 1961).

Following up on the lead of the English study group, an American team initially studied 10 companies. These companies were in three industries—plastics, consumer foods, and standardized containers. The team was concerned about how to design departments in organizations faced with distinct environments.[9]

According to the American team, there are two crucial concepts associated with designing an organization: differentiation and integration. **Differentiation** is the degree of difference between the knowledge and feelings of managers in different departments—for example, the differences between the knowledge and feelings of a marketing manager and the knowledge and feelings of a production manager. **Integration** refers to the degree to which members of various departments work together effectively.

The study found that the certainty or uncertainty of the environment affected the degree of differentiation. For example, departments in plastics firms, which operated in a relatively uncertain environment, were more differentiated than departments in container firms, which operated in a more certain environment. The team also discovered that not all departments were affected similarly by environmental conditions. In a generally uncertain external environment, research and development departments might use an organic or flexible type of design. On the other hand, the production departments operating in a certain environment of the same organizations might use a mechanistic or more classical design.

The contingency approach is reflected in the researchers' conclusion:

> The internal functioning of organizations must be consistent with the organization task, technology, or external environment, and the needs of its members if the organization is to be effective.[10]

Technology

Joan Woodward was a leading researcher who found that an organization's technology is of major importance in selecting an appropriate design.[11] In one study, Woodward classified technologies as unit, mass, or process production. *Unit production* referred to production to meet a customer's specific order. Here the product is developed after an order is received. The manufacture of custom-made shirts is an example of unit production technology. *Mass production* refers to the production of large quantities, such as on an assembly line. Zenith Corp. uses a mass production technology to make television picture tubes. *Process production* refers to producing materials or goods on the basis of weight or volume. Processing

---

[9] Paul R. Lawrence and Jay W. Lorsch, *Organization and Environment* (Homewood, Ill.: Richard D. Irwin, 1967).

[10] Ibid., p. 85.

[11] Joan Woodward, *Industrial Organization: Theory and Practice* (London: Oxford University Press, 1965).

3 million barrels of oil or producing vats of paint at Sherwin-Williams are examples of production in this category.

Woodward found that a strong relationship existed between performance and both organizational design and technology. The highest performing organizations with unit and process technologies used open and flexible structures, or System 4 structures. However, the highest performing organizations with mass production technologies used a more rigid or System 1 design.

Woodward's research findings are offered as evidence that technology influences the design used. Woodward encouraged managers to consider the role that technology plays in influencing work behavior and to recognize that appropriate design decisions require consideration of the technological complexities that management must address.

Woodward's research has resulted in a number of principles that suggest how technology influences organizational design. They are:

1. The more complex the technology—going from a unit system to a more process system—the greater are the number of managerial personnel and the levels of management.
2. The more complex the technology, the larger is the number of clerical and administrative personnel.
3. The span of control of first-line managers increases from unit production systems to mass production systems and then decreases from mass production systems to process production systems.

The successful firms in each technology category seem to employ the design characteristics suggested by the three principles.

Hybrid organization designs

Two organizational designs, project and matrix, are attempts to combine the advantages of both System 1 and System 4.

Project design

The **project design** has become popular in a number of organizations. A project manager directs a job or a set of job tasks through to completion. Lockheed Aircraft Corporation won a government contract to build 58 giant C–5A military air transports. For this purpose, it created a whole new project design which included more than 11,000 employees. To complete the multibillion-dollar project, Lockheed managers had to coordinate the work of their own employees and of subcontracting firms. In all, 6,000 companies were involved in producing the more than 120,000 parts needed for the C–5A. At the conclusion of the C–5A project, the 11,000 employees were reassigned.

In a project design, people are brought together to complete various phases of the project. The design is temporary, yet very flexible. Specialists enter and leave the project, depending on needs and the completion of work. The specialists are borrowed from functional divisions of the company. The project team generally works together until specific objectives are accomplished. Project teams are transient, but they can be used effectively in many different situations. They have been used in aerospace, research and development, consulting firms, and engineering construction organizations. A project manager describes his view of project design assignments:

> *I have the most exciting job in the organization. My record shows that in the past eight years I worked on six projects. Three of these projects were in the Middle East, one in Texas, and two in California. All of them were different and challenging. I dread going back into the line management pool, and I can't wait for my next project assignment.*

A project design is shown in Figure 8–2. The specialists from the functional areas are assigned to the Randall and Southworks projects. When

Figure 8–2

A project design

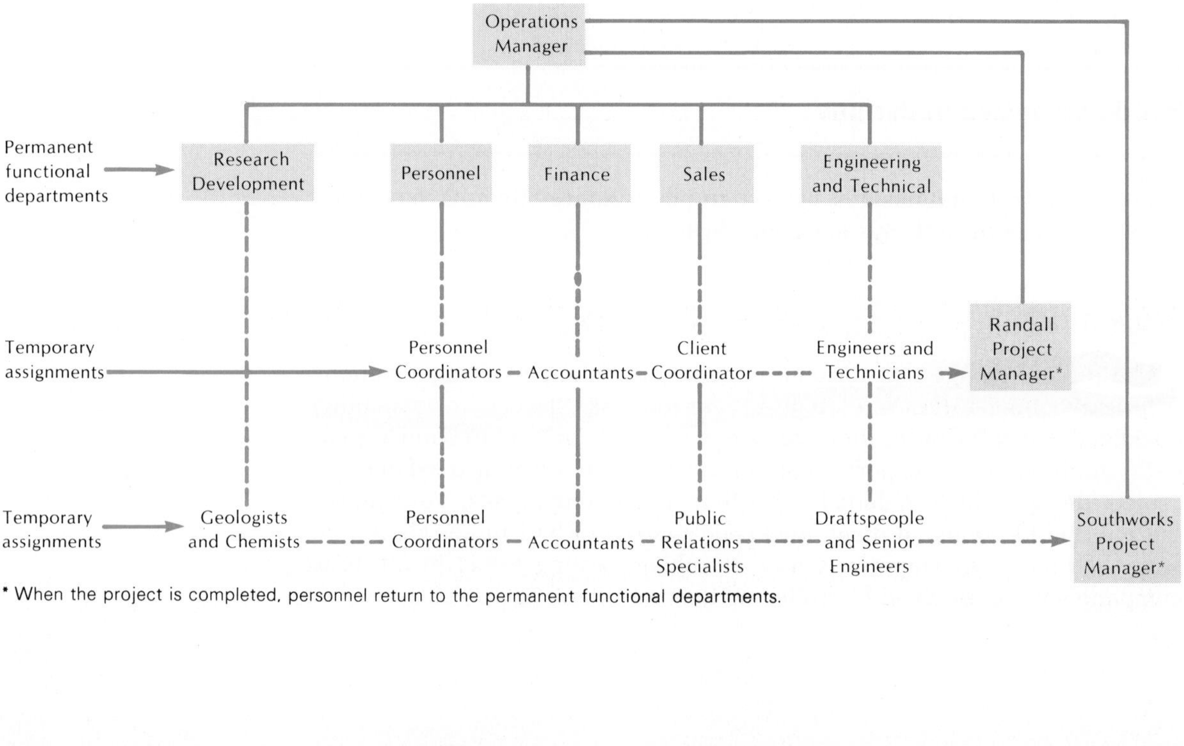

* When the project is completed, personnel return to the permanent functional departments.

the specialists' work on the projects is completed, they return to their permanent functional departments. This type of design seems to be effective in situations in which there is a need to accomplish technologically complex projects without totally disrupting the permanent organizational design.

Matrix design

A special type of project design is called **matrix design.** The matrix design is generally found in technical organizations in which technical, engineering, scientific, and craft specialists are grouped together to work on highly complex projects. Basically, a project-type design is superimposed on a functional structure to create the matrix design.

In a matrix design, the functional department managers have authority over the specialists in their units. These specialists are assigned to particular projects. A person works for two managers, which sometimes becomes frustrating. The assignments are usually made at the start of the projects when the functional and project managers arrange the flow of work. Figure

Figure 8–3

Matrix design for an engineering power division

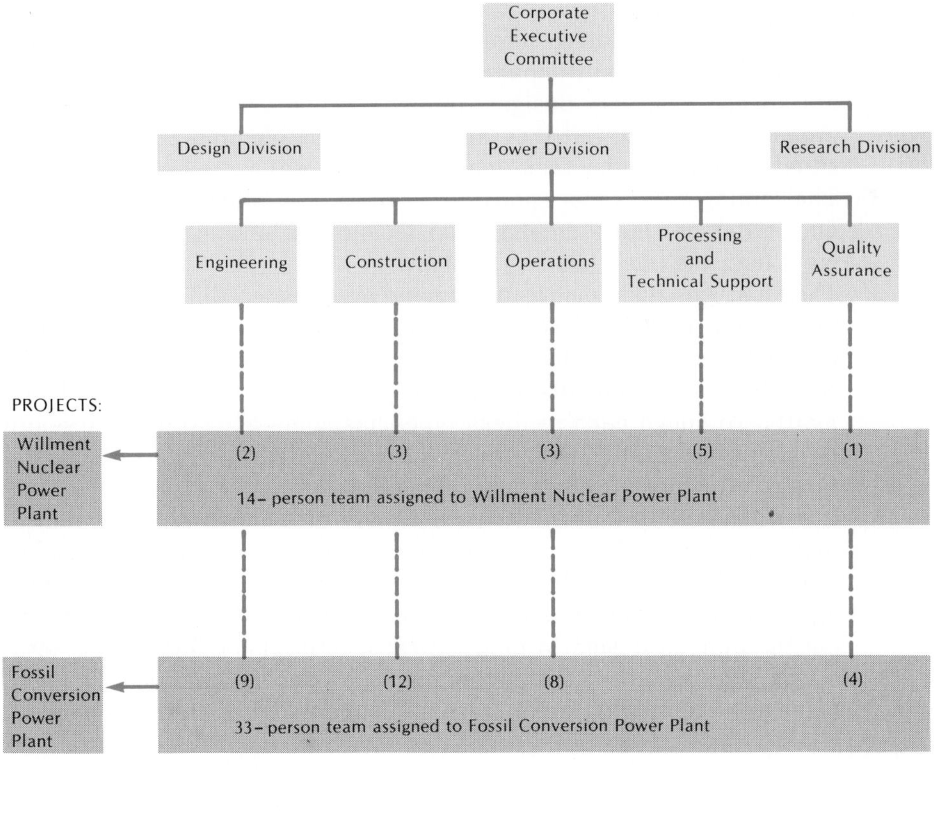

8–3 presents a matrix design for an engineering power division. Across the top are the permanent functional departments into which specialists are hired, and down the left side are two power plant projects that are currently being constructed. As shown in Figure 8–3, in a matrix design, two types of structure exist at the same time—functional departments and project teams.

In a matrix design, the classical principles of hierarchy and unity of command are typically violated. In addition, problems may arise if project team members seek help from the functional departments over the course of the project. Obtaining such help requires skill in bargaining and negotiating. On the other hand, the matrix design gives an organization the flexibility to work on important projects. It brings together the specialized talent needed to complete the job and brings that talent to bear on the project when and where it is needed. Texas Instruments has adopted the ideas of matrix organization as the means for achieving responsiveness to changing environmental demands.

Management summary

1. The bureaucratic design offered by Weber, the classical suggestions of Fayol, and the participative theme offered by Likert and Argyris are all one best way designs. In some stituations, these designs are probably excellent, but they are rather inflexible, and changes in the situation often render them inadequate.
2. The contingency design approach borrows from other design approach and introduces more emphasis on technology, strategy, and environment than the one best way designs.
3. The ideas on mechanistic and organic systems, on differentiation and integration, and on technology have provided the bases for contingency organizational design decision making among managers.
4. Specific designs that are contingency in nature include project and matrix. Although each of these types has some appeal, there are still problems associated with them, such as unfamiliarity, conflict, and lack of structure for some individuals.
5. If performance is the crucial determinant of managerial competence, then awareness of organizational design alternatives and the ability to make changes must be included in the manager's tool kit. The manager needs knowledge, energy, and a willingness to make changes to put the optimal design in place. After it is in place, fine tuning, total revamping, or starting over again may soon become realities. The best managers are able to make these adjustments when they are needed.

Review and discussion questions

1. Why are many of the ideal bureaucracy principles suggested by Weber still used in organizations that employ contingency design principles?
2. Are the behavioralists as narrow in their design approaches as the classicists or Weber? Explain.
3. Why is the project organizational design so popular in organizations with a technical and research orientation?
4. Is a focus on technology more important than a focus on organizational strategy in the contingency design approach?
5. Are you a System 1- or a System 4-oriented person? Why is this type of self-knowledge important for a manager?
6. Some believe that Argyris's concern about having the organization help people grow psychologically is misguided. They state that an organization in the profit sector is an economic institution and not a religious or counseling center. What do you think?

Suggested reading

Briscoe, D. R. "Organizational Design: Dealing with the Human Constraint." *California Management Review,* Fall 1980, pp. 71–80.

Cleland, D. I. "The Cultural Ambience of the Matrix Organization." *Management Review,* November 1981, pp. 24–27, 37–39.

_______. "Matrix Management: A Kaleidoscope of Organizational Systems." *Management Review,* December 1981, pp. 48–56.

Galbraith, J. R. "Designing the Innovative Organization." *Organizational Dynamics,* Winter 1982, pp. 5–25.

Mills, P. K., and B. Z. Posner. "The Relationships between Self-Supervision, Structure, and Technology in Professional Service Organizations." *Academy of Management Journal,* June 1982, pp. 437–43.

Pitts, R. A. "Toward a Contingency Theory of Multibusiness Organization Design." *Academy of Management Review,* April 1980, pp. 203–10.

Poza, E. J. and M. L. Markus. "Success Story: The Team Approach to Work Restructuring." *Organizational Dynamics,* Winter 1980, pp. 2–25.

Applying what you have learned about designing the organization

Cases:

Organization design at General Motors
What organization design is best?

Organization design at General Motors*

General Motors is the only U.S. auto manufacturer which has a clearly identified strategy to compete in the world market. The strategy was formulated in the 1970s in response to worldwide consumer demand for fuel efficient, quality automobiles. The most important characteristic of GM's strategy is to replace its entire line of cars with smaller ones, most of them to have front-wheel drive and to compete in the world market. The company plans to introduce a new product every six months beginning with the subcompact J car in May 1981.

The innovativeness of GM's strategy is all the more striking when compared to its history and reputation. Throughout its earlier years, GM was not known as an innovator or a risk taker. Its advantage was in manufacturing technology through which it reduced unit costs of production by spreading machinery and tooling expenses over larger volume. That strategy was so successful that GM's return on equity averaged almost 20 percent per year during the 1950s and 1960s. The company apparently did not need to innovate to maintain profitability. Consequently, it acquired a reputation as a "lumbering organization" most recently popularized in former GM Group Executive, John Z. DeLorean's book, *On a Clear Day You Can See General Motors.*

The idea of GM as a lumbering, or perhaps slumbering, giant doesn't seem to square with its recent history. Yet, observers close to the scene at GM believe that the popular view of

* This case is adapted from Charles G. Burck, "How GM Stays Ahead," *Fortune,* March 9, 1981, pp. 43–56.

the company has always been a false one. Although product innovation has not been a focus of change, the company has, in fact, been through numerous and significant changes. The mobilization of the company during World War II is a striking example of significant change.

In addition, GM's organization structure changes frequently. It has added vice presidents for consumer relations and service, for quality and reliability, and for technical operations, all since 1977. These changes reflect the company's adaptation to growing concerns for consumers, quality, and technology as important strategic factors during the decade of the 1980s.

Probably the most important source of structural change is the almost constant shifting balance between decentralized operations and centralized controls. As a divisionalized structure, GM's operating divisions must have considerable autonomy to make key decisions. Yet, that same autonomy must be counterbalanced by accountability to corporate headquarters. In practice, the optimal balance is never achieved. Consequently, a continual state of flux exists as divisions and headquarters negotiate the terms of the balance.

Recently, a major thrust of GM's production strategy has been to achieve greater economies of scale and flexibility in assembly operations. That emphasis caused the company to centralize all vehicle assembly operations into one assembly division. As a result, Chevrolet, for example, no longer assembles its own cars. But the car divisions are granted greater freedom to modify components that will give their cars distinctive handling and ride qualities. Research and development is also being decentralized into the car divisions to reinforce the importance of dealing with specific problems at the operating level.

The formal organization structure is not the only source of flux. Inherent in the way that GM makes decisions is its committee system, but in recent years, these formal committees meet to confirm and communicate decisions that have been made in the informal system consisting of lunch meetings and other casual settings. It is in sessions such as these that decisions are reached which are important as the one to downsize the 1977 big cars. The informal system simply works faster and is more responsive to circumstances requiring immediate action. The formal system of regular committees coexists with the informal system, but its purpose is to inform, not to deliberate.

Thus, the organization structure facilitates strategic redirection of GM's resources. The structure is far too complex to be simply described, but it does seem to encourage change in the midst of stability and informality along with formality.

Questions:

1. How can an organization be both stable and dynamic as is suggested in the case?
2. How does GM's organizational structure enable it to achieve its corporate strategy?
3. What does the GM case suggest about the existence of "pure" types, such as bureaucracy, mechanistic, or organic, of organizations in the real world?

What organization design is best?

The design of any organization is based on many different factors. Listed below are two sets of information about two differing organizations. Read the sets carefully and then answer the questions.

Organization A Jasper Corporation manufactures a number of agribusiness products such as fertilizers, pest sprays, plant food, and "weed-be-gone" chemicals for lawns. There are over 120 employees in the plant working on a morning shift and an afternoon shift (eight hours each). Approximately 100 of the employees operate the machines and perform the processes for manufacturing the products, which are sold to garden stores, supermarkets, and department stores. The employees are unionized, and they have a very specific set of job descriptions. The executive committee of Jasper has recently bought a pet food manufacturing plant, which includes 70 unskilled employees and six managers.

Organization B The Human Resource Division of a large multiindustry corporation has been involved in creating and implementing training and development programs for 17,000 managers in the firm. The division is a part of the personnel department, and it requires approval for operating funds from the corporate executive committee. The executive committee consists of 12 vice presidents of various functional units, such as marketing, personnel, finance, and legal. The Human Resource Division has over the past three years conducted in-house training programs for managers on such subjects as management practices, capital budgeting, performance appraisal, strategic planning, and career development.

Questions:

1. Why would the designs of these two organizations probably differ?
2. How would the external environments of these two organizations differ?
3. Which forces would have the most effect on how these two organizations are designed?

9

Chapter nine
Staffing the organization

Performance objectives

- **Define** what staffing means to a manager.
- **State** why each manager has a vital responsibility for matching people to jobs.
- **Describe** why managers may require the services and opinions of experts to do a better job of staffing.
- **Explain** the increased role which the government plays in staffing decisions.
- **Discuss** why even small business owners should be familiar with staffing procedures.

Management update*

Recruiting, selecting, and placing people in jobs are key activities of the staffing responsibility of managers. Successful staffing often requires innovative approaches, especially in those times of short supply of qualified people. Such a situation exists today for those organizations which are in the market for computer workers. According to R. A. McLaughlin of Trans Telecommunications Corporation, there has always been a shortage of data processing workers, but it now appears that the situation is getting worse. The turnover rate for such workers now runs about 28 percent per year, which means that the data processing staff completely changes every four years.

The costs of this turnover for those companies are a significant part of operating expenses. Not only are there costs associated with having jobs unfilled, but in addition there are the costs associated with training new hirees as well as the increased salaries. In the experience of one company, it now takes six to seven months to hire someone where once it took 30 to 60 days. The training period is 12 to 18 months, and the starting salaries have increased by $140 per month for new graduates. One effect of this situation is that some companies pay bonuses of up to $2,000 to an employee for each qualified applicant he or she brings in. One result is that people will raid their former employers and thus encourage even higher turnover.

Other companies have attempted to combat the problems of high turnover rates among computer personnel by changing their personnel practices. For example, they have promoted from within rather than hiring from the outside. They have also attempted to upgrade the jobs of data processing employees by giving them more authority and responsibility. The larger jobs often mean higher salaries, yet the increased costs of salaries for their loyal employees are offset by the savings from reduced turnover and the associated costs of staffing the organization with new employees.

---

* This Management Update is based on "Data Managers Sing the Turnover Blues," *Management Review*, March 1980, pp. 4–5.

Once the most suitable organizational design is in place, people must perform the activities and tasks which will result in the accomplishment of objectives. There is no more important managerial responsibility than filling positions with people who can and will make necessary contributions to the organization. Finding and developing the right people to perform the positions are central managerial concerns in staffing the organization.

In more specific terms, staffing is concerned with determining, maintaining, and retaining the quality and quantity of the people needed to accomplish objectives. Staffing in a large organization is the dual responsibility of the personnel department and the manager of the unit being staffed. In a small organization, managers have the full responsibility for staffing because there is usually no personnel department.

In this chapter, we will describe the steps in the staffing process as they are conducted in organizations. Many of the steps in the staffing process are conducted by experts, but there are many principles that managers need to be aware of.

The staffing process

The determination of what types and quantities of personnel are needed to operate an organization is part of staffing. The **staffing process** includes the forecasting, recruitment and selection, placement, and training and development of employees. Both managerial and nonmanagerial jobs must be staffed.

The focus in this chapter will be on the eight main steps of the staffing process:

1. *Human resource planning*—estimating the size and composition of the future work force.
2. *Recruitment*—acquiring the best-qualified applicants to satisfy the organization's human resource plans.
3. *Selection*—evaluating applicants and choosing the best candidates to fill jobs.

4. *Orientation*—introducing the selected individuals to their unit and the organization.
5. *Training and management development*—conducting activities that will prepare employees to contribute to the organization.
6. *Performance evaluation*—attempting to allocate resources, reward employees, provide feedback, and maintain relationships and communications between managers and subordinates.
7. *Compensation*—attempting to pay employees in accordance with the contributions they make to the organization.
8. *Promotion, demotion, and termination*—developing systems that involve shifting employees to higher-level positions (promotion) or to lower-level positions (demotion) or asking them to leave the organization (discharge).

The staffing process brings together the human assets and organizational design. Without human assets, there is simply no need to even consider the practice of management. Thus, staffing adds muscles, abilities, and other human characteristics to the organizational design. In essence, it adds life to the organization. Figure 9–1 outlines the staffing process.

Human resource planning

Human resource planning involves estimating the size and composition of the future work force. It is the process by which the organization estimates what numbers and kinds of human assets will be needed. Human resource planning requires forecasting. Experience indicates that the longer the period predicted, the less accurate the prediction will be. Other compli-

Figure 9–1
Staffing process

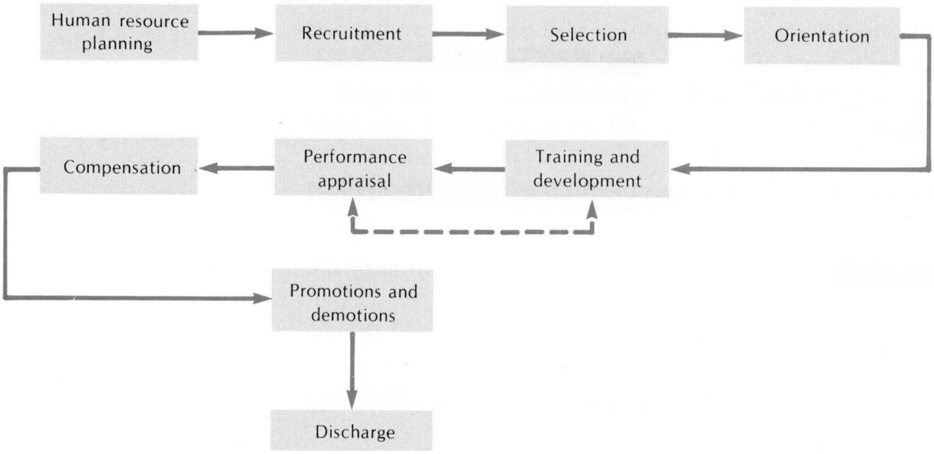

cating factors include changes in the environment in such areas as economic conditions, the labor supply, and competition.

The effort to anticipate future business and environmental demands on the organization requires the use of a planning system. The activities that a manager can follow in such a system include:

1. *Human resource inventory*—assessing the personnel skills, abilities, and potential that are present in the organization.
2. *Forecasting*—predicting future personnel requirements.
3. *Human resource plans*—developing a strategy for recruiting, selecting, placing, transferring, and promoting personnel.
4. *Development plans*—assuring that a continuing supply of properly trained managers is ready to take over vacant or new jobs.

Managers use formal and informal approaches to human resource planning to conduct these four activities. For example, some organizations use mathematical projections. Data are collected on such factors as the available supply of human resources, labor-market composition, the demand for products, new research breakthroughs, and competitive wage and salary programs. From these data and previous records, managers can use statistical procedures to make forecasts. Of course, unpredictable events can alter past trends, but with a minimum number of such events, fairly reliable forecasts are possible.

Estimating based on experience is a more informal forecasting procedure. Department managers and team leaders may be asked for opinions about future human resource needs. Some managers are confident in human resource planning, whereas others are reluctant to offer an opinion or are just not reliable forecasters.

The J. C. Penney Company, a large retail merchandiser, plans its human resource needs from information supplied by each retail store. Store managers from around the country provide information to a central data center that develops five-year projections for each position in the organization. The company's human resource needs are met primarily by promotion because of low turnover. The company recruits recent college graduates for lower-level managerial and staff positions. All J. C. Penney employees are called *associates* to give them a sense of commitment to the organization. Each employee is evaluated on his or her potential for being promoted. These evaluations give the company a readily available company-wide inventory of human resources. A computer is used to match present and anticipated vacancies with available associates.

Recruitment

Recruiting is a crucial step in staffing the organization. Its primary objective is to acquire the best-qualified applicants to fill vacancies. However, even before seeking applicants, managers must clearly understand the jobs. The methods and procedures that are used to acquire an understanding about jobs are called *job analysis.*

Job analyses: Description and specification

Job analysis is the process of determining the tasks that make up the job and the skills, abilities, and responsibilities that are required of an individual in order to successfully accomplish the job. The information for obtaining the facts about a job are shown in what are called a *job description* and a *job specification.* These terms are used to describe the information for nonmanagerial jobs. When discussing managerial jobs, we use the terms *position description* and *position specification.* The relationship between job analysis, job description, and job specification is presented in Figure 9–2.

Job analysis programs provide information that can be used by every manager within the organization. For example, to recruit and select effectively, it is necessary to match qualified personnel with job requirements. The relevant set of job information is provided by the job description and the job specification. Another use of job information is to establish proper

Figure 9–2

A manager's guide for job information

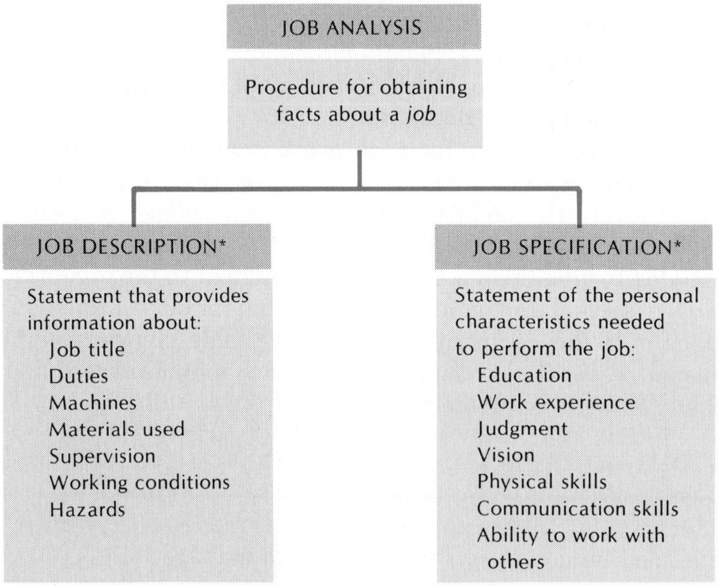

JOB ANALYSIS
Procedure for obtaining facts about a *job*
JOB DESCRIPTION*
Statement that provides information about:
Job title
Duties
Machines
Materials used
Supervision
Working conditions
Hazards
JOB SPECIFICATION*
Statement of the personal characteristics needed to perform the job:
Education
Work experience
Judgment
Vision
Physical skills
Communication skills
Ability to work with others

* Terms used primarily for nonmanagerial jobs. For managerial jobs, *position description* and *position specification* are the usual terms.

Figure 9–3

Job description and job specification

Classification: Manager — Power Division (Eastern Base)

Title: Project General Manager

Summary: Manages engineering, procurement, operations, and construction of single-responsibility power project.

Specific duties:

1. Establishes with Owner and Power Division, Engineering, Operations, and Construction the basic criteria for project plan and schedules.
2. Reviews project status to measure performance and minimize delays.
3. Continually monitors project to identify and resolve potential or real problem areas.
4. Administers contract and coordinates contract changes.
5. Reviews and issues progress reports to Owner and Division management.
6. Reviews and issues Engineering and Construction change notices.
7. Reviews and issues estimates and cash flow schedules to provide financial information to Owner.
8. Arranges and conducts project status meetings with Owner, Engineering, Procurement, and Construction management.
9. Prepares Project Management Office procedures.
10. Performs other duties as assigned.

Supervisory responsibilities:
Directly supervises four or more project coordinators; indirectly supervises three or more project team leaders.

Desirable qualifications: Specifications
College degree in Engineering with 10 or more years of related experience or equivalent and professional registration in Illinois; with knowledge of power plant design and construction, planning and scheduling, cost engineering, procurement, estimating, and utility practices and requirements.

rates of pay. In order to have an equitable pay system, it is necessary to have a complete job description. An example of a job description and a job specification for a project general manager is provided in Figure 9–3.

Performing an informative and accurate analysis of managerial jobs is no easy task. The duties of managers, such as those presented in the job description for the project general manager in Figure 9–3, are difficult to spell out. However, because of the range and types of managerial behaviors and duties, there must be a careful analysis of each managerial job. Suggested steps for gathering relevant information on managerial or nonmanagerial jobs include the following:

1. Accumulate systematic observations, reports, or record of many job behaviors of individuals carrying out the job.
2. Analyze these job behaviors and group them in sets; define the behaviors in the various sets.
3. Try to observe the job behaviors of job occupants, using the various sets developed in step 2.
4. Modify the behaviors, definitions, and sets after making new observations.

By gathering information in this manner, better and more meaningful job descriptions can be created.

The job description shown in Figure 9–3 was the topic of discussion between one of the authors and a project general manager. The manager stated:

> *The job description is not very revealing. An outsider has no idea about the features of my job if the description is read. For example, 60 percent of my time is spent on one job facet, yet it is just mentioned in a matter-of-fact way. The job description is for the personnel manager. It serves little purpose in my opinion.*

The project general manager believed that the job description was not useful for any purpose. However, the personnel manager believed that it was especially useful for showing applicants and new engineers information about jobs. The description was also used to calculate salary rates and to establish criteria for the performance appraisal system.

A good job analysis can provide the basic information needed for the recruitment and placement of people. Particular circumstances and laws affect the recruitment and placement of personnel. For organizations with low turnover that promote and transfer from within, external recruitment is rarely used. However, in high-turnover situations, external recruitment is essential. The company image also influences recruitment. Companies such as Alcoa, Tenneco, Rockwell, TRW, and General Mills have such good reputations in the labor market that they have a steady flow of qualified job applicants who can perform the duties specified in the job descriptions.

Legal issues in recruiting

Managers responsible for recruiting are faced with legal requirements. The legal requirement of recruiting a larger percentage of minority group members and women for positions that have seldom been filled by such employees is enforced by the Equal Employment Opportunity Commission

(EEOC). Through Title VII of the Civil Rights Act of 1964 and through the Equal Employment Opportunity Act of 1972, the federal government attempts to provide equal opportunities for employment without regard to race, religion, age, creed, sex, national origin, or disability.

These laws have broad coverage. They apply to any activity, business, or industry in which a labor dispute would hinder commerce. They also apply to state and local governments, governmental agencies, and agencies of the District of Columbia.

At first, the EEOC attempted to encourage organizations to follow the guidelines of the law. Now, the EEOC is more aggressive—it asks employers to prepare affirmative action programs. This requires the employer to identify what the company will be doing to improve the distribution of employees—that is, to state how the company will increase the number of minority and female employees. If EEOC investigators do not accept the employee distribution, they can propose adjustments.

The legal procedures regarding equal employment opportunities and recruitment are important issues in the staffing process. In the 1980s, it is almost essential that organizations adjust and work within these laws. Although adjustments are sometimes difficult, they seem to be a better alternative than becoming involved in a long and costly court battle. Providing equal opportunities to all qualified job applicants makes sense legally and morally. The vast majority of managers in organizations believe that all citizens have a right to any job they can perform reasonably well after a reasonable amount of training.

Recruiting activities

If needed human resources are not available within the company, outside sources must be tapped. An attractive organization such as Alcoa keeps a file on applicants who sought employment over the past year. Even though these applicants were not hired, they frequently maintain an interest in working for a company with a good reputation and image, such as Alcoa. By carefully screening these files, some good applicants can be added to the pool of candidates.

Advertisements in newspapers, trade journals, and magazines are a means to secure applicants. Responses to advertisements will be received from qualified individuals and from some who are unqualified. Occasionally, a company will list a post office box number and not provide the company name. This form of advertisement is called a *blind ad*. Such advertisements are used to eliminate the necessity of contacting every applicant. However, they do not permit a company to use its name or logo as a form of promotion.

One of the most important sources for recruiting lower-level managers is the *college campus*. Many colleges and universities have placement centers that work with organizational recruiters. The applicants read advertisements and information provided by the companies and then are interviewed. The most promising students are invited to visit the companies, where other interviews are conducted.

In locating experienced employees in the external market, organizations can also use private employment agencies, executive search firms, or state employment agencies. Some private employment agencies and executive search firms are called *no-fee agencies,* which means that the employer pays the fee instead of the applicant. An organization is not obligated to hire any person referred by the agency, but the agency is usually informed when the right person has been located.

Selection

The **selection** of people depends largely on organizational needs and compliance with legal requirements. Discriminatory practices in recruiting, testing, and offering a job are illegal, as stated earlier in discussing the Civil Rights Act of 1964 and the Equal Employment Opportunity Act of 1972. A few of the important legal guidelines affecting the selection step of staffing that managers must follow are described in Figure 9–4.

The actual selection process is a series of steps starting with initial screening and ending with the orientation of newly hired employees. Figure 9–5 presents each step in the process. Recognizing human resource needs

Figure 9–4

Some legal guidelines for the selection step in staffing

Selection screening steps	Legal activities	Illegal activities
Tests	Can be used if they have been validated	Cannot be used when there is no relationship between test results and performing the job
Interview information	To ask if a person is U.S. citizen	To require citizenship or to ask proof of citizenship
	To ask about convictions for crime	To ask if person has ever been arrested
Age	To require proof of age after hiring	To require birth certificate
Racial identity	To keep records on racial and ethnic identity for purposes of reporting	To ask for race, creed, or national origin in application or interview

Figure 9–5

Selection steps

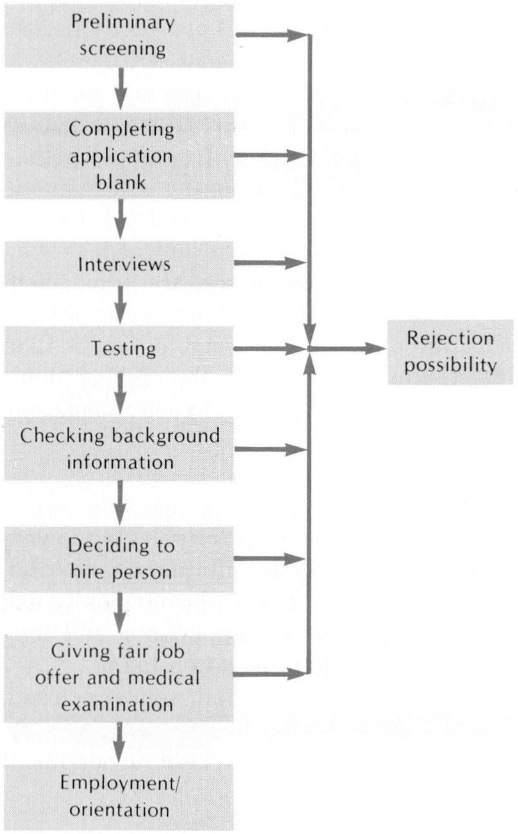

through the planning phase of staffing is the point at which selection begins. Preliminary interviews are used to screen out unqualified applicants. This *screening* is often the first personal contact a person has with an organization. If the applicant passes the preliminary screening, he or she usually completes an application blank.

Applications

The *application blank* is used to obtain information that will be helpful in reaching an employment decision. It is important to ask questions that can be used, even in a general sense, to predict job success. The appropriate questions should be developed only after a careful job analysis. It is important to have an application form that is complete yet concise so as not to burden the selection step with unnecessary information.

Two approaches are widely used to analyze application blank responses.

In the *clinical method,* the interviewer carefully analyzes answers. This analysis attempts to determine clues about a person's attitudes, personality, or career goals. Clinical analysis should not be used by untrained personnel. It should also not be considered a procedure that always provides a perfect analysis of an applicant's credentials.

The *weighted application method* is also used. It appears that for some jobs and organizations, certain items in a person's background—such as education and previous work experience—may be more important than other items in differentiating successful employees from unsuccessful employees. Suppose that through careful analysis it is determined that the most successful sales personnel for an engineering firm are college educated, have at least eight years of field sales experience, are in excellent health, and have been raised in the sales territory. Managers could use this information as part of the selection process. The weighted application blank approach is not perfect. It can, however, increase the organization's ability to employ those individuals who have the best chance to succeed.

Interviews

Interviews are used throughout the selection step. First, interviewers usually acquaint themselves with the job analysis information. Second, they review the application blank information. Third, they typically ask questions that can provide better insight about the applicants, and they add this information to what is included on the application blank.

Three general types of interviews are used: structured, semistructured, and unstructured. In the **structured interview,** the interviewer asks specific questions of all interviewees. A director of human resource development described how his unit used structured interviews:

> *We use the same set of questions for all individuals. This is very restrictive, but we want every person to answer the same questions. We then compare answers and make some rather difficult selection and training decisions.*

In the **semistructured interview,** only some questions are prepared in advance. This approach is less rigid than the structured interview and allows for more flexibility by the interviewer.

The **unstructured interview** allows the interviewer the freedom to cover what he or she thinks is important. Comparing answers across interviewees is rather difficult if the unstructured approach is used. One manager described his frustration with the unstructured interview approach:

> *We have to hire people who are willing to relocate rather frequently. It is important to probe into a college*

graduate's interest in, and inclination for, travel. I've noticed that only some of our campus recruiters ask questions about relocation attitudes. When the candidates arrive for the headquarters interview, some have no idea about relocation needs. They should have been told about this in the screening interview on campus. Half are told, and the other half are not told. We simply have no uniformity in our system.

Testing

In recent years, *selection tests* have become widely used to screen applicants. Selection tests are costly and time consuming, have legal implications, and should be conducted by experts.

The advantages of a testing program include:

1. *Improved accuracy in selecting employees.* Individuals differ in skills, intelligence, motivation, interests, needs, and goals. If these differences can be measured, and if they are related to job success, then performance can be predicted to some extent by test scores.
2. *Objective means for judging.* Applicants answer the same questions, under test conditions, and their responses are scored. One applicant's score can then be compared to the scores of other applicants.
3. *Information on the needs of present employees.* Tests given to present employees provide training, development, or counseling information.

Despite these advantages, tests have been and will probably remain controversial. Important legal rulings and fair employment codes have resulted in strict procedures for developing tests. The following criticisms have been directed at testing programs:

1. *Tests are not infallible.* Tests may reveal what persons can do, but not what they will do. Some of the best test performers may be the poorest job performers.
2. *Tests are given too much weight.* Tests cannot measure everything about a person. They can never substitute for judgment.
3. *Tests discriminate against minorities.* Ethnic minorities, such as blacks and Chicanos, may score lower on certain paper and pencil tests because of cultural bias. The Civil Rights Act of 1964 prohibits employment practices which artificially discriminate against individuals on the basis of test scores.

The U.S. Supreme Court in 1971 made an important ruling in the *Griggs v. Duke Power Company* case.[1] In 1965, Duke Power established a policy

[1] Bently Baranabus, "What Did the Supreme Court Really Say?" *Personnel Administrator*, July–August 1971, pp. 22–25.

that job applicants had to obtain a satisfactory score on a number of tests and have a high school education to qualify for placement and promotion. A group of black employees challenged these requirements on the basis that they were denied promotion opportunities because of the testing policy. The Supreme Court ruled that neither the high school requirement nor the test scores showed a relationship to successful job performance.

Because of the *Duke Power* decision, organizations using any test must carefully examine how the scores are used and be sure that there is a relationship between test scores and job performance. Basically, this means that tests must be validated. That is, there must be statistical proof that test scores are related to job performance.

In summary, testing is a part of the recruiting process. It is one of the tools that can assist managers in making decisions. Test results provide some information that can be used, but they do not provide a total picture of how well the person will perform.

The hiring decision

Once the preliminary screening steps are completed—evaluating the application blank, interviewing, and testing—and the organization considers making an offer, a **background check** is usually made. The background check consists of verifying various information and collecting additional data from references. An important group of references are previous employers. The organization also attempts to gather facts about the applicant's previous record of job performance.

If reference checks yield favorable information, the line manager and an employment division representative usually meet to decide the type of compensation and benefit offer that will be made.

Orientation

Most large companies have a formal **orientation** for employees. Although most new employees usually know something about the organization, they often do not have specific information. It is customary to provide information about the working hours, pay, parking facilities, rules, and available facilities. The orientation information should be furnished by line managers. The personnel department is usually the coordinator in providing orientation information, but the manager of the new hiree is the key individual in the process.

If new employees are properly oriented, a number of objectives can be accomplished. First, start-up costs can be minimized. If not properly oriented, a new employee can make costly mistakes. Explaining tasks, expectations, and procedures and answering questions can reduce start-up costs.

Second, anxieties can be reduced by a good orientation. Finally, orientation can help create realistic job expectations. Explaining and discussing organizational expectations is very important in that a clear understanding of those expectations can help reduce new-job tensions and anxieties.

The manager of an insurance office described the type of orientation used for new employees:

> *I carefully make it a point to explain the office organization, our objectives, and some of the history of the office. I then explain working conditions—hours of work, expense accounts, overtime policies, payday, protocol, and routes. Then I discuss our performance appraisal system and how it is tied to promotion, merit increases, and development. Then the new employee and I go over the job. I ask the new person to go home and study the job content and see me in two days. We discuss the job at this time in detail. Finally, I introduce the new person to every one of our employees.*

Training and development

Training

Training begins the first day a person starts to work. The training may occur at the place of work or offsite at a special training facility. Training as part of staffing is done to aid employees in improving performance. Training is a continuous process that should be managed by experts. To be effective, training programs must accomplish a number of objectives. First, they must be based on organizational and individual needs. Second, training should address problems that need to be solved. Third, training programs should be based on theories of learning. Finally, training must be evaluated. Through evaluations, modifications in training programs can be made.

Before a specific training program can be developed, specific problem areas must be pinpointed. Once problems are identified, objectives can be established and programs initiated. The implemented programs can then be evaluated. Organizations have a number of techniques available to pinpoint problems. Some of them are:

Reviewing management performance reports. Data on production, safety, cost, and efficiency can reveal positive or negative trends.

Reviewing personnel performance indicators. Data on grievances, turnover, absenteeism, and suggestions can reveal educational needs.

Developing job descriptions. These reveal what the employee needs to know in order to do a good job.

Administering attitude surveys. Data from attitude surveys can pinpoint areas, skills, or abilities that need improvement.

Reviewing opinions of managers. Managers work with subordinates and thus learn what is troubling employees.

Using exit interviews. Interviews with employees leaving the organization can reveal problem areas that exist in a department or a work unit.

Once training needs have been identified, the objectives of training need to be stated in writing. These objectives serve as the framework for the training program. The objectives should be concise, accurate, meaningful, and challenging. There are usually two major categories of objectives—*skills* and *knowledges.* The skill objectives focus on developing physical abilities, while the knowledge objectives are concerned with understanding, attitudes, and concepts. An example of a *skill objective* is:

To reduce operation costs for PXY project by 18 percent by June 15.

A *knowledge objective* is:

To improve the customer service coordinators' knowledge of customer needs.

A large number of methods are available to accomplish skill or knowledge training objectives. The particular method selected is determined by considering such factors as cost, the time available, the number of persons to be trained, the background of the trainees, and the skill of the trainees. Some of the more widely used training methods include:

1. On-the-job training A manager or other worker may take a new employee and show him or her how to perform the job. The new employee will then try to do the job while being closely observed by the manager. The activities of explaining, demonstrating, performing, and correcting may continue until the new employee can do the work in the absence of the manager.

2. Vestibule training This term is used to describe training away from the actual work area. An attempt is made to duplicate as nearly as possible the equipment and the general conditions of the real work area.

3. Classroom training Numerous classroom methods are used by organizations. The *lecture,* or a formal organized presentation, is one method. A *conference,* or small discussion group, is used to get the student more involved than the lecture method. *Case analysis* can be used to discuss a particular situation or a group of problems. *Role playing* is another method that is used to provide insight into behavior. In role playing, two or more trainees are assigned parts to play before the class. They are provided with either written or oral descriptions of a situation, and they act these out. For example, one person may be assigned a manager's role and another person may be assigned the role of a subordinate. The two may then be asked to discuss the complaints of the subordinate about the performance appraisal system. The training class will observe and comment on what happened in the role play.

Determining who will serve as the trainer and what methods will be used are difficult decisions. Sound learning principles should always be used. The trainer should have knowledge of such learning principles as feedback, transfer of learning, whole versus part learning, and motivation. *Feedback*, or knowledge of one's success, is necessary for learning to occur. Individuals learn faster when they receive immediate feedback on their performance. This allows them to direct their energy and effort toward what they do not know. The effect of what is learned in one situation on learning in other situations is called *transfer*. Transfer of learning is especially important when the vestibule or classroom methods are used. Thus, a trainer must make the learning realistic, allowing the students to practice and to test their skill or knowledge on the job.

Trainers should consider the issue of *whole versus part learning*, the issue being whether the entire operation should be taught or whether individual segments of the operation should be taught separately and then combined after the segments have been mastered. In many cases, the trainer provides an overview of the entire subject to be learned. Then, he or she divides the subject into parts for the student to learn. Finally, the whole is reviewed again and the parts are combined. This is typically done in teaching management courses. Perhaps at the beginning of this course, the instructor provided an overview, and now one of the important management processes, staffing, is being studied.

Management development

Training is generally associated with operating employees or first-level managers, while management development is discussed in terms of managerial personnel. **Management development** refers to **the process of educating and developing selected employees so that they have the knowledge, skills, attitudes, and understanding needed to manage in future positions.** The process starts with the selection of a qualified individual, and it continues throughout that individual's career.

Whether an organization has a management development program depends to some extent on its size. Larger organizations usually have a more formalized management development effort than do smaller companies. In fact, some of the larger organizations have in-house programs that are conducted either on the job or in some development center. The U.S. Civil

Service Commission, Exxon, and General Motors combine on-the-job development with off-the-job development.

The objectives of management development are (1) to insure the long-run success of the organization, (2) to furnish competent replacements, (3) to create an efficient team whose members work well together, (4) to enable each individual manager to utilize his or her full potential, and (5) to reduce or prevent managerial obsolescence. In addition, there may be managerial turnover and a shortage of available management talent, and management development can provide the skills to operate under such conditions.

There are two principal methods by which individuals can acquire the knowledge, skills, attitudes, and understanding necessary to become successful managers. One is through on-the-job development, and the other involves formal development programs. Examples of on-the-job programs include:

> *An understudy program.* An individual works as an understudy so that eventually he or she can assume the full responsibilities and duties of the job. This program emphasizes experience.
>
> *Job rotation.* This involves transferring managers from job to job on a systematic basis. The assignments on each job generally last about six months.
>
> *Coaching.* This is a method by which a manager teaches job knowledge and skills to subordinates. The manager instructs, directs, corrects, and evaluates subordinates.

Each of these on-the-job development steps emphasizes actual job experience. The steps are taken to increase not only the manager's skill and knowledge but also his or her confidence. Through the development of confidence and actual on-the-job experience, managers usually progress enough so that some of them can be promoted as vacancies occur.

Management development in formal programs covers a wide range of subjects and methods. There are programs covering management functions such as planning, decision making, organizing, leading, and controlling; programs on topics such as conflict resolution, team building, motivation, and leadership; programs concerning the environmental impact on organizations, which cover business ethics, economics, consumerism, social responsibilities, and the government; and programs for developing such personal skills as report writing, conducting meetings, and giving verbal presentations.

These formal programs are conducted within organizations by training units or consultants from universities and in specialized training facilities around the country. In corporations such as General Electric, Westinghouse, International Harvester, and AT&T, full-time training units conduct regular management development courses. For example, one major course offered at General Electric is called the Advanced Management Course. This course is designed for the four highest levels of management and is conducted over a period of 13 weeks. Its content includes business policy, economics, social issues, and management principles.

The American Management Association (AMA) conducts many management development programs. The manager is taken off the job to develop abilities and skills. These programs are usually also supposed to reduce job obsolescence. A recent participant in an American Management Association program stated:

> *You have to stay ahead of the game. I appreciate the opportunity to attend AMA programs so that my skills can meet the changing job requirements. Even if the company didn't pay for these programs, I would pay the fee. I just do not ever want to be considered one of the old antiques. The AMA has helped me prevent this kind of image.*

Performance evaluation

The evaluation or appraisal system and the reward structure of an organization will have a significant impact on the behavior of employees. In Chapter 17, considerable attention will be given to performance evaluation. We introduce evaluation here only because it also plays a vital role in the staffing process. **Performance evaluation** is a formal managerial activity that determines in the most objective manner possible the extent to which each employee is making a performance contribution.

Compensation

Through compensation programs, organizations are able to attract, maintain, and motivate employees. Therefore, although compensation is a source of motivation and will be covered in Chapter 13, it is also mentioned here because of its importance to staffing.

Promotion, demotion, and discharge

Advancement to a position of greater authority and responsibility is a **promotion**. For most persons, promotions do not occur often. The social and psychological fulfillments inherent in a promotion are meaningful to many employees. Often with the promotion there is an increase in pay, which is also gratifying. The promotion decision is similar to the selection decision in many respects. The manager attempts to match the best person with the job.

In some organizations, promotions are based on merit and/or seniority. Seniority on a job or in the organization is used by some organizations because it shows loyalty to employees. Unions support basing promotions on seniority. On the other hand, management prefers to base promotions on merit. A merit determination can be based on the performance evaluations collected on the candidate over a period of time.

If a person is not able to perform adequately on a job, he or she may be demoted or discharged. A **demotion** is likely to bring about dissatisfaction and discouragement, since losing status and in some cases pay is interpreted by many as a form of punishment. As more organizations achieve a state of controlled growth in the size of their work force, promotional opportunities will decrease. The pressure to fill jobs with the best-qualified people has continued to increase, especially with the increased competition being faced by most organizations. In addition to domestic competitors, foreign firms are now putting pressure on U.S. organizations to have the best-qualified people perform the job.

Discharge is the most drastic staffing action that a manager can take. It is used only for the most serious offenses. When a person is discharged, he or she loses all seniority standing and privileges. Since discharge is such a drastic form of termination, careful documentation and consideration of the events justifying discharge should be done by the manager.

At the nonmanagerial level in unionized organizations, discharge is often not possible because of seniority rules, union-management contractual agreements, a limited supply of replacements, or the overall philosophy of the organization. In general, managers are reluctant to discharge employees. Altercations, theft, gambling, insubordination, and inability to perform the job are the most common causes of discharge action.

Management summary

1. The staffing responsibility must be accepted by all managers if qualified personnel are to be attracted, selected, and encouraged to perform well in an organization.
2. Staffing involves human resource planning, recruitment, selection, orientation, training and development, performance appraisal, compensation, promotion, demotion, and discharge. It is a series of steps that are taken in working with the human assets of an organization.
3. Government legal requirements are so vital to effective staffing that

experts in law are often called on to make judgments so that violations do not occur.

4. Because of legal, validity, and interpretation problems, selection tests must be used with care.
5. Downward transfer is now being used as a form of demotion. It is a painful measure, but often it is the only alternative to discharge. The best success with demotion has occurred when the employee's salary has not been reduced.

Review and discussion questions

1. What are the potential problems with a program which results in a significant amount of discharge for unacceptable performance?
2. Why is it important for all managers, not only personnel specialists, to be familiar with the staffing process?
3. Do the owners of small business organizations have to be concerned with staffing? Why?
4. Some experts believe that training and development is a lifelong process? Do you agree? Why?
5. Why is human resource planning an important part of the staffing process?
6. How could a new hiree use the information provided in the job description?
7. Do you feel that it is realistic and fair to an organization to bar it from engaging in the activities that are listed as illegal in Figure 9–4?
8. Do you believe that experienced managers who are joining another organization should have to be tested? Why?
9. Why is job analysis an important feature of staffing?
10. Should staffing be given a place of importance in a situation in which qualified job applicants are in unlimited supply? Why?

Suggested reading

Barrett, R. S. "Is the Test Content Valid: Or, Does It Really Measure a Construct?" *Employee Relations Law Journal,* Winter 1980–81, pp. 459–75.

Bowen, D. E. "Some Unintended Consequences of Intention to Quit." *Academy of Management Review,* April 1982, pp. 205–11.

Bucknall, W. L. "Executive Continuity Planning: An Idea Whose Time Has Come." *Management Review,* February 1981, pp. 21–23.

Cronin, R. J. "Executive Recruiters: Are They Necessary?" *Personnel Administration,* February 1981, pp. 31–34.

Dreher, G. F. "The Role of Performance in the Turnover Process." *Academy of Management Journal,* March 1982, pp. 137–47.

Hubsch, D. M. "Planning the Staffing of a Growing Business." *Management Review,* August 1981, pp. 59–61.

Mackey, C. B. "Human Resource Planning: A Four-Phased Approach." *Management Review,* May 1981, pp. 17–22.

Applying what you have learned about staffing the organization

Cases:

Executive recruitment as practiced at Korn/Ferry International
A heart attack victim fights back

Executive recruitment as practiced at Korn/Ferry International*

Head-hunting is a big business. The largest executive recruiting firm, Korn/Ferry International, had revenues of $12.6 million in 1977 and $30 million in 1980. That increase in revenues represents a jump of 138 percent in four years. The average increase for the largest six firms in this business is 110 percent. Thus, the evidence strongly suggests that recruiting and placing executives for big business is big business.

The practice of hiring an outside firm to search out candidates for high-level executive jobs is an extension of the more traditional employment placement business. The difference is that finding a qualified candidate for an executive position ordinarily involves enticing the candidate away from another firm. Thus the term *head-hunting* was coined to refer to the practice of raiding the executive ranks of one company to staff those of other companies. In a sense, the executive search firm serves as an intermediary between talented managers and firms requiring that talent, but without that talent in their present managerial staff. In exchange for its services, the executive recruiter will charge the client company a fee equal to approximately 33 percent of the recruited manager's starting salary.

The increasing importance of executive recruitment in staffing executive positions is reflected in nonmonetary terms as well. More and more, successful firms such as Korn/Ferry have positioned themselves as human resource

* This case is adapted from Herbert E. Meyer, "Headhunters Cast a Wider Net," *Fortune,* September 7, 1981, pp. 65–67.

advisors, as private consultants on all personnel matters. The resultant relationship between Korn/Ferry and its clients does not depend upon whether an active search for executive talent is either active or contemplated. Yet, in most instances, the search for managerial talent is continuous, particularly when the full range of management positions—from lower level through middle and top management—is the focus of attention. The more traditional executive search consultant specializes in top-level positions only and does business with a large number of clients. Korn/Ferry, on the other hand, believes that continued growth in its business can come only by doing more for fewer clients. Korn/Ferry has about 750 clients compared to 2,000 clients of the second largest firm, Heidrick and Struggles.

The underlying basis for the relative success of the Korn/Ferry strategy is the increasing importance of personnel issues on the agendas of chief executives. In recent years, more and more managerial time and attention have been taken up by personnel issues, including promotion, compensation, and affirmative action issues. Consequently, firms that use executive search consultants are likely to insist that they enlarge their function to that of human resource consultants.

Questions:

1. Evaluate the practice of using executive recruiting firms such as Korn/Ferry International.
2. What staffing steps as indicated in Figure 9–1 would a firm turn over to Korn/Ferry International should it become a client?
3. What dangers do you see in the practice of using executive recruiters as "human resource consultants"?

A heart attack victim fights back

Mike Matson was a senior project engineer for a large manufacturing company. He had worked for the firm for nine years and had received promotions on four different occasions. Mike supervised 15 project engineers and worked closely with 6 other senior project engineers and the vice president of engineering. In the company, Mike was viewed as a comer who would probably become a vice president in the near future. He was considered a superstar among the project engineers.

In July, Mike, at the age of 36, had a heart attack. He was hospitalized for 4 weeks and then spent 12 more weeks recovering at home. Since the position of senior project engineer was vital in the flow of its work, the company replaced Mike while he was away. It promoted Don Watts from a West Coast affiliate of the firm to assume Mike's position.

After regaining his strength, approximately four months after the heart attack, Mike resumed work. The first month back he worked about three hours a day in the corporate headquarters. When he was back to full strength, he visited with the vice president of engineering. Mike had assumed that his old job would be available. However, the vice president informed him that the strenuous nature of the job and Don Watts's excellent performance made it necessary to work out another job assignment. In essence, Mike was informed that he no longer matched the job requirements. Mike felt that the clean bill of health he had received from his doctor, his loyalty to the company, and his nine-year performance record had not been given full consideration in the vice president's decision. Mike also pointed out that in the past three years, a number of executives had been out for extended periods and that all of them had returned to their previous assignments.

Questions:

1. How do you rate the company's handling of Mike's situation? Why?
2. Is the vice president discriminating against a heart attack victim? Explain.
3. What type of staffing policy could prevent such a situation from occurring in the future?

10

Chapter ten Developing careers and human resources

Performance objectives

- **Define** career development in terms of individual and organizational processes.
- **State** the specific problems which recent hirees and midcareer managers face.
- **Describe** the practices and policies which managers can use to counteract career problems.
- **Explain** why managing dual-careers employees is becoming a widespread managerial issue.
- **Discuss** the difficulties associated with devising career paths for a specific individual.

Management update*

Parsons, Brinckerhoff, Quade & Douglas, Inc., a consulting engineering and architectural firm which employs 1,400 professional and support people, recently initiated a unique career development program. The program is designed to provide its technical staff with opportunities for career growth without having to become managers or giving up their technical orientation. In most companies, the only way to gain decision-making authority, status, and other rewards is to become a manager. The consequence of this practice is that talented technical and engineering personnel are diverted into management, and the company loses a technical resource. As Henry L. Michel, president of Parsons, Brinckerhoff, states: "We are losing some of our very best people in the technical areas where they are badly needed without necessarily gaining the best qualified managers." To counter the problem, opportunities for advancement must be available to those on technical career paths.

The Parsons, Brinckerhoff program created a series of three senior professional titles that are awarded to employees who fulfill specific and stringent criteria. Each title requires an increasing degree of expertise and contributions in a specific technical area and at least 10 years of experience in that area. The last title in the series is equivalent in status, authority, compensation, and benefits to that of vice president.

An employee who wishes to pursue career development meets with his or her supervisor to determine personal career objectives and to identify appropriate training, experience, and other developmental activities consistent with the objectives. No employee is forced to participate, and in fact, the company encourages individual initiative in the pursuit of career objectives.

The company is not concerned that its program will create more qualified people than it can use. Because of its size and growth and its recent change to a *matrix* organization design, there is a shortage of qualified people to fill senior positions.

---

* This Management Update is based upon "Providing Career Prospects for Engineers and Technicians," *Management Review*, February 1981, 29–31.

A key management responsibility is to develop subordinates to their full potential. Organizational change and growth require managers to pay attention to developing people and placing them in key positions. Organizational growth through expansion, mergers, and acquisitions *creates* new management positions and *changes* the responsibilities of existing positions. Capable people must be available to fill the new and bigger jobs. Even organizations facing a stable or a contracting future recognize that a key to performance is the development of human resources.

As organizations change, so do their employees. A recently hired manager has different needs and aspirations than does the midcareer or the preretirement manager. All of us move through a fairly uniform pattern of phases during our careers. The different phases produce different opportunities and stresses which have implications for job performance. Effective managers comprehend these implications and facilitate the efforts of employees who wish to confront and deal with their careers and life needs.

Managers should be concerned with their own career goals and with the paths that are most likely to lead to those goals. Yet, managers often lack the ability and the information that are needed to develop their career plans in systematic and explicit ways. But we see more and more evidence of growing interest in providing individuals with information that will help them to identify their goals and to understand what they should do to reach them.

This chapter reviews some of the issues related to human resource and career development. The subject matter is a natural extension of many of the topics introduced in the previous chapter. The framework which guides the presentation is shown in Figure 10–1. Note that two aspects of human resource and career development are human resource planning and formal training and development programs. Each of these topics was covered extensively earlier and need not be discussed here except to stress the interrelationships between those two aspects of staffing and career and human resource development. Chapter 9 emphasized organizational needs and opportunities; this chapter emphasizes individual needs and aspirations. To the extent that the organizational and individual needs are matched and mutually achieved, the organizing process will contribute to overall performance.

Figure 10–1

Career and human resource development

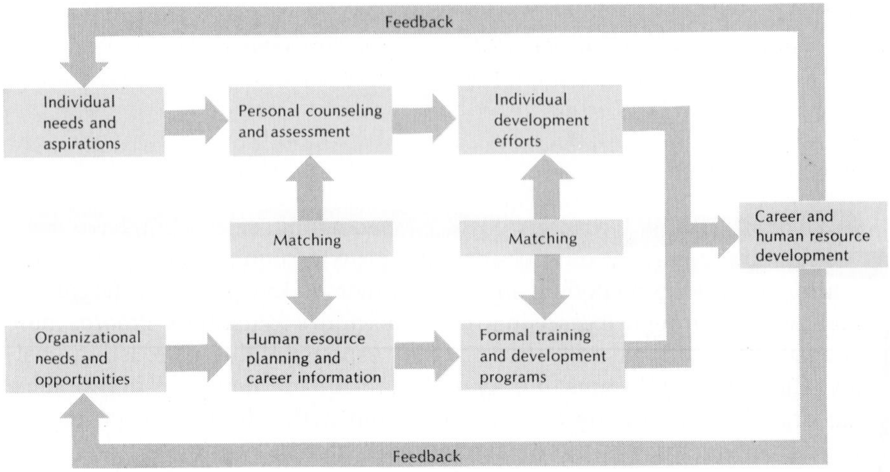

SOURCE: Based on John C. Aplin and Darlene K. Gerster, "Career Development: An Integration of Individual and Organizational Needs," *Personnel,* March–April 1978, p. 25.

The concept of career

The concept of career has many meanings. The popular meaning is probably reflected in the idea of moving upward in one's chosen line of work—making more money; having more responsibility; acquiring more status, prestige, and power. Although typically restricted to lines of work which involve gainful employment, the concept of career can apply to other life pursuits. For example, we can think of homemakers, mothers, and volunteer workers as having careers. For they too advance in the sense that their talents and abilities to take on larger responsibilities grow with time and experience. It goes without saying that the mother of married children plays a far different role than she did when the children were preschoolers.

Here, our discussion will center on the careers of those in occupations and professions. The definition of career that we will use follows closely the one recently devised by an important contributor to this field. Accordingly:

> The career is the individually perceived sequence of attitudes and behaviors associated with work-related experiences and activities over the span of the person's life.[1]

[1] Douglas T. Hall, *Careers in Organizations* (Pacific Palisades, Calif.: Goodyear Publishing, 1976), p. 4.

This definition emphasizes that the term **career** does not imply success or failure except in the judgment of the individual, that a career consists of both attitudes and behaviors, and that it is an ongoing sequence of work-related activities. Yet, even though the concept of career is clearly work related, it must be understood that a person's nonwork life and roles play a significant part in it. For example, the attitudes of a midcareer manager 50-years-old about a job advancement involving greater responsibilities can be quite different from those of a manager nearing retirement. A bachelor's reaction to a promotion involving relocation is likely to be different from that of a father of school-age children.

Now that you have read some introductory material on careers, it would be useful for you to consider your own career aspirations. The exercise which follows will enable you to think about a career and its meaning. Although you can do the exercise without inputs from others, it would be helpful to share and compare the results. The exercise is presented in a step-by-step format, and it can be completed on a separate sheet of paper.

1. Draw a horizontal line which depicts the past, present, and future of your *career*. On that line, mark an *X* to show where you are now.

2. To the left of the *X*, that part of the line which represents your *past*, identify the events in your life which gave you genuine feelings of fulfillment and satisfaction.

3. Examine these historical milestones and determine the specific factors which seem to have caused those feelings. Does a pattern emerge? Did the events occur when you were alone or when you were with other people? Did you accomplish some objective alone or with other people? Write down as much as you can about the events and your reactions to them.

4. To the right of the *X*, that part of the line which represents your *future*, identify the career-related events from which you expect to realize genuine fulfillment and satisfaction. You should describe these events as explicitly as possible. If you are only able to write such statements as "Get my first job" or "Get my first raise," you probably have ill-defined career expectations.

5. After you have identified these future career-related events, rank them from high to low, in terms of how much fulfillment and satisfaction you expect to derive from them.

6. Now go back to step 3 and rank the historical events from high to low in terms of the actual fulfillment and satisfaction you derived from them. Compare your two sets of ranked events. Are they consistent? Are you expecting the future to be the same as, or different from, the past? If you expect the future to be considerably different from the past, are you being realistic about the fulfillment and satisfaction that you think the future events will provide?

7. Discuss your results with your classmates and your instructor. How do you compare with your classmates in terms of your self-understanding and your understanding of the role of a career in providing personal fulfillment and satisfaction?

Career stages

The idea that individuals go through distinct but interrelated stages in their careers is widely recognized. The simplest version would include four stages: (1) the prework stage (attending school), (2) the initial work stage (moving from job to job), (3) the stable work stage (maintaining one job), and (4) the retirement stage (leaving active employment). Most working people prepare for their occupation by undergoing some form of organized education in high school, trade school, vocational school, or college. They then take a first job, but the chances are that they will move to other jobs in the same organization or in other organizations. Eventually, they settle into a position in which they remain until retirement. The duration of each stage varies among individuals, but most working people go through all of these stages.

Studies of career stages have found that needs and expectations change as the individual moves through the stages.[2] Managers in American Telephone and Telegraph (AT&T) expressed considerable concern for security during the initial years on their jobs. This phase, termed the *establishment* phase, ordinarily lasted during the first five years of employment. Following the establishment phase is the *advancement* phase, which lasts approximately from age 30 to age 45. During this period, the AT&T managers expressed considerably less concern for security and more concern for achievement, esteem, and autonomy. Promotions and advancement to jobs with responsibility and opportunity to exercise independent judgment are characteristics of this phase.

The *maintenance* phase follows the advancement phase. This period is marked by efforts to stabilize the gains of the past. Although no new gains are made, the maintenance phase can be a period of creativity, since the individual has satisfied many of the psychological and financial needs associated with earlier phases. Although each individual and each career will be different, it is reasonable to assume that self-fulfillment would be the most important need in the maintenance phase. But, as we will see, many people experience what is termed the *midcareer* crisis during the maintenance phase. Such people are not achieving satisfaction from their work, and consequently, they may experience physiological and psychological discomfort.

The maintenance phase is followed by the *retirement* phase. The individual has, in effect, completed one career, and he or she may move on to another one. During this phase, the individual may have opportunities to experience self-fulfillment through activities that it was impossible to pursue while working. Painting, gardening, volunteer service, and quiet reflection are some of the many positive avenues that are available to retirees.

[2] Douglas T. Hall and Khalil Nougaim, "An Examination of Maslow's Need Hierarchy in an Organizational Setting," *Organizational Performance and Human Behavior* (1968), pp. 12–35.

The relationship between career stages and needs is summarized in Figure 10–2.

The fact that individuals pass through different stages during their careers is evident. It is also understandable that individual needs and motives are different from one stage to the next. But managing the careers of others requires a more complete description of what happens to individuals during these stages. One group of individuals whose careers are of special significance to the performance of modern organizations are the *professionals*. Knowledge workers—such professionals as accountants, scientists, and engineers—are the fastest growing segment of the work force. This segment constitutes 32 percent of the work force at present (blue-collar workers make up 33 percent).[3] These professionals spend their careers in large, complex organizations after having spent several years in obtaining advanced training and degrees. The organizations that employ them expect them to provide the innovativeness and creativity that are necessary for organizational survival in dynamic and competitive environments. Obviously, the performance levels of professional employees must be of the utmost concern for the organization's leaders.

Figure 10–2

Career stages and important needs

Important needs	Safety, security, physiological	Safety, security	Achievement esteem, autonomy	Esteem, self-fulfillment	Self-fulfillment
Age	0 ⟷ 25	25 ⟷ 30	30 ⟷ 45	45 ⟷ 65	65 ⟵
Career stage	Prework	Establishment	Advancement	Maintenance	Retirement

The effective management of professionals begins with understanding the crucial characteristics of the four stages of professional careers. Professional employees could avoid some disappointments and anxieties if they also understood more about their career stages.

Stage I Young professionals enter an organization with technical knowledge, but not with an understanding of the organization's demands and expectations. Consequently, they must work fairly closely with more experienced persons. The relationship that develops between the young professionals and their supervisors is an *apprenticeship*. The central activities in which apprentices are expected to show competence include *learning*

[3] Gene W. Dalton, Paul H. Thompson, and Raymond L. Price, "The Four Stages of Professional Careers—A New Look at Performance by Professionals," *Organizational Dynamics*, Summer 1977, pp. 19–42.

and *following directions.* To move successfully and effectively through Stage I, professionals must be able to accept the *psychological state of dependence.* And some professionals cannot cope with being placed in a situation similar to that which they experienced while in school. They find that they are still being directed by an authority figure, just as they were in school. Yet they had anticipated that their first job would provide considerably more freedom. Those who do not cope successfully can compromise their careers if they engage in sloppy and slipshod work behavior.

One professional, Bob, is a CPA employed by a large manufacturer. He reflected upon his first years with the company:

> *I really felt that all I had to do was what I was told to do. It seems like all I was expected to do was the nitty-gritty detailed jobs of a bookkeeper. I soon saw that my future in the company depended on doing the junk work without complaining.*

This young person had the foresight to see that his progress depended on his performance of the routine work. He moved on to Stage II.

Stage II Once through the dependent relationship characteristic of Stage I, the professional employee moves into Stage II, which calls for working independently. But passage to this stage depends on having demonstrated competence in some specific technical area. The technical expertise may be in a content area, such as taxation, product testing, or quality assurance, or it may be in a skill area, such as computer applications. The professional's primary activity in Stage II is to be an *independent contributor* of ideas in the chosen area. The professional is expected to rely much less on direction from others. The *psychological state of independence* may pose some problems because it is in such stark contrast to the state of dependence required in Stage I. Stage II is extremely important for the professional's future career growth. Those who fail at this stage do so either because they do not have the requisite technical skill to perform independently or because they do not have the necessary self-confidence to do so.

When Bob moved to Stage II, the move was marked by a promotion which placed him in charge of cost accounting for a special project. As he recalls:

> *I got the job because I knew what I was doing. In my early years with the company, I was always having to ask for answers on company accounting procedures. But soon I was able to answer the questions myself. I showed that I knew my stuff.*

The promotion not only enabled Bob to become even more expert in product costing, but it also placed him in charge of six other people, including four recently hired college graduates with CPAs. The managerial experience that Bob gained on this assignment, coupled with the need to deal with other professionals, such as the engineers and scientists assigned to the project, was the basis for Bob's move to Stage III.

Stage III Professionals who enter Stage III are expected to become the mentors of those in Stage I. They also tend to broaden their interests and to deal more and more with people outside the organization. Thus, the central activities of professionals at this stage are *training* and *interactions* with others. Stage III professionals assume *responsibility for the work of others,* and this characteristic of the stage can cause considerable psychological stress. In previous stages, the professional was responsible for his or her own work. But now it is the work of others which is of primary concern. Individuals who cannot cope with this new requirement may decide to shift back to Stage II. Individuals who derive satisfaction from seeing other people move on to bigger and better jobs may be content to remain in Stage III until retirement.

Bob's experience in Stage III revolved around his assignments on product development teams. More and more, he found himself teaching the younger accountants "the ropes to know and the ropes to skip." He derived considerable satisfaction from the success of these younger accountants. As he said:

> *Our company grew tremendously during the 60s. We simply had to maintain a steady stream of able people to do the high-level accounting work required in our product development efforts. I have trained most of the ones now heading up the accounting side of the teams. They got where they are by doing what I did—first learn the routine, then become an ace.*

At present, Bob is the chief cost system analyst at corporate headquarters, a Stage IV assignment in his career.

Stage IV Some professional employees remain in Stage III; for these professionals, Stage III is the career maintenance phase. Other professionals progress to yet another stage. This stage is not experienced by all professionals because its fundamental characteristic is that it involves *shaping the direction of the organization itself.* Although we usually think of such activity as being undertaken by only one individual in an organization—its chief executive—in fact it may be undertaken by many others. For example, key personnel in product development, process manufacturing, or technological research may be Stage IV types. As a consequence of their performance in Stage III of their careers, Stage IV professionals direct their attention to long-range strategic planning. In doing so, they play the roles of manager, entrepreneur, and idea generator. Their primary job relationships are to *identify* and *sponsor* the careers of their successors and to interact with key people outside the organization. The most significant shift for a person in Stage IV is to accept the decisions of subordinates without second guessing them. Stage IV professionals must learn to influence events and others through such indirect means as idea planting, personnel selection, and organizational design. These shifts can be difficult for an individual who has relied on direct supervision in the past. As noted in the Management Update, this stage can create problems for the organization.

Bob, whose career we have been following, attained his position at corporate headquarters at 43, a relatively early age. At first, he had difficulty with the job:

> *When I first arrived at headquarters, I was struck by how far away from the action I was. I was always a hands-on kind of person. But at headquarters I found that I had to work to get my ideas across. After all, changes in systems can cause people a lot of trouble, particularly when the changes disrupt the way they have been doing things. I soon learned who I had to work on to get my ideas accepted. Most of the time, they are the same people I worked with when I was on the product development teams.*

The concept of career stages is fundamental for understanding and managing career development. It is necessary to comprehend **life** *stages* as well. Individuals go through career stages as they go through life stages, but the interaction between career stages and life stages is not easy to understand.

Life stages

Our understanding of the stages of life for children and youth is relatively well developed as compared to our understanding of adult life stages. Psychology has provided much insight into the problems of childhood, but far less insight into the problems of adulthood. More and more, however, we are finding that adulthood is defined by rather distinct phases. The demands, problems, and opportunities presented in these phases must be taken into account by managers who are concerned with developing the careers of their subordinates.

One view of the life stages emphasizes developmental aspects. That is, each life stage is marked by the need to work through a particular developmental task before the individual can move successfully into the next stage.[4] The stages and their developmental tasks are as follows:

Adolescence For most people, this stage occurs from age 15 to age 25. Prior to this stage is *childhood,* but since our primary concern is the life stages as related to the career stages, childhood is relatively unimportant for our purposes. Essential for normal progression through adolescence is the achieving of *ego identity.* Adolescents are much concerned with settling on a particular career or occupational choice. They can become confused by the apparent gaps between what they think they can do and what they think they must do to succeed in a career. The latter years of the adolescent stage usually coincide with initial employment, and if ego identity has not been achieved, one can expect difficulties during this first employment opportunity.

Young adulthood The years between 25 and 35 ordinarily entail the development of *intimacy and involvement with others.* During this life stage, individuals learn to become involved not only with other persons but also with groups and organizations. The extent to which individuals pass through this phase successfully depends on how successful they were in establishing their ego identities as adolescents. In terms of career stages, young adulthood corresponds with the *establishment* of a career and the initial stages of *advancement.* Conflicts may develop between life stage demands and career stage demands if, for example, the demands of the career stage include behaviors that are inconsistent with the development of relationships with others.

Adulthood The 30 years between 35 and 65 are devoted to *generativity,* a term that implies concern for actions and achievements which will benefit *future generations.* Individuals experiencing this life stage emphasize the productive and creative use of their talents and abilities. In the context of work experience, adulthood involves building organizations, devising new and lasting products, coaching younger people, and teaching others. This life stage coincides with the later years of the advancement career stage and the full duration of the maintenance stage. Successful development of the adulthood stage depends on having achieved ego identity and commitment to others, the developmental tasks of the preceding two stages.

Maturity The last life stage is maturity, and people pass through this stage successfully if they achieve *ego integrity,* that is, if they do not despair of their lives and of the choices they have made. In a sense, this stage represents the culmination of a productive and creative life served in the interests of others to the satisfaction of self. This life stage coincides with the retirement career stage.

The relationships between life stages and career stages are shown in Figure 10–3. Successful careers are evidently a result, in part, of achieving

[4] Erik H. Erikson, *Childhood and Society,* 2d ed. (New York: W. W. Norton, 1963), as presented in Hall, *Careers in Organizations,* pp. 48–52.

certain career stages at certain ages. For example, a study of scientists in two research and development companies attempted to determine the relationship between performance and career stage for those over 40. The results are shown in Table 10–1. In these two companies, it is apparent that individuals whose career stages were not in step with their life stages were relatively low performers. Notice that 100 percent of the employees over 40 who were classified as at Stage I of their careers were considered to be below-average performers. For whatever reasons, these employees were unable to establish themselves as independent contributors of ideas and thus to move on to Stage II. Perhaps they had been unable to achieve ego identity during the early stages of their lives. Managers must recognize the interaction between career stages and life stages in designing effective career development programs.

Figure 10–3

The relationships between career stages and life stages

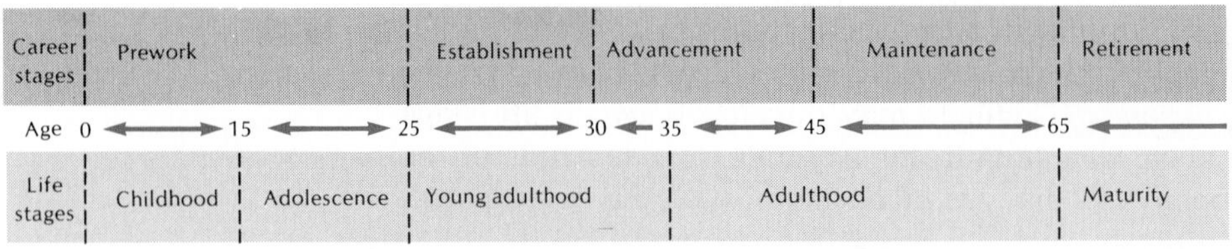

Two points in the careers of individuals are particularly crucial for career development. The *recent hiree* begins his or her career with a particular job and position. Experiences on this first job can have considerable positive and negative effects on future performance. The *midcareer* person is subject to pressures and possibilities different from those of the recent hiree, but he or she is also at a critical point. The following sections describe some career development problems of recent hirees and midcareer managers.

Career development for recent hirees

Recently hired employees face many anxious moments. They have selected their positions on the basis of expectations regarding the demands that the organization will make of them and what they will receive in exchange for meeting those demands. Young managers, particularly those with college training, expect opportunities to utilize their training in ways which lead to recognition and advancement. In too many instances, recently

Table 10–1

Relationship between age, career stage, and performance (40 years or older)

	Stage I	Stage II	Stage III	Stage IV
Above-average performance	0%	18%	79%	100%
Below-average performance	100%	82%	21%	0%

Based on Gene W. Dalton, Paul H. Thompson, and Raymond L. Price, "The Four Stages of Professional Careers—A New Look at Performance by Professionals," *Organizational Dynamics*, Summer 1977, p. 37.

hired managers are soon disappointed with their initial career decisions. Although the specific causes of early-career disappointments vary from person to person, some general causes have been identified.

Causes of early-career difficulties

Studies of the early-career problems of young managers typically find that those who experience frustration are victims of "reality shock." These young managers perceive a mismatch between what they thought the organization was and what it actually is. Several factors contribute to reality shock, and it is important for young managers and their managers to be aware of them.

The initial job challenge The first jobs of young managers often demand far less of them than they are able to deliver. Consequently, young managers believe that they are unable to demonstrate their full capabilities and that in a sense they are being stifled. This particular cause is especially damaging if the recruiter has been overly enthusiastic in selling the organization to the managers when they were recruited.

Kim D. majored in marketing as an undergraduate and then went on to earn an M.B.A. Her first job was with a market research firm. After being with the company for less than a year, she contacted the college placement office at the school where she earned the M.B.A. She told the placement office director that she was looking for a new job because:

> *Since being with this company, I have done nothing but gather data on phone surveys. All day long I sit and talk on the phone, asking questions and checking off the answers. In graduate school, I was trained to design research studies, but here I am doing what any*

high school graduate can do. I talked to my boss, and he said that all employees have to pay their dues. Well, not me!

Some young managers are able to *create* challenging jobs even when their assignments are fairly routine. They do this by thinking of ways to do their jobs differently and better. They may also be able to persuade their managers to give them more leeway and more to do. Unfortunately, many young managers are unable to create challenge. Their previous experiences in school were typically experiences in which challenge had been given to them by their teachers. The challenge had been created for them, not by them.

Initial job satisfaction Recently hired managers with college training often believe that they can perform at levels beyond those of their initial assignments. After all, they have been exposed to the latest managerial theories and techniques, and in their minds at least, they are ready to run the company. Disappointment and dissatisfaction are the sure outcomes, however, when they discover that their self-evaluations are not shared by others in the organization.

Kim D.'s experience on her first job illustrates how low job challenge can cause dissatisfaction. She was able to exercise some freedom and to seek employment elsewhere. In other instances, such freedom is unavailable. For example, George W. is a graduate engineer employed in a state health department's water control division. One of the division's responsibilities is to control the quality of the water in public swimming pools. In addition to periodic checking of actual purification procedures, the division must also approve the design specifications of each new swimming pool. George's reaction to his work follows:

My primary responsibility is to check blueprints of proposed new swimming pools. The regulations which builders must follow spell out the design characteristics to the nth degree. Day in and day out, I sit and look at the blueprints and OK them. A draftsman can easily do my job. But where am I going to go? I have a wife and three children to support, and every year I will get a raise just because I am still around. Lately I have been doing things that make me ashamed of myself, like taking two-hour lunches and 45-minute coffee breaks—anything to get away from these blueprints.

Initial job performance feedback Feedback on performance is an important managerial responsibility. Yet, many managers are inadequately trained to meet this responsibility. They simply do not know how to evaluate the performance of their subordinates. This management deficiency is especially damaging to new managers. They have not been in the organization long enough to be socialized by their peers and other employees. They are not as yet sure of what they are expected to believe, what values to hold, or what behaviors are expected of them. They naturally look to their own managers to guide them through this early phase. But when their managers fail to evaluate their performance accurately, they remain ignorant and confused as to whether they are achieving what the organization expects of them.

Anthony J.'s first job after graduating with a B.B.A. in finance was in the consumer loan department of a large bank. While attending the first reunion of his class, he told his favorite finance professor the following story:

> *My first boss is really a nice guy, too nice. He never tells any of us how we are doing. He treats all of us the same way, super-nice. The trouble is I know that some of the people in the loan department are real doughheads. They spend half of their time making a mess of things, the other half cleaning up the mess. But he still just smiles and says we are* all *doing a great job. Well, I know better than that, but if the bank tolerates this level of performance from employees, I won't be around long enough to see it fail.*

Certainly, not all young managers experience problems associated with their initial assignments. But those who do and who leave the organization as a consequence of their frustrations represent a waste of talent and money. Thus, it is apparent that the cost of losing capable young managers outweighs the cost of efforts and programs designed to counteract initial job problems.

Programs and practices to counteract early-career problems

Managers who wish to improve the retention and development of young management talent have several alternatives.

Realistic job previews One way to counteract the unrealistic expectations of new recruits is to provide realistic information during the *recruiting* process. This practice is based on the idea that people should know both the bad and the good things to expect from their jobs and their organizations. Through **realistic job previews** (RJPs), recruits are given opportunities to learn not only the benefits that they may expect but also the disbenefits. Studies have shown that the recruitment rate is the same for those who receive RJPs as for those who do not. More important, those who receive RJPs are more likely to remain on the job and to be satisfied with it than are those who have been selected in the usual manner. The practice of telling it like it is, is used by a number of organizations, including the Prudential Insurance Company, Texas Instruments, and the U.S. Military Academy.

A challenging initial assignment Managers of newly hired people should be encouraged to assign them the most demanding of the available jobs. Successful implementation of this policy requires managers to take some risks because managers are accountable for the performance of their subordinates. If the assignments are too far beyond the ability of the subordinates, both the managers and the subordinates share the cost of failure. Thus, most managers prefer to bring their subordinates along slowly by giving them progressively more difficult and challenging jobs, but only *after the subordinates have demonstrated their ability.* Newly hired managers have *potential for performance,* but not *demonstrated performance.* Thus, it is risky to assign an individual to a task for which there is any probability of failure. But studies have indicated that managers who experienced initial job challenge were more effective in their later years.[5]

Demanding bosses A practice which seems to have considerable promise for increasing the retention rate of young managers is to assign them initially to demanding supervisors. In this context, demanding should not be interpreted as autocratic. Rather, the type of boss most likely to get new hirees off in the right direction is one who has high but achievable expectations for their performance. Such a boss instills in the young managers the understanding that high performance is expected and rewarded and, equally important, that the boss is always ready to assist them through coaching and counseling.

The programs and practices that are intended to retain and develop young managers—particularly recent hirees with college training—can be used separately or in combination. A manager would be well advised to establish policies that would be most likely to retain those recent hirees who have the highest potential to perform effectively. The likelihood of that result is improved if the policies include realistic job previews coupled with challenging initial assignments supervised by supportive, performance-oriented managers. Although such practices are not perfect, they are helpful not only in retaining young managers but also in avoiding the problems which may arise during the middle phases of a manager's career.

Career development for midcareer managers

Managers in the midstages of their careers are ordinarily key people in their organizations. They have established a place for themselves in

[5] Hall, *Careers in Organizations,* p. 67.

society as well as at work. They occupy important positions in the community, often engage in civic affairs, and are looked upon as model achievers in our achievement-oriented culture. Yet, popular and scholarly articles and books appear yearly which discuss the midcareer crisis and the middle-aged dropout. Executives disappear from their jobs and are later found driving taxis, teaching in ghettos, or at worst, on skid row. Such lost talent is expensive to replace, and more and more organizations are initiating practices to deal with the problems of the midcareer manager.

The midcareer plateau

Managers face the midcareer plateau during the adult stage of life and the maintenance phase of careers. At this point, the likelihood of additional upward promotion may be quite low. Two reasons account for the plateau. First, there are simply fewer jobs at the top of the organization, and even though the manager has the ability to perform at that level, no opening exists. Second, openings may exist, but the manager may lack either the *ability* or the *desire* to fill them.[6]

Managers who find themselves stifled in their present jobs tend to cope with the problems in fairly consistent ways. They suffer from depression, poor health, and fear and hostility toward their subordinates. Eventually, they may "retire" on the job or leave the organization physically and permanently. Any one of these ways of coping results in lowered job performance and, of course, lowered organizational performance.[7]

The midcareer, middle-age crisis has been depicted in novels, movies, dramas, and psychological studies. Although each individual's story is different and unique, the scenario has many common features. A successful sales executive for a well-known business machine corporation stated:

> *Something happened when I was 45 or so. The kids were married and gone. The house was too big for me and the wife—what can two people do with a four-bedroom house? We had more money than we could spend, and I knew that I could stay with the firm for as long as I wanted to. But I asked myself what was so important about selling typewriters. The world would hardly be better off if we met our sales quota. I began to think about leaving the company and doing something else. But what could I do? For 20 years, I had been selling something or other to someone or other. I reread* Death of a Salesman *and thought, Is*

[6] Thomas P. Ference, James A. F. Stoner, and E. Kirby Warren, "Managing the Career Plateau," *Academy of Management Review,* October 1977, p. 604.

[7] Duane Schultz, "Managing the Middle-Aged Manager," *Personnel,* November–December 1974, pp. 8–17.

that where I'm headed? I still don't know. I try not to think about it, but sometimes . . .

Of course, not all managers respond to their situations in the same ways. Some, perhaps most, cope constructively. But to the extent that effective managers experience disruptive psychological, physical, and professional traumas, organizational performance will suffer. The cost of impaired managerial effectiveness indicates that organizations should implement programs to counteract midcareer plateau problems.

Programs and practices to counteract midcareer problems

Counteracting the problems that managers face at midcareer involves providing *counseling* and *alternatives.*

Midcareer counseling Organizations such as IBM, Du Pont, Alcoa, and Western Electric employ full-time staff psychiatrists to assist employees in dealing with career, health, and family problems.[8] In the context of such counseling, midcareer managers are provided with professional help in dealing with the depression and stress they may experience. Since midcareer managers are usually well educated and articulate, they often only need someone to talk to, someone skilled in the art of listening. The process of verbalizing their problems to an objective listener is often enough to enable midcareer managers to recognize their problems and to cope with them constructively.

Midcareer alternatives Effective resolution of the problems of midcareer crises requires the existence of acceptable alternatives. The organization cannot be expected to go beyond counseling on personal and family problems. But when the crisis is precipitated primarily by career-related factors, the organization can be an important source of alternatives. In many instances, the organization simply needs to accept career moves that are usually viewed as unacceptable.

Three career moves which have potential for counteracting the problems of midcareer managers are lateral transfers, downward transfers, and fallback positions.[9]

Lateral transfers involve moves at the same organizational level from one department to another. A manager who has plateaued in production

[8] Manfred F. R. Kets de Vries, "The Midcareer Conundrum," *Organizational Dynamics,* Autumn 1978, p. 58.

[9] Douglas T. Hall and Francine S. Hall, "What's New in Career Management," *Organizational Dynamics,* Summer 1976, pp. 21–27.

could be transferred to a similar level in sales, engineering, or some other area. The move would require the manager to learn quickly the technical demands of the new position, and there would be a period of reduced performance as this learning occurred. But once qualified, the manager would bring the perspectives of both areas to bear on decisions.

Downward transfers are associated in our society with failure; an effective manager simply does not consider a move downward to be a respectable alternative. Yet downward transfers are in many instances not only respectable alternatives but entirely acceptable alternatives, particularly when one or more of the following conditions exist:

The manager values the quality of life afforded by a specific geographic area and may desire a downward transfer if this is required in order to stay in or move to that area.

The manager views the downward transfer as a way to establish a base for future promotions.

The manager is faced with the alternatives of dismissal or a downward move.

The manager desires to pursue time-consuming non-job-related activities—such as religious, civic, or political activities—and for that reason may welcome the reduced responsibility (and demands) of a lower-level position.

The use of *fallback positions* is a relatively new way to reduce the risk of lateral and downward transfers. The practice involves identifying in advance a position to which the transferred manager can return if the new position does not work out. By identifying the fallback position in advance, the organization informs everyone who is affected that some risk is involved but that the organization is willing to accept some of the responsibility for it and that returning to the fallback job will not be viewed as failure. Companies such as Heublein, Procter & Gamble, Continental Can, and Lehman Brothers have used fallback positions to remove some of the risk of lateral and upward moves. The practice appears to have considerable promise for protecting the careers of highly specialized technicians and professionals who make their first move into general management positions.

The suggestion that organizations initiate practices and programs to assist managers through midcareer crises does not excuse managers from taking responsibility for themselves. Individuals who deal honestly and constructively with their lives and careers will early on take steps to minimize the risk of becoming obsolete or redundant. At the outset of their management careers, they can begin to formulate their *career plans and paths.* Often they will be assisted in this process by the organization which employs them.

Career planning and pathing

Career planning involves matching an individual's career aspirations with the opportunities available in an organization. **Career pathing** is the sequencing of the specific jobs that are associated with those opportunities. The two processes are intertwined. Planning a career involves the identification of the means for achieving desired ends, and in the context of career plans, career paths are the means for achieving aspirations. Although career planning is still a relatively new practice, many organizations are turning to it as a way to *proact* rather than *react* to the problems associated with early and midcareer career crises.

Successful career planning and the career pathing process place equal responsibility on the individual and the organization. The individual must identify his or her aspirations and abilities and, through counseling, recognize what training and development are required for a particular career path. The organization must identify its needs and opportunities through human resource planning, and provide the necessary career information and training to its employees. Such companies as Weyerhaeuser, Nabisco, Gulf Oil, Exxon, and Eaton use career development programs to identify a broad pool of talent that is available for promotion and transfer opportunities. Companies often restrict career counseling to managerial and professional staff, but IBM, GE, TRW, and Gulf Oil provide career counseling for both blue-collar and managerial personnel.

Career planning

Individual and organizational needs and opportunities can be matched in a variety of ways. Two widely used approaches are (1) informal counseling by the personnel staff and (2) career counseling by supervisors. These approaches are often quite informal. Somewhat more formal and less widely used practices involve workshops, seminars, and self-assessment centers.

Informal counseling The personnel staffs of organizations often include counseling services for employees who wish to assess their abilities and interests. The counseling process can also move into personal concerns, and this is proper, since as we have already seen, life concerns are important factors in determining career aspirations. In this context, career counseling is viewed by the organization as a service to its employees, but not as a primary service.

Career counseling by supervisors is usually included in performance appraisals. The question of where the employee is going in the organization arises quite naturally in this setting. In fact, the inclusion of career information in performance appraisal predates the current interest in career planning. A characteristic of effective performance evaluation is to let the employee know not only how well he or she has done, but also what the future holds. Thus, supervisors must be able to counsel the employee in terms of organizational needs and opportunities not only within the specific department but throughout the organization. Since supervisors usually have limited information about the total organization, it is often necessary to adopt more formal and systematic counseling approaches.

Formal counseling Workshops, assessment centers, and career development centers are being used increasingly in organizations. Typically, such formal practices are designed to serve specific employee groups. Management trainees and high-potential or fast-track management candidates have received most of the attention to date. However, women employees and minority employees have been given increasing attention. Career development programs for women and minority employees are viewed as indications of an organization's commitment to affirmative action.

One example of a formal organizational career planning system is Syntex Corporation's Career Development Center. The center was the result of the realization that the managers in Syntex were unable to counsel their subordinates because they were too caught up in their own jobs. The center's staff first identifies the individual's strengths and weaknesses in eight skill areas which Syntex believes to be related to effective management. These eight areas are (1) problem analysis; (2) communication; (3) goal setting; (4) decision making and conflict handling; (5) selecting, training, and motivating employees; (6) controlling employees; (7) interpersonal competence; and (8) the use of time. On the basis of scores in the eight areas, each manager sets career and personal goals. The center's staff assists the manager to set realistic goals which reflect his or her strengths and weaknesses in the eight areas.

Organizations can use a variety of practices to facilitate their employees' career plans. One of the oldest and most widely used practices is some form of **tuition aid program.** Employees can take advantage of educational and training opportunities available at nearby schools, and the organization pays some or all of the tuition. J. I. Case, a Tenneco company with corporate offices in Racine, Wisconsin, is but one of many organizations that provide in-house courses and seminars as well as tuition reimbursement for courses related to the individual's job.

Another practice is **job posting;** that is, the organization publicizes job openings as they occur. The employees are thus made aware of the opportunities. Effective job posting requires more than simply placing a notice on the company bulletin board. At a minimum, job posting should meet the following conditions:

1. It should include promotions and transfers as well as permanent vacancies.
2. The available jobs should be posted at least three to six weeks prior to external recruiting.

3. The eligibility rules should be explicit and straightforward.
4. The standards for selection and the bidding instructions should be stated clearly.
5. Vacationing employees should be given the opportunity to apply ahead of time.
6. Employees who apply but are rejected should be notified of the reason in writing, and a record of the reason should be placed in their personnel files.[10]

Whatever approach is used, the crucial measure of its success will be the extent to which *individual and organizational* needs are satisfied.

Career pathing

The result of career planning is the placement of an individual into a job which is the first of a sequential series of jobs. From the perspective of the organization, career paths are important inputs into work force planning. An organization's future work force depends on the projected passage of individuals through the ranks. From the perspective of the individual, a career path is the sequence of jobs which he or she desires to undertake in order to achieve personal and career goals. Although it is virtually impossible to completely integrate the organizational and individual needs in the design of career paths, systematic career planning has the potential for closing the gap between the needs of the individual and the needs of the organization.

Traditional career paths have emphasized upward mobility in a single occupation or functional area. When recruiting personnel, the organization's representative will speak of engineers', accountants', or salespersons' career paths. In these contexts, the recruiter will describe the different jobs that typical individuals will hold as they work progressively upward in an organization. Each job, or rung, is reached when the individual has accumulated the necessary experience and ability and has demonstrated that he or she is ready for promotion. Implicit in such career paths is the attitude that failure has occurred whenever an individual does not move on up after a certain amount of time has elapsed. Such attitudes make it difficult to use lateral and downward transfers as alternatives for managers who no longer wish to pay the price of upward promotion.

An alternative to traditional career pathing is to base career paths on real-world experiences and individualized preferences. Paths of this kind would have several characteristics:

1. They would include lateral and downward possibilities as well as upward possibilities, and they would not be tied to normal rates of progress.

[10] David R. Dahl and Patrick R. Pinto, "Job Posting: An Industry Survey," *Personnel Journal*, January 1977, pp. 40–42.

2. They would be tentative, and they would be responsive to changes in organizational needs.
3. They would be flexible enough to take into account the qualities of individuals.
4. Each job along the paths would be specified in terms of *acquirable* skills, knowledge, and other specific attributes, not merely in terms of educational credentials, age, or work experience.[11]

Realistic career paths, rather than traditional ones, are necessary for effective employee counseling. In the absence of such information, the employee can only guess at what is available.

An example of a career path for general management in a telephone company is depicted in Figure 10–4. According to the path, the average

Figure 10–4

Career path, general management

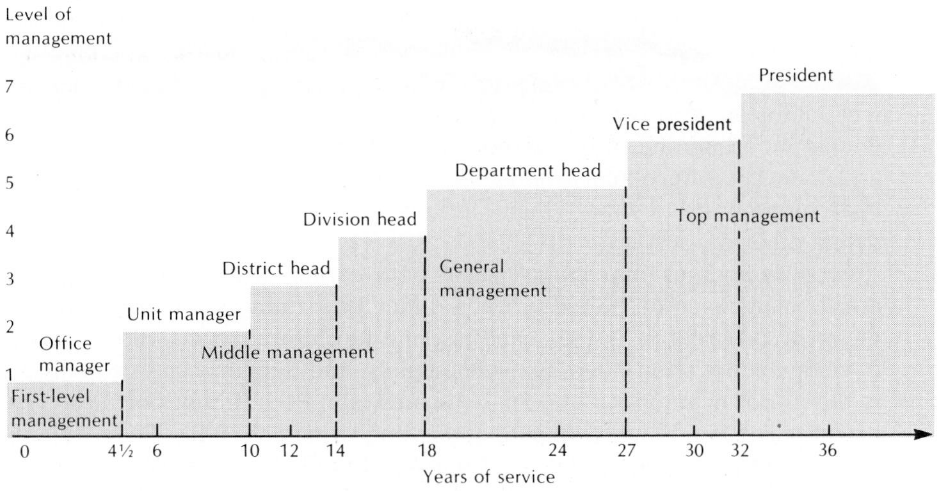

SOURCE: Based on William F. Glueck, *Personnel: A Diagnostic Approach* (Plano, Tex.: Business Publications, 1978), pp. 272–73. © 1978 by Business Publications, Inc.

duration of a manager's assignment in first-level management is 4 years—2½ years as a staff asistant in the home office and 1½ years as the manager of a district office in a small city. By the 14th year, the average manager should have reached the fourth level of management. The assignment at this level might be that of division manager of the Commercial Sales and Operations Division. Obviously, not all managers reach the fifth level, much

[11] James W. Walker, "Let's Get Realistic about Career Paths," *Human Resource Management*, Fall 1976, pp. 2–7.

less the seventh, president. As one nears the top of the organization, the number of openings declines and the number of candidates increases.

Some difficult career and human resource development issues

Organizations which undertake career development programs are certain to encounter some difficult issues along the way.[12] The following problems are based on the actual experiences of some organizations.

Integrating career development and human resource planning

The relationship between career development and human resource planning is obvious. Career development provides a *supply* of talents and abilities; human resource planning projects the *demand* for talents and abilities. It would seem that organizations which undertake one of these activities would undertake the other. Surely, it makes little sense to develop people and then have no place to put them, *or* to project needs for people but have no program to supply them. In fact, some organizations do have one or the other but not both.

Even companies that make use of both career development programs and human resource planning have difficulty in integrating the efforts of the two. One reason is that each is done by different specialties. Career development is often done by psychologists, and human resource planning is the job of economists and systems analysts. Practitioners of these two disciplines have difficulty in communicating with each other. Their training and backgrounds create potential barriers to effective communication.

A second reason for failure to integrate the efforts of career development and human resource planning is related to the *organization structure*. Career planning is usually the function of *personnel departments*. Work force planning is the function of *planning staffs*. The two activities are carried out in two organizationally distinct units. The manager who is responsible for both units may be the chief executive officer or a group executive.

Managing dual careers

As more and more women enter the working world and pursue careers, managers will increasingly confront the problems of **dual careers**. The prob-

[12] This section is based on Hall and Hall, "What's New in Career Management," pp. 27–30.

lems arise because the careers of husbands and wives may lead them in different directions. An obvious problem can arise when the organization offers the husband or wife a transfer (involving a promotion), but it is rejected because the required relocation is incompatible with the spouse's career plans. One study reports that one in three executives cannot or will not relocate because this would interfere with the career of the spouse.[13] Thus, organizations *and* individuals lose flexibility as a consequence of dual careers.

The incidence of dual careers will probably rise as more women enter the labor force. At present, more than 46 million employed men and women are two-career couples. There is not reason to believe that the number will decrease with time; in fact, the reasonable assumption to make is that both the number and the proportion of dual-career couples will increase. The problems associated with this phenomenon are relatively new, but those who have studied these problems offer the following advice:

1. An organization should conduct an employee survey which gathers statistics and information regarding the incidence of dual careers in its *present* and *projected* work force. The survey should determine (*a*) how many employees are at present part of a two-career situation, (*b*) how many people interviewed for positions are part of a dual-career situation, (*c*) where and at what level in the organization the dual-career employees are, (*d*) what conflicts these employees now have, and (*e*) whether dual-career employees perceive company policy and practices to be helpful to their careers and careers of their spouses.
2. Recruiters should devise methods which present realistic previews of what the company offers dual-career couples. Orientation sessions conducted by personnel departments should include information which helps such couples identify potential problems.
3. Career development and transfer policies must be revised. Since the usual policies are based on the traditional one-career family, they are inapplicable to dual-career situations. The key is to provide more flexibility.
4. The company should consider providing career couples with special assistance in career mangement. Couples are typically ill prepared to cope with the problems posed by two careers. Young, recently hired couples are especially naive in this regard.
5. The organization can establish cooperative arrangements with other organizations. When one organization desires to relocate one dual-career partner, cooperative organizations can be sources of employment for the other partner.
6. The most important immediate step is to establish flexible working hours. Allowing couples the privilege of arranging their work schedules

[13] Francine S. Hall and Douglas T. Hall, "Dual Careers—How Do Couples and Companies Cope with the Problem?" *Organizational Dynamics,* Spring 1978, p. 58.

so that these will be compatible with family demands is an effective way to meet some of the problems of managing dual-career couples.[14]

It would be a mistake to believe that dual-career problems exist only for managerial and prefessional personnel. More and more nonmanagerial personnel are also members of two-career families. Managers will confront problems in scheduling overtime for these people and in transferring them to different shifts. Like the needs of managerial and professional people, the needs of blue-collar individuals must be considered.

One company which has responded to the needs of its dual-career employees is Morgan Adhesives Company in Stow, Ohio. Tom and Vickie Barker are employed by the company. In 1977, Vickie won her bid to run a machine which applies an adhesive coating to films, foils, foams, and papers. She is responsible for monitoring and controlling the machine's output and for directing the work of two helpers. One of her helpers is her husband Tom. After Vickie had won her bid, Tom put in a bid to be her helper so that they could be on the same shift. The company has no difficulty with the arrangement. As Bill Wyers, Morgan Adhesives' personnel manager said, "Our only policy is performance, and the Barkers are delivering."[15]

The issues of managing dual careers both from the couple's and the organization's viewpoint are only beginning to emerge. Managers of the 1980s will find these issues to be among their most significant career development challenges.

Dealing with EEO problems

The initial thrust of affirmative action programs is to recruit and place women and minority employees into managerial and professional positions. Many organizations have been successful in that effort, but their success has created additional problems. For example, the career development needs of women and minority employees require nontraditional methods. A potentially explosive additional problem is coping with the reactions of white male employees.

Apparently, the key to meeting the career development needs of women and minority employees is to integrate recruitment, placement, and development efforts. For example, Virginia National Bankshares, the holding company of Virginia National Bank (VNB), has 155 offices throughout Virginia. Despite the fact that 72 percent of its employees are women, only 25 percent of them are in management positions. To correct the imbalance, VNB started a program which is designed to move more women into management. VNB

[14] Ibid., pp. 72–76.

[15] "At Home on the Coating Line," *Management Review*, September 1978, p. 46.

appointed an advisory board consisting of eight women from various specialties within the bank. The advisory board interviewed all present female managers to determine what women considered to be their problems. The board then surveyed 109 nonmanagerial women to find out how many actually aspired to be managers.

The advisory board discovered a large number of women who stated that they were willing to undergo whatever training was necessary to move into management. The board also identified three crucial problem areas which had to be resolved before these women could realize their aspirations: (1) misconceptions about women and outdated attitudes toward women, (2) lack of lending experience among women, and (3) lack of management skills among women. The bank's management accepted the advisory board's recommendation that a rotational program be implemented. Women would be placed in all major credit areas throughout the bank. They would be trained in three lending skills: accounting, economics/finance, and financial statement analysis. They would spend one month in each credit area: branch management, credit review, marketing, branch lending, commercial loans, mortgage loans, and national accounts. In addition to the rotational program, the bank sponsors seminars prepared by the National Association of Bank Women and conducts life planning seminars to help women function effectively in their careers and in other areas of their lives.[16]

The VNB program is representative of career development that is designed to meet the specific needs of specific employees in a specific situation. Traditional programs are directed toward mainstream employees and are too general in focus and content to meet the needs of women and minority employees. Although the VNB program's target group was women, its principles could be equally applicable to minority employees.

In the midst of EEO and affirmative action concerns, the employees most likely to feel threatened are white males of average competence. The threat is most keenly felt when the economy slows down and what few promotions are available go to women and minority employees. White males are not much comforted to be told that such practices are temporary and are intended to correct past injustices. The white male of average competence is the one who often loses the promotion, and he is the one who is most threatened. Above-average white males will usually progress; below-average performers will always lag behind. So what can managers do to help the average performers?

No company practice can guarantee that average male employees will go along with affirmative action programs. But some practices offer promise. First, the company should provide open and complete information about promotions. Instead of being secretive about promotions (in the hope that

[16] "Making Room at the Top," *Management Review*, April 1978, p. 45.

if white males aren't told that they are being passed over for promotion, they won't notice it), the organization should provide information which permits white males to see precisely where they stand. If given such information, they will be less likely to overestimate their relative disadvantage and will be able to assess their position in the organization more accurately.

A second practice that seems promising is to make sure that white males receive as much career development assistance as other groups. White males may also need information about occupational opportunities *outside the company.* Since their upward mobility may be temporarily stifled by the company's affirmative action efforts, the average white males should be given the opportunity to seek career mobility elsewhere. But the management of any company that is sincerely pursuing affirmative action through career development must not expect all employees to go along with and support the effort. Vested interests are at stake when one group progresses at the expense of another.

Management summary

1. Providing career development programs for employees is an important managerial responsibility. The effective performance of individual tasks depends, in part, on the balance between individual ability and task demands.
2. Career development recognizes the changing needs of the organization and the individual. Organizations change in response to environmental pressures and opportunities; these changes alter the organizations' need for management talent. Individuals typically change as they grow and develop their abilities and talents.
3. The unique career problems of recent hirees should be counteracted by the use of specifically designed practices and policies. The cost of replacing young managers justifies considerable organizational effort to hold them.
4. Midcareer employees often face severe personal stress. Enlightened management practices will encourage such employees to face their situations and to exercise options offered by the organization.
5. Effective career development involves matching organizational needs and individual aspirations. Through counseling, educational opportunities, and career path information, individuals can more systematically plan their careers and lives.
6. Several issues loom as difficult future career development problems. The most significant are dual careers, meeting the developmental needs of women and minority employees, and integrating human resource planning and career development.

Review and discussion questions

1. What is your career plan? How many of your friends seem to know what they want from their careers? For what reasons do young people typically have difficulty with the question "What do I want to do?"
2. What conflicts do you think you will have when you take your first job upon graduation? For which of these conflicts can you now plan and anticipate appropriate coping responses?
3. Do you believe that you can cope with the personal and career problems of a dual-career situation? If so, what experiences in life have prepared you to cope with the problems? If not, why not?
4. As the authors define the term *career,* who is the sole judge of career success? Why is this proper? Unrealistic?
5. Why do young hirees into management positions experience problems? How could a business school prepare students to have realistic expectations?
6. Is it possible that some managers are satisfied with the experience of midcareer plateaus? Explain.
7. Explain why white males of average competence consider affirmative action programs to be reverse discrimination. Do you share this view?
8. Explain the interrelationships between the staffing process (Chapter 9) and career development.
9. University colleges and departments typically employ secretaries to assist professors. Visit the personnel department of the university you attend and determine whether career paths have been developed for these secretaries. If no career paths exist, how would you go about preparing them?

Suggested reading

Barr, E. E. "Experiencing Success: Breaking Them in at Sun Chemical." *Business,* September–October 1980, pp. 9–14.

Conarroe, R. R. "Climbing the Corporate Success Ladder: A Self-Marketing Program for Executives." *Management Review,* February 1981, pp. 24–28, 42–44.

Heier, W. D. "Company Loyalty: A Zero-Based Asset?" *Management Review,* April 1980, pp. 57–61.

Lee, N. "The Dual Career Couple: Benefits and Pitfalls." *Management Review,* January 1981, pp. 46–52.

Lewicki, R. J. "Organizational Seduction: Building Commitment to Organizations." *Organizational Dynamics,* Autumn 1981, pp. 5–22.

Lyman, D.; F. Luthans; and N. Carter. "For Managers in New Jobs: An Accountability and Appraisal System." *Management Review,* January 1980, pp. 46–51.

Morrison, A. M. "Job-Hopping to the Top." *Fortune,* May 4, 1981, pp. 127, 129–30.

Seligman, D. "Luck and Careers." *Fortune,* November 16, 1981, pp. 60–66, 70, 72.

Applying what you have learned about developing careers and human resources

Cases:

Career development practices at AT&T, IBM, and Hewlett-Packard
Success has a price

Career development practices at AT&T, IBM, and Hewlett-Packard*

The contemporary emphasis on career development includes career mobility. Where once it was thought that factors such as dedication, allegiance, and loyalty were important in career success, it is now thought that *concern for results* and *desire for responsibility* are key factors. And, of course, the latter two factors can be achieved in any company where the opportunity exists. The deemphasis of company loyalty has accelerated during the decade of the 1970s to the point that companies are now becoming concerned for consequences of the change.

Some of the consequences are directly measurable. For example, since 1960, the turnover among managers out of college less than five years has increased by 500 percent. The typical company can expect to lose 50 percent of its college recruits within five years of hiring them. These numbers translate into higher training costs, higher salaries, and lower productivity. The economic effects of these consequences are sufficiently large to stimulate countermeasures in some of America's best-known corporations.

AT&T attempts to match its needs for future executive leadership with the needs of individuals who seek that kind of leadership. AT&T's campus recruiters are directed to seek out those individuals who are predisposed to accept the company's operating style and fundamental beliefs. AT&T had compared its current group of recruits with those it had hired 20 years ago. Both groups expressed strong desire for achievement, but the current group

---

* This case is adapted from Roy Rowan, "Rekindling Corporate Loyalty," *Fortune*, February 9, 1981, pp. 54–58.

scored only half as high in "deference to authority" and twice as high on "loyalty to peers." The results were interpreted to mean that the 1980's college recruit has little regard for where the achievement is realized, whether AT&T or in some other company. Thus, AT&T turned the attention of its campus recruiters toward those who are "our [AT&T] kind of people."

IBM, long noted for its success in imbuing its executives with the corporate credo, has had no particular difficulty with managerial turnover. In fact, IBM's turnover has been cut in half since 1960. The philosophy at IBM is that company loyalty has to be earned. W. E. Burdick, vice president for personnel, states: "We'd be foolish to expect an M.B.A. to walk in through the door and be loyal. Loyalty is something you've got to win." One feature of the IBM career development program is that each promotion up the executive ladder requires an additional training visit to the company's management-development center in Armonk, N.Y. The newly promoted manager is not only trained in the job requirements of the new position but also reindoctrinated in company philosophy: "Dignity and Respect for the Individual. Pursuit of Excellence. Dedication to Service." And, one might add, loyalty to IBM.

Hewlett-Packard's approach to acquiring company loyalty places emphasis on sharing company successes with those who produce those successes. The company is headquartered in an area of California known popularly as Silicon Valley. It is in this area that the business of producing microprocessors has flourished and where the turnover of engineering personnel averages 60 percent. Yet, Hewlett-Packard's turnover is but 10 percent. The secrets, according to David Packard, chairman of the board, are profit participation and decentralized operating control. The company has 40 divisions, and each has its own research and development resources. According to Packard, creative people need the freedom to create technological breakthroughs that contribute to company profitability; those who developed the breakthrough share in that profitability.

These practices are successful means for instilling loyalty in career-oriented individuals. However, as one crusty CEO states: "When it comes to establishing loyalty, I have yet to find a substitute for fear." The fear referred to is the fear of unemployment brought about by a prolonged recession. As 1981 drew to a close, holiday and seasonal news was being pushed off the evening news by reports of mass layoffs of white-collar employees. One must wonder whether loyalty was a criterion for keeping one's job in those reported instances.

Questions:

1. Compare the practices of the three companies. In what specific ways are they different, the same?
2. Is company loyalty a necessary condition for achieving career effectiveness from the individual's perspective? From the organization's perspective?
3. What specific factors would cause you to be loyal to a particular organization?

Success has a price

Joseph Arthur had reached the top! He was 43 years old, and he had passed all the competition in what he called "the fast lane." He had graduated with honors from two prestigious universities, and he had an undergraduate degree in chemical engineering and a master's degree in business administration. He took his first job with a major chemical firm at the age 21. His first job, following completion of the company's management training program, was in the operations division as supervisor of bulk processing. His performance caught the attention of his supervisor, and he was soon transferred to a larger facility.

At the age of 35, Joseph had held managerial positions in every functional area and his reputation as the company whiz kid was widespread. Everyone seemed to know about him. He was the comer, the achiever. When the board of directors reviewed the candidates for the position of chief executive officer, it was no contest. At the age of 40, Joseph reached the top spot in the organization. His was a career to emulate, or so many thought. But after three years in the job, Joseph was not so sure.

Sure, the job offered challenges, and the salary was more than he had ever dreamed possible. Yet, the job soon became uneventful. After all, Joseph had made his reputation by accepting challenge and successfully meeting it. Moreover, he had always been goal oriented. For him a job well done meant a promotion and new challenges. But where could he go now? He was at the top. And he still had more than half of his working life ahead of him.

Joseph decided that he should seek employment outside the company. Surely, he thought, I can get a similar job with greater challenge at another company. But he soon discovered that other companies were not so appreciative of his potential. Companies in industries other than chemicals were particularly uninterested in employing him except in positions far below that of chief executive officer and at far lower salaries. He was considered competent but narrowly trained. Despite his record of achievement, he discovered that other companies had their own superstars. Joseph was approached by other firms in the chemical industry, but he saw no reason to simply move his "desk across the hall."

When discussing his situation with a lifelong friend, Joseph confided that he now wished that he had gone slower. "I should have taken my time and smelled the roses. I'm 43, and I have nowhere to go except the golf course or the racquetball court. I can't stand the thought of 20 more years of going nowhere. But how can I start all over again with another company?"

Questions:

1. What do you believe Joseph will do? Do you think that his performance as CEO will suffer if he remains in the job?
2. What would you suggest that Joseph do if he were to ask you for advice?
3. What do you think of Joseph's idea that he should have gone slower? Is his case typical of high achievers? Explain.

Applying what you have learned about the organizing function

Learning exercise:

Designing the new venture

Comprehensive case:

Chandler's Restaurant

Learning exercise Designing the new venture

Purpose: The purpose of this exercise is to provide students with first-hand experience in organizing a new business venture.

Setting up the exercise:

I. A few years ago, George Ballas got so frustrated trying to keep his lawn neatly trimmed around the roots of oak trees that he developed what is now called the Weed Eater. The original Weed Eater was made from a popcorn can which had holes in it and was threaded with nylon fishing line. Weed Eater sales in 1972 totaled $568,000, but by 1978, sales were in excess of $100 million. There are now 20 or so similar devices on the market.

Two brothers from Pittsburgh, George and Jim Gammons, are starting a new venture called Lawn Trimmers, Inc. They are attempting to develop an organization that makes a profit by selling Lawn Trimmers which do not wear out for over 2,000 trimming applications. The Weed Eaters and similar products often have breaks in the nylon lines which require the user to turn off the trimmer and readjust the line. The Gammons have developed a new type of cutting fabric that is not physically harmful and cuts for over 2,000 applications.

In order to sell the Lawn Trimmers, the Gammons brothers will have to market their products through retail establishments. They will make the products in their shop in Pittsburgh and ship them to the retail establishments. The profits will come entirely from the sales of the Lawn Trimmers to retail establishments. The price of the product is already set, and it appears that there will be sufficient market demand to sell at least 6,000 Lawn Trimmers annually.

II. The instructor will set up teams of five to eight students to serve as organizational design experts who will provide the Gammons brothers with the best structure for their new venture. The groups should meet and establish a design that would be feasible for the Gammons at this stage in their venture.

III. Each group should select a spokesperson to make a short presentation of the group's organizational design for the Gammons.

IV. The class should compare the various designs and discuss why there are similarities and differences in what is presented.

A learning note: This exercise will show that organizational design necessitates making assumptions about the market, competition, labor resources, scheduling, and profit margins, to name just a few areas. There is no one best design that should be regarded as a final answer.

Chandler's Restaurant*

In discussing the kitchen as a status system, we have only incidentally taken account of the fact that the kitchen is part of a communication and supply system, which operates to get the food from the range onto the customer's table. Looking at it this way will bring to light other problems.

Where the restaurant is small and the kitchen is on the same floor as the dining room, waitresses are in direct contact with cooks. This does not eliminate friction, but at least everybody is in a position to know what everybody else is doing, and the problems of communication and coordination are relatively simple.

When the restaurant is large, there are more people whose activities must be coordinated, and when the restaurant operates on several floors, the coordination must be accomplished through people who are not generally in face-to-face contact with each other. These factors add tremendously to the difficulty of achieving smooth coordination.

The cooks feel that they work under pressure—and under a pressure whose origins they cannot see or anticipate.

As one of them said,

> It's mostly the uncertainty of the job that gets me down, I think. I mean, you never know how much work you're going to have to do. You never know in advance if you're going to have to make more. I think that's what a lot of 'em don't like around here. That uncertainty is hard on your nerves.

For a cook, the ideal situation is one in which she always has a sufficient supply of food prepared ahead so that she is never asked for something she does not have on hand. As one of them said, "You have to keep ahead or you get all excited and upset."

Life would be simpler for the cook if she were free to prepare just as much food as she wanted to, but the large and efficiently operated restaurant plans production on the basis of very careful estimates of the volume of business to be expected. Low food costs depend in part upon minimizing waste or left-over food. This means that production must be scheduled so as to run only a little ahead of customer demand. The cook therefore works within a narrow margin of error. She can't get

* This case was prepared by William F. Whyte and is reprinted here by permission of the author.

far ahead, and that means that on extra-busy days she is certain sometimes to lose her lead or even to drop behind.

When the cook drops behind, all the pressures from customer to waitress to service pantry to runner descend upon her, for no one between her and the customer can do his job unless she produces the goods. From this point of view, timing and coordination are key problems of the organization. Proper timing and good coordination must be achieved in human relations or else efficiency is dissipated in personal frictions.

While these statements apply to every step in the process of production and service, let us look here at the first steps—the relations of cooks to kitchen runners to the service pantry.

When the restaurant operates on different floors, the relations must be carried on in part through mechanical means of communication. There are three common channels of this nature, and all have their drawbacks. Use of a public address system adds considerably to the noise of the kitchen and service pantries. The teleautograph (in which orders written on the machine on one floor are automatically recorded on the kitchen machine) is quiet but sometimes unintelligible. Orders written in a hurry and in abbreviated form are sometimes misinterpreted so that sliced ham arrives when sliced toms (tomatoes) were ordered. Besides, neither of those channels operates easily for two-way communication. It is difficult to carry on a conversation over the public address system, and, while kitchen runners runners can write their replies to orders on the teleautograph, this hardly makes for full and free expression. The telephone provides two-way communication, but most kitchens are so noisy that it is difficult to hear phone conversations. And then in some restaurants there is only one telephone circuit for the whole house, so that when kitchen and pantry runners are using it, no one else can put in a call.

The problems that come up with such communication systems can best be illustrated by looking at a particular restaurant, Chandler's, where teleautograph and phone were used.

A kitchen supervisor was in charge of Chandler's kitchen, and pantry supervisors were in charge of each pantry, under her general supervision. There was also an assistant supervisor working in the kitchen.

The supplying function was carried on in the kitchen by two or three runners (depending upon the employment situation) and by a runner on each of the service-pantry floors. Food was sent up by automatic elevator.

The kitchen runners were supposed to pick up their orders from storage bins, iceboxes, or direct from the cooks. When the order was in preparation, the cook or salad girl was supposed to say how long it would be before it was ready, and the runner would relay this information by teleautograph to the service pantries. When the cooking or salad making had not been begun, the runner had no authority to tell the cook to hurry the order. Before each meal, the cook was given an open order (a minimum and maximum amount) on each item by the kitchen supervisor. She worked steadily until she had produced the minimum, and, from then on, she gauged her production according to the demands that came to her from the runner. That is, if the item was going out fast, she would keep producing as fast as she could until she had produced the maximum. Beyond this point she could not go without authorization from her supervisor. Ideally, the supervisor and cook would confer before the maximum had been reached in order to see whether it was necessary to set a new figure, but this did not always happen.

While the runner could not order the cook to go beyond her maximum, his demands did directly influence her behavior up to that point. He originated action for her.

That was at the base of his troubles. Among kitchen employees, as we have seen, the cooks have the highest status. In Chandler's, runners had a low status, just above potwashers and sweepers. The jobs were filled by inexperienced employees, women or men who, if they performed well, were advanced to something of higher status. Their wages were considerably lower than the cooks', and the cooks also had a great advantage in seniority. In this particular case, the age difference was important too. The runners were a young man, a teen-aged boy, and a young girl, while the cooks were middle-aged women.

The runners would have been in a more secure position if they had been in close touch with a supervisor, but here the communication was sporadic and ineffective. The supervisor was inclined to let the runners fend for themselves.

When the runners put pressure on them, the cooks were inclined to react so as to put the runners in their place. For example, we observed incidents like this one. One runner (Ruth) asked another to get some salmon salad from the salad girl. The second runner found that the salad girl had no more on hand.

> "They want me to get some more of that salmon salad," he said. "Could you make it, please?"
>
> "Who told you that?" she asked.
>
> "Ruth did."
>
> "You can tell Ruth that I don't take no orders from her. I have a boss, and I don't take no orders from nobody else. You can just tell her that."

Now it may have been that the salad girl had made her maximum and could not go on without authorization from her supervisor, but the runner had no way of knowing that this was the case. He put his request to her politely, and she could have responded in kind by saying she was sorry that she could not make more without consulting the supervisor. Instead she responded aggressively, as if she felt a need to make it clear that no mere runner was going to originate action for her.

Even when they complied with the runner's requests, the cooks sometimes behaved so as to make it appear as if it were really they who originated the action. They always liked to make it clear that they had authority over the foods after they had been prepared, and that they could determine what should be done with them. While this was a general reaction, the salad girl was most explicit in such cases.

A runner went to look for some boiled eggs. The salad girl was not present at the moment, so he could not ask her, but after he had got the eggs from the icebox, he saw that she was back at her station. He showed her the pan of eggs, asking, "What about that?"

> "I don't like that," she said belligerently. "You have no business taking them eggs out of the icebox without asking."
>
> "Well, I'm asking you now."
>
> "I have to know how much there is. That's why I want you to tell me. . . . Go on, you might as well take them now that you have them."
>
> On other occasions when he asked her for salad, she would say "Why don't you people look in the icebox once in a while?"

In such a case, whatever the runner did was wrong. The salad girl's behavior was irrational, of course, but it did serve a function for her. Behaving in this way, she was able to originate action for the runner instead of being in the inferior position of responding to his actions.

The runners also had difficulty in getting information out of the cooks. When there was a demand from the service pantries, and the food could not be sent up immediately, the runners were always supposed to give an estimate as to when they could furnish the item. This information they were expected to get from the cooks. The cooks sometimes flatly refused to give a time and were generally reluctant to make an estimate. When they did give a time, they nearly always ran considerably beyond it.

Incidentally, time seems to be used as a weapon in the restaurant. It is well known that customers feel and complain that they wait for a table or for service far longer than they actually do. Waitresses, as we observed them, estimated their waiting time on orders as much as 50 to 100 percent more than the actual time. While they were not conscious of what they were doing, they could express impatience with the service-pantry girls more eloquently by saying, "I've been waiting 20 minutes for that order," than by giving the time as 10 minutes. In the front of the house, time is used to put pressure on people. In the back of the house, the cooks try to use time to take pressure off themselves. They say that an item will be done "right away," which does not tell when it will be done but announces that they have the situation well in hand and that nobody should bother them about it. Giving a short time tends to have the same effect. It reassures the runner, who reassures the service pantries. When the time runs out, the pantry runners begin again to demand action, but it may take a few minutes before the pressure gets back to the cooks, and by that time the item may really be ready for delivery. Furthermore, the cooks' refusal to give a time turns the pressure back on runners and other parts of the house—a result that they are not able to accomplish in any other way.

In the case of some of the inexperienced cooks, it may be that they simply did not know how to estimate cooking time, but that would hardly explain the persistent failure of all the cooks to cooperate with the runners in this matter.

The management was quite aware of this problem but had no real solution to offer. One of the pantry supervisors instructed a kitchen runner in this way:

> "You have to give us a time on everything that is going to be delayed. That is the only way we can keep things going upstairs. On our blackboards we list all our foods and how long it will take to get them, and most of the time we have to list them 'indefinite.' That shouldn't be. We should always have a definite time, so the waitress can tell the guest how long he will have to wait for his order. We can't tell the guest we're out of a certain food item on the menu and that we don't know how long it will take to replace it. They'll ask what kind of a restaurant we're running."
>
> The runner thought that over and then went on to question the supervisor. "But sometimes we can't get that information from the cooks . . . They won't tell us, or maybe they don't know."
>
> "Then you should always ask the food-production manager. She'll tell you, or she'll get the cook to tell you."
>
> "But the cooks would think we had squealed."
>
> "No, they wouldn't. And if they did, all right, it's the only way they'll ever learn. They've got to learn that, because we must always have a time on all delayed foods."
>
> "Yes, surely we couldn't tell on them if they refused to give the information."

"Yes, you could. You have to. They'll have to learn it somehow."

The efficiency of this system depended upon building up a cooperative relationship between cooks and runners. For runners to try to get action by appealing to the boss to put pressure on the cooks is hardly the way to build up such a relationship. It is clear that, considering their low status in relation to the cooks, runners are not in a position to take the lead in smoothing out human-relations difficulties.

Some of the runner's problems arise out of failure to achieve efficient coordination and communication between floors. For example, on one occasion one of the upstairs floors put in a rush order for a pan of rice. With some difficulty, the kitchen runner was able to fill the order. Then, 15 minutes later, the pan came back to the kitchen again, still almost full, but apparently no more was needed for the meal. The cooks gathered around the elevator to give vent to their feelings. This proved, they said, that the rice had not been needed after all. Those people upstairs just didn't know what they were doing. After the meal was over, the kitchen runner went up to check with the pantry runner. The pantry man explained, "I ran out of creole, and there wasn't going to be any more, so I had no use for any more rice."

This was a perfectly reasonable explanation, but it did not reach the cooks. As a rule, the cooks had little idea of what was going on upstairs. Sometimes there would be an urgent call for some food item along toward the end of the meal-time, and it would be supplied only after a considerable delay. By the time it reached the service pantries, there would no longer be a demand for it, and the supply would shortly be sent back. This would always upset the cooks. They would then stand around and vow that next time they would not take it seriously when the upstairs people were clamoring for action.

"In the service pantries," one of the cooks said, "they just don't care how much they ask for. That guy, Joe [pantry runner], just hoards the stuff up there. He can't always be out of it like he claims. He just hoards it."

A kitchen runner made this comment:

> Joe will order something and right away he'll order it again. He just keeps calling for more. Once or twice I went upstairs, and I saw he had plenty of stuff up there. He just hoards it up there, and he has to send a lot of stuff downstairs. He wastes a lot of stuff. After I caught on to the way he works, I just made it a rule when he called for stuff and the first floor was calling for stuff at the same time, I divided it between them.

On the other hand, when Joe was rushed and found that he was not getting quick action on his orders, his tendency was to make his orders larger, repeat the orders before any supply had come up, and mark all his orders *rush.* When this did not bring results he would call the kitchen on the phone. If all else failed, he would sometimes run down into the kitchen himself to see if he could snatch what he needed.

This kind of behavior built up confusion and resentment in the kitchen. When orders were repeated, the kitchen runners could not tell whether additional supply was needed or whether the pantry runners were just getting impatient. When everything was marked rush, there was no way of telling how badly anybody needed anything. But most serious of all was the reaction when the pantry runner invaded the kitchen.

One of them told us of such an incident:

> One of the cooks got mad at me the other day. I went down there to get this item,

> and boy, did she get mad at me for coming down there. But I got to do *something!* The waitresses and the pantry girls keep on yelling at me to get it for them. Well, I finally got it, or somehow it got sent upstairs. Boy, she was sure mad at me, though.

Apparently the cooks resented the presence of any upstairs supply man in the kitchen, but they were particularly incensed against Joe, the runner they all suspected of hoarding food.

One of them made this comment:

> That guy would try to come down in the kitchen and tell us what to do. But not me. No sir. He came down here one day and tried to tell me what to do. He said to me, "We're going to be very busy today." I just looked at him. "Yeah?" I said, "who are you? Go on upstairs. Go on. Mind your own business." Can you beat that! "We're going to be very busy today!" He never came down and told *me* anything again. "Who are you?" I asked him. That's all I had to say to him.

Here the runner's remark did not have any effect upon the work of the cook, but the implication was that he was in a superior position, and she reacted strongly against him for that reason. None of the cooks enjoy having the kitchen runners originate action for them, but, since it occurs regularly, they make some adjustment to it. They are not accustomed to any sort of relationship with the pantry runners, so when they come down to add to the pressure and confusion of the kitchen, the cooks feel free to slap them down.

It was not only the pantry runners who invaded the kitchen. The pantry supervisors spent a good deal of time and energy running up and down. When an upstairs supervisor comes after supplies, the kitchen reaction is the same as that to the pantry runners—except that the supervisor cannot be slapped down. Instead, the employees gripe to each other.

As one kitchen runner said,

> I wish she would quit that. I wonder what she thinks she's doing, running down here and picking up things we're waiting for. Now like just a minute ago, did you see that? She went off with peaches and plums, and we'd never have known about it if I hadn't seen her. Now couldn't she have just stepped over here and told us? . . . She sure gets mad a lot, doesn't she? She's always griping. I mean, she's probably a nice person, but she's hard to get along with at work—she sure is!

There were other pantry supervisors whose presence in the kitchen did not cause such a disturbance. The workers would say that so-and-so was really all right. Nevertheless, whenever a pantry supervisor dashed into the kitchen for supplies, it was a sign to everybody that something was wrong—that somebody was worried—and thus it added to the tension in the atmosphere and disturbed the human relations of the regular supply system—such as they were.

In this situation, the kitchen runner was the man in the middle. One of the service-pantry girls we interviewed put it this way:

> Oh, we certainly are busy up here. We don't stop even for a moment. I think this is the busiest place around here. It's bad when we can't get those foods, though. We get delayed by those supply people downstairs all the time. I could shoot those runners. We can be just as busy up here—but down there it's always slow motion. It seems like they just don't care at all. They always take all the time in the world.

On the other hand, the cooks blamed the inefficiency of the runners for many of their troubles. They felt that the runners were constantly sending up duplicate orders just through failure to consult each other on the progress of their work. Actually, according to our observation, this happened very rarely, but whenever a runner was caught in the act, this was taken as proof that duplication was common practice. The failure of the runners to coordinate their work efficiently did annoy the cooks in another way, as they were sometimes asked for the same order within a few seconds by two different runners. However, while this added to the nervous tension, it did not directly affect the flow of supplies.

Such were the problems of supply in one restaurant where we were able to give them close attention. However, as it stands, this account is likely to give a false impression. The reader may picture the restaurant as a series of armed camps, each one in constant battle with its neighbor. He may also get the impression that food reaches customers only intermittently and after long delays.

To us it seemed that the restaurant was doing a remarkable job of production and service, and yet, in view of the frictions we observed, it is only natural to ask whether it would not be possible to organize the human relations so as to make for better teamwork and greater efficiency.

According to one point of view, no basic improvement is possible because "you can't change human nature."

But is it all just personalities and personal inefficiency? What has been the situation in other restaurants of this type (operating on several floors) and in other periods of time?

Unfortunately we have no studies for other time periods, but we do have the testimony of several supervisors who have had previous experience in restaurants facing similar problems, and who have shown themselves, in the course of our study, to be shrewd observers of behavior in their own organizations. Their story is that the friction and incoordination we observed were not simply a war-time phenomenon. While increased business and inexperienced help made the problem much more acute, the friction came at the same places in the organization—between the same categories of people—that it used to. The job of the kitchen runner, apparently, has always been a "hot spot" in such an organization.

This, then, is not primarily a personality problem. It is a problem in organization design. When the organization operates so as to stimulate conflict between people holding certain positions within it, then we can expect trouble.

Questions:

1. What kind of coordination problems existed at Chandler's Restaurant?
2. Are differences in status of cooks, runners, potwashers, and sweepers related to their positions in the organizational hierarchy? Explain.
3. What are the career satisfaction possibilities for a cook working at Chandler's Restaurant?

Part IV
The leading function

11. Elements of leading
12. Interpersonal and organizational communications
13. Motivation and performance
14. Work groups and performance

A management profile
George E. Johnson

George E. Johnson was born in Richton, Mississippi, in a three-room sharecropper's shack. At the age of three, with his mother and two brothers, he moved to Chicago in the era of the Great Depression. Though times were bleak, George and his brothers were blessed with a devoted, self-sacrificing mother, from whom he learned the virtues of hard work.

By school age, George helped support the family by shining shoes at a local hotel and collecting bottles and junk to sell for spare change. At 17, he dropped out of high school to take a full-time job. He started as a busboy, became a waiter, and in the evenings, worked as a pinsetter in a bowling alley.

A major turning point in George's life was the decision he made to join his brother in working for the Fuller Products Company, a prominent black-owned cosmetics manufacturer. George progressed quickly under the direction of S. B. Fuller, George's role model and mentor.

Starting in sales and later moving into research and development, George familiarized himself with product formulations, management techniques, and general business knowledge of the industry to which he would dedicate his life. He prepared himself to be a leader who would be respected by fellow employees and subordinates.

While working at Fuller Products, George fortuitously met a barber who wanted to have developed a chemical hair straightener superior to anything then available. Intrigued with the challenge, George spent nearly a year working nights and weekends developing the product.

Finally in 1954, when George was 27, he perfected his new product, and he made the big move. With $250, George launched his own business venture, initially in partnership with the Chicago barber, and began manufacturing the company's first product, Ultra Wave Hair Culture.

The business was not an overnight success; sales were steady, but not spectacular. To minimize overhead, he and his wife, Joan, worked out of a rented storefront, and George traveled from town to town selling the product from his station wagon. What profits they made were put back into product development, manufacturing equipment, and personnel to produce quality products for black hair-care needs.

Their years of persistence and commitment to quality ultimately paid off. Today, Johnson Products Company is the recognized leader in the ethnic personal-care industry, with sales exceeding $45 million and over 500 employees. The company, listed on the American Stock Exchange, markets over 100 hair-care and cosmetic products on four continents. Its administrative offices and manufacturing facilities are spread over 23 acres on Chicago's South Side, in the heart of the black community. The company also has a manufacturing facility in Lagos, Nigeria.

Despite his success, George Johnson has not forgotten his early struggles and remains deeply committed to helping black youth and prospective entrepreneurs achieve their goals. Because of his guiding spirit, Johnson Products is often called the "company with a conscience." George Johnson has been a leader with a deep concern for people.

Through the George E. Johnson Educational Fund, which Johnson established in 1972 with a personal gift of $1.5 million, more than 500 inner-city youth have received grants for college study. The Johnson Foundation supports a variety of civic and social-welfare organizations whose goals are to improve the quality of life for disadvantaged Americans.

Introduction to part IV

Part IV, the leading function, contains four chapters. They are:

Chapter 11—Elements of leading
Chapter 12—Interpersonal and organizational communications
Chapter 13—Motivation and performance
Chapter 14—Work groups and performance

The inclusion of the material contained in the four chapters is based upon the following rationale:

The leading function is defined as attempts of managers to influence through interpersonal and organizational communications the behavior of individuals and groups to achieve performance objectives. The **elements of leading,** presented in Chapter 11, consist of task and person-oriented influence attempts. The effective leadership attempt is contingent upon the leader's personality, the needs of individuals and groups, and factors in the situation itself. Numerous theories have been proposed to identify the circumstances in which a particular kind of influence attempt will be effective.

Leaders **exercise influence through communications.** Although the most apparent communication channels are interpersonal ones, more formal organizational channels such as memorandums, written directives, and policies are also important. Chapter 12 reviews some of the more important ideas on communication from the perspective of the leading function.

Finally, Chapters 13 and 14 present relevant information on the objects of leadership influence—individuals and groups. Chapter 13 describes theory and practice in the use of **motivation to influence individual performance.** Methods such as job enrichment, behavior modification, and pay programs are presented. Chapter 14 deals with the positive and negative **effects of work groups on performance objectives.**

The figure below depicts the four aspects of the leading function.

The leading function

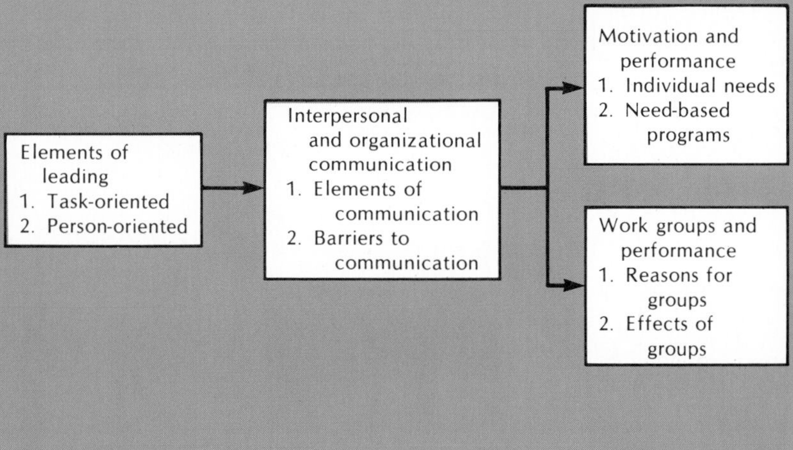

11

Chapter eleven Elements of leading

Performance objectives

- **Define** leadership in terms which are meaningful to managers.
- **State** the three general approaches to the study of leadership.
- **Describe** the two primary functions of leadership.
- **Explain** why leadership is a necessary management function.
- **Discuss** the primary conclusions to be drawn from each of the three general approaches to the study of leadership.

Management update*

Many people believe that effective leadership is a personal quality. It is assumed by some that unless one possesses that quality, he or she is doomed to failure as a leader. The search for people with this quality is often frustrating, confusing, and difficult.

Winston Churchill is a good example of one who had the right leadership quality. He was a good manager first. He could identify problems, weigh alternatives, and make decisions. He sent people into action when many didn't want to go. And here is where a distinction between leadership and managership can be seen. For the people who perceived Churchill as correct in his assessment and his plan, he was both a manager and a leader. But for the dissenters, he was only their manager until the moment when they could agree that what was good for England was also good for them as individuals.

Organizations today continue to search for talented people who possess leader and manager attributes. They need these multitalented, creative, inspirational individuals to point the way and influence others. Just as was true with Winston Churchill, leadership exists in the eye of the beholder. Becoming the top executive at a company like Dr Pepper illustrates a recent search for the best leader.

W. W. (Foots) Clements, president and CEO of Dr Pepper, sought his eventual successor for about five years. During the 1970s, he tried to groom two executive vice presidents—Joe K. Hughes and Frederick F. Avery—as candidates. It was a contest to see who was the best man. However, in the end, Clements startled everyone by picking Charles L. Jarvie from Procter & Gamble as his successor.

Why did Dr Pepper look for its leader from outside? Clements indicated that he'd have preferred to promote someone from within the firm. However, he concluded that inside candidates didn't have all the right qualities. Jarvie seemed to have the qualities that Clements wanted.

Jarvie is described this way. "He's a people man, and he knows the business of marketing and distributing consumer products from A to Z. He started in bar-soap sales at P&G and rose from there through the ranks." Dr Pepper valued Jarvie's sensitive understanding of human nature. It was this characteristic which put Jarvie at the top of the talent pool.

---

* This Management Update is based on William G. Smith, "Dr Pepper Picks a President," *Texas Business*, May 1980, pp. 15–16.

Leadership is important and necessary for achieving individual, group, and organizational performance. Managers, whether they are chief executive officers or first-level supervisors, influence attitudes and expectations that encourage or discourage performance, secure or alienate employee commitment, reward or penalize achievement. Despite the growth of large, impersonal organizations, people still relate to leaders. We see this in our everyday lives, and we make judgments about the leaders of our business, governmental, and educational organizations. Leadership does make a difference.

This chapter reviews some of the current theories and ideas about leadership. We will see that efforts to analyze effective leadership have focused on three general areas: (1) **the personal characteristics of leaders,** (2) **the behavior of leaders,** and (3) **the situations in which leaders are found.** A great deal of effort has been expended to understand leadership, yet it is impossible to state that there is a one best way to lead. Rather, the contingency view is that the best way to lead varies with the forces that exist in specific situations.

Ideas about leadership are held by practicing managers. And what they believe will certainly affect how they practice management. As stated by a commissioner of public health:

> *Leadership is the process of creating a work environment in which people can do their best work.*

The commissioner acted on his belief by attempting to train the managers of his organization in the application of good human relations.

A superintendent of a component part subassembly line stated her view of leadership as:

> *Leadership is getting people to do their work willingly, even when they don't really want to do it at all. Most of the time they don't want to work at the necessary pace, and my job is to convince them that they should do it anyway.*

The superintendent's idea about leadership reflects in part her assumptions about individuals.

Leadership involves other people; therefore, as there are leaders, there must also be followers. Leadership can arise in any situation in which people have combined their efforts to accomplish a task. Thus, leaders may or may not be managers. Within the organization, informal groups develop, and within those groups are people who influence the behavior of other group members. Such people are the **informal leaders.** Managers who influence the behavior of their assigned groups are the **formal leaders** of organizations. Our emphasis in this chapter is formal leadership; that is, managers who must exhibit leadership behavior.

Functions of leaders

Leadership involves simultaneous attention to (1) the tasks to be accomplished by groups and individuals and (2) the needs and expectations of groups and individuals.

The two broad leadership functions and the intended effects of those functions are shown in Figure 11–1. Leaders exercise influence through **communication** to specify the task-related activities of the individuals and

Figure 11–1

A concept of leadership

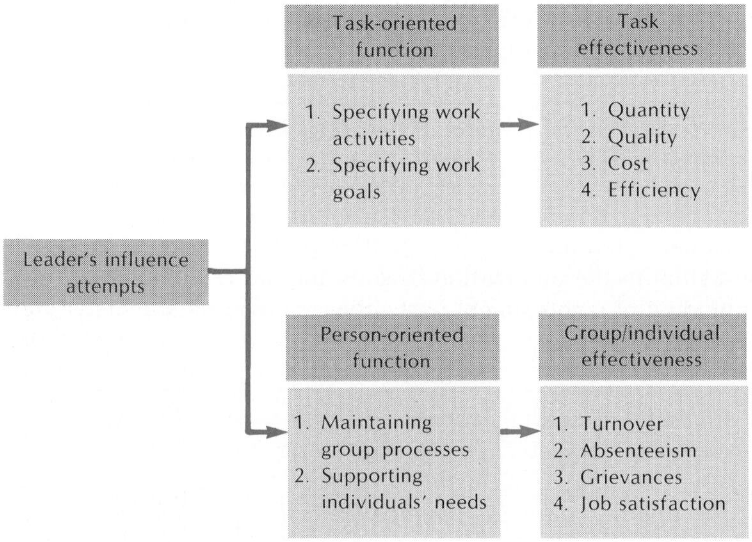

groups. These activities are, in turn, required to achieve effective performance. At the same time, leaders exercise influence to maintain their groups' ability to work as units and also to support the specific needs of individuals. Performance criteria such as turnover, absenteeism, grievances, and job satisfaction are achieved through effective leadership.

A manager in specific situations may not recognize that effective leadership requires attention to *tasks* and *people*. No doubt, experienced managers develop in time a particular style which reflects their own ideas and perspectives on the relative importance of tasks and people. As stated by one successful nurse administrator:

> *When I first became a manager of other nurses, it was easy for me to believe that our work was the most important responsibility I had. As I grew older, I began to realize that I was responsible for the well-being of my nurses as well as our patients. In fact, I believe I am now wise enough to see that effective nursing management does not require a choice between patients and nurses.*

Thus, we can think about leadership as consisting of influence attempts. These attempts are intended to achieve two separate yet related types of functions: (1) task-oriented functions and (2) person-oriented functions. Task-oriented functions are achieved by specifying work activities and work goals of the group as a whole and of each individual member of the group. Person-oriented functions require leaders to maintain group processes and to support individuals' needs and aspirations. Figure 11–1 summarizes our concept of leadership.

Personal characteristics of effective leaders

Leaders are different from other people. If they were not different, we wouldn't be interested in them. We observe them, and we note that they are able to influence other people to do things that those people would perhaps not want to do. It is then natural to ask whether the secret of leadership is to be found in the characteristics of leaders. Are there differences between leaders and nonleaders in terms of personality traits, physical characteristics, motives, and needs?

The systematic study of the personal characteristics and traits of leaders began as a consequence of the need for military officers during World

War I. Many business and governmental organizations also began to attempt to discover the characteristics which distinguished their most effective managers from the least effective ones.

The studies that attempt to identify the characteristics of effective leaders have produced a lengthy list of traits. These traits can be grouped into six categories as follows:

1. Physical characteristics—age, height, weight.
2. Background characteristics—education, social class or status, mobility, experience.
3. Intelligence—ability, judgment, knowledge.
4. Personality—aggressiveness, alertness, dominance, decisiveness, enthusiasm, extroversion, independence, self-confidence, authoritarianism.
5. Task-related characteristics—achievement need, responsibility, initiative, persistence.
6. Social characteristics—supervisory ability, cooperativeness, popularity, prestige, tact, diplomacy.

As noted in the Management Update, many executives involved in the recruitment and selection of managers believe that the trait approach is as valid as any other method. However, the comparison of leaders by various physical, personality, and intelligence traits has resulted in little agreement.

Physical traits

Some advocates of the trait theory contend that the physical stature of a person affects ability to influence followers. For example, an extensive review of 12 leadership investigations determined that 9 of the studies found leaders to be taller than followers; 2 found them to be shorter; and one concluded that height was not the most important factor.[1] Other physical traits that have been studied with no conclusive results include weight, physique, and personal appearance.

Personality

Some studies have found several personality factors to be related in some, but not all, cases of effective leadership.[2] These studies have found that leaders with the drive to act independently and with self-assurance (e.g., with confidence in their leadership skills) are successful in achieving task and group performance.

One study suggests that successful leaders may be more perceptive than

---

[1] Ralph Stogdill, "Personal Factors Associated with Leadership," *Journal of Applied Psychology,* January 1948, pp. 35–71.

[2] Edwin E. Ghiselli, "Managerial Talent," *American Psychologist,* October 1963, pp. 631–41.

nonsuccessful leaders.[3] Accordingly, effective leaders are more proficient in differentiating their best from their poorest followers than are the less effective leaders. The leaders of high-performing groups maintain greater psychological distance between themselves and their followers than do the leaders of less effective groups.

Intelligence

After surveying the literature, one scholar concluded that leadership ability is associated with the judgment and verbal facility of the leader.[4] Another researcher concluded that an individual's intelligence is an accurate predictor of managerial success within a certain range.[5] Above and below this range, the chances of successful leadership decrease significantly. It should be noted, however, that the leader's intelligence should be close to that of the followers. The leader who is too smart or not smart enough may lose the followers' respect.

An example of leadership trait studies

Edwin E. Ghiselli, an important student of leadership, has studied eight personality traits and five motivational traits.[6] The traits he studied are:

Personality traits:
- Intelligence.
- Initiative.
- Supervisory ability.
- Self-assurance.
- Affinity for the working class.
- Decisiveness.
- Masculinity-femininity.
- Maturity.

Motivational traits:
- Need for job security.
- Need for financial reward.
- Need for power over others.
- Need for self-actualization.
- Need for occupational achievement.

---

[3] Fred Fiedler, "The Leader's Psychological Distance and Group Effectiveness," in *Group Dynamics*, ed. Dorwin Cartwright and Alvin Zander, (New York: Harper & Row, 1968) pp. 586–605.

[4] Stogdill, "Personal Factors."

[5] Ghiselli, "Managerial Talent."

[6] Edwin E. Ghiselli, *Explorations in Management Talent* (Pacific Palisades, Calif.: Goodyear Publishing, 1971).

Ghiselli's research findings suggest the relative importance of the traits as noted in Figure 11–2.

There are some shortcomings in the method of employing a trait approach and assuming, for example, that a manager who is decisive, self-assured, and intelligent will be an effective leader. First, the trait theory of leadership ignores the subordinates. The followers have a significant effect on the job accomplished by the leader. Second, except for Ghiselli, trait theorists have not specified the relative importance of the various traits. Should an organization attempt to find managers who are confident or managers who act independently—which trait should be weighted more? Third, the evidence is inconsistent. For every study that supports the idea that a particular trait is positively related to leadership effectiveness, another study finds a negative or no relationship. Finally, although large numbers of traits have already been uncovered, the list grows annually, suggesting that still others will be found in the future.

Figure 11–2

The relative importance of leader characteristics and effective leadership

Very important characteristics	Moderately important characteristics	Unimportant characteristics
1. Supervisory ability 2. Occupational achievement 3. Intelligence 4. Self-actualization 5. Self-assurance 6. Decisiveness	1. Lack of need for security 2. Working-class affinity 3. Initiative 4. Lack of need for financial reward 5. Maturity	1. Masculinity-femininity

Traits and characteristics are not completely valid indicators of leadership ability, yet some managers insist that they can size up candidates for jobs. The personnel manager of a paper products manufacturer stated the following:

> *I have had good success in selecting college graduates for jobs in the company. I look for a lot of things when I interview them on campus, but the most important thing is whether they have a record of achievement. I ask them to tell me what they have done to be proud of. If they have difficulty recalling accomplishments, I start thinking about the next name on the interview sheet.*

Behavior of effective leaders

The disappointing results of efforts to identify the characteristics of effective leaders have led to a somewhat different line of thought. Rather than focusing on the *characteristics* of effective leaders, an alternative is to focus on their *behavior*. The question then becomes: What do effective leaders *do* that ineffective ones *do not do?* For example, are effective leaders democratic rather than autocratic, permissive rather than directive, person oriented rather than task oriented? Or are effective leaders characterized by some balance of these behaviors? This line of questioning is based on the reasoning shown in Figure 11–3.

Terms such as *permissive-directive, democratic-autocratic, and person oriented–production-oriented* are nearly synonymous. Generally, these terms refer to whether the leader's behaviors reflect primary concern for the work or for the people who are doing the work. We noted earlier that the essence of leadership is getting work done through other people. One point of view holds that the one best way to lead is to be task oriented.

Task-oriented leadership

Scientific management techniques such as motion and time study, work simplification, and piece-rate incentive pay plans emphasize the need for leaders to plan each worker's job tasks and job outcomes. The leader is assumed to be the most competent individual in planning and organizing the work of subordinates. According to a major proponent of scientific management:

> The work of every workman is fully planned out by the management at least one day in advance, and each man receives . . . complete written instructions, describing in detail the task which he is to accomplish, as well as the means to be used in doing the work.[7]

Figure 11–3

Behavior of effective leaders

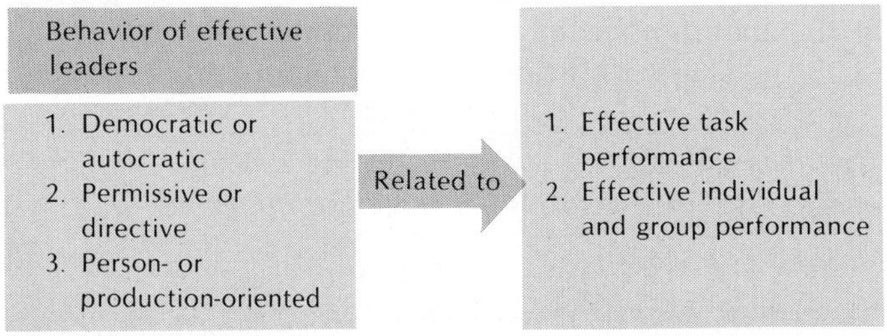

[7] Frederick W. Taylor, *Scientific Management* (New York: Harper & Row, 1911), p. 39.

To assure that each task is performed according to the plan, the worker is paid on an incentive basis. The performance standards are stated in terms of quantity and quality of output, and the worker is paid for each unit of acceptable quality.

The terms used to refer to leader behaviors which are concerned primarily with task goals and activities, i.e., the task function of leadership, include *directive, production oriented, autocratic,* and *initiating structure.* Each of these terms is used in the literature of contemporary management and leadership. Although the origins of task-oriented leadership are to be found in literature first published some 70 years ago, some modern leaders still believe that task-oriented behavior is the most effective for obtaining performance. As stated by the superintendent of a metal fabricating shop:

> *My most effective foremen know what their people should be doing, and they tell them how to do it. In our business, people have to produce or we are not in business.*

Person-oriented leadership

A pioneer in the development of the idea that the behaviors of the most effective leaders are person oriented is Rensis Likert. He and his associates at the University of Michigan have conducted studies in various organizational settings—industrial, governmental, educational, and health care. These studies have led Likert to believe that the most effective leaders focus on the human aspects of their groups. They attempt to build effective teamwork through supportive, considerate, *employee-centered* behavior. Such leaders were found to be more effective than those who emphasized task-centered behavior, that is, those leaders who specifically detailed the work of subordinates,[8] closely supervised them, and rewarded them only with financial incentives.

The idea that effective leaders are person oriented is an outgrowth of the behavioral approach to management, particularly the human relations branch. The concept that people seek a wide array of satisfactions through work is at the core of many management practices. It is not surprising that it should also be the underpinning of a popular point of view regarding leadership. As the chief executive officer of a major corporation stated:

> *The quality of leadership in business* [in the 1980s] *will depend to a great extent on securing the informed*

[8] Rensis Likert, "Management Styles and the Human Component," *Management Review,* October 1977, pp. 23–28 and 43–45.

consent of those who are led. . . . The day of the autocratic taskmaster is over.

Thus, it would seem that we are left with the choice that the effective leader is *either* task oriented *or* person oriented, *but not both.* And if this is the case, then aspiring leaders need only a narrow range of skills. If the most effective leaders are task oriented, then leaders need only be skilled in the technical aspects of planning and organizing the work of others. But if the most effective leaders are person oriented, then human relations and interpersonal skills are required. But what if both points of view are correct? Some believe that effective leaders are equally task and person oriented in their behavior toward subordinates.

The idea that the one best way to lead effectively requires a balance between task- and person-oriented behavior has considerable appeal. Two approaches to studying this idea have become well known in the theory and practice of leadership. The first is the **two-dimensional theory** and the second is the **managerial grid theory.**

Two-dimensional theory

One of the most significant investigations of leadership has been an ongoing program at The Ohio State University that began immediately after World War II. The researchers associated with this program have produced many studies of leadership effectiveness. The two key concepts in the two-dimensional theory are **initiating structure** and **consideration.** Initiating structure refers to task-oriented behavior in which the leader organizes and defines the relationships in the group, establishes patterns and channels of communications, and directs the way in which work is to be done. Consideration refers to person-oriented behavior in which the leader exhibits friendship, trust, respect, and warmth toward subordinates.

Generally, the behaviors of leaders who emphasize initiating structure fall into a consistent pattern. They tend to insist that subordinates follow standard ways of doing things in every detail; they insist on being informed; they push their subordinates for greater effort; they decide in detail what shall be done and how it shall be done. Considerate leaders express appreciation for jobs well done, stress the importance of high morale, treat everyone as equals, and are friendly and approachable.

One study of the relationship between initiating structure and consideration and leadership effectiveness focused on first-level management—supervisors in a manufacturing facility. The measures of leadership effectiveness included proficiency ratings made by top management, absenteeism, accident rates, grievances, and turnover. The study found that supervisors of line departments (production) scored high on proficiency ratings if they also scored high on initiating structure and low on consideration. However, supervisors of staff departments were most proficient when they scored low on initiating structure and high on consideration. Subsequent studies tended to conclude that supervisors who score high on both dimensions are generally more effective than those who score low.[9]

Managerial grid theory

According to the proponents of the managerial grid theory, leaders are most effective when they achieve a high and balanced concern for people and for task.[10] Each leader can be rated somewhere along each of the axes from 1 to 9 depending on his or her orientation. This idea is shown in Figure 11–4.

Although there are 81 possible positions in the grid, attention is drawn to 5 of them:

1. *The 9, 1 leader* is primarily concerned for production and only minimally concerned for people. This type of leader, termed *task management,* believes that the primary leadership responsibility is to see that the work is completed.
2. *The 1, 9 leader* is primarily concerned for people and only incidentally concerned for production. This leader, termed *country club management,* believes that a supervisor's major responsibility is to establish harmonious relationships among subordinates and to provide a secure and pleasant work atmosphere.
3. *The 1, 1 leader,* termed *impoverished management,* is concerned for neither production nor people This leader would attempt to stay out of the way and not become involved in the conflict between the necessity for production and the attainment of good working relationships.
4. *The 5, 5 leader* reflects a middle-ground position and is thus termed *middle-of-the-road management.* A leader so described would seek to compromise between high production and employee satisfaction.
5. *The 9, 9 leader's* behavior is the most effective—it is the one best way. This style, termed *team management,* is practiced by leaders who achieve high production through the effective use of participation and involvement of people and their ideas.

The managerial grid is used to assess the actual leadership styles of men and women prior to training. An important assumption of this approach is that people can be trained to become 9, 9 leaders. Thus a 1, 9 or a 9, 1 leader can change and become more effective by learning the behaviors associated with 9, 9 leadership.

---

[9] Edwin A. Fleishman and James G. Hunt, eds., *Current Developments in the Study of Leadership* (Carbondale: Southern Illinois University Press, 1973), pp. 1–37.

[10] Robert S. Blake and Jane S. Mouton, *The Managerial Grid* (Houston: Gulf Publishing, 1964).

Figure 11–4

Managerial grid®

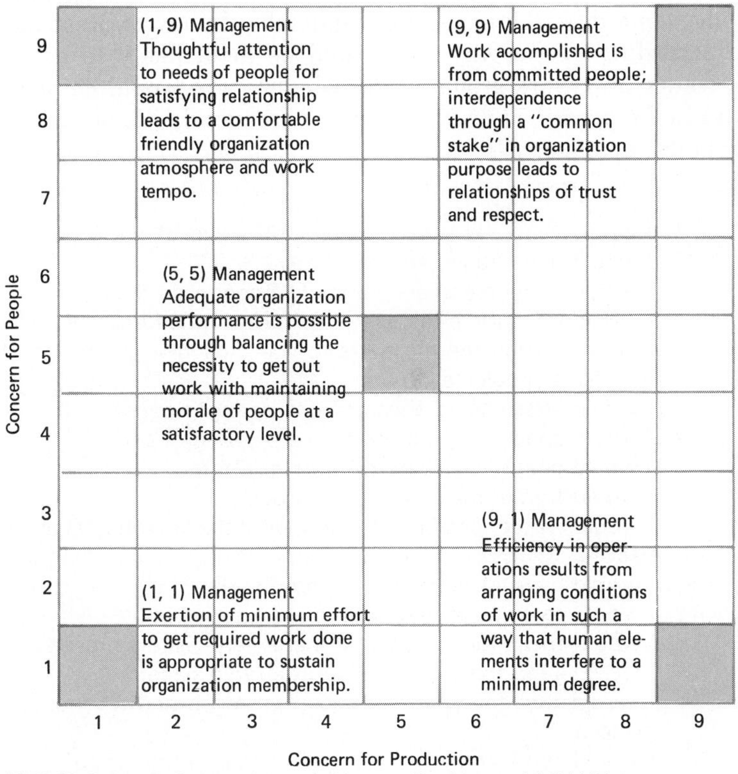
(1, 9) Management
Thoughtful attention to needs of people for satisfying relationship leads to a comfortable friendly organization atmosphere and work tempo.
(9, 9) Management
Work accomplished is from committed people; interdependence through a "common stake" in organization purpose leads to relationships of trust and respect.
(5, 5) Management
Adequate organization performance is possible through balancing the necessity to get out work with maintaining morale of people at a satisfactory level.
(9, 1) Management
Efficiency in operations results from arranging conditions of work in such a way that human elements interfere to a minimum degree.
(1, 1) Management
Exertion of minimum effort to get required work done is appropriate to sustain organization membership.
Concern for People
Concern for Production
1
2
3
4
5
6
7
8
9

SOURCE: Robert R. Blake and Jane S. Mouton, *The Managerial Grid* (Houston: Gulf Publishing, 1964), p. 10.

The significant contribution of the two-dimensional and managerial grid theories is that they force us to seek more complete answers to the question "What is effective leadership?" The trait theory simply requires the leader to have the appropriate characteristics; the one best way behavior theories require the leader to choose between person- and task-oriented behavior. But the answer may be more complex than even that suggested by the balanced 9, 9 approach. As yet we have not considered the impact of different *situations* on effective leadership.

The reader may at this point wish to assess his or her own leadership style. The following questionnaire is based on two-dimensional leadership theory and, specifically, the managerial grid. By completing the questionnaire and scoring your answers, you can get a fairly good idea of your leadership style tendencies at this point in your life.

The task-people (T-P) leadership questionnaire

The following items describe aspects of leadership behavior. Respond to each item according to the way you would be most likely to act if you were the leader of a work group. Circle whether you would be most likely to behave in the described way: always (A), frequently (F), occasionally (O), seldom (S), or never (N).

A F O S N	1. I would most likely act as the spokesman of the group.
A F O S N	2. I would encourage overtime work.
A F O S N	3. I would allow members complete freedom in their work.
A F O S N	4. I would encourage the use of uniform procedures.
A F O S N	5. I would permit the members to use their own judgment in solving problems.
A F O S N	6. I would stress being ahead of competing groups.
A F O S N	7. I would speak as a representative of the group.
A F O S N	8. I would needle members for greater effort.
A F O S N	9. I would try out my ideas in the group.
A F O S N	10. I would let the members do their work the way they think best.
A F O S N	11. I would be working hard for a promotion.
A F O S N	12. I would tolerate postponement and uncertainty.
A F O S N	13. I would speak for the group if there were visitors present.
A F O S N	14. I would keep the work moving at a rapid pace.
A F O S N	15. I would turn the members loose on a job and let them go to it.
A F O S N	16. I would settle conflicts when they occur in the group.
A F O S N	17. I would get swamped by details.
A F O S N	18. I would represent the group at outside meetings.
A F O S N	19. I would be reluctant to allow the members any freedom of action.
A F O S N	20. I would decide what should be done and how it should be done.
A F O S N	21. I would push for increased production.
A F O S N	22. I would let some members have authority which I could keep.
A F O S N	23. Things would usually turn out as I had predicted.
A F O S N	24. I would allow the group a high degree of initiative.
A F O S N	25. I would assign group members to particular tasks.
A F O S N	26. I would be willing to make changes.
A F O S N	27. I would ask the members to work harder.
A F O S N	28. I would trust the group members to exercise good judgment.
A F O S N	29. I would schedule the work to be done.
A F O S N	30. I would refuse to explain my actions.
A F O S N	31. I would persuade others that my ideas are to their advantage.

A F O S N 32. I would permit the group to set its own pace.
A F O S N 33. I would urge the group to beat its previous record.
A F O S N 34. I would act without consulting the group.
A F O S N 35. I would ask that group members follow standard rules and regulations.

T _____ P _____

Scoring the T-P questionnaire To score your responses, follow these directions:

1. Circle the item number for items 8, 12, 17, 18, 19, 30, 34, and 35.
2. Write the number 1 in front of a *circled item number* if you responded S (seldom) or N (never) to that item.
3. Also write a number 1 in front of *item numbers not circled* if you responded A (always) or F (frequently).
4. Circle the number 1's which you have written in front of the following items: 3, 5, 8, 10, 15, 18, 19, 22, 24, 26, 28, 30, 32, 34, and 35.
5. *Count the circled numbers 1's.* This is your score for concern for people. Record the score in the blank following the letter *P*.
6. *Count the uncircled number 1's.* This is your score for concern for task. Record this number in the blank following the letter *T*.

Shared leadership results from balancing concern for task and concern for people

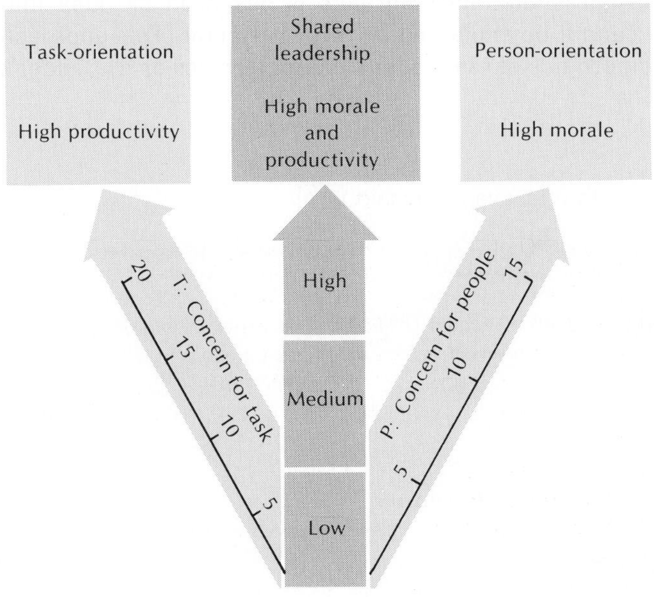

The T-P leadership-style profile sheet To determine your style of leadership, mark your score on the concern for task dimension (T) on the left-hand arrow shown on page 295. Next, move to the right-hand arrow and mark your score on the concern for people dimension (P). Draw a straight line that intersects the P and T scores. The point at which that line crosses the shared leadership arrow indicates the extent to which you have a balanced concern for tasks and people.

Situational leadership

Efforts to find the one best set of leadership traits and the one best set of leadership behaviors have been largely unsuccessful. Contemporary managers are more and more prone to believe that the practice of leadership is too complex to be represented by unique traits *or* behaviors. Rather, the idea that effective leadership behavior depends on the situation is a current theme. But even this idea is not now fully settled. One variation of the idea assumes that leaders must change the behaviors to meet situational needs. A second variation assumes that leaders' behaviors are difficult to alter and that the situation itself must be changed to make it compatible with the leaders' behavior.

The situational approach to leadership is considerably more complex than either the trait approach or the behavioral approach. As indicated in Figure 11–5, effective leadership depends on the interaction of the leader's personal characteristics, the leader's behavior, and factors in the leadership situation. In a sense, the situational approach is based on the idea that effective leadership cannot be explained by any one factor. This approach does not deny the importance of the leader's characteristics or the leader's

Figure 11–5

The situational approach to effective leadership

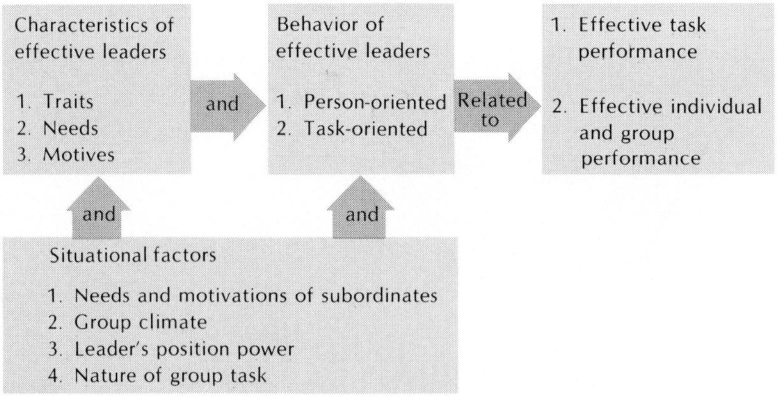

behavior. Rather, it states that *both* must be taken into account and considered in the context of the situation in which the leader must lead.

Leadership flexibility: Fit the style to the situation

A recurring theme in leadership theory and practice is the concept of *participation* by subordinates in decision making. This theme originated in the writings of the behavioral approach to management, and it has held a prominent place in the thinking of managers for the last 40 years. The fundamental idea is shown in the leadership continuum of Figure 11–6.[11]

Figure 11–6

Continuum of leadership behavior

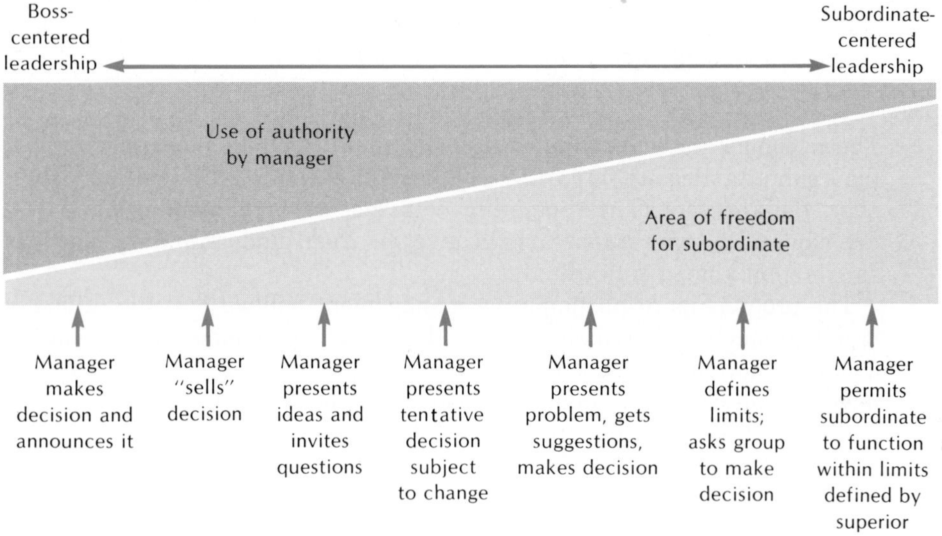

At the extremes of this continuum are boss-centered leadership and subordinate-centered leadership. Between these extremes are five points representing various combinations of managerial authority and subordinate freedom. One of the extreme positions, boss-centered leadership, represents a manager who makes a decision and announces it. As the director of a policy and budget division in a state government stated:

> *I believe in getting things done. I cannot afford to waste time on meetings deciding what we should be doing.*

[11] Robert Tannenbaum and Warren H. Schmidt, "How to Choose a Leadership Pattern," *Harvard Business Review*, May–June 1973, pp. 162–80.

The policy and budget analysts are here to work. Somebody needs to call the shots, and the governor says I'm that person.

We would expect this director to make decisions regarding the division's work activities and to announce the decision. But there is an exactly opposite position, subordinate-centered leadership.

The subordinate-centered leader permits subordinates to participate fully in decision making. Within prescribed limits, the subordinates act as partners with the leader. The manager of a secretarial pool in a major university stated:

Whenever we have to make a change in our operations or when we receive an excessive work load, I put the problem squarely to them. I try to help them make the decision by helping them understand their own thoughts and feelings. It takes time.

These comments reflect the attitude of many leaders who believe that their subordinates are important sources of job-related information. Moreover, the very act of participating with the leader in making important decisions can bring about a high level of trust, understanding, and job satisfaction among subordinates.

The proponents of participative management believe that the difficulty is not so much in convincing people that they must change their behavior as the situation changes, but in teaching leaders how to recognize the need for the change. A number of guidelines have been proposed to help leaders identify situations which lend themselves to participative decision making.

Whether a leader should make the decision and announce it (boss centered) or share the problem with subordinates and seek group consensus (subordinate centered) depends on the interaction of factors related to the problem and to the subordinates. Factors related to the *problem* are:[12]

1. The likelihood that one solution to the problem is more effective than another.
2. The extent to which the leader has sufficient information to make a high-quality decision.
3. The extent to which alternative solutions are known with some certainty.

[12] Victor Vroom and Arthur Jago, "Decision-Making as a Social Process: Normative and Descriptive Models of Leader Behavior," *Decision Sciences*, 1974, pp. 743–70.

Factors related to *subordinates* are:

1. The likelihood that effective implementation of the solution depends on subordinates accepting it as appropriate.
2. The likelihood that if the leader makes the decision, the subordinates will accept it.
3. The extent to which subordinates recognize and accept the organizational objectives to be attained by the solution.
4. The likelihood that conflict among subordinates will result if the preferred solution is adopted.

In a practical sense, combining these seven factors results in different situations. At one extreme are situations for which a number of solutions exist, none of which require the acceptance by subordinates for effective implementation. The manager should make the decision and announce it. On the other hand, participation is warranted to the extent that only one solution is likely and its consequences are not known with certainty *and* subordinates have relevant information *and* their acceptance is necessary for implementation. The effective leader changes style whenever demanded by the situation. That is, the leader is flexible enough to be relatively task centered or employee centered as situations change. Whether leaders can be flexible is arguable. Indeed, one influential leadership theory is based on the idea that leaders cannot easily change their behaviors and that it is therefore better to change the situation.

Leadership inflexibility: Fit the situation to the leader's style

Based on a considerable body of research evidence, Fiedler has developed an important contribution to the situational theory of leadership.[13] The theory identifies three important *situational factors* or *dimensions,* which are assumed to influence the leader's effectiveness. The dimensions identified are:

1. *Leader-member relations.* This refers to the degree of confidence which the subordinates have in the leader. It also includes the loyalty shown to the leader and the leader's attractiveness.
2. *Task structure.* This refers to the degree to which the subordinates' jobs are routine rather than nonroutine.
3. *Position power.* This refers to the power inherent in the leadership position. It includes the rewards and punishments typically associated with the position, the leader's official authority (based on ranking in the managerial hierarchy), and the support that the leader receives from superiors and the overall organization.

[13] Fred E. Fiedler and Martin M. Chemers, *Leadership and Effective Management* (Glenview, Ill.: Scott, Foresman, 1974).

Fiedler has obtained data which relate leadership style to the three-dimensional measures of different situations. Fiedler's measure of leadership style distinguishes between leaders who tend to be permissive and considerate and to foster good interpersonal relations among group members and leaders who tend to be directive, controlling, and more oriented toward task than toward people. Fiedler suggests that leaders who are directive and leaders who are permissive can function best in certain types of situations. Instead of stating that a leader must adopt this or that style, Fiedler identifies the type of leader who functions best in a given situation. According to Fiedler, we should not talk simply about good leaders or poor leaders. A leader who achieves effectiveness in one situation may not be effective in another. The implication of this logic is that managers should think about the situation in which a particular leader (subordinate manager) performs well or badly. Fiedler assumes that managers can enhance subordinates' effectiveness if they carefully choose situations that are favorable to the subordinates' style.

Figure 11–7 presents some of Fiedler's findings about the relationship of the three dimensions to leadership style for such groups as bomber crews, management groups, high school basketball teams, and steel mill crews. A review of Figure 11–7 indicates a relationship between effective task performance and directive leadership under conditions 1, 2, 3, and 8, and a relationship between effective task performance and permissive leadership under conditions 4 and 5. These results indicate that in certain situations a particular leadership style achieves the best results.

Figure 11–7

Summary of Fiedler's investigations of leaderships

	Group situation			
Condition	Leader-member relations	Task structure	Position power	Leadership style correlating with performance
1	Good	Structured	Strong	Directive
2	Good	Structured	Weak	Directive
3	Good	Unstructured	Strong	Directive
4	Good	Unstructured	Weak	Permissive
5	Moderately poor	Structured	Strong	Permissive
6	Moderately poor	Structured	Weak	No data
7	Moderately poor	Unstructured	Strong	No relationship found
8	Moderately poor	Unstructured	Weak	Directive

An example of an effective leader under condition 1 could be the following:

> *A well-liked head nurse in a university medical center is in charge of getting the nursing team ready for open-heart surgery. The tasks which must be performed by the head nurse are very tightly structured. There is no room for error or indecision, and the duties of everyone on the nursing team are clearly specified. The head nurse has complete power to correct any personnel or performance problems within the nursing team.*

An example of a leader who is working under condition 5 would be the following:

> *A recent college graduate's first job assignment was to supervise 18 technicians in a manufacturing plant in Chicago. Most of the technicians had little education past the eighth grade and had worked for more than 10 years in the plant. They generally believed that college kids were either wise guys or good people, but they took their time deciding. Because they were genuine experts on their job, a formal leader had very little control over sequencing or structuring the job. The job was structured by the experts, and the manager actually concentrated on paperwork, not technical work.*

Some pragmatic procedures for improving a leader's relations, task structure, and position power are as follows:

1. Leader-member relations could be improved by restructuring the leader's group of subordinates so that the group is more compatible in terms of background, educational level, technical expertise, or ethnic origin. It should be noted that this would be extremely difficult in a unionized group, since the group may assume that this restructuring is a management plan to weaken the union.
2. The task structure can be modified in the structured or the nonstructured direction. A task can be made more structured by spelling out the jobs in greater detail. A task can be made less structured by providing only general directions for the work that is to be accomplished. Some workers like minimum task structure, while others want detailed and specific task structure.
3. Leader position power can be modified in a number of ways. A leader can be given a higher rank in the organization or more authority to do

the job. In addition, a leader's reward power can be increased if the organization delegates authority to evaluate the performance of subordinates.

Thinking about leadership

A framework for understanding and integrating contemporary leadership theory is proposed in Figure 11–8. The framework emphasizes the effect of the *leader's background and experiences* on (1) the *leader's qualities,* such as communicative ability, self-awareness, and confidence; and (2) the *leader's perceptions* of subordinates, the situation, and the self. The interaction of all these factors is important in determining the *leader's ability* to *influence* others. The manner in which these variables interact and the proportionate weight of each are not known with certainty, but there is no doubt of their importance.

The leader should consider a number of important organizational and environmental variables, as illustrated in Figure 11–8. In the context of the leadership framework, the effective leader influences followers in such a manner that high productivity, high group morale, low absenteeism and turnover, and the development of followers are achieved. Figure 11–8 specifies only three personal qualities which contribute significantly to a leader's ability to influence others. The three qualities are suited for most leadership

Figure 11–8

A framework for thinking about leadership

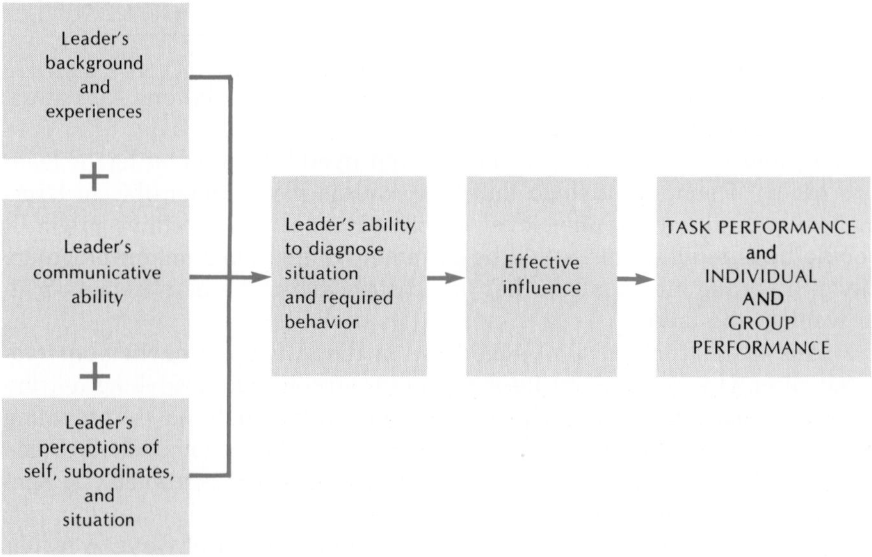

styles and are especially compatible with the situational, or contingency, theory of leadership.

One of the most important factors in the situational approach to leadership centers on leader self-awareness. Leaders should be aware of the impact of their behaviors on those they lead even though they cannot predict accurately in every situation how those behaviors will affect followers. Leaders should attempt to learn more about their influence on others.

Every leader must be able to communicate with followers. The leader who fails to communicate with followers may become ineffective as an influencer of others. As noted in the Management Update, Winston Churchill was a great leader who had great skills as a communicator. The following chapter examines in detail the problems and potential of communications.

Apparently, an important ability of effective leaders is to understand themselves, their subordinates, and their situations. They must understand the causes and effects of individual motivation and behavior and group dynamics and behavior. Leadership training programs should stress diagnostic and adaptability skills. It should not be concluded that managers can be easily trained to diagnose work situations accurately and to develop appropriate leadership abilities. Rather, patience is essential if leaders are to become flexible enough to change their leadership styles.

Management summary

1. Leadership is the ability to influence followers through the use of power. The use of different bases of power will elicit different reactions from followers.
2. The trait approach to leadership has attempted to relate personal characteristics and effective leadership. Despite much study and effort, no conclusive results are available to guide managers in selecting future leaders.
3. The idea that effective leaders behave differently from ineffective leaders has led to inconclusive results. An important issue is whether an individual can shift between person-oriented behavior and task-oriented behavior.
4. The situational approaches to leadership are more complex than the trait and behavior approaches. The complexity arises from the necessity to consider the interactions of the leader, behavior, and the situation.
5. The situational approaches are based on two different assumptions about leadership flexibility. One approach assumes that leaders can and must change their behavior to fit the situation; the other approach assumes that leaders cannot change their behavior but must change the situation.

6. The most important conclusion from leadership theory is that managers must understand their own abilities and their impact on others.

Review and discussion questions

1. Do you believe that a manager can be effective if he or she is not considered by subordinates to be a leader? Explain.
2. Can leadership concepts be applied in the classroom setting? That is, can the teaching styles of your professors be described as person oriented and task oriented? Are these distinctions useful for analyzing why some professors are more effective than others? Explain.
3. Leadership is obviously one factor that contributes to the performance of a group or an organization. What other factors can you think of, and how important are they in comparison to leadership?
4. It is often said that . . . leaders are born, not trained. . . . In light of what you have studied about the trait theory of leadership, how would you respond to that statement?
5. "Person-oriented leadership is OK if you are only interested in employee satisfaction, but if you want to get the job done, then task-oriented leadership is the only way." Evaluate this quotation.
6. What is your reaction to the idea that an effective leader must be able to shift from person orientation to task orientation as the situation dictates? Do you believe that you can be flexible in your behavior? Explain.
7. Describe in practical terms the ways in which a manager's job can be altered to fit his or her leadership style.
8. In how many of the eight situations described in Fiedler's theory have you had work experience? Describe in detail one of those experiences and determine whether the manager was using the "appropriate" style.
9. "The failure of many organizations is not due to the absence of leadership, but rather to the absence of the followership." What does this statement mean? Comment on the statement.

Suggested reading

Broder, D. S. *Changing of the Guard: Power and Leadership in America.* New York: Simon & Schuster, 1980.

Howard, A. and D. W. Bray. "Today's Young Managers: They Can Do It, but Will They?" *Wharton Magazine,* Summer 1981, pp. 23–28.

Loomis, C. J. "Archie McCardells' Absolution." *Fortune,* December 15, 1980, pp. 89–98.

Maccoby, M. *The Leader.* New York: Simon & Schuster, 1981.

Margerison, C. "Leadership Paths and Profiles." *Leadership & Organization Development Journal,* Winter 1980, pp. 12–17.

Marth, D. "How the Top Bulldog Learned His Way Up." *Nation's Business,* December 1981, pp. 56–60.

Owens, J. "A Reappraisal of Leadership Theory and Training." *Personnel Administrator,* November 1981, pp. 75–84, 98–99.

Placky, R. J. "Leading vs. Managing: A Guide to Some Crucial Distinctions." *Management Review,* September 1981, pp. 58–61.

Watson, K. M. "An Analysis of Communication Patterns: A Method for Discriminating Leader and Subordinate Roles." *Academy of Management Journal,* March 1982, pp. 107–20.

Applying what you have learned about elements of leading

Cases:

Leadership at Revlon, Inc.
Changing a leadership style

Leadership at Revlon, Inc.*

Michel Bergerac is chairman and chief executive of Revlon, Inc. As head of one of the world's largest cosmetic companies, he's asked and paid to be a skillful manager and an inspirational leader. He makes about $1.1 million a year for a company with sales of about $2.5 billion a year. Bergerac has taken a company that was identified with one man—its autocratic founder, Charles Revson—and made it his own. Revson started the cosmetics empire on a $300 nail-enamel business and built it by his own unfailing intuition for what women would perceive as glamorous.

And what has Bergerac done? Since 1975, the year he took over, Revlon's sales have increased at a compound annual rate of 24 percent and are now over $2.5 billion annually. The company's beauty business in the United States is now somewhat sluggish. Bergerac faced this sluggishness by pushing Revlon harder into the health care area. The revenues in health care have multiplied eight times since Bergerac arrived. Revlon is now the major collector of human blood in the United States, after the Red Cross. It breaks down the blood chemically, selling elements like the clotting factor for treating hemophiliacs and the much-touted but unproved anticancer substance interferon.

Bergerac is pushing health care harder than ever, and some people question this strategy. However, one fact is not questioned at Revlon and that is Bergerac's leadership style. He is given high marks for bringing professional management to a company that had none. One executive recalls that when Bergerac first asked his managers for five-year plans, "we

* This case is adapted from Ann M. Morrison, "Revlon's Surprising New Face," *Fortune*, November 2, 1981, pp. 72–80.

looked at him like he was speaking Hindustani. For us, planning meant the next season, the next look."

Now, every part of Revlon is run on an annual budget, and the head of every department reports on it in a monthly management letter. The letter always begins with an "action alert"—a short paragraph flagging the trouble spots in an executive's operation. "I try not to shoot the messenger," Bergerac says. "If someone has bad news, he (1) should know that he's got bad news, (2) have a plan to correct it, and (3) be prepared to do it within a reasonable time frame."

Once a month, Bergerac holds a management meeting at Revlon's corporate headquarters. The meetings take place around a custom-built 38-foot conference table with built-in speakers and microphones. Sessions begin promptly at 10:00 A.M. and often don't break up until after midnight. Bergerac and his staff sit on one side of the table, and the operations people sit on the other.

One by one, executives defend their business in front of their peers and their boss. A screen at one end of the room shows the financial information that goes along with the business under discussion. Bergerac wants the words being expressed to match the data. He also wants to hear from each manager that he or she has accomplished a 8.5 percent aftertax return on sales.

After some success in his first five years at Revlon, some critics are beginning to question Bergerac's style and decisions. He is being accused of neglecting the bread and butter of Revlon, the cosmetics business. His style is said to provoke a high degree of anxiety on managers who are asked to perform in front of peers. Some also feel that Revlon is making a mistake by becoming involved with human blood products. They claim that Bergerac's leadership skills will be tested when there is a consumer backlash to Revlon's step into the health care field.

Questions:

1. What leader traits and behavior describe Michel Bergerac of Revlon?
2. How do you rate Bergerac's communication ability as the top executive at Revlon?
3. Should Bergerac's managers be asked to perform in front of peers? What do you think?
4. Is a leader like Bergerac worth the salary he receives—about $1.1 million a year? Explain.

Changing a leadership style

The thermocoupling research group was a subunit of the nuclear engineering department of a large corporation. The group contained 20 persons, most of whom had or were working toward Ph.D.s. The organization of the group was well defined, and the manager had insisted on following the formal rules and procedures of the company whenever problems occurred.

The group was currently working on a project to develop coupling units that would withstand the wear, tear, and temperature changes of space travel. The manager was Marianne Newley, a 35-year-old Ph.D. physicist. The 19 other employees in the group were assigned to three sections: analysis, experimental, and testing and quality control. The section leaders were Marla Beeler, Allen Samuels, and Jason Martin.

Marianne was known around the company as a competent, but often abrasive, manager. She worked long hours and was assigned difficult projects because of her record of doing excellent work. Subordinates, however, often complained about her lack of concern for them and about her obsession with finishing the job on time and within the allocated budget.

Marianne's superior, Mark Neeley, was aware of the complaints and wanted Marianne to reconsider her leadership style. He called her into his office and asked her to attend a three-week leadership training program. The training program covered the managerial grid theory of leadership. The bulk of the training focused on self-diagnosis through the managerial grid and discussions of leadership behavior and effectiveness.

Marianne's attendance at the training program occurred just before her present assignment in the thermocoupling group. Twelve of the group's members had worked with her on other projects and were aware of her task-oriented behavior. After attending the training course, Marianne's style became somewhat more people oriented. She asked for more advice from subordinates, and she also encouraged them to voice complaints about her methods of running the project. In the past, she would never ask subordinates for advice and she would become angry when subordinates questioned her decisions. She still insisted, however, that the rules and policies regarding work hours, time off, and bid preparation be followed exactly as stated in the company operating manual.

The individuals who had worked for Marianne previously were puzzled by her sudden change of behavior. They were skeptical about accepting her suggestion that they voice their complaints. One of the section leaders, Marla Beeler, visited with Mark Neeley and informed him that the group was disorganized because of Marianne's behavior. The conversation between them proceeded as follows:

Mark: Hi, Marla. Can I help you with anything?

Marla: I sure hope so. Mark, we just do not know what to do in our project group. Marianne is completely different than before, and her attitudes toward us seem strange.

Mark: What do you mean, strange?

Marla: Well, she is asking for advice, and in six years, this has never happened.

Mark: Perhaps the training program she attended is paying off.

Marla: Come on, Mark. We think it is the quiet before the storm, and we are not buying any of it. You just cannot teach or train a person so rapidly.

Mark: Are you familiar with the managerial grid and the power of this technique?

Marla: The behavioralists have really brainwashed you. The grid is something I studied in college. I know it is not as powerful as you believe. You just can't change a leader's style with a broad-brush approach.

This meeting with Marla puzzled Mark, and he reexamined what was said in the conversation. He then called in Marianne, and their discussion proceeded as follows:

Mark: Marianne, how are things going?

Marianne: Fine, I'm on schedule and rounding the turn for home on the project.

Mark: How was the training program?

Marianne: Interesting, but not very challenging. They talked about leadership and the "mystery zone" of effective leadership behavior. I found out that my predominate style is 9, 1. I ended up a 6, 5 after the program. However, when I'm pressed, I may become 100, 1.

Mark: Do you feel any differently about your subordinates now?

Marianne: No, except I know that they expect me to be more employee centered after attending the training program. Thus, I have made some gradual changes in my style. If they work, who knows, I may change permanently.

Mark: What do you mean?

Marianne: My group is superintelligent, and they know that you do not change overnight. You just do not become a 9, 9 without a long period of trial and error. In fact, 9, 9 would be a disaster in my group.

Mark was taken aback once again. He had learned a lot about leadership style just by discussing the topic with two intelligent and articulate people.

Questions

1. Do you believe that any change in Marianne's leadership style has occurred?
2. What does Marianne mean when she states, "In fact, 9, 9 would be a disaster in my group"?
3. Should Marianne have been sent to the training program in the first place? Why?

12

Chapter twelve Interpersonal and organizational communications

Performance objectives

- **Define** the concept of communications from a leadership perspective.
- **State** the basic elements of communications.
- **Describe** the typical communication flows in an organizational setting.
- **Explain** how a leader can minimize the barriers to effective communication.
- **Discuss** the important psychological variables that affect interpersonal communications.

Management update*

Many companies, large and small, are reluctant to discuss salary-related information with employees. A survey conducted by Hewitt Associates, a management consulting firm, verified this reluctance in 248 companies. The survey focused on management's willingness to communicate with employees about salaries.

In general, the survey found that companies avoid telling employees more than the bare minimum about salaries and the corporate salary structure. Why? Many employers indicated they fear that disclosing salary information could violate the confidentiality of individual salaries, or that most employees would not understand the complexities of a salary administration program. On most of the 14 salary issues included in the survey, the responding companies indicated they communicate with employees about salary information "only when asked to do so" or "not at all."

The survey revealed three general salary communication patterns. First, companies seem most inclined to share general information about the salary administration process and individual salaries. According to respondents, performance appraisal is the salary topic most communicated about. Over half of all respondents said they routinely communicate with employees about performance standards.

How frequently the salary structure is updated to keep pace with inflation is another "routinely" discussed salary matter. Over 60 percent of the responding companies tell top and middle managers about salary structure updating, while 41 percent share this information with lower-level salaried employees.

Second, companies communicate more openly about salary issues with top executives and middle managers than with lower-level salary employees. Among all companies, 27 percent routinely tell top executives what an "average raise" is for their position or level, versus 11 percent who explain the average raise to lower-level salaried employees.

Third, medium-sized companies seem to be more willing to discuss and communicate salary information with employees than large companies are. On nearly all the salary issues (e.g., size of raises, average raise per level), medium-sized companies were more open communicators than large companies.

---

* This Management Update is based on "More Communication," *Personnel Journal*, September 1981, p. 668.

Communicating and communication are vital aspects of the managerial function of leading. In the managerial leadership perspective, communications are the means for *influencing* individuals and groups to attain performance objectives. The pervasive use of communications to attain effective performance is underscored by the chief executive officer of a medium-sized utility:

> *There is no more important managerial responsibility than to communicate effectively. We must continually strive to convince the public that our actions are in the interests of providing efficient energy, that we are not gouging our customers, that our wages are fair, and that our profits are not excessive. No matter what is, in reality, the case, if we cannot get our message across, then reality becomes whatever customers, employees, and government officials want to believe.*

Effective communication is so important for managerial performance that our discussion of what it is and how it is achieved should reflect its full complexity. A framework for understanding the complexity of communications is presented in the following section. Next, the topic of organizational communications is presented, followed by consideration of some of the problems associated with interpersonal communications. The chapter concludes with a discussion of the causes and cures of communication breakdowns.

A framework for understanding communications

Communication is defined as **the transmission of mutual understanding through the use of symbols.** The definition underscores the fact that unless mutual understanding results from the transmission of symbols, there is

Figure 12–1

A framework for communication

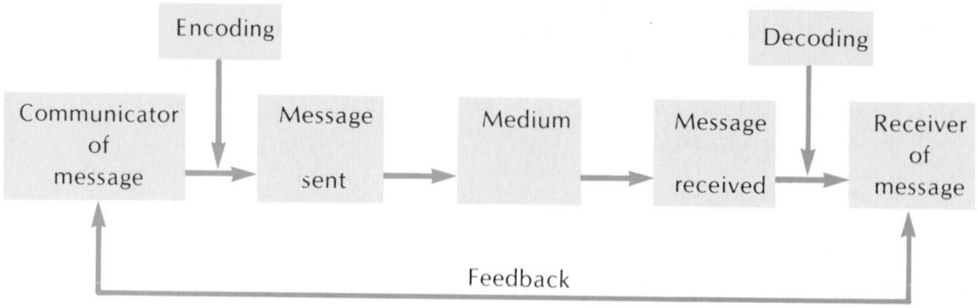

no communication. Figure 12–1 reflects the definition and identifies the important elements of communication.

As shown in Figure 12–1, the basic elements of communication are the *communicator, encoding,* the *message,* the *medium, decoding,* the *receiver,* and *feedback.* In simple terms, an individual or a group of individuals (the communicator) has an idea, message, or understanding to transmit to another individual or group of individuals (the receiver). To transmit the idea, the communicator must translate the idea into a language (encoding) and send the message by verbal, nonverbal, or written means (the medium). The message is received through the senses of the receiver and translated (encoded) into a message received. By a nod of the head, a facial expression, or action, the receiver acknowledges whether understanding has been achieved (feedback). Let us examine each element more closely.

The communicator

Communicators in an organization can be managers, nonmanagers, departments, or the organization itself. Managers communicate with other managers, subordinates, supervisors, clients, customers, and parties outside the organization. Nonmanagers likewise communicate with managers and nonmanagers, clients, customers, and external parties. People in sales departments communicate with people in production departments, and engineering personnel communicate with product design teams. Communications within the organization are important means for coordinating the work of separate departments. And more and more organizations communicate with employees, unions, the public, and government. Each of these communicators has a message, an idea, or information to transmit to someone or some group.

Encoding

The communicator's message must be translated into a language which reflects the idea; that is, the message must be encoded. The reader of spy novels is familiar with the scene in which the enemy (or friendly) agent has a message to send to headquarters. To prevent friendly (or enemy) agents from obtaining the message and understanding it, the agent transmits the message in *code,* a language persumably known only by the agent and headquarters. In less dramatic and intriguing situations, encoding is usually the selection of language specific to the purpose of the communicator's message. The encoding action produces the message.

The message

The result of the encoding process is the message. The purpose of the communicator is expressed in the form of the message—either verbal or nonverbal. Managers have numerous purposes for communicating, such as to have others understand their ideas, to understand the ideas of others, to gain acceptance of themselves or their ideas, and to produce action. The message, then, is what the individual hopes to communicate, and the exact form that the message takes depends to a great extent on the medium used to carry it. Decisions relating to the two are inseparable.

The medium

The medium is the carrier of the message. Organizations provide information to their members by a variety of means, including face-to-face communication, telephone, group meetings, computers, memos, policy statements, reward systems, production schedules, and sales forecasts.

Not as obvious, however, are *unintended messages* that can be sent by silence or inaction on a particular issue as well as decisions on which goals and objectives are *not* to be pursued and which methods are *not* to be utilized. Finally, such nonverbal media as facial expressions, tone of voice, and body movements also communicate.

Decoding

The decoding element refers to the process by which receivers *translate* the message into terms that are meaningful to them. If headquarters uses the same code book that the agent used in preparing the coded message, then the message that headquarters receives will be the same as the message that the agent sent. But if the code is known only to the agent, then no common understanding can be reached. In a business organization, if the message that the chief executive receives from the accounting department includes many technical terms that are known to accountants, but not to nonaccountants, no communication exists. An often cited complaint in organizations which employ staff specialists is that they cannot communicate. Each staff group has a language and symbols that persons outside the group cannot decode.

The problem of decoding is reflected in the complaint of a project team leader:

> *My team includes representatives from all the functional units—production, accounting, engineering, computing, and legal. The first three months of this project were a fiasco. We were assigned the responsibility of preparing a bid for a big government contract, but you would think that we represented the interests of five different firms. Accountants would present their analyses in jargon; engineers would use every technical phrase they learned in school; the legal beavers spoke in Latin. Finally, I said that anyone who could not use words that could be understood by a high school student would be kicked off the team. We then made some progress because everybody understood me.*

The receiver

Communication requires a receiver. The foregoing discussion of decoding difficulties underlines the importance of taking the receiver into account when a communicator attempts to transmit information. "Telling isn't teaching" if the teacher uses language that the student cannot understand (cannot decode). Engineers cannot expect to communicate to nonengineers if the symbols they use are beyond the receivers' training and ability to comprehend. Effective communication requires the communicator to anticipate the receiver's decoding ability, to know where the receiver comes from. Effective communication is receiver oriented, not sender oriented.

Feedback

Feedback enables the communicator to determine whether the message has been received and has produced the intended response. *One-way* communication processes do not allow receiver-to-communicator feedback. *Two-way* communication processes provide for such feedback. For the manager, communication feedback may come in many ways. In face-to-face situations, *direct* feedback is possible through verbal exchanges as well as through such subtle means as facial expressions that indicate discontent or misunderstanding. In addition, communication breakdowns may be indicated by *indirect* means, such as declines in productivity, the poor quality of production, increased absenteeism or turnover, and conflict or a lack of coordination between units.

Organizational communications

Managers must provide for communication in four distinct directions: downward, upward, horizontal, and diagonal. Since these four directions establish the framework within which communication takes place in an organization, let us briefly examine each of them. This examination will enable the manager to better appreciate the barriers to effective organizational communication and the means for overcoming those barriers.

Downward communication

Downward communication flows from individuals at higher levels of the organization to those at lower levels. The most common forms of downward communications are job instructions, official memos, policy statements, procedures, manuals, and company publications. In many organizations, downward communication is often both inadequate and inaccurate, as noted in the results of the survey reported in the Management Update. The absence of information can create unnecessary stress among organization members.

Philips Industries, a British firm, communicates downward with members of its seven unions through annual conferences of management and labor. The principal purpose of the conferences is to allow the firm to give a "state-of-the-company" report to the union leadership. The focus of the report is the broad economic problems facing Philips. The communication of ideas and views between the management and union officials is carried on without reference to salaries and contracts. The proceedings of the conference are videotaped and made available to all personnel in the 25 Philips plants in the United Kingdom.

An American company, Pitney Bowes, has made special efforts to develop effective downward communications. One of its most successful practices is its annual "jobholders' meeting." The annual employees' meetings have much the same purpose as stockholders' meetings, and that is to give the persons who attend a face-to-face management accounting on the progress of the business. The employees not only hear from management, but they are also invited to raise questions on matters of specific concern to them. The use of open, scheduled meetings between management and employees is a growing practice in the United States.

In large organizations, the practice of employee communications is typically undertaken by a staff of communication experts. The usual function of the staff is to produce a publication aimed at these three purposes: (1) to explain the organization's plans and programs as they are implemented, (2) to answer complaints and criticisms, and (3) to defend the status quo and those who are responsible for it. The medium often selected to accomplish these purposes is a periodic publication. The publication's intended messages are those which present the organization's side of issues. Large organizations are more and more viewed with distrust and suspicion. Although they may not always be successful in convincing the general public that their actions are public minded, it has become increasingly necessary for them to win the support of their employees.

Upward communication

A high-performing organization needs effective upward communication as much as it needs effective downward communication. Effective upward communication is difficult to achieve, especially in larger organizations. However, effective upward communication is often necessary for sound decision making. Widely used upward communication devices include suggestion boxes, group meetings, and appeal or grievance procedures. In the absence of these flows, employees find ways to adapt to nonexistent or inadequate upward communication channels, as is evidence by the emergence of underground employee publications in many large organizations.

The practices of ESCO Corporation of Portland, Oregon, reveal the company's commitment to upward communications. Employees in this company who wish to communicate directly with top management—whether to express complaints, suggestions, questions, compliments, or comments—simply dial a listed telephone number and state their views. The calls are recorded, transcribed, and reviewed by ESCO's vice president of industrial relations in charge of personnel. The vice president forwards the transcriptions to the appropriate department managers for reply and action. If callers give their names, they receive a written answer; if they choose to be anonymous, the answers are posted on the bulletin board. No call is unanswered, and each call is answered within 48 hours.

Effective upward communications are important because they provide employees with opportunities to have a say. They are equally important because top management depends on subordinates for vital information. The dependence of top management on upward communications is well illustrated by the comments of the dean of the business school in a state university:

> *I sit at the top of an organization that has a bewildering variety of activities. We teach graduate and undergraduate students, undertake executive and continuing education, provide assistance to small business, and do contract research. The faculty and professional staff must represent every scientific discipline from mathematics to management to economics. Now it is impossible for me to know what is going on in all these activities. I depend completely on what my chairpersons and directors tell me. I have*

to trust them to be honest and honorable in communicating with me. Funny thing is, I know that the university president is in the same boat with me. It makes you wonder who manages who around here.

Horizontal communication

Often overlooked in the design of most organizations is provision for the horizontal flow of communication. When the supervisor of the accounting department communicates with the director of marketing concerning advertising budget expenditures, the flow of communication is horizontal. Although vertical (upward and downward) communication flows are the primary considerations in organizational design, effective organizations also need horizontal communication. Horizontal communication—for example, between production and sales in a business organization and between different departments within a hospital—is necessary for the coordination of diverse organizational functions.

Managers who recognize the need for horizontal communication can appoint committees of representatives from the departments. One plant manager routinely meets each Monday at 7:30 A.M. with each department head to go over the upcoming week's work schedule, to review progress toward objectives, and to anticipate any problems that will require the attention of more than one department. The use of routinely scheduled staff meetings can facilitate horizontal communication. The more interdependent the work of the departments, the greater is the need to formalize horizontal communication.

Figure 12–2

Organizational information flows

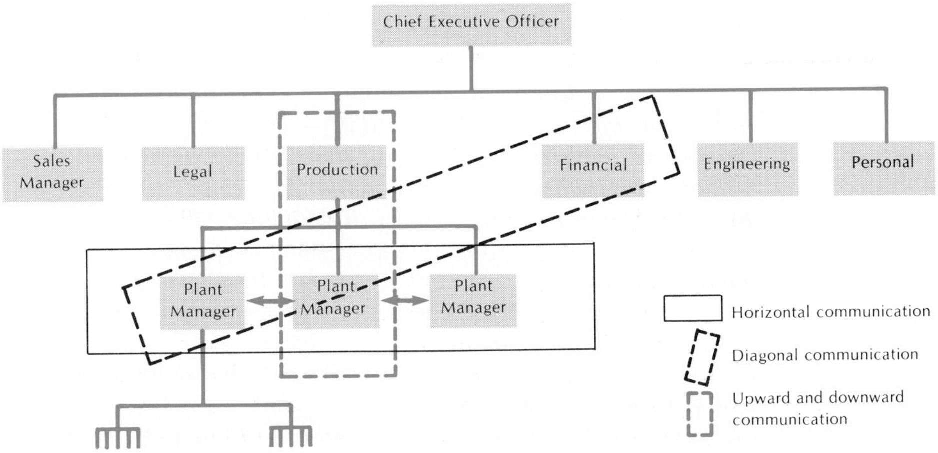

Diagonal communication

Although diagonal communication is probably the least-used channel of communication in organizations, it is important in situations in which members cannot communicate effectively through other channels. For example, the comptroller of a large organization may wish to conduct a distribution cost analysis, and one part of the analysis may involve having the sales force send a special report directly to the comptroller rather than go through the traditional channels in the marketing department. Thus, the flow of communication would be diagonal rather than vertical (upward) and then horizontal. In this case, the use of a diagonal channel would minimize the time and effort expended by the organization.

The four directions of organizational communication flows are depicted in Figure 12–2. The flows shown are representative only. Many others can and do exist.

Interpersonal communications

Communication flows from individual to individual in face-to-face and group settings. Such flows are termed *interpersonal communications,* and they vary in form from direct orders to casual expressions. A review of the typical manager's daily activities bears out the importance of interpersonal communication. One study of the work of managers determined that they receive and transmit a large quantity of information and that they favor *verbal* rather than *written* means of communication. But we need not rely on studies to appreciate the importance of communication for achieving high-managerial performance. For example, the store manager of a fast-food franchise stated:

> *It seems like all I do is talk, tell, relate, debate, or whatever you want to call it. Day in and day out, I am constantly talking to the people who are supposed to be working for me. I have a daily—yes, daily—meeting of each shift crew. I tell them what has been going on and what needs to be done. And then I have to go back and tell each one of them again. Maybe I am not a very good communicator, but I sure get a lot of practice.*

Whether the store manager is a good communicator is not the point. The fact is that he does a lot of communicating.

The problems which arise when managers attempt to communicate with

Figure 12–3

Interpersonal styles and communication

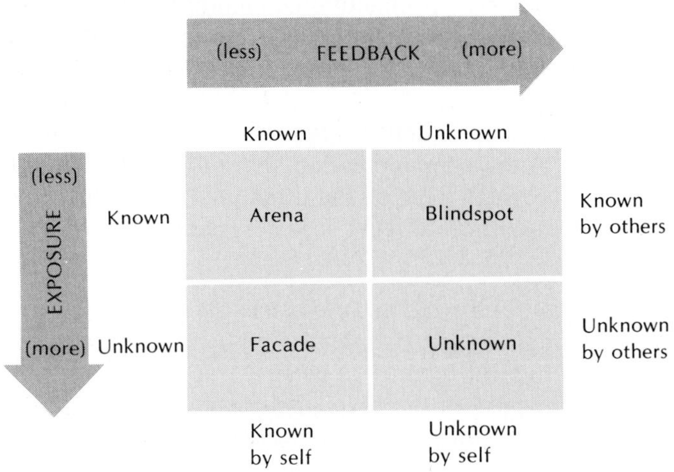

other people can be traced to *perceptual* and *interpersonal style differences.* Each manager perceives the world in terms of his or her background, experiences, personality, frame of reference, and attitude. The primary manner in which managers relate to and learn from the environment (including people in that environment) is through information received and transmitted. And the way in which managers receive and transmit information depends, in part, on how they relate to two important *senders* of information, *themselves* and *others.*

Interpersonal styles

Interpersonal styles differ among individuals, and these differences are important for managerial and organizational performance. **Interpersonal style refers to the way in which an individual prefers to relate to others.** The fact that much of the relationship among people involves communication indicates the importance of interpersonal style.[1]

We begin by recognizing that information is held by self and by others, but that you and I do not fully have or know that information. The different combinations of knowing and not knowing information are shown in Figure 12–3. The figure identifies four regions, or combinations, of information known and unknown by self and others.

---

[1] This discussion is based on Jay Hall, "Communication Revisited," *California Management Review,* 1973, pp. 58–67.

The arena The region which is most conducive for effective interpersonal relationships and communications is termed the *arena*. In this setting, all the information necessary to carry on effective communication is known to both the sender (self) and the receivers (others). As expressed in the current cliché, each party to the communication knows where the other comes from.

In practical terms, if a communication attempt is in the arena region, this means that the parties to the communication share identical feelings, data, assumptions, and skills which bear on the attempt. The arena region is reflected in the words of a corporate legal services manager:

> *When I have to go to our plants to discuss the implications of the Robinson-Patman Act for our pricing policies, the highlight of the day is when I discuss the issues with the lawyers in the plant. They know what I am talking about, and they understand the importance of compliance. But trying to tell the marketing group what is going on is a futile exercise. They simply cannot relate to the issue because they are not knowledgeable. They are trying to sell the product; I am trying to keep us out of court.*

The blindspot When relevant information is known to others, but not to self, a blindspot area results. In this context, a person (self) is at a disadvantage when communicating with others because he or she cannot know their feelings, sentiments, and perceptions. Consequently, interpersonal relationships and communications suffer.

The blindspot results when one party is unable to know his or her true feelings or sentiments about an issue and is thus unable to perceive accurately the information received from others. The idea of *selective perception* relates to blindspot problems, since when a blindspot exists, an individual is likely to be unable to receive and decode information properly. The greater the blindspot, the smaller the arena, and vice versa. One individual expressed her difficulty in communicating to her subordinates as follows:

> *The women I manage have no ambition. They do not want to get ahead. They tell me that they work simply to get the money to help their families stay ahead of inflation. But why should they be content with their situation? Why should they not seek more responsibility? After all, there is more to life than raising kids and pleasing husbands.*

The supervisor who expressed the above viewpoint was blinded by her own perceptions and biases. Consequently, she had considerable difficulty in communicating with her subordinates.

The facade When information is known to the self but unknown to others, person (self) may resort to superficial communications; that is, he or she may present a facade. A facade is a false front. The facade area is particularly damaging when a subordinate "knows" and an immediate supervisor "does not know." The facade, like the blindspot, diminishes the area and reduces the possibility of effective communication.

An example of the facade in interpersonal relations and communications is reflected in the words of a university department chairperson who said of the dean:

> *The dean doesn't really understand the kind of research we do in the economics department. He is a psychologist by training, and his inability to recognize good economic research prevents him from appreciating the work done in the economics department. But I can't challenge him because he has the final say on salary administration, so I try to get what I can by playing up to his ego. I tell him that the economics faculty strongly support his efforts. Thus, I never have to tell him that he is ignorant of research.*

Why the economics department chairperson doesn't level with the dean is difficult to understand.

The unknown If neither party knows the relevant feelings, sentiments, and information, each party is functioning in the unknown region. As is often stated, "I can't understand them, and they don't understand me." In such situations, interpersonal communications are sure to suffer. The unknown problem often results in organizations when individuals in different technical areas must coordinate their activities through communications.

An example of this problem was provided by a commissioner of public health who had to meet with a commissioner of environmental quality on the matter of solid waste disposal:

> *I went to the meeting with the commissioner of environmental quality fully prepared to talk about the health implications of solid waste disposal. He came in all set to go on the environmental aspects. Three hours later, we had made no progress toward developing an integrated cross-departmental effort. I didn't understand him, and he didn't understand me.*

We left the matter unresolved, and we still don't have an effective program.

Thus, we see that the larger the areas affected by blindspots, facades, and unknowns, the smaller the arena. But how can we reduce those areas and enlarge the arena?

Exposure and feedback

Interpersonal communication problems are the results of unsound relationships. An individual can improve unsound relationships by adopting two strategies—exposure and feedback.

Exposure Increasing the arena area by reducing the facade area requires that the individual be open and honest in sharing information with others. The unwillingness of companies to discuss salary matters as reported in the Management Update is an example of inadequate exposure. The process that the self uses to increase the information known to others is termed *exposure* because it leaves the self in a vulnerable position. Exposing one's true feelings and sentiments is a ploy that involves some risk. A contemporary sports announcer takes considerable pride in telling it like it is. Most readers will recognize who this announcer is and will also recognize that he is truly controversial.

Feedback When the self does not know or understand, more effective communications can be developed through feedback from those who do know. Thus, the blindspot can be reduced with a corresponding increase in the arena. Whether feedback is possible depends on the individual's willingness to hear it or the willingness of others to give it. Thus, the individual is less able to control the provision of feedback than the provision of exposure. Obtaining feedback is dependent on the active cooperation of others, while exposure requires the active behavior of the individual and passive listening by others.

Management styles and interpersonal styles

The day-to-day activities of managers place a high value on effective interpersonal communications. Managers provide *information* (which must be *understood);* they give *commands* and *instructions* (which must be *obeyed* and *learned*); they make *efforts to influence* and *persuade* (which must be *accepted* and *acted upon*). Thus, the way in which managers communicate, both as senders and receivers, is crucial for obtaining effective performance.

Managers who desire to communicate effectively can theoretically use both exposure and feedback to enlarge the area of common understanding, the arena. As a practical matter, such is not the case. Managers differ in their ability and willingness to use exposure and feedback. At least four different managerial styles can be identified:

Type A Managers who use neither exposure nor feedback are said to have a Type A style. The unknown region predominates in this style because the manager is unwilling to enlarge the area of his or her own knowledge or the knowledge of others. Such managers exhibit anxiety and hostility and give the appearance of aloofness and coldness toward others. If an organization has a large number of Type A managers in key positions, then we would expect to find poor and ineffective interpersonal communications and a loss of individual creativity. Type A managers often display the characteristics of autocratic leaders.

Type B Some managers desire some degree of satisfying relationships with their subordinates, but because of their personalities and attitudes these managers are unable to open up and express their feelings and sentiments. Consequently, they cannot use exposure and they must rely upon feedback. The facade is the predominant feature of interpersonal relationships when managers overuse feedback to the exclusion of exposure. The subordinates are likely to distrust such managers because they realize that these managers are holding back their own ideas and opinions. Type B behavior is often displayed by managers who desire to practice some form of permissive leadership.

Type C Managers who value their own ideas and opinions, but not the ideas and opinions of others, will use exposure at the expense of feedback. The consequence of this style is the perpetuation and enlargement of the blindspot. Subordinates will soon realize that such managers are not particularly interested in communicating, only in telling. Consequently, Type C managers usually have subordinates who are hostile, insecure, and resentful. Subordinates soon learn that such managers are mainly interested in maintaining their own sense of importance and prestige.

Type D The most effective interpersonal communication style is one which uses a balance of exposure and feedback. Managers who are secure in their positions will feel free to expose their own feelings and to obtain feedback from others. To the extent that the manager practices Type D behavior successfully, the arena region becomes larger and communication becomes more effective.

To summarize our discussion, we should emphasize the importance of interpersonal styles in determining the effectiveness of interpersonal communication. The primary force in determining the effectiveness of interpersonal communication is the attitude of managers toward exposure and feedback. The most effective approach is that of the Type D manager. Type A, B, and C managers resort to behaviors which are detrimental to the effectiveness of communication and to organizational performance.

Why communications break down

Communications in organizations take place among people and within the structure. Communications flow upward, downward, horizontally, and diagonally. Managers communicate with their managers, their peers, and their subordinates. A manager has no greater responsibility than to develop effective communications. However, communications often break down. Various problems account for breakdowns both in formal organizational communications, such as public relations press releases, and in interpersonal communications. In general, managers should recognize that a breakdown can occur whenever any one of the elements of communication—sender, encoding, media, decoding, receiver, or feedback—is defective.

Conflicting frames of reference

Individuals can interpret the same communication differently, depending on their previous experiences. This type of communication breakdown is related to the *encoding* and *decoding* elements. When the receiver and the sender use the same encoding and decoding language, then they achieve common understanding. But because each of us have a certain uniqueness in background and experience, words take on different meanings for different people. In terms of interpersonal communication, the arena area is relatively small when compared to blindspots, facades, and unknown area. To the extent that individuals have distinctly different frames of reference, communications among those individuals will be difficult to achieve.

One result of different frames of reference is that communications become distorted. For example, teenagers have different experiences than do their parents (the oft-cited generation gap?); district sales managers have different perceptions than do salespersons. In an organization, the *jobs* that people perform will create barriers and distortions in communications. For example, a pricing problem will be viewed differently by the marketing manager than by the plant manager. An efficiency problem in a hospital will be viewed by the nursing staff from its frame of reference and its experiences, and this may result in interpretations that differ from those of the staff physicians.

Different *levels* in the organization will also have different frames of reference. First-line supervisors have frames of reference that differ in many respects from those of vice presidents. First-line supervisors and vice presidents are in different positions in the organization's structure, and this influences their respective frames of reference. As a result, the needs, values, attitudes, and expectations of these two groups will differ, and this will often result in unintentional distortions of the communications between them. Neither group is wrong or right. In any situation, individuals will choose that part of their own past experiences which relates to their current experiences and is helpful in forming conclusions and judgments. Unfortunately, such incongruities in encoding and decoding result in barriers to effective communication.

Selective perception

Selective perception occurs when people block out new information, especially if it conflicts with what they believe. Thus, when people receive information, they are apt to hear only those words that reaffirm their beliefs. Information that conflicts with preconceived notions is either not noted or is distorted to confirm our preconceptions.

For example, a notice may be sent to all operating departments that costs must be reduced if the organization is to earn a profit. Such a communication may not achieve its desired effect because it conflicts with the "reality" of the receivers. Operating employees may ignore or be amused by the notice in light of the large salaries, travel allowances, and expense accounts of some managers. Whether these expenditures are justified is irrelevant; what is important is that such preconceptions result in breakdowns in communication. In other words, if people hear only what they want to hear, they cannot be disappointed.

An example of selective perception in action was related by the director of training of a government contractor:

> *When I announced to the staff that I planned to schedule in-house training programs to upgrade our ability to respond to federal affirmative action directives, the staff was up in arms because they heard me say that some of them were going to be replaced by minorities. Now that is not at all what I meant.*

Value judgments

In every communication situation, receivers make **value judgments** by assigning an overall worth to a message prior to receiving the entire communication. Such value judgments may be based on the receiver's evaluation of the communicator, the receiver's previous experiences with the communicator, or the message's anticipated meaning. Thus, a hospital administrator may pay little attention to a memorandum from a nursing team leader because "she's always complaining about something." An employee may consider a merit evaluation meeting with the supervisor as going through the motions because the employee perceives the supervisor as being concerned about administrative matters to the exclusion of performance.

Source credibility

Source credibility refers to the trust, confidence, and faith that the receiver has in the words and actions of the communicator. The level of credibility that the receiver assigns to the communicator, in turn, directly affects how the receiver views and reacts to the words, ideas, and actions of the communicator.

Thus, how subordinates view a communication from their manager is affected by their evaluations of the manager. The degree of credibility which they attach to the communication is heavily influenced by their previous experiences with the manager. A group of hospital medical staff who view the hospital administrator as less than honest, manipulative, and not to be trusted is apt to assign nonexistent motives to any communication from the administrator. Union leaders who view managers as exploiters and managers who view union leaders as inherent enemies are likely to engage in little real communication.

The problem of source credibility was aptly illustrated by this statement of a plant manager who was in the midst of a violent strike:

> *I cannot believe these guys. Whenever an employee comes to work for me, I assume that he becomes my enemy the moment he signs on. After all is said and done, we are at different ends of the spectrum. My interest is a quality product at competitive prices; the employees' interests are minimal quality and maximum wages. How can I believe that we have any common ground? It is in their interests to lie. I let my actions speak for me, and I am going to whip them this time.*

Semantic problems

Communication is the transmission of *information* and *understanding* through the use of *common symbols.* Actually, we cannot transmit understanding. We can only transmit information in the form of words, which are the common symbols. Unfortunately, the same words may mean entirely different things to different people. The understanding is in the receiver, not in the words.

When a plant manager announces that a budget increase is necessary for the growth of the plant, the manager may have in mind the necessity for new equipment, and expanded parts inventory, and more personnel. To the existing personnel, however, growth may be perceived as excess funds that can be used for wage and salary increases.

Again, because different groups use words differently, communication can often be impeded. This is especially true with abstract or technical terms or phrases. A *cost-benefit study* would have meaning to persons involved in the administration of the hospital but would probably mean very little to the staff physicians. In fact, it might even carry a negative meaning to the latter. Such concepts as *trusts, profits,* and *Treasury bills* may have concrete meaning to bank executives but little or no meaning to bank tellers. Thus, because words mean different things to different people, it is possible for a communicator to speak the same language as a receiver but still not transmit *understanding.*

Occupational, professional, and social groups often develop words and phrases that have meaning only to group members. Such special language can serve many useful purposes. It can provide group members with feelings of belongingness, cohesiveness, and, in many cases, self-esteem. It can also facilitate effective communication *within* the group. The use of in-group language can, however, result in severe semantic problems and communication breakdowns when outsiders or other groups are involved. Technical and staff groups often use such language in an organization, not for the purpose of transmitting information and understanding, but rather in order to communicate a mystique about the group or its function.

Filtering

Filtering communications amounts to "manipulating information" so that the information is perceived as positive by the receiver. Subordinates cover up unfavorable information in messages to their superiors. The reason for such filtering should be clear. Management makes merit evaluations, grants salary increases, and promotes individuals based on what it receives by way of the upward channel. The temptation to filter is likely to be strong at every level in the organization.

The design of the organization determines the extent to which information can be filtered. An organizational design with many levels of management (a "tall" organization) will experience more information filtration than will one with fewer levels (a "flat" organization). The reason is fairly simple: The more levels through which upward communications must flow, the greater is the opportunity for each successive layer of management to take out what it does not want the next level to know. An advantage of flat organizational designs is that they minimize the problem of filtration.

Time pressures

The pressure of time is an important barrier to communication. An obvious problem is that managers do not have the time to communicate frequently with every subordinate. However, time pressures can often lead to serious problems. *Short-circuiting* is a failure of the formally prescribed communication system which often results from time pressures. What it means is simply that someone has been left out of the formal channel of communication who normally would be included.

For example, suppose that a salesperson who needs a rush order for a very important customer goes directly to the production manager with the request, since the production manager owes the salesperson a favor. Other members of the sales force get word of this and become upset over this preferential treatment and report it to the sales manager. Obviously, the sales manager would know nothing of the deal, since the sales manager has been short-circuited. However, in some cases, going through formal channels is extremely costly or is impossible from a practical standpoint. Consider the impact on a hospital patient if a nurse had to report a malfunction in some critical life-support equipment in an intensive care unit to the nursing team leader, who in turn had to report it to the hospital engineer, who would then instruct a staff engineer to make the repair.

Communication overload

One of the vital tasks performed by a manager is decision making. One of the necessary conditions for effective decisions is *information.* Because of the advances in communication technology, difficulties may arise, not from the absence of information, but from excessive information. In fact, the last decade has often been described as the Information Era or the Age of Information. Managers are often deluged by information and data. As a result, they cannot absorb or adequately respond to all of the messages directed to them. They screen out the majority of messages, which in effect means that these messages are never decoded. Thus, the area of organizational communication is one in which "more" is not always "better."

The barriers to communication discussed here, though common, are by no means the only ones which exist. Examining these barriers indicates that they are either *within individuals* (e.g., frame of reference, value judgments) or *within organizations* (e.g., in-group language, filtering). This point is important because attempts to improve communications must focus on changing people and/or changing the organization structure.

How communications can be improved

Managers who are striving to become better communicators must accomplish two separate tasks. First, they must improve their messages—the information they wish to transmit. Second, they must improve their own *understanding* of what other people are trying to communicate to them; they must become better encoders and decoders. *They must strive not only to be understood but also to understand.* The techniques discussed here will help managers to accomplish these two important tasks.

Following up

This technique involves assuming that you are misunderstood and, whenever possible, attempting to determine whether your intended meaning was actually received. As we have seen, meaning is often in the mind of the receiver. An accounting unit leader in a government office communicates notices of openings in other agencies to the accounting staff members. Although this action may be understood among longtime employees as a friendly gesture, a new employee might interpret it as an evaluation of poor performance and a suggestion to leave.

The use and value of follow-up were learned by a young engineering department head. When asked what the most important lesson was that he had learned about communicating with the engineers, he said the following:

> *When I first became department head, it was necessary to have a lot of meetings with the staff engineers. I assumed, at first, that the entire department understood what we were deciding about technical and departmental matters. But then I discovered that that was not the case. I then began to make a written record of our decisions and circulated it to the staff. After I started doing that, the instances of people not knowing what was going on decreased.*

Regulating information flow

Regulating the flow of communications insures an optimum flow of information to managers, thereby eliminating the barrier of communication overload. Both the quality and quantity of communications are regulated. The idea is based on the **exception principle** of management, which states that only significant deviations from policies and procedures should be brought to the attention of managers. In terms of formal communication, then, managers should be communicated with only on matters of exceptions and not for the sake of communication.

Certain types of organizational designs are more amenable to this principle than are other types. Certainly, in Likert's System 4 organization, with its emphasis on free-flowing communication, the principle would not apply. However, System 1 organizations would find the principle useful.

Utilizing feedback

Feedback is an important element in effective two-way communication. It provides a channel for receiver response which enables the communicator to determine whether the message has been received and has produced the intended response.

In face-to-face communication, direct feedback is possible. In downward communication, however, inaccuracies often occur because of insufficient opportunity for feedback from receivers. Thus, distributing a memorandum on an important policy statement to all employees does not guarantee that communication has occurred. One might expect feedback in the form of upward communication to be encouraged more in System 4 organizations, but the mechanisms discussed earlier which can be utilized to encourage upward communication are found in many different organizational designs. An organization needs effective upward communication if its downward communication is to have any chance of being effective. The point is that developing and supporting feedback involves far more than following up on communications.

Empathy

Empathy is the ability to put oneself in the other person's role and to assume the viewpoints and emotions of that person. This involves being receiver oriented rather than communicator oriented. The form of communication should depend largely on what is known about the receivers. Empathy requires communicators to place themselves in the receivers' positions for the purpose of anticipating how the message is likely to be decoded.

It is vital that a manager understand and appreciate the process of decoding. Decoding involves perceptions, and the message will be filtered through the perceptions of the receiver. For vice presidents to communicate effectively with supervisors, for faculty to communicate effectively with students, and for government administrators to communicate effectively with students, and for government administrators to communicate effectively with minority groups, empathy is often an important ingredient. Empathy can reduce many of the barriers to effective communication that have been discussed above. The greater the gap between the experiences and background of the communicator and the receiver, the greater is the effort which must be made to find a common ground of understanding—ground on which there are overlapping fields of experience.

Simplifying language

Complex language has been identified as a major barrier to effective communication. Students often suffer when their instructors use technical jargon that transforms simple concepts into complex puzzles.

Schools are not the only places, however, where complex language is used. Government agencies are also known for their often incomprehensible communications. We have already noted instances in which professional people attempt to use their in-group language in communicating with individuals outside their group. Managers must remember that effective communication involves transmitting *understanding* as well as information. If the receiver does not understand, then there has been no communication.

In fact, many of the techniques discussed in this section have as their sole purpose the promotion of understanding. Managers must encode messages in words, appeals, and symbols that are meaningful to the receiver.

Effective listening

To improve communication, managers must seek not only to be understood, but also to *understand.* They must *listen.* One way to encourage someone to express true feelings, desires, and emotions is to listen. Just listening is not enough; one must listen with understanding. Can managers develop listening skills? Numerous pointers for effective listening have been found useful in organizational settings. For example:

1. STOP TALKING.
2. Put the listener at ease.
3. Demonstrate that you want to listen.
4. Remove distractions.
5. Empathize with the speaker.
6. Be patient.
7. Hold your temper.
8. Don't argue.
9. Ask questions.
10. STOP TALKING.

Such guidelines can be useful for managers. More important, however, is the *decision to listen.* The above guidelines are useless unless the manager makes the conscious decision to listen. Only when the manager realizes that effective communication involves understanding as well as being understood can such guidelines become useful.

Using the grapevine

The grapevine is an important informal communication channel that exists in all organizations. It serves basically as a bypassing mechanism, and in many cases it is faster than the formal system it bypasses. Because it is flexible and because it usually involves face-to-face communication, the grapevine transmits information rapidly. Through the grapevine, the resignation of an executive may become common knowledge long before it has been announced officially.

The grapevine is likely to have a stronger impact on receivers than formal communications because it is face-to-face and because it permits feedback. The grapevine will always exist. No manager can do away with it. If the grapevine is inevitable, managers should seek to utilize it or at least should attempt to increase its accuracy. One way to minimize the undesirable aspects of the grapevine is to improve other forms of communication. If managers provide information on issues relevant to subordinates, then damaging rumors are less likely to develop.

In conclusion, it would be hard to find an aspect of a manager's job that does not involve communication. If all members of the organization had a common point of view, communicating would be easy. Unfortunately, each member comes to the organization with a distinct personality, background, experience, and frame of reference. The structure of the organization itself influences status relationships and the distance (levels) between individuals, and these in turn influence the ability of individuals to communicate.

Although business organizations are not the sole producers of rumors, rumors certainly abound in such organizations. As the manager of a large landscape nursery said:

> *The fastest way to find out how the people in the firm will react to a policy change is to say something about it when the mail clerk is picking up the morning mail. By midafternoon, I will have had a dozen phone calls from unit managers. Usually their version of the policy is inaccurate and more drastic than the one I am thinking about. So when I finally get around to announcing the actual policy, it is viewed as a modified version, reflecting the managers' inputs.*

In this chapter, we have tried to convey the basic elements in the process of communication and what it takes to communicate effectively. These elements are necessary whether the communication is face-to-face or written and whether it occurs vertically, horizontally, or diagonally within an organization. Several common communication barriers and several means to improve communications were discussed. We realize that there is often insufficient time to utilize many of the techniques for improving communications, and such skills as empathy and effective listening are not easy to develop. Communicating is a matter of transmitting and receiving, and managers must be effective at both. They must understand as well as be understood.

Management summary

1. Communication is the process of achieving common understanding, and for managerial purposes, it is undertaken to achieve an effect.
2. If the intended effect is not achieved, communication has not taken place, "Telling" is not communication; "telling" is but one of several communication elements, specifically the medium.
3. The elements of communication are the sender, encoding, the message,

the medium, decoding, the receiver, and feedback. All of these elements must be in harmony if communication is to achieve understanding and effect.

4. A crucial factor in determining the effectiveness of communications in organizations is the way in which the organizations are structured. Upward, downward, diagonal, and horizontal flows are more likely to occur in nonbureaucratic than in bureaucratic structures.
5. The critical factors in determining the effectiveness of interpersonal communications are such psychological factors as perception, personality, and interpersonal style.
6. The extent to which individuals share understandings depends on their use of feedback and exposure. People differ in this regard, with some preferring feedback and others preferring exposure. The balanced use of both is the most effective approach.
7. Communication barriers can be identified in organizations and in people. Effective management attempts to remove or at least to minimize these barriers, especially those that are under managerial control.

Review and discussion questions

1. Explain why no communication occurs if the manager does not achieve the purpose or effect that he or she desired as a consequence of sending the message.
2. Explain the relationship between organization structure and communication flows within the structure.
3. In your experience, which communication element has often been the cause of your failures to communicate? What can you do to improve your ability to communicate?
4. It is often said that the public relations efforts of business firms are little more than propaganda. What is your opinion?
5. If you were the public information officer for a large petroleum company, what would you do to combat the public's belief that your company's profits are way out of line with what the public considers a fair return?
6. Do you tend to be a Type A, Type B, Type C, or Type D person when you engage in interpersonal communications? Are you content to be what you think you are? If not, how could you change?
7. In your experience, what kinds of people in terms of personality, needs, and motivation are most likely to use one-way communication?
8. Which barriers to communication are most controllable by managers? Explain.
9. What, if anything, can managers do to remove barriers to communication that are beyond their control?

10. To what extent do you believe it possible to be empathetic? Do you really believe that you can understand another person's feelings, sensitivities, and needs? Why do you hold this opinion?

Suggested reading

Baird, J. E., Jr. "Supervisory and Managerial Training through Communication by Objectives." *Personnel Administrator,* July 1981, pp. 28–32.

Dulek, R. "Six Sacrosanct Writing Guidelines." *Personnel Journal,* December 1981, pp. 932–933.

Flacks, N., and R. W. Rasberry. *Power Talk.* New York: Macmillan, 1982.

Hatfield, J. D., and R. C. Huseman. "Perceptual Congruence about Communication as Related to Satisfaction: Moderating Effects of Individual Characteristics." *Academy of Management Journal,* June 1982, pp. 349–58.

Katz, E.; D. Dayan; and P. Motly. "Communications in the 21st Century: In Defense of Media Events." *Organizational Dynamics,* Autumn 1981, pp. 68–80.

Kotter, J. P. *The General Managers.* New York: Macmillan, 1982.

Rader, M. H. "Dealing with Information Overload." *Personnel Journal,* May 1981, pp. 373–75.

Applying what you have learned about interpersonal and organizational communications

Cases:

Safety communications at Stow/Davis Furniture
Get the job done

Safety communications at Stow/ Davis Furniture*

According to Allen Hunting, president of Stow/Davis Furniture, based in Grand Rapids, Michigan, a furniture factory is a never-ending series of booby traps. "There's lots of exposed tubing," he explains, "and quick setups and takedowns for assembly." He adds, "It's mighty easy to cut your hand on a saw. Haven't technological innovations done anything to improve safety? Hell, there hasn't been anything new in this industry since the Romans."

The accident rate in this kind of industry is significantly higher than the average for all industries. And at Stow/Davis, the rate is twice the average even for the furniture industry. The company searched and searched for a solution.

Stow/Davis workers suffered 145 accidents last year requiring medical attention (among an employee population of 600, scattered throughout six plants in Grand Rapids). The box score looks like this—1,400 workdays lost to accidents and compensation claims totaling $250,000.

Stow/Davis simply had no safety program. This wasn't necessarily unique in the furniture industry. Since the furniture industry is made up primarily of smaller, less elaborate businesses, comprehensive safety programs are difficult to find. Employees at Stow/Davis were not aware of the safety hazards around them on the job. Even supervisors weren't very concerned about accident prevention.

The result of Hunting's concern about safety is the Safety Communications Program, SCP. These are the phases of the program:

* Adapted from "Safety Communications at Stow/ Davis," *Personnel Journal,* December 1981, p. 39.

1. A preliminary audiovisual presentation of safety management was made to all employees—one plant at a time. All employees were bused to the Grand Rapids Care Theater to see the presentation. Now, when a new employee joins Stow/Davis, he or she is presented with the audiovisual presentation.
2. A full-time safety officer was hired to audit safety procedures and to communicate findings.
3. Supervisors attend a 10-part series of one-hour training sessions that stress accident prevention.
4. Spot safety checks are made by supervisors of all work areas. These checks are made daily.
5. Safety box scores are posted in key areas, recording accidents over a period of time—and naming the employees involved. At the end of the year, a bonus is awarded to the plants having the lowest number of accidents and the greatest percentage drop of accidents from the previous year.

The SCP emphasizes awareness, teamwork, and pride. The president feels that it will do the job and improve a very dangerous and negative atmosphere in Stow/Davis plants. He will be closely watching the lost workdays and workers' compensation claims to see if the SCP is working.

Questions:

1. Do you believe that there is a communication overload problem with the Stow/Davis SCP program? Explain.
2. Will the Stow/Davis SCP program be successful? Make a prediction and explain.
3. Why would Stow/Davis use safety box scores in the SCP program?

Get the job done

Jack Forrester, 35, is a bloodstock agent in the Thoroughbred horse industry. As bloodstock agent, he locates and brings together buyers and sellers of Thoroughbred horses and breeding rights. He has achieved tremendous success through his hard work and his knowledge of Thoroughbred bloodlines. He started his business five years ago, and he now employs eight other agents, three secretaries, an office manager, and me. Jack hired me four months ago and told me that I was the "assistant office manager." I thought that was (and is) a grand job title, even though no one ever told me what I was supposed to do. But the pay is great for a part-time job (I am a junior in college), and I am learning a lot about an interesting industry. I am also learning a lot about people.

I stood by the door of Forrester's office. Forrester was on the phone, and before I could knock, he motioned for me to come in and sit down. His desk was covered by numerous reports, memos, horse sale catalogs, telephone messages, and racing results. Other reminders on bits of paper were taped to the wall, and a "to do" list with at least 10 entries on it was taped to the base of the telephone. Evidently these were things that he had "to do" immediately. While talking on the phone, he added another item to this list.

As he continued the phone conversation, he was shaking his head and signing letters at the same time. Finally, he put his hand over the phone and said to me, "This is Robinson in Florida on that two-year-old filly deal. All the tests on her are not in yet, but he insists on giving me every detail on the entire test procedure. The guy is going to drive me nuts."

Turning his attention back to the phone, Forrester removed his hand and resumed talking. "Right, Robbie, OK. . . . Great. . . .

OK. . . . Sure. . . . Call me back on that. . . . Terrific. . . . Bye."

Forrester hung up the phone with a sigh of relief and looked at me. "Do you know what I like about you, Tinsley?" I didn't have time to answer, nor did he, because the phone rang again. "Yeah. . . . Fine. . . . Terrific. . . . Count me in. . . . Bye." At this point, his secretary looked in and said, "John Towne of Winthrop Farms is on hold. It sounds urgent."

Forrester shook his head again and went back to the telephone. After a few minutes of conversation, he put his hand over the receiver and called to his secretary. "Get Johnson and Burke in here, fast." Johnson was the office manager, and Burke was an agent. They arrived as he hung up the phone.

"Burke," he said, "you know that deal you put together for the syndication of that three-year-old, Ol' Blue? Well, they don't like it. Put this information into it and tell me what effect the changes will have on us. When you get it finished, bring it to me so I can call Towne back." Burke left.

"Johnson, I want all of the training fees, jockey expenses, and all other expenses on that horse. Don't give them to me by the month like you did last time. I need totals in all categories, and for crying out loud, this time break out the 'other' category a little better. I looked real bad last week when Towne asked me what the $6,300 in 'other expenses' was for. I want all the information at my fingertips in case we've got to go to war with these people." Johnson left.

"Now, Tinsley, what did you need me for?"

"Just sign this bill of sale," I said. "No reason to spend a lot of time on it. It's for the sale of that yearling you asked me to take care of."

"That's what I like about you, Tinsley," he said as he leaned back in his chair and signed the bill of sale. "When I give you a job, you listen, and then you do it right the first time, and then you tell me when it's done. You don't tell me how you did it, the problems you're having doing it, who you met while doing it, and every other Mickey Mouse detail. If the rest of the people around here had that ability, I might be able to get some work done. I think I got more work done five years ago when I had nobody working for me."

As I left his office, I didn't have time to thank him because the phone began ringing.

Questions:

1. Explain why Forrester communicates as he does with his employees.
2. Identify barriers to communication in the interactions described in the case.
3. What kinds of personalities, needs, and motivations must people have to work effectively with Forrester?

13

Chapter thirteen Motivation and performance

Performance objectives

- **Define** the meaning of motivation.
- **State** why individuals react differently to being frustrated or blocked in satisfying their needs.
- **Describe** why money is not always a powerful motivator of employee behavior in organizations.
- **Explain** the differences between expectancy theory and behavior modification.
- **Discuss** the types of rewards used in job enrichment, pay, behavior modification programs, and quality circles.

Management update*

Steel and autos are two industries in the United States which are presently not known to have profitable firms. However, John H. McConnell has had success with his Columbus, Ohio-based, Worthington Industries. Worthington's core business is selling steel to auto companies. His philosophy and practice of motivation are very simple and straightforward. "Treat your workers and customers as you want to be treated." This may sound pretty corny if one thinks about all of the complex and sophisticated theories of motivation found in textbooks.

The McConnell theory of motivation may sound corny, but it works at Worthington. He actually does treat his workers well—he believes that money is a powerful motivator. Employees at Worthington receive quarterly profit-sharing checks that can and often do double a production worker's wages. He treats his customers to reliable, fast deliveries of steel—and they pay a premium price for the service.

It is McConnell's view that employees are partners in the business. After a six-month probationary period, workers are eligible for profit sharing. Furthermore, McConnell boasts that he never lays off anybody once they've passed the six-month probationary period.

The McConnell motivational program includes lectures about the meaning of profit and loss, the cost of absenteeism, the cost of scrap and the importance of productivity. Peer pressure is also important in keeping everyone busy. Absenteeism at Worthington's profit-sharing operations is 2 percent, compared with 5 percent at comparable shops; the reject rate is 1 percent, compared with 3 percent to 4 percent for the industry.

McConnell makes no pretense that his ideas and plans of generating better performance are based on a democratic or participative approach to creating a motivational climate. Employee councils review and can veto promotion of a probationary employee to permanent status. McConnell wants to give workers authority and responsibility and let them do the job.

---

* The Management Update is based on William Baldwin, "Spreading The Wealth," *Forbes,* April 27, 1981, pp. 116 and 118.

Motivation is concerned with the causes of human behavior. An understanding of motivation is a necessity for the student of management because whenever we ask managers what their biggest problem is, the answer in the vast majority of cases comes back—motivating subordinates. How can I motivate people to achieve high levels of performance? This challenging question is not easily answered. Nevertheless, this chapter will provide some bases for answering the question generally, but managerial judgment will always be required to devise means for motivating a specific individual.

Motivation is defined as "all those inner striving conditions described as wishes, desires, drives, etc. . . . It is an inner state that activates or moves.[1] Motivation cannot be seen, heard, or felt but can only be inferred from behavior. In other words, we can judge how motivated a person is only by observing his or her behavior; managers cannot measure motivation directly because it is unobservable. For example, if one salesperson consistently achieves higher sales than other salespersons with similar abilities, we might infer that he or she is highly motivated. If a typist completes more purchase orders than other typists with comparable skills, we might infer that the typist is motivated. However, note that in each case we did not measure motivation directly; we observed a presumed indicator of motivation (sales and purchase orders completed) and made inferences from our observations.

Motivation and behavior

Behavior is motivated because people have reasons for doing what they do or for behaving in the manner that they do. Thus, human behavior is directed toward certain goals and objectives. Such goal-directed behavior revolves around the desire for **need satisfaction.**

[1] Bernard Berelson and Gary A. Steiner, *Human Behavior: An Inventory of Scientific Findings* (New York: Harcourt Brace Jovanovich, 1964), p. 239.

The motivation process

An unsatisfied need is the starting point in the process of motivation as shown in Figure 13–1. An unsatisfied need causes tension (physical or psychological) within the individual, leading the individual to engage in some kind of behavior (seek a means) to satisfy the need and thereby reduce the tension. Note that this activity is directed toward a goal; arrival at the goal satisfies the need, and the process of motivation is complete. For example, a thirsty person *needs* water, is *driven* by thirst, and is *motivated* by a desire for water in order to satisfy the need. Thus, the continuous process begins with an unsatisfied need and ends with need satisfaction, with goal-directed behavior as a part of the process.

The importance of understanding the relationships between motivation and behavior was understood by McGregor who proposed that managers usually assume that employees are motivated by one of two ways. The traditional way, or view, is referred to as **Theory X.** This view suggests that managers assume that they must coerce, control, and threaten in order to motivate subordinates. These managerial actions are needed because employees:

1. Inherently dislike work.
2. Dislike responsibilities for decision making.
3. Have little ambition and want job security above all.

Thus, a manager who accepts Theory X would engage in authoritarian and directive practices. These practices result from the manager's assumptions about how and why subordinates behave.

The opposite of Theory X is **Theory Y.** McGregor believed that Theory Y was a reasonable alternative to the more traditional Theory X approach. The manager using Theory Y assumes that employees are:

1. Not lazy and want to do challenging work.
2. Interested under proper conditions in accepting responsibility.
3. Interested in displaying ingenuity and creativity.

Figure 13–1

The process of motivation

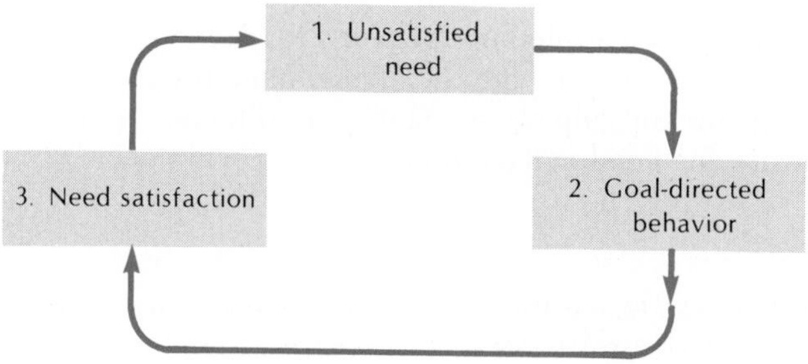

Thus if Theory Y assumptions are made about subordinates, managers would probably seek to create an environment in which a full range of needs can be satisfied; an example of Theory Y management is reported in the Management Update.

One problem of attempting to fit all people into two categories such as Theory X or Theory Y is that not everyone fits. Three managers provided some descriptions of what they thought about people. It is obvious that the managers do not exactly fit either Theory X or Theory Y.

> *A plant superintendent: I like people because I'm always able to learn from others. If the work is challenging, people will pitch in. However, with the unemployment rate so high, people are too cautious and concerned about losing their jobs.*
>
> *A restaurant owner: Without good people I have to close my doors. Trust, respect, and confidence are what everyone wants.*
>
> *A nursing supervisor: The nurses are too independent. They are not as professional as they should be. I have to put up with complaints and absenteeism because there are plenty of other nursing jobs available.*

Individual needs and motivation

Needs may be classified in different ways. Many of the early writers on management regarded monetary incentives as prime means for motivating the individual. These writers were influenced by the classical economists of the 18th and 19th centuries, who emphasized the rational pursuit of economic objectives and believed that economic behavior was characterized by rational economic calculations. Today, many psychologists hold that while money is obviously an important motivator, people seek to satisfy other than purely economic needs. In fact, Freud was the first psychologist to state that much of a person's behavior may be influenced by needs of which the individual is not aware.

Although most psychologists agree that human beings are motivated by the desire to satisfy many needs, there is a wide difference of opinion as to what those needs and their relative importance are. Most psychologists, however, emphasize many different types of needs whose satisfaction is a key determinant of behavior. Maslow's need hierarchy is an important motivation theory.

Maslow's need hierarchy is widely accepted in management theory and practice. This theory of motivation is based upon two important assumptions:

1. Each person's needs depend on what he or she already has. Only needs not yet satisfied can influence behavior. A satisfied need cannot influence behavior.
2. Needs are arranged in a hierarchy of importance. Once one need is satisfied, another emerges and demands satisfaction.

Maslow believed that five levels of needs exist. These levels are (1) physiological, (2) safety, (3) social, (4) esteem, and (5) self-actualization.[2] He placed them in a framework referred to as the *hierarchy of needs.* This framework is presented in Figure 13–2.

Figure 13–2

The hierarchy of needs

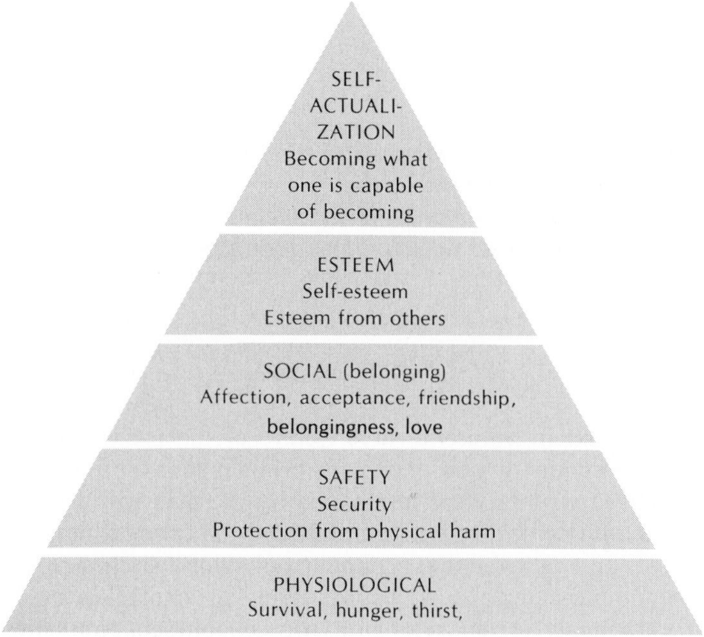

Maslow stated that if all of a person's needs are unsatisfied at a particular time, the most basic needs will be more pressing than the others. Needs at a lower level must be satisfied before higher-level needs come into play, and only when they are sufficiently satisfied do the next needs in line become significant. Let us briefly examine each need level.

Physiological needs This category consists of the basic needs of the human body, such as food, water, and sex. Physiological needs will dominate when all needs are unsatisfied. In such a case, no other needs will serve

[2] Abraham H. Maslow, *Motivation and Personality* (New York: Harper & Row, 1954), pp. 93–98.

as a basis for motivation. As Maslow states, "A person who is lacking food, safety, love, and esteem would probably hunger for food more strongly than for anything else."[3]

Safety needs These needs include protection from physical harm, ill health, economic disaster, and the unexpected. From a managerial standpoint, safety needs manifest themselves in attempts to insure job security and to move toward greater financial support.

Social needs These needs are related to the social nature of people and to their need for companionship. This level in the hierarchy is the point of departure from the physical or quasi-physical needs of the two previous levels. Nonsatisfaction of this level of needs may affect the mental health of the individual.

Esteem needs These needs comprise both the awareness of one's importance to others (self-esteem) and the actual esteem of others. The satisfaction of esteem needs leads to self-confidence and prestige.

Self-actualization needs Maslow defines these needs as the "desire to become more and more what one is, to become everything one is capable of becoming."[4] The satisfaction of self-actualization needs enables the individual to realize fully the potentialities of his or her talents and capabilities. Maslow assumes that the satisfaction of self-actualization needs is possible only after the satisfaction of all other needs. Moreover, he proposes that the satisfaction of self-actualization needs will tend to increase the strength of those needs. Thus, when people are able to achieve self-actualization, they will tend to be motivated by increased opportunities to satisfy that level of needs.

When completed and scored, Figure 13–3 will provide you with an approximate idea about the relative importance of your needs.

Nonsatisfaction of needs

As noted previously, unsatisfied needs produce tensions within the individual. When the individual is unable to satisfy needs (and thereby reduce the tension), **frustration** is the result. The reactions to frustration vary from person to person. Some people react in a positive manner (constructive behavior), others in a negative manner (defensive behavior).

Constructive behavior

The reader is undoubtedly familiar with the constructive behavior in which people engage when attempts to satisfy needs have been frustrated.

[3] Ibid., p. 82.

[4] Ibid., p. 92.

Figure 13–3

Motivation survey

Directions: The following statements have seven possible responses:

Strongly agree	Agree	Slightly agree	Don't know	Slightly disagree	Disagree	Strongly disagree
+3	+2	+1	0	−1	−2	−3

Please mark one of the seven responses by circling the number that fits your opinion. For example, if you "Strongly agree," circle the number "+3." Complete every item.

1.	Special wage increases should be given to employees who do their jobs very well.	+3 +2 +1 0 −1 −2 −3
2.	Better job descriptions would help employees to know exactly what is expected of them.	+3 +2 +1 0 −1 −2 −3
3.	Employees need to be reminded that their jobs are dependent on the company's ability to compete effectively.	+3 +2 +1 0 −1 −2 −3
4.	A supervisor should give a good deal of attention to the physical working conditions of his employees.	+3 +2 +1 0 −1 −2 −3
5.	The supervisor ought to work hard to develop a friendly working atmosphere among his people.	+3 +2 +1 0 −1 −2 −3
6.	Individual recognition for above-standard performance means a lot to employees.	+3 +2 +1 0 −1 −2 −3
7.	Indifferent supervision can often bruise feelings.	+3 +2 +1 0 −1 −2 −3
8.	Employees want to feel that their real skills and capacities are put to use on their jobs.	+3 +2 +1 0 −1 −2 −3
9.	The company retirement benefits and stock programs are important factors in keeping employees on their jobs.	+3 +2 +1 0 −1 −2 −3
10.	Almost every job can be made more stimulating and challenging.	+3 +2 +1 0 −1 −2 −3
11.	Many employees want to give their best in everything they do.	+3 +2 +1 0 −1 −2 −3
12.	Management could show more interest in the employees by sponsoring social events after-hours.	+3 +2 +1 0 −1 −2 −3
13.	Pride in one's work is actually an important reward.	+3 +2 +1 0 −1 −2 −3
14.	Employees want to be able to think of themselves as "the best" at their own jobs.	+3 +2 +1 0 −1 −2 −3
15.	The quality of the relationships in the informal work group is quite important.	+3 +2 +1 0 −1 −2 −3

Figure 13–3 (*concluded*)

16.	Individual incentive bonuses would improve the performance of employees.	+3 +2 +1 0 −1 −2 −3
17.	Visibility with upper management is important to employees.	+3 +2 +1 0 −1 −2 −3
18.	Employees generally like to schedule their own work and to make job-related decisions with a minimum of supervision.	+3 +2 +1 0 −1 −2 −3
19.	Job security is important to employees.	+3 +2 +1 0 −1 −2 −3
20.	Having good equipment to work with is important to employees.	+3 +2 +1 0 −1 −2 −3

Scoring instructions are at the end of the chapter.

SOURCE: This survey was developed by University Associates, La Jolla, California, 1973.

An assembly line worker who has been frustrated in attempts for esteem because of the nature of the job may seek esteem off the job by winning election to leadership posts in fraternal or civic organizations. In order to satisfy frustrated social and belonging needs, a worker may conform to the norms and values of a group which bowls on weekends. Each of these is an example of constructive adaptive behavior which individuals employ to reduce frustration and satisfy needs.

Defensive behavior

Individuals who are blocked in attempts to satisfy their needs may exhibit defensive behavior instead of constructive behavior. All of us employ defensive behavior in one way or another because such behavior performs an important protective function in our attempts to cope with frustration. In most cases, defensive behavior does not handicap the individual to any great degree. Ordinarily, however, it is not adequate for the task of protecting the self. As a result, adults whose behavior is continually dominated by defensive behavior usually have great difficulty in adapting to responsibilities of work and of social relationships.

What happens when needs are not satisfied is difficult to understand but is worth considering. Some general patterns of defensive behavior have been identified, of which some of the more common are discussed below.

Withdrawal One obvious way to avoid reality is to withdraw or avoid situations which will prove frustrating. The withdrawal may be physical (leaving the scene), but more than likely it will be expressed as apathy. Workers whose jobs provide little in the way of need satisfaction may withdraw, and this is reflected by excessive absences, latenesses, or turnover.

Aggression A common reaction to frustration is aggression. In some cases, this may take the form of a direct attack on the source of the frustration. Unfortunately, aggression is often directed toward another object or party unrelated to the cause of the frustration. For example, a supervisor may direct aggression toward a subordinate production worker who, in turn, may direct his aggression toward his wife.

Substitution This occurs when the individual puts something in the place of the original object. An employee whose attempts to achieve a promotion have been frustrated may substitute for promotion the achievement of leadership status in a work group whose objectives are to resist management policies.

Compensation When a person goes overboard in one area or activity to make up for deficiencies in another, this defense mechanism is being evoked. A manager whose personality is disagreeable may compensate with attempts to practice good "human relations" with subordinates.

Repression Many individuals repress frustrating situations and problems. Repression may be an almost automatic response whereby the individual loses awareness of incidents that would cause anxiety or frustration if they were allowed to remain at the conscious level of the mind. Thus, an unpleasant encounter with a manager may be quickly "forgotten" by a subordinate.

Regression When confronted with frustration, some individuals will revert (regress) to childlike forms of behavior in their attempts to avoid the unpleasant reality. In the work situation, regression often manifests itself in some form of horseplay.

Projection This involves attributing one's own feelings to someone else. A subordinate who dislikes a superior for some reason may attempt to make the superior appear ineffective whenever possible. The subordinate may attempt to justify this behavior by saying, "My boss never liked me from the moment I got here."

Rationalization This behavior enables an individual to present a reason that is less ego deflating or more socially acceptable than the true reason. An example of this defense mechanism is perceiving one's own poor performance as the result of obsolete equipment rather than personal deficiency.

Every person relies to some extent on defense mechanisms. However, subordinates' overreliance on defensive behavior can be minimized if managerial decisions provide conditions which encourage constructive behavior. In addition, a manager who understands defensive behavior will have greater empathy with those who use it and will realize that such behavior may not be a true indication of the person's actual character.

What has been said thus far about motivation is summarized in Figure 13–4. The diagram indicates that an unsatisfied need results in tensions within the individual and motivates a search for ways to relieve the tensions. The diagram also indicates that if a person is successful in achieving a goal, the next unsatisfied need emerges. If, however, attempts are met with frustration, the person either engages in constructive behavior (note the plus sign to indicate its adaptive/positive nature) or resorts to defensive behavior (indicated with a minus sign because of its often negative effects). In either case, the person returns to the next unsatisfied need which emerges.

Personality and motivation

Personality differences influence the process of motivation in the following ways:

Strength of needs The strength and importance of various needs will differ from one individual to another, depending on their personalities. For example, strong esteem needs may lead some people to seek different kinds of employment or career paths than are sought by people whose esteem needs are not as strong.

Aspiration level Aspiration levels differ among individuals, depending on the personality. One individual may not be satisfied until a position of power and influence in an organization is reached, while another may be quite satisfied in a middle-management position. The aspiration levels of two junior engineers reveal significant differences:

> *I have trained myself to be the best engineer in my discipline. The only thing that will prove that I made it will be to become the youngest vice president in the firm.*
>
> *I work to acquire power. Unless I'm able to exert influence over others, my day is incomplete. I'm not talking about power in a negative sense, but in a positive way—that is, power to lead others.*

Figure 13–4

A motivational model

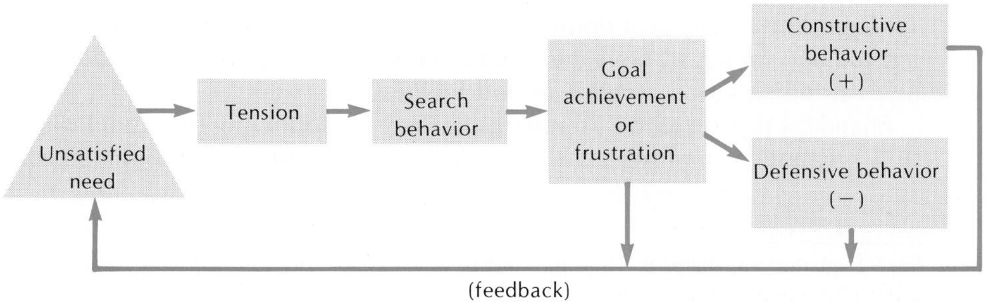

Types of behavior Although individuals may experience the same needs, the specific behaviors which an individual utilizes to achieve need satisfaction are a function of personality. For example, one person may satisfy esteem needs by gaining on-the-job recognition from superiors, while another person may satisfy the same needs by striving to become a respected member of a professional or peer group. The need is the same, but the behaviors to satisfy them differ.

Reaction to frustration How a person reacts to nonsatisfaction of needs is also a function of personality. Personality differences affect the types of situations which cause frustration, the degree to which defense mechanisms are evoked, and the kinds of defense mechanisms that are employed. For example, one individual who has been frustrated in attempts to express herself to co-workers and management might seek to become a spokesperson for a community cause, such as public support for a teenage community center (constructive behavior), while another individual who has experienced the same frustration might engage in unfounded criticism of the organization and its management (defensive behavior).

In this section, we have presented a motivational model based on the need hierarchy framework. We have also noted that both motivation and behavior will vary from person to person as a result of differences in personality. Other explanations of motivation are found in Herzberg's two-factor model and in the expectancy model.

The two-factor theory of motivation

Frederick Herzberg advanced a theory of motivation based on a study of need satisfactions and on the reported motivational effects of those satisfactions on 200 engineers and accountants. His approach is termed the **two-factor theory of motivation.**[5]

Herzberg asked the subjects of his study to think of times when they felt especially good and especially bad about their jobs. Each subject was then asked to describe the conditions which caused those feelings. Significantly, the subjects *identified different work conditions for each of the feelings.* For example, if managerial recognition for doing an excellent job led to good feelings about the job, the lack of managerial recognition was seldom indicated as a cause of bad feelings.

Based on this research, Herzberg reached the following two conclusions:

1. Although employees are dissatisfied by the absence of some job con-

[5] See Frederick Herzberg, B. Mausner, and B. Snyderman, *The Motivation to Work* (New York: John Wiley & Sons, 1959).

ditions, the presence of those conditions does not cause strong motivation. Herzberg called such conditions **maintenance factors,** since they are necessary to maintain a minimal level of need satisfaction. He also noted that these factors have often been perceived by managers as factors which can motivate subordinates, but that they are, in fact, more potent as dissatisfiers when they are absent. He concluded that there were 10 maintenance factors, namely:

a. Company policy and administration.
b. Technical supervision.
c. Interpersonal relations with supervisor.
d. Interpersonal relations with peers.
e. Interpersonal relations with subordinates.
f. Salary.
g. Job security.
h. Personal life.
i. Work conditions.
j. Status.

2. Some job factors cause high levels of motivation and job satisfaction when present. However, the absence of these factors does not prove highly dissatisfying. Herzberg described six of these motivational factors.

a. Achievement.
b. Recognition.
c. Advancement.
d. The work itself.
e. The possibility of personal growth.
f. Responsibility.

The motivational factors are job centered; that is, they relate directly to the job itself, that is, the individual's job performance, the job responsibilities, and the growth and recognition obtained from the job. The maintenance factors are peripheral to the job itself and are more related to the external environment of work. The distinction between motivational and maintenance factors is similar to the distinction between *intrinsic* and *extrinsic* rewards. Intrinsic rewards are part of the job and occur when the employee performs the work; the work itself is rewarding. Extrinsic rewards are external rewards that have meaning or value after the work has been performed or away from the workplace. They provide little, if any, satisfaction when the work is being performed.

Since conducting the original study, Herzberg has cited numerous and diverse replications which support his position.[6] These studies were conducted on professional women, hospital maintenance personnel, agricultural administrators, nurses, food handlers, manufacturing supervisors, engineers, scientists, military officers, managers ready for retirement,

[6] Frederick Herzberg, *Work and the Nature of Man* (Cleveland: World Publishing, 1966).

teachers, technicians, and assemblers; and some of the studies were conducted in other cultural settings—Finland, Hungary, Russia, and Yugoslavia.

There is much similarity between Herzberg's and Maslow's models. A close examination of Herzberg's ideas indicates that what he is actually saying is that some employees may have achieved a level of social and economic progress in our society such that the higher-level needs of Maslow (esteem and self-actualization) are the primary motivators. However, these employees must still satisfy their lower-level needs in order to maintain their current state. Thus, we can see that money might still be a motivator for nonmanagement workers (particularly those at a minimum wage level) and for some managerial employees. Herzberg's model adds to the need hierarchy model because it draws a distinction between the two groups of motivational and maintenance factors and because it points out that the motivational factors are often derived from the job itself. Figure 13–5 compares the two models.

Figure 13–5

A comparison of the Maslow and Herzberg models

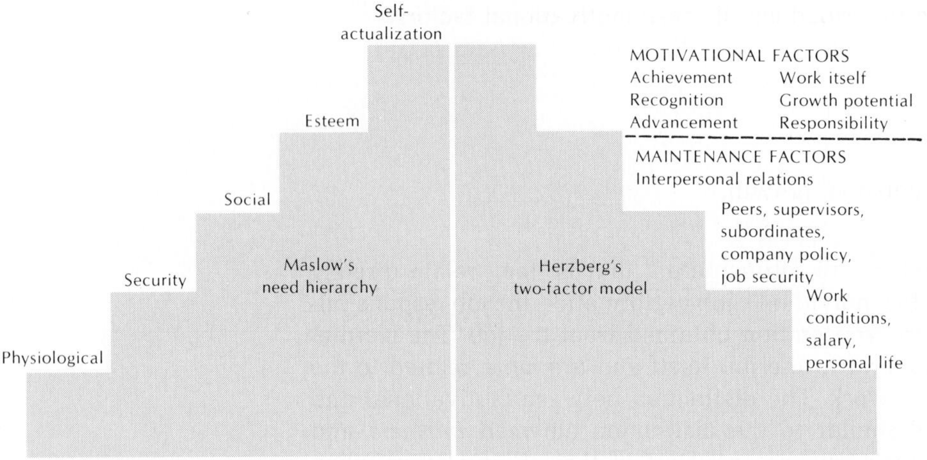

The expectancy theory of motivation

A theory of motivation has been developed by Vroom that expands on the work of Maslow and Herzberg.[7] The expectancy theory views motiva-

[7] Victor H. Vroom, *Work and Motivation* (New York: John Wiley & Sons, 1964).

tion as a process governing choices. Thus, an individual who has a particular goal must perform some behavior in order to achieve the goal. The individual, therefore, weighs the likelihood that various behaviors will achieve the desired goal, and if a certain behavior is expected to be more successful than others, that behavior will probably be selected.

An important contribution of the expectancy theory is that it explains how the *goals* of individuals influence their *effort* and that the behavior individuals select depends on their assessment of whether it will successfully lead to the goal. For example, the members of an organization may not all place the same value on such job factors as promotion, high pay, job security, and working conditions. Vroom believes that what is important is the perception and value that the individual places on certain goals. Suppose that one individual places a high value on salary increases and perceives high performance as instrumental in reaching that goal. Accordingly, this individual will strive toward superior performance in order to achieve the salary increases. However, another individual may value a promotion and perceive knowing the right person as related to achieving it. This individual, therefore, is not likely to emphasize superior performance to achieve the goal. The reader is now encouraged to think of this in terms of student motivation, where one student has the goal of an A grade and another the goal of a C grade in a particular course. How might their respective efforts and behaviors in the course vary?

Some examples of how goals influence behavior were collected from individuals. A few of them are summarized:

> *Technician: My goal is to enjoy myself off the job flying airplanes. To accomplish this expensive goal, I have to work hard and earn a good living.*
>
> *Medical technologist: My goal is to work and keep from being bored. Whenever something difficult comes up, I volunteer. New challenges keep me from boredom.*
>
> *Manager: As I said before, I work to get ahead. To me, getting ahead means promotions and more money. These are my goals and the things that my work performance can get me.*
>
> *Scientist: My goal is to be recognized as a good researcher. This recognition must come from respected colleagues, or it means nothing.*

Each of these people described some of their goals and how work could help achieve those goals. What is important is that what the individual perceives as the consequence of a particular behavior is far more important than what the manager (or professor) believes the individual should perceive.

The expectancy theory is certainly more abstract than the need hierarchy and the two-factor theories. However, the expectancy theory adds insight into the study of motivation at work, since it attempts to explain how *individual goals* influence *individual performance.* But note that the common thread running through each of these three theories is **that behavior is goal directed.** Thus, the process of motivation as it was presented earlier in the chapter (Figure 13–1) serves as the cornerstone of the Maslow, Herzberg, and Vroom theories of motivation.

Managerial approaches for improving motivation

A number of approaches are available to managers who desire to motivate workers to perform more effectively. Four approaches which have been relatively effective are job enrichment, linking pay to job performance, behavior modification, and quality circles. Although other approaches could be cited, these four appear to be among the most widely used.

Job enrichment

Job enrichment, as described by one of its leading proponents,

> seeks to improve both task efficiency and human satisfaction by means of building into people's jobs, quite specifically, greater scope for personal achievement and recognition, more challenging and responsible work, and more opportunity for individual advancement and growth. It is concerned more incidentally with matters such as pay and working conditions, organizational structure, communications, and training, important and necessary though these may be in their own right.[8]

Thus, job enrichment is based upon the two-factor theory of motivation.

In a series of experiments, Herzberg sought to determine, among other things, the generality of his original findings.[9] The studies covered widely different business areas and company functions as well as many types and levels of jobs including laboratory technicians in a research and development department, sales representatives, design engineers, production

[8] Frederick Herzberg, "One More Time: How Do You Motivate Employees?" *Harvard Business Review,* January–February 1968, p. 53.

[9] William J. Paul, Jr., Keith B. Robertson, and Frederick Herzberg, "Job Enrichment Pays Off," *Harvard Business Review,* March–April 1969, p. 61.

supervisors on shift work, and engineering supervisors on day work. There were three main features to the study:

1. The maintenance factors were held constant. This means that no deliberate changes were made in pay, security, and other maintenance factors because the researchers were only interested in determining gains which were brought about through changes in motivation factors.
2. An experimental group was formed for whom the specific changes in motivation factors were made, and a control group was formed whose motivation factors remained the same.
3. The fact that the studies were being done was kept confidential to avoid the tendency of people to behave differently when they are aware that they are part of a study.

The researchers sought to measure job satisfaction and performance for both the experimental group and the control group over the study period, which lasted one year. The performance measures were specific to the group concerned and were determined by the local management of the participating company.

How were the jobs "enriched"? Rather than examine all five groups, let us review the program of action devised and implemented for the sales representatives.

> Sales representatives were no longer obliged to write reports on every customer call. They were asked simply to pass on information when they thought it appropriate or request action as they thought it was required.
>
> Responsibility for determining call frequencies was given to the representatives themselves, who kept the only records for purposes such as staff reviews.
>
> The technical service department agreed to provide service on demand from the representatives; nominated technicians regarded such calls as their first priority. Communication was by direct contact, paperwork being cleared after the event.

After the changes, the sales representatives' sales increased by 19 percent over the same period for the previous year. Sales declined by 5 percent during the study period for the sales representatives whose jobs were not enriched. The equivalent change for both groups during the previous year had been a decline of 3 percent.

The jobs in the remaining four groups were enriched in a fashion similar to that for the sales representatives. The specific changes are not detailed here. However, similar positive results were found for each of the other four types of jobs when specific changes were made in the motivational factors. The researchers concluded that tasks have to be motivational—that is, the more they draw upon the motivators, the more likely they are to produce an effective contribution to organizational objectives.

The core dimensions of jobs Recent refinements in the concept and application of job enrichment emphasize that changes in motivational factors involve changes in the **core dimensions of jobs.**[10] Core dimensions of jobs are those specific attributes which, when present, produce positive motivation and, consequently, high levels of satisfaction and performances. Five job attributes, or core dimensions, which tend to have the potential for producing motivation to perform are *variety, task identity, task significance, autonomy,* and *feedback.*

Variety allows employees to perform different operations using several procedures and perhaps different equipment. Jobs that are high in variety are often viewed as challenging because they require the use of the full range of an employee's skills.

Task identity allows employees to perform a complete piece of work. Overspecialized jobs tend to create routine duties. A worker performs only one part of the entire job, and this results in a sense of loss or of nonaccomplishment. Broadening the task to provide the worker with the feeling of doing a whole job is what is meant by task identity.

Task significance is the amount of impact that the work being performed has on other people. This impact may be within the organization or in the community. The feeling of doing something worthwhile is important to many people. For example, a respected supervisor may tell an employee that she has done an outstanding job and has contributed to the overall success of the department. Her task then has significance because it has been recognized by a superior.

Autonomy refers to the idea that employees have some control over their job duties and their work area. This seems to be an important dimension in stimulating a sense of responsibility. One way to provide autonomy is to give individuals authority to establish their own work and career goals.

Feedback refers to the information that workers receive on how well they are performing. People in general have a need to know how they are doing. They need feedback frequently so that they can make necessary improvements.

Diagnosing jobs These five core dimensions must be modified to accomplish job enrichment. Managers can study jobs to determine the quantity and quality of the core dimensions for each job. By analyzing the core dimensions, they can identify and perhaps modify the weak dimensions.

The comments of two employees reveal some interesting differences in the core dimensions:

Technician: I really like my job. It keeps me busy, and I'm also able to tell how good my performance is. This

[10] J. Richard Hackman, Greg Oldham, Robert Janson, and Kenneth Purdy, "A New Strategy for Job Enrichment," *California Management Review,* Summer 1975, pp. 57–71; and Richard Hackman and Gred Oldham, "Development of the Job Diagnostic Survey," *Journal of Applied Psychology,* April 1975, pp. 159–70.

is important. I don't like the checking that is done by the new foreman. He is always bothering me and slowing me down. I am also a little upset by the new quality control procedure. Before, I took the job from the beginning to the warehouse, but now I turn it over to inspection before it is sent into inventory.

Assembly line operator: My job is easy to learn and soon becomes boring. I really think it is harder to work on this job than on some of the lab work. Because the job is so easy, management doesn't care about it or the workers. They do watch us, but they never try to improve the working conditions.

Effective job enrichment requires managers to examine the employees' readiness for enrichment and the special problems that may hinder any job redesign. Employees who do not have a need for autonomy and feedback may not respond favorably to job enrichment. Thus, the employees' need strength is an important factor in developing the most appropriate job enrichment strategy.

A special problem of job enrichment is how the program can be continued after it has been started. How far will management go in changing each core dimension? What are the limits of the autonomy that management is willing to build into the job? If management is reluctant to continually diagnose and modify the job enrichment program, further improvement will be difficult. The management team needs to consider the following questions when reviewing job enrichment:

1. Can the employee accept more responsibility?
2. Can the employee work with more autonomy?
3. Is management able to accept changes in jobs that may result in more worker autonomy and more feedback?

Organizational applications of job enrichment One attempt to implement job enrichment occurred at Saab-Scandia in the 1960s.[11] The engine assembly group was organized into teams. Each team consisted of employees who assembled the entire engine and were in charge of their work area. There was no mechanical assembly line. Each team was able to control its own work pace and team arrangement. Workers rotated job duties to minimize boredom. Following this team arrangement, Saab-Scandia reported increased productivity, higher job satisfaction, reduced turnover, and fewer work stoppages.

An attempt to enrich jobs was built into a General Foods pet food plant

[11] Noel M. Tichy, "Organizational Innovations in Sweden," *Columbia Journal of World Business*, Summer 1974, pp. 18–27.

that opened in 1971.[12] The new plant management established work teams of 7 to 14 employees. The teams were given large amounts of autonomy and frequent feedback. A high degree of variety was also built into each job. Most of the routine work was mechanized. The five core dimensions appear to have been modified to a large extent.

The preliminary results indicated that the pet food plant compared favorably to more traditionally operated plants. Productivity was greater, and absenteeism and turnover were less in the pet food plant than in nonenriched jobs in similar plants. It has been suggested that the positive results may have occurred because the pet food facility was new. These results began to weaken a few years after enrichment occurred.

The Non-Linear Systems experiment offers a caution to advocates of job enrichment.[13] The firm manufactures digital electrical measuring instruments. Management replaced an assembly line with teams of 3 to 12 employees. The managers of each team provided minimal supervision. The teams decided how the instruments would be produced. Work could be rotated and the pace controlled by the team. Each group was also responsible for resolving conflicts and handling disciplinary problems.

The early results at Non-Linear Systems revealed increased productivity and higher satisfaction. Over a period of years, however, productivity and satisfaction began to decline. The teams were not able to make quick decisions because there was little structure within the units. The team members became dissatisfied. After approximately four years of experimenting with job enrichment, the firm reverted to its previous managerial practices.

These experiences suggest that the implementation of job enrichment principles can be successful in some situations but not in others. There is also the question of how long performance improvements can continue. This is an important issue in the General Foods example. Job enrichment should not be viewed as a universally desirable program. Some workers and managers cannot perform effectively under job enrichment conditions. Therefore, both worker and managerial reactions need to be considered by managers before job enrichment is implemented.

Pay and job performance

Pay can often be used to motivate employee performance.[14] In order for a pay plan to motivate, it must (1) create a belief that good performance

[12] Richard E. Walton, "How to Counter Alienation in the Plant," *Harvard Business Review*, November–December 1972, pp. 70–81.

[13] Erwin L. Malone, "The Non-Linear Systems Experiment in Participative Management," *Journal of Business*, January 1975, pp. 52–64.

[14] The best available discussion of pay and performance appears in Edward E. Lawler III, *Pay and Organizational Effectiveness* (New York: McGraw-Hill, 1971).

leads to high levels of pay, (2) minimize the negative consequences of good performance, and (3) create conditions in which desired rewards other than pay are seen to be related to good performance. These three conditions follow from the expectancy theory of motivation which states that individuals will be motivated to seek goals that they value and that they can attain.

Relating pay to performance Managers use numerous methods in their attempts to relate pay to performance. One survey of personnel practices reported high dissatisfaction with pay plans.[15] It seems that many pay plans are disliked because they are implemented poorly or because they are not well suited for a particular job.

Incentive pay plans can be rated on three separate criteria. First, each plan can be rated in terms of how effective it is in creating the perception that pay is tied to performance. Second, the plans can be evaluated in terms of their success in minimizing negative side effects, such as disruptive competition, conflict, and grievances. Third, each plan can be rated in terms of whether it contributes to the perception that important rewards other than pay (e.g., feelings of esteem and increased responsibility) result from high performance.

Table 13–1 summarizes the relative effectiveness of different types of pay plans in terms of the three criteria. The six basic plans are straight salary on (1) individual, (2) group, and (3) organization-wide bases and salary plus bonus on (4) individual, (5) group, and (6) organization-wide bases. Moreover, salary and salary plus bonus plans can be based upon different performance measures. For example, an individual's salary or salary plus bonus plan can be based upon his or her productivity, cost-effectiveness, or superior's rating. Similar performance measures are applicable to group-based salary and salary plus bonus plans. Organization-wide salary and salary plus bonus plans can be based upon productivity and cost-effectiveness, but also profits, as at Worthington Industries as noted in the Management Update. Thus, when these three performance measures are linked to the six basic pay plans, 18 different variations are possible. Each of these 18 variations can range from very effective (+3) to very ineffective (−3) in relation to each of the three criteria, as summarized in Table 13–1.

The most effective plan for producing the perception that pay is in fact related to performance is the individual salary plus bonus based upon productivity. However, this same plan is least effective in minimizing negative side effects. Highly productive employees are often ostracized by their fellow employees for being rate-busters. Thus, as is the case of many other managerial practices, the alternative that is most effective for one purpose, is least effective of other purposes. Clearly, the choice of pay plan involves

[15] John P. Campbell, Marvin D. Dunnette, Edward E. Lawler III, and Karl E. Weick, Jr., *Managerial Behavior, Performance, and Effectiveness* (New York: McGraw-Hill, 1970), pp. 51–59.

compromise and the direction of the decision will be affected by factors specific to a situation, including the relative ease of developing valid performance measures.

In many situations, it is difficult to develop valid, equitable, and accepted measures of performance. Therefore, it is difficult to relate pay to performance. For example, measures of college teaching effectiveness are quite controversial. No widely accepted objective measure of college teaching performance exists, although subjective peer or student evaluations are often used.

In other situations, too much emphasis may be placed on objective measures of performance. If only objective measures are used in determining pay increases, then the employee may emphasize only these and disregard others that are also important. Management must balance the objective and subjective evaluations of performance.

Another important issue involved in tying pay to performance is that of the amounts. Motivating high performers may cost a lot of money. A company that cannot afford large increases may not want to use pay to

Table 13–1

Ratings of selected pay-incentive plans

	Type of plan	Performance measure	Tie pay to performance	Minimize negative side effects	Tie other rewards to performance
Salary	Individual plan	Productivity	+2	0	0
		Cost effectiveness	+1	0	0
		Superiors' rating	+1	0	+1
	Group	Productivity	+1	0	+1
		Cost effectiveness	+1	0	+1
		Superiors' rating	+1	0	+1
	Organization-wide	Productivity	+1	0	+1
		Cost effectiveness	+1	0	+1
		Profits	0	0	+1
Bonus	Individual plan	Productivity	+3	−2	0
		Cost effectiveness	+2	−1	0
		Superiors' rating	+2	−1	+1
	Group	Productivity	+2	0	+1
		Cost effectiveness	+2	0	+1
		Superiors' rating	+2	0	+1
	Organization-wide	Productivity	+2	0	+1
		Cost effectiveness	+2	0	+1
		Profits	+1	0	+1

SOURCE: Edward E. Lawler III, *Pay and Organizational Effectiveness* (New York: McGraw-Hill, 1971) pp. 164–65.

motivate exceptional performance. Moreover, some individuals are not motivated by even large increases in pay. Management needs to determine what value employees place on pay before tying pay increases to performance.

In summary, before pay is used to motivate performance, management needs to consider a number of issues. They are:

1. Methods of measuring individual job performance.
2. The subjective-objective criteria for evaluating job performance.
3. The size of pay rewards for high performers.
4. The preferences of the employees.

Behavior modification

Another method for improving employee productivity which has emerged in recent years is **behavior modification.** This method is based largely on the theory and research of B. F. Skinner[16] who believes that behavior can be modified by changing the environment in which the behavior occurs. In terms of motivation theory, behavior modification applies both need and expectancy theory in the sense that individuals *learn* how to achieve need satisfaction from cues provided by the environment.

Skinner distinguishes between **respondent behavior** and **operant behavior.** Respondent behavior occurs because of some prior stimulus. It is unlearned, instinctive behavior. One does not learn to sneeze or to cough. Operant behavior, on the other hand, must be learned.

The fundamental difference between respondent behavior and operant behavior can be further illustrated by the relationship between response and the environment. In respondent behavior, the environment acts on the person and there is a response. The doctor taps a knee and the leg moves—respondent behavior. However, the patient must first call the doctor for an appointment—operant behavior.

In studying this distinction, Skinner introduced the concept of **operant conditioning.** In Skinner's theory, operant behavior is learned on the basis of its consequences. Thus, learned behavior operates on the environment to produce a change. If the behavior causes the desired change, then Skinner states that this behavior is reinforced and will probably be repeated. For example, being permitted to drive across a toll bridge is contingent on inserting the proper change in a coin meter. If the proper change is inserted, the green light will flash and the gate will go up. The *behavior* is inserting the coin, and the *consequence* is the gate going up. Thus, behavior can be conditioned by adjusting its consequences.

Over the years, scientific experimentation has produced the information needed to implement behavior modification in organizations. Three specific

[16] B. F. Skinner, *Contingencies of Reinforcement* (New York: Appleton-Century-Crofts, 1969).

strategies have emerged from this work—positive reinforcement, negative reinforcement, and punishment. The strategies can and are used singly or in various combinations to improve performance.

Positive reinforcement refers to an increase in the frequency of a response which is followed by a positive reinforcer. Such reinforcers are often called *rewards.* For example, employees repeatedly produce large quantities of parts (a frequent response) because they are paid on a piece-rate basis. Something is reinforcing the behavior to produce the large quantities. In this example, pay is the positive reinforcer (reward) that increases the frequency with which the workers produce large quantities.

A bank president described his use of positive reinforcers:

> *The reinforcement we now use focuses on the positive or reward forms controlling behavior. Positive control has paid off for our employees and the bank. Our bank rewards performance through increased merit salary increments, bonuses, days off, and educational benefits. In most cases, the employees have become advocates of our positive reward program. I have heard person after person express the wish that the program had been introduced years ago. We are more than pleased with the program and plan to continue using it with all employees. Our emphasis will remain on influencing behavior by altering conditions within the control of the manager. By managing in this manner, higher levels of performance can be achieved.*

This president had become so enthusiastic about positive reinforcement that he wrote articles in the bank newsletter on the topic and asked all managers to attend seminars on what the bank called *behavior management.*

Negative reinforcement refers to the increased frequency of a response which is brought about by removing a disliked event immediately after the response occurs. An example would be an employee whose supervisor continually nags about producing more units. By producing more, the worker causes the supervisor to stop nagging. The elimination of the nagging results in more production.

Punishment decreases the frequency of a response by introducing something disliked or removing something liked following that response. A worker may tell the supervisor that she has discovered a way to reduce machine downtime. The supervisor publicly reprimands her for wasting time and tells her to get back to work. The actions of the supervisor are punishment oriented and will probably reduce the tendency of the worker to be creative.

Organizational applications of behavior modification Emery Air Freight has used positive reinforcement as a behavior modification strategy. Under the direction of Edward J. Feeney, a vice president when behavior modification was introduced at Emery, the company reported a saving of $2 million over a three-year period. Feeney developed what he called a *Performance Audit* for identifying performance-related behaviors and strengthening them with positive reinforcement.

An audit was conducted to find the job behaviors that were most closely linked to profit. The strategy was to tell the individuals who were responsible for profit-oriented behaviors how they were doing. This feedback was a part of learning for the employees. They found out on a regular basis how they were doing and what the company thought about their work.

The Emery program is kept simple in each unit. First, the audit identifies the key performance behaviors. Second, management establishes a realistic goal and gives the employees frequent feedback on how they are performing. Third, improved performance is strengthened by positive reinforcement such as praise and recognition. The main thrust of the Emery program is to provide timely feedback and to use positive reinforcement that is contingent on performance improvement.

B. F. Goodrich Chemical Company uses a positive reinforcement program. One production section in a B. F. Goodrich plant in Ohio was not performing well. After identifying some problems, the production manager introduced a positive reinforcement program. The program provided cost, scheduling, and goal accomplishment information directly to the first-line supervisors once a week. Daily meetings were also held to discuss how each group in the section was doing. This program allowed the supervisor and the subordinates to look at the performance of the group on a regular basis. Illustrative charts were developed that showed achievements as compared to objectives in terms of sales, costs, and production.

The evaluation of this program by company representatives indicated that production increased over 300 percent in five years. Production costs went down. The company believed that these impressive results were largely the result of providing the supervisors and employees with feedback about their performance.

Criticisms of behavior modification Despite impressive results from behavior modification, there have been many critics of this approach.[17] Some of the major criticisms of behavior modification are:

It is coercive.

It is bribery.

It is dependent on extrinsic reinforcers.

It requires continual reinforcement.

[17] Fred L. Fry, "Operant Conditioning in Organizational Settings: Of Mice or Men," *Personnel,* July–August 1974, pp. 17–24.

One means to avoid coercion is to have employees participate in the development of the reinforcement program. Participative behavior modification programs are certainly possible.

In some programs, tokens are used to reward employees for being present or for performing well. The critics charge that this practice is an improper use of rewards and also that it demeans the persons who receive them. They point out that mental institutions sometimes give tokens to patients who display socially acceptable behavior, and they argue that tokens ought not to be applied to employees.

Some critics object that reinforcement leads to a dependence on reinforcers. As a result, extrinsic reinforcers might always be required in order to secure acceptable performance. The issue here is whether enough extrinsic reinforcers can be found to continue the program. If the same reinforcers are used over and over again, they become boring and lose their effect.

The final criticism focuses on the necessity for continual reinforcement. To be successful, behavior modification requires that supervisors closely monitor the performance of their subordinates and reward desired behavior. However, in many organizations, managers simply do not have sufficient time for such close supervision.

Behavior modification, like the use of a good pay plan or of job enrichment, will work in some organizations but not in others. The evidence of success is not overwhelming, but it does appear promising. Of course, failures are usually not as widely publicized as successes. It appears that Skinner's ideas may be used by some managers to obtain some degree of performance improvement.

Quality circles

During the past 10 years, American and Canadian industry has been experiencing a quiet revolution. Faced with sluggish productivity, an increasingly competitive world market, and inflation, some managers have discovered and experimented with quality circles (QCs). Quality circles are small groups of workers (7 to 12) who meet regularly (weekly in most cases) with their supervisor as the circle leader to solve work-related problems (e.g., quality, quantity, cost).

From management's point of view, the QC is a motivational program that has significant potential. One expert stated that "There is scarcely a study in the entire literature that fails to demonstrate that . . . productivity increases accrue from a genuine increase in decision making power. . . . The participative worker is an involved worker, for his job is an extension of himself and by his decisions he is creating his work, modifying and regulating it." Circles leave time for managers to manage. The motivation is assumed to be in the task itself, as Herzberg's theory predicts.

QCs give the employee opportunity for involvement, social need satisfaction, participation in work improvement, challenge, and opportunity for growth. They are in essence a vehicle for providing employees with opportunities to satisfy lower- and upper-level needs as stated by Maslow and the motivators as described in Herzberg's theory. Participation in QCs provides the vital Herzberg-type motivators to even the lowest-level employee. Members assume responsibility to identify and analyze problems in their work areas.

Although in most cases QCs meet for only about an hour a week, this meeting carries over into the rest of the week. Circle activities are carried to break and lunchtimes. Also, members continue to think about the points raised in the meetings. Frequently, circle members meet on their own time to complete QC assignments such as charting its progress to that of other QCs.

The QC provides employees with an opportunity to be a part of a team seeking common goals. Matching the worker's needs to company goals can be accomplished in a QC. Organizational goals can be reached while personal needs keep the process moving forward.

Like any managerial program that has motivational overtones, QCs have some risks. Assuming that QCs are the answer to all motivational problems is, of course, misleading and untrue. The Japanese popularized the use of QCs. A report by the Japanese Union of Scientists and Engineers indicates that 100,000 QCs are now registered in the country. Toyo Kogyo, maker of the Mazda, alone has 1,800 QCs.[18] A concern is whether a method of motivation which works in Japan can work in the United States or Canada. Japan differs in many important ways from the United States or Canada. For example, Japan has a homogeneous culture which treats organizational life as an extension of family life. This, of course, is not the case in plants, offices, and construction projects in Detroit, Chicago, Los Angeles, Toronto, and elsewhere in North America.

Culture is certainly a powerful force that must be considered. However, there is also the need to determine whether labor and management are willing to work together in QCs. Instead of initiating the Japanese style of QCs, it seems more realistic to develop an American style QC, a Canadian style of QC, and so forth. The appropriate QC style must be developed by labor and management through a cooperative team effort. If such cooperation is not possible, then QCs, no matter how they are designed, have little chance to be successful in motivating participants.

The American aerospace industry has used QCs successfully. This industry is concerned with quality because one small error can have a devastating effect on human lives. There is also a history of labor-management cooperation in the aerospace industry. The results of QCs in the industry have been positive—higher productivity and morale. The industry is well suited for QCs.

On the other hand, in the auto industry, the use of QCs has been much

[18] Ron Zemke, "What's Good for Japan May Not Be Best for Your Training Department," *Training/HRD*, October 1981, p. 62.

more difficult. For years, the labor-management relationship has been antagonistic. This relationship is difficult to overcome through the use of QCs. The common good, common interest, and common goals are extremely difficult to accomplish if labor and management are not inclined to cooperate and work together.

Another potential problem with QCs is managerial resistance. QCs encourage people to voice opinions, make suggestions, and display their ideas about work. This practice theoretically reduces the "administrative distance" between worker and manager. The result is that some managers often feel threatened by what they perceive as a loss of power, status, prestige, and authority. They may consciously or subconsciously hinder the work and processes of the QC.

Still another potential area of difficulty is the role of the QC leader. In organizations, leadership roles are taken by managers and supervisors. However, in the QC, the leader is not in an authority position. He or she is instead a facilitator, a discussion leader who helps the group reach solutions. The leader who attempts to enforce autocratically his or her viewpoints quickly loses the respect, cooperation, and attention of the QC members. Many managers have a difficult time making the transition from a legitimate authority position in the formal hierarchy to the role of a facilitator in a QC.

The continued introduction and research of QCs in American and Canadian industry will undoubtedly continue in the 1980s. Whether or not QCs can work as well in North America as they have in Japan remains to be tested in the next few years. They are worth a look from managers and organizations who are willing to allow employees to participate in job-related problem solving.[19]

Management summary

1. Unsatisfied needs initiate the process of motivation. These needs initiate goal-directed behavior. An important management task is to identify the goals of subordinates. This information would help managers understand the behavior of the subordinates.
2. Maslow's hierarchy is a useful explanation of needs. Managers often use it when analyzing motivational problems.
3. Need frustration often results in the use of defense mechanisms. Aggressive behavior, rationalizing behavior, and withdrawal may be explained in terms of frustration.
4. Although Herzberg's two-factor theory is open to criticism, it appeals

[19] Edwin G. Yager, "The Quality Explosion," *Training and Development Journal,* April 1981, p. 98–99, 101–5.

to practicing managers. Herzberg discusses satisfaction by using work-oriented terms which managers can identify with.

5. The best explanation of the connection between goals and effort is provided by the expectancy theory of motivation. The value or preference that a person places on goals is important in interpreting the degree of effort that is being expended.
6. Job enrichment, pay, behavior modification, and quality circles all possess motivation potential if used correctly and in the right situations. They are actually contingency-type plans which can be successful. Unfortunately, overzealous proponents give the impression that they always work well. Managers must always guard against such claims. If used correctly, these three application programs can provide benefits for organizations and employees.

Review and discussion questions

1. Why do some writers claim that if management enriches the job's core dimensions, a worker may become more motivated?
2. Are there any differences between expectancy theory and behavior modification?
3. The manager of a fast-food restaurant was overheard saying, "I believe that money is the best of all possible motivators. You can say what you please about all that other nonsense, but when it comes right down to it, if you give a guy a raise, you'll motivate him. That's all there is to it." In light of what we have discussed in this chapter, advise this restaurant manager.
4. Think of a situation from your personal experience in which two individuals reacted differently to frustration. Discuss each situation and the reactions of the two individuals. Can you give a possible explanation of why the two individuals reacted differently?
5. Some critics of job enrichment and behavior modification programs state that most of the declared successes are based on short-term results. These critics contend that a proper evaluation over a longer period of time would show less positive results for these programs. Comment.
6. How can the performance of a manager be validly measured so that pay can be more closely tied to performance?
7. In this chapter, it was emphasized that managers must be familiar with the fundamental needs of people in order to motivate employees successfully. Select two individuals with whom you are well acquainted. Do they differ, in your opinion, with respect to the strength of various needs? Discuss these differences and indicate how they could affect behavior. If you were attempting to motivate those persons, would you use different approaches for each? Why?

8. Can a student's "job" be enriched? Assume that your professor has asked you to consult with him/her about applying the two-factor motivation theory in your class. You are to answer these questions for him/her: (1) Can you apply this approach to the classroom? Why? (2) If so, differentiate between maintenance and motivational factors and develop a list of motivational factors that your professor can use to enrich the student's job.
9. Assume that you have just read that the *goals* of individuals influence their *effort* and that the behavior which they select depends on their assessment of the probability that the behavior will successfully lead to the goal. What is your goal in this management course? Is it influencing your effort? Do you suppose that another person in your class might have a different goal? Is his or her effort (behavior) different from yours? Could this information be of any value to your professor?
10. What is the difference between intrinsic and extrinsic rewards? What types of rewards are used in job enrichment, pay, and behavior modification programs?

Suggested reading

Archibald, D. "Incentive Carrots: Make Them Large and Plentiful." *Training/HRD,* March 1981, p. 14.

Crystal, G. S. "Pay for Performance—Even If It's Just Luck." *The Wall Street Journal,* March 2, 1981, p. 16.

Delong, D. "Creative People Can Meet Deadlines." *Inc.,* December 1981, pp. 97–98.

Flamion, A. "The Dollars and Sense of Motivation." *Personnel Journal,* January 1980, pp. 51–52, 61.

Gardner, J. "Creating Motivating Workplaces." *Personnel Journal,* May 1981, pp. 406–8.

Haynes, R. S., R. C. Pine, and H. G. Fitch. "Reducing Accident Rates with Organizational Behavior Modification." *Academy of Management Journal,* June 1982, pp. 407–16.

Kazdin, A. E. *Behavior Modification in Applied Settings.* Homewood, Ill.: Dorsey Press, 1980.

Odiorne, G. S. "An Uneasy Look at Motivation Theory." *Training and Development Journal,* June 1980, pp. 106–12.

"Quality of Work Life: Catching On." *Business Week,* September 21, 1981, pp. 72–76, 80.

Skinner, B. F. "Reward or Punishment: Which Works Better." *U.S. News & World Report,* November 3, 1980, pp. 79–80.

Steers, R. M., and L. W. Porter, eds. *Motivation and Work Behavior.* New York: McGraw-Hill, 1979.

Scoring instructions for the motivation survey in Figure 13–3

1. Transfer the numbers you circled in Figure 13–3 to the appropriate places in the chart below:

Statement number	Score	Statement number	Score
10	______	2	______
11	______	3	______
13	______	9	______
18	______	19	______
Total (self-actualization needs)	______	Total (safety needs)	______

Statement number	Score	Statement number	Score
6	______	1	______
8	______	4	______
14	______	16	______
17	______	20	______
Total (esteem needs)	______	Total (physiological needs)	______

Statement number	Score
5	______
7	______
12	______
15	______
Total (social needs)	______

2. Record your total scores in the chart below by marking an *X* in each row next to the number of your total score for that area of needs motivation.

	−12	−10	−8	−6	−4	−2	0	+2	+4	+6	+8	+10	+12
Self-actualization													
Esteem													
Social													
Safety													
Physical													

Low use — High use

Once you have completed this chart, you can see the relative strength of each of these needs.

Applying what you have learned about motivation and performance

Cases:

A motivational program at General Motors Inland plant
Motivating different individuals

A motivational program at General Motors Inland plant*

In a cramped noisy section of General Motors Inland plant in Dayton, Ohio, an eight-member work crew is testing the effectiveness of a new way to motivate employees. The crew is stationed at the end of a production line in which foam-rubber car seats are formed in aluminum molds. Bending over a hot conveyor line, the workers use short hoelike tools to scrape off excess rubber that has extruded through holes in the molds. Then they remove the cushions and toss them on another conveyor for shipping. Many employees consider the job dull, boring, and demeaning.

About three months ago, management implemented a new system that brings together workers' suggestions and technical engineering requirements. A committee of 30 hourly and salaried workers meet as a work process task force. The committee studies and recommends ways to improve jobs like the one described above.

Local 87 of the United Rubber Workers, which represents 5,400 workers at Inland, is cooperating with management's use of the work process task force. Management promised not to lay off employees when and if recommendations of the task force are used.

The task force proposals for job improvement are passed on to a redesign committee consisting of plant superintendents and the Local 87 president Red Hutchins. Before the task force was started, Red described the entire plant climate as hostile, "us (the union) against them (management). Now it seems to be only us."

---

* This case is adapted from "The New Industrial Relations" and "A New Way of Managing People," *Business Week,* May 11, 1981, pp. 84–85, 89, 94–96.

Management generally believes the morale has improved in the seat cushion department. There is now talk of expanding the task force idea to other departments. However, some skeptics still exist. One manager stated that, "It's too early to say it is good or bad. Don't jump to conclusions." A union member stated, "Some of our views are still not listened to by the task force. This is just another gimmick to keep us under control."

Although some skeptics question the task force program, most workers like the new atmosphere at Inland. They are making more suggestions for changes, they seem happier, and there is a new sense of job involvement. Most workers believe their views are being heard.

Labor and management have through the task force program created a more positive motivational climate. One union member stated, "It's better to work around here, even though the job is still pretty boring." Inland's management now is considering the expansion of the task force program into other divisions. It feels that the program could even be used to cut down on absenteeism in the shipping division. The plan is to put together a shipping division task force to study the jobs in the department and to address the excessive unexcused absenteeism problem.

The shipping supervisor Mark Gallat feels that the task force idea as used in the seat cushion department is not feasible to improve absenteeism in the shipping division. It is not the way to decrease absences. Furthermore, he feels that the union will not cooperate on absenteeism reduction approaches with management. He feels that the monotony and boredom of working on a shipping platform are work conditions that can't be changed. His method of motivating workers in shipping is to pay them more. This, in his opinion, will cut back on absenteeism.

Questions:

1. What is your opinion of the motivational impact of the task force program in the seat cushion department? Do you like the program? Why?
2. Evaluate the management and union skeptics' comments about the task force program.
3. Does Mark Gallat make sense when he criticizes the use of the task force program in shipping and his claim about the motivational impact of money?

Motivating different individuals

Below are brief descriptions of several individuals. Assume that you are their manager. Select from the following the strategy that you feel would be most likely to motivate each person to improve performance. Explain your reasons for selecting it.

a. An individual incentive plan.
b. Recognition for achievement.
c. A salary increase.
d. The threat of demotion or discharge.
e. Additional status (e.g., a bigger office, a title, carpeting in the office, a secretary).
f. A group profit-sharing plan.
g. Job enrichment.
h. Additional fringe benefits.
i. More participation in management decisions.
j. More freedom of action (i.e., less supervision).

1. Jim Hammer is a marketing representative for a large pharmaceutical firm. His job involves calling on physicians to promote the firm's line of prescription drugs. He is 31-years-old, married, has one child, and

holds a college degree in business administration. He has been with the firm five years and earns $17,300 annually.

2. Barbara Oldeck is the head pediatrics nurse at a large public hospital. She is 24-years-old, married, has two children, and is currently pursuing a master's degree. She has a reputation among staff physicians as an extremely competent nurse. Her yearly salary is $13,300.
3. John Ekard is vice president of operations for one of the nation's largest fast-food franchisers. He is 49-years-old, divorced, and has three children—two attend college, and one is married. He has been with the company for nine years, and he earns a salary of $62,500 per year. He is among a group of top-level executives in the company who share in company profits through a bonus system.
4. Dave Noe is a part-time employee for a large supermarket chain. He is 26-years-old and an Air Force veteran, and he worked for the firm before entering the Air Force and has worked for it since being discharged. He is a highly valued employee, and he earns approximately $6.40 per hour. He attends a local university and at present is completing the final 15 hours for a degree in business administration.
5. Marie Glass is assistant director of market development for a new space industry firm. She is 32-years-old, single, bright, witty, and energetic. She exemplifies the "new woman." Her annual salary is $18,000. She has just completed her master's degree.

14

Chapter fourteen Work groups and performance

Performance objectives

- **Define** the work group from a manager's perspective.
- **State** the reasons why groups are formed within organizations.
- **Describe** the difference between formal and informal groups.
- **Explain** how work groups can apply pressure to an individual which can result in conformity.
- **Discuss** management strategies that can be implemented to deal with intergroup conflict.

Management update*

At a Siemens plant in Karlsruhe, West Germany, workers assembling electronics products used to perform simple tasks over and over. Each task required about one minute of a worker's attention and effort. Today, many employees work in groups of three to seven at well-designed "work islands," where they can avoid boredom by rotating jobs, socializing, and working in cycles of up to 20 minutes rather than a few seconds. In auto and appliance assembly plants, the Germans appear to be using the group-oriented work island effectively to improve performance.

American management and labor groups have visited German factories to see the work islands in action. Germany has a history of labor-management cooperation on the shop floor. American visitors have been impressed with the West German use of work islands.

The group concept also works to perfection at the Mercedes Benz plant in West Germany. Teams of workers who rotate jobs follow the product to the last step in the assembly process. They are linked together by a group-incentive pay plan. The workers at the Benz plant like group work because it permits and even requires socializing on the job.

In group assembly, each worker learns to handle several jobs instead of a few simple tasks. Boredom, fatigue, and dissatisfaction seem to be lower at the West German plants using the work island concept. Of course, West Germany doesn't have a patent on the work island notion. It is used in Japan and the United States with varying degrees of success. In Japan, workers respond enthusiastically, even though the work pace for the groups is heavily engineered and under management control.

The fact that U.S. management and labor representatives have taken notice and regularly visit foreign plants using group assembly teams is in itself interesting. These representatives are interested in any method or procedure that can improve the quality of worklife and performance. This is not to say that work islands will be successful in every U.S. plant or situation. The point is that the U.S. management and labor community is willing to observe, analyze, and experiment with various group or team efforts to enhance performance.

---

* This Management Update is based on "Moving beyond Assembly Lines," *Business Week*, July 27, 1981, pp. 87–88.

This chapter is concerned with the issues of managing work groups and group processes in organizations. Managers and researchers have paid special attention to the group processes which affect individuals and organizations. Thus, any presentation of management would certainly be incomplete if the reader were not provided with a framework for understanding the nature and characteristics of work groups. An appropriate definition of the term *work group* is as follows: **A work group is a collection of employees (managerial or nonmanagerial) who share certain norms and are striving toward member need satisfaction through the attainment of group goals.**

The purposes of this chapter are to provide (1) a classification of the different types of groups, (2) some knowledge about the reasons for the formation and development of groups, (3) an understanding of some characteristics of groups, and (4) some insights into the results of group membership.

Students often ask why work groups should be studied in a management text. Many different answers could be provided. Two of the more relevant responses are:

1. The formation of work groups is inevitable in organizations. Thus, it is in management's interest to understand what happens within and among work groups because they are found throughout the organization.

2. Work groups strongly influence the behavior and performance of their members. Understanding the influences exerted by such groups requires a systematic analysis.

The common thread found in most answers is that work groups exist and that they are a force which affects the work performance of employees. This is the most obvious and pragmatic reason for the study of groups.

Classification of groups

Managers and nonmanagers belong to a number of different groups within organizations. The memberships in groups often overlap. In some instances, individuals are members of a group because of their position in the organization. However, through contacts they make in the group, they begin to affiliate with some of its members on an informal basis.

Formal work groups

Employees will be members of at least one group based on their positions in the organization. These **formal groups** are the departments, units, and so on, that the organization forms to do the work. The demands and processes of the organization lead to the formation of these groups. Two specific types of formal groups are command and task groups.

The command group The **command group** is specified by the organization chart. The subordinates who report directly to a given supervisor make up a command group. The relationship between the department manager and the three supervisors in a machine shop is indicated in the organization chart. As the span of control of the department manager increases, the command group increases in number. A marketing manager described how he ended up in a particular unit:

> *I had the statistical background needed to round out the project team. I knew it, and so did my boss. Consequently, nine months ago, I was assigned to it. I'm happy now because the group is really quite exciting, and the project is challenging. I guess I was the right guy in the right place at the right time.*

The task group A number of employees who work together to complete a specific project or a job are considered a **task group.** The work island described in the Management Update is a task group. A manufacturing or office work process that requires a great deal of interdependence is an example of a task group. Assume that three office clerks are required for (1) securing the file of an automobile accident claim; (2) checking the accuracy of the claim by contacting the persons involved; and (3) typing the claim, obtaining the required signatures of those involved, and refiling the claim.

The activation of the file and the steps that must be taken before the claim is refiled constitute required tasks. These tasks create a situation in which three clerks must communicate and coordinate with one another if the file is to be handled properly. Their activities and interactions facilitate the formation of the task group.

Committees are very common in organizations. Committees are actually task groups that are established for such purposes as:

1. Exchanging views and information.
2. Recommending action.
3. Generating ideas.
4. Making decisions.

Committees can achieve all of these purposes. However, a group may have difficulty in making decisions. Thus, the fourth purpose cited is often hard to achieve in a committee. Managers can see that a committee is kept relatively small, since size affects the quality of a group's decisions. Increasing a committee's size tends to limit the extent to which its members want to or can communicate. As the size of committees increases, members tend to feel threatened and less willing to participate actively. The perceived threat can lead to increased stress and conflict. Of course, these types of outcomes do not encourage the generation of good committee decisions.

The committee chairperson is expected to provide proper direction. Ordinarily, successful committees have chairpersons who understand group processes. Such chairpersons see that the committee's objectives and purposes remain clear, encourage committee members to participate, and know how to keep the committee moving toward its objectives.

A committee chairperson must follow a fine line. A chairperson who is too non-directive may lose the members' respect. On the other hand, a chairperson who exerts tight control may alienate the members. The chairperson needs to be directive without alienating the committee members. A dominating chairperson will not usually acquire the group's acceptance. Without group acceptance, the chairperson is a leader without a following.

Managerial experience on committees has led to some guidelines that can aid committee chairpersons. Some of these are:

1. Be a careful listener and listen with an open mind.
2. Allow each member to voice opinions and do not place your opinion above those of others.
3. Get everyone involved in the committee's activities.
4. Display an active interest in the purpose of the committee and in the ideas of its members.
5. Help the committee focus on the task at hand and on the progress being made.

Committee members must also be responsible for creating an atmosphere of cooperation within the group. Management experience indicates that in cooperative groups as distinguished from competitive groups, one finds:

1. Stronger motivation to accomplish the task.
2. More effective communication.
3. More ideas generated.
4. More membership satisfaction.
5. More group performance.

Thus, when cooperation prevails, there are generally positive results. Communication, satisfaction, and productivity are generally all more positive in the cooperative committee. Both the committee's chairperson and its members are important determinants of cooperative committee efforts.

Informal work groups

Whenever employees associate on a fairly continuous basis, there is a tendency for groups to form whose activities may be different from those required by the organization. These **informal groups** are natural groupings of people in the work situation. They do not arise as a result of deliberate design but evolve naturally. Two types of informal work groups are interest and friendship groups.

The interest group Groups often form because their members share a common interest in some particular job-related event or possible outcome. This type of group can be viewed as an **interest group,** since the members have joined together to achieve some objective, such as an equitable pension payment. The members of the group may or may not be members of the same command or task group.

Figure 14–1

Informal-formal group types

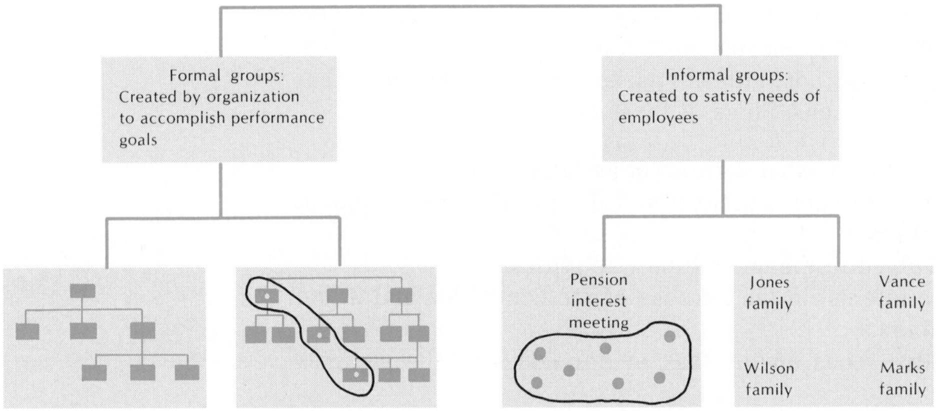

Command group | Task group | Interest group | Friendship group

The friendship group In the workplace, because of some common characteristic such as age, ethnic background, political sentiment, or an interest in sports, employees often form **friendship groups.** These groups often extend their interaction and communication to off-the-job activities. For example, their members, having become friends in the workplace, then bowl together, or attend sporting events together, or take their families on picnics together.

Figure 14–1 classifies groups on the basis of formality-informality and type. Many individuals are members of all of these groups at the same time. Thus, managers must think about the multiple group memberships of their subordinates.

The formation of work groups

Explanations of the reasons for group formation center on a number of location, economic, and sociopsychological factors.

Location

When people are in close proximity, they tend to interact and communicate. Some degree of interaction and communication is necessary for group formation, particularly informal groups.

In organizations, a typical procedure is to position workers in similar occupations together. For example, in the construction of a home, the bricklayers perform their jobs in close proximity to one another. The same situation exists in offices, where clerks or secretaries are located next to one another. An office manager of an insurance company provided a vivid picture of how proximity influences people:

> *The office is like a large family room in a home. Everyone is so close that we learn everything about each other. This occasionally shocks some of the timid types. They can't believe they say what they do. In my opinion, one way to get people to talk and level with each other is to let them work right next to each other. When clerks are at odds, I often nudge them to work with each other. In most cases, the results are tremendous for everyone concerned.*

Economic reasons

In some cases, work groups form because individuals believe that they can derive more economic benefits on their jobs if they form groups. For example, individuals working at different stations on an assembly line may be paid on a group-incentive basis. Whatever the particular group produces determines the wages of each member. Because of the interest of the workers in their wages, they will interact and communicate with one another. By working as a group instead of as individuals, they may actually obtain higher economic benefits.

Another example of the economic motive for the formation of informal work groups might be a nonunion organization, in which the workers might form a group to bring pressure on management for more economic benefits. The group members would have a common interest—increased economic benefits—which would lead to group affiliation. A nurse described how her group was pressuring management:

> *We have no intention of unionizing in the near future. However, we want better benefits and more time off. The grind is just unrealistic. We are professionals and will not stand being pushed around. We are all going to visit with our supervisor and make our point once and for all. Unionizing is not a threat but leaving the hospital is certainly being considered.*

The nurses' demands were expressed, but little was done about them. The final result of this situation was unionization. The nurses' leaders were approached by a union organizer, and soon afterward, a union was voted in. The hospital had to increase its fringe benefits, but it also cut turnover significantly after the nurses became unionized.

Sociopsychological reasons

Workers in organizations are also motivated to form work groups so that certain needs can be more adequately satisfied. The safety, social, esteem, and self-actualization needs can be satisfied to some degree by work groups.

Safety Work groups protect members from management pressures such as demands for better quality and quantity of production, insistence that they punch the clock on time, and recommendations for changes in individual work area layouts. By being members of a group, individual employees can openly discuss these management demands with other workers, who usually support their viewpoint. Without the group to lean on, individuals often assume that they are alone against management and the entire organization. The interactions and communications that exist among members of a work group serve as a buffer to management demands.

Social Employees often join work groups because of their need for affiliation. The basis of affiliation ranges from wanting to interact with and enjoy other employees to more complex desires for group support of the self-image. A management atmosphere which does not permit interaction and communication suppresses the desire of employees to feel a sense of belongingness. A lawyer for inner-city clients described a social interaction problem she experienced:

> *We were once all located in one office—six lawyers, seven paralegals, and three clerk-typists. Now the restructuring has placed all of us in neighborhood offices. This move has effectively broken up the group. Before, we exchanged ideas and complaints, but now I talk to myself. I really didn't appreciate our group until they set us up in these isolated field offices. What a change!*

Esteem Some employees are attracted to a work group because they gain prestige by being in it. A particular group in an organization may be viewed by employees as being a top-notch work group. Consequently, membership in the elite group bestows prestige on the members which is not enjoyed by nonmembers. This prestige is conferred on the members by other employees (nonmembers), which leads to more gratification of the esteem need. By sharing in the activities of a high-prestige work group, the individual identifies more closely with the group. This form of identification is valued highly by some employees.

Self-actualization The desire of individuals to grow and develop psychologically on the job expresses the self-actualization need. Employees often believe that rigid job requirements and rules do not enable them to satisfy this need sufficiently. One reaction to rigid requirements, rules, and regulations is to join a work group, which is viewed as a vehicle for communicating among friends about the use of job-related skill. The jargon utilized and the skill employed are appreciated by the knowledgeable group members. This appreciation can lead to the feeling of accomplishing a worthwhile task. This feeling, and similar feelings which are related to the belief that one is creative and skillful, often lead to more satisfaction of the self-actualization need.

The development of work groups

The development of work groups is distinctly related to learning—learning to work together and learning to accept and trust each other. These phases are referred to as the maturation of a group. The following account of a four-phase group development process points out clearly some of the problems and frustrations inherent in group development.[1]

First phase: Mutual acceptance

Employees are often hampered by their mistrust of each other, of the organization, and of their superiors. They are fearful that they do not have the necessary training or skill to perform the job or compete with others. These feelings of insecurity motivate employees to seek out others in the same predicament and to express their feelings openly. A group results,

[1] The discussion of the development of groups is based largely on Bernard Bass, *Organizational Psychology* (Boston: Allyn & Bacon, 1965), pp. 197–98. A number of alterations were made by the authors. Also see J. Stephen Heiner and Eugene Jacobson, "A Model of Task Group Development in Complex Organizations and a Strategy of Implementation," *Academy of Management Review*, October 1976, pp. 98–111.

and the mistrust is significantly reduced. Thus, after an initial period of uneasiness and learning about the feelings of others, individuals typically begin to accept each other.

In some groups, however members never accept each other as reflected in the following comments about a training session on performance evaluation:

> *Plant superintendent: Throughout the three days of training, there was a deadly silence. The sessions included raters and ratees—what more could be expected? I don't remember much trust or openness. Everyone was very careful so as not to offend someone that he or she would be working with after the completion of the training.*
>
> *First-line supervisor: I disliked everything about the training, especially my boss sitting next to me. The training program didn't solve any of the performance evaluation problems. I think we could have done a better job by having raters and ratees trained in different groups.*
>
> *Organizational trainer: I was never able to get the people to level with each other. I felt that there would be some problems, but never expected such a problem throughout the three days. What a mess—a group that never became a group.*

Although these three statements involved a temporary training group, there is one important message for managers: Do not expect a group to just naturally reach a point of mutual acceptance.

Second phase: Decision making

During this phase, open communication and expression of thoughts concerning the job are the rule. Problem solving and decision making are undertaken. The members trust one another's viewpoints and beliefs; they develop strategies to make the job easier, to help one another perform more effectively.

Third phase: Motivation

The group has reached maturity, and the problems of its members are known. It is accepted that it is better for the group to have cooperation instead of competition among the members. Thus, the emphasis is on group solidarity in the form of cooperating with one another so that the job is more rewarding both economically and sociopsychologically.

Fourth phase: Control

The group has successfully organized itself, and its members contribute according to their abilities and interests. The group exercises sanctions, when control is needed to bring members into line with the group's norms.

The structures and processes that are found in work groups develop over a period of time. The motivation of group members and the control of their behavior are not an overnight occurrence. Through observing, listening, and working with a group, a manager can acquire some awareness about the stage of the group's development. This would allow the manager to better understand and cope with the group's behavior and performance.

Characteristics of work groups

The creation of an organization structure results in such characteristics as specified relationships among subordinates, superiors, and peers; leaders assigned to positions; standards of performance; a status rank order according to the positions that individuals are filling; and group politics. Work groups have characteristics which are similar to those of organizations, including leaders, standards of conduct, reward and sanction mechanisms, and political maneuvering. These and other characteristics of groups are discussed below.

The group leader

As a group attempts to complete some objective and the individual members begin to know one another, the members begin to fill one or more of the many group roles. One of the most important roles is that of the group leader. The leader emerges from within the informal group and is accepted by the group members. In the formal group, the leader is appointed.

Leaders in formal groups are followed and obeyed because employees perceive them as possessing power and influence to reward or punish them for not complying with requests. The formal leaders possess the power to regulate the formal rewards of the work group members. Here is what an engineer on a project stated:

> *One of the biggest myths in construction engineering is that the CE* [chief engineer] *has little control. I've heard that since day one, and it is pure bull. The CE*

has the clout to stop anyone dead. He can block promotions, suspend people for poor performance, transfer people, and hold up merit increases. Don't tell me about CEs—I know what they can do.

The informal leader emerges from within the group and serves a number of functions. First, any group of individuals that does not have a plan or some coordination becomes an ineffective unit. The individuals are not directed toward the accomplishment of goals, and this leads to a breakdown in group effectiveness. The leader serves to initiate action and provide direction. If there are differences of opinion on a group-related matter, the leader attempts to settle the differences and to move the group toward accomplishing its goals.

Second, some individual must communicate the group's beliefs about policies, the job, the organization, the supervision, and other related matters to nonmembers. The nonmembership category could include members of other groups, supervisory personnel, and the union. In effect, the group leader communicates the values of the group.

Thus, the characteristics of informal group leaders can be summarized as follows:

1. The leadership role is filled by an individual who possesses the attributes which the members perceive as being critical for satisfying their needs.
2. The leader embodies the values of the group and is able to perceive those values, organize them into an intelligible philosophy, and verbalize them to nonmembers.
3. The leader is able to receive and interpret communication relevant to the group and to effectively communicate important information to group members.

An informal leader in a South Chicago packaging plant described his informal leadership role in the following terms:

They have hired all new shift supervisors with college degrees. What management has found out is that working with blue-collar people takes an ability to understand different kinds of people. Thirty to 40 percent of the workers here were born in foreign countries. The college graduates don't understand these people. I do. I am one of them. These foreign-born employees want respect and someone to listen to them. The union steward is too busy politicking around. I'll never become a foreman. I have more respect than any manager and enjoy being a part of the working team and will never become an official bigwig.

Group status

Managers have relative status depending upon their positions in the hierarchy; that is, the top managers of the firm have more status than middle managers, and the middle managers have more status than lower-level managers. The top-level positions have more authority, responsibility, power, and influence and thus are accorded more status.

A similar type of status system develops in groups. For many different reasons, individuals are accorded status by the group in which they interact and communicate. Individuals who perform leadership roles possess status because of their roles. Consequently, they are ranked highly in the group-status hierarchy.

Other factors influence the status systems of groups. Many groups consider the seniority of a member to be important. A worker having more seniority is often thought of as being "organizationally intelligent," which means that the person knows how to adapt to the demands of supervisors, subordinates, or peers. This ability to adjust is an important status factor with group members.

The skill of an individual in performing a job is another factor related to status. An individual who is an expert in the technical aspects of the job is given a high status ranking in some groups. This type of status does not mean that the individual actually utilizes the skill to perform more effectively, but that the group members perceive this skill in the individual.

Group norms and compliance

A **norm** is an implicit or explicit agreement among the group members as to how the members of the group should behave. The more a person complies with norms, the more the person accepts the group's standards of behavior.

Work groups can utilize norms to bring about job performance that is acceptable to the group. The following are examples of production-related norms: (1) don't agree with management in its effort to change the wage structure, (2) present a united front to resist the directives of the new college graduate assigned to the group's work area, (3) don't produce above the group leader's level of production, (4) help members of the group to achieve an acceptable production level if they are having difficulty and if you have time, and (5) don't allow the union steward to convince you to vote for his favorite union presidential candidate in the upcoming election.

Three specific social processes bring about compliance with group norms, namely, group pressure, group review and enforcement, and the personalization of the norms.

Group pressure The pressure to adhere to a specific group norm can result in conformity to the behavior of the group's membership. Conformity occurs when the behavior of a person complies with a group's wishes because of the pressure being applied or the fear of future group pressure. Complying to group pressure is not a signal that the person agrees with the group's wishes. A plant manager expressed how the group can make a person conform:

> *On the assembly line, the idea among group members is to dance quietly. This means that the group members will conform to the production norm. Everyone supports a reasonable, steady level of production—or dancing quietly as a team. Winning the dance contest means that a person is acting against the group-set norm. The consequences of winning the contest are isolation, being cussed at, and just plain cold-shouldered treatment. Working alone in isolation for even a short period brings them back into line, and they begin to dance quietly.*

Group review and enforcement If group members, either veterans or newcomers, are not complying with generally accepted norms, a number of different approaches may be employed. A soft approach would be a discussion between respected leaders and the persons who are deviating from the norms. If discussion does not prove effective, more rigorous corrective action is used, such as private and public scolding by the members. The ultimate type of enforcement would be to ostracise the nonconforming members.

Personalization of norms The behavioral patterns of people are influenced significantly by their values. Their values, in turn, are influenced by the events occurring around them; values are learned and become personalized. For example, the norm of a work group may be to treat college graduates and persons who did not go to college equally and courteously. This norm may be accepted by a group member as morally and ethically correct. Prior to group affiliation, the member may have displayed little interest in whether an individual attended college. However, based on a feeling of fairness, the member personalizes this group-learned norm and it becomes a standard of behavior.

The group norms can be either positive or negative as far as a manager is concerned. However, both types of norms are typically encountered when compliance is the issue of concern. Figure 14–2 illustrates some examples of work conditions for which norms are often established by groups. Positive and negative norms are presented to portray what managers often face. A keypunch supervisor discussed her frustrations with group norms:

> *I just can't predict the way the operators are going to react. They asked for a longer rest break. They get*

it, and all of a sudden production decreases. We get in the new machines, and they still use their old ways of completing jobs. They ask for training and then are afraid to volunteer. No one wants to go to school.

Group cohesiveness

Cohesiveness is another important characteristic of groups. Briefly, this concept involves the stick-together characteristic of groups. It is the attraction of members to the group in terms of the strength of the forces on the individual member to remain active in the group and to resist leaving it.[2]

Figure 14–2

Positive and negative group norms

Condition	Positive group norm	Negative group norm
Performance		
Output	Members work hard to produce at optimal skill levels	Members work just hard enough to get by
Quality	Members take pride in producing quality products	Members pay enough attention to quality to keep management minimally happy
Absenteeism	Members pride themselves on being present	Members not interested in good attendance
Supervisory relations	Members respect supervisors and are honest in their interactions	Members distrust management and hold back vital information
Honesty	Members are against stealing and slowdowns	Members encourage some pilferage and slow down the line when everyone seems tired
Wages/salaries	Members expect a fair day's pay for a good day's work	Members expect to be taken care of despite a lack of effort—the "organization owes me" attitude

All of the above characteristics of groups are influenced in some degree by the cohesiveness within a group. For example, the greater the attraction

[2] This definition is based on the group cohesiveness concept presented by Stanley E. Seashore, *Group Cohesiveness in the Industrial Work Group* (Ann Arbor: University of Michigan, Institute for Social Research, 1954).

within the group, the more likely it is that the members will adhere closely to a group norm such as a production level.

Some of the conditions which influence cohesiveness are presented in Figure 14–3. The factors identified are representative of the types of factors that can enhance or reduce the cohesiveness of work groups.

The size of the work group Among the necessary conditions for the existence of a group is that its members interact and communicate with one another. If a group is so large that the members do not get to know one another, there is little likelihood that the group will be high in cohesiveness. Managers have learned that an inverse relationship does exist between group size and group cohesiveness.[3] As the size of a group increases, its cohesiveness decreases.

Figure 14–3

Factors contributing to group cohesiveness

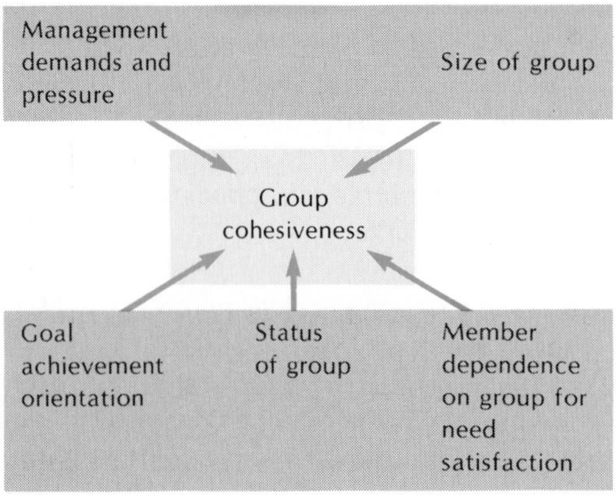

The dependence of the members on the work group The greater the individual's dependency on the group, the stronger will be the attraction. Individuals join groups because they can help them satisfy economic and sociopsychological needs. A group that is able to satisfy a significant portion of an individual's needs will appear attractive to that individual. Group processes such as interaction with co-workers and overall friendship make the group a key factor in the individual's life. Thus, what the group stands for, its norms, and its membership are bonds which tie the individual to the group.

The achievement of goals The attainment of some set of group-established goals (e.g., better production than another group) influences the group's members. For example, if a work group attains a highly desired rating

[3] Ibid., pp. 90–95. Also see Robert C. Cummins and Donald C. King, "The Interaction of Group Size and Task Structure in an Industrial Organization," *Personnel Psychology,* Spring 1973, pp. 87–94.

for completing a task, then the value of belonging to that group is enhanced. Its members feel pride in being part of a group that has performed in a manner that is recognized as superior.

Work groups that have successfully attained preestablished goals are likely to be highly cohesive units, the members tending to be more attracted toward one another because they have worked together in the past and because their efforts have resulted in achieving desired goals. Thus, success and cohesiveness are interrelated: Success in goal achievement encourages cohesiveness and cohesive work groups are more likely to attain goals. Managers know, however, that although group cohesiveness can lead to the achievement of goals, cohesiveness can prove detrimental when group and organization goals are incompatible. A manager explained the consequences of such incompatibility:

> *It sure isn't a bed of roses. The troops want to reach the same level of output as the last quarter of this past year, while management wants a 25 percent improvement. It's like a war. Them and us. It is really a bad situation because the group is as thick as thieves—one for all and all for one. Management is going to lose this one. Maybe we can fire all 30 of them.*

Managers must clearly recognize that they will have a difficult job if a group is highly cohesive but has performance goals that are different from those of the organization. On the other hand, a cohesive group whose goals are similar to those of management can be a very enjoyable unit to manage. The possible relationships between cohesiveness and goal similarities are illustrated in Figure 14–4. The best situation occurs when the highly cohesive group has performance goals similar to those of the organization, which is shown as the ●● cell in Figure 14–4.

The status of the group In an organizational setting, groups are typically ranked in a status hierarchy. A status hierarchy may develop among groups for many different reasons, including the following:

1. The group is rated higher than another group in overall performance; this rating measures success in an organization.
2. To become a member of the group, individuals must display a high level of skill.
3. The work being done by the group is dangerous, or financially more rewarding, or more challenging, than other work.
4. The group is less closely supervised than other groups.
5. In the past, members of the group have been considered for promotion more often than members of other groups.

These are only some of the criteria which affect the status hierarchy of groups. Generally, the higher a group ranks in the intergroup status hierar-

Figure 14–4

Cohesiveness and goal similarities: Similarity between
group and organization performance goals

	High similarity	Little similarity
HIGH LEVEL	● ●	– –
Group cohesiveness degree		
	●	–
LOW LEVEL		

KEY: ● ● = Achievement of goals is enhanced.
    ● = Achievement of goals is adequate.
    – = Achievement of goals is slightly hindered.
    – – = Achievement of goals is almost impossible.

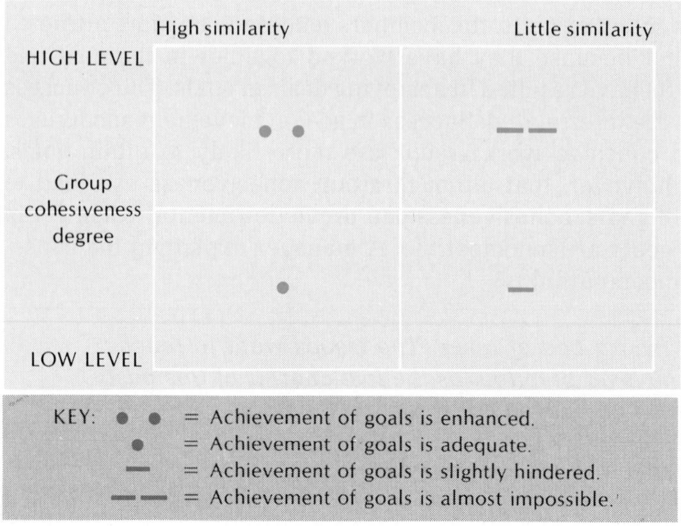

chy, the greater is its cohesiveness. However, the higher-status groups appear attractive only to some nonmembers. Individuals outside the group
may very well not want to become members of a high-status group because
membership entails close adherence to group norms.

Management demands and pressure Another cause of group cohesiveness
is management demands and pressure. It is certainly true that in many
organizations, management has a significant impact on group cohesiveness.
The members of groups tend to stick together when they are pressured
by superiors to conform to some organizational norm.

The group cohesiveness attributed to managerial demands may be either
a short-run or a long-run phenomenon. In some cases, a loosely knit group
(low in cohesiveness) may interpret a company policy statement as a threat
to the job security of the group's members. Consequently, the members
of the group may become a more cohesive and unified whole to withstand
the perceived management threat. After the danger is past (i.e., the policy
statement is rescinded), the group may drift back toward low cohesiveness.
In other cases, the cohesiveness may be a longer-lasting phenomenon.

When groups possess high conformity and cohesiveness, there is a possibility that a phenomenon called **groupthink** will occur.[4] The process of

---

[4] Irving L. Janis, *Victims of Groupthink: A Psychological Study of Foreign Policy Decisions
and Fiascos* (Boston: Houghton Mifflin, 1972); and Irving L. Janis and Leon Mann, *Decision
Making: A Psychological Analysis of Conflict, Choice, and Commitment* (New York: Macmillan, 1977).

groupthink can occur when a group believes that it is invincible, rationalizes away criticism, believes that everyone should comply with a group norm, and is characterized by unanimity among its members. The group of policy-makers who considered the pros and cons of the Bay of Pigs invasion believed that with the talent around the table studying the situation, any problem could be solved (invincibility). They viewed outside criticism as illogical and not based on good information (rationalization). Experts were called in to silence dissenters (conformity pressure).

The results of the Bay of Pigs invasion are now history. Managers must guard against groupthink in their organizations. Managers are in a position to encourage criticism, fresh ideas, and open discussion. If they do this, cohesiveness and conformity can be better used to accomplish organizational and personal goals and groupthink can be minimized.

Intergroup conflict

Management prefers to have groups work cooperatively toward the accomplishment of organizational and individual goals. However, conflicts often develop among groups. If the groups are working on tasks that are interdependent (i.e., Department A's output flows to Department B, and Department B's output flows to Department C), the coordination of the groups and the effectiveness with which they work together are crucial managerial issues. The relationships among groups can become antagonistic and so disruptive that the entire flow of production is slowed or even stopped. However, cooperation is not always the most desirable result of group interaction. For example, two groups may cooperate because they both oppose the introduction of new equipment that is being installed to improve cost control. In this instance, the cooperation of the groups can make the trial period of testing the new equipment a bad experience for management.

Many reasons account for conflict among groups. Some of the more important reasons relate to limited resources, communication problems, differences in interests and goals, different perceptions and attitudes, and lack of clarity about responsibilities.

Limited resources Groups that possess an abundance of materials, money, and time are usually effective. However, when a number of groups are competing for limited resources, conflict often results. The competition for the limited equipment dollars or merit increase money or new positions can become fierce. Thus, when resources are limited, people compete and the result can be conflict.

Communication problems Groups often become very involved with their own areas of responsibility. Each group tends to develop its own unique vocabulary. Paying attention to an area of responsibility is a worthy endeavor, but it can result in communication problems. The receiver of information should be considered when a group communicates an idea, a proposal, or a decision. Misinformed receivers often become irritated and then hostile.

Different interests and goals A group of young workers may want management to do something about an inadequate promotion system. However, older workers may be accusing management of ignoring improvements in the company pension plan. Management recognizes the two different goals but believes that the pension issue is the more pressing and addresses it. The groups want management to solve both problems, but this may not be currently possible. Thus, one group, the young workers, may become hostile because it has been ignored.

Different perceptions and attitudes Individuals perceive differently. The groups to which they belong can also have different perceptions. Groups tend to evaluate in terms of their backgrounds, norms, and experiences. Since each of these can differ, there is likely to be conflict among groups. Most groups tend to overvalue their own worth and position and to undervalue the worth and position of other groups.

Lack of clarity Job clarity involves knowing what others expect in terms of task accomplishment. Yet, in many cases, it is difficult to specify who is responsible for a certain task. For example: Who is responsible for the loss of a talented management trainee—the personnel department or the training department? Who is responsible for the increased sales revenue—marketing or research and development? The inability to pinpoint positive and negative contributions causes groups to compete for control over the activities that are more easily associated with specific effort.

The causes of conflict just cited are among the more common ones. Each of these causes exists and needs to be managed. The management of intergroup conflict involves determining strategies to minimize such causes.

Management reaction to disruptive intergroup conflict can take many different forms.[5] There is a typical sequence of events. Management will first try to minimize the conflict indirectly, and if this fails, it will become directly involved.

Managing group conflict indirectly Initially, managers often avoid direct approaches to solving conflict among groups. Unfortunately, *avoidance* does not always minimize the problem. Matters get worse because nothing is being done about the problem, and the groups become more antagonistic and hostile.

Another indirect strategy is to encourage the groups to meet and discuss their differences and to work out a solution without management involvement. This strategy can take the form of bargaining, persuasion, or working on a problem together.

Bargaining involves having the groups agree about what each will get and give to the other. For example, a group may agree to give another group quick turnaround time on the repairs of needed equipment if the other group agrees to bring complaints about the quality of repairs to it

[5] Alan Filley, *Interpersonal Conflict Resolution* (Glenview, Ill.: Scott, Foresman, 1975); and Louis Pondy, "Organizational Conflict: Concepts and Models," *Administrative Science Quarterly*, September 1972, pp. 296–320.

before going to management. Bargaining between two groups can be successful if both groups are better off (or at least no worse off) after an agreement has been reached.

Persuasion involves having the groups find areas of common interest. The groups attempt to find points of agreement and to show how these are important to each of the groups in attaining organizational goals. Persuasion is possible if clashes between group leaders do not exist.

A problem can be an obstacle to a goal. For groups to minimize their conflicts through *problem solving,* they must generally agree on the goal. If there is agreement, then the groups can propose alternative solutions that satisfy the parties involved. For example, one group may want the company to relocate the plant in a suburban area and the other group may want better working conditions. If both parties agree that a common goal is to maintain their jobs, then building a new facility in an area that does not have a high tax rate may be a good solution.

Managing group conflict directly Management may use *domination* to minimize conflict. It may exercise authority and require that a problem be solved by a specific date. If management uses authority, the groups may join together to resist its domination. Management thus becomes a common enemy, and the groups forget their differences in order to deal with their opponent.

Another direct approach is to *remove* the *key figures* in the conflict. If a conflict arises because of personality differences between two individuals, this may be a possible alternative. Three problems exist with this approach. First, the key figures who are to be removed may be leaders of the groups. Removing them could make the groups more antagonistic and lead to greater conflict. Second, it is difficult to pinpoint accurately whether the individuals in conflict are at odds because of personal animosities or because they represent their groups. Third, removal may create martyrs. The causes of the removed leaders may be remembered and fought for, even though the leaders themselves are gone.

A final direct strategy to minimize conflict is that of finding *superordinate goals.* These goals are desired by two or more groups but can only be accomplished through the cooperation of the groups. When conflicting groups are faced with the necessity of cooperating in order to accomplish a goal, conflict can be minimized. For example, a company-wide profit-sharing plan may encourage groups to work together. If company profits are distributed among employees at the end of the year, conflict among groups can reduce the amount of profits that each employee receives. Thus, the superordinate goal, generating profit, may take precedence over group conflict.

Group politics

One increasingly recognized characteristic of groups is political maneuvering to obtain limited resources. Since organizations typically work with scarce resources, group politics is a problem that managers become involved with on a regular basis.

Group politics exists when the behavior of the group is specifically self-serving. When a group is acting to enhance its own position, regardless of the costs of the action, it is acting politically. Often self-serving group behavior creates such a strained relationship among groups that both organizational performance and group performance suffer. When a situation becomes an "us" versus "them" controversy or a "my group" versus "your group" controversy, there are self-serving overtones. Through their actions and their dealings with groups, managers set the tone for the degree of political maneuvering that will emerge.

Two types of managerial behaviors can create the atmosphere for group politics—offensive and defensive. **Offensive political behavior** by a manager of a group includes power building, exploiting or calling attention to the weaknesses of others, and sabotaging the work of others. An example of power building is highlighted by the comments of a project team leader:

> *The philosophy at this company is number of people. The more people on your project, the more people upstairs will listen to you. So, we all build big teams, run the costs up, and try to throw our weight around. I asked for three more engineers just to keep my unit larger than Mike's. I know the numbers game, and so does Mike.*

The project team leader was then asked whether this maneuvering hurt the organization. His reply was:

> *I guess it does, but who is going to stop it? We have to remain aggressive to be promoted, and one way to do so is to build a large team and be recognized for the building job.*

Defensive political behavior by a group manager includes maneuvers in response to others. Placing the blame on another group, covering up mistakes, or even working hard to direct attention away from weaknesses are examples of defensive political behavior. A lab worker described a tactic she faced:

> *Everyone knows that the lab supervisor blames us for being inaccurate, or for any slowdowns. Why management is not able to see behind the smoke screen is beyond me. This is really not the best way to run an organization.*

Offensive and defensive political behaviors exist among groups and among individuals. By example, managers can often create the environment for the degree and kind of politics in organizations. Subordinates look to managers for direction. When managers use political maneuvers, subordinates tend to imitate these behaviors. Managers can start the process of becoming less political by examining their own political tendencies:

Is this action only self-serving?

Will this action hurt another group or person?

Will organizational performance be improved by this action?

Confronting these questions can help managers become more aware of the political impact of their behavior. When the behavior initiated by a manager involves working together with other groups, organizational performance can be improved.

End result: Group performance

The end result of group membership is group performance. In recent years, social psychologists have increased their efforts to understand the causes of group performance. Some specific causes are (1) perceived freedom to participate, (2) perceived goal attainment, and (3) status consensus.

Perceived freedom to participate

A group member's perception of freedom to participate influences need satisfaction and performance. Supposedly, work group members who perceive themselves as active participators report themselves more satisfied, whereas those who perceive their freedom to participate to be insignificant are typically the least-satisfied members in a work group.

The freedom-to-participate phenomenon is related to the entire spectrum of economic and sociopsychological needs. For example, the perceived ability to participate may lead individuals to believe that they are valued members of the group. This assumption can lead to the satisfaction of social, esteem, and self-actualization needs and to behavior that leads to high levels of performance.

Perceived goal attainment

The perception of progress toward the attainment of desired goals is an important factor in the performance of group members. Groups that progress toward the attainment of goals indicate higher levels of member satisfaction, whereas the members of groups that were not progressing adequately toward the attainment of group goals indicate lower satisfaction levels. Goal attainment is effective performance.

Status consensus

This concept is defined as agreement about the relative status of all group members. When the degree of status consensus is high, satisfaction and performance tend to be high; when status consensus within the group is low, they tend to be low.

Figure 14–5

Checklist for learning about groups

Area of concern	Questions to answer
1. Activities	Who does what job in the group?
2. Interactions	Who initiates contact? How frequently? On what issues?
3. Norms	What are the task and the behavioral norms? How clear are the norms to the members?
4. Leaders	Who are the informal leaders?
5. Status	What is the status order?
6. Cohesiveness	How cohesive is the group? On what issues is its cohesiveness greatest?
7. Group politics....	How much political maneuvering goes on in the group?
8. Performance	How does the group's performance compare to that of other groups? Has its performance fluctuated? When?

The discussion emphasizes that managers must work with groups and that it is important for managers to know how groups function and perform. Managers who understand groups will have a better chance of being able to turn inevitable group characteristics into positive forces to accomplish desirable performance objectives. Without a solid understanding of group structure, processes, development, and consequences, the manager is placed at an uncomfortable disadvantage. Figure 14–5 presents guidelines that managers can use to learn more about their groups.

Management summary

1. Managers must deal with formal and informal groups. Despite the most efficient management practices, informal groups will emerge.
2. Groups are formed to satisfy needs—organizational, economic, and sociopsychological.
3. Groups develop over a period of time and because of interaction. This suggests that if a mature group is what a manager wants, then the group will have to be kept together.
4. The different types of groups that managers are involved with as members or leaders include task, command, friendship, and interest groups. Each of these types satisfies some set of needs of the group members.
5. Group characteristics include emergent leaders, norms, cohesiveness, status, and politics. These are areas that managers must learn about through careful observation. Failure to understand these characteristics and their link to performance places a manager at a disadvantage.
6. Groups can have a significant influence on individuals. In seeking explanations for behavioral or performance problems, a manager should examine the group-individual interaction.
7. Group cohesiveness and conformity may result in groupthink—everyone goes along with the group because it is all-powerful. Managers should try to encourage open debate and differences of opinions among group members.
8. Group politics can have a negative impact on performance. Providing a good model that minimizes political maneuvering is one procedure that a manager can adopt in order to minimize the dysfunctions of group politics.
9. In order to improve the ability to work effectively with groups, it is important for the manager to observe and to ask the right questions. The questions should address the formation, characteristics, and performance of the groups. Observing, asking, and listening are steps that improve a manager's ability to accomplish organizational goals without manipulating or degrading groups.

Review and discussion questions

1. Why does a manager need to know how groups can influence the behavior of subordinates?
2. A manager stated that if he were doing a good job of managing, no

informal groups would be formed by subordinates. Do you agree? Explain.

3. Why is it better for managers to use indirect methods of resolving intergroup conflict before becoming directly involved?
4. Why do most people comply with group norms?
5. Is status the same in both informal and formal groups?
6. Is the mutual acceptance phase of a group's development the point in time at which the group exercises control most effectively?
7. Why is proximity a factor that can encourage the formation of groups?
8. Should a manager be excited about having a highly cohesive group of subordinates?
9. Why is self-serving group behavior usually viewed as group politics?
10. Why is being a good listener an important requirement of serving as the chairperson of a committee?

Suggested reading

Cathey, P. "Reaching out to the Worker." *Iron Age,* June 10, 1981, pp. 61–75.

Farrell, D. and J. C. Petersen. "Patterns of Political Behavior in Organizations." *Academy of Management Review,* July 1982, pp. 403–12.

Herzberg, F. "Group Dynamics at the Roundtable." *Industry Week,* November 16, 1981, pp. 39–40.

Littlejohn, R. F. "Team Management: A How-to Approach to Improved Productivity, Higher Morale, and Lasting Job Satisfaction." *Management Review,* January 1982, pp. 23–28.

McManus, G. J. "Team Concept Stressed at Productivity Confab." *Iron Age,* December 7, 1981, pp. 45–47.

Soloman, S. "How a Whole Company Earned Itself a Roman Vacation." *Fortune,* January 15, 1979, pp. 80–83.

Zemke, R. "Conflict Resolution: Fighting off the Urge to Fight On." *Training,* July 1981, pp. 38–41.

Applying what you have learned about work groups and performance

Cases:

The work team approach at Texas Instruments
The underperforming group

The work team approach at Texas Instruments*

Any chief executive in organizations from small job shops to large firms regularly faces problems that defy easy or quick answers. How can our market share be increased? What foreign markets should we enter? Should we buy a company that is for sale? How can productivity and individual performance be improved? The chief executive can turn to old standbys like hiring a management consultant or appoint a committee to study the problem. Or he or she can do what more and more firms are doing: set up short-term task forces or work teams to come to grips with the broad and important problems.

Task forces are groups of people who typically focus on a single issue and not a laundry list of issues. On the other hand, a *work team* is a group of workers who spring into action when a need arises. But the team is not disbanded like a task force is once a problem has been solved.

At Texas Instruments (TI), work teams are considered the best way to solve work-related problems. More than two thirds of TI's 89,000-plus employees worldwide participate in work teams. TI feels that task forces can't be assembled fast enough to deal with problems requiring quick response. TI wanted something more permanent. Thus, workers are grouped, based on work area, into work teams.

After study and deliberation, the work teams at TI have drastically changed a number of work procedures. For example, TI workers now use hair dryers instead of paper towels to dry silicon components (which reduces the drying

---

* Adapted from Michael A. Verespej, "Mission Extraordinary? Call for a Task Force," *Industry Week,* October 19, 1981, pp. 6–72.

time to about one tenth of what it had been). Work teams also came up with a new drill device and developed a computerized communication network for managers and employees to use to exchange technical information.

The TI work teams are given credit for increasing the company's productivity by 15 percent. In addition, TI's management believes that the work teams break down barriers of mistrust between workers and management. Also, more workers think about and work at problem solving. These problem-solving concerns are job related and meaningful to the workers. There is also at TI a feeling of being in on things and taking pride in helping the team do something.

Under the TI work team approach, the choice of solutions is left to the workers—except example, a TI plant in Malaysia was experiencing excessive scrap rates—a work team came up with a solution. The team responsible for production now affixes labels bearing the team name on parts shipped to customers. The team feels pride in seeing its tag on products being shipped to customers.

Most managers at TI believe that work teams are good for morale, productivity, and cost control. However, a few critics believe that work teams are taking away the need for managers. What will happen if the work teams become even more effective? Some feel that many managers will have to be terminated. If the work team idea works too well, management morale and attitudes may become serious problems at TI.

Questions:

1. Are the TI work teams a formal or informal group?
2. Do you see any possibilities for work team intergroup conflict at TI? Explain.
3. Should TI stop the work team experiment if managers are going to have to be terminated? Explain.

The underperforming group

Dan Vance was recently transferred to the company's largest plant. Dan wanted to do the best job possible, and he thought about the kind of strategy that was needed to start off on the right foot. During his first two months on the job, he observed the work of his 12 subordinates and took notes on how they worked together, who the informal leaders were, and how task oriented they were. He decided that the average group production level of 4,100 units per week was lower than it could be if the group were motivated properly. Dan also noticed that the output of the individual group members ranged from 338 units to 347 units per week. That is, the highest performer produced 347 units and the lowest performer produced 338 units. Everyone else was producing an amount between these two figures.

After the observation period and some careful analysis, Dan believed that the way to increase production was to work through the two informal leaders of the group, Randy Bice and Chet Galic. He called Randy and Chet into his office to discuss the group and its production output. Both of them expressed the opinion that the group was at its limit of endurance and performance. Dan, in a tactful manner, disagreed and expressed the opinion that if the group were inclined to do so, it could increase the average group output by at least 1,000 units a week. He pointed out the following production levels of the six groups working in the manufacturing department.

Group leaders	Average group weekly output
Bruce	4,900
Tony	6,100
Marcus	5,300
Tyrone	4,800
Julio	4,900
Dan	4,100

Dan also hinted that the skills and abilities of the members of the other groups were no better than those of the members in his group.

Randy and Chet seemed surprised about the figures. They did not commit the group to a higher production level, but they did state that they wanted to check a few things and to meet with Dan in about a week.

Questions:

1. What do you think Randy and Chet were going to check?
2. How do you rate Dan's approach to this situation?
3. What could be the next step for Dan to take?

Applying what you have learned about the leading function

Learning exercises:

Ranking motivators
Group and conflict resolution

Comprehensive case:

Work group ownership of an improved tool

Learning exercise

Ranking motivators

Purpose: The purpose of this exercise is to compare the importance of various individual motivational factors with other people so that an awareness of differences and similarities is brought into focus.

Setting up the exercise:

I. Individually complete the ranking priority form shown below using Table 1. The 12 factors in Table 1 were identified by Herzberg in developing his two-factor theory of motivation.

II. After the ranking has been individually completed, the instructor will form groups of four to six students to discuss their rankings.

III. Each group will appoint a spokesperson to report to the entire class how individual rankings differed in his or her group.

A learning note: This exercise will illustrate that there are major individual differences in motivational preferences. The difficulties faced by managers in addressing such individual differences should become clear.

Priority of motivation factors
(most influential first)

1. ____________________
2. ____________________
3. ____________________
4. ____________________
5. ____________________
6. ____________________
7. ____________________
8. ____________________
9. ____________________
10. ____________________
11. ____________________
12. ____________________

Table 1

Motivation factors

Rate the following factors in the order of their actual or assumed (if not currently working) influence on your job performance.

Factors	Description
Recognition	Recognition could be from anyone—a superior, another individual in management, a peer, the general public. Could be either positive or negative recognition.
Achievement	Successful completion of a job, solutions to problems, seeing the results of one's work. Includes its opposite, failure, and the absence of achievement.
Possibility of growth	The potential of moving up in the organization or enlarging skills and responsibilities. Objective evidence that the possibilities for personal growth are increased or decreased.
Advancement	An actual change in status or position within the company.
Salary	Events in which compensation plays the dominant role. Could be increases or unfulfilled expectations for increases.
Interpersonal relations	Events in which the interaction with a superior, subordinates, or peers is the major factor.
Responsibility	Factors relating to the assignment of responsibility and authority or the lack thereof.
Company policy and administration	Covers adequacy or inadequacy of company organization and management. Also covers harmfulness or beneficial effects of company policies, usually personnel policies.
Working conditions	Physical conditions for work, the facilities available for doing work. Adequacy or inadequacy of ventilation, lighting, tools, space, and other environmental factors.

Table 1 (*concluded*)

Work itself	The actual doing of the job or the task as a source of good or bad feelings about it. Routine, creative, and so forth.
Status	Having a secretary in a new position, flying first class while on company work, being assigned a "prestige" parking spot, and so forth, or the deprivation of such status items.
Security	Objective signs of the presence or absence of security, such as tenure and company stability or instability.

Learning exercise
Groups and conflict resolution

Purpose: The purpose of this exercise is to compare individual versus group problem salary and to examine conflict.

Setting up the exercise:

I. Each individual has 15 minutes to read the story and answer the 11 questions about the story. Individuals may not refer to the story when answering the questions and may not confer with anyone else. Each person should circle T if the answer is clearly true; F if the answer is clearly false; or ? if it isn't clear from the story whether the answer is true or false.

II. Next, form small groups of four to five and make the same decisions using group consensus. No one should change his or her answers on the individual questions. The ground rules for group decisions are:

a. Group decisions should be made by consensus without reference to the story. It is illegal to vote, trade, average, flip a coin, and so forth.

b. No individual group member should give in only to reach agreement.

c. Every group member should be aware that disagreements may be resolved by facts. Conflict can lead to understanding and creativity if it does not make group members feel threatened or defensive.

III. After 20 minutes of group work, the instructor should announce the correct answers. Scoring is based on the number of correct answers out of a possible total of 11. Individuals are to score their own individual answers, and someone should score the group-decision answers. The exercise leader should then call for:

a. The group-decision score in each group

- *b.* The average individual score in each group
- *c.* The highest individual score in each group

IV. Responses should be posted on the tally sheet. Note should be taken of those groups in which the group score was (1) higher than the average individual score (2) higher than the best individual score. Groups should discuss the way in which individual members resolved disagreements and the effect of the ground rules on such behavior. They may consider the obstacles experienced in arriving at consensus and the possible reasons for the difference between individual and group decisions.

The story: A businessman had just turned off the lights in the store when a man appeared and demanded money. The owner opened a cash register. The contents of the cash register were scooped up, and the man sped away. A member of the police force was notified promptly.

Statements about the story:

1. A man appeared after the owner had turned off his store lights. T F ?
2. The robber was a man. T F ?
3. A man did not demand money. T F ?
4. The man who opened the cash register was the owner. T F ?
5. The store owner scooped up the contents of the cash register and ran away. T F ?
6. Someone opened a cash register. T F ?
7. After the man who demanded the money scooped up the contents of the cash register, he ran away. T F ?
8. While the cash register contained money, the story does *not* state *how much.* T F ?
9. The robber demanded money of the owner. T F ?
10. The story concerns a series of events in which only three persons are referred to: the owner of the store, a man who demanded money, and a member of the police force. T F ?
11. The following events in the story are true: Someone demanded money, a cash register was opened, its contents were scooped up, and a man dashed out of the store. T F ?

Tally sheet

GROUP NUMBER	GROUP SCORE	AVG. INDIVIDUAL SCORE	BEST INDIVIDUAL SCORE	GROUP SCORE BETTER THAN AVG. INDIV.?	GROUP SCORE BETTER THAN BEST INDIV.?

Comprehensive case
Work group ownership of an improved tool*

The Whirlwind Aircraft Corporation was a leader in its field and especially noted for its development of the modern supercharger. Work in connection with the latter mechanism called for special skill and ability. Every detail of the supercharger had to be perfect to satisfy the exacting requirements of the aircraft industry.

In 1941 (before Pearl Harbor), Lathe Department 15–D was turning out three types of impeller, each contoured to within 0.002 inch and machined to a mirrorlike finish. The impellers were made from an aluminum alloy and finished on a cam-back lathe.

The work was carried on in four shifts, two men on each. The personnel in the finishing section were as follows:

1. *First Shift*—7 A.M. to 3 P.M. Sunday and Monday off.
   a. Jean Latour, master mechanic, French Canadian, 45 years of age. Latour had set up the job and trained the men who worked with him on the first shift.
   b. Pierre DuFresne, master mechanic, French Canadian, 36 years of age. Both these men had trained the workers needed for the other shifts.
2. *Second Shift*—3 P.M. to 11 P.M. Friday and Saturday off.
   a. Albert Durand, master mechanic, French Canadian, 32 years of age; trained by Latour and using his lathe.
   b. Robert Benet, master mechanic, French Canadian, 31 years of age; trained by DuFresne and using his lathe.
3. *Third Shift*—11 P.M. to 7 A.M. Tuesday and Wednesday off.

---

* From *Personnel Administration: A Point of View and a Method*, 1956 ed. by Pigors & Myers. Copyright © McGraw-Hill Book Company, 1956. Used with permission of McGraw-Hill Book Company.

a. Philippe Doret, master mechanic, French Canadian, 31 years of age; trained by Latour and using his lathe.
b. Henri Barbet, master mechanic, French Canadian, 30 years of age; trained by DuFresne and using his lathe.

4. *Stagger Shift*—Monday, 7 A.M. to 3 P.M.; Tuesday, 11 P.M. to 7 A.M.; Wednesday, 11 P.M. to 7 A.M.; Thursday, off; Friday, 3 P.M. to 11 P.M.; Saturday, 3 P.M. to 11 P.M.; Sunday, off.

   a. George MacNair, master mechanic, Scotsman, 32 years of age, trained by Latour and using his lathe.
   b. William Reader, master mechanic, English, 30 years of age; trained by DuFresne and using his lathe.

Owing to various factors (such as the small number of workers involved, the preponderance of one nationality, and the fact that Latour and DuFresne had trained the other workers), these eight men considered themselves as members of one work group. Such a feeling of solidarity is unusual among workers on different shifts, despite the fact that they use the same machines.

The men received a base rate of $1.03 an hour and worked on incentive. Each man usually turned out 22 units a shift, thus earning an average of $1.19 an hour. Management supplied Rex 95 High-Speed Tool-Bits, which workers ground to suit themselves. Two tools were used: one square bit with a slight radius for recess cutting, the other bit with a 45-degree angle for chamfering and smooth finish. When used, both tools were set close together, the worker adjusting the lathe from one operation to the other. The difficulty with this setup was that during the rotation of the lathe, the aluminum waste would melt and fuse between the two toolbits. Periodically the lathe had to be stopped so that the toolbits could be freed from the welded aluminum and reground.

At the request of the supervisor of Lathe Department 15–D, the methods department had been working on his tool problem. Up to the time of this case, no solution had been found. To make a firsthand study of the difficulty, the methods department had recently assigned one of its staff, Mr. MacBride, to investigate the probelm in the lathe department itself. Mr. MacBride's working hours covered parts of both the first and second shifts. MacBride was a young man, 26 years of age, and a newcomer to the methods department. For the three months prior to this assignment, he had held the post of "suggestion man," a position which enabled newcomers to the methods department to familiarize themselves with the plant setup. The job consisted in collecting, from boxes in departments throughout the plant, suggestions submitted by employees and making a preliminary evaluation of these ideas. The current assignment of studying the tool situation in Lathe Department 15–D, with a view to cutting costs, was his first special task. He devoted himself to this problem with great zeal but did not succeed in winning the confidence of the workers. In pursuance of their usual philosophy: "Keep your mouth shut if you see anyone with a suit on," they volunteered no information and took the stand that, since the methods man had been given this assignment, it was up to him to carry it out.

While MacBride was working on this problem, Pierre DuFresne hit upon a solution. One day he successfully contrived a tool which combined the two bits into one. This eliminated the space between the two toolbits which in the past had caught the molten aluminum waste and allowed it to become welded to the cutting edges. The new toolbit had two advantages: it eliminated the frequent machine stoppage for cleaning and regrinding the old-type tools; and it enabled the operator to run the lathe at a higher speed. These advantages made it possible for the operator to increase his efficiency 50 percent.

DuFresne tried to make copies of the new tool, but was unable to do so. Apparently the new development had been a "lucky accident" during grinding which he could not duplicate. After several unsuccessful attempts, he took the new tool to his former teacher, Jean Latour. The latter succeeded in making a drawing and turning out duplicate toolbits on a small grinding wheel in the shop. At first the two men decided to keep the new tool to themselves. Later, however, they shared the improvement with their fellow workers on the second shift. Similarly it was passed on to the other shifts. But all these men kept the new development a closely guarded secret as far as "outsiders" were concerned. At the end of the shift, each locked the improved toolbit securely in his toolchest.

Both DuFresne, the originator of the new tool, and Latour, its draftsman and designer, decided not to submit the idea as a suggestion but to keep it as the property of their group. Why was this decision made? The answer lies partly in the suggestion system and partly in the attitude of Latour and DuFresne toward other features of company work life and toward their group.

According to an information bulletin issued by the company, the purpose of the suggestion system was to "provide an orderly method of submitting and considering ideas and recommendations of employees to management; to provide a means for recognizing and rewarding individual ingenuity; and to promote cooperation." Awards for accepted suggestions were made in the following manner: "After checking the savings and expense involved in an adopted suggestion [the suggestion committee] determined the amount of the award to be paid, based upon the savings predicted upon a year's use of the suggestion." "It is the intention of the committee . . . to be liberal in the awards, which are expected to adequately compensate for the interest shown in presenting suggestions." In pursuance of this policy, it was customary to grant the suggestor an award equivalent to the savings of an entire month.

As a monetary return, both DuFresne and Latour considered an award based on one month's saving as inadequate. They also argued that such awards were really taken out of the workers' pockets. Their reasoning was as follows: All awards for adopted suggestions were paid out of undistributed profits. Since the company also had a profit-sharing plan, the money was taken from a fund that would be given to the workers anyway, which merely meant robbing Peter to pay Paul. In any case, the payment was not likely to be large and probably would be less than they could accumulate if increased incentive payments could be maintained over an extended period without discovery. Thus there was little in favor of submitting the new tool as a suggestion.

Latour and DuFresne also felt that there were definite hazards to the group if their secret were disclosed. They feared that once the tool became company property, its efficiency might lead to layoff of some members in their group, or at least make work less tolerable by leading to an increased quota at a lower price per unit. They also feared that there might be a change in scheduled work assignments. For instance, the lathe department worked on three different types of impeller. One type was a routine job and aside from the difficulty caused by the old-type tool, presented no problem. For certain technical reasons, the other two types were more difficult to make. Even Latour, an exceptionally skilled craftsman, had sometimes found it hard to make the expected quota before the new tool was developed. Unless the work was carefully balanced by scheduling easier and more difficult types, some of the operators were unable to make standard time.

The decision to keep the tool for their own group was in keeping with Latour's work philosophy. He had a strong feeling of loyalty to his own group and had demonstrated this in the past by offering for their use several improvements of his own. For example, he made available to all workers in his group a set of special gauge blocks which were used in aligning work on lathes. To protect himself in case mistakes were traced to these gauges, he wrote on them: "Personnel (*sic*) Property—Do not use. Jean Latour."

Through informal agreement with their fellow workers, Latour and DuFresne "pegged production" at an efficiency rate that in their opinion would not arouse management's suspicion or lead to a restudy of the job, with possible cutting of the rate. This enabled them to earn an extra 10 percent incentive earnings. The other 40 percent in additional efficiency was used as follows: The operators established a reputation for a high degree of accuracy and finish. They set a record for no spoilage and were able to apply the time gained on the easier type of impeller to work on the other types which required greater care and more expert workmanship.

The foreman of the lathe department learned about the new tool soon after it was put into use but was satisfied to let the men handle the situation in their own way. He reasoned that at little expense he was able to get out production of high quality. There was no defective work, and the men were contented.

Mr. MacBride was left in a very unsatisfactory position. He had not succeeded in working out a solution of his own. Like the foreman, he got wind of the fact that the men had devised a new tool. He urged them to submit a drawing of it through the suggestion system, but this advice was not taken, and the men made it plain that they did not care to discuss with him the reasons for this position.

Having no success in his direct contact with the workers, Mr. MacBride appealed to the foreman, asking him to secure a copy of the new tool. The foreman replied that the men would certainly decline to give him a copy and would resent as an injustice any effort on his part to force them to submit a drawing. Instead he suggested that MacBride should persuade DuFresne to show him the tool. This MacBride attempted to do, but met with no success in his efforts to ingratiate himself with DuFresne. When he persisted in his attempts, DuFresne decided to throw him off the track. He left in his lathe a toolbit which was an unsuccessful copy of the original discovery. At shift change, MacBride was delighted to find what he supposed to be the improved tool. He hastily copied it and submitted a drawing to the tool department. When a tool was made up according to these specifications it naturally failed to do what was expected of it. The workers, when they heard of this through the "grapevine," were delighted. DuFresne did not hesitate to crow over MacBride, pointing out that his underhanded methods had met with their just reward.

The foreman did not take any official notice of the conflict between DuFresne and MacBride. Then MacBride complained to the foreman that DuFresne was openly boasting of his trick and ridiculing him before other workers. Thereupon, the foreman talked to DuFresne, but the latter insisted that his ruse had been justified as a means of self-protection.

When he was rebuffed by DuFresne, the foreman felt that he had lost control of the situation. He could no longer conceal from himself that he was confronted by a more complex situation than what initially he had defined as a "tool problem." His attention was drawn to the fact that the state of affairs in his department was a tangle of several interrelated problems. Each problem urgently called for a decision that involved understanding and practical judgment. But having for so long failed to see the situation as a whole, he now found himself in a dilemma.

He wished to keep the goodwill of the work group, but he could not countenance the continued friction between DuFresne and MacBride. Certainly, he could not openly abet his operators in obstructing the work of a methods man. His superintendent would now certainly hear of it and would be displeased to learn that a foreman had failed to tell him of such an important technical improvement. Furthermore, he knew that the aircraft industry was expanding at this time and that the demand for impellers had increased to such an extent that management was planning to set up an entire new plant unit devoted to this product.

Questions:

1. In your opinion, what were the causes of the high degree of group cohesion in Lathe Department 15–D?
2. If you were the manager (foreman), how would you get the improved tool from the group?
3. Was the lathe department a motivated group? Explain.

Part V
The controlling function

15. Elements of controlling
16. Production-operations and financial control
17. Human resource performance evaluation
18. Organizational change

A management profile
Robert McNamara

Anyone who thinks that an accountant's life has to be dull could never have known Robert McNamara. For years, McNamara dazzled Detroit as one of the famous "whiz kids" whose sharp statistical skills turned around the problems of the Ford Motor Company. Though often characterized as scholarly and bookish, the onetime Harvard accounting professor was in touch with the tastes of the American consumer.

It was McNamara who developed the first compact family car, the Ford Falcon. He championed the 12,000-mile warranty and promoted safety belts, and he changed Ford's sporty Thunderbird to a four-seater and tripled its sales. To insiders, it wasn't surprising when in November of 1960, at the comparatively young age of 44, Robert Strange McNamara became the first person outside the Ford family to be named president of the motor company.

Six weeks later, he received a request from John F. Kennedy to serve the nation as secretary of defense. In accepting his place among "the best and the brightest," McNamara willingly let go of his Ford holdings, at a loss estimated at $3 million.

During the next seven years, McNamara brought the Defense Department under what has been called the strongest civilian control in history. Some Capitol Hill observers contend that he single-handedly shaped the military and domestic policies of Kennedy's and Johnson's administrations. By the end of his tenure at the Pentagon, U.S. military prestige was firmly established throughout the world.

Yet throughout the Kennedy and Johnson administrations, McNamara maintained that the greatest threat to world security was the poverty of developing nations. In 1968, he committed himself to this belief and left the Defense Department to head the World Bank.

Based on funds donated by over 125 member countries, the World Bank provides financial and technical assistance to developing countries. Its funds have built roads in Brazil, modernized farming in Africa, and tackled population problems in Pakistan. It is no surprise to McNamara-watchers that under his leadership, the World Bank has doubled its lending funds and is now the largest development agency in the world.

McNamara used control to monitor and evaluate the performance of the Defense Department. Control became an important function in managing the day-to-day operations of the department. Without control systems, any organization would be unable to check its progress toward accomplishing objectives. In this section of the book, *control* is the main topic of concern. How control influences people and the direction that an organization takes will be discussed. Planning, decision making, organizing, and leading without proper controls often result in failure. The reasons for such failures will become more obvious as you complete this part of the book.

Photograph by Fabian Bachrach, courtesy of World Bank

Source: Elizabeth J. Kenny for P. S. Associates, Inc., Sterling, Massachusetts.

Introduction to Part V

Part V, The controlling function, contains four chapters. They are:

Chapter 15—Elements of controlling
Chapter 16—Production-operations and financial control
Chapter 17—Human resource performance evaluation
Chapter 18—Organizational change

The inclusion of the material contained in the four chapters is based upon the following rationale:

The controlling function involves comparing actual results with planned results and, consequently, *making changes* in individual and group behavior, in financial and technical processes and, often, in the organization itself. Consequently, the essential feature of managerial control is *change.*

The four chapters which comprise the part cover various aspects of the activities of managerial control. Chapter 15 presents the **elements of controlling** with emphasis on the informational requirements for effective control. The following chapter, Chapter 16, presents control in the context of **production and operations activities.** The focus of management in controlling production and operations include the material, machines, and financial resources necessary to achieve the objectives of the organization. Chapter 17 stresses control from the perspective of **human resource performance.** The focus of the discussion in that chapter is the work performance of employees and the extent to which their actual performances are consistent with performance standards. The last chapter, Chapter 18, examines the problems and potential associated with actions to **change the total organization.** Here, the focus is not on any one aspect of the organization, its human and nonhuman resources, but on the entity itself. Managers must at times consider the possibility that planned results can be achieved only after significant change in the total organization.

The figure below depicts the four aspects of the controlling function.

The controlling function

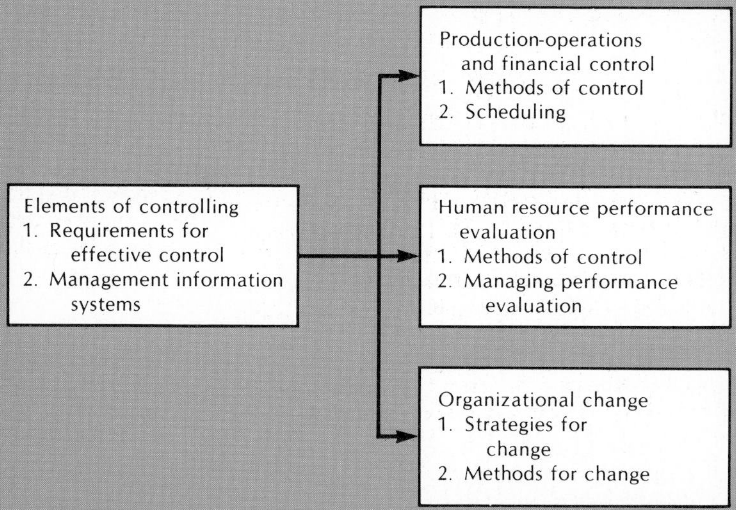

15

Chapter fifteen Elements of controlling

Performance objectives

- **Define** the concept of managerial control.
- **State** the necessary conditions for effective control.
- **Describe** the features of an effective management information system (MIS).
- **Explain** the roles of management information in managerial control decisions.
- **Discuss** the functions of a management information system.

Management update*

Technological innovations have typically created human problems. The development of assembly line manufacturing methods, for example, is cited as a cause of considerable management-labor conflict. Although technological innovation often results in dislocation of working people as their skills and abilities are no longer needed, more often the change is in the nature of relationships between managers and those they manage. The current rapidly changing technology in information and word processing can cause major problems for companies that adopt the automated office environment.

The most serious human problems to be confronted in the automated office are the new required roles and relationships of managers and secretaries. As a consequence of the new technology, secretaries no longer perform routine tasks. Those tasks are now automated. One consequence is that secretaries now have time to take on tasks previously performed by managers. But in order to take advantage of both the technological and the human sources of increased productivity requires training in the new roles. In fact, both managers and secretaries must be *retrained.*

A company with over 70 years of experience as a training and finishing school for secretaries, Katharine Gibbs School Inc., recently announced a new program which focuses on solving the problems of the automated office. The director of the group established by Gibbs to provide the service is Randy J. Goldfield. She states that a key to retraining for the office of the future is to convince managers that their time is better spent on conceptual issues. The retrained secretaries, with the aid of state-of-the-art technology, are capable of dealing with routine managerial tasks.

* This Management Update is adapted from "Retraining for the Automated Office," *Business Week,* April 27, 1981, p. 102.

The controlling function consists of actions and decisions which managers undertake to assure that actual results are consistent with desired results. The key to effective control is the explicit predetermination of desired results through planning; unless managers decide in advance what level of performance is desired, they have no basis for judging actual performance. As described in earlier chapters, when managers plan, they establish the ways and means to achieve objectives. These objectives are the targets, the desired results, which management expects the organization to achieve.

Subsequent to planning, managers must employ their organizations' resources to perform activities which are necessary to achieve the results. Although these resources and activities can be planned and anticipated, managers recognize that unforeseen events such as fuel shortages, strikes, machine breakdowns, competitive actions, and governmental influence can cause the organization to move away from the path that leads to the targeted results. Thus, managers must be prepared and able to adjust their organization's activities so that these return to the desired paths.

Necessary conditions for control

The implementation of control requires three basic conditions: (1) *standards* must be established; (2) *information* which indicates deviations between actual and standard results must be available; and (3) *action* to bring about the correction of any deviations between actual and standard results must be possible. The logic is evident: Without standards, there can be no basis for evaluating actual performance; without information, there can be no way of knowing the situation; without provision for action to correct deviations, the entire control process becomes a pointless exercise.

Standards

Standards are derived from objectives and have many of the characteristics of objectives. Like objectives, they are targets; to be effective, they must be clearly stated and logically related to strategic objectives. Standards are the criteria against which future, current, or past actions are compared. They are measured in a variety of ways, including physical, monetary, quantitative, and qualitative terms. The various forms which standards take depend on what is being measured and on the managerial level responsible for the controlling decision.

As a manager moves up in the organization, the performance standards for which he or she is accountable become more abstract and the causes for deviations become more difficult to identify. The plant manager of a concrete products manufacturer recollected:

> *When I first joined the firm as the manager of the concrete block division, it was fairly easy to know when something was wrong and what caused it. A defective concrete block is due to bad material or workmanship. I could correct that problem. But now I am responsible for the profitability of the entire operation, and even though the profit figure is easy to read on a profit and loss statement, I am never sure that I know why it was not higher, or lower, for that matter.*

Information

Information which reports actual performance and which permits appraisal of that performance against standards must be provided. Such information is most easily acquired for activities which produce specific results; for example, production and sales activities have end products which are easily identifiable and for which information is readily obtainable. The performance of legal departments, research-and-development units, and personnel departments is quite difficult to appraise because the outcomes of their activities are difficult to measure.

Corrective action

Managerial actions to correct deviations are stimulated by the discovery of the need for action and by the ability to implement the necessary action. The people responsible for taking the corrective action must know (1) that they are indeed responsible and (2) that they have the assigned authority to take those steps. Unless the jobs and position descriptions include specific statements which clearly delineate these two requirements, the control function will surely fall short of its objective.

Responsibilities which fall between two jobs of two individuals are undesirable, but sometimes unavoidable. Managers who work in organizations which face uncertain and unpredictable environments often confront situations which have not been previously anticipated and provided for by job specifications. A former corporate-level executive of a successful fast-food franchise business recollected:

> *When we first started out, we knew we had a good product and that its acceptance by the customers would make up for our management mistakes. At the time, I thought that the biggest mistake we were making was not specifying the precise responsibility of the corporate staff. Things were happening so fast that we couldn't keep up with the opportunities. Many of these opportunities were lost because no one had been assigned the responsibility for doing so. In retrospect, I now know that there was no other way to go. If we had not had people willing to work 80-hour weeks, we wouldn't have made it.*

The essential elements of management control are diagramed in Figure 15–1. The control function, then, involves the implementation of methods which provide answers to three basic questions, namely: What are the planned and expected results? By what means can the actual results be compared to the planned results? What corrective action is appropriate from which authorized person?

Figure 15–1

Management control

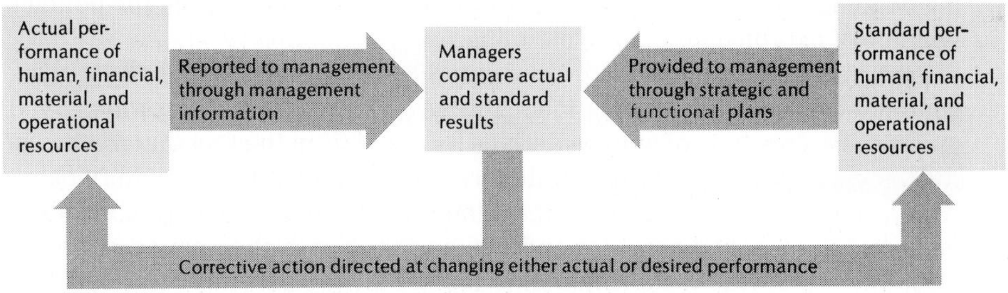

Three types of control

The control function can be broken down into three types on the basis of the focus of control activity. Figure 15–2 describes the three types.

Precontrol focuses on the problem of *preventing* deviations in the quality and quantity of the resources used in the organization. Human resources

Figure 15–2

The controlling function

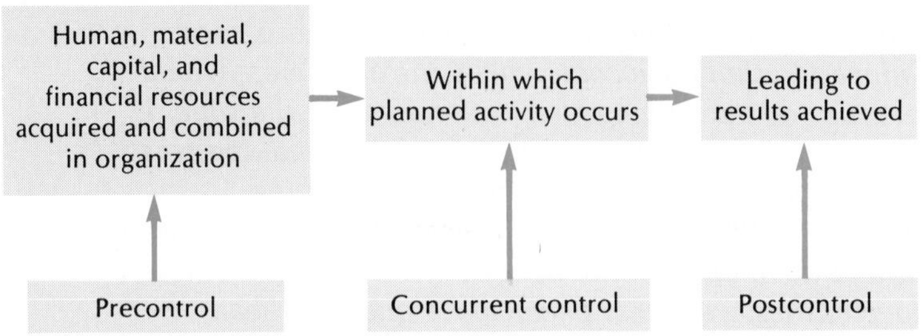

must meet the job requirements as defined by the organization structure; employees must have the capability, whether physical or intellectual, to perform the assigned tasks. The materials must meet acceptable levels of quality and must be available at the proper time and place. In addition, capital must be on hand to assure the adequate supply of plant and equipment. Finally, financial resources must be available in the right amounts and at the right times.

Concurrent control monitors ongoing operations to assure that objectives are achieved. The principal means by which managers implement concurrent control are their directing or supervisory activities. Through personal, on-the-spot observation, managers determine whether the work of others is proceeding in the manner defined by policies and procedures. The delegation of authority provides managers with the power to use financial and nonfinancial incentives to achieve concurrent control. The standards guiding ongoing activity are derived from job descriptions and from the policies which are established during planning.

Postcontrol methods focus on end results. The corrective action, if taken, is directed at improving either the resource acquisition process or the actual operations. This type of control derives its name from the fact that *historical* results guide *future* actions. An illustration of postcontrol is a thermostat, which automatically regulates the temperature of a room by constantly measuring actual temperature and comparing it with the desired temperature. Since the thermostat maintains the preset temperature (standard) by constantly monitoring the actual temperature, future results (temperature) are directly and continuously determined by actual results (again, temperature). The postcontrol methods employed in business include budgets, standard costs, financial statements, and quality control.

At this point, the three types of control can be described and distinguished by examining the *focus* of corrective action. As shown in Figure 15–3, precontrol methods are based on information which measures some attribute or characteristic of resources; the focus of corrective action is directed, in turn, at the resources. That is, the variable *measured* is the variable *acted upon.* Similarly, concurrent control methods are based on

Figure 15–3

The three types of control as distinguished by the focus of corrective action

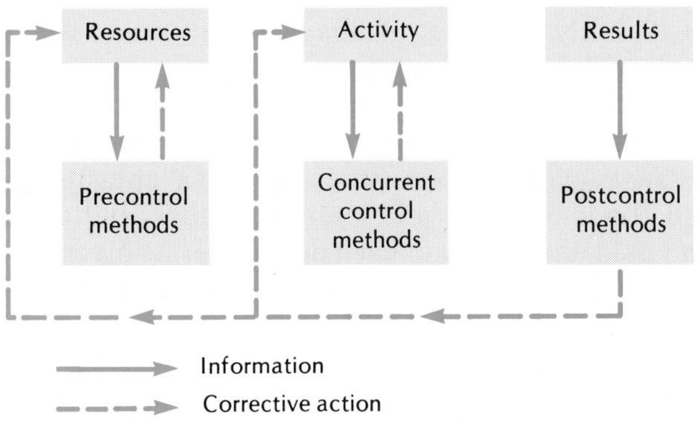

information related to activity, and it is activity that is acted upon. However, the focus of corrective action associated with postcontrol is not that which is measured—results. Rather, resources and activity are acted upon.

Precontrol

Precontrol procedures include all managerial efforts to increase the probability that future actual results will compare favorably with planned results. From this perspective, we can see that policies are important means for implementing precontrol, since policies are guidelines for future action. Setting policy is included in planning, whereas implementing policy is a part of controlling. The concept of precontrol can be illustrated in terms of human, capital, and financial resources.

Precontrol of *human resources* depends on job requirements which predetermine the skill requirements of the jobholders. These requirements vary in their degree of specificity, depending on the nature of the task. At the shop level, the skill requirements can be specified in terms of physical attributes and manual dexterity. On the other hand, the job requirements of management and staff personnel are more difficult to define in terms of concrete measurements.

The acquisition of *capital* reflects the need to replace existing equipment or to expand the firm's productive capacity. Capital acquisitions are precontrolled by establishing criteria of potential profitability which must be met before the acquisitions are authorized. The decisions which involve the commitment of present funds in exchange for future funds are termed *investment decisions;* and the methods which serve to screen investment proposals derive from financial analysis, as will be shown in Chapter 16.

An adequate supply of *financial* resources must be available to assure the payment of obligations arising from current operations. Materials must be purchased, wages paid, interest charges and due dates met. Budgets—particularly cash and working capital budgets—are the principal means for precontrolling the availability and cost of financial resources. These budgets anticipate the ebb and flow of business activity when materials are purchased, finished goods are produced and inventoried, goods are sold, and cash is received. This cycle of activity, the operating cycle, results in a problem of *timing* the availability of cash to meet the obligations. As inventories of finished goods increase, and materials, labor, and other expenses are incurred and paid, the supply of cash decreases. As inventory is sold, the supply of cash increases. Precontrol of cash requires that cash be available during the period of inventory buildup and that it be used wisely during periods of abundance. This requires the careful consideration of alternative sources of short-term financing during periods of inventory buildup and of alternative short-term investment opportunities during periods of inventory depletion.

Organizations which operate with fairly stable technology can predict with relative certainty the effects of input changes on results. Dynamic technologies, however, are less conducive to precontrol methods. Consequently, the standards against which management compares potential inputs are relatively loose. An executive employed by a chemical manufacturer stated:

> *We have a difficult time knowing the impact of what we do now on future operations. The chemical industry is constantly in a state of flux, with new processes, synthetics, and products appearing daily. We try to plan and budget for the future, but our contingencies are so unpredictable that our planning horizon is at most a year. Consequently, we rely on monitoring current activities and try to make immediate adjustments to our resources as the needs arise.*

Concurrent control

Concurrent control consists primarily of actions of supervisors who *direct* the work of their subordinates. *Direction* refers to the acts which managers undertake (1) to instruct subordinates in the proper methods and procedures and (2) to oversee the work of subordinates to assure that it is done properly.

Direction follows the formal chain of command, since the responsibility of each manager is to interpret for subordinates the orders received from higher echelons. The relative importance of direction depends almost entirely on the nature of the tasks which are performed by subordinates.

The manager of an assembly line which produces a component part requiring relatively simple manual operations may seldom engage in direction. On the other hand, the manager of a research-and-development unit must devote considerable time to direction. Research work is inherently more complex and varied than manual work, thus requiring more interpretation and instruction.

Directing is the primary activity of the first-line supervisor, but every manager in an organization engages at some time in directing employees. As a manager moves up the hierarchy, the relative importance of directing diminishes and other responsibilities become relatively more important.

As noted above, the scope and content of direction vary, depending on the nature of the work being supervised. Other factors determine differences in the form of direction. For example, since direction is basically the process of *interpersonal communication,* the amount and the clarity of information are important factors in direction. Subordinates must receive sufficient information to carry out the task and must understand the information that they receive. On the other hand, too much information and too much detail can be damaging. The manager's mode and tone of expression greatly influence the effectiveness of direction.

Effective direction depends on effective communication. To be effective, a directive must be reasonable, intelligible, and appropriately worded, and consistent with the overall objectives of the organization. It is the subordinate rather than the manager who decides whether these criteria have been met. Many managers have assumed that their directives were straightforward and to the point, only to discover that their subordinates had failed to understand them or to accept them as legitimate.

The process of direction includes not only the manner in which directives are communicated but also the mannerisms of the person who directs. Whether the supervisor is autocratic or democratic, permissive or directive, considerate or inconsiderate has implications for the effectiveness of direction as a concurrent control technique. Direction involves day-to-day overseeing of the work of subordinates. As deviations from standards are identified, managers take immediate corrective action by demonstrating and coaching their subordinates to perform their assigned tasks appropriately.

Postcontrol

The distinguishing feature of postcontrol methods is focusing attention on *historical* outcomes as the bases for correcting *future* actions. For example, the financial statements of a firm are used to evaluate the acceptability of historical results and to determine the desirability of making changes in future resource acquisitions or operational activities. Four postcontrol methods are widely used in business: financial statement analysis, standard cost analysis, quality control, and employee performance evaluation. Subsequent chapters will go into greater detail in discussing these important control methods.

A principal source of information from which managers can evaluate historical results is the firm's accounting system. Periodically, the manager receives a set of *financial statements* which usually include a balance sheet, an income statement, and a sources and uses of funds statement. These statements summarize and classify the effects of transactions in terms of assets, liabilities, equity, revenues, and expenses—the principal components of the firm's financial structure.

Standard cost accounting systems are a major contribution of scientific management. A standard cost system provides information that enables management to compare actual costs with predetermined (standard) costs. Management can then take appropriate corrective action or assign others the authority to take action. The first uses of standard costing were concerned with manufacturing costs, but in recent years standard costing has been applied to selling, general, and administrative expenses.

Quality control information reports the attributes and characteristics of output to ascertain whether the manufacturing process is "in control," that is, producing acceptable output. To make this determination, the manager must specify the product characteristic that is considered critical. The critical characteristic may be weight, length, consistency, or defects. Once the characteristic has been defined, it must be measured.

No doubt, the most difficult postcontrol technique is *performance evaluation*. It is important because the most crucial resource in any organization is its people. As is so often said, "People make the difference." Effective business firms, hospitals, universities, and governments are staffed by people who are effectively performing their assigned duties. Evaluation is difficult because the standards for performance are seldom objective and straightforward; many managerial and nonmanagerial jobs do not produce outputs which can be counted, weighed, and evaluated in objective terms.

Each control method, whether precontrol, concurrent control, or postcontrol, requires the same three fundamental elements: *standards, information,* and *corrective action*. Although each of these elements is necessary for effective control, information is the most critical element. Managers act on the basis of information—reports, documents, position papers, and analyses. Without information, standards could not be set and corrective action could not be taken. Thus, it is important for managers to develop information systems which facilitate their controlling activities.

Management information for control

Effective controlling requires relevant, accurate, and timely information. Unfortunately, an organization has no memory other than the memory of the people who manage it. Because individuals come and go, managers must out of necessity develop some type of information system. The development of information systems obviously recognizes the need for information in support of managerial control, but also of planning. The need arises for (1) managing existing information and (2) utilizing the vast data generating capacity of the computer.

Managing existing information

The ability of organizations to generate information is really not a problem, since most organizations are capable of producing massive amounts of data. Why, then, do so many managers complain that they have insufficient or irrelevant information on which to base their everyday decisions? Specifically, most managers' complaints fall into the following categories:

1. There is too much of the wrong kind of information and not enough of the right kind.
2. Information is so scattered throughout the organization that it is difficult to locate answers to simple questions.
3. Vital information is sometimes suppressed by subordinates or by managers in other functional areas.
4. Vital information often arrives long after it is needed.

Historically, managers did not have to deal with an overabundance of information. Instead, they gathered a bare minimum of information and hoped that their decisions would be reasonably good. In fact, in some business organizations, marketing research came to be recognized as an extremely valuable staff function in the 1930s and 1940s because it provided information for marketing decisions where previously there had been little or none. Today, by contrast, most managers often feel buried by the deluge of data that comes across their desks. As noted in the Management Update, managers face the necessity of retraining employees to deal with new information processing technology.

The feeling of being inundated with information is often a sense of anxiety. This feeling results when managers believe that they should be using the information, though often they have neither the time nor the inclination to even read it. The manager of a regional store of a major paint manufacturer stated:

> *Each month I get 30 or 40 pages of computer printout from the central office. These reports tell me all about sales and costs data from all the regional offices, including this one. They tell me what paints are selling all across the country, so I can compare how my sales are doing. But after I find out what is going on in the other stores, I still don't know how to sell more paint in my store.*

Utilizing the capacity of computers

The means for the greater production of information are certainly available. New and better computers and numerous other types of information-handling equipment are being developed at a rapid rate. Still, managers complain of information losses, delays, and distortions. Apparently, many managers have been so concerned about the abundance of new types of information-handling equipment and their potential that they have overlooked the planning necessary for the effective use of these developments. This has happened to such an extent that many people believe that gathering, storing, manipulating, and organizing information for the management decisions of business firms costs as much as or more than direct factory labor.

Unfortunately, in some organizations, computers are not being utilized effectively to provide managers with the best information for decision making. This results in many nonmeasurable (but extremely important) costs because more often than not the effectiveness of organizations is at the mercy of the information available to managers. In the dynamic environment faced by most managers, the need is great for swift and effective correcting action. Thus, though the cost of managing information may be high, the cost of mismanaging it (bad decisions) is even higher.

Managers who are unable to use computer technology effectively sometimes believe that managerial needs are compromised in favor of computer needs. One exasperated store manager of a large retail chain stated:

> *When we got the computer, we in management thought that we had finally solved some of our pressing inventory control and accounts receivable problems. But now that the computer is in place, we are often told by the data processing center manager that suggested changes in inventory and credit policies and procedures are not possible because the computer can't handle it.*

The information requirements of managers have changed greatly in the past decade, but within most organizations the basic information arrangements have remained essentially the same. The problem of generating the right information at the right time must now be viewed in a much broader perspective than it was viewed previously. The task of generating data for managerial control decisions must be viewed as the function of a *management information system* rather than as the function of the individual managers in the various areas of an organization.

Organization structure and information needs

Managers face either programmed or nonprogrammed control decisions, depending on the type of problem. As one moves higher in the organization, the problems faced become less structured, with a great deal of uncertainty, and the procedures used for dealing with the different types of problems vary. At this point, it should be clear that the information requirements would also vary, depending on the level in the organization and the type of control decision being made. Note that in every instance, however, it is vital that an appropriate information flow be directed to the proper decision managers.

The types as well as the sources of information will vary by level in the organization.

Strategic control information

This type of information relates to the top-management tasks of formulating objectives for the organization, the amounts and the kinds of resources necessary to attain the objectives, and the policies that govern the use of those resources. Much of this information will come from external sources and will relate to such factors as the present and predicted state of the economy, the availability of resources (nonhuman as well as human), and the political and regulatory environment. This information forms the input for the nonprogrammed types of decision made at this level in the organization.

Functional control information

This information helps middle managers to make decisions consistent with the achievement of organizational objectives as well as to see how efficiently resources are being used. It enables middle managers of manufacturing, marketing, engineering and other functional units to determine whether "actual results" are meeting "planned-for results" (objectives). Functional control relies heavily on internal sources of information (often interdepartmental), and it involves such problems as developing budgets and measuring the performance of first-line supervisors. The problems faced at this level may result in either programmed or nonprogrammed decisions.

Operational control information

This information relates to the day-to-day activities of the organization. It includes routine and necessary types of information such as financial accounting, inventory control, and production scheduling. The information is generated internally, and since it usually relates to specific tasks, it often comes from one designated department. First-line supervisors are the primary users of this information. Since decision making at this level in the organization usually involves structured types of problems, many decisions at the operational level can be programmed.

Designing a management information system (MIS)

An appreciation of the importance and complexity of MIS can be gained by understanding the various information flows with which we must deal and the various functions that an MIS must perform.

Understanding information flows

Two broad types of information flows in a management information system can be distinguished. One type is an *external information flow,* that is, information flowing to the organization *from* its outside environment or from the firm *to* its outside environment; the other type is an *intraorganization flow,* that is, information flowing within the organization.

External information flows Again, the external information flows from the organization to its environment and from the environment to the organization. We shall label the inward flow *intelligence information* and the outward flow *organizational communications.*

Intelligence information includes data on the various elements of the organization's operating environment, such as clients, patients, customers, competitors, suppliers, creditors, and the government, for use in evaluating short-run trends in the immediate external environment. Intelligence information also includes long-run strategic planning information on the economic environment, such as consumer income trends, the spending patterns of business organizations, and developments in the social and cultural environment in which the organization operates. This type of information has long-run significance to the organization and aids in long-range planning and strategic control.

An organization learns about its operating environment in various ways. Often, managers discover that their clients' needs have changed only after sales have dropped off. The management of a medium-sized concrete products firm attempted to stay ahead of changes in customer needs by training sales representatives to be information gatherers. As gatherers of intelligence information, the sales representatives were concerned not only with selling the firm's present products but also with projecting what products customers would be needing in the future. The owner of the firm stated:

> *We try to stay ahead of the competition by knowing what is going to sell tomorrow. We use a simple system of field reports from the sales reps. We ask them to tell us a few key things. I am particularly interested in why we lose a sale; I want to know why we lost it.*

Organizational communications flow outward from the organization to the various components of its external environment. In the case of a business organization, any advertising or other promotional efforts are considered organizational communications. Whatever the type of organization, the content of this information flow is controlled by the organization. Although an important information flow, it is nevertheless an *outward flow* with which we will not be concerned in this book.

Intraorganization flows In order to be useful, intelligence information which enters the organization must, along with internally generated information, reach the right manager at the right time. Thus, information must flow through as well as to the organization. Unfortunately, many managers believe that once information is within the organization it will somehow find its way to the proper person at the proper time. It must be recognized that within every organization there are *vertical* (both upward and downward) as well as *horizontal* information flows. The rationale of MIS is that all information flows must become part of the master plan of an MIS and not be allowed to function without a formal scheme and direction. Figure 15–4 illustrates the various information flows and information types that have been discussed thus far.

The purposes of an MIS

All management information systems share several purposes in varying degrees. An MIS should provide management with three major information services: determinations of information needs, information gathering and processing, and information utilization.

The determination of information needs Management must answer such questions as How much information is needed? How, when, and by whom will it be used? In what form is it needed? In other words, management must begin with an examination of the output requirements. One way is to classify information based on the level in the organization at which it will be used. Thus, the output requirements would be based on the answers to such questions as What information is necessary for planning and controlling operations at different organizational levels? What information is needed to allocate resources? What information is needed to evaluate per-

Figure 15–4

Management information flows and types of information

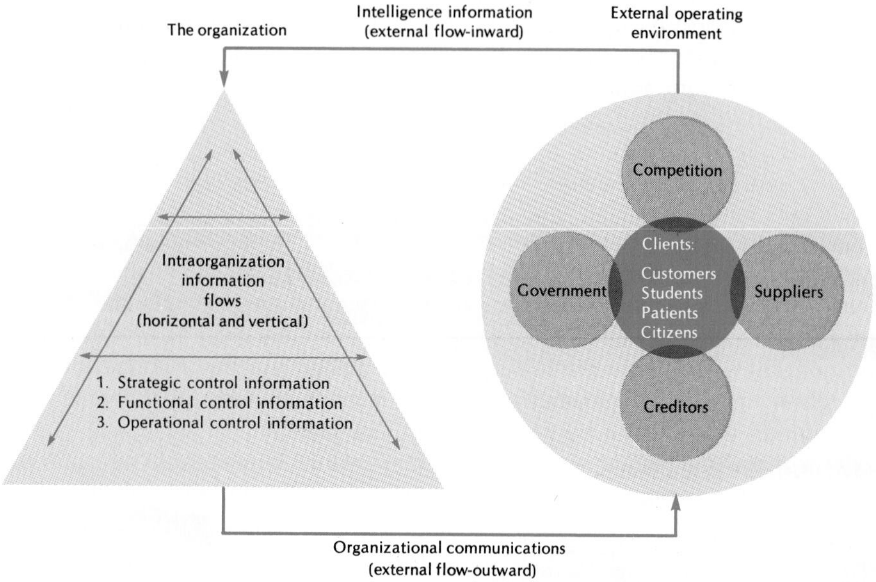

formance? Such questions recognize that a different kind of information is needed for formulating organizational objectives than for scheduling production. They also recognize that too much information may actually hinder managerial performance. It is at this point that we must distinguish "need to know" types of information from "nice to know" types of information. One of the important reasons for using MIS is that *more information does not mean better performance.*

Information gathering and processing The purpose of this service is to improve the overall quality of information. The service includes five component services. *Evaluation* involves determining how much confidence can be placed in a particular piece of information. For example, the credibility of the source and the reliability and validity of the data must be determined. *Abstraction* involves editing and reducing incoming information in order to provide managers with only the information that is relevant to their particular tasks. Once information has been gathered, the service of *indexing* is important in order to provide classifications for storage and retrieval purposes. *Dissemination* entails getting the right information to the right manager at the right time. Indeed, this is the overriding purpose of an MIS. The final information processing service is *storage.* As noted earlier, an organization has no natural memory, so every MIS must provide for the storage of information to permit its use again if it is needed. Modern electronic information storage equipment has greatly improved the "memory" capabilities of organizations.

Information use How information is utilized depends greatly on its quality (accuracy), its form (how it is presented), and its timeliness. If the system is planned carefully, the user will be provided with relevant information. The major goal is to provide the right information to the right decision maker at the right time. Timeliness may take precedence over accuracy. If information is not available when it is needed, then its accuracy is not important. In most cases, however, both timeliness and accuracy are critical. Timeliness is determined by the nature of the decisions that must be made. For example, a sales manager may find accurate weekly product sales reports adequate, whereas an air-traffic controller needs accurate information every second. The functions of an MIS are presented in Figure 15–5.

In this section, we have implied that a central management information unit is needed for the purpose of facilitating information flows both to and within the organization. An MIS does not focus on specific problems. Instead, it monitors the external environment of the organization and it facilitates information flows within the organization.

The information center

If a truly integrated management information system is to become a reality, a single, separate information center must exist in the organization so that one individual can be made responsible for the system. Such a center is also necessary because both the users and the suppliers of man-

Figure 15–5

Functions of a management information system

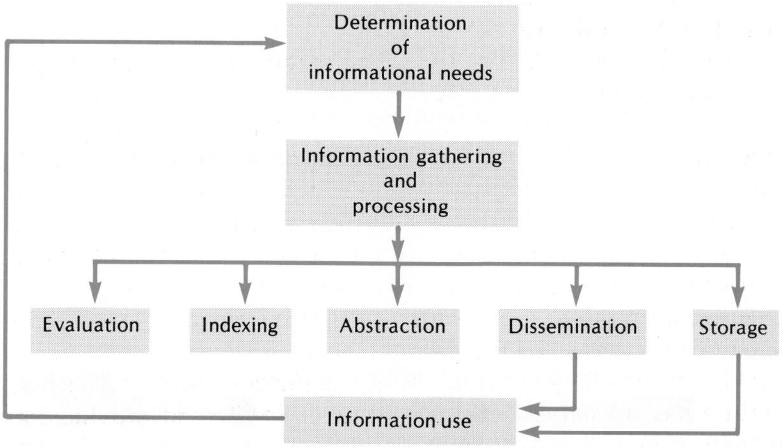

agement information are scattered throughout the organization, and some unit is needed to oversee the operation of the information system. In fact, a basic weakness in many organizations has been the absence of a central unit for the gathering and processing of information. A top-level executive expressed this problem as follows:

> *Before we created the data center, I would receive reports from every functional unit—marketing, production, research, the whole gamut. The reports would be in different formats, information would be duplicated, and the reports were sent to me on what seemed a random basis. Now that the data center is in place, I get reports that meet my needs.*

The information requirements of most managers have greatly changed in the past decade, whereas the information arrangements within most organizations have remained essentially the same. Specifically, three tasks are necessary:

1. Dispersed information activities must be identified throughout the organization.
2. These activities must be viewed as parts of a whole.
3. These activities must be managed by a separate centralized information center.

The information center must be responsible for determining information needs, information gathering, information processing, and information use. In order to justify its existence, the center must facilitate improved managerial performance through more and better information availability and use.

Many information-oriented organizations have established a separate, centralized information office. This practice is probably most widespread in highly competitive, volatile, consumer goods industries. However, as we noted earlier, the need for such an office is becoming more recognized in other areas of private industry and in the public sector. This organizational arrangement offers several advantages, such as increased efficiency and the more effective use of information. It makes all computer, knowledge, and storage and retrieval facilities available to all other units in the organization.

Information as an organizational resource

A frequent problem in many organizations is that a great deal of information is generated for no real purpose. Such information should be eliminated. There seems to be a tendency to generate large quantities of information on the assumption that a direct relationship exists between the amount of information and the quality of decisions. As we have seen, this can only be true if the information is relevant and if it is provided to the right decision maker—that is, if it is provided to the right person at the right time. One useful approach to the effective design and utilization of an MIS is to think of information as a basic resource of the organization, as we think of money, materials, personnel, and plant and equipment. As a basic resource, information:

1. Is vital to the survival of the organization.
2. Can only be used at a cost.
3. Must be at the right place at the right time.
4. Must be used efficiently for an optimal return on its cost to the organization.

Each user of information should consider the cost of the information relative to its utility for decision making. For example, the cost of complete information for a control decision must be weighed against the expected loss that would occur if a control decision were made with incomplete information.

Management summary

1. Effective control depends on managerial actions and decisions that correct deviations between actual and planned results.
2. The three necessary elements of control are predetermined standards, information, and corrective action. *Each* of these elements must be in place before a control system or method can be considered effective.
3. Three general types of control systems and methods can be identified on the basis of (1) the source of information and (2) the focus of corrective action.
4. Precontrol methods and systems depend on information about characteristics and qualities of inputs—materials, capital, financial, and human resources. The focuses of corrective action are the inputs themselves.
5. Concurrent control methods and systems depend on information about ongoing activities and operations. The focuses of corrective action are the activities and operations *or* the inputs, depending on the identified causes of the deviations between actual and desired performance.
6. Postcontrol methods and systems use the information which measures characteristics and qualities of actual results and performance and take corrective action on activities, operations, *and* inputs.
7. Accurate, valid, and timely information must be available to managers who are responsible for control decisions.

8. Organizations frequently use management information systems which utilize the capacity of computers to obtain internal and external sources of data.
9. Integrated management information systems take into account the different informational needs of managers at different organizational levels.
10. The functions of a management information system are to determine information needs, to gather and process needed information, and to provide information to those who need and use it.

Review and discussion questions

1. Explain why predetermined standards are necessary for effective managerial control. Does the fact that management has set standards for crucial aspects of the organization guarantee that control will be effective? Explain.
2. Explain why the standards which chief executive officers (top management) must consider are more subjective and ambiguous than those which subordinates (first-level management) must consider.
3. Explain how the college or university you attend controls the teaching performance of the faculty. Organize your answer in terms of the three types of control.
4. Explain why control is a pointless exercise if it is impossible to take corrective action.
5. In most large organizations, the preparation of control reports is the responsibility of staff personnel, such as accountants, engineers, and other professional employees. How can a manager not trained in these specialties judge the accuracy and interpretation of the reports?
6. Explain how the organizational level of managers affects their informational needs.
7. In what ways does planning information differ from controlling information? Can both types of information be provided by an integrated management information system? Explain.
8. Some managers complain that once a computer system is installed, the computer system rather than management determines what information is to be produced for managerial use. Explain why this complaint may have merit.
9. If information is, in fact, a scarce resource that is demanded by managers throughout the organization, how can you justify the suggestion that the information functions be centralized in one unit, thus giving it monopoly power over this scarce resource?
10. Describe how a manager's leadership style will be reflected in his or her attitudes and behavior toward the controlling process.

Suggested reading

Alexander, T. "Computers on the Road to Self-Improvement." *Fortune,* June 14, 1982, pp. 148–52, 156, 160.

Brinberg, H. R. "Tailor Specific Data to Specific Needs: New Thrusts of Information Management." *Management Review,* December 1981, pp. 8–11.

Cheney, P. H., and G. W. Dickson. "Organizational Characteristics and Information Systems." *Academy of Management Journal,* March 1982, pp. 170–84.

Ebenstein, M., and L. Krauss. "Strategic Planning for Information Resource Management." *Management Review,* June 1981, pp. 21–26.

Murr, D. W.; H. B. Bracey; and W. K. Hill. "How to Improve Your Organization's Management Controls." *Management Review,* October 1980, pp. 56–63.

Rowe, D. L. "How Westinghouse Measures White Collar Productivity." *Management Review,* November 1981, pp. 42–47.

Tom, P. L. "Management Information Systems—History and Future." *Cost and Management,* September–October 1980, pp. 6–15.

Applying what you have learned about elements of controlling

Cases:

Managerial control at Intel Corporation
Precontrolling purchasing decisions

Managerial control at Intel Corporation*

Intel Corporation of Santa Clara, California, is in the business of selling microchips to manufacturers of office equipment. The company has been successful in terms of profitability—it earned $2.21 per share in 1980 on sales of $855 million. But the chip business is highly competitive, and in one year, the price of a widely used programmable memory chip dropped from $25 to $7. That kind of market pressure puts a premium on cost control.

The major cost component in the chip business is labor, and the major labor component is nonproduction workers. When Intel recognized the necessity for cost control, it found that half of its 10,000 employees were in administration. When engineers and salespersons were added, the nonproduction employees accounted for 64 percent of the total work force. Intel's president, Andrew S. Grove, believed that the company's future profitability depended on its ability to control nonproduction labor cost. Yet, he also recognized that these categories of jobs are the most difficult ones to control because of the difficulty in establishing performance standards. Administrative, scientific, and sales personnel, unlike production personnel, do not typically produce tangible and measurable outcomes that can be standardized. Nevertheless, Grove directed that Intel's top management begin a program which would enable the company to control the quantity and quality of nonproduction work.

By 1981, the cost control program had achieved some notable successes:

* This case is adapted from Jeremy Main, "How to Battle Your Own Bureaucracy," *Fortune,* June 29, 1981, pp. 54–58.

1. Two years ago, 12 forms and 95 administrative steps were required to order one $2.79 mechanical pencil; today, the pencil can be ordered with 1 form and 8 steps.

2. Two years ago, 364 administrative steps were required to hire a new employee; today 250 steps are needed.

3. Two years ago, four weeks were required to process expense accounts; only a few days are now required to do the job.

Although these illustrations appear trivial, the director of the program points out that savings such as these and others could increase profits by $60 billion.

The method that Intel uses to determine standards for nonproduction jobs relies upon ideas of scientific management. The company takes each administrative procedure, such as ordering office supplies, hiring new employees, or processing expense vouchers, and examines it methodically. The procedure is laid out systematically with each step identified and examined. The basic idea is to shorten the procedure by eliminating needless or redundant steps, combining steps, and reducing delays. The standard for doing the procedure is the most simplified way of doing it. Thus, the Intel program applies principles of work simplification to nonproduction jobs.

A particular feature of the Intel program is the company's belief in participative management. Consequently, the people whose jobs are to be simplified are asked to do it. The office which performs the job sets up a group of five to seven employees, including the office manager and nonmanagers. The group is responsible for simplifying the job procedures with assistance from the program director's staff. Despite the effort to involve employees in the process, work simplification and standard setting create change and uncertainty and many employees apparently experienced stress and frustration. One unhappy result of the program was an initial increase in employee turnover. Yet, many employees were enthusiastic about the changes which simplified their jobs and enabled them to work more productively.

Questions:

1. In terms of necessary conditions for effective control, what specific problems is Intel Corporation encountering in its effort to control nonproduction labor costs?

2. Why is it so difficult to determine standards of performance for administrative personnel.

3. What standards would you consider valid to measure the performance of personnel in MIS units?

Precontrolling purchasing decisions

The Jason Corporation was in trouble. In each of the last five years, the rate of return on equity had dropped steadily until it had reached its present 5 percent. As one executive observed: "We might as well sell out and let the stockholders put their money in CDs. After all, they could get at least 12 percent on their money and take no risks." The company had been an industry leader in the manufacture of high-quality, high-price accessories for recreational vehicles. The latest financial information reflected the firm's operations through December 1979.

Top management decided that it was unable to analyze the situation without outside help.

The chief executive, Jason Jones, suggested that a nationally known management consulting firm be hired to evaluate the corporation from top to bottom. After a thorough study, the consulting firm submitted a report containing several recommendations. One of the most strongly worded recommendations dealt with the corporation's information system (or the absence thereof). The following is an excerpt from the consultant's report:

Decision makers do not now have the information they need to make decisions. We strongly recommend that Jason Corporation design and install a management information system to satisfy informational needs at all levels of the organization. The design of the system must begin with the identification of informational needs.

Jason Jones agreed with the recommendation and instructed the data processing manager, Bill Knoblett, to work with the consultants in designing the system. Knoblett's first step was to ask each major decision maker to study the informational needs of his or her unit. The study was to result in reports which specified the types of information that were required by each decision maker on a regular basis.

Janet Lea, the chief purchasing agent, did her homework and told Knoblett that she would like to discuss her draft report. The report is summarized as follows:

Informational Needs and Sources of Information for the Purchasing Function

In order to make effective purchasing decisions, an industrial buyer needs a certain amount and quality of information. Our informational needs are related primarily to the following:

1. Price of the items.
2. Quantities to be purchased.
3. Number of sources of supply.
4. Urgency of the purchase.
5. Complexity of the items.
6. Current market situation relative to the items.
7. Authority over details of the purchase decision.

Our specific informational needs will be, for the most part, of two types: technical and quantitative. The technical informational needs relate to such things as dimensional prints, engineering specifications, and quality requirements. The quantitative informational needs concern such things as lot sizes, estimated prices, and terms of shipment.

A careful analysis of the purchasing task reveals numerous and diverse sources of information. Some of our most important and widely used sources are the following:

1. Engineering department.
2. Research and development department.
3. Production control.
4. Supplier literature.
5. Trade papers and magazines.
6. Supplier salespersons.
7. Accounting department.
8. Receiving department.
9. Competitors.
10. Other buyers in the purchasing department.
11. Production department.
12. Legal department.

When Janet and Bill met to discuss the report, Bill was most enthusiastic about what she had done. "A really first-rate job!" he said, "But after reading what information you need, I can't help but wonder how you ever made decisions." Janet, somewhat ruffled by the remark, responded: "Well, we did, and not too badly at that! I can tell you one thing, though—we won't need to be making them if the price of gasoline keeps going up!"

Questions:

1. What postcontrol standards underlie Jason Jones's decision to hire a consulting firm?
2. What does Janet Lea mean by her comment regarding the price of gasoline?
3. What standards can Janet Lea develop from the information she includes in her report?

16

Chapter sixteen Production-operations and financial control

Performance objectives

- **Define** production-operations and financial control in terms of managerial control.
- **State** the necessary conditions for effective *internal control* of financial resources and assets.
- **Describe** the methods that managers can use to precontrol the quality and quantity of financial and production resources.
- **Explain** how statistical quality control can be used to control the quality of input.
- **Discuss** the various production scheduling applications of network and linear programming models.

Management update*

The contemporary concern for raising the level of productivity in American industry has encouraged managers to consider practices which elevate in importance the functions of production planning and control. General Electric and 3M are but two of several companies that have introduced an organizational concept which gives complete responsibility and authority to production planning and control staff for all manufacturing activities from master scheduling and order entry to shipment of the final product to the customer.

This organizational concept is distinctly different from the typical line-staff concept which has been the prevalent practice since the early days of the Industrial Revolution. According to the line-staff concept, the authority for all manufacturing decisions rests with line personnel—production supervisors and managers. The staff personnel have no authority and can only advise the line personnel. Thus, production planning and control experts often have their plan and schedules rejected by line managers. In practice, conflicts between staff and line personnel result in delays and breakdowns, equipment failures, late deliveries from suppliers, and unrecognized changes in customer demand. Clearly, these costs cannot be tolerated in a period of declining productivity, increasing price levels, and intensive competition from foreign companies.

One result is the organizational concept that has emerged which delegates full authority for production and operations to experts in technical planning. Line managers no longer have the authority to accept or reject the directives of these experts. In those plants which have adopted the new concept, it has been necessary to develop entirely new relationships among production planners and production managers. For example, the production planner now has complete authority to determine what job is to be produced and in what sequence it will be produced. The production manager has the authority to select the workers to produce the product. Thus, the staff manager has responsibility for the technical apsects of production, and the line manager has responsibility for the human aspects of production. Despite the significant psychological costs associated with striking these new relationships, it can be anticipated that increasingly more American companies will be willing to experiment with new organizational forms which place greater emphasis on the roles of production planning and control.

---

* This Management Update is based on Eugene F. Baker, "Management Giving Production Planning Bigger Role in Shopfloor Operations," *Management Review*, July 1980, pp. 34–35.

Managerial control of production-operations and financial activities is critical to organizational performance. Although modern organizations must undertake numerous activities, their ultimate fates depend in large part on how well managers allocate financial and productive resources. All other organizational activities, such as engineering, personnel, marketing, and research and development, are supportive of, and supported by, the primary activity of producing goods and services.

This chapter presents several methods which managers use to control productive and financial resources. The presentation is organized around the three basic types of control—precontrol, concurrent control, and postcontrol. The primary focus of the discussion is on the three necessary conditions for effective control, namely standards, information, and corrective action. Production-operations controls are presented first, followed by financial controls.

Production-operations control

All organizations produce outputs, whether those outputs are goods, services, or ideas. The outputs are obtained by transforming certain basic inputs—materials, capital, and labor—through *production,* or *operations,* processes. Manufacturing, publishing, and construction firms produce tangible, physical outputs, and in such cases it is customary to refer to the transformation process as production. Other organizations, such as retailers, wholesalers, banks, railroads, universities, newspapers, and television stations, produce intangible outputs—services and ideas. The transformation process in such organizations is referred to as *operations.*

As was noted in Chapter 15, control methods can be discussed in terms of the focus of their corrective action. Accordingly, production-operations control methods can be described as focusing on inputs (precontrol), transformation (concurrent), or outputs (postcontrol). That basis for discussion is followed in this section.

Precontrol of inputs

Operations management involves acquiring resources and allocating them among all the competing uses for those resources. Precontrol methods focus specifically on the acquisition of resources. The three major types of resources are labor, capital, and materials. Precontrol requires the predetermination of standards for the *quantity* and *quality* of resources. That is, materials, capital, and labor in sufficient quantity and of acceptable quality must be available when needed. Precontrol of labor will not be presented here. The reader should recognize that staffing the organization is intended to assure the availability of labor, and that aspect of organizing was presented in Chapter 9. Here, precontrol of materials and capital is discussed.

Precontrol of materials quality The raw material which is converted into the finished product must conform to standards of quality. At the same time, a sufficient inventory of raw materials must be maintained to insure a continuous flow of the finished product to meet customer demands. The techniques of inventory control are discussed later; at this point, we are concerned only with the quality of incoming materials.

In recent years, numerous statistical sampling methods have been devised to control the quality of materials by inspecting samples rather than the entire lot. These methods require less inspection time, but they entail the risk of accepting an excessive quantity of defective material.

A complete discussion of statistical sampling is beyond the scope of this text, but the essence of the procedure is easily explained. Suppose, for example, that management sets a standard 3 percent level of defective items as the maximum that it will accept from the supplier. A random sample of the items is then inspected, and the percentage of defective items in that sample is calculated. The decision that must then be made, based on the sample, is whether to accept or reject the entire order or to take another sample. Errors can be made in sampling, so that a lot may be accepted when in fact it contains more than 3 percent defectives or a lot may be rejected when in fact it contains less than 3 percent defectives. The sampling procedures will be based on a careful balancing of the relative costs of these two types of errors.

Maintaining quality control of materials often creates difficult human relations problems for managers. The superintendent of a manufacturing facility expressed this problem:

> *The quality control people are rightly concerned with the dollars and cents of our inspection efforts. But I see it as balancing the potential loss of goodwill of suppliers and customers. For example, if we accept material which is defective even though the samples were OK, then we have some disgruntled customers who will be buying the defective product. If we reject*

material which is otherwise acceptable, then the suppliers are mad.

The characteristics of materials precontrol are illustrative of control decisions which are quite routine. The decision to accept or reject materials occurs frequently, and it must be made on a fairly routine basis. The standard is easily measured, and the information (the sample) is readily available. The decision to accept or reject (or to take another sample) is based on straightforward instructions; given the sample results, the decision is automatic. The inspector's instructions may read: "If sample defectives are equal to or less than 3 percent, accept the lot; if sample defectives are equal to or more than 5 percent, reject the lot; if sample defectives are between 3 and 5 percent, take another sample." If a second sample is required, the inspector's actions will be determined by another set of instructions.

Precontrol of materials quantity Production managers make two key control decisions. They are (1) how *many* of each lot or batch to order and (2) how *often* to order each lot or batch. In resolving inventory problems, the manager must initially identify the cost factors which affect the choices being considered. First, there are the **ordering costs** which are incurred each time a lot is ordered from a supplier. They are the clerical and administrative costs per order, which also include the costs of placing the lot into inventory.

Second, there are the **carrying costs** which are incurred whenever items are held in inventory. These include the interest on money invested in inventory and the cost of storage space, rent, obsolescence, taxes, protection, and insurance on losses due to theft, fire, and deterioration. The carrying cost component is usually expressed as an annual figure and as a percentage of the average inventory.

To minimize inventory costs, a manager must minimize both ordering and carrying costs. These two costs are related to each other in opposing directions, as is shown in Figure 16–1. That is, as ordering costs decrease, carrying costs increase. As the size of each order increases, the number of orders and the cost of ordering decreases, but since larger quantities are being ordered and placed in inventory, the cost of carrying the inventory increases.

The number of orders for a given period of time is equal to usage (U) for the period divided by the size of each order (Q), or U/Q. The total ordering cost per period (week, month, or year) is equal to the cost of ordering each lot (J) *multiplied by the number of orders per period, or*

$$\frac{U}{Q}(J)$$

It should be evident now that as the order size (Q) increases, fewer orders are required to meet the usage (U) for a period, and consequently, the

Figure 16–1

The relationship between ordering costs and carrying costs

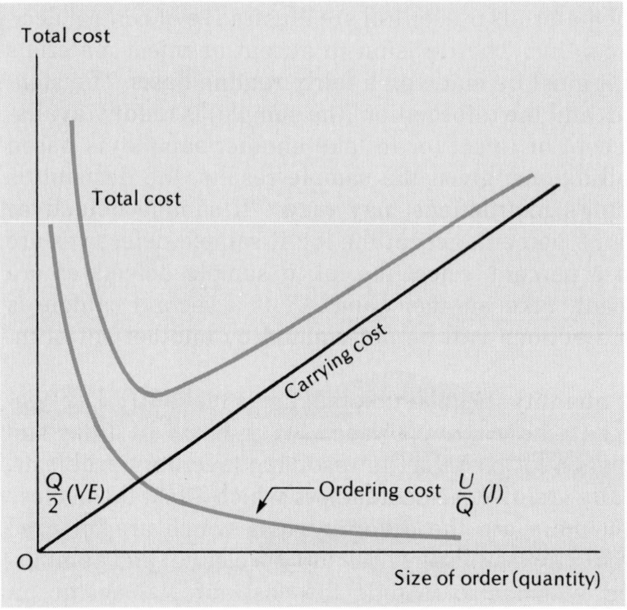

ordering cost component will decrease. This is illustrated graphically by the downward-sloping ordering cost curve in Figure 16–1.

The cost of carrying an item in inventory is calculated by multiplying the cost of the item (V) by a percentage figure (E), or VE, which is management's estimate of taxes, insurance, and so on, per period as a percentage of the cost of inventory. The total carrying costs are equal to the cost of carrying one item (VE) multiplied by the average inventory $Q/2$. Note in Figure 16–1 that unlike ordering costs, carrying costs increase as the size of the order increases.

An example will illustrate why average inventory is $Q/2$. Assume that an organization orders and receives 500 items and that it uses 100 of them each week; at the midpoint of the first week, it has 450 on hand. Table 16–1 illustrates the number in inventory at the midpoint of each week over a period of five weeks. Thus, an average of 250 (1,250 ÷ 5) parts is on hand over the five-week period. The average (250) can also be found by utilizing the formula $Q/2$, that is, 500/2. Note, however, that the formula, $Q/2$, as an approximation of average inventory, depends upon how constant is the rate of usage.

Assume that a production manager is attempting to solve an order quantity problem involving a component part. The yearly usage, which is con-

Table 16–1

Average inventory analysis

Week	Number in inventory at midpoint of week
1	450
2	350
3	250
4	150
5	50
	1,250

stant for the part, is established as 1,000. The administrative and clerical costs of each order are $40. The manager estimates insurance and taxes to be 10 percent per year. The cost of a single part is $20. Thus, the variables involved are: usage (U) = 1,000; setup costs (J) = $40; insurance and taxes (E) = 10 percent; cost of the item (V) = $20.

Referring to Figure 16–1, we see that the minimum total inventory cost is at the intersection of the carrying cost and the ordering cost. Total cost decreases as the size of the order increases up to the intersection, but increases beyond the intersection. Thus, the first step is to set the carrying cost and the ordering cost equal to each other:

$$\frac{Q}{2}(VE) = \frac{U}{Q}(J)$$

Solving for Q yields:

$$Q(VE) = \frac{2\,UJ}{Q}$$

$$Q^2(VE) = 2\,UJ$$

$$Q^2 = \frac{2\,UJ}{VE}$$

$$Q = \sqrt{\frac{2\,UJ}{VE}}$$

The final equation is commonly referred to as the **economic order quantity** (EOQ) formula, and it can be used to solve the inventory problem we have outlined. Using the data in our problem, we can determine the economic order quantity where U = 1,000, J = $40, E = 10 percent, and V = $20.

$$Q = \sqrt{\frac{2(1{,}000)(\$40)}{(\$20)(0.10)}}$$

$$Q = \sqrt{\frac{\$80{,}000}{\$2}}$$

$$Q = \sqrt{40{,}000}$$

$$Q = 200$$

The EOQ formula notes that placing five lots of 200 each will be least costly.

The EOQ model was illustrated here in the context of ordering an item in a job, lot, or batch manufacturing setting. It should be recognized, however, that a retail establishment could also use the approach. In fact, the general approach used in the EOQ model is applicable whenever an organization must purchase, or manufacture, a resource to hold in inventory.

Precontrol of capital In this section, a number of methods in widespread practice will be discussed. Each of these methods involves the formulation of a standard which must be met in order to purchase capital equipment.

The **payback method** is the simplest and apparently the most widely used standard. This approach calculates the number of years that it will take for the proposed capital acquisition to repay its original cost out of future cash earnings. For example, a manager is considering a machine which will reduce labor costs by $8,000 per year for each of the four years of its estimated life. The cost of the machine is $16,000, and the tax rate is 50 percent. The additional aftertax cash inflow from which the machine cost must be paid is calculated as follows:

Additional cash inflow before taxes (labor cost savings) . . .		$8,000
Less additional taxes:		
Additional income	$8,000	
Less depreciation ($16,000 ÷ 4)	4,000	
Additional taxable income	$4,000	
Tax rate	0.5	
Additional tax payment		2,000
Additional cash inflow after taxes		$6,000

After the additional taxes are deducted from the labor savings, the payback period can be calculated as follows:

$$\frac{\$16{,}000}{\$6{,}000} = 2.67 \text{ years}$$

The proposed machine will repay its original cost in $2\frac{2}{3}$ years. If the standard requires a payback of at most three years, the machine would be deemed an appropriate investment.

An effect of economic uncertainty is the tendency of managers to shorten the required payback period. For example, the financial analyst for a major electronics manufacturer said:

> *In recent years, we have become very cautious with our commitments to long-term capital expenditures. Oil shortages, inflation, and talk of recession have made us wary of putting money in any project which won't pay out in two or three years. If economic conditions stabilize, then we can begin to consider longer-term payback projects, but for now we are playing it close to the vest.*

The payback method suffers many limitations as a standard for evaluating capital resources. It does not produce a measurement of profitability, and more important, it does not take into account the time value of money; that is, it does not recognize that a dollar today is worth more than a dollar at a future date. Other methods can be employed which include these important considerations.

The **rate of return on investment** produces a measure of profitability which is consistent with methods ordinarily employed in accounting. Using the above example, the calculations would be as follows:

Additional gross income		$8,000
Less depreciation ($16,000 ÷ 4)	$4,000	
Less taxes	2,000	
Total additional expenses		6,000
Additional net income after taxes		$2,000

The rate of return is the ratio of the additional net income to the original cost:

$$\frac{\$2{,}000}{\$16{,}000} = 12.5\%$$

The calculated rate of return would then be compared to some standard of minimum acceptability, and the decision to accept or reject would depend on that comparison.

The measurement of the simple rate of return has the advantage of being easily understood. It has the disadvantage, however, of not including the time value of money. The discounted rate of return method overcomes this deficiency.

The **discounted rate of return** is a measure of profitability which takes into account the time value of money and can be used as a standard for screening potential capital acquisitions. This method is similar to the payback method in that it considers only cash inflows and outflows. The method is widely used because it is regarded as the "correct" method for calculating the rate of return. Based on the above example, it proceeds as follows:

$$\$16{,}000 = \frac{\$6{,}000}{(1+r)} + \frac{\$6{,}000}{(1+r)^2} + \frac{\$6{,}000}{(1+r)^3} + \frac{\$6{,}000}{(1+r)^4}$$

$$r = 18\%$$

The discounted rate of return (r) is 18 percent, which is interpreted to mean that a \$16,000 investment which repays \$6,000 in cash at the end of each of four years yields a return of 18 percent.

The rationale of the method can be understood by thinking of the \$6,000 inflows as cash payments received by the firm. In exchange for each of these four payments of \$6,000, the firm must pay \$16,000. The rate of return, 18 percent, is the factor which equates future cash inflows with the present cash outflow.

The time value of money is explicitly considered in the method in the following way: If we remember that 18 percent is the rate of return and that there are four distinct and separate future receipts of \$6,000, we can see that \$16,000 is the present value of the future proceeds:

\$5,085 = Present value of \$6,000 to be received in one year,
or $\$5{,}085 \times (1.18) = \$6{,}000$
\$4,309 = Present value of \$6,000 to be received in two years,
or $\$4{,}309 \times (1.18)^2 = \$6{,}000$
\$3,652 = Present value of \$6,000 to be received in three years,
or $\$3{,}652 \times (1.18)^3 = \$6{,}000$
\$3,095 = Present value of \$6,000 to be received in four years,
or $\$3{,}095 \times (1.18)^4 = \$6{,}000$
\$16,141 = Present value of (error due to rounding)

Whether managers are controlling materials or capital, the decision is essentially go or no-go. If the standard is met, the decision is go; if the standard is unmet, the decision is no-go. Similarly, if an applicant for a vacant position meets the standard, that is, has the requisite skills, abilities, and experience, he or she is hired; if not, then he or she is not hired. Once acquired, resources must be allocated. The techniques of resources allocation are presented next.

Concurrent control of operations

The operations decisions which are based on concurrent control methods relate to how much and when outputs will be produced. These decisions are typically termed *production scheduling,* and two general types of models can be used—network models and linear programming models. These methods are typically used by production schedulers who, as noted in the Management Update, prepare production schedules which line managers implement.

Network models Managers can use **network models** to combine and schedule resources or to control activities in order to see that plans are carried out as stated. Such models are especially suited for, but not restricted to, nonroutine projects which will be conducted only once or a few times. In such projects, there is a great need for some type of coordination to insure that tasks which must be completed prior to other tasks are actually completed on time. Some idea is also needed of approximately how long the entire project will take. In summary, some method is needed to avoid unnecessary conflicts and delays by keeping track of all the events and activities on a specific project—and their interrelationships. Network models provide the means to achieve these goals. A widely used network model is the **Program Evaluation and Review Technique (PERT).**

PERT (and variations of it) is probably one of the most widely used production management methods. After the Special Projects Office of the U.S. Navy introduced it on the Polaris missile project in 1958, PERT was widely credited with helping to reduce by two years the time originally estimated for the completion of the engineering and development programs for the missile. By identifying the longest paths through all of the tasks necessary to complete the project, PERT enabled the program managers to concentrate their efforts on these tasks that vitally affected the total project time. During the last two decades, PERT has spread rapidly throughout the defense and space industries. Today, almost every major government military agency involved in the space program utilizes PERT. In fact, many government agencies require contractors to use PERT and other network models in planning and controlling their work on government contracts.

While the aerospace business faces peculiar problems, one-of-a-kind development work is also an important element in many other kinds of organizations and industries. In addition to developing space vehicles and putting a man on the moon, PERT has also been utilized successfully in:

1. Constructing new plants, buildings, and hospitals.
2. Designing new automobiles.
3. Coordinating the numerous activities (production, marketing, etc.) involved in introducing new products.
4. Planning sales campaigns.
5. Planning logistic and distribution systems.
6. Coordinating the installation of large-scale computer systems.
7. Coordinating ship construction and aircraft repairs.

In addition to its use in engineering-oriented applications, PERT has also been used successfully in coordinating the numerous activities necessary to complete mergers between large organizations, for economic planning in underdeveloped countries, and even for smaller specific applications, such as coordinating and planning all the tasks necessary for organizing large-scale conventions and meetings.

PERT networks are developed around two key concepts: activities and events. An **activity** is the work necessary to complete a particular event. An **event** is an accomplishment at a particular point in time. In PERT networks, an event is designated by a circle and an activity is designated by an arrow connecting two circles. This is shown in Figure 16–2.

Figure 16–2

Two events and one activity

In Figure 16–2, there are two events connected by one activity. The events are assigned numbers, and the activity is designated with an arrow. Each of the two events occurs at a specific point in time. Event 1 could represent the specific point in time "project begun," and event 2 could represent the specific point in time "project completed." The arrow connecting the two events represents the activity—the actual work done—and the time necessary to complete it. Thus, the two events in Figure 16–2 designate the beginning and the end of the activity. The activity is what requires time, not the events.

In constructing the network, emphasis is placed on identifying events and activities with enough precision so that it is possible to monitor accomplishment as the project proceeds. There are four basic phases in constructing a PERT network:

1. Define each activity that must be done.
2. Estimate how long each activity will take.
3. Construct the network.
4. Find the critical path—that is, the longest path in time—from the beginning event to the ending event.

All events and activities must be sequenced in the network under a strict set of logical rules (for example, no event can be considered complete until all predecessor events have been completed) which allows for the determination of the critical path.

The paramount variable in a PERT network is time—the basic measure of how long a project will take. Estimating how long each activity will take is extremely difficult, since the manager has no experience to rely on in most cases.

Estimating activity time requirements is designed to deal specifically with the problem of uncertainty in making the job estimates. For example, assume that you are trying to estimate how long it will take to complete a term project for your management class. You know that one activity will be to collect certain information. If all goes well and you do not encounter any obstacles, you believe that you could complete this one activity in eight weeks. However, if a situation occurred in which you encountered numerous obstacles (dates, parties, illness, materials not available in the library, etc.), the chances would be greater that this one activity would take much longer to complete. Thus, you could estimate a variety of possible completion times for this part of your term project.

For PERT projects, *three time estimates are required for each activity.* Each time estimate should be made by the individual or group that is most closely connected with, and responsible for, the particular activity under consideration. The three time estimates needed are:

1. *Optimistic time* (a). This is the time in which the project can be completed if everything goes exceptionally well and no obstacles or problems are encountered.
2. *Most likely time* (m). This is the most realistic estimate of how long an activity might take. It is the time that would be expected to be required most often if the activity were repeated numerous times.
3. *Pessimistic time* (b). This is the time that would be required if everything went wrong and numerous obstacles and problems were encountered. A PERT network consisting of eight events is depicted in Figure 16–3. The three time estimates for each activity are also indicated.

Obviously, it would be extremely difficult to deal simultaneously with the optimistic time, the most likely time, and the pessimistic time. Fortunately, a way has been developed to arrive at one time estimate. It has been determined that an **expected time (t_e)**, can be estimated satisfactorily for each activity by using the following formula:

$$\text{Expected time } (t_e) = \frac{a + 4m + b}{6}$$

Figure 16–4 depicts the network (Figure 16–3) after the expected time (t_e) has been calculated for each activity. It is now possible to calculate the critical path, the sequence of events which takes the longest time. Note that the sequence along the path 1, 2, 3, 5, 6, 7, 8 takes 17 weeks, whereas the sequence along the path 1, 2, 4, 6, 7, 8 takes 16 weeks. The critical path, then, is the one which takes the longest time (17 weeks).

Figure 16–3

PERT network

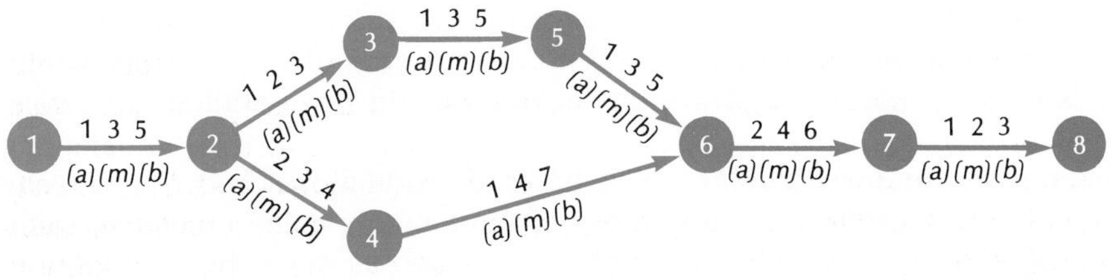

Figure 16–4

Expected time (t_e) for each activity

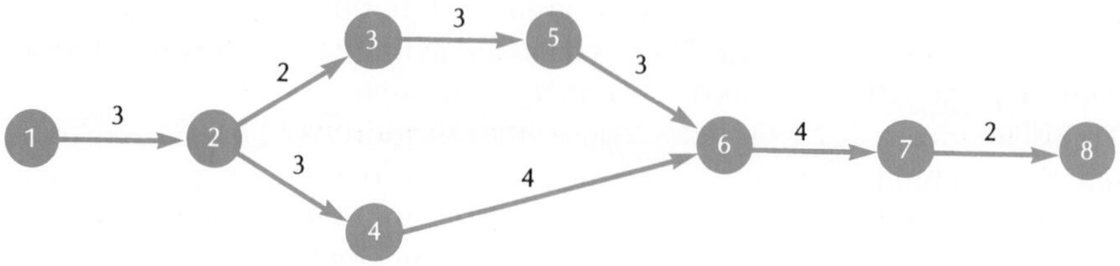

A major advantage of PERT is that the tremendous planning involved in constructing the network contributes significantly to the *concurrent control* of the project. The construction of the network is a very demanding task which forces the manager to visualize the number and kinds of necessary activities and this sequence. In most cases, this kind of thinking cannot help but be a benefit in and of itself.

Effectively used, PERT can be a valuable control device. It provides time schedules for each activity, and it therefore permits networks to be revised if unforeseen difficulties occur. Resources can be shifted, and activities can be rescheduled with a minimum of delay in the completion of the project.

The owner-manager of a construction company specializing in commercial buildings said the following:

> *Our volume of business puts a high premium on knowing where we are on every job. Our PERT system gives me the information I need to keep alert to when we are on schedule and when to shift people to sites where we are behind. Delays cost money, and when the drywall people are waiting for the electricians, the cost of that building is going up, and I have to absorb that cost.*

In projects where subcontractors are used, the necessity for meeting scheduled dates can be stressed by showing subcontractors the negative effects that a delay would have on the entire project. When subcontractors are involved, it is vital that they meet their scheduled delivery dates. For example, the Polaris project involved some 250 prime contractors and almost 10,000 subcontractors. The failure of any one of the subcontractors to deliver a piece of hardware on schedule could have stalled the entire project.

Linear programming models These types of production scheduling models are extremely useful for the purpose of maximizing some objective, such as profits, or of minimizing some objective, such as costs, by determining what the future values of certain variables affecting the outcome should be in order to achieve the objective. The manager has some control over these variables.

The models are called linear because the mathematical equations employed to describe the particular systems under study, as well as the objectives to be achieved, are in the form of linear relations between the variables. A linear relationship between two or more variables is one which is directly and precisely proportional. **Linear programming models** are used in a variety of situations in which numerous activites are competing for limited resources. The manager must find the optimum way to allocate the limited resources, given an objective and any relevant constraints. A complete discussion of the mathematics involved in linear programming models is beyond the purposes of this text. Here, the emphasis is placed on the applications of these models for concurrent control in production-operations management.

Product-mix problems arise when managers must determine the levels for a number of production activities for the planning period. For example, managers face a problem of this nature if a firm manufactures two products which must both go through the same three production processes. The two products compete for time in the three production processes, and the task of the linear programming model in this case would be to allocate the limited resources (the available time in the three processes) in such a way as to produce that number of each product which will maximize the firm's profits.

Feed-mix problems confront large farming organizations which purchase and mix together several types of grains for different purposes. Each grain may contain different amounts of several nutritional elements. For one situation, the production manager must blend the different grains for the purpose of producing a mixture for feeding livestock. The mixture must meet the minimal nutritional requirements at the lowest possible cost. Linear programming can be used to allocate the various grains (each containing different amounts of the nutritional elements) in such a way that the resulting mixture will meet the nutritional and diet specifications at the minimum cost.

Fluid-blending problems are variations of the feed-mix problem. In this case, the manager seeks to blend fluids such as molten metals, chemicals, and crude oil into finished products. Steel, chemical, and oil companies make wide use of linear programming models for problems of this type. Computing the right mixture of octane requirements in the blending of different gasolines is an example of such a problem in the oil industry.

Transportation problems arise when manufacturers and large retail chains face the following situation: Given a number of sources of supply (e.g., warehouses) and a number of destinations (e.g., customers), and given the cost of shipping a product from each source to each destination, select those routes that will minimize total shipping costs. The reader can imagine the complexity of the problem if the firm has many warehouses in different parts of the country and thousands of geographically dispersed customers. Linear programming provides a means for arriving at the optimum shipping program.

Advertising media-mix problems have the following characteristics: Given an advertising budget, how can the budgeted funds be allocated over the various advertising media in order to achieve maximum exposure of the product or service. This type of problem lends itself to the use of linear programming. A number of media (e.g., five magazines) may be competing for a limited advertising budget. Linear programming is widely used in many advertising agencies to solve problems of this type.

Although the above problems are probably the most popular areas of application, linear programming has proven its worth in handling a multitude of other practical problems. For example:

1. The allocation of materials to machines in order to minimize production time.
2. The allocation of cargoes to ships and aircraft.
3. The allocation of coal to power stations to minimize shipping costs.
4. Production scheduling.
5. Personnel assignments.

Linear programming models can result in improved production and operations decisions. Once a linear programming model has been constructed, there is no room for management judgment, since a computer often performs the computations and manipulations and provides a solution which maximizes or minimizes the stated objective within the given constraints. However, before the model is ready to be solved and after it has been solved, human judgment and creativity are necessary. For example, once a solution has been selected, the manager may alter or add a constraint or change the objective. The computer can then provide a new solution under the revised set of conditions. Only a manager, however, can determine which of the two solutions is best.

Postcontrol of outputs

Effective production-operations control requires managers to establish standards for the finished good or service. Precontrol and concurrent control procedures increase the chances that high-quality, efficiently produced outputs will result. But the real test must be based on analysis of the output. If the output fails to meet acceptable standards, production managers can pinpoint causes in the inputs or the transformation process. Two techniques which have been widely used for postcontrol of outputs are standard cost analysis and statistical quality control.

Standard cost analysis The three elements of manufacturing costs are direct labor, direct materials, and overhead. For each of these, an estimate must be made of the element's cost per unit of output. For example, the direct labor cost per unit of output consists of the standard usage of labor and the standard price of labor. The standard usage derives from time studies which determine the expected output per worker-hour; the standard price of labor will be determined by the salary schedule appropriate for the kind of work necessary to produce the output. A similar determination is made for direct materials. Thus, the standard labor and standard materials costs might be as follows:

Standard labor usage per unit	2 hours
Standard wage rate per hour	$3.00
Standard labor cost (2 × $3.00)	$6.00
Standard material usage per unit	6 pounds
Standard material price per pound	$0.30
Standard material cost (6 × $0.30)	$1.80

The accounting information system produces data which enable the manager to compare incurred costs with standard costs. For example, if during the period covered by the report, 200 units of output were produced, the standard labor cost is $1,200 (200 × $6.00) and the standard material cost is $360 (200 × $1.80). Assume that the actual payroll cost for that same period was $1,500 and that the actual material cost was $400. That is, there was an *unfavorable labor variance* of $300 and an *unfavorable material variance* of $40. Management must determine the reasons for the variances and decide what corrective action is appropriate.

Assuming that the standards are correct, the manager must analyze the variance and fix the responsibility for restoring the balance between standard and actual costs. It is obvious that if the actual labor cost exceeds the standard cost, the reason for the difference will be found in labor usage and labor wage rates. Either the actual labor usage exceeded the standard labor usage or the actual wage rates exceeded the standard wage rates, or both. Suppose that in this example the accountant reports that the actual payroll consisted of 450 actual hours at an average wage rate of $3.33. The questions management must resolve are now narrowed to two: What happened during the period to cause output per worker-hour to go down (it should require 400 worker-hours to produce 200 units of output) and why was the average wage rate higher than the standard wage rate? The answers to these questions are found in the resources and activity stages of the production cycle.

Similar analyses are made to discover the causes for the unfavorable material variance. The first step is to discover the relationships between the actual usage and the standard usage and between the actual price and the standard price. As with the labor usage, the manager may find that the actual material usage exceeded the material usage specified by the standard, and/or the manager may find that the actual price exceeds the standard price. Once the cause has been isolated, the analysis must proceed to fix responsibility for corrective action.

Quality control Every production manager dreams of a manufacturing process which produces output with zero defects. But for any number of reasons, 100 percent perfect goods are usually impossible; the quality of raw materials varies, machines operate imperfectly, employees have different levels of skills. Thus, production managers are aware that defective parts will be produced. Exactly how many or what percentage of defective parts or products should be permitted through a manufacturing process depends on such factors as economy, safety, and the firm's reputation for quality. In recent years, quality of output has become an increasingly important control issue. The public has been made more sensitive to the issue as Japanese products are often thought to be of higher quality than some American products.

The cost of having defective, low-quality outputs must be balanced against the cost of not having them. Strictly speaking, the cost of defective output includes spoilage, rework, and warranty expenses. Spoilage occurs when defective output cannot be reworked; for example, some food and drug products cannot be remade if errors occur in mixing or packaging. Rework expenses are the additional labor, materials, and overhead that are required to correct a defective output; for example, if a refrigerator door doesn't seal properly, it would be placed on a repair line and reworked. Warranty expenses are the costs of repairing the product after it has been sold. To avoid such costs, production managers can establish inspection and quality control procedures, but these procedures also cost money, primarily the salaries of inspectors and quality control technicians and engineers.

In most applications of quality control, inspectors do not inspect 100 percent of the output. For example, consider one problem of a manufacturer of peanut butter: maintaining a minimum quantity of peanut butter in each container, say 12 ounces. One approach would be to weigh each container when it is filled—that is, 100 percent of the output could be inspected. An alternative is to inspect samples of the output and to make inferences about the process based on the sample information. This approach is termed **statistical quality control.** This method makes use of statistical sampling theory, and since it reduces the amount of time devoted to inspection, it also reduces the cost of inspection.

If the proportion of sampled peanut butter which contains less than 12 ounces is below some specified standard, say 3 percent, the manufacturing process is allowed to continue in operation. But if the proportion exceeds the allowable proportion, the process is considered out of control. A decision must then be made to shut down the process and to determine and correct the cause of the quality defect. The underlying idea is much the same as the idea which underlies the sampling of raw materials. That is, the cost of inspection is minimized through sampling, but at the risk of permitting a process to continue producing more than 3 percent defective when a sample happens to contain less than 3 percent.

Northrup Corporation's Defense Systems Division pays special attention to quality control. The management of the division initiated the concept of the Quality Visibility Center, which is, in effect, a room set aside to show the quality performance of each production unit. At the center, a record is kept of the quality performance of each unit along with the results of actions to correct deviations from standard. The purpose of the center is to publicize the company's commitment to quality and to develop awareness of that commitment among employees.

The theory and practice of statistical quality control is quite complex, and a complete discussion goes far beyond the scope of this book. The point for the aspiring manager to understand is that statistical sampling methods exist which enable organizations to control the quality of outputs at minimum cost. These methods require predetermined standards of acceptable quality, information obtained from actual output, and corrective action which focuses on the input and transformation elements of production and operations. In many instances, defective outputs can be reworked prior to delivery to customers. But warranty expenses will necessarily be incurred for those defective products which reach the ultimate customer.

Financial controls

Financial control methods aid managers in acquiring, allocating, and evaluating the use of financial resources—cash, accounts receivable, accounts payable, inventories, and long-term debt. The methods also enable managers to achieve acceptable liquidity, solvency, and profitability standards. Regardless of their size and type, organizations must be able to pay short-term obligations (liquidity) and long-term obligations (solvency). They must also pay dividends or distribute profits to the owners (profitability). In addition, the assets of an organization must be protected from theft, unlawful conversion, and misuse. Our discussion is not intended to provide a complete treatment of financial control. Rather, a survey of some methods will be presented to highlight the general principles of all such methods.

Precontrol of financial resources

A primary means for precontrolling financial resources are the various plans prepared during the planning phase. Each of these plans is supported by *budgets* which allocate funds to each major expense category and organizational unit. A primary responsibility of accounting personnel is to develop the procedures and processes which enable management to keep track of how financial resources are allocated and who is accountable for expending and safeguarding them.

The importance of budgeting is illustrated by these comments of the owner-manager of a retail boat and outboard motor outlet:

When I decided to go into business for myself three years ago, the man at the Small Business Administration office told me of the importance of staying on top of cash flow. I took him seriously, and I have set up cash flow budgets for every segment of my company. I pay particular attention to due dates for payables so as not to miss discounts. Every employee knows that spending cash wisely and within budgeted amounts is the key to our survival.

A discussion of the different types of budgets was presented in Chapter 3. Among the important types are flexible and moving budgets. There is no need to repeat that discussion here. The management functions of planning and controlling overlap, and budgeting is one of those areas of overlap.

Concurrent control of financial resources

Planning and budgeting are ineffective unless they are supported by policies and procedures which define how and by whom ongoing transactions are to be handled. Concurrent control of financial resources is implemented primarily through **internal control.**

Internal control is an accounting function and responsibility. Through the efforts of the organization's accounting unit, policies and procedures are adopted which safeguard assets and verify the accuracy and reliability of accounting data. The characteristics of effective internal control include the following:

1. No one person should have complete control over all phases of an important transaction. For example, the same individual should not be responsible for preparing purchase orders and for making out the checks in payment of those purchases.
2. The flow of work from employee to employee should not be duplicative, but the work of the second employee should provide a check on the work of the first. For example, the check drawn to pay the vendor of materials should be cosigned by a second employee who verifies the accuracy and legitimacy of the transaction.
3. Employees who handle assets should not also be responsible for the record-keeping on those assets. This provision is implemented when employees who receive and store materials do not also verify the receipt of those materials.
4. Definitions of job responsibilities must be clearly established so as to fix accountability for each and every aspect of a financial transaction. The organizing function of management must be the primary source for this important aspect of internal control.

Effective internal control procedures can be established for each distinct financial resource. Cash, accounts receivable, interest, inventories, investments, accounts payable, sales, payrolls, and purchases must be safeguarded through procedures which conform to the four characteristics of effective internal control.

Postcontrol of financial resources

A principal source of information from which managers can evaluate historical results is the firm's accounting system. Periodically, the manager receives a set of financial statements which usually includes a balance sheet, an income statement, and a sources and uses of funds statement. These statements summarize and classify the effects of transactions in terms of assets, liabilities, equity, revenues, and expenses—the principal components of the firm's financial structure.

A detailed analysis of the information contained in the financial statements enables management to ascertain the adequacy of the firm's earning power and its ability to meet current and long-term obligations; that is, the manager must have measures of and standards for profitability, liquidity, and solvency.

Profitability The discussion of strategic planning in Chapter 5 described profitability measures. Whether the manager prefers the rate of return on sales, on owners' equity, or on total assets, or a combination of all three, it is important to establish a meaningful standard—one that is appropriate to the particular firm, given its industry and its stage of growth. An inadequate rate of return will negatively affect the firm's ability to attract funds for expansion, particularly if a downward trend over time is evident.

Liquidity The measures of liquidity reflect the firm's ability to meet current obligations as they become due. The widest known and most often used measure is the *ratio of current assets to current liabilities.* The standard of acceptability depends on the particular firm's operating characteristics. Bases for comparison are available from trade associations which publish industry averages. A more rigorous test of liquidity is the *acid test ratio,* which is the ratio of cash and near-cash items (current assets excluding inventories and prepaid expenses) to current liabilities.

The relationship between current assets and current liabilities is an important determinant of liquidity. Equally important is the *composition* of current assets. Two measures which indicate composition and which rely on information found in both the balance sheet and the income statement are the *accounts receivable turnover* and the *inventory turnover.* The accounts receivable turnover is the ratio of credit sales to average accounts receivable. The higher the turnover, the more rapid is the conversion of accounts receivable to cash. A low turnover would indicate a time lag in the collection of receivables, which in turn could strain the firm's ability to meet its own obligations. The appropriate corrective action might be a tightening of credit standards or a more vigorous effort to collect outstanding accounts. The inventory turnover also facilitates the analysis of appropriate balances in current assets. It is calculated as the ratio of the cost of goods sold to the average inventory. A high ratio could indicate a dangerously low inventory balance in relation to sales, with the possibility of missed sales or production slowdowns; conversely, a low ratio might indicate an overinvestment in inventory to the exclusion of other, more profitable, assets. Whatever the case, the appropriate ratio must be established by the manager, based on the firm's experience within its industry and market.

Current obligations must be paid on a timely basis. Consequently, many managers insist on periodic reports of liquidity measures. One manager of a family-owned laundry and dry cleaning firm stated:

> *Sound financial management demands my constant attention. In fact, each month my accountant prepares a report which compares key ratios and account balances with those of a year ago and with those we believe we should have. In this way, I can see where we are out of line and can make some adjustments. I used to have the report sent to me every six months, but that interval was too long.*

Solvency Another financial measure is solvency, the ability of the firm to meet its long-term obligations—its fixed commitments. The solvency measure relates the claims of creditors and owners on the assets of the firm. An appropriate balance must be maintained—a balance which protects the interests of the owners, yet does not ignore the advantages of long-term debt as a source of funds. A commonly used measure of solvency is the *ratio of profits before interest and taxes to interest expense.* This indicates the margin of safety, and ordinarily a high ratio is preferred. However, a very high ratio combined with a low *debt to equity ratio* could indicate that management has not taken advantage of debt as a source of funds. The appropriate balance between debt and equity depends on a number of factors, and the issue is an important topic in financial management. As a general rule, however, one can say that the proportion of debt should vary directly with the stability of the firm's earnings.

The ratios discussed above are only suggestive of the variety of methods that are used to evaluate the financial results of the firm. Figure 16–5 conveniently summarizes profitability, liquidity, and solvency ratios. Accounting as a tool of analysis in management has a long history predating scientific management. Our point here is that financial statement analysis as a part of the management process is clearly a postcontrol method.

Figure 16–5

A summary of key financial ratios, how they are calculated, and what they show

Ratio	How calculated	What it shows
Profitability ratios:		
1. Gross profit margin	$\frac{\text{Sales} - \text{Cost of goods sold}}{\text{Sales}}$	An indication of the total margin available to cover operating expenses and yield a profit.
2. Operating profit margin	$\frac{\text{Profits before taxes and before interest}}{\text{Sales}}$	An indication of the firm's profitability from current operations without regard to the interest charges accruing from the capital structure.
3. Net profit margin (or return on sales)	$\frac{\text{Profits after taxes}}{\text{Sales}}$	Shows aftertax profits per dollar of sales. Subpar profit margins indicate that the firm's sales prices are relatively low or that its costs are relatively high, or both.
4. Return on total assets	$\frac{\text{Profits after taxes}}{\text{Total assets}}$ or $\frac{\text{Profits after taxes} + \text{Interest}}{\text{Total assets}}$	A measure of the return on total investment in the enterprise. It is sometimes desirable to add interest to aftertax profits to form the numerator of the ratio, since total assets are financed by creditors as well as by stockholders; hence, it is accurate to measure the productivity of assets by the returns provided to both classes of investors.
5. Return on stock-holders' equity (or return on net worth)	$\frac{\text{Profits after taxes}}{\text{Total stockholders' equity}}$	A measure of the rate of return on stockholders' investment in the enterprise.

Figure 16–5 (*continued*)

Ratio	How calculated	What it shows
6. Return on common equity	(Profits after taxes − Preferred stock dividends) / (Total stockholders' equity − Par value of preferred stock)	A measure of the rate of return on the investment which the owners of common stock have made in the enterprise.
7. Earnings per share	(Profits after taxes − Preferred stock dividends) / Number of shares of common stock outstanding	Shows the earnings available to the owners of common stock.
Liquidity ratios:		
1. Current ratio	Current assets / Current liabilities	Indicates the extent to which the claims of short-term creditors are covered by assets that are expected to be converted to cash in a period roughly corresponding to the maturity of the liabilities.
2. Quick ratio (or acid test ratio)	(Current assets − Inventory) / Current liabilities	A measure of the firm's ability to pay off short-term obligations without relying on the sale of its inventories.
3. Inventory to net working capital	Inventory / (Current assets − Current liabilities)	A measure of the extent to which the firm's working capital is tied up in inventory.
Solvency ratios:		
1. Debt to assets ratio	Total debt / Total assets	Measures the extent to which borrowed funds have been used to finance the firm's operations.
2. Debt to equity ratio	Total debt / Total stockholders' equity	Provides another measure of the funds provided by creditors versus the funds provided by owners.

Figure 16–5 (*concluded*)

Ratio	How calculated	What it shows
3. Long-term debt to equity ratio	$\frac{\text{Long-term debt}}{\text{Total stockholders' equity}}$	A widely used measure of the balance between debt and equity in the firm's overall capital structure.
4. Times-interest-earned (or coverage ratios)	$\frac{\text{Profits before interest and taxes}}{\text{Total interest charges}}$	Measures the extent to which earnings can decline without the firm becoming unable to meet its annual interest costs.
5. Fixed charge coverage	$\frac{\text{Profits before taxes and interest + Lease obligations}}{\text{Total interest charges + Lease obligations}}$	A more inclusive indication of the firm's ability to meet all of its fixed charge obligations.

SOURCE: Arthur A. Thompson, Jr., and A. J. Strickland, *Strategy and Policy: Concepts and Cases* (Plano, Tex.; Business Publications, 1981), pp. 216–19. © 1981 by Business Publications, Inc.

Management summary

1. Effective control of production-operations and financial resources requires an appropriate mix of precontrol, concurrent control, and postcontrol methods and policies.
2. Production-operations control requires methods, procedures, and policies for the input, transformation, and output elements.
3. Precontrol of inputs attempts to assure the appropriate quantity and quality of each resource. Labor, materials, and capital are the principal resources subject to precontrol.
4. Concurrent control in production-operations management is fundamentally a scheduling problem. Managers can use network and linear programming models to schedule the allocation of resources to different outputs.
5. The quality and costs of outputs can be controlled through statistical quality control and standard cost analysis. The purpose of these methods is to avoid low-quality outputs by monitoring actual production.
6. Precontrol of financial resources is implemented through budgets which specify standard levels of expenditures for expense categories and orga-

nizational units. The specified levels are based on planned objectives that are included in planning documents.

7. Concurrent control of financial resources depends on effective internal control procedures and policies. The development of these procedures is a primary responsibility of the accounting unit.
8. Financial statement and ratio analyses are important means for achieving postcontrol of financial resources. Liquidity, solvency, and profitability standards must be established, and corrective action must be taken when the actual results deviate from the standards.

Review and discussion questions

1. Describe the financial and production operations control system you would set up if you were the manager of a fast-food establishment. Be as specific as possible.
2. Refer to Chapter 9, "Staffing the Organization," and discuss the differences between precontrol of labor and precontrol of materials. Your answer should take into account the differences in setting standards, obtaining information, and taking corrective action.
3. Describe how you would go about determining whether a firm has an adequate internal control system for sales, cash, and accounts receivable.
4. The EOQ model is a useful technique for controlling the quantity of materials purchased. Explain how the model could be used to control the quantity of materials to be manufactured.
5. Explain how a company might purchase a carload of defective materials even if a sample of the items contains no defective items.
6. Liquidity, solvency, and profitability measure different aspects of an organization's financial condition. Explain how it would be possible for an organization to have an imbalance of these three measures.
7. Explain why production scheduling is fundamentally a problem of resource allocation.
8. Distinguish between the types of scheduling problems for which PERT is applicable and those for which linear programming is applicable.
9. Explain why a manufacturing firm cannot achieve perfect quality of output. If *perfect* quality is impossible, explain how a production manager could establish *acceptable* quality.
10. Explain *possible* causes of favorable and unfavorable labor variances and favorable and unfavorable material variances.

Suggested reading

Andrew, C. G., and G. A. Johnson. "The Crucial Importance of Production and Operations Management." *Academy of Management Review,* January 1982, pp. 143–47.

Buffa, E. S. *Modern Production-Operations Management.* New York: John Wiley & Sons, 1980.

Camillus, J. C. and J. H. Grant. "Operational Planning: The Integration of Programming and Budgeting." *Academy of Management Review,* July 1980, pp. 369–80.

Gallagher, G. R. "Materials Requirements Planning: How to Develop a Realistic Master Schedule." *Management Review,* April 1980, pp. 18–25.

Lubar, R. "Rediscovering the Factory." *Fortune,* July 13, 1981, pp. 52–56, 60, 64.

Wu, F. H. "Incrementalism in Financial Strategic Planning." *Academy of Management Review,* January 1981, pp. 133–43.

Applying what you have learned about production-operations and financial control

Cases:

Inventory control at PPG Industries
Strategic control

Inventory control at PPG Industries*

"When you are facing a 20 percent prime, you can't rely on the hope that the day after tomorrow you will get enough orders to use the stuff up," says Malcolm G. Slaney, vice president and general manager of the coatings and resins division of PPG Industries. The *stuff* that Slaney refers to is inventory. The *prime* is the interest rate that banks charge preferred customers for short-term loans of the type required to carry inventory in stock. The effect of rising interest rates is to increase the cost of carrying inventory and thereby reduce the production of inventory. As Slaney's statement implies, controlling inventory size becomes even more acute during periods of rising interest rates.

PPG's recent experience with inventory control procedures suggests that inventory control is possible even under the most unfavorable circumstances. The largest customers of the division that Slaney manages are the automobile companies. The purchases of these companies in 1980–81 was at best erratic. Yet in 1980, the coatings and resins division maintained a better inventory-sales balance than it had in earlier years when sales were steady and relatively more predictable.

The significance of PPG's inventory control success can be readily understood by considering some basic facts of economic life. In 1974, companies such as PPG could borrow money at interest rates below 10 percent (the prime) to finance stocks of materials, parts, and finished goods. Other carrying costs such as storage, insurance, pilferage, and obsolescence were between 5 percent and 10 percent

* This case is adapted from Lewis Beman, "A Big Payoff from Inventory Controls," *Fortune*, July 27, 1981, pp. 76–80.

annually. At the same time, inflation was adding about 15 percent a year to the value of that inventory. Consequently, for the economy as a whole, the cost of carrying an inventory that averaged about $332 billion was less than $10 billion.

In 1981, however, interest rates were higher than inflation rates. In the first quarter of 1981, inventories for all companies totaled $710 billion (twice as large as in 1974), but the cost to carry that inventory was running at an annual rate of $110 billion (*10 times* higher than in 1974). From another perspective, $110 billion is more than half of the total pretax profit for the year 1980. Thus, for the economy as a whole and for individual firms, inventory control is a significant managerial issue.

The success of PPG in holding the line on inventory costs is a computer-based inventory-control system. Each of the company's 11 plants in the United States and Canada has a Burroughs B–4700 computer that keeps track of 5,000 different raw materials and 10,000 finished products. The computer enables the company to process and integrate information from all the various functions which determine the usage and availability of inventories. Purchasing, shipping and receiving, sales, manufacturing, and warehousing decisions and actions must be integrated to achieve lowest-cost inventory levels. But the required integration was impossible prior to the development of computer technology.

Questions:

1. Explain how the PPG Industries experience reflects the importance of inventory control from both a company and a societal perspective.
2. What is the role of computer technology in inventory control?
3. What alternatives are available to companies that cannot afford computer technology, but which must control inventory costs?

Strategic control

The plant manager of a major electronics manufacturer called a meeting with his immediate subordinates to discuss a major strategic control decision. The issue to be resolved concerned whether to go into the full-scale production and marketing of a new product, a miniature thermostat. The miniature thermostat, MT, had been under development for the past three years, and the manager believed that it was time to make a decision. The meeting was to be attended by the marketing manager, the production superintendent, the purchasing manager, and the plant cost accountant. The plant manager instructed each official to bring appropriate information and to be prepared to make a final decision regarding the MT.

Prior to the meeting, the plant manager noted the following facts concerning the MT:

1. Developmental efforts had been undertaken three years ago in response to the introduction of a similar product by a major competitor.
2. Initial manufacturing studies had indicated that much of the technology and know-how to produce the MT already existed in the plant and its work force.
3. A prototype model had been approved by Underwriters' Laboratories.
4. A pilot production line had been designed and installed. Several thousand thermostats had already been produced and tested.
5. Market projections indicated that the trend toward the miniaturization of such components as thermostats was likely to continue.

6. The competitor who had introduced the product was successfully marketing it at a price of $0.80 each.
7. The cost estimates derived by the cost accountant over the past two years consistently indicated that the firm could not meet the competitor's price and at the same time follow its standard markup of 14 percent of the selling price.

Because of his concern for the cost of the MT, the plant manager asked the cost accountant to brief the group at the outset of its meeting. The accountant's data are shown below:

	Actual costs	Standard costs
Direct labor	$0.059	$0.052
Direct material	0.340	0.194
Manufactured overhead (438% of standard direct labor)	0.228	0.228
Total manufacturing cost	$0.627	$0.474
Spoilage (10%)	0.063	0.047
Selling and administrative costs (40% of direct labor and overhead)	0.115	0.112
Total cost per MT ...	$0.805	$0.633
Required price to achieve 14% markup on selling price	$0.936	$0.736

The accountant noted for the group that the firm would not be able to manufacture and sell the MT for less than $0.805 each, given the present actual costs. In fact, meeting its markup objective would require a selling price of approximately $0.94 each, but that would be impossible, since the competitor was selling the same product for $0.80. She explained that if the MT could be manufactured at standard costs, it could compete successfully with the competitor's thermostat. She said that the company should abandon the MT if it could not be made at standard costs.

The marketing manager stated that the MT was an important product and that it was critical for the firm to have an entry in the market. He said that in a few years the MT would be used by all of the company's major customers and that the competition had already moved into the area with a strong sales program. He added that he did not place too much reliance on the cost estimates because the plant had had so little experiemce with full-scale production of the MT and that in any case standard costs, though appropriate for cost containment, were inappropriate for decisions of this type.

The manufacturing superintendent stated that he was working with engineers to develop a new method for welding contacts and that if it proved successful, the direct labor cost would be reduced significantly. This would have a cumulative effect on costs, since overhead, spoilage, and selling and administrative expenses were based on direct labor. He also believed that with a little more experience, the workers could reach standard times on the assembly operations. He said that much progress in this direction had been made in the past four weeks.

The purchasing manager stated that material costs were high because the plant had not procured materials in sufficient quantities. She said that with full-scale production, material costs should decrease to standard.

Questions:

1. If you were the plant manager, what decision would you make regarding the MT?
2. If you decided to manufacture the MT, would your decision indicate that the standard of 14 percent markup was not valid?
3. Trace the relationships between precontrol, concurrent control, and postcontrol as revealed by the facts of the case.

17

Chapter seventeen Human resource performance evaluation

Performance objectives

- **Define** the process of performance evaluation in terms of managerial purposes.
- **State** the necessary conditions for human resource performance standards.
- **Describe** the important traditional performance evaluation methods.
- **Explain** how behaviorally anchored rating scales and results-oriented evaluation methods differ from traditional methods.
- **Discuss** the key decisions which managers must make when administering a performance evaluation program.

Management update*

Effective performance evaluation systems do not just happen. They require investments not only in procedures but also in people, particularly those people who have responsibilities for evaluating the performance of other people. Sybron Corporation, a major manufacturer of scientific and photographic equipment and instruments, recently developed and implemented a training program for managers with performance evaluation responsibility. According to Ben Harper, training coordinator at Sybron's headquarters in Rochester, New York, "Many managers did not know how to set measurable objectives. Nor did they know how to evaluate subordinates effectively and objectively." According to Harper, the company's system is fundamentally sound, but the managers had to be trained to work within it.

The training staff prepared and implemented a two-phase program. The first phase teaches managers interpersonal skills for setting goals, substantiating goal accomplishment, and carrying out performance and salary reviews. They practice the skills and review their own performance on videotape. The managers are then required to return to their work stations and use their newly learned skills. They subsequently report back to the group on their progress.

The second phase of the program instructs the managers in the five general principles that the company believes are conducive to high levels of performance. The principles are:

1. Maintain and enhance the self-esteem of others.
2. Focus on the behavior of others, not their personalities.
3. Use positive reinforcement to shape behavior.
4. Listen actively to what others are saying.
5. Maintain communications and set specific follow-up dates.

These principles are applicable not only in the context of performance appraisals, but they are also applicable in interactions with peers, customers, and suppliers according to Sybron's training staff.

---

* This Management Update is based on "Sybron Trains Managers to Improve Performance Appraisals," *Management Review*, January 1981, pp. 32–33.

The responsibility of managers for working with people to achieve organizational purposes involves a range of managerial issues. In previous chapters, issues related to motivation, individual differences, group behavior, leadership, communications, and career development have been discussed in terms of human resources. In addition, our discussion of organizational and job design and of organizational staffing has emphasized people issues. Thus, a continuing theme in any discussion of management is the human perspective.

This chapter presents the problems and potentials of evaluating the performance of individuals. Effective performance evaluation is not only a critical managerial responsibility but also an inevitable one. Managers inevitably engage in evaluating performance because they must decide on hirings, promotions, transfers, and pay. As noted in the Management Update, organizations make investments in training managers to be effective evaluators of performance.

Because performance evaluation is inevitable, effective management of the process requires managers to gather relevant information. Managers who attempt to gather such information will eventually have to answer several questions: (1) What are the purposes of performance evaluation? (2) What performance standards are applicable to an individual's job? (3) What potential problems are associated with performance evaluation? (4) What performance evaluation methods can best accomplish the purposes of performance evaluation and minimize its potential problems?

An overview of performance evaluation

The four basic questions of performance evaluation must be viewed in the context of the people and the procedures that it involves. From Figure 17–1, we see that the focal people are the managers who must make the evaluation decisions, the individuals who perform the work, and the individuals who define the performance standards. In many organizations, these three sets of people are distinctly different. Staff individuals in personnel and industrial engineering units define the standards for each job. They use techniques of work measurement such as motion and time study to arrive at the standard quantity and quality of output for each job. In some organizations, the standards are defined by managers who then evaluate performance; in other organizations, setting standards is a joint process involving managers, the individuals doing the work, and staff personnel.

However standards are set, performance evaluation requires that managers receive information about each individual's job performance. That information can be gleaned from direct observation; from such reports as check sheets, rating forms, and production reports; or from interview sessions with the individual. Typically, the manager must prepare some form of written evaluation of the employee's performance as a basis for corrective action.

The corrective action that is taken subsequently is directed toward either the individual performing the work or the standards. When the individual is the focus, the manager attempts to reward high performance and improve low performance. Pay, promotion, advancement, and development opportunities are means by which the manager can achieve the purposes of performance evaluation. The manager would attempt to revise standards if he or she believed they were invalid.

Thus, performance evaluation shares the characteristics of other techniques of managerial control. Specifically, standards, information, and corrective action are necessary elements of effective performance evaluation.

Purposes of performance evaluation

Performance evaluation processes and procedures accomplish two broad purposes and several specific purposes. The two broad purposes are termed (1) *judgmental* and (2) *developmental.*[1]

Judgmental purposes

When performance evaluation results are the bases for salary, promotion, and transfer decisions, judgmental purposes are being served. The immediate objective is to improve performance by rewarding those individuals who are deemed high performers. Managers who use performance evaluation for judgmental purposes must evaluate performance accurately and precisely and distribute rewards on the basis of performance; failure to

[1] The following discussion is based on Larry L. Cummings and Donald P. Schwab, *Performance in Organizations* (Glenview, Ill.: Scott, Foresman, 1973), pp. 4–7.

do so undermines the judgmental purposes and causes employees to be cynical about the process.

Many employees who work in organizations which use grade and step salary plans view the annual performance evaluation with distaste and cynicism. One accounting clerk with many years of service in a state government agency stated:

> *Every year my supervisor comes around and tells me that I have been a top producer. Then the salary announcements are released, and* everybody *has moved up another step in grade. Getting to the next step in your grade comes with putting in another year, not with being a top producer. I really don't see why performance evaluation is necessary unless it is to give my supervisor something to do.*

The role of managers is that of judge when judgmental purposes are sought. Because the subordinates being evaluated recognize that their vital and vested financial and career interests are at stake, they tend to play passive, reactive roles and they frequently engage in defensive behavior. The atmosphere in which performance evaluations are undertaken is often colored by suspicion and distrust. Managers and subordinates alike are uncomfortable about the process, particularly when the information about performance is potentially inaccurate and when the performance standards are invalid.

The comments of the director of a data processing center illustrate some of the difficulties of performance evaluation that is done for judgmental purposes:

Figure 17–1

The performance evaluation process

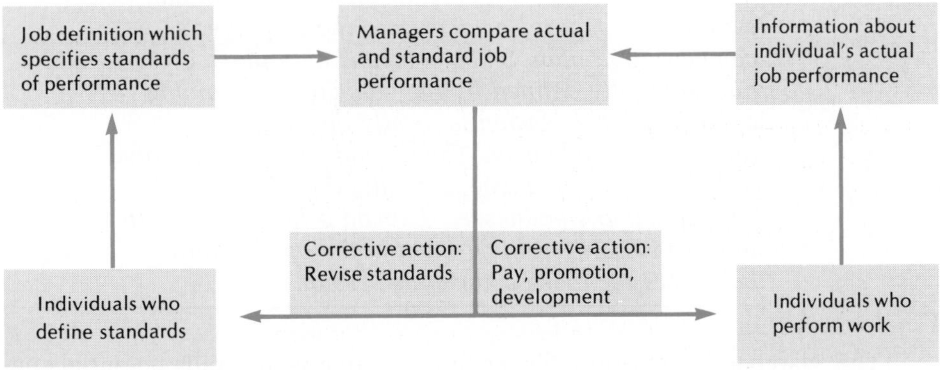

> *Each year I have to evaluate each of the 15 people in the unit. The two weeks during which I must do it are the longest of the year. It seems like all my efforts to be a good guy and to get along with my people go down the tubes. They keep their distance for weeks before and after we go through the exercise. I don't like to do it, and they don't like to do it.*

These comments are not presented as representative of the typical case. Many organizations are able to remove some of the stresses of performance appraisal, particularly when there are straightforward and objective standards, accurate information, and clear-cut linkages between performance and pay and promotion.

Developmental purposes

The second broad purpose of performance evaluation is to improve performance through self-learning and personal growth. This developmental purpose is accomplished when employees are made aware of their strengths and weaknesses and of ways to improve their skills and abilities.

The focus of attention is not so much on the appraisal of past performance as on the improvement of future performance. The managers' roles in the process are to counsel, guide, and be generally helpful as subordinates, through active involvement, seek better understanding of their potential for improved performance. Managers would avoid judgmental terms such as *good-bad, positive-negative,* and *right-wrong.* Instead of making judgments about employees' past performances, managers assist employees in identifying areas of improvement.

The warehouse manager of a paper products manufacturer expressed her philosophy of performance evaluation:

> *I encourage the supervisors to hold two distinctly different sessions with each of their people. In one session, the supervisor discusses the employee's compensation plan. Since compensation plans are almost wholly defined by the collective bargaining agreement, this session is mostly devoted to information exchanges. The second session is devoted to helping the employee understand performance strengths and weaknesses. I spend a lot of time with the supervisors, training them in the appropriate behaviors for these counseling sessions.*

This warehouse manager believes that this approach avoids potential conflict between developmental and judgmental purposes.

The two general purposes of performance evaluation are not mutually exclusive. Managers must, however, identify the purposes of performance evaluation and provide for those purposes by adopting appropriate procedures. In addition to judgmental and developmental purposes, some specific purposes can be identified.

Specific purposes

Managers are continually faced with the need to make judgments concerning the job performance of subordinates. For example, they must make judgments about promotions and pay raises. Most experts recommend that the evaluation sessions which address salary or promotion be kept separate from those dealing with personal and career development, a point of view that was adopted by the warehouse manager mentioned above. This separation is recommended because of the differences between the judgmental and developmental purposes of performance evaluation.

A well-designed and well-implemented performance evaluation program can have a *motivational* impact on employees. It can encourage improvement, develop a sense of responsibility, and increase organizational commitment. Performance evaluation can also be motivational if it can provide the employees with some understanding of what is expected of them.

Another specific purpose of performance evaluation is to improve *managerial understanding.* A formal performance evaluation program encourages managers to observe the behavior of subordinates. Through increased and more thorough observations, improved mutual understanding between supervisors and subordinates can result.

Performance evaluation information also provides a basis for *planning, training,* and *development.* Areas requiring improvement, such as technical competence, communication skills, and problem-solving techniques, can be identified and analyzed.

A *research purpose* can also be accomplished through performance evaluation. The accuracy of selection decisions can be determined by comparing performance evaluations with such selection devices as test scores and interviewers' ratings.

An important and often forgotten purpose of performance evaluation is to reduce *favoritism* in making important managerial decisions. This purpose is extremely important to many employees. It is a subjective factor, whereas the other purposes cited are related to the broad judgmental and developmental categories. The negative effects of perceived favoritism include strained supervisor-subordinate relationships, low morale, and dissatisfaction with company policies. Valid performance standards are an important means for reducing perceptions of favoritism.

Perceptions of favoritism are often the bases for unionization efforts. The personnel manager of a surgical bandage manufacturer stated:

We came close to losing a recognition election when the union publicized numerous complaints of favoritism. Unfortunately, there was just enough of it going on to give the union a strong position with the employees. We won the recognition election, but rather than sitting on our hands, we immediately developed a performance evaluation process that gave us the bases for our personnel decisions. In a sense, the union accomplished its purpose, although it lost the election.

Performance standards

The performance evaluation program at any level within the organization hierarchy must at some point focus on the performance standards issue. In performance evaluation, the standard is the basis for appraising the effectiveness of an individual employee.

Requirements of a performance standard

A number of requirements should be met before a measure qualifies as a performance standard. First, a performance standard must be *relevant* to the individual and the organization. Determining what is relevant is itself controversial. Some person or group must make a judgment about what constitutes relevance.

Second, the standard must be *stable,* or reliable. This involves agreement between different evaluations at different points in time. If the results from two different evaluations show little agreement, there would be some uncertainty about whether the standard was stable.

Third, a performance standard must *discriminate* between good performers and poor performers. If all employees are good performers, then there is no need to discriminate. If, however, there are good, average, weak, and poor performers, then the evaluation standard must discriminate.

Finally, the standard must be *practical.* The standard must mean something to the rater and the ratee. If the standard serves no useful function, then it has no meaning to either the rater or the ratee.

Single or multiple standards

In general, there is ample evidence to support the argument for either single or multiple standards. In some situations, especially at the policy-making level, a single standard is needed to reach a managerial decision. In cases involving promotion, salary and wage decisions, transfer, and counseling, multiple standards can be useful in illustrating why a particular decision is made or why a specific development program is recommended.

It would be extremely difficult to make a promotion decision on the basis of a single criterion.

Managers ordinarily evaluate performance in several key factors of work activity. Table 17–1 summarizes a survey which sought to determine the extent to which such factors as quantity and quality of work were used in performance evaluation. The results clearly indicate the importance of quality and quantity of work for both white-collar and blue-collar workers; 90 percent or more of the respondents to the survey indicated that they used these two factors. Notice also the extensive use of personality traits and characteristics (initiative, cooperation, dependability, and need for supervision).

Table 17–1

Percentage use of factors for which standards are set

	White-collar workers	Blue-collar workers
Quality	93%	91%
Quantity	90	91
Job knowledge	85	85
Attendance	79	86
Initiative	87	83
Cooperation	87	83
Dependability	86	86
Need for supervision	67	77

SOURCE: Bureau of National Affairs, "Employee Performance: Evaluation and Control," *Personnel Policies Forum,* February 1975.

Activities or results standards

Another controversial issue involves the use of activities versus results as standards. The job performance of any person can be viewed in terms of the activities performed and the effort made by the individual. Any performance evaluation program that concentrates on either activities or results to the exclusion of the other often produces problems because employees learn what is important and focus on this aspect of the job. For example, if production output is the standard for assessing performance, assembly line workers may produce as many units as possible so that they receive a good evaluation. The production quantity orientation may result in the manufacture of low-quality products at high costs because of the excessive amount of rejects.

The danger of relying solely on quantity standards is noted by the manager of a plant producing seat belts for the automobile industry:

We are under great pressure to keep costs down in the midst of inflation. The more belts we get out, the lower the unit cost. But a side effect of that emphasis is product failure. We recently had to rework a very large shipment which Detroit rejected because buckles were improperly installed. It was a failure of quality control to catch it, but the root cause was our emphasis on quantity at the expense of workmanship.

On the other hand, a program of performance evaluation which appraises only activities would have some limitations. First, it would encourage only activities and disregard accomplishments. For example, if assembly line workers are only evaluated on whether safety rules are followed and work areas are properly prepared for production, too few units may be made.

It seems appropriate to suggest that performance evaluation standards for both activities and results should be established whenever possible. If any performance evaluation program addresses either activities criteria or results criteria to the exclusion of the other, little attention may be paid to the accomplishment of organizational and personal goals.

Production standards

Production standards may be used for some jobs, such as assembly line, clerical, and sales jobs. The manager can count the number of generators manufactured, the number of accident claims filed per day, or the number of used cars sold. These are certainly worthwhile indicators of job performance for some jobs.

Even when objective measures such as the quantity and quality of output seem appropriate, there may be some problems. Objective results are often not stable from day to day or from month to month. A high performer this week may be an average performer next week. If the supervisor bases the evaluation on the data showing poor performance time, the employee would be rated low. Thus, it is important to base performance evaluation conclusions on a representative sample of performance data collected over a normal time period.

Another potential problem with using production standards is that employees often cannot control factors that influence the criteria. The equipment may be obsolete, receipt of the resources needed to do the job may be erratic, or the employee may be asked to train an understudy during the workday.

Personnel standards

Personnel standards are often used for various jobs. These standards include absences, tardiness, accident frequency, and rate of wage or salary advancement. Each of these standards must be treated with caution. For example, it is necessary to examine "excused" and "unexcused" absenteeism. These two types of absences indicate different behaviors on the part of employees. Also, the rate of wage or salary advancement can be influenced by market position, union demands, and the financial position of the organization.

Many jobs are just not suited for either production or personnel performance standards. This means that the performance on some jobs must be evaluated on the basis of judgment standards.

Judgment standards

Since qualified production and personnel criteria are not available for evaluating employee performance for some jobs, there is a need to rely on rater judgments. These judgments may take the form of rating scales, comparisons, checklists, or critical incidents. Most performance evaluations of managerial, technical, and professional employees use judgment standards. When using such standards, it is important to minimize rater subjectivity.

The specification of purposes and standards is an important first step in devising performance evaluation procedures. Four additional issues to be resolved relate to the administration of the procedures.

Administering performance evaluation

Although developing a systematic program for performance evaluation is extremely important, there are other managerial practices regarding performance evaluation which are just as significant. It is extremely important to decide (1) who will do the rating, (2) who will be rated, (3) when the rating should take place, and (4) how to carry on the evaluation interview. These decisions set the general tone for the overall administration of the performance evaluation program.

Who should rate?

Five possible parties can serve as raters: (1) the supervisor or supervisors of the ratee, (2) organizational peers, (3) the ratee, (4) subordinates of the ratee, and (5) individuals outside the work environment. In most situations, the rater is the immediate supervisor of the person rated. Because of frequent contact, he or she is assumed to be most familiar with the employee's performance. In addition, many organizations regard performance evaluation as an integral part of the immediate supervisor's job.

The supervisor's evaluations are often reviewed by higher management, thereby maintaining managerial control over the evaluation program.

A form of peer evaluation is in use at Romac Industries, Inc., in Seattle. This company permits all employees with six months on the job to vote on the raises of other employees. When an individual requests a raise, his or her picture is put on the bulletin board along with the information about the raise. The employees then vote whether to grant the raise. Management reserves the right to veto the results, but the essence of the policy is to allow peers to evaluate peers. Since pay raises are related to performance, peers are judging the performance of peers and reflecting their judgments in the way they vote on the requested raises.

There is some interest in using self-evaluations. The major claims in support of this approach are that it improves the employee's understanding of job performance, increases the personal commitment of employees because of their participation in the performance evaluation process, and reduces the hostility between superiors and subordinates over ratings. Some employers fear that self-ratings will be unusually high. One study of the effects of self-ratings provides some support for the practice. In the study, 40 subordinates completed self-evaluations and 41 were rated in the usual manner by their managers. More defensiveness about the ratings was noted among the individuals who were rated by their supervisors than among the individuals who rated themselves. In a three-month follow-up after the evaluation interviews, supervisors reported that 16 of the 41 manager-appraised subordinates were not performing well, as compared to only 8 of the 40 self-rated employees.[2]

There is some support for increased use of multiple evaluators. The major advantage of using superior, peer, and self-ratings is that this provides a great deal of information about the ratee. In making decisions about promotion, training and development, and career planning, as much information as possible is needed to suggest the best alternative courses of action for the employee.

When to rate

There is no specific schedule for rating employees. In general, one formal evaluation a year is provided for older or tenured employees. Recent hirees are usually evaluated more frequently than other employees. The time to rate will depend on the situation and on the intent of the evaluation. If performance evaluations are too far apart or occur too frequently, the ratee may not be able to use the feedback received to make improvements.

Recently, EEO and affirmative action directives and guidelines have encouraged more frequent performance evaluations. The concern for compli-

---

[2] G. A. Bassett and H. H. Meyer, "Performance Appraisal Based on Self-Review," *Personnel Psychology,* Winter 1968, pp. 421–30.

ance with these guidelines is reflected in the comments of a paper products distributor:

> *Since 1975, we have evaluated our people twice a year—three times a year for new employees. We do this to obtain as much performance data as possible as bases for our personnel actions. I realize that frequent evaluations do not completely eliminate the biases of the supervisors, but the more they have to evaluate, the more familiar they become with the abilities of their people. Even though we spend a lot of time and money doing it, a judicial award for failure to meet antidiscrimination guidelines would probably cost a whole lot more.*

An evaluation program that is conducted solely for the sake of rating employees will soon lose any potential value or motivational impact unless it becomes integrated with the main emphases of the organization. The judgmental and developmental purposes will show through when both the ratee and the rater understand each other's roles in the process. The rater must clarify, coach, counsel, and provide feedback. On the other hand, the ratee must understand rater expectations, his or her own strengths and weaknesses, and the goals that need to be accomplished. These various roles can become clear if the performance evaluation program is considered a continual process that focuses both on task accomplishment and on personal development.

The evaluation interview

Regardless of how individual job performance information is collected, the rater must provide formal feedback to the ratee. Without formal feedback, the ratee will have difficulty in making the modifications necessary to improve performance, in matching his or her individual job performance expectations with those of the rater, and in assessing the progress that is being made toward the accomplishment of career goals.

The feedback interview should be a part of any performance evaluation program from the beginning. The interview should focus on the job performance of the ratee. Generally, raters feel uncomfortable about discussing ratee weaknesses or problems. On the other hand, ratees often become defensive when personal weaknesses or failures are pointed out by a rater. As critical comments increase, the defensiveness of subordinates increases. Furthermore, praise in the feedback sessions is often ineffective, since most raters first praise, then criticize, and finally praise to end the feedback session and ratees become conditioned to this sequence.

Too often, performance evaluation interviews focus on the past year or on plans for the short run. Rarely do a manager and a subordinate discuss careers.[3] It is important for managers to have knowledge about the requirements for the various career tracks that are available within the organization. The manager should be able to help create challenging but not unattainable job tasks for subordinates. This will help prepare subordinates for future jobs which require the use of more skills and abilities. Basically, it seems worthwhile for managers to consider and be prepared to discuss the lifelong sequence of job experiences of subordinates as part of the performance evaluation feedback interview. Only through managerial consideration of career goals can the evaluation process become a developmental experience as well as a judgmental analysis of job performance.

Although the needs of each organization, manager, and individual must be considered, some general guidelines can be suggested. In Figure 17–2, suggestions for preparing and conducting the appraisal interview are stated.

Traditional performance evaluation methods

Managers usually attempt to select a performance evaluation procedure that will minimize conflict with ratees, provide relevant feedback to ratees, and contribute to the achievement of organizational objectives. Basically, the manager attempts to develop and implement the performance evaluation program that can benefit the employee, other managers, the work group, and the organization.

As is the case with most managerial procedures, there are no universally accepted methods of performance evaluation that fit every purpose, person, or organization. What is effective in IBM will not necessarily work in General Mills. In fact, what is effective within one department or for one group in a particular organization will not necessarily be right for another unit or group within the same company.

Graphic rating scales

The oldest and most widely used performance evaluation procedure, the graphic scaling technique, appears in many forms. Generally, the rater is supplied with a printed form, one for each subordinate to be rated. The form contains a number of job performance qualities and characteristics to be rated. The rating scales are distinguished by (1) how exactly the categories are defined; (2) the degree to which the person interpreting

[3] G. W. Dalton, P. H. Thompson, and R. L. Price, "A New Look at Performance by Professionals," *Organizational Dynamics,* Summer 1977, pp. 19–42.

Figure 17–2

Guidelines for preparing and conducting an appraisal interview

Preparing for the interview:

1. Hold a group discussion with employees to be evaluated to describe the broad standards for their appraisals.
2. Discuss your employees with your own manager and several of your peers.
3. Clarify any differences in language between the formal written appraisal and the interview.
4. If you are angry with an employee, talk about it before the interview, not during the interview.
5. Be aware of your own biases in judging people.
6. Review the employee's compensation plan and be knowledgeable of his or her salary history.
7. If you have already given the employee a number of negative appraisals, be prepared to take action.

Conducting the interview:

1. Focus on positive work performance.
2. Remember that strengths and weaknesses usually spring from the same general characteristics.
3. Admit that your judgment of performance contains some subjectivity.
4. Make it clear that the responsibility for development lies with the employee, not with you (the rater).
5. Be specific when citing examples.

SOURCE: John Cowan, "A Human-Factors Approach to Appraisals," *Personnel,* November–December 1975, pp. 49–56.

the ratings (e.g., the superior) can tell what response was intended by the rater; and (3) how carefully the performance dimension is defined for the rater.

Each organization devises rating scales and formats that suit its needs. Figures 17–3 and 17–4 are examples of types of rating forms that are used in many organizations. The one shown in Figure 17–3 is a more general form than that in 17–4, which is used by a state university to evaluate technical and staff personnel. Each form attempts to clarify the meanings of each of the rating factors. Users of the form in Figure 17–4 know that the rating scale is 1 (unacceptable) to 4 (superior) for each of the three factors. Note also that Figure 17–3 contains many of the factors that are typically used in business organizations, as found in the study cited earlier and listed in Table 17–1. The rating form in Figure 17–4 makes explicit the weights of each factor, and when it has been completed, the employee would receive an overall score which is indicative of performance during the period covered by the evaluation.

Figure 17–3

Typical graphic rating scale

Name ________________ Dept. ________________ Date ______________

	Outstanding	Good	Satisfactory	Fair	Unsatisfactory
Quantity of work Volume of acceptable work under normal conditions Comments:	☐	☐	☐	☐	☐
Quality of work Thoroughness, neatness, and accuracy of work Comments:	☐	☐	☐	☐	☐
Knowledge of job Clear understanding of the facts or factors pertinent to the job Comments:	☐	☐	☐	☐	☐
Personal qualities Personality, appearance, sociability, leadership, integrity Comments:	☐	☐	☐	☐	☐
Cooperation Ability and willingness to work with associates, supervisors, and subordinates toward common goals Comments:	☐	☐	☐	☐	☐
Dependability Conscientious, thorough, accurate, reliable with respect to attendance, lunch periods, reliefs, etc. Comments:	☐	☐	☐	☐	☐

Figure 17–3 (*concluded*)

	Out-standing	Good	Satis-factory	Fair	Unsatis-factory
Initiative Earnest in seeking increased responsi-bilities; self-starting, unafraid to proceed alone Comments:	☐	☐	☐	☐	☐

SOURCE: William F. Glueck, *Personnel* (Plano, Tex.: Business Publications, 1978), p. 302. © 1978 by Business Publications, Inc.

Ranking methods

Some managers use a rank order procedure to evaluate all subordinates. The subordinates are ranked according to their relative worth to the company or unit on one or more performance dimensions. The procedure followed usually involves identifying the best performer and the worst performer. These are placed in the first and last positions on the ranking list. The next best and next poorest performers are then filled in on the list. This rank ordering continues until all subordinates are placed on the list. The rater is forced to discriminate by the rank-ordering performance evaluation method.

There are some problems with the ranking method. One problem is that ratees in the central portion of the list are likely not to be much different from one another on the performance rankings. Another problem involves the size of the group of subordinates being evaluated. Large groups of subordinates are more difficult to rank validly than small groups.

Weighted checklists

A **weighted checklist** consists of a number of statements that describe various types and levels of behavior for a particular job or group of jobs. Each statement has a weight or value attached to it. The rater evaluates each subordinate by checking those statements that describe the behavior of the individual. The check marks and the corresponding weights are summated for each subordinate. Figure 17–4 illustrates a form of the weighted checklist.

The weighted checklists makes the rater think in terms of specific job behavior. However, this procedure is difficult to develop and very costly.

Figure 17–4

Personnel evaluation

Name ______________ Social Security No. ______________

Job title ______________

Bureau/center ______________

	Rating	× Weight	= Score
1. Demonstrated personal characteristics Consideration should be given to job knowledge, judgment, communication skills, attitude, ability to deal with people (superiors, subordinates, clients, and other university personnel), initiative, etc.	____	20%	____
2. Performance of assigned duties Consideration should be given to the degree of program goal accomplishment, quality service provided, quantity of program activities (work load and clients generated), degree of supervision and/or guidance required, quality of reports, contribution to public relations, improvements generated in program to which assigned, clients'/students' reactions, etc.	____	60%	____
3. Contribution outside area of assigned duties Consideration should be given to suggestions for furthering the Office for Research, contribution to new program development, public relations activities, contribution to improving relations with the college and university, and state agencies.	____	20%	____
		Total score	____

Comments: ______________

____

____

______________ Date ______________ Signature

Separate checklists are usually established for each different job or group of jobs.

Descriptive essays

The essay method of performance evaluation requires the rater to describe each ratee's strong and weak points. Some organizations require every rater to discuss specific points, while others allow the rater to discuss whatever he or she believes is appropriate. One problem of the unstructured essay evaluation is that it provides little opportunity to compare ratees on specific performance dimensions. Another limitation is the variations in the writing skills of raters. Some individuals are effective writers, while others are not very good at writing descriptive analyses of subordinates' strengths and weaknesses with regard to job performance.

Rating errors

The above descriptions of just four of the numerous types of traditional performance evaluation methods point out problems and potential errors of each. The major problems and errors can be **technical** in the form of poor reliability, validity, and practicality or rater misuse. In some situations, raters are extremely harsh or easy in their evaluations. These are referred to as *strictness* or *leniency* rater errors. The harsh rater tends to give ratings which are lower than average ratings usually given to subordinates. The lenient rater tends to give higher ratings than the average level usually given to subordinates. These kinds of rating errors typically result because the rater is applying personal standards to the particular performance evaluation system being used. For example, the words *outstanding* or *average* may mean different things to various raters.

The dean of a business school reflected some dismay in comments regarding the performance evaluation of faculty:

> *Every year the chairpersons submit performance evaluations for their faculty, and every year the average is almost 3.5 on a scale from 1 to 4, with 4 representing outstanding performance. Now I know we have good faculty, but surely some are better than others. The bind comes from having a fixed amount of money to distribute in salary, and the chairpersons know that the only way to get top-dollar raises for their faculty is to give top evaluation scores. But it is self-defeating, because everyone ends up getting the same, average, raises.*

Another type of rater error is called the **halo error.** The term *halo* suggests that there is a positive or negative aura around an individual employee. This aura influences the rater's evaluation in about the same way for all of the performance dimensions considered. The halo error is caused by the rater's inability to discriminate among the different dimensions being rated. It is also caused by the rater's assumption that a particular dimension is extremely important. The rating on this dimension influences the rater's evaluations for all of the other dimensions.

The **central tendency error** occurs when a rater fails to assign extremely high or extremely low ratings. That is, the rater tends to rate almost all ratees around the average. Such ratings provide little guidance for decisions on promotions, compensation, training, career planning, and development. Everyone is about the same—average. Playing it safe by rating everyone average does not enable the manager to integrate performance evaluation with reward or employee development programs.

In many performance evaluation programs, the most recent behaviors of ratees tend to bias ratings. Using only the most recent ratee behaviors to make evaluations can result in what is called the **recency of events error.** Forgetting to include important past behaviors can introduce a strong bias into the evaluation. Ratees are often aware of this tendency and become visible, interested, productive, and cooperative just before the formal evaluation occurs.

Such rating errors as leniency, strictness, halo, central tendency, and recency of events are likely to be minimized if:

1. Each dimension addresses a single job activity rather than a group of activities.
2. The rater can observe the behavior of the ratee on a regular basis while the job is being accomplished.
3. Terms such as *average* are not used on rating scales, since different raters react differently to such terms.
4. The rater does not have to evaluate large groups of subordinates. Fatigue and difficulty in discriminating among ratees become major problems when large groups of subordinates are evaluated.
5. Raters are trained to avoid such errors as the leniency, harshness, halo, central tendency, and recency of events errors.
6. The dimensions being evaluated are meaningful, clearly stated, and important.

Another possibility would be to use forms of performance evaluation that attempt to minimize rating errors. Two of the more recently developed approaches are behaviorally anchored rating scales (BARS) and management by objectives (MBO).

Nontraditional performance evaluation methods

In an effort to improve on traditional performance evaluations, some organizations have used various behaviorally based and goal-setting programs. The behaviorally based programs attempt to examine what the employee does in performing the job. The objective, or goal-oriented, programs typically examine the results of accomplishments of the employee.

Behaviorally anchored rating scales

Behaviorally anchored rating scales (BARS) are constructed through the use of "critical incidents."[4] *Critical incidents are examples of specific job behaviors which determine various levels of performance.* Once the important areas of performance are identified and defined by employees who know the job, critical incident statements are used to discriminate among levels of performance. The form for a BARS usually covers 6 to 10 specifically defined performance dimensions, each with various descriptive behaviors. Each dimension is based on observable behaviors and is meaningful to the employees being evaluated.

An example of a BARS for the engineering competence performance dimension for engineers is presented in Figure 17–5. The dimension is defined for the rater, the behaviors define the particular response categories for the rater, and the response made by the rater is specific and easy to interpret. The feedback provided by the BARS is specific and meaningful. For example, if the ratee is given a 1.5 on this dimension, he or she is provided with the specific performance behavior that the rater used to make the rating.

A number of advantages are associated with the use of BARS. It is assumed that since job-knowledgeable employees participate in the actual development steps, the final evaluation form will be reliable, valid, and practical and will cover the full domain of the job. A common problem of traditional performance evaluation programs is that they do not tap the full domain of the job.

The use of BARS also provides valuable insights about developing training programs. The skills to be developed are specified in terms of actual behavioral incidents rather than abstract or general skills. Trainess in a BARS-based program could learn expected behaviors and how job performance is evaluated.

A behaviorally anchored evaluation system may minimize leniency, halo, and central tendency errors. There are, however, some critics of BARS who present results which indicate that this approach is not always the most reliable, valid, and practical. These critics also suggest that more research is needed comparing BARS with the traditional evaluation methods on such factors as leniency, central tendency, halo error, and dimension independence.[5]

Despite the time, the cost, and the procedural problems of developing and implementing BARS, this system seems to possess some advantages.

---

[4] P. C. Smith and L. M. Kendall, "Retranslation of Expectations: An Approach to the Construction of Unambiguous Anchors for Rating Scales," *Journal of Applied Psychology,* April 1963, pp. 149–55.

[5] D. P. Schwab, H. G. Henneman III, and T. A. DeCotiis, "Behaviorally Anchored Rating Scales: A Review of the Literature," *Personnel Psychology,* Winter 1975, pp. 549–62.

Figure 17–5

A BARS performance dimension

Engineering Competence
(the technical ability and skill utilization as applied to any assigned job)

Place a single *X* on the appropriate point on the vertical scale.

________________ (Ratee's name)

	2.00—This engineer is recognized as an expert and can be expected to help others and to provide advice and counsel to others working on the team.
Highest performance Always displays an understanding of difficult engineering problems	1.75—
	1.50—This engineer can be expected to know almost everything about the job and can provide answers to some of the difficult problems.
	1.25—
Average performance Displays an understanding of engineering job requirements when doing normal job	1.00—This engineer can be expected to work diligently on normal projects and to contribute positively to completing these tasks on time.
	0.75—This engineer can be expected to work late on projects and to make every effort to complete projects
	0.50—This engineer has difficulty in working on nonroutine projects and on many normal projects.
Lowest performance Is interested only in routine jobs that require minimum engineering skills	0.25—
	0.00—This engineer is confused and can be expected to hinder the completion of projects because of a lack of engineering knowledge.

Specifically, a BARS program could minimize subordinate or ratee defensiveness toward evaluation. By being involved in the development of BARS, subordinates can make their inputs known. These inputs can be incorporated into the final BARS. The BARS development steps could include both superiors and subordinates. In a sense, then, all of the parties involved can contribute to the creation of the evaluation criteria (dimensions) and the behavioral incidents that are used to define each level of performance.

Another advantage of using BARS is that the evaluation program concentrates on job-specific and job-relevant behaviors. Many performance evaluation programs are abstract and not meaningful to either the ratees or the raters. Thus, when providing feedback to ratees, the raters must convert the ratings to examples of actual job behavior. There are in many cases variances in the raters' ability to make these conversions from the rating scale to meaningful job behaviors. The BARS already contain behaviors that the superior can use in developing the evaluation counseling interview.

Objectives or goal performance evaluations

In the traditional and BARS evaluation programs, the rater is making judgments about the performance of *activities*. As noted earlier in this chapter, many managers believe that a *results-based* program is more informative. One popular results-based program is called management by objectives (MBO). This program typically involves the establishment of objectives by the supervisor alone or jointly by the supervisor and the subordinate.

MBO is far more than just an evaluation approach. It is usually a part of an overall motivational program, planning technique, or organizational change and development program. Because of its importance in modern management practice, an entire chapter (Chapter 6) is devoted to MBO. Here we will only introduce the idea of MBO as an alternative to traditional performance evaluation methods.

An MBO performance evaluation program focuses on what the employee achieves. The key features of a typical MBO program are as follows:

1. The superior and the subordinate meet to discuss and jointly set goals for the subordinate for a specified period of time (e.g., six months or one year).
2. Both the superior and the subordinate attempt to establish goals that are realistic, challenging, clear, and comprehensive. The goals should be related to the needs of both the organization and the subordinate.
3. The standards for measuring and evaluating the goals are agreed upon.
4. The superior and the subordinate establish some intermediate review dates when the goals will be reexamined.
5. The superior plays more of a coaching, counseling, and supportive role and less of a judgmental role.

6. The entire process focuses on results and on the counseling of the subordinate, and not on activities, mistakes, and organizational requirements.

MBO-type programs have been used in organizations throughout the world. Approximately 40 percent (200) of *Fortune's* 500 largest industrial firms report using MBO-type programs. As with each of the performance evaluation programs already discussed, there are both benefits and potential costs associated with the use of MBO. The fact that MBO stresses results is a benefit that can also be a problem. Focusing only on results may take attention away from how to accomplish the objectives. A subordinate receiving feedback about what has been achieved may still not be certain about how to make performance corrections. A manager may tell a subordinate that the quality control goal was missed by 3.5 percent, but this type of feedback is incomplete. The subordinate who has failed to meet the quality control goal needs feedback or guidance on how to accomplish it in the future.

Other problems that have been linked to MBO programs include improper implementation, lack of top-management involvement, too much emphasis on paperwork, failing to use an MBO system that best fits the needs of the organization and the employees, and inadequate training preparation for employees who are asked to establish goals.[6]

A final limitation of MBO is that comparisons of subordinates are difficult. In traditional performance evaluation programs, all subordinates are rated on common dimensions. Since in MBO each individual usually has a different set of objectives, it is difficult to make comparisons across a group of subordinates. The superior must make reward decisions not only on the basis of objectives achieved but also on the basis of his or her conception of the kinds of objectives that were accomplished. The feeling of achieving objectives will generally wear thin among subordinates if the accomplishment is not accompanied by meaningful rewards.

A review of potential performance evaluation programs

Figure 17–6 summarizes the main points of the various approaches discussed. A system may be more useful in some organizations than in other

[6] J. M. Ivancevich, "Different Goal-Setting Treatments and Their Effects on Performance and Job Satisfaction," *Academy of Management Journal,* September 1977, pp. 406–19; and J. M. Ivancevich, J. H. Donnelly, Jr., and J. L. Gibson, "Evaluating MBO: The Challenges Ahead," *Management by Objectives,* Winter 1976, pp. 15–24.

organizations because of the types of individuals doing the rating or because of the criteria being used. All of the programs discussed have both costs and benefits. Since performance evaluation is such an integral part of managing within organizations, recognizing the strengths, weaknesses, and best uses for a particular program is an important job for managers.

Management summary

1. Evaluating the performance of human resources is an important managerial responsibility. Effective performance evaluation accomplishes such purposes as increased motivation, improved knowledge, the validation of selection and placement decisions, the identification of training needs, and overall employee development.
2. As a management control activity, performance evaluation requires the specification of standards. These performance standards must be relevant, stable, practical, and capable of distinguishing different levels

Figure 17–6

Managerial points of interest when selecting a performance evaluation program

	Programs					
Point of interest	Graphic rating scales	Ranking	Checklists	Essay	BARS	MBO
Acceptability to subordinates	Fair	Fair/poor	Fair	Poor	Good	Generally good
Acceptability to management	Fair	Fair/poor	Fair	Poor	Good	Generally good
Useful in reward allocations	Poor	Poor	Fair	Fair	Good	Good
Useful in counseling and developing subordinates	Poor	Poor	Poor	Fair	Good	Good
Meaningful dimensions	Rarely	Rarely	Sometimes	Rarely	Often	Often
Ease of developing actual program	Yes	Yes	Yes	No	No	No
Development costs	Low	Low	Low	Moderately high	High	High

of performance. Performance standards are ordinarily production standards, personnel standards, or judgmental standards.

3. The administration of a performance evaluation program requires managers to make several key decisions, including who should do the rating, when to rate, and how the evaluation interview will take place.
4. Traditional performance evaluation methods use some form of rating scale which requires managers to rate their subordinates on a number of dimensions. Common rating errors include strictness and leniency, halo, central tendency, and recency of events biases. These errors can be reduced, but not completely eliminated.
5. In reaction to some of the problems inherent in traditional performance evaluation methods, two recently developed methods have been widely adopted. These two methods are behaviorally anchored rating scales and management by objectives.
6. Behaviorally anchored rating scales use critical incidents or specific job behaviors which determine different levels of performance. This method is costly, but the required joint effort between managers and their subordinates can result in increased mutual acceptance of the evaluation process.
7. Management by objectives requires that managers and their subordinates mutually set objectives and standards for specified time periods. The role of the manager in management by objectives is that of coach and teacher, rather than judge and evaluator.

Review and discussion questions

1. Explain why both developmental and judgmental purposes are difficult to achieve in performance evaluation.
2. In your view, if a manager must choose between using performance evaluation for either developmental or judgmental purposes, which should be chosen? Explain.
3. Explain why the common rating errors occur and why they cause problems in performance evaluation.
4. In your view, what is the proper role of subordinates in developing the evaluation system which managers will then use?
5. Explain the necessary conditions which performance standards should meet.
6. Describe and distinguish between the various traditional performance evaluation methods.
7. Explain the differences between behaviorally anchored rating scales and traditional rating scales.
8. Explain the importance of each key decision that managers must make when administering a performance evaluation program.

9. Why do all performance evaluation methods include some element of managerial subjectivity?
10. Explain the basic features of a management by objectives performance evaluation program.

Suggested reading

Beldt, S. F., and D. O. Jewell. "Where Have the Promotions Gone?" *Business,* March–April 1980, pp. 24–30.

Cederblom, D. "The Performance Appraisal Interview: A Review, Implications, and Suggestions." *Academy of Management Review* April 1982, pp. 219–27.

Ellig, B. "Pay Strategies during Inflationary Times." *Management Review,* September 1981, pp. 23–28, 37.

Ivancevich, J. M., and J. T. McMahon. "The Effects of Goal Setting, External Feedback, and Self-Generated Feedback on Outcome Variables: A Field Experiment." *Academy of Management Journal,* June 1982, pp. 359–72.

Lawler, E. E. "Merit Pay: Fact or Fiction?" *Management Review,* April 1981, pp. 50–53.

Louis, M. R. "Managing Career Transition: A Missing Link in Career Development." *Organizational Dynamics,* Spring 1982, pp. 68–77.

Moravec, M. "Performance Appraisal: A Human Resource Management System with Productivity Payoffs." *Management Review,* June 1981, pp. 51–54.

Applying what you have learned about human resource performance evaluation

Cases:

Performance appraisal at Gulf Oil
Evaluating managerial performance

Performance appraisal at Gulf Oil*

Typical performance evaluation methods involve the superior appraising the performance of subordinates. But seldom does performance evaluation involve subordinates appraising the performance of superiors. Gulf Oil Corporation recently completed an experiment in which employees were asked to rate the performance of the senior vice president of human resources, their overall supervisor. The process thus reverses the typical roles of subordinates and superiors in performance evaluation.

The process consisted of several steps, the first of which was to develop a rating form that included the key elements of the vice president's position. Rating forms for lower-level positions existed, but since senior executives had never been evaluated by this process, it was necessary to develop an appraisal rating form. The basis for the form was a series of interviews with the vice president who described his position's requirements. The rating form which was developed from these interviews and which was acceptable to the vice president identified six job components, each broken down into subcomponents and evaluated on a five-point scale. The form also included a section which permitted evaluators to make suggestions for specific performance improvement (see Exhibit 1).

The second step of the process was to send the form to 21 senior-level human resource people who the vice president believed would have a useful perspective on his performance.

---

* This case is adapted from Gerald W. Bush and John W. Stinson, "A Different Use of Performance Appraisal: Evaluating the Boss," *Management Review,* November 1980, pp. 14–17.

The group was balanced between headquarters and field personnel to insure that both views were incorporated in the evaluation. Each individual receiving the form was informed of the nature of the experiment and the names of the other members of the group.

The raters were told to complete the form without discussing it with anyone else. Anonymity was assured because raters were told to return the completed form unsigned. The process was unique in that subordinates had never before evaluated their managers, and the company believed that anonymity was essential to obtain true expressions of feelings and opinions.

The results of the survey were then summarized by the project coordinator and made known to the senior vice president. The feedback session between the vice president and the project coordinator focused on differences in ratings of headquarters and field personnel and on the degree of consistency among all raters on specific job components. The vice president expressed satisfaction with the process's success in obtaining results which he found useful in improving his performance. He also stated that the most useful information was contained in the open-ended section of the form. It was there that he was able to see specific examples and suggestions for improving his performance.

The experiment in multiple subordinate ratees produced positive results in this instance. The senior vice president accepted the information as valid bases for his own performance improvement plan. Whether other managers in Gulf Oil would have the same positive reaction is not now known.

Questions:

1. What primary purpose was served by Gulf Oil's performance evaluation experiment?
2. What specific circumstances must exist in an organization to make effective the use of subordinates' appraisals of their superior's performance.
3. Evaluate the rating form used in the Gulf Oil experiment.

Evaluating managerial performance

Steven Patrick was anxiously waiting for the Monday morning staff meeting to begin. He had only recently been promoted to corporate director of personnel, and today he would present a new idea to the rest of the corporate staff. This would be the first time that he had done so. In the six months since Steven had taken the new job and had begun attending the weekly staff meetings, he had remained silent except when responding to a direct question from one of the other corporate-level managers.

The staff meeting convened, and its chairperson, the executive vice president, called upon Steven to present his idea. "As you know," said Steven, "the Personnel Division has the responsibility for developing procedures to evaluate the performance of line managers throughout the company. We view this responsibility in terms of the larger issue of developing the skills and abilities of line managers. Historically, this company has relied on evaluation by superiors, but I would like to suggest that the real source of information about how managers perform is their subordinates. As a company, we have not attempted to obtain information from the people who report to managers. Many companies, including some of our competitors, attempt to obtain information from subordinates.

"I am proposing that we consider a

Exhibit 1

The appraisal rating form

SECTION I, II

From your perspective and working relationship with Gerry Bush over the time span you have worked with him, you are asked to rate his performance in all of the following JOB COMPONENTS and INTERPERSONAL RELATIONSHIP areas. Please use the five point scale provided by placing an "X" in the appropriate box.

SECTION 1—PRINCIPAL JOB COMPONENTS

I. HUMAN RESOURCES FUNCTIONAL LEADER

	LOW 1	2	3	4	HIGH 5
1. Appropriate involvement in each H.R. functional area:					
Labor Relations	[ ]	[ ]	[ ]	[ ]	[ ]
Salary Administration	[ ]	[ ]	[ ]	[ ]	[ ]
Benefits	[ ]	[ ]	[ ]	[ ]	[ ]
EEO	[ ]	[ ]	[ ]	[ ]	[ ]
Personnel Planning	[ ]	[ ]	[ ]	[ ]	[ ]
International Personnel	[ ]	[ ]	[ ]	[ ]	[ ]
Career Development	[ ]	[ ]	[ ]	[ ]	[ ]
Annuitants	[ ]	[ ]	[ ]	[ ]	[ ]
Placement	[ ]	[ ]	[ ]	[ ]	[ ]
2. Directing and coordinating Strategy Center/Corporate Human Resources projects where there is a need for a common view point.	[ ]	[ ]	[ ]	[ ]	[ ]
3. Resolving unproductive conflict between Strategy Centers and Corporate Human Resources Departments.	[ ]	[ ]	[ ]	[ ]	[ ]
4. Understanding of Corporate Executive view points regarding future Human Resources Policy development and providing direction to Human Resources groups accordingly.	[ ]	[ ]	[ ]	[ ]	[ ]
5. Promoting the Human Resources function with Corporate and Strategy Center Executives and building support for proposed Human Resources Policy and strategy recommendations.					

II. CORPORATE HUMAN RESOURCES MANAGER

	1	2	3	4	5
1. Focuses attention of subordinates on important work priorities.	[ ]	[ ]	[ ]	[ ]	[ ]
2. Encourages/leads inter-Human Resources discussion, collaboration between Corporate Human Resources groups on work projects or in resolving day-to-day issues.	[ ]	[ ]	[ ]	[ ]	[ ]
3. Follows up on work projects.	[ ]	[ ]	[ ]	[ ]	[ ]
4. Rejects inadequate work.	[ ]	[ ]	[ ]	[ ]	[ ]
5. Rewards good work.	[ ]	[ ]	[ ]	[ ]	[ ]
6. Handles unproductive conflict between Corporate Human Resources groups.	[ ]	[ ]	[ ]	[ ]	[ ]
7. Ensures that subordinates are kept informed on important developments affecting their functions.	[ ]	[ ]	[ ]	[ ]	[ ]

III. H.R. CONSULTANT/ADVISOR—CORPORATE EXECUTIVE

	1	2	3	4	5
1. Keeps Corporate Executive informed on internal and external H.R. issues of major significance to the Corporation.	[ ]	[ ]	[ ]	[ ]	[ ]

Exhibit 1 (*concluded*)

	LOW 1	2	3	4	HIGH 5
2. Directs H.R. personnel's attention to important issues raised by the Executive and requiring immediate action.	[ ]	[ ]	[ ]	[ ]	[ ]
IV. H.R. CONSULTANT/ADVISOR—STRATEGY CENTER EXECUTIVE					
1. Understands major H.R. issues or concerns of the Strategy Center Executives.	[ ]	[ ]	[ ]	[ ]	[ ]
2. Provides advice or marshalls internal or external consulting resources to address major Strategy Center H.R. issues.	[ ]	[ ]	[ ]	[ ]	[ ]
V. COMPANY REPRESENTATIVE					
1. Handles interactions with government regulatory agencies effectively on behalf of the Corporation.	[ ]	[ ]	[ ]	[ ]	[ ]
2. Represents the Corporation effectively internally with employee groups.	[ ]	[ ]	[ ]	[ ]	[ ]
3. Represents the Corporation effectively externally with business or educational institutions.	[ ]	[ ]	[ ]	[ ]	[ ]
SECTION II—INTERPERSONAL RELATIONSHIPS					
I. The effectiveness of leadership style exhibited in such business situations as Human Resources Council meetings.	[ ]	[ ]	[ ]	[ ]	[ ]
II. The extent to which appropriate functional or business information is communicated, measured in terms of:					
Quantity	[ ]	[ ]	[ ]	[ ]	[ ]
Quality	[ ]	[ ]	[ ]	[ ]	[ ]
III. The level of trust existing in your relationship with him.	[ ]	[ ]	[ ]	[ ]	[ ]
IV. The level of openness existing in your relationship with him.	[ ]	[ ]	[ ]	[ ]	[ ]
V. The "ease" of interaction existing in your relationship with him.	[ ]	[ ]	[ ]	[ ]	[ ]
VI. The level of support he gives you on assignments/projects.	[ ]	[ ]	[ ]	[ ]	[ ]
VII. The level of supervision and encouragement he gives you on assignments/projects.	[ ]	[ ]	[ ]	[ ]	[ ]

SECTION III—PERFORMANCE IMPROVEMENT INFORMATION

Considering the rating analysis you completed in Sections I and II and thinking more specifically about the job performance, complete the following sub-sections:

A. Identify minimally three work activities or practices which the Senior Vice President could do *more of* to improve job performance.

B. Identify minimally three work activities or practices which the Senior Vice President should do *less of* that would improve job performance.

C. Identify minimally three work activities or practices which the Senior Vice President is currently handling *just about right.*

procedure for obtaining information that will enable us to know the strengths and weaknesses of each manager as viewed by those who report to him or her. The procedure is relatively simple. Each manager will meet with his people. A trainer from the Personnel Division will also be present at this initial meeting. The manager must assure his people that the purpose of the meeting is to obtain their cooperation in a process which will help him become a better manager. Any subordinate must feel free to refuse to take part in the process.

"Once the manager has met with his people and has explained what is going on, one of my trainers will meet with each subordinate who has agreed to participate and will have the subordinate complete a questionnaire. The specific questions to be included in the questionnaire will relate to the manager's performance of assigned activities, including his or her manner of dealing with people. Each subordinate will rate the manager on each activity on a numerical scale and will explain the basis for the rating to the trainer. To protect the subordinates from any real or imagined threat for participating, the responses will remain anonymous when they are reported to the manager. Only the trainer will know the source of any comments.

"After the trainers have obtained information from the subordinates, they will meet with each manager. The managers will be given all of the information obtained, and they will discuss it with the trainer. The purpose of this session and of others to follow is to prepare a plan that will enable each manager to take corrective action. The corrective action can range from a simple change in the manager's behavior if he or she has unknowingly been relating to people in objectionable ways to a training program designed to develop the manager's skills and knowledge.

"Let me conclude my remarks by saying that we in Personnel believe that this procedure will provide valuable information to our managers. It will also be possible to take the corrective action necessary to improve the performance of line managers. The only unresolved issue is that of standards. We will obtain numerical ratings for each manager, but we will have nothing to compare them to except those of other managers. If this group accepts the feasibility of this plan, our next step is to develop standards for managerial performance. I believe that to be the responsibility of top management, as represented by this group."

Questions:

1. If you were a line manager, how would you react to Steven's plan? Would you consider it threatening? Why?
2. Do you see any problems in a procedure that attempts to obtain data for performance evaluation *and* personal development?
3. If you were Steven, how would you go about obtaining the performance standards? What type of control does Steven's plan represent?

18

Chapter eighteen Organizational change

Performance objectives

- **Define** the meaning of organizational change from the perspective of a manager.
- **State** why a framework is useful for understanding the characteristics of organizational change.
- **Describe** the differences between the structural, behavioral, and technological change approaches.
- **Explain** why employees resist change in organizations.
- **Discuss** the timing and scope dimensions of implementation.

Management update*

A sizable part of Westinghouse Electric Corporation is converting to "Japanese style management." The change is occurring in the company's construction group, a unit which employs 7 percent of Westinghouse's total work force. As a consequence of the change, Westinghouse expects to obtain better ideas, better decisions, better execution, and increased productivity. The inspiration for the change is the much publicized *Theory Z,* a term which identifies a number of management practices which, in one form or another, apply participative management theory. Although not a new idea, participative management has become a symbol of Japanese management and, more important, of Japanese productivity and quality. As American managers sought solutions to the productivity problem in their own plants, they quite naturally looked to the Japanese.

What they found in Japanese plants were management practices styled after the ideas of *American* management writers. Maslow, McGregor, and Likert are standard sources in American management literature for ideas on participative management, management-labor collaboration, and group-centered leadership. And these ideas have found their way into many American firms. The significance of the Westinghouse experience is not so much that participative management is being implemented, or that a change per se is occurring. The significance is that participative management is being adopted at *Westinghouse.*

As noted by many observers of the American business scene, Westinghouse is an unlikely place to attempt participative management. The company has the reputation for being directive in its orientation with an established chain of command and a staff of tradition-minded engineers. Thus, participative management is a less-than-obvious basis for a significant organizational change in Westinghouse. Nevertheless, the company has embarked on a serious effort to change the way it manages, with the expectation that tangible signs of performance improvement will occur only after a two-year period. In the meantime, the company is going through an intensive training and reeducation process throughout the construction group's management and nonmanagement personnel. Subsequently, the change will be implemented throughout the company.

* Jeremy Main, "Westinghouse's Cultural Revolution," *Fortune,* June 15, 1981, pp. 74, 76, 80, 84, 88, 93.

Organizational change is the planned attempt by management to improve the overall performance of individuals, groups, and the organization by altering structure, behavior, and technology. Organizational change involves the **total organization as the focus of corrective action.** The magnitude of the deviation between actual and desired performance is too great to be closed by correcting operations or individual and group behavior. A larger focus is required.

A model for managing change

The management of change implies a systematic process which can be broken down into subprocesses, or steps. Figure 18–1 describes this process. The process consists of eight steps which are linked in a logical sequence. A manager needs to consider each of these steps, either explicitly or implicitly, in undertaking a change program. The prospects for initiating successful change are enhanced when the manager goes through each successive step explicitly and formally.

It is our purpose to describe alternative change techniques and strategies, but not to propose that some alternatives are superior to others. No one change technique or change strategy can be assumed to be superior without considering the specific situation.

The knowledgeable manager is one who recognizes the possible alternatives and is not committed to one particular approach to the exclusion of all others. At the same time, the effective manager avoids the pitfalls of stagnation. The sign of decay is "managerial behavior that (*a*) is oriented more to the past than to the future, (*b*) recognizes the obligations of ritual more than the challenges of current problems, and (*c*) owes allegiance more to department goals than to overall company objectives."[1] Thus, the management of change implies a flexible, forward-looking stance for the

[1] Larry E. Greiner, "Patterns of Organization Change," *Harvard Business Review,* May–June 1967, p. 119.

manager. Such a stance is an essential basis for the use of the change process outlined in Figure 18–1. Each step of the process is discussed in this chapter.

Forces for change

The forces for change are of two types, external forces and internal forces. The **external** forces for change are changes in the marketplace, the technology, and the environment; such forces are usually beyond the control of the manager. **Internal** forces operate inside the firm and are to some extent within the control of managers.

External forces

Managers of business firms must respond to changes in the *marketplace.* Competitors introduce new products, increase advertising, reduce prices, or improve customer service. In each case, a response is required unless a manager is content to permit the erosion of profit and market share. Changes also occur in customer tastes and incomes. The firm's products may no longer have customer appeal; customers may be able to purchase more expensive, higher-quality forms of the same products.

Another source of market forces for change is the supply of resources to the firm. A change in the quality and quantity of human resources can dictate changes in the firm. For example, the adoption of automated processes can be stimulated by a decline in the supply of labor. The techniques of coal mining and tobacco farming have changed greatly during recent

Figure 18–1

The management of change

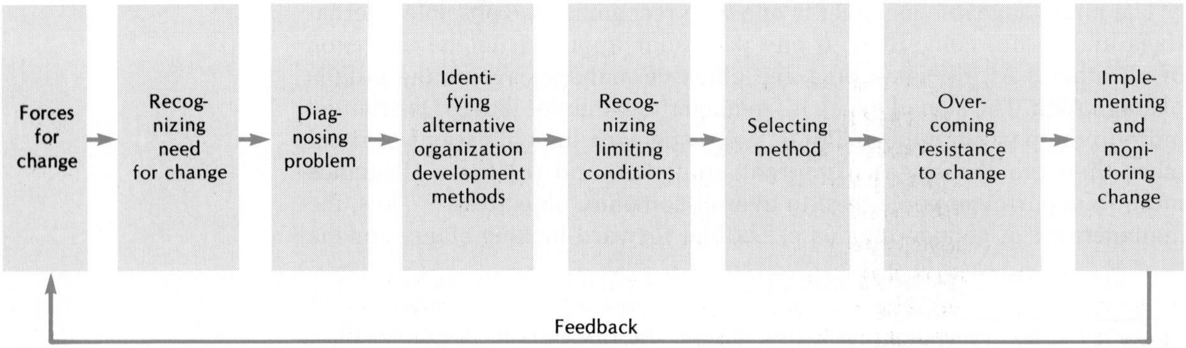

years because of labor shortages. We can also understand how changes in the materials and energy supply can cause the firm to attempt to substitute one material for another. Rayon stockings and synthetic rubber tires were direct outgrowths of the shortages of raw materials induced by World War II. Oil and gas shortages are changing the ways in which people live. The 1980s will probably be an era of energy conservation, increased exploration for energy supplies, and increased review of alternative energy sources.

Changes in *technology* are the second external force for change. The knowledge explosion that has taken place since World War II has introduced new technology for nearly every management activity. Computers have made possible high-speed data processing and the solution of complex production problems. New machines and new processes have revolutionized the ways in which many products are manufactured and distributed. Computer technology and automation have affected not only production techniques but also the social conditions of work. New occupations have been created, and old occupations have been eliminated. Sooner or later, slowness in adopting new technology which reduces costs and improves quality will be reflected in the financial statement. Technological advance is a permanent fixture in contemporary society, and it will continue to demand attention as a force for change.

Environmental changes are the third external force for change. Managers must be tuned in to great movements over which they have no control but which control the fates of their firms. The 1960s and 1970s witnessed a distinct increase in social activity. The drive for social equality posed new issues for managers. In addition, the relationship between government and business became much more involved as new regulations were imposed. Sophisticated mass communications and international markets created enormous potential, but they also posed a great threat to those managers who were unable to understand what was going on. These pressures for change reflect the increasing complexity and interdependence of modern living.

Internal forces

The forces for change which occur within the organization can be traced to *processes and people.* Processes which act as forces for change include decision making, communications, and interpersonal relations. Breakdowns or problems in any of these processes can also create forces for change. Decisions may not be made, may be made too late, or may be of poor quality. Communications may be short-circuited, redundant, or simply inadequate. Tasks may not be undertaken or may not be completed because the person responsible did not get the word. Because of inadequate or nonexistent communications, a customer order is not filled, a grievance is not processed, an invoice is not filed, or a supplier is not paid. Conflicts between people and groups reflect breakdowns in the interaction among individuals.

Low levels of morale and high levels of absenteeism and turnover are symptoms of people problems that must be diagnosed. A wildcat strike or a walkout may be the most tangible sign of a problem, yet such tactics are usually employed because they arouse the management to action. There is in most organizations a certain level of employee discontent; a great danger is to ignore employee complaints and suggestions. But the process of change includes the *recognition* step, and it is at this point that management must decide to act or not to act. An executive expressed his opinion about recognizing employee discontent and the need for some changes in the following manner:

> *When my best people complain about working conditions, our outdated fringe benefit package, and the lack of respect shown by some managers toward employees, I have to listen long and hard. Some complaints are going to always exist, but when I spot a pattern, it is time to pay attention. I always recognize complaints, and then I look for patterns.*

Recognizing the need for change

Information is the basis on which managers are made aware of the magnitude of the change forces. Financial statements, quality control data, and budget and standard cost information are important media through which both external and internal forces for change are communicated. These sources of information are often integrated elements of a refined management information system. Declining profit margins and market shares are tangible signs that the firm's competitive position is deteriorating and that change may be required.

Unfortunately, the need for change goes unrecognized in many organizations until some major catastrophe occurs. The employees strike or seek the recognition of a union before management finally recognizes the need for action. Talented managers leave the organization because they are not delegated authority and responsibility. A plant is forced to close because of government fines for polluting the environment. The need for change must be recognized by some means, and the exact nature of the problem must be diagnosed.

Diagnosing the problem

Before appropriate action can be taken, managers must diagnose the symptoms of the problem, then discover the problem itself. Experience and judgment are critical at this stage unless the problem is readily apparent to all observers. However, managers often disagree as to the nature of the problem. There is no magic formula. The objectives of this step can be described by three questions:

1. What is the problem, as distinct from the symptoms of the problem?
2. What must be changed to resolve the problem?
3. What outcomes (objectives) are expected from the change, and how will their attainment be measured?

The answers to these questions can come from management information systems in some organizations. However, it may be necessary to generate specific information through the creation of committees or task forces. Meetings between managers and employees provide a variety of points of view which can be sifted through by a smaller group. Technical operational problems may be easily diagnosed, but subtler problems usually entail extensive analysis. One approach to diagnosing such problems is the attitude survey.

An attitude survey questionnaire can be administered to the entire work force or to a sample of it. The questionnaire permits the respondents to evaluate and rate (1) management, (2) pay and pay-related items, (3) working conditions, (4) equipment, and (5) other job-related items. The appropriate use of an attitude survey requires that the data be collected from members of an organization, analyzed in detail, and fed back to various organization members. The objective of the survey is to pinpoint the problem or problems as perceived by the members of the organization. Subsequent feedback discussions of the survey results at all levels of the organization can add insights into the nature of the problem.

A questionnaire survey on the characteristics of a recently implemented goal-setting program allowed the participants to evaluate and rate the goal-setting program. A sample of a part of the survey is presented in Figure 18–2. After reviewing the survey responses, the committee in charge of implementing the program interviewed a sample of the participants. It then combined the interview responses and the questionnaire answers to identify problems, strengths, and topics for further review.

The approach which management uses to diagnose the problem is a crucial part of the total strategy for change. As will be seen in a later section, the manner in which the problem is diagnosed has clear implications for the success of the proposed change.

Finally, the diagnostic step must specify *objectives* for change. Given

Figure 18–2

Goal factors*

Having gone through several work-planning and goal-setting (WP&G) sessions with your supervisor, you have established a set of goals for your job which are in your WP&G contract. Listed below is a set of statements which may or may not describe your feelings about the entire WP&G process. Please read each statement carefully and then circle the one number from the seven alternatives which *best* describes your degree of agreement or disagreement with the statement. Please remember that there are no right or best answers. We would like your first impression to the question. Please answer each of the questions.

	Strongly disagree		Neutral			Strongly agree	
1. I receive a considerable amount of feedback concerning my overall performance on goals.	1	2	3	4	5	6	7
2. I am allowed a significant degree of influence in determining the results for my work.	1	2	3	4	5	6	7
3. The results expected for my work are extremely clear and help me know exactly what my job is.	1	2	3	4	5	6	7
4. The feedback I receive concerning my performance is well organized and helpful.	1	2	3	4	5	6	7
5. It takes a high degree of skill on my part to attain the results expected for my work.	1	2	3	4	5	6	7
6. I am not very committed to the WP&G goal-setting process.	1	2	3	4	5	6	7
7. It takes a lot of effort on my part to attain the results expected for my work.	1	2	3	4	5	6	7

* The complete questionnaire contains 34 questions.

the diagnosis of the problem, it is necessary to define objectives to guide the change and to evaluate its outcome. The objectives can be stated in terms of financial and production data, such as profits, market shares, sales volume, productivity, and scrappage. They can also be stated as attitude and morale objectives that are derived from attitude survey information or as a personal development objectives that are meaningful to the members of an organization. For example, objectives can focus on the personal growth or reeducation of one employee or a group. Whatever the objectives, they must be explicit, understandable, challenging, and meaningful. They must also contribute to the strategic objectives of profitability, competitiveness, flexibility, and efficiency.

Identifying alternative change techniques

The choice of the particular change technique depends on the nature of the problem that management has diagnosed. Management must determine which alternative is most likely to produce the desired outcomes. As we have noted above, diagnosis of the problem includes specification of the outcomes which management desires from the change. In this section, we will describe a number of change techniques. They will be classified according to the major focus of the technique, namely, to change structure, people, or technology.[2] This classification of organizational change techniques in no way implies a distinct division among the three types. On the contrary, the interrelationships among structure, people, and technology must be acknowledged and anticipated. Most of the literature on organizational change indicates the relative weakness of efforts to change only structure (e.g., job design), only people (e.g., sensitivity training), or only technology (e.g., introducing new equipment or a new computer).

Behavioral scientists have conducted studies examining the impact of structure on attitudes and behavior. Some of the results show that overspecialization and narrow spans of control can lead to low levels of satisfaction and low productivity. In addition, the technology of production, distribution, and information processing affects the structural characteristics of the firm as well as the attitudes and sentiments of its people. The fact that the interrelationships among structure, people, and technology are so pronounced might suggest a weakness in our classification scheme; but in defense of that scheme, the techniques described below can be distinguished on the basis of their major thrust or focus—structure, people, or technology.

Structural change

Logically, organizing follows planning, since the structure is a means for achieving the objectives established through planning. Structural change

[2] See Harold J. Leavitt, "Applied Organizational Change in Industry: Structural, Technological, and Humanistic Approaches," in *Handbook of Organizations,* ed. James G. March (Skokie, Ill.: Rand McNally, 1965), pp. 1144–68.

in the context of organizational change refers to managerial action which attempts to improve performance by altering the formal structure of task and authority relationships. At the same time, we must recognize that the structure creates human and social relationships which can gradually become ends for the members of the organization. Members of the organization may resist efforts to disrupt these relationships.

Structural changes alter some aspects of the formal task and authority system. The design of an organization involves the specification of jobs, the grouping of jobs in departments, the determination of the size of the groups reporting to a single manager, and the distribution of authority including the provision of staff assistance. Changes in the nature of jobs, bases for departmentation, and line-staff relationships are, therefore, structural changes.

Changes in the nature of jobs Changes in the nature of jobs originate with new methods and new machines. Work simplification and job enrichment are two examples of methods changes. Work simplification narrows job content and scope, whereas job enrichment widens them. Through the use of motion and time studies, scientific management introduced significant changes in the ways work is done. These methods tend to create highly specialized jobs. Job enrichment, however, moves in the opposite direction, toward despecialization.

Changing a job can occur by changing (1) the job description, (2) the role expectations of a position, (3) the relationships among positions, and (4) work flow patterns. For example, a change in a job description means that the duties to be performed and the expectations of the manager about the duties are changed. A purchasing agent had her job description changed in an area involving her latitude to make purchasing decisions. After the change, she was able to make any purchasing decision without checking immediately with her manager. This change was a structural change. Her increased purchasing authority also meant that she would have to work on Saturday evenings. This was a role expectation for purchasing agents who had full purchasing decision authority.

Changes in the bases for departmentation In Chapter 7, the process of combining jobs into groups was discussed. There is a growing opinion among managers and researchers that grouping jobs on the basis of function, territory, product, and customer doesn't occur in an orderly fashion. The classification system of various departmental arrangements is not a very accurate description of the organization of the 1980s. What is found at Tenneco, Shell Oil, the Buick Division of General Motors, Zenith, and other organizations is a hodgepodge of various types of departmental bases.

Departmentation in the 1980s seems to be based largely on a contingency perspective. The situation, people, resources, and external organizational forces appear to dictate largely what form or variety of departmentation will be used. The multiproducts and multiindustry organization requires a significant amount of managerial coordination. Thus, experiments with different forms of departmentation with various managerial hierarchies are being conducted.[3]

Changes in line-staff relationships These changes ordinarily include two techniques. The first and the usual approach is to create staff assistance as a temporary or permanent solution. One response of manufacturing firms to the problem of market expansion is to create separate staff and service units. These units provide the technical expertise to deal with the production, financial, and marketing problems posed by expansion.

An illustrative case is a company which had grown quite rapidly since its entry into the fast-foods industry. Its basic sources of field control were area directors who supervised the operations of the sales outlets of a particular region. During the growth period, the area directors had considerable autonomy in making the advertising decisions for their regions. Within general guidelines, they could select their own advertising media and formats and set their own advertising budgets. But as their markets became saturated and as competitors appeared, corporate officials decided to centralize the advertising function in a staff unit located at corporate headquarters. Consequently, the area directors' authority was limited and a significant aspect of their jobs was eliminated.

A final illustration of changes in line-staff relationships is based on a consulting situation.[4] A large insurance company hired a management consulting firm to analyze the problems created by a deteriorating market position. The consulting firm recommended that the company undertake a program of decentralization by changing a staff position to a line position. This recommendation was based on the consultants' belief that in order to increase premium income, the company must have its best personnel and resources available at the branch office level. Accordingly, the consultants recommended that assistant managers become first-level supervisors reporting to branch managers. The reorganization required a significant change in the jobs of assistant managers and of managers throughout the organization.

These examples indicate the range of alternatives that managers must consider. Certainly, we have not exhausted the possibilities. Elements of structural change often include plans, procedures, the span of control, staff-line functions, and levels of organization. The point that should be made in concluding this discussion, however, is not that any list of structural change approaches is incomplete, but that students and managers must recognize the interrelationships of structural parts. A change in the content of a job does not take place in a vacuum; on the contrary, the change

[3] Charles G. Burck, "What's Good for the World Should Be Good for G.M.," *Fortune*, May 7, 1979, pp. 125–36.

[4] Jeremiah O'Connell, *Managing Organizational Innovation* (Homewood, Ill.: Richard D. Irwin, 1968), p. 119.

affects all other directly related jobs. The management of structural change must be guided by the point of view that all things are connected.

Behavioral change

Behavioral change techniques are efforts to redirect and increase employee motivation, skills, and knowledge bases. The major objective of such techniques is to enhance the capacity of individuals and groups to perform assigned tasks in coordination with others. The early efforts to effect behavioral changes date to scientific management work improvement and employee training methods. These attempts were primarily directed at improving the skills and knowledge bases of employees. The employee counseling programs which grew out of the Hawthorne studies were (and remain) primarily directed at improving employee motivation.

Training and development programs for managers have typically emphasized supervisory relationships. These programs attempt to provide supervisors with basic technical and leadership skills. Since supervisors are primarily concerned with overseeing the work of others, these traditional programs emphasize techniques for dealing with people problems: how to handle the malcontent, the loafer, the troublemaker, the complainer. The programs also include conceptual material dealing with communications, leadership styles, and organizational relationships. The training methods include role playing, discussion groups, lectures, and organized courses offered by universities, consultants, and training corporations.

Training continues to be an important technique for introducing behavioral changes. In some applications, training has taken on a form quite different from that which developed in classical management theory. The vast majority of what are called organizational development (OD) change techniques have been directed at changing the behavior of individuals and groups through the processes of problem solving, decision making, and communication. Some of the more popular behavior change approaches are sensitivity training, transactional analysis, survey feedback, team building, and process consultation.

Survey feedback is a method of assessing the attitudes of organizational members, identifying differences in attitudes and perceptions, and solving crucial differences by using survey information in feedback groups. **Team building** involves having team members interact with one another to learn how others in the team think, solve problems, and work. The team attempts to identify problems and processes for improving team performance. **Process consultation** involves using an outside consultant to help a manager perceive, understand, and act out various job situations. The consultant is used to help the manager gain insight into his or her work situation; into his or her personality, attitudes, and perceptions; and into the work habits, attitudes, and goals of his or her subordinates.

Sensitivity training and transactional analysis will be discussed in more detail because they are two of the more controversial behavior change approaches.

Sensitivity training This change technique attempts to make the participants more aware of themselves and of their impact on others. "Sensitivity" in this context means sensitivity to self and to relationships with others. An assumption of sensitivity training is that poor task performance is caused by the emotional problems of the people who must collectively achieve a goal. Thus, if these problems can be removed, a major impediment to task performance is eliminated. Sensitivity training stresses "the *process* rather than the *content* of training and . . . *emotional* rather than *conceptual* training."[5] We can see that this form of training is quite different from the traditional forms which stress the acquisition of a predetermined body of concepts which have immediate application to the workplace.

The process of sensitivity training includes a group of managers (the training group, or T-group) who in most cases come together at some location other than their place of work. Under the direction of a trainer, the group usually engages in a dialogue which has no agenda and no focus. The objective is to provide an environment which produces its own learning experiences. The unstructured dialogue encourages one to learn about self in dealing with others. One's motives and feelings are revealed through behavior toward others in the group and through the behavior of others.

The research evidence to date on the effectiveness of sensitivity training as a change technique suggests mixed results. A detailed review of 100 research studies found that sensitivity training was most effective at the personal level.[6] The studies reviewed compared the influence of 20 or more hours of training on the participants' attitudes or behaviors. The review concluded that sensitivity training:

Stimulated short-term improvement in communication skills.

Encouraged trainees to believe that they controlled their behavior more than did others.

Was likely to increase the participative orientation of trainees in leadership positions.

Improved the perceptions of others toward the trainee.

Managers should critically examine this technique in terms of the kinds of behavioral changes which are desired and are possible. There are conditions which limit the range of possible changes. In this light, managers must determine whether the changes induced by sensitivity training are instrumental for organizational purposes and whether the prospective participant is able to tolerate the potential anxiety generated by the training.

[5] Henry C. Smith, *Sensitivity to People* (New York: McGraw-Hill, 1966), p. 197.

[6] P. B. Smith, "Controlled Studies of the Outcome of Sensitivity Training," *Psychological Bulletin,* July 1975, pp. 597–622.

Transactional analysis Transactional analysis (TA) is another behavioral change approach. It was first developed by Eric Berne for use in group therapy. TA is a method for analyzing and understanding human behavior. The areas of attention are the personality, the manner in which people interact (transactional analysis), the ways in which people structure their time, and the roles which people learn to play in life (life scripts).

Transactional analysis training is used by organizations to bring about desirable changes in understanding and interaction. Typically, a training program is used to examine the features and types of transactional analysis. Trainers attempt to change the participants' use of inappropriate interaction patterns so that personal development and organizational performance are improved. A first step in TA training is to increase the participant's understanding of his or her ego state.

The personality of each person is assumed to be made up of three ego states. Berne defines ego as "a consistent pattern of feeling and experience directly related to a corresponding consistent pattern of behavior."[7] Managers cannot direct ego states, but they can observe behavior and make inferences.

One ego state is called the Parent. This ego state arises from the ways in which our parents reared us. The Parent in us provides advice, guidelines, regulations, and discipline for others. The Adult ego state is our dispassionate and objective side. It uses facts, information, and analysis to reach the best decision. The Child ego state reflects the natural impulses, attitudes, and activities that are learned from childhood experiences. This ego state can range from listening and responding to whining and hostility.

Each of these three ego states (Parent, Adult, Child) exists in every individual. Ideally, if our Adult state is in control, we are aware of our Child and Parent states. However, as Berne emphasizes, all three ego states are necessary.

The Adult develops later in life than the Parent and the Child. The usual response to some stimulus is a Child or Parent reaction. Therefore, Berne recommends that the best way to become Adult (objective and analytic) is to become aware of Parent and Child signals. Some Parent signals include sighing and patting someone on the head or back; using such words as *pal, lazy, stupid,* and *nonsense;* or exclaiming, "Not again!" A few typical child signals include tears, pouting, temper tantrums; and such statements as I wish, I want, and I don't care. The more aware a person is of such Parent- and Child-type signals, the stronger becomes that person's Adult, which is more applicable to work and co-worker relationships in organizations.

Transactional analysis has only recently been applied in organizations as a behavioral change approach. Most of the research results are anecdotal

[7] Eric Berne, *Transactional Analysis in Psychotherapy* (New York: Grove Press, 1961); and Eric Berne, *What Do You Say after You Say Hello?* (New York: Grove Press, 1972).

or self-report responses after one- to three-day TA training sessions. Therefore, it is not possible to strongly recommend or discourage the use of TA in organizations. There appears to be a significant amount of both criticism and support for TA training.

Technological change

This category of change includes any application of new ways to transform resources into the product or service. In the usual sense of the word, technology means new machines—lathes, presses, computers, and the like. But we should expand the concept to include all new techniques, whether or not they include new machines. From this perspective, the work improvement methods of scientific management can be considered technological breakthroughs. However, in this section, only those changes which are induced by the introduction of a machine or a worker-machine process are discussed.

The changes in organizational efficiency brought about by a new machine are calculable in economic and engineering terms. Determining whether the machine is a good investment is a matter of estimating its future profitability in relation to its present cost. Such calculations are an important part of the managerial control function. Here, however, we are interested in the impact of the new machine on the structure of the organization and on the behavior of the people in the organization. As we noted in Chapter 8, technology is a key determinant of organizational design. Firms with simple and stable technology should adopt a structure that tends toward System 1 design, whereas firms with complex and dynamic technology ought to tend toward System 4 design. Thus, it would appear that the adoption of new technology involves a concurrent decision to adapt the organizational design to that technology.

A recent example of a change in technology occurred in a hospital. The dietary department had the responsibility for planning and preparing the meals and delivering them to hospital patients, employees, and visitors.[8] A change in the assembly and delivery of meals was initiated. This was a technological change. Before the change, patient meals were assembled and delivered by a diet aide with the use of a delivery cart. The aide assembled each meal in the kitchen according to the prescribed menu.

The pressure for change came from the difficulty and expense of repairing and replacing the delivery carts as well as the frustration of the aides because of broken delivery carts. An outside consultant recommended the use of a conveyor belt in the kitchen. Trays with patient menus attached were fed into the belt. Diet aides stood at various food stations along

[8] R. Billings, R. Klimoski, and J. Breaugh, "The Impact of a Change in Technology on Job Characteristics: A Quasi Experiment," *Administrative Science Quarterly*, June 1977, pp. 318–39.

the belt and placed the appropriate food item on each tray as it passed. The trays were loaded on a stacking cart (different from the delivery cart), and delivery was made to the patients.

The technological change led to less running around the kitchen completing menus, less frustration because of broken delivery carts, and a steady flow of work at mealtime. The aides appeared to enjoy the new technology and to be more satisfied with the pattern of work that accompanied its introduction. The technological change, the conveyer belt, caused a change in the organization structure, specifically a change *toward* System 1 since it is more compatible with the new, more routine, technology.

In order to catalog the impact of technological change on organization structure and behavior, Floyd Mann analyzed a number of actual cases and concluded that the adoption of new machines in the factory involves:

1. Major changes in the division of labor and the content of jobs.
2. Changes in the social relations among workers.
3. Improvements in working conditions.
4. The need for different supervisory skills.
5. Changes in career patterns, promotion procedures, and job security.
6. Generally higher wages.
7. Generally higher prestige for those who work.
8. Around-the-clock operations.[9]

The degree and extent of these observed changes in structure and behavior depend on the magnitude of the technological change. Obviously, the introduction of a new offset printing press would not cause great dislocations and changes, but the complete automation of a previously worker-paced manufacturing process would entail many, if not all, of the above changes.

The decision to adopt a technological change must include consideration of the potential structural and behavioral impacts. Those impacts must, in turn, be reconciled with the conditions which limit the scope and magnitude of the proposed change.

The three major alternative change approaches attempt to improve performance by improving communication, decision making, attitudes, and skills. These approaches are based on the assumption that changes in structure, behavior, and technology can result in improvements for the organization, individuals, and groups. The three change approaches are presented in Figure 18–3 as a system. That is, changes in one area are related to changes in other areas. The anticipated outcomes of this system of interrelated changes include the factors shown in Figure 18–3. Accomplishing all of the anticipated outcomes would be worthwhile for any manager. However, any successes may be limited because of problems of implementation, resistance to change, and various other conditions.

---

[9] Floyd C. Mann, "Psychological and Organizational Impacts," in *Automation and Technological Change,* ed. John T. Dunlop (Englewood Cliffs, N.J.: Prentice-Hall, 1962), pp. 50–55.

Recognizing limiting conditions

The selection of the change technique is based on diagnosis of the problem, but it is also tempered by certain conditions that exist at the time. Three such conditions are the leadership climate, the formal organization, and the organizational culture.

Leadership climate refers to the nature of the work environment which results from the leadership style and the administrative practices of managers. Any change program which does not have the support and commitment of management has only a slim chance of success. Management must be at least neutral toward the change. By not supporting the change or by being unenthusiastic about it, a manager can undermine the change because he or she is in an authority position. We also understand that the style of leadership itself may be the subject of change; for example, sensitivity training is a direct attempt to move managers toward a certain style—open, supportive, and group centered. But it must be recognized that the participants in sensitivity training may be unable to adopt such styles if these are incompatible with the styles of their own superiors.

The **formal organization** must be compatible with the proposed change.

Figure 18–3

Three change approaches

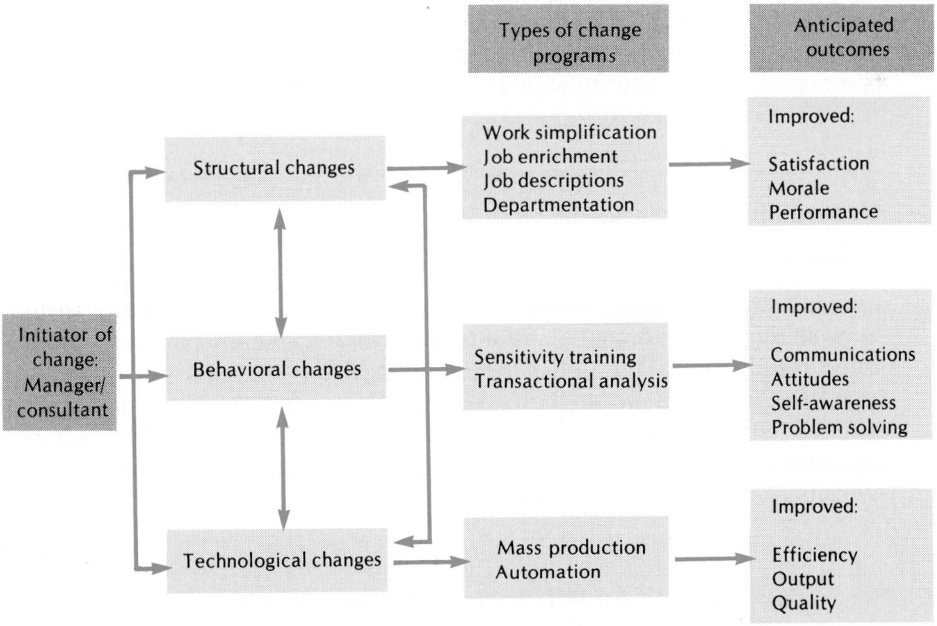

This includes the effects on the organizational environment that result from the philosophy and policies of top management, as well as legal precedent, organizational design, and the system of control. Of course, each of these sources of impact may be the focus of the change effort; the important point is that a change in one must be compatible with all of the others. For example, a change in technology which will eliminate jobs contradicts a policy of guaranteed employment.

The **organizational culture** refers to the impact on the organizational environment that results from group norms and values and from informal activities. The impact of traditional behavior, sanctioned by group norms but not formally acknowledged, was first documented in the Hawthorne studies. A proposed change in work methods or the installation of an automated device can run counter to the expectations and attitudes of work groups. If such is the case, the manager who implements the change must anticipate the resulting resistance.

When managers evaluate the strength of limiting conditions, they are simultaneously considering the problem of objective setting. Many managers have been disappointed by change efforts which fell short of their expectations. Particularly frustrated are those managers who cannot understand why the simple issuance of a directive does not produce the intended response. Thoughtful managers will recognize that even as they are attempting to be forces for change, other conditions are forces for stability. The realities of limiting conditions are such that managers must often be content with modest change or with no change at all.

The implementation of change which does not consider the constraints imposed by prevailing conditions within the present organization may only make the original problem worse. Such change may prepare the ground for subsequent problems. Taken together, these constraints constitute the climate for change and this climate can be positive or negative.

Overcoming resistance to change

People tend to resist change. A combination of factors usually results in some resistance to change. In a recent training seminar, the participants were asked to recall the most recent change that they had faced in their organizations. They were then asked to state why they had or had not resisted the change. Some of the participants stated that they had not opposed or resisted the most recent change. However, the comments of other participants indicated some resistance.

> *A superintendent of a finishing mill: My company changed the purchasing requisition procedure. For six years, there has not been a single complaint or foul-*

up in purchasing materials. Now an efficiency expert has put together a system that I have to use. The idea is untested, unsound, and unnecessary.

Loading supervisor in a food plant: The new automated load system meant that I would not work every other Saturday. Since I was promoted to supervisor three years ago, I have worked at least 20 Saturdays a year. Now with automation, I lose the extra pay for the Saturdays. You bet I resisted, and I still am resisting. I've lost some money because of the new system.

Managers must then recognize the possibility that change will be resisted and devise means for minimizing the resistance.

An approach which has the greatest likelihood of minimizing resistance to change involves the participation of superiors and subordinates in the entire process. But there is no guarantee that the approach will work in all cases. Indeed, some very basic preconditions must exist before employees can meaningfully participate in the change process. These are:

1. An intuitively obvious precondition is that employees must want to become involved. For any number of reasons, they may reject the invitation to participate. They may have other, more pressing needs, such as getting on with their own work. Or they may view the invitation to participate as a subtle (but not too subtle) attempt by managers to manipulate them toward an already predetermined solution. Perhaps they do not want to become associated with a program whose success is uncertain.

2. The employees must be willing and able to voice their ideas. They must also have expertise in some aspect of the analysis. The technical problems associated with a computer installation or automated processes may be beyond the training of assembly line workers, yet they may have valuable insights into the impact of the machinery on their jobs and on the jobs of their co-workers.

3. The managers must be secure in their own positions. Insecure managers would perceive any participation by employees as a threat to their authority. They might view employee participation as a sign of personal weakness or as undermining their status. They must be able to give employees credit for good ideas and to explain their rejection of ideas of questionable merit.

4. Finally, the managers must be open to employees' suggestions. If the managers have arrived at a predetermined solution, the employees will soon recognize the meaninglessness of their participation. Certainly, the managers have the final responsibility for the outcome and they are entitled to control the situation by specifying beforehand the latitude of the employees: They may define objectives, establish constraints, or whatever, so long as the employees know the rules prior to their participation.

If any of the conditions which limit effective employee participation are present, the use of the shared or delegated authority approaches must be viewed with caution. As we have seen, the same factors which limit the range of viable alternative change techniques also limit the range of alternative change strategies. Leadership style, the formal organization, and the organizational culture, along with the characteristics of the employees, are key variables which constrain the entire change process.

Implementing and monitoring the change process

The implementation of the proposed change has two dimensions—*timing* and *scope*. *Timing* is the selection of the appropriate time to initiate the change. Introducing a new electronic cash register system in a retail store would not be desirable during the Christmas season. *Scope* is the selection of the appropriate scale of the change. The matter of timing is strategic, and the proper timing depends on a number of factors, particularly the organization's operating cycle and the groundwork which has preceded the change. It is certainly desirable to avoid having a change of considerable magnitude compete with ordinary operations. Thus, such a change might well be implemented during a slack period. On the other hand, if the change is critical to the survival of the organization, then immediate implementation is in order.

The scope of the change depends on the change strategy. The change may be implemented throughout the organization, and it thus becomes an established fact in a short period of time. Or it may be phased into the organization level by level, department by department. The strategy of successful changes makes use of a phased approach which limits the scope but provides feedback for each subsequent implementation. An example of a phased approach was described by a plant supervisor:

> *We decided to implement the changeover to automated testing equipment over a six-month period instead of pushing our people too quickly. The six-month phase-in will help the testers get used to the equipment and to become the experts on testing procedure.*

The provision of feedback information is termed the *monitoring* phase. From Figure 18–1, we see that information is fed back into the forces-for-change phase because the change itself establishes a new situation that will create problems.

As we have come to understand, the stimulus for change is the deterioration of performance objectives and standards which mangement traces to structural, behavioral, or technological causes. The standards may be any number of indicators, including profit, sales volume, productivity, absenteeism, turnover, scrappage, and costs. The major source of feedback on those variables is the firm's management information system. But if the change includes the objective of improving employee attitudes and morale, the usual sources of information are limited if not invalid.

To avoid the danger of overreliance on productivity data, the manager can generate ad hoc information which measures employee attitudes and morale. A benchmark for evaluation would be available if an attitude survey had been used in the diagnosis phase. The definition of acceptable improvement is difficult when attitudinal data are evaluated, since the matter of "how much more" positive the attitudes of employees should be is quite different from the matter of "how much more" productive they should be. Nevertheless, if a complete analysis of results is to be undertaken, attitudinal measurements must be combined with productivity measurements.

Management summary

1. Organizational change is often inevitable and necessary. It is necessary to improve the overall performance of the organization. Research has shown that planned change has a greater probability of achieving performance improvement objectives than unplanned change.
2. The introduction of changes in structure, behavior, and technology generates resistance from employees. People resist change for economic reasons and because of insecurity and other psychological reasons. Managers have to be alert to resistance indicators or clues and should probably also do some preliminary priming to prepare subordinates for change.
3. Before selecting change techniques, a manager must first recognize the need for change and conduct a thorough diagnosis so that problems can be uncovered.
4. The approach to change which appears to create the least resistance is the participative approach. This approach involves subordinates in defining problems and solutions or at least in defining solutions after management has zeroed in on the problems.
5. Monitoring change requires that managers acquire data about whether objectives are being accomplished. Judging a major change a success even after as long a time as one year is often premature.

Review and discussion questions

1. Some experts believe that resistance to change is a natural human tendency that is based primarily on the fear of the unknown. Why do people resist structural, behavioral, and technological changes?
2. Do you believe that planned change is more effective and generally successful than unplanned change? Why?
3. Why is it important for a manager to recognize the need for change?
4. How does a manager become attuned to the internal and external sources of change in an organization?
5. The following comment was overheard: "Structural, behavioral, and technological changes are all geared toward one major outcome, improved productivity. Thus, the best way to improve production output is to use the optimal mix of change strategies and this means everything available." Why is this statement incorrect?
6. Timing is the selection of the appropriate moment to initiate a change. Why is timing so important in implementing change?
7. Is a change in mass production procedures considered a technological change or a behavioral change? Explain.
8. The initiator of change may be a manager or an outside consultant. Does it matter whether the initiator is an employee of the organization or an outside consultant?
9. Why is sensitivity training a behavioral change technique that is often criticized for creating stress and anxiety?
10. Why should organizational changes be monitored?

Suggested reading

Arnold, J. D. "The Why, When and How of Changing Organizational Structures." *Management Review,* March 1981, pp. 17–20.

Calish, I. G., and R. D. Gamache. "How to Overcome Organizational Resistance to Change." *Management Review,* October 1981, pp. 21–28, 50.

Cobb, A. T., and N. Margulies. "Organization Development: A Political Perspective." *Academy of Management Review,* January 1981, pp. 49–59.

Davis, S. M. "Transforming Organizations: The Key to Strategy is Context." *Organizational Dynamics,* Winter 1982, pp. 64–80.

Herzog, E. L. "Improving Productivity via Organization Development." *Training and Development Journal,* April 1980, pp. 36–39.

March, J. G. "Footnotes to Organizational Change." *Administrative Science Quarterly,* December 1981, pp. 563–77.

McAvoy, R. "How to Integrate People's Needs with Development Strategies." *Management Review,* August 1981, pp. 55–59.

Ouchi, W. "Going from A to Z: Thirteen Steps to a Theory Z Organization." *Management Review,* May 1981, pp. 9–16.

Pati, G. C. "AAP and OD: Not Such an Odd Couple." *Management Review,* May 1980, pp. 58–62.

Tita, M. A. "Internal Consultants: Captive Problem Solvers." *Management Review,* June 1981, pp. 21–26.

Waterman, R. H.; T. J. Peters; and J. R. Phillips. "Structure is Not Organization." *Business Horizons,* June 1980, pp. 14–26.

Applying what you have learned about organizational change

Cases:

Organizational change at Johnson & Johnson International
Resisting better working conditions

Organizational change at Johnson & Johnson International*

Johnson & Johnson International has devised an approach which it believes to be the primary cause of its success in managing organization change. The approach focuses on integrating and coordinating the roles of all participants in the change effort, including consultants, managers, supervisors, peers, and pertinent members of the work force. The company uses various techniques in change efforts, depending upon their applicability to a specific situation. For example, the company has used MBO, behavior modification, transactional analysis, group and individual training, job redesign, and confrontation meetings. Regardless of the technique used, the approach is the same and it is the approach, not necessarily the technique, that assures successful change.

The approach identifies the key participants in a change effort as the department manager whose department is the focus of the change, the superintendent who is the department manager's boss, and an internal or external consultant. Next, the roles and expectations for each participant are specified in detail. Exhibit 1 portrays the general responsibility of the three key participants, but each change effort requires more specific definition of those responsibilities.

The central participant in the change process is the department manager. The consultant and superintendent assist the manager in bringing his or her department up to the desired level of performance. All three work together as a team, and as indicated in Exhibit 1, they have

* This case is adapted from Richard D. Babcock and William B. Alton, "A Systematic Approach to Managing Corporate Change," *Management Review*, December 1979, pp. 24–27.

Exhibit 1

Joint and individual responsibilities in organizational change programs

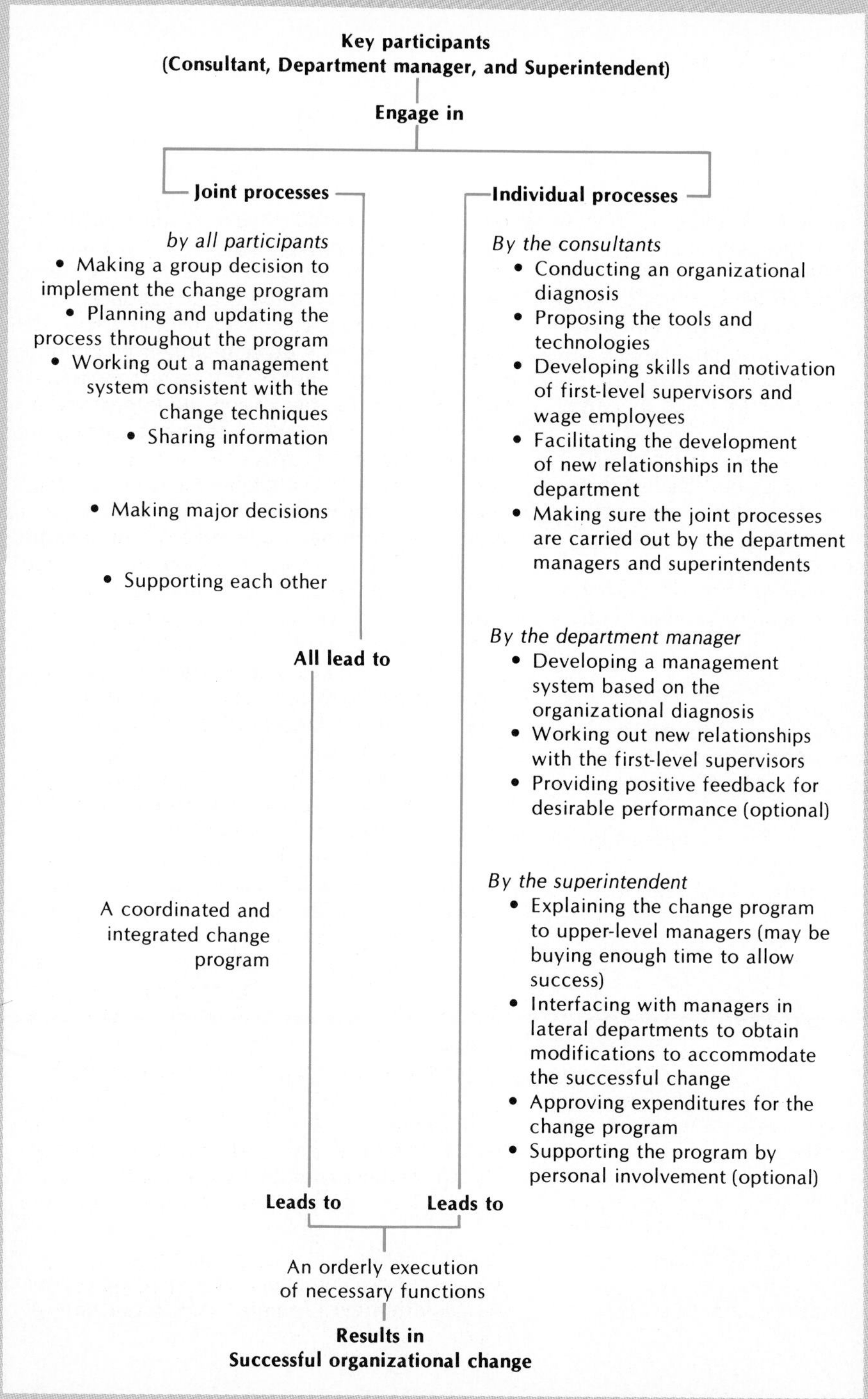
Key participants
(Consultant, Department manager, and Superintendent)
Engage in
Joint processes
by all participants
• Making a group decision to implement the change program
• Planning and updating the process throughout the program
• Working out a management system consistent with the change techniques
• Sharing information
• Making major decisions
• Supporting each other
All lead to
A coordinated and integrated change program
Leads to
Individual processes
By the consultants
• Conducting an organizational diagnosis
• Proposing the tools and technologies
• Developing skills and motivation of first-level supervisors and wage employees
• Facilitating the development of new relationships in the department
• Making sure the joint processes are carried out by the department managers and superintendents
By the department manager
• Developing a management system based on the organizational diagnosis
• Working out new relationships with the first-level supervisors
• Providing positive feedback for desirable performance (optional)
By the superintendent
• Explaining the change program to upper-level managers (may be buying enough time to allow success)
• Interfacing with managers in lateral departments to obtain modifications to accommodate the successful change
• Approving expenditures for the change program
• Supporting the program by personal involvement (optional)
Leads to
An orderly execution of necessary functions
Results in
Successful organizational change

individual as well as joint (team) responsibilities. The participation by the superintendent is crucial to successful change because the change must be coordinated with other departmental activities. For example, if successful change occurs in a production unit so that output is increased, the sales department must be geared up to sell the larger volume of output.

Thus, the Johnson & Johnson approach to managing change recognizes that change in one part of the organization must be taken into account in other parts of the organization. In fact, the company's organizational change staff recommends against change in one department if the results cannot be accommodated in other departments.

Questions:

1. What are the primary reasons behind Jonnson & Johnson's approach to organizational change?
2. How does the company's approach implement the model for managing change as shown in Figure 18–1?
3. Evaluate the company's approach to managing change.

Resisting better working conditions

Sixteen employees of an engineering drafting company worked in the Southgate office of the firm. The office was a single room 36 feet by 46 feet. The drafting technicians, as they were called, liked their cozy office because they worked close to other technicians and away from the engineers, who were housed two miles away at an office in the Northline shopping mall.

The company completed construction of a new office complex that housed all of its drafting technicians, engineers, and clerical personnel. Finally, after three years of being separated, all 96 of the organization's employees were able to work together under one roof. The new office complex was modern and had new furniture, full carpeting, a cafeteria, and a relaxation reading room. An architectural design firm set up the work area and decorated the offices. The drafting technicians and the engineers worked next to each other and in fact had small private offices for four- to six-person teams. The president of the firm, Jon Thorton, was very pleased with the appearance of the new offices and thanked the architectural designers for doing such an outstanding job.

Six months passed after the new offices were opened, and Thorton was puzzled about the poor performance of all the drafting technicians and many of the engineers. Absenteeism and turnover had increased, and the quality of completed work was generally poor.

Thorton met with Ralph Stello, the engineering supervisor, and Sherry Caldwell, the director of technical services, to analyze what had gone wrong. Sherry believed that the routine and the work pattern had been broken by the new office arrangement and that the technicians were resisting the change. Ralph agreed with her analysis. It was also Ralph's opinion that the engineers and the technicians should be assembled to discuss the problems.

Questions:

1. Why is the organization faced with the problems presented in this case?
2. Is Sherry Caldwell accurate in her assessment of what went wrong with the change?
3. What recommendation should be followed at this time to improve the situation?

Applying what you have learned about the controlling function

Learning exercises:

Paper Plane Corporation
Controlling the appearance of employees
The need for change

Comprehensive case

Supra Oil Company

Learning exercise Paper Plane Corporation

Purpose: To work on a task and use the functions of planning, organizing, leading, and controlling.

Setting up the exercise:

Unlimited groups of six participants each are used in this exercise. These groups may be directed simultaneously in the same room. Approximately a full class period is needed to complete the exercise. Each person should have assembly instructions and a summary sheet, which are shown on the following pages, and ample stacks of paper (8-½ by 11 inches). The physical setting should be a room large enough so that the individual groups of six can work without interference from the other groups. A working space should be provided for each group.

- The participants are doing an exercise in production methodology.
- Each group must work independently of the other groups.
- Each group will choose a manager and an inspector, and the remaining participants will be employees.
- The objective is to make paper airplanes in the most profitable manner possible.
- The facilitator will give the signal to start. This is a 10-minute, timed event utilizing competition among the groups.
- After the first round, everyone should report their production and profits to the entire group. They also should note the effect, if any, of the manager in terms of the performance of the group.
- This same procedure is followed for as many rounds as there is time.

Paper Plane Corporation: Data sheet

Your group is the complete work force for Paper Plane Corporation. Established in 1943, Paper Plane has led the market in paper plane production. Presently under new management, the company is contracting to make aircraft for the U.S. Air Force. You must establish an efficient production plant to produce these aircraft. You must make your contract with the Air Force under the following conditions:

1. The Air Force will pay $20,000 per airplane.
2. The aircraft must pass a strict inspection made by the facilitator.
3. A penalty of $25,000 per airplane will be subtracted for failure to meet the production requirements.
4. Labor and other overhead will be computed at $300,000.
5. Cost of materials will be $3,000 per bid plane. If you bid for 10 but only make 8, you must pay the cost of materials for those you failed to make or which did not pass inspection.

Summary sheet

Round 1:

Bid: ________ Aircraft @ $20,000.00 per aircraft = ____________________

Results: ________ Aircraft @ $20,000.00 per aircraft = ____________________

Less: $300,000.00 overhead

____________ × $3,000 cost of raw materials

____________ × $25,000 penalty

Profit: ____________________

Round 2:

Bid: ________ Aircraft @ $20,000.00 per aircraft = ____________________

Results: ________ Aircraft @ $20,000.00 per aircraft = ____________________

Less: $300,000.00 overhead

____________ × $3,000 cost of raw materials

____________ × $25,000 penalty

Profit: ____________________

Round 3:

Bid: ________ Aircraft @ $20,000.00 per aircraft = ____________________

Results: ________ Aircraft @ $20,000.00 per aircraft = ____________________

Less: $300,000.00 overhead

____________ × $30,000 cost of raw materials

____________ × $25,000 penalty

Profit: ____________________

Learning exercise
Controlling the appearance of employees

Purpose: This exercise should increase the students' understanding of organizational control and how it can control behavior.

Setting up the exercise:

I. The class will be divided into groups of about six students each. Each group will be assigned to one of the following organization types:
   A. Computer sales organization.
   B. Fire department.
   C. Restaurant.
   D. Insurance organization.
   E. Charity (e.g., American Heart Association).
   F. Bank
   G. Lawn and gardening retail store.
   H. Stereo equipment store.
   I. Real estate firm.
   J. Medical outpatient clinic.

II. Each group should develop a set of organizational policies that focus on the appearance of employees. Appearance refers to the overall appropriateness of the dress and hairstyle of employees.

Instructions for aircraft assembly

Step 1: Take a sheet of paper and fold it in half, then open it back up.

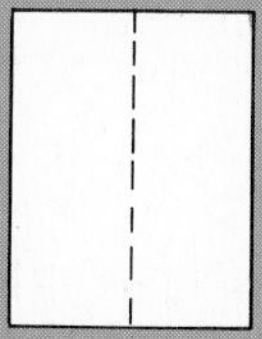

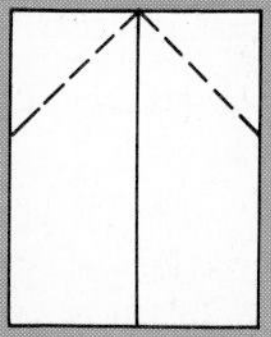

Step 2: Fold upper corners to the middle

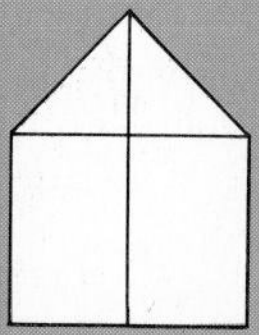

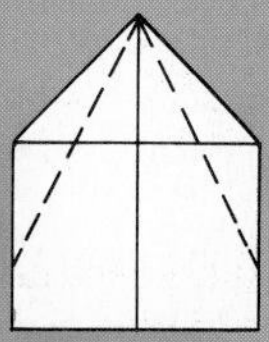

Step 3: Fold the corners to the middle again.

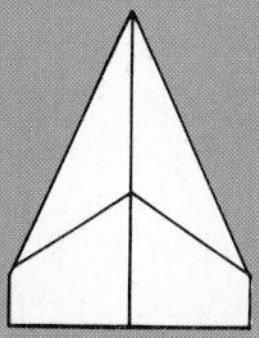

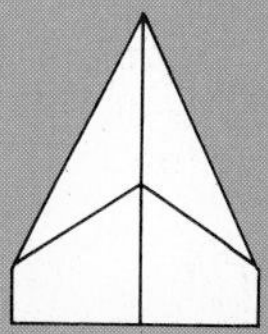

Step 4: Fold in half.

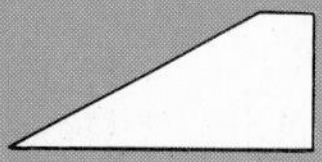

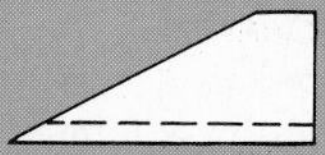

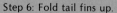

Step 5: Fold both wings down.

Step 6: Fold tail fins up.

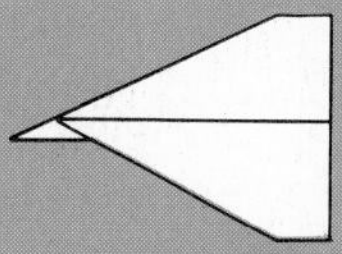

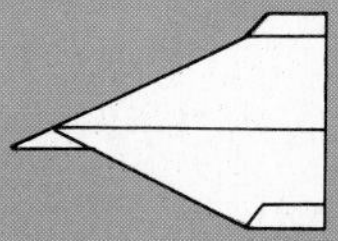

Completed aircraft

III. A spokesperson will be appointed by each group to make a report of the appearance policies to the entire class. The spokesperson should present the group's recommendations, the factors used as guidelines in reaching the group decision, and how the group felt about organizations being involved in the formulation of appearance policies.

A learning note: This exercise should illustrate that appearance is a nonquantifiable characteristic. That is, the policy will be difficult to reach agreement on and to effectively communicate to others.

Learning exercise
The need for change

Purpose: To develop an understanding of how various change techniques can be used to solve a staffing problem and to illustrate how resistance to change can affect the outcome of an organizational change.

Setting up the exercise:

I. Establish groups of five or fewer students. Each group is to prepare a short consultant's report concerning the Southeast Par Telephone staffing situation. Specifically, the president wants the consultants to determine the organization's problem and to develop a solution that results in the fewest complaints.

The exercise is more informative if one group of students from the class serves as evaluators of the presentations. This group would be the panel reviewing the analysis of the other groups.

II. The Southeast Par Telephone situation is as follows:

Over the past three years, Southeast Par Telephone Co. has had a terrible record of recruiting young, qualified management trainees for positions in the accounting, operations, traffic, and maintenance departments. The company has a reputation of paying well and treating employees well, but it is also considered to be an organization with limited advancement opportunity.

The company is searching for young men and women between 21 and 35 years old, with college degrees (preferably some graduate education), who are willing to work different shifts during the two-year training cycle.

The unemployment rate in the city is 5.1 percent, which is below the national average, and the company is located eight miles west of the city. Management is puzzled about the company's inability to bring in qualified people for well-paying trainee positions.

III. Each group should develop a consultants' report which emphasizes the problem, the diagnosis that should be used, the most feasible change strategy, and the anticipated resistance consequences of any change strategy.

IV. Each group should select a spokesperson to make a short presentation emphasizing the points in III to the evaluating group.

V. The evaluating group should then select the best consultants' report and discuss with the entire class why this particular report was selected.

A learning note: This exercise will illustrate how different diagnoses result in the adoption of different change techniques.

Supra Oil Company*

John Nichols, a university research worker, had a talk with Mr. Bennet[1] about the headquarters sales organization of the Supra Oil Company, one of the larger integrated oil companies in the country. Excerpts from the conversation follow:

Nichols: You mentioned that you're planning to make some organizational changes here at headquarters. I wonder if you could tell me something about that.

Bennett: Well, sure I will. I don't want to take too much credit for this thing, but it sort of got started because in the last couple of years I've been doing some beefing around here about the fact that I was being kept terribly busy with a lot of the operating details of the sales organization. You can see what I mean by looking at the organization chart we have been working under. [Mr. Bennett produced a chart from his desk drawer and indicated all the people that were currently reporting to him.] [See Exhibit 1 for a copy of this chart.]

You can see that with all these people looking to me for leadership I am not in a position to give them the right kind of guidance that I think they should have on their jobs. I just couldn't take the time. It didn't work too badly some time ago, but since I've been made a member of the board of directors, those activities have taken more of my time. What with being on additional committees and things of that kind, I just couldn't give 17 headquarters' division managers the amount of help and attention that they really need. I think one of the things that they miss is that they're not in close enough touch with me or anybody else higher up the line so that we can be in a good position to appraise their work. We hear about it from some of the field people when they are doing a lousy job, but we don't hear much about it if they're doing a good job. Occasionally, a field man will report that he is getting a lot of help from some staff outfit here, but that's rather rare. So we don't have a very good basis for appraising the good things that they do. So we started talking about what might be done to straighten this out.

Our plans are taking pretty definite shape now. Let me show you what we have in mind. [Mr. Bennett sketched on a pad of paper a diagram to indicate the planned organizational changes.] [See Exhibit 2.] You see, we will have two regional managers instead of three. We'll be making one of the present regional managers the manager of the headquarters sales divisions. Those are the divisions that specialize in promoting and selling our different specialty products. Then we'll set up a new job for Wingate, who has been acting as an administrative assistant here at headquarters. He'll take charge of a good number of headquarters sales staff divisions that were reporting directly to me. Those are staff divisions like price analysis and advertising. We will also give each of the two remaining regional managers an assistant manager. Those will be new positions too.

* *Supra Oil Co.* (9–557–005) Copyright © 1957 by the President and Fellows of Harvard College. Reprinted by permission of the Harvard Business School. This case was prepared by Paul R. Lawrence under the supervision of Milton P. Brown.

[1] Mr. Bennett was assistant general manager of sales.

Exhibit 1

Partial organization chart of the sales department

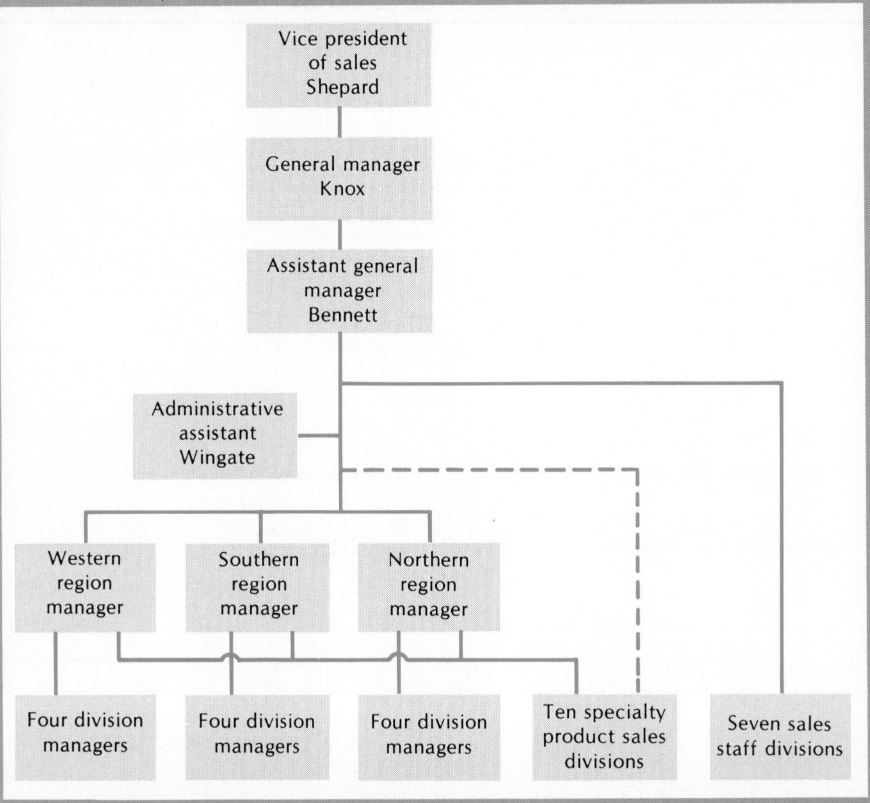

Nichols: How did you get these plans started?

Bennett: I raised it with Shepard [vice president of sales] quite a while back.

Nichols: Would you say that was maybe six months ago?

Bennett: I think it probably was six months ago. Shepard's first reaction was unfavorable. You see, I expected him to feel that way because he was the one that had the most to do with setting up our current organizational plan. But I approached him on it two or three times and complained a little bit and kept raising the question, and finally he said, "Well, I'm going to be leaving here pretty soon.

Exhibit 2

Proposed organization chart of the sales department

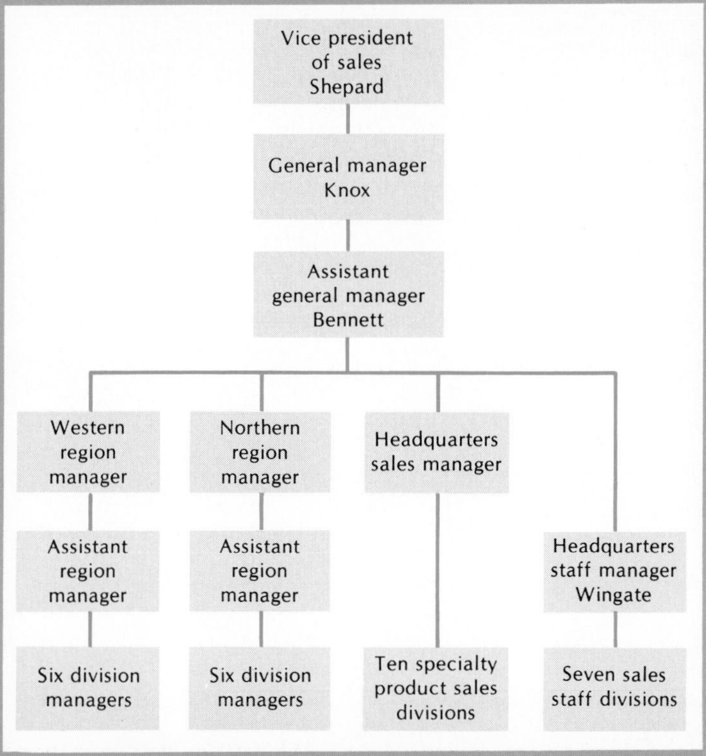

You people have got to live with the organization. If you think it would work better some other way, I certainly won't object to your changing it." Well, that sort of thing gave me the green light, so then I went ahead and raised the question with Mr. Weld [president]. That is, Mr. Knox [general sales manager] and I did. The first time we went to him we talked about it in general terms. He said he thought it sounded like a pretty good idea and asked that we come back with two or three alternative ways of doing the thing in very specific terms. We talked to him once since then and, as a matter of fact, I'm going to see him this afternoon to see if he'll give us a final OK to go ahead with these plans.

Nichols: If you get his approval, what would you predict—that it might be another month before the change actually takes place?

Bennett: Well, I would say so. I think if we've got this thing going in a month that we will be doing pretty well. I'm going to want to talk to my regional managers and then the headquarters divisional managers about this, but they should buy it all right. I think it will be a fairly simple job to sell it to them. You see, they will in effect be getting more chance to have access to their boss. I think it will work out much better, and they will see the point to it.

Nichols: You say that you are making one less region and making the third regional manager the head of—I guess you are calling him the headquarters sales manager. Are all three of those jobs going to continue to be on an equal level?

Bennett: Yes, they will, but actually this job of headquarters sales manager will be sort of a training position for somebody to step into my job here as assistant general sales manager. That's what we have in mind. I think it will be a good assignment for training for my job. Then too, we're going to be able to open up a couple of new positions here, the assistant regional managers. I think that is going to be very useful from a management development standpoint. You see, one of our problems is that a number of the top executives here are all about the same age. You see, Knox and myself and the three regional managers are all about the same age, and then the heads of a lot of our headquarters divisions here are men of about our age who—well, they won't retire immediately, but they don't have a terribly long time to go. So we can't look to too many of those people to be our successors here at headquarters. We want to bring in some people from the field who will step in here as assistant regional managers in training for the job of regional managers.

Nichols: I take it then that you will be picking the people for those jobs from your field division men on the basis of talent and ability rather than on the basis of seniority.

Bennett: Yes, that's right, we're going to pay very little attention to seniority in picking them. As a matter of fact, the two people we have in mind are two of our newest division managers, but they are both very able people. We think this will give us a chance to give them a good training for future development here.

This change that we are proposing, however, will not drastically change anybody's status here at headquarters, and I don't think it is going to cause as much trouble to put it in. You see, nobody will be jumped over the head of anybody else ahead of them in the management line. We think it's going to help a lot to have an assistant regional manager in here because that means that both he and the regional manager will be able to spend more time out with the field organization. One will be able to cover matters here at headquarters while the other is gone.

Nichols: Does that mean that your field people will be getting more top-level supervision as a result of this change?

Bennett: Well, in a sense that's true of course, but it won't be taking any authority or responsibility from the field people. We just feel that they will be in closer personal contact with the people here at headquarters. We think it is very necessary that we do more of that. You see, if our regional managers and assistant managers can get out in the field and meet with the people, they will have a better basis for appraising different people that come along, and they can make sure we get the best people in the jobs that open up. Sometimes it's pretty hard to tell here at headquarters just who some of the best people are out in the field. You see, some division may have a job open up, and they will have a candidate for that job whom they will recommend highly for the promotion. That may be all well and good, but we want to know whether or not there may be a better man in some other division whom we aren't hearing about who might be shifted over for that promotion. You can't blame the division people for that sort of thing because they will have their favorite candidate and will of course be recommending him. We've made a few mistakes along the way because of this sort of thing, and if we have more personal contact we will be able to do a better job of it.

Nichols: Will this mean that you will be able to spend more time in the field?

Bennett: Yes, I do hope that it will mean that. I want to do that very much. I think I ought to get out in the field more to keep in touch with what's going on in the market. It's really pretty hard to keep in touch with things while you are spending your time here at headquarters. You know, I want to get out and talk to people and see what they are talking about and see what kind of problems they are up against.

Nichols: I've heard several comments on this business of getting a feel for the market by getting out in the field. I take it that this is quite a different process from keeping in touch with the market on what you might call a statistical basis?

Bennett: Well, yes, it is. You see, I can look at the reports here in the office, and I may see that some district or some division is not doing too well at all on the basis of the figures in comparison with the competition. But I don't know just what the story is behind those figures. On a personal basis I could probably begin to get some answers to it. It could be any one of a number of things. I might go out there and find that it's a temporary situation because the competition is in effect going out and buying the business away from us, or I might find out that our people are not being very smart or aggressive about promoting our products, or I might find out that they do not know some of the facilities we have available that would help them compete for the business. You see, one way we can compete for the business is the fact that this company has available some pretty good capital resources; and if we don't have good outlets in a given district, we're often in a position to offer to put up some capital to get some better outlets. That way we can do a better job of competing for the business, and sometimes the local people don't know that these possibilities exist, or perhaps they're a little reticent about putting up proposals. Or even if they do put up proposals, if we haven't been out in the field to see for ourselves what's going on, we probably don't do as good a job of appraising the proposals they do put up.

Nichols: In other words, the figures tell you that maybe something ought to be checked into, but you've got to go out and talk to people to find out what is really going on?

Bennett: Yes, that's right. You have to take a personal look. You can find out a lot faster than you can by correspondence just what is going on and what can be done about it.

Nichols: Won't this reorganization mean that some of the people both here and in the field will have new bosses now?

Bennett: Yes, that's right, but it's not too drastic a change. You see, we used to have only two regional managers some time ago. I guess we shifted off that system some four or five years ago. When I was out in the field as manager of a division, I was reporting in to the northern regional manager, who was Mr. Shepard at that time. Then I was brought in here as his assistant for the whole region. It was about that time that we set up this business of having three regions and I was named one of the regional managers, and at that time Mr. Shepard became general manager.

Nichols: Well, it sounds as if that previous move might have been motivated somewhat by a desire to develop people and perhaps give you a chance to take over a regional managership before you might otherwise have had a chance to.

Bennett: Yes, I think that's right. At that time, that move was the way we could open things up for further management development, and now we are sort of doing it the other way around. Everybody knows that the arrangement we are now proposing may well be changed again in a few more years.

We like to change the organization around a little bit like this from time to time just to let people know that we are not going to be static about things. Of course, we want to do it in a way so that some of our senior people do not get bypassed or jumped over by some of the younger ones, because that not only bothers the individual but it also hurts morale further down in the organization. You see, when some of the people further down see some of that sort of thing happening, they are apt to conclude that it might happen to them some day, and it's pretty discouraging to them. The way we are doing it now we can bring up some younger people without jumping over anybody's head who is senior.

I think an organization change of this kind is also useful in that it indicates to some of our younger people that they need not feel discouraged if they are in a position where someone is above them in line who shows no signs of being promoted on up. This situation might make a person feel that he is being blocked from future promotion by his boss. But he is encouraged when he sees an occasional organizational shift of this kind because it makes him realize that things can happen in the future that might shift the organization around to a point where he can be sprung loose for a move on up even though his boss may not be promotable.

Nichols: Then I take it that one of the predominant thoughts in this whole reorganization was one of management development?

Bennett: Oh, that's certainly true. That was one of the prime reasons we're proposing this, because we think it will help us develop our managers and this gives us a way of doing it without upsetting the organization too much.

That afternoon Mr. Bennett kept the appointment with Mr. Weld that was mentioned in the conversation above. Upon entering Mr. Weld's office, Mr. Bennett handed Mr. Weld a copy of the revised sales organization chart.

Bennett: Here's a final version of our reorganizational plans. Do you think it is all right to go ahead on this?

Questions:

1. Will the changes at Supra Oil be viewed as change just for the sake of change? As Bennett stated, "We like to change the organization around a little bit like this from time to time. . ."
2. How will the proposed changes effect the control systems at Supra Oil?
3. Suppose the change takes place at Supra, would Bennett's performance as assistant general manager be easier to evaluate under the new system?

Part VI Managing for performance: Trends and perspectives

19. Managing the multinational company
20. Managing work-related stress
21. Managing future challenges and responses

A management profile
Mary Kay Ash

Mary Kay Ash likes to tell people that a "little miracle" launched the cosmetics company that bears her name. Those who know her will tell you that there were no miracles—just a lot of hard work.

Born in a small town in Texas, Mary Kay (as she prefers to be known) acquired her drive and independence the hard way. As a child, she stayed home to care for her invalid father while her mother worked long hours to support the family.

Married right out of high school, Mary Kay soon found herself divorced and with three children to support. For 13 years, she sold kitchen utensils from her home with dazzling success, regularly winning her company's top sales award. Later, she took her talent and experience to another company, where she rose to the position of national sales training director.

And then, out of the blue, Mary Kay was struck with a rare form of paralysis, ending her long success in the business world. Or so she thought. Adversity was nothing new for Mary Kay, and she resolved to recover. She conquered her affliction through surgery, and then she began looking for a new marketing project.

At a demonstration party similar to the ones at which she had once sold utensils, Mary Kay was introduced to a facial cream that seemed to produce what she called a *peaches and cream* complexion. With $5,000 of her savings, she bought the rights to the formula, and Mary Kay Cosmetics was born.

The first-year sales were $200,000. Sales quadrupled the next year, and Mary Kay never looked back. Right from the start, Mary Kay Cosmetics were sold exclusively by women at home demonstration parties, where saleswomen show customers—usually a group of neighbors—how to apply Mary Kay products. Today, they are sold the same way all over America as well as in several overseas locations. Sales are measured in millions of dollars, and the company's stock is traded on the New York Stock Exchange. As Mary Kay says, "You know, women can do anything once they put their minds to it."

The Mary Kay Ash story will be repeated numerous times in the 1980s. As more women take over top-management positions and enter the professional ranks in greater numbers, organization members will become more accustomed to female leadership. The 1980s will be the era in which competence, energy, and creativity will be more important than whether a person is a woman, a Chicano, or a Protestant. This part of the book will point out trends and perspectives that are occurring and what organizations are doing to cope with them. Like Mary Kay Ash, the manager of tomorrow will have to work hard to stay ahead of the pack.

Photograph by Bradford Bachrach, courtesy of Mary Kay Cosmetics, Inc.

Source: Elizabeth J. Kenny for P. S. Associates, Inc., Sterling, Massachusetts.

Introduction to Part VI

Part VI, Managing for performance: Trends and perspectives, contains three chapters. They are:

Chapter 19—Managing the multinational company
Chapter 20—Managing work-related stress
Chapter 21—Managing for performance: Challenges and responses.

The inclusion of the material contained in the three chapters is based upon the following rationale:

The last section of a management textbook should integrate the main ideas that have been developed in the preceding chapters. Ideally, the integration of ideas should be in the context of important issues that managers confront. The authors endeavor to achieve this ideal by presenting the contributions and relevance of the management functions to the issues of managing multinational companies, managing work-related stress, and managing future challenges and responses.

The **multinational company** is an increasingly important form of organization. Managers who must plan, organize, lead, and control organizations which cross national boundaries face diverse cultures, governmental practices, and employee attitudes. Although the elements of the managerial functions are applicable regardless of setting, the form they take must be compatible with the setting. The importance of multinational corporations will be an important management issue during the 1980s.

Work-related stress has commanded public attention for many years. But it has been only recently that managers have come to accept its importance to corporate performance. Increasing numbers of organizations have implemented programs designed to reduce the incidence and severity of stress that can be traced to work-related causes. The concern for work-related stress is part of the larger concern for individual well-being. That concern will accelerate during the 1980s.

The era of the 1980s will present numerous challenges. The **responses of managers to those challenges** cannot be known with certainty, but it is certain that issues such as energy, ethics, equal opportunity, scarcity, productivity, and foreign competition will call for the very best in management performance. The authors believe that the ideas we have developed in this text can contribute to that performance.

The figure below summarizes the concept of this, the last part of the text:

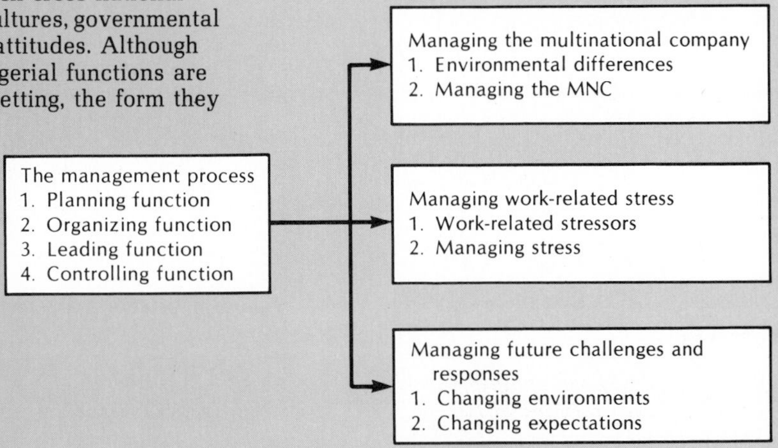

19

Chapter nineteen Managing the multinational company

Performance objectives

- **Define** what is meant by a multinational company (MNC).
- **State** the general reasons why a firm decides to become an MNC.
- **Describe** the evolution of an MNC.
- **Explain** the impact of culture, economics, and politics on managerial performance in an MNC.
- **Discuss** the performance of the management functions in an international environment.

Management update*

When a business firm decides to leave its national borders and do business in other countries, it becomes a multinational company (MNC). With the decision to become a MNC, the environmental component takes on an increasingly important and more complex role in managerial performance. The organization becomes subject to the perils of different cultures, economies, and political whims. A good case in point took place recently in France.

Without warning, French customs officers held up thousands of imported Japanese automobiles at dockside and in warehouses as part of a campaign by the industry minister to pressure the Japanese into limiting shipments of automobiles into Europe. Officially, France allows Japan only a 3 percent share of the French car market and the previous year had achieved just 2.93 percent. However, the Japanese were hurting the French in other European countries such as West Germany and Belgium which the French view as their prime export markets.

As the new Japanese autos were unloaded, they were held up until they received certificates of conformity to local technical standards. For example, one entire model was held up because its bumper was slightly longer than it had been the previous year. The Japanese attributed the French minister's action to "pure politics." With an election only about two months away, they claimed the French were using Japanese cars as a scapegoat in an attempt to get votes.

* This Management Update is based on "The Sneak Attack on Japanese Automobiles," *Business Week*, March 2, 1981, p. 42.

It is safe to say that most American business organizations would prefer doing business domestically. Domestic business is, for the most part, simpler and safer. For example, there is no need to alter the firm's products to different sets of expectations and needs, and managers need not deal with different currencies, political uncertainties, or learn different languages.

Why then do so many American business organizations become involved in international business? There are usually one or two major factors. First, the firm might be forced into it by weakening opportunities at home. Economic growth may decline, taxes may increase, or legislation may become too burdensome. Second, the firm might be drawn into it by outstanding opportunities to market its products in other nations while continuing to do business at home. Whatever the causes, once a firm makes the decision to do business abroad, it confronts a whole new set of circumstances. Performance of the managerial functions in an international setting is the subject of this chapter.

The multinational company

Although American exports are less than 7 percent of the nation's gross national product, America is the world's largest exporter in absolute dollar terms. Other nations are not as fortunate. For example, Great Britain, the Netherlands, New Zealand, and Belgium must sell well over half of their output in international markets in order to maintain a stable economy with high employment. For firms in these countries, experience in conducting business worldwide is, therefore, common.

A business firm doing business in two or more countries is referred to as a **multinational company** (MNC). Typically, however, most such firms have sales offices and in many cases manufacturing facilities in many different countries. Indeed, they view their scope of operation as global in nature. For example, American firms such as Pfizer, Hoover, Otis Elevator, Mobil Oil, and Gulf Oil currently sell the majority of their output outside the United States. American firms such as Xerox, Coca-Cola, Dow Chemical, IBM, and Chrysler currently earn more than half their profits outside the United States.

Another way to appreciate the truly multinational nature of many business firms is to examine foreign companies that have entered the United States and American firms that are owned by foreign multinationals. Figure 19–1 presents some recognizable names in each of these categories.

It is safe to say that as competition intensifies, American firms will find it necessary to become increasingly proficient in international business. The necessity of avoiding costly mistakes and pressure from experienced competitors will demand managers who can bring about effective performance in an MNC. The importance of effective performance by American MNCs was stated very strongly by the president of the international division of a medical supply manufacturer.

> *We are now in the age of the multinational company. Most of your larger American firms receive a substantial amount of sales and/or profits from outside the United States. Both management practice and education cannot afford a policy of isolation any longer.*

The decision to become a MNC

When a firm becomes a MNC, it enters a situation quite different from the one it presently operates in. The last three decades have presented American business with new opportunities as well as new problems relating to international business. Some of the most important are (1) the internationalization of the world economy as evidenced by the rapid growth in world trade and investment, (2) the less dominant position of the United States and a falling value of the dollar in world money markets, (3) the rapid rise in the economic power of Japan, (4) the establishment of an international financial system providing improved currency convertibility; (5) the shift in world income to the oil-producing countries, (6) the increasing trade barriers to protect domestic markets against foreign competition, and (7) the gradual opening of major new markets, namely China, the USSR, and the Arab countries.[1]

Thus, the decision to become an MNC is truly a major one. The experience of many firms indicates that becoming a MNC is, in most cases, a sequence of different strategies. Each strategy involves greater involvement in, and commitment to, becoming a global enterprise.

[1] Warren J. Keegan, "Multinational Product Planning: New Myths and Old Realities," in *Multinational Product Management* (Cambridge, Mass.: Marketing Science Institute, 1976), pp. 1–8.

Figure 19–1

Foreign multinationals and American firms owned by foreign multinationals

Some foreign multinationals operating in America	
Unilever	Toyota Motors
Royal Dutch/Shell	Sony
Nestle	Volkswagen
Datsun	Perrier
Honda	Norelco
Some American firms owned by foreign multinationals	
Saks Fifth Avenue	Capitol Records
Bantam Books	Kiwi Shoe Polish
Baskin-Robbins	Lipton
Six of the 10 largest California banks are foreign owned	
Midland Bank Limited	Standard Chartered Bank Limited
Rothschild	Lloyds Bank Group
The Bank of Tokyo	The Sumitomo Bank

Alternative entry strategies

The evolution to a MNC begins when a firm decides to enter a foreign market. This decision is usually the result of a determination that a particular foreign market represents a good opportunity for the firm. Once this decision is made, there are three basic entry strategies. These strategies are illustrated in Figure 19–2. Each strategy results in greater involvement in international business.

Export The simplest way for a firm to enter a foreign market is by exporting. This strategy involves little or no change in the basic mission, objectives, and strategies of the organization, since it continues to produce all of its products at home. The firm will usually secure an *agent* in the particular foreign market who facilitates the transactions with foreign buyers.

Foreign subsidiary As exports increase in importance to the firm, it may decide that it can now justify its own foreign subsidiary. This decision

Figure 19–2

The evolution of an MNC: Alternative Energy Strategies

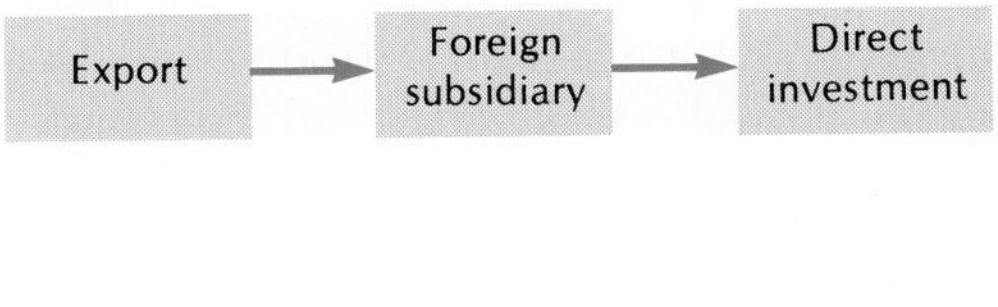

usually involves joining with nationals in the foreign country to establish production and/or marketing facilities. It differs from direct investment in that some type of association is formed with a local firm or individual. This type of association usually takes the form of licensing or joint-venture arrangements. *Licensing* is granting the right to produce and/or market the firm's product in another country to an outside firm. Gerber and Coca-Cola have used this arrangement to enter foreign countries. *Joint-venture* arrangements involve foreign investors forming a group with local investors to begin a local business with each group sharing ownership. Several U.S. banks are jointly owned by both U.S. and foreign interests.

Direct investment The strongest commitment to becoming a global enterprise is when management decides to begin producing the firm's products abroad. This strategy enables the firm to maintain full control over production, marketing, and other key functions. Volkswagen made such a decision when it decided to construct an assembly plant in Pennsylvania.

Whichever entry strategy is utilized, effective international management will be required. The degree and kind of involvement might vary depending upon whether foreign agents, subsidiaries, or direct investment is utilized. Regardless of which alternative is used, performance of the management functions will still be necessary.

The MNC and the management functions

At this point, we should address the question of whether international enterprises involve unique requirements for effective managerial performance and the management functions. Certainly, the management functions of planning, organizing, leading, and controlling must be performed effectively. The management functions are required regardless of business setting. However, the differences between peoples may be such that international managers will be forced to learn about special environmental factors and institutions or to change some of their basic assumptions about people, organizations, and roles of management. In the opening section of our book, we discussed the importance of environmental factors in managerial performance. As important as these factors are to domestic management, they are magnified many times in the international setting. We now turn our attention to a discussion of the most important environmental differences in international management.

Environmental differences in international management

Effective managerial performance in an international setting requires careful consideration and appreciation of differences in **culture, economics,** and **politics.** While other differences could be identified, these three have the greatest impact on managerial performance in MNCs. How effectively managers respond to these differences very often determines the success or failure of an MNC.

Culture

Culture is a very complex environmental influence which includes knowledge, beliefs, law, morals, art, customs, and any other habits and capabilities an individual acquires as a member of society. Customs, beliefs, habits, and values can vary greatly. If an MNC is global in nature, then management will be required to adapt managerial practices to the specific and unique aspects of culture in each nation. It is important to be aware that cultures are **learned,** cultures **vary,** and cultures **influence behavior.**

Cultures are learned Cultures include all types of learning and behavior, the customs that people have developed for living together, their values, and their beliefs of right and wrong. It is the total of what humans learn in common with other members of the society to which they belong.

Cultures vary Different societies have different cultures. Different objects are prized, and behavior that is valued in one society may be much less important in another. This cultural diversity affects individual perception and, therefore, individual behavior. Cultural diversity, then, results in a diversity of human behavior among different cultures.

Cultures influence behavior Diversity in human behavior can be found in almost every activity in which human beings engage. Religious ceremonies, beliefs, values, work habits, food habits, and social activities vary endlessly with cultural environment. In other words, the differences in behavior between peoples of different nations are due to differences in culture rather than to differences between the people. Although human needs may be inherently similar, the cultural environment determines the relative importance of needs and means through which they are satisfied.

Thus, depending upon the cultural influences, attitudes of individuals will differ concerning such subjects as the importance of work, authority, material possessions, competition, introducing change, time, risk taking, and profit. A manager cannot assume that the attitudes toward these and similar subjects in the company will be consistent in all nations. For example, in some areas of the world, hard work is viewed as good, while in others it is viewed as something to be avoided. Authority is viewed as a right in some nations, for example, Japan, but must be earned by demonstrated ability in others, for example, the United States. Figure 19–3 presents attitudes in three different cultures (American, European, and Japanese) toward competition and indicates how these attitudes influence managerial behavior, motivational approaches, reward systems, staffing practices, and leadership styles. The impact of management's inability to adjust to cultural differences was strongly stated by a vice president of international communications.

Figure 19–3

Attitudes toward competition in three different cultures

Nature and effect of competition	Typical American viewpoints	Typical European viewpoints	Typical Japanese viewpoints
Nature of competition	Competition is a strong moral force: it contributes to character building.	Competition is neither good nor bad.	There is conflict inherent in nature. To overcome conflicts, man must compete but man's final goal is harmony with nature and his fellowman.
Business competition compared	Business competition is like a big sport game.	Business competition affects the livelihood of people and quickly develops into warfare	The company is like a family. Competition has no place in a family. Aggressive action against competitors in the marketplace is in order for the survival and growth of the company.
Motivation	One cannot rely on an employee's motivation unless extra monetary inducements for hard work are offered in addition to a base salary or wage.	A key employee is motivated by the fact that he has been hired by the company.	Same as the European viewpoint.

Figure 19–3 (*concluded*)

Reward system	Money talks. A person is evaluated on the basis of his image (contribution) to the company. High tipping in best hotels, restaurants, etc., is expected.	An adequate salary, fringe benefits, opportunities for promotion, but no extra incentives—except in sales. Very little tipping (service charge is included in added-value tax).	Same as the European viewpoint.
Excessive competition	Competition must be tough for the sake of the general welfare of society. No upper limit on the intensity and amount of competition is desirable.	Too much competition is destructive and is in conflict with brotherly love and Christian ethic.	Excessive competition is destructive and can create hatred. Only restrained competition leads to harmony and benefits society.
Hiring policy	Aggressive individuals who enjoy competition are ideal employees. Individuals who avoid competition are unfit for life and company work.	Diversity of opinion. How competitiveness or aggressive behavior of an individual is viewed varies with national ideology and the type of work. In England, it is not a recommendation to describe a job applicant as being aggressive.	Individuals are hired usually not for specific jobs but on the basis of their personality traits and their ability to become an honorable company member. Team play and group consensus are stressed.

SOURCE: Hugh E. Kramer, "Concepts of Competition in America, Europe, and Japan," *Business and Society*, Fall 1977, pp. 22–23.

In my opinion, the majority of management mistakes made in foreign countries are caused by a lack of understanding and appreciation of cultural differences. We read every day of outrageous marketing mistakes caused by insensitivity to cultural differences. But I'm also talking about mistakes inside the company: mistakes dealing with superiors and subordinates that ultimately influence performance. So many are caused by insensitivity to cultural differences. We assume that our way is the only way.

Economics

The economic environment in the nations in which it conducts business is obviously important to the MNC. Income levels, growth trends, inflation rates, balance of payments, and economic planning agencies can vary greatly among nations. The MNC must be constantly aware of the economic stability as reflected by the nation's rate of inflation and the degree of stability of its currency.

The nations of the world are classified as either a **developed country** or a **less developed country** (LDC). An LDC has a very low gross national product, very little industry, or an unequal distribution of income with a very large number of poor. However, the majority of MNC investment is located in these developing nations. This diversity of economies in which the MNC must operate has a strong impact on the management function of planning as indicated by a vice president for planning:

My biggest challenge is developing ways to respond to totally different economies with some type of consistent organizational plan. We certainly cannot develop a separate strategy for each economic area.

Economic relations between MNCs and LDCs have often been the subject of controversy. Many LDCs have strong feelings of nationalism. During the last 30 years in their drives for political independence and freedom from foreign domination, many developing nations felt the need to consolidate control of their economies by altering the past pattern of relationships with foreign firms. In some LDCs, extensive government regulations were adopted with the ultimate purpose of limiting the growth of MNCs. More recently, however, there has been a movement away from this trend. The reasons for the shift are changing attitudes and rising direct investment.[2]

[2] This section is based on *Transnational Corporations and Developing Countries: New Policies for a Changing World Economy* (New York: Committee for Economic Development, 1981), pp. 1–3.

Changing attitudes Although charges of exploitation by MNCs still appear quite frequently, changes have taken place in the attitudes of both host governments and MNCs that have led to greater mutual understanding and accommodation in their relations. Although host-country fear of foreign domination still exists, it has eased substantially. Apparently, there is now an appreciation that the relationship with MNCs need not be a no-win situation, but rather one of mutual gain.

Rising direct investment With improved relations, direct investment, the third-entry strategy, in LDCs has doubled in recent years, in comparison with the early 1960s. Apparently, many MNCs believe the possible returns are worth the risk. Also, these direct investments do not reflect the flow of other resources, such as managerial skills, technology, and marketing skills, which may overshadow the monetary contribution.

Despite greater mutual trust and understanding and a greater volume of investment, it would be wrong to assume that total agreement has been achieved between MNCs and developing countries on the questions of exploitation of resources and threats to sovereignty. These issues have divided them for years and, even today, a wide variety of opinions still exists within each group. At the heart of the controversy, a basic difference in perceptions and objectives remains. The MNCs, although giving greater recognition to their social responsibilities, still tend to concentrate on short-run performance criteria. Efficient and profitable operation is regarded as automatically benefiting workers, customers, and suppliers directly and the rest of the host country indirectly through the payment of taxes. Critics in the host country on the other hand often stress undesirable political, social, and economic effects which MNCs often cause in developing countries struggling to achieve political and economic autonomy. The reader should recognize these differences in perceptions and objectives of the social role of the business organization. Similar arguments are brought up in every discussion of the social responsibilities of business firms in our own country.

Politics

Political differences can have a large impact in international management. Nations differ greatly in the favorableness of their political and legal environment for imports and direct investment by foreigners. Managers in MNCs must be aware of the potential problems and risks associated with business activities that span different political systems.

Some governments subsidize MNCs. Japan, Great Britain, and France actively support exporters with subsidies. On the other hand, some nations seek to penalize political adversaries through economic boycotts, prohibiting trade with another country. Thus, it is possible for an MNC in the United States to face competitors in Japan, Great Britain, and France, which are being subsidized by their governments, while at the same time not be able to do business in other countries (e.g., Cuba) boycotted by the United States.

Managers of MNCs must be sensitive to the changing political and legal environments in those nations in which they operate. Differences in politics and law can influence all of the managerial functions. Consequently, they can make the difference between succeeding and failing. Managers should consider at least three factors when evaluating the political environment in a particular country. They are the attitudes toward imports and direct investment, stability of government, and efficiency of government.

Attitudes toward imports and direct investment As we noted above, some nations support and encourage foreign investment. Others are very hostile and may force import quotas on foreign firms, impose heavy taxes on foreign firms, and require that a large proportion of top management be nationals. Coca-Cola for example no longer operates in India for these reasons.

Stability of government In numerous cases, a foreign firm's property has been taken, its money held, or new duties or quotas instituted when a government changes. In some countries unfortunately, governments often change quite rapidly and violently. Some countries with quite stable governments for long periods of time have become quite unstable rapidly. The stability of government can influence many decisions from the entry strategy chosen and the scope of operation to the amount of direct investment. The impact of local political conditions was noted by a division director of an appliance manufacturer who stated:

> *Developing countries with quick-changing governments make life difficult for my managers. Most of the governments in these nations really do not know how inexperienced they are in managing government.*

Efficiency of government Many American businessmen are disillusioned by the inefficient bureaucracies which they must deal with in many countries. Often, little assistance is provided to businessmen, customs-handling procedures are inefficient and burdensome, and market information is nonexistent. Systems of law in each country can also be quite different. For example, the United States has developed its legal system by means of English *common law.* The courts are guided by principles derived from previous cases. In much of Europe and Asia, the legal system is one of *civil law.* In such systems, judges are less important and the bureaucrat (civil servant) is extremely important. Unfortunately, American managers have found that many of the inefficiencies and obstacles in local governments tend to disappear when a suitable payment is made to some civil servant. In many nations such bribes are considered a part of doing business. For example, during the late 1970s, the Northrop Corporation was accused of spending a substantial part of $30 million over approximately five years for bribes and kickbacks. One factor which became evident during Congressional hearings was that such payments were considered in the Middle East to be traditional peculiarities of business practice.[3]

Out of the above and some 400 other cases came the Foreign Corrupt Practices Act, which President Carter signed into law in 1977. For the first time in U.S. history, it is a crime for corporations to bribe an official of a foreign government in order to obtain, or retain, business in another country. More specifically, the law requires publicly held companies to institute internal accounting controls to insure that all transactions are made in accordance with management's specific authorization and are fairly recorded. Meanwhile, in West Germany, France, and Great Britain, payments of bribes abroad remain not only legal but tax deductible. This practice obviously places the United States at a disadvantage in certain areas. The complexity of the relationship between international management and politics was summarized extremely well by Henry Kissinger when he said:

> We have come a long way, and very rapidly, to the . . . proposition that international business depends decisively on international politics. . . . We have come a long way from the 19th century when the United States accounted for very little in the scale of world economies. . . . The future of American business will require the highest degree of sensitivity to the political framework in which it functions and to the great coming changes in the world political process.[4]

The management functions in international management

In the opening chapter of this book, we identified the management functions of planning, organizing, leading, and controlling. We noted that these functions were applicable (as adapted to the particular situation) to all managerial situations. In this chapter, we have indicated that these functions are equally important and applicable in international management, although the environment in which the manager performs will differ. Now that we have discussed the most important environmental differences, it is time to focus our attention on the management functions.

[3] For an excellent account, see "Northrop Corporation: Development of a Policy on International Sales Commissions," in *Marketing and Society,* ed. R. D. Adler, L. M. Robinson, and J. E. Carlson (Englewood Cliffs, N.J.: Prentice-Hall, 1981), pp. 329–51.

[4] Henry Kissinger, "The Future of Business and the International Environment" (Address to the Future of Business Project for Strategic and International Studies at Georgetown University, Washington, D.C., June 28, 1977).

Planning

There would appear to be no reason why the types of objectives of an MNC should not be the same if it were operating only in the United States. The objectives of profitability, competitiveness, efficiency, and flexibility outlined in Chapter 3 are certainly valid objectives to pursue whether operating domestically or internationally.

Unfortunately, however, there is an important difference. There is potential for conflict between corporate objectives and objectives of the economic and political systems of the various countries in which the firm operates. This potential conflict exists because of the role played by government in planning in many nations. For example, the Ministry of International Trade and Industry in Japan plans that nation's economy to the point of specifying five-year percentage growth rates in exports of specific products.

In certain situations, therefore, it is possible that the country may have certain objectives, for example, an improved standard of living for its population, a favorable balance of payments, and economic growth, which may not coincide with the corporate objectives of the MNC. A common source of conflict is, when in order to achieve a profitability objective, some amount of earnings of a subsidiary must be returned to the headquarters of the MNC in the United States. This flow of earnings out of the country could have a negative impact on the balance of payments of the host country. It is because of this and similar-type conflicts that some nations place restrictions on MNCs. Bolivia, Chile, Colombia, Ecuador, and Peru for example, stipulate that a majority of the stock in manufacturing plants must be held by citizens of the host country within 20 years of the start of operations. The chief executive of a drug company offered the following observation on planning in an MNC:

> *In my opinion, the most exciting challenge in international management is planning. You face a completely new set of economic factors, business conditions, competition, and their impact on your business strategy. Developing plans to respond to these factors and still be consistent with corporate objectives is quite a challenge.*

As noted earlier, civil servants such as engineers, budget analysts, and other staff specialists hold influential positions in foreign governments. Thus, they often dominate the planning activities of many foreign nations. Managers of MNCs must be acquainted with the attitudes and practices of these individuals because it is they who often establish the conditions under which the managers must do their own planning. It is hoped that the economic power of the MNC and the political power of individuals in the host country result in accommodations whereby both partially achieve their objectives.

Organizing

We already know that the purpose of the organizing function is to provide a structure of jobs and authority for achieving organizational objectives as specified in the planning function. The planning function specifies *what* will be accomplished by *when*. Organizing specifies *who* will accomplish what and *how* it will be accomplished. As with planning in international management, organization structures must often be adapted to local conditions. A smooth functioning organization structure in the United States may not be so in another country.

MNCs employ the basic organizational structures discussed earlier in the book, that is, *functional, territorial, product,* and *customer.* Recently some have also began experimenting with the *matrix* design. The major difference, of course, would be the scope of operation. For example, in a *product* design, each product unit would be given international responsibilities. In a *territorial* design, a specific unit would be assigned to Europe, North America, South America, and so forth.

As is the case at home, no organization structure is suitable in all cases. Organization design is contingent on numerous factors as we discovered in Chapter 7. An MNC in a high-technology industry probably would not organize around territories, and one with relatively inexperienced managers would probably not use a product design.

One factor that apparently does influence the organizational design of an MNC is the degree to which the management is home-country oriented, host-country oriented, or world oriented. Thus, how the management views itself and the organization will influence how it organizes the firm in foreign countries. Figure 19–4 indicates how this orientation will influence the organizing function. Figure 19–4 also indicates the resulting impact the orientation will have on decision making, the management function of control, performance evaluation, and staffing.

Leading

Leadership approaches will vary in effectiveness across nations because styles of leadership and motivation incentives are influenced by a variety of factors. As with domestic organizations, the effective management of an MNC requires managers to understand the needs and expectations of the people in the nations in which they operate. In our discussion of culture earlier, we noted that attitudes toward work, competition in the workplace, and authority vary greatly among cultures. Thus, leadership styles that might be effective in America, Canada, Great Britain, and parts of Western Europe would probably not be in Mexico, Africa, Turkey, Taiwan, or South America. In other words, differences among cultures not only differ greatly, but so do the dominant needs of people in different countries. The impact of culture on the leading function was noted by an international product manager:

Figure 19–4

Management orientation and impact on the organizing function

Organizational design	Home-country oriented	Host-country oriented	World oriented
Complexity of organization	Complex in home country, simple in subsidiaries	Varied and independent	Increasingly complex and interdependent
Authority; decision making	High in headquarters	Relatively low in headquarters	Aim for a collaborative approach between headquarters and subsidiaries
Evaluation and control	Home standards applied for persons and performance	Determined locally	Find standards which are universal and local
Rewards and punishments; incentives	High in headquarters, low in subsidiaries	Wide variations; can be high or low rewards for subsidiary performance	International and local executives rewarded for reaching local and worldwide objectives
Communication; information flow	High volume to subsidiaries; orders, commands, advice	Little to and from headquarters, little between subsidiaries	Both ways, and between subsidiaries; heads of subsidiaries part of management team
Staffing, recruiting, development	Recruit and develop people of home country for key positions everywhere in the world	Develop people of local nationality for key positions in their own country	Develop best people everywhere in the world for key positions everywhere in the world

SOURCE: Adapted from Howard V. Perlmutter, "The Tortuous Evolution of the Multinational Corporation," *Columbia Journal of World Business,* January–February 1969, p. 12.

I find that effective communication and employee motivation directed at a common purpose are very difficult to achieve. I think this is because of differences in leadership style produced by differences in culture.

Nowhere is the difference in leadership styles more evident as it is in Japan. Since World War II, Japan has experienced increased prosperity, job security, and growing, successful, and stable business organizations. Seeking to discover the secrets of Japan's high productivity has become almost an obsession in U.S. business circles. New books and articles on the subject of Japanese labor management relations are appearing almost daily. While several reasons have been cited, there appears to be one upon which there is widespread agreement. It relates directly to leadership and is simply that Japanese managers *trust* not only their workers but also their peers and superiors.

Managers in Japan assume that the average person finds work natural and pleasant, is productive, and will exercise control. They believe, therefore, that suitable goals and reasonable motivation—never intimidation or threat—are appropriate for encouraging good work habits and the achievement of organizational objectives.[5] Apparently, the existence of this *trust* has resulted in simplified organizational structures which have helped Japanese companies become low-cost producers. There is no need to employ additional layers of high-paid executives whose only job is to review and pass on the work of other managers.

Clearly, the Japanese utilize with great effectiveness the Theory Y approach to motivation. This approach has enabled them to manage quite effectively without cadres of supervisors. For example, the presidents of two of Japan's larger companies, Quasar Co. and Matsushita Industrial Co., work with only one vice president and may have 10 or more managers reporting to them. The Japanese approach to the leading function is summarized very well in the following three statements:[6]

> Instinctively, the Japanese recognize that a Theory Y approach must be a two-way street. Japanese companies are as conscious of their employees' interests as they expect employees to be of theirs. Work force layoffs are rare, and similarly, Japanese managers are almost never pushed out. Promotions and raises are based as much on seniority and teamwork as on individual performance.
>
> The Japanese managers do not feel they must constantly cover themselves or be caught up in an individually competitive position to get ahead.

[5] Mitz Noda, "Business Management in Japan," *Technology Review*, June–July 1979, pp. 20–30.

[6] From "Trust: The New Ingredient in Management," *Business Week*, July 6, 1981, pp. 104–5.

There is pride and even sibling rivalry, but there is a family consciousness. Everyone believes that his colleagues and superiors care about his welfare.

This discussion of Japanese leadership approaches is not meant to imply that American approaches to leadership are inferior. Its purpose is to illustrate that what is effective in one nation may not be in another because of attitudes, values, and philosophy. It is interesting to note, however, that many individuals believe that improvements in productivity of American firms will only come about with changes in approaches in business leadership. This currently rather widely held opinion was strongly expressed by an executive of an automobile manufacturer.

For some reason which I do not understand, our government spends next to nothing studying how to effectively manage people at work. However, it continues to spend for technological and economic research. Unfortunately, in my opinion, the same old solutions are not going to solve our nation's productivity problems. They will be solved when we learn how to manage people more effectively.

Controlling

Evaluating and controlling performance is extremely important in MNCs. Obviously, the more global the operation, the more difficult the controlling function becomes. The control concepts discussed in earlier chapters are also applicable to MNCs; however, the control function is not used in some countries to the same degree it is used in the United States because of cultural differences. For example, such things as performance appraisals and quality control may have little meaning in certain countries. The implementation of control in the international environment requires the same three basic conditions required domestically: standards, information, and action.

In establishing **standards** for MNCs, consideration must be given to overall corporate objectives but also to local conditions. This often involves bringing local managers into the planning process. As citizens of the country in which they work, these individuals can provide the type of input which can be used in establishing standards of performance which contribute to organizational objectives without causing interculture conflict.

Information which reports actual performance and which permits appraisal of that performance against standards must be provided. Problems can occur here which may not appear in domestic organizations. For example, should profitability be measured in local currency or the home currency? The value of different currencies may result in the headquarters arriving at different performance measures than local managers. Finally, long distances can fill information systems with a great deal of irrelevant information or too much information. Management information systems must be designed or altered to minimize the amount of information necessary for control.

Managerial **action** to correct deviations is the final step of the controlling function. The range of possibilities is between total centralization of decisions where all operating decisions are made at corporate headquarters to a situation where international units are independent and autonomous. In the majority of cases, most action is taken by international managers with specific guidelines from corporate headquarters.[7] Effective managerial control of a global enterprise is extremely important but at the same time extremely complex. One difficulty was outlined clearly by a vice president for international affairs.

> *My major concern is establishing the limits of authority for foreign operations so that the managers onsite have sufficient control. You want some control at headquarters, but you also do not want to delay the process of decision making by forcing managers into frequent consultations up through the corporate chain of command.*

The MNC and the contingency approach to management

The MNC is the type of organization that virtually demands a contingency approach to management. In fact, it presents a special challenge to managers. Effective managerial performance in the international environment requires the manager to give careful consideration to the same factors we outlined in the opening section of the book. In this chapter, we have seen how performance of the planning, organizing, leading, and controlling functions can be influenced by the peculiarities of the environment in which the manager performs. The fact is what works in one part of the globe may be a failure or worse, disastrous, in another part. The contingency approach to management with its emphasis on adaptability will be the key to effective international management. Consider the following statement by the vice president of the international division of a tool manufacturer:

[7] See Guvene G. Alpander, "Multinational Corporations: Hombase-Affiliate Relations," *California Management Review,* Spring 1978, pp. 47–53, for some examples.

In my opinion, the effective international manager of the future will possess three distinct skills. First, extremely good general management skills—planning, organization, motivation, and control. Second, language skills. Third, and perhaps most important, high cultural understanding and adaptability.

Management summary

1. The global enterprise, or MNC, presents a challenge to future managers. That challenge is performing effectively the management functions in an international environment.
2. The decision to become an MNC is very often a gradual sequence of stages. Each stage—exporting, establishing a foreign subsidiary, direct investment—involves greater involvement in, and commitment to, becoming a global enterprise.
3. The management functions of planning, organizing, leading, and controlling will be the same in international management. However, the differences among peoples may be such that international managers may be forced to learn special environmental factors and institutions or to change their basic assumptions about people, organizations, and management.
4. Culture, economics, and politics are likely to be the environmental factors that will differ in international management.
5. Differences in culture can result in differing attitudes toward the importance of work, authority, competition, introducing change, authority, material possessions, risk taking, and profits. These attitudes can influence the effective performance of the managerial functions.
6. Economic factors such as income levels, growth trends, inflation rates, economic planning, balance of payments, and the stability of the currency and overall economy can vary widely between nations. Each can influence organizational performance.
7. Political differences can have a great impact on organizational performance in an MNC. In fact, it is difficult to separate politics and the MNC. The attitudes in host countries toward imports and direct investment, the stability of government, and the efficiency of government vary widely between nations. Each may also change rapidly in those nations where governments change rapidly.
8. The MNC requires a contingency approach to management. The contingency approach to management with its emphasis on adaptability will be the key to effective international management.

Review and discussion questions

1. What are the major factors which cause a business to become involved in international business? Discuss and give examples where possible.
2. Relate the discussion of the contingency approach to management (Chapter 1) to managing an MNC.
3. "How effective an individual is in international management will be determined by how well he or she can adjust to local conditions." Discuss.
4. Do you believe that you would be effective in an overseas assignment? If so, discuss why. If not, identify and discuss the reasons why.
5. Much is presently being written on the differences between Japanese and American styles of management. Consult the business publications in your library and contrast the two styles of management.
6. Culture, economics, and politics are three environmental factors that greatly influence managerial performance in an MNC. Are these factors unimportant for a manager operating solely in the United States? Discuss.
7. Briefly discuss the three alternative entry strategies a firm may use in international management.
8. Would the social responsibility aspects of managerial actions differ between domestic and international managers? Discuss.
9. Discuss the applicability of the management functions of planning, organizing, leading, and controlling to international management.
10. What features do you believe the United States has which might make it attractive to foreign multinationals?

Suggested reading

Bradway, M. K. "Styles of Mideastern Managers." *California Management Review,* Spring 1980, pp. 51–58.

Galbraith, J. K. "The Defense of the Multinational Company." *Harvard Business Review,* March 1978, pp. 83–93.

Ouchi, W. *Theory Z: How American Business Can Meet the Japanese Challenge.* Reading, Mass.: Addison-Wesley Publishing, 1981.

Pascale, R. T., and A. G. Athos. *The Art of Japanese Management: Applications for American Executives.* New York: Simon & Schuster, 1981.

Schonberger, R. J. "The Transfer of Japanese Manufacturing Management Approaches to U.S. Industry." *Academy of Management Review,* July 1982, pp. 479–87.

Tanaka, H. "The Japanese Method of Preparing Today's Graduate to Become Tomorrow's Manager." *Personnel Journal,* February 1980, pp. 109–12.

Applying what you have learned about managing the multinational company

Case:

General Metropolitan Ltd., expands to the United States

General Metropolitan Ltd., expands to the United States*

In 1948, Sir Maxwell Joseph purchased a hotel in London. From that beginning, he has build General Metropolitan Ltd., into one of Great Britain's largest and most diversified companies. In 1980, it achieved $6.2 billion in sales from a broad range of businesses: hotels, liquor, food, gaming, and leisure products. In fact, the company has been so successful that Sir Maxwell Joseph has decided it is too big for Great Britain. In 1980, 88 percent of its profits came from its home base, and it has been blocked by law from making any new significant acquisitions. Besides, Great Britain's economy holds little promise for growth anyway.

As a result, Grand Met has decided to enter the largest consumer market in the world: the United States. In 1980, Grand Met acquired Liggett Group Inc., which will be its vehicle for expansion into the United States. Liggett is a consumer-oriented firm, with Liggett & Myers Tobacco Company, Alpo dog food, sporting goods operations, and soft drink bottling and liquor distribution businesses.

Grand Met has a three-part plan for expansion in the United States. First, it hopes to broaden its U.S. sales of liquor which includes Grand Met's own brands such as J&B Rare scotch. Second, Liggett will be the base for adding companies in the food ingredients industry (it has already added three U.S. ingredient producers). Third, it plans to buy upper-class hotels in major U.S. cities and

---

* This case is adapted from "Grand Metropolitan: A British Giant Expands into U.S. Consumer Markets," *Business Week,* August 24, 1981, pp. 54, 59.

convert them to the Grand Met format that has been successful in Great Britain and Europe.

Grand Met management believes that its expertise in consumer markets will be an asset to it in the United States. However, it plans to use U.S. management, which is a new approach for Grand Met. During the 1970s, Grand Met attempted direct expansions into Italy and France. It was unable to compete with local industry. An executive stated, "We learned the sheer danger of assuming you can understand another country from here. We learned you have got to go in and make a partnership."

At present, Grand Met has made no major management changes in Liggett, although its top executive is expected to soon retire. Most observers agree that in keeping with its policy of decentralized, local management, Grand Met will replace the top executive with a U.S. manager rather than a British manager.

Questions:

1. What is your opinion of Grand Met's entry strategy into foreign markets? What other approaches could it have used? Do they offer any advantages?
2. What is your opinion of Grand Met's policy of utilizing local managers? Can you foresee any problems?
3. What are some of the problems Grand Met faced before the acquisition and will face as a result of the acquisition that are similar to those faced by American MNCs?

20

Chapter twenty Managing work-related stress

Performance objectives

- **Define** what is meant by the term *work stress.*
- **State** what the term *Type A behavior pattern* means.
- **Describe** why we are not able to state that stress *causes* illness.
- **Explain** the inverted-J explanation of stress and performance.
- **Discuss** different types of stressors that may produce a stress response in some individuals.

Management update*

This is a true account provided by Frederick B. Michael about his stay in a coronary care unit.

A coronary care unit is a strange place. It is a vast jungle of electronic equipment, with medical technicians who move around the unit very quietly so that the most noticeable noise is that of various unseen beeps and buzzes apparently coming from the huge computerized console in the center of the unit. As you lie there watching the incessant display of your heartbeat on the monitor beside your bed (I wonder if doctors know how disconcerting those things are to the patient), you realize that you can alter the pattern traced on the screen just by raising and lowering your arm (it's amazing what you will do to entertain yourself when there is very little to do). You never realize just how much salt adds to the taste of food until you sample the hospital's salt-free "cuisine."

You constantly are told to rest, but I never did figure out how they thought that was possible, since they check your blood pressure and temperature quite frequently. I did figure out how they entertain themselves. They wait until you fall asleep, and then they send in the lab technicians for a blood sample. Wild thoughts race through your mind. You wonder if their work performance is measured in average patients cared for and if they are keeping your blood supply purposely low so they can keep you from moving to the regular care unit and not hurt their performance statistics. I've always loved to sleep on my stomach, but you learn quickly that you can't roll over completely without half-strangling yourself in the assorted wires and intravenous tubes attached to you. You also would be surprised at how long you can go when a bedpan is your only source of relief. What you do is stare at the ceiling a lot and wonder how you got there, and how it is going to affect your life. According to my cardiologist, I got there because of too much stress.

In retrospect, I should have seen some of the symptoms, such as the periods of extreme hypertension and several incidents of severe vertigo, but I ignored them, falsely assuming I was indestructible. I was slightly past 40 at the time of my attack—mild coronary problems—the first week of October.

As I found out, stress affects the individual and the organization he or she works for. What is work-induced stress, and what can be done to minimize it?

---

* Adapted from Frederick B. Michael, "Stress: Race to the Bottom Line," *Management Accounting*, April 1981, pp. 15–20.

The poet W. H. Auden has called ours the Age of Anxiety. Actually, he fixed that label on our times more than 30 years ago; since then inflation, shortages, unemployment, and societal revolutions—among other changes—have compounded the anxieties of everyday life. The Age of Anxiety is, in the 1980s, being retitled the Age of Stress.

This chapter is about work-related stress. Specifically, we will examine occupational or work-related stress. Since work is a major part of our lives, it contains the potential for many forms of gratification and challenge—as well as harm. Work, life, and family stress are so interrelated that it is somewhat artificial to separate them in any discussion. However, we elect to focus on the work stress that each of us feels, experiences, and reacts to every day.

First, let's take a brief stress quiz. Please answer the 10 questions and then read on. We will provide the answers a little later in the chapter.

Stress Fact or Fiction Quiz

How much do you know about stress? Answer the following statements to test your knowledge:

1. *People who feel stress are nervous to start with. True or False?*
2. *You always know when you're under stress. True or False?*
3. *Prolonged physical exercise will weaken your resistance to stress. True or False?*
4. *Stress is always bad. True or False?*
5. *Stress can cause unpleasant problems, but at least it can't kill you. True or False?*
6. *Stress can be controlled with medication. True or False?*
7. *Work-related stress can be left at the office and not brought home. True or False?*
8. *Stress is only in the mind; it's not physical. True or False?*
9. *Stress can be eliminated. True or False?*

10. *There's nothing you can do about stress without making drastic changes in your lifestyle. True or False?*

What is stress?

The word *stress* has been defined in medical, biological, engineering, and behavioral terms. One popular definition claims that stress is the force acting on a person that causes discomfort or pain.[1] This definition doesn't indicate how individuals subjected to the same force may react differently.

Another definition states that stress is the response an individual makes to stressors. A **stressor** is an event or situation that may be harmful. Again, individual differences in response are not recognized in this definition.

A third definition claims that **stress is the consequence of the interaction between an event or situation and the individual.**[2] This definition focuses on a person's response to potential stressors. The response can be positive or negative. An important determining factor is the individual, his or her perceptions, experiences, and ability to cope with the potential stressors.

In a stress-management training program, we asked participants to list on a three-by-five index card examples of work stress. The lists helped shape the initial discussions in the training program. They also reveal that the third definition—the one that addresses the interaction of the person and the environment—makes a lot of sense. A few of the cards read:

Stress is:

> Not knowing how well I'm doing on my job.
>
> Being afraid of losing my job.
>
> Having to work and interact with an incompetent boss.
>
> Knowing that the company is not going to remain competitive in the market.
>
> Having to make promotion choices and then tell good people they weren't promoted.
>
> Not being able to relax after work. I'm always thinking about the job.

Most of the cards tend to portray stress in negative or unpleasant terms. Of course stress has a positive side. We are stressed when we receive a promotion, a raise, personal recognition, asked to give a speech, receive

[1] T. Cox, *Stress* (Baltimore: University of Park Press, 1978), p. 15.

[2] John M. Ivancevich and Michael T. Matteson, *Stress and Work: A Managerial Perspective* (Glenview, Ill.: Scott, Foresman, 1980), pp. 8–9.

a gift, embrace a loved one. We have said that stress is a consequence of the interaction between an event or situation and the individual. Whether stress is positive or negative depends on the person and how he or she interprets and responds to the event or situation. In this chapter, we will address primarily negative interpretations or responses that affect performance and other work outcomes.

Researchers have shown that moderate levels of work stress can be beneficial. At moderate levels, employees remain alert to the event or situation.[3] This point is important to remember. Working without stress is not a goal of management or an individual. As Hans Selye has aptly stated, "Life without stress is death."[4] On the other hand, life with too much stress can mean problems.

Returning to our Stress Quiz. The correct answers for all 10 questions is False. If you answered True to even one, you're a victim of a stress myth.

General adaptation syndrome

Two medical researchers discovered in 1943 a man named Tom who was forced, through the circumstances of a freak accident, to live most of his adult life with his stomach open and connected to the surface of his body.[5] They found that Tom's moods, feelings, and even his thoughts had a significant effect on his stomach function. In one reported example, the researchers were working with Tom about 24 hours after he'd had a particularly unpleasant encounter with a hospital administrator. During preparation for one experiment, Tom began to relate his argument with the administrator to the researchers. As he relived the incident, the redness of Tom's stomach lining, the volume of free stomach acid, and the acid secretion all increased.

The researchers made an effort to have Tom's attention diverted from what was a stressful encounter with the administrator. Within 30 minutes, most of the stomach conditions had reversed themselves. This early pioneering research demonstrated that mental, emotional, and behavioral events have an impact on the body. The body is alarmed and responds.

The pattern of alarm and response is termed the **general adaptation syndrome.** The syndrome has three stages:

[3] J. Horn, "Peak Performance—The Factors that Produce It," *Psychology Today* (1978), p. 110; and A. T. Welford, "Stress and Performance," *Ergonomics* (1973), pp. 567–80.

[4] Hans Selye, *The Stress of Life,* 2d ed. (New York: McGraw-Hill, 1976), p. 12.

[5] Stewart Wolf and Harold G. Wolff, *Gastric Function: An Experimental Study of a Man and His Stomach* (New York: Oxford University Press, 1943).

1. *Alarm* When the body is initially stressed, it responds with an alarm reaction; it mobilizes. This is the stage that was observed in Tom.
2. *Resistance* After a persistent and prolonged exposure to a stressful situation, the body begins to resist its alarm reaction.
3. *Exhaustion* If the stress continues too long or if the stress load increases substantially, the body goes on alert again. This second arousal reaction continues until the defenses are drained or exhausted. If the stress remains unabated, the only remaining outcome is death.

Two points should be made about the general adaptation syndrome (GAS). First, few people reach the exhaustion stage. Arctic explorers, people trapped in a coal mine, exessively abused prisoners of war reach the exhaustion stage, but not typical employees in General Electric, IBM, Proctor & Gamble or other organizations. Second, even when a person reaches the exhaustion stage, he or she is seldom in any immediate danger—unless, of course, he or she chooses not to heed, or can't heed, the built-in warning signals to slow down.

Consequences of stress

The mobilization of the body's defense mechanisms are not the only consequences of stress. Rather, there are a series of consequences which can result.[6] They are:

Subjective effects: anxiety, guilt, moodiness, low self-esteem, and fatigue.

Behavioral effects: accident proneness, increased drug use or alcohol intake, impaired speech, and emotional outbursts.

Cognitive effects: inability to make timely decisions, forgetfulness, mental blocks.

Physiological effects: increased heart rate and breathing, dryness of mouth, elevated blood pressure.

Organizational effects: increased absenteeism, poorer productivity, increased job dissatisfaction.

These five categories of possible effects of stress have not been proven beyond doubt. They are suggested by the research being conducted on work stress. The possibility that work-induced stress is a direct or indirect contributor to these effects is why managers are studying the topic. They want to understand and explain the impact of work stress on their employees and themselves. The five categories of the possible effects of stress

[6] Seyle, *The Stress of Life.*

are each important. However, managers pay more attention to a few specific consequence areas such as health, alcoholism, smoking, drug abuse, absenteeism and turnover, and performance.

Stress and health

Of all the possible consequences of stress, the physical health effects are perhaps the most challenging, controversial, and debilitating. Years ago, those who boldly suggested a relationship between stress and physical disease were, more often than not, ignored. Today, virtually no health authority would deny a link between stress and disease. Most current medical textbooks, for example, attribute from 50 to 70 percent of illness to stress-related origins.

Stress contributes to ill health and feeling below par. The stresses encountered on the job add up. Most of these stresses, as individual events, have no impact on health. However, it seems important to consider the stress-health connection in terms of the duration of the stressors. Figure 20–1 breaks down stress events in terms of duration.

The important point to keep in mind is that an ongoing stream of relatively minor stresses, none of which by themselves are particularly harmful, can

Figure 20–1

Duration of stress events

How long an event remains stressful is important. Duration can be determined from the following categories:

Short stress situations. This category includes the many, usually mild, stress situations that almost everyone faces daily. It includes enduring of traffic jams, sitting next to a smoker, and receiving criticism. Their common denominator is their duration; they are events lasting from a few seconds to a few hours at most. Unless you experience a continuous chain of these events, the stress they provoke is unlikely to cause significant harm.

Moderate stress situations. These are events which last from several hours to a number of days. Examples are periods of work overload, new job responsibilities, a continuing unresolved disagreement with a family member, and other events of moderate duration. This category is important to your health in the role it may play in precipitating the onset of physical problems where a predisposition already exists.

Severe stress situations. These are chronic situations. They may last weeks, months, or even years. Examples include sustained reactions to the death of a loved one, protracted financial difficulties, prolonged physical illnesses, and inordinate and sustained demands in a work situation. While there is no certainty that these severe stress situations will lead inevitably to negative health outcomes, evidence strongly implicates stress as a contributor.

produce negative health outcomes. Ideally, your body and mind adapt perfectly to each and every stressor. In reality, however, perfection in adapting is rarely achieved. Instead, diseases of adaptation are the result of your imperfect attempt(s) to meet the threat of stressors.

The diseases of adaptation are sometimes referred to as *postponable diseases.* They include hypertension, heart disease, rheumatoid arthritis, inflammatory diseases of the skin, ulcers, headaches, mental malfunction, some sexual dysfunction, and other similar diseases of resistance.[7]

Does stress really cause all these diseases? To say that stress is *the* cause of a particular disease is much like saying that the alcohol consumed by the driver was the cause of an automobile accident. It would be safer to say that alcohol contributed to the accident. The stress and disease link is similar. Stress appears to be a contributor to the early onset of postponable diseases.

In 1981, over one million people died from forms of coronary heart disease. This disease has been linked to over 52 million lost workdays annually. Stress is implicated in coronary heart disease. We know that stress tends to increase the frequency of heart beat.[8] The faster the heart rate, the greater the heart's requirements for oxygenated blood. Stressors such as heavy work loads, time pressures, and responsibility for people elevate the heart's activities and demands. These demands strain the heart muscle unless it is in excellent shape.

Of course, a manager isn't expected to understand how the heart muscle functions. But he or she can be expected to understand that heart disease means more days absent, disability, reduced performance. The bill for stress and health is high. A conservative estimate is that stress-related diseases cost industry over $100 billion annually. This represents about 10 percent of the gross national product.[9]

Absenteeism and turnover

Absenteeism and turnover are ways that some workers use to withdraw from stressful jobs. One survey found that while there has been a 22 percent increase in a 15-year period attributable to physical diseases, absenteeism attributable to psychological problems, many of which are job stress related, increased by 152 percent for men and 302 percent for women.[10] Absenteeism and turnover add to the costs of production.

---

[7] Cox, *Stress.*

[8] For a discussion of health and disease, see John M. Ivancevich and Michael T. Matteson, "Optimizing Human Resources: A Case for Preventive Health and Stress Management," *Organizational Dynamics,* Autumn 1980, pp. 5–25.

[9] Berkeley Rice, "Can Companies Kill?" *Psychology Today,* June 1981, pp. 78, 80–85.

[10] Frances M. Stern and Ron Zemke, *Stressless Selling* (Englewood Cliffs, N.J.: Prentice-Hall, 1981), pp. 273–74.

Figure 20–2

Performance and stress

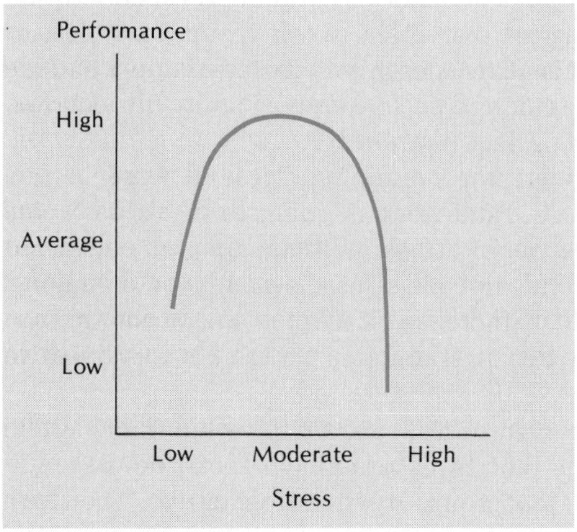

Performance

A major concern of any manager are the effects of work stress on job performance. The performance relationship is not simple. People are different, situations vary, and management's impact on performance differs. The relationship is similar to an inverted-J curve, as presented in Figure 20–2. When work stress is low, employees work at their regular or current levels of performance. At a moderate stress level, employees are motivated to increase their performance. The challenge of solving a problem, making a difficult sale, pushes the person to performance. Under a condition of high stress, performance decreases. The person pays attention to the stress and not job performance.

Furthermore, it is difficult to predict the effects of stress on performance without knowing a person's tolerance for stress. What are moderate and high levels of stress? This is why we caution against quick answers about the stress-performance relationship. The inverted-J curve is simply offered to show a general picture of the relationship. Individual differences should never be excluded from a manager's analysis and interpretation of stress-performance links.

A stress framework

We have talked in general terms about work stress, but what is really needed is a focused view. One way of outlining such a view is to use a framework which will identify specific causes and consequences of stress.

Such a framework should include the relationship between the individual's personality and the organization's policies and practices. Consideration of the person without examining job variables, work group variables, or career variables is insufficient. It is also necessary to include factors outside of work which influence job behavior and performance. Family life, community activities, and leisure habits affect one's work.

Figure 20–3 presents a framework for examining stress at work. A few points should be made. First, any framework is going to leave out some important causes and consequences of stress; neither comprehensive nor total coverage is possible. Second, not all stress is costly or damaging. When stress is linked to alcoholism, increased absenteeism, or poor performance, it is costly. However, when it stimulates or results in a push to do a better job, it is beneficial.

The framework presented in Figure 20–3 should be read from left to right, A, B, C, D. What it says is this: Stressors at work can be placed in one of five categories—physical, job, group, organization, career. The stressors outside of work interact with these work stressors. Stressors are interpreted by each employee. What is stress for one may be pure excitement for a co-worker. Each individual has a built-in stress-processing network that helps determine when stress is excessive. The built-in network is displayed in the form of individual characteristics (B). Personality, needs, values, and mental view of work (C) influence the way a person interprets stressors.

Finally, the framework distinguishes between three sets of potential results of stress (D). There are physical, psychological, and organizational results to be considered. Each is important and each is potentially costly.

Stressful occupations: Fact or Fiction?

Certain occupations are thought to be more stressful than others. There is some evidence that the stressful consequences of these occupations can be measured. The measurement of the results of stress typically looks at the type of factors shown in Figure 20–3.

Some studies show that stressors such as responsibility for people, work overload, time pressure, and family responsibilities contribute to physical, psychological, and organizational problems. It is important to recognize that whether these stressors actually become stressful depends on the way people interpret them. Every occupation has its own unique stress for some people. In fact, there is no such thing as a sample of stressful occupations. All occupations have people who are highly stressed, become ill, quit work, and even try to hurt themselves. They also have people who are not stressed, are happy, and enjoy life. Let's first look at two frequently studied occupations.

The intensive care nurse A nurse in the intensive-care unit of a hospital is often present when patients die. This is what intensive care nursing is

Figure 20–3

Stress framework*

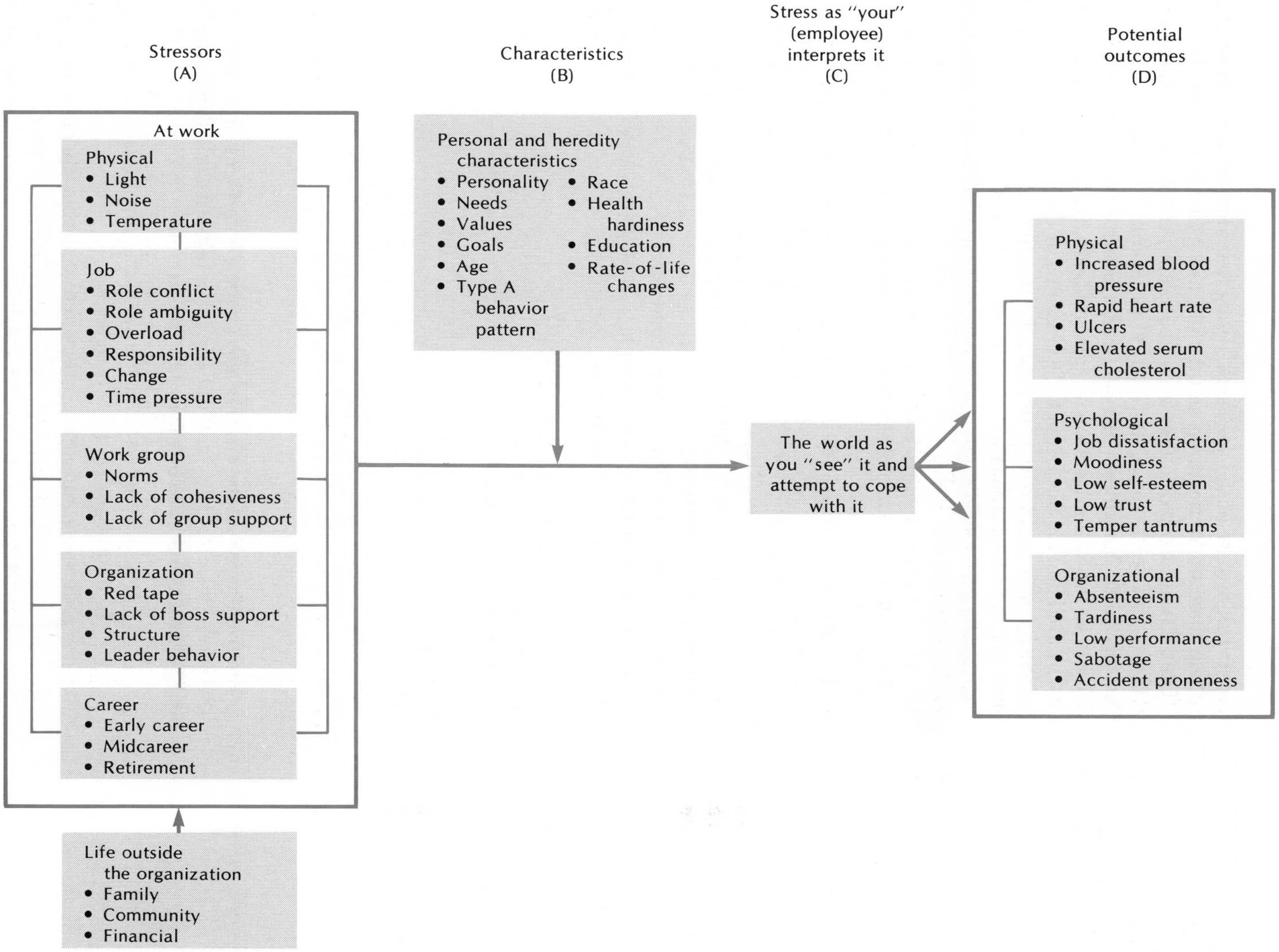

* Adapted from Michael T. Matteson and John M. Ivancevich, *Managing Job Stress and Health* (New York: Macmillan, 1982).

about. Taking care of the very sick, trying to make them comfortable, trying to help them maintain some self-dignity are parts of the job.

On a day-to-day basis, they are exposed to people with problems, people with life-and-death struggles. This takes its toll.

The air traffic controller An air traffic controller in one of the busiest airports in the United States directs landings every 30 seconds and near misses are common occurrences. Avoidance of the disasters requires quick thinking and a cool head. The flow of aircraft is never ending; controllers must be alert at all times.

The jobs of nurse and air traffic controller are usually considered high-stress occupations. There are, however, others in these same occupations who are not experiencing these difficulties. Similarly, other so-called low-stress occupations harbor many people who are highly stressed.

Think, for example, about the stress potential of individuals in some of the underpublicized, yet very important occupations:

- Salesperson (especially car or insurance salesperson in a declining economy).
- Medical technologist.
- Oil rig worker.
- Stockbroker/investment counselor.
- Steelworker in an economically depressed area of the country (Chicago, Youngstown, Pittsburgh).
- Nuclear power plant employee.
- Secretary.
- Filing clerk.

The important point being made here is that the degree of stress and its consequences depend to a large extent on the person. In some occupations, there may be a higher frequency of problems, but in all occupations, from performing janitorial service to conducting delicate coronary surgery, there are some individuals who are stressed.

Points to remember

The framework offered in this section can help focus attention on stress at work. It can also help point out a number of issues which have individual and organizational importance. The issues are:

- Stressors play a role in the onset of many physical, psychological, and organizational problems.
- Stressors and stress are different things. Stress at work is perceived by each of us in a very personal way.
- Individual characteristics such as needs, values, and personality play a role in the outset of physical, psychological, and organizational problems.

Stressors outside of work are associated with stress at work and vice versa. Realistically, we can't neatly separate family and work or economic conditions and work.

Some sources of work-related stress

The stress framework, Figure 20–3, draws from numerous behavioral and medical research studies. Coverage of all potential sources of work stress is not possible. Instead, we highlight a few in each major category (A and B) of the framework.

Organizational structure

Organization structure refers to the arrangement of jobs and work units. Where an employee's job is located in the arrangement can affect the kinds of stressors experienced. If a person is at the top level (president or vice president), he or she may be stressed by competition, winning a new market share, not receiving a large order from a customer, or some new government regulations restricting the sale of your firm's product. If an employee's job is at the middle level (supervisor, district manager), he or she may be stressed by requests received from the the top, complaints from the next lower level, and not having qualified subordinates and enough say in decision making. If an employee is at the lower level (first-level supervisor, clerk, machinist), he or she is probably stressed by too many policies, lack of support from the immediate boss, and not being able to participate in decisions that affect the job.

Studies indicate that low participation or little say in important decisions is associated with job dissatisfaction, low self-esteem, and high absenteeism. It also results in less flow of important information between employees.[11]

Change

One of the most common work situations producing discomfort and stress is organizational change.[12] *Stress* and *change* are almost synonymous

[11] J. R. P. French and R. D. Caplan, "Organizational Stress and Individual Strain," in *The Failure of Success,* ed. Alfred J. Marrow (New York: AMACOM, 1972).

[12] The remainder of the discussion on sources is adapted and modified based on Michael T. Matteson and John M. Ivancevich, *Managing Job Stress and Health* (New York: Macmillan, 1982).

terms. Change often disrupts the flow of work as well as relationships between people. Even a change for the better, like new equipment or opening a brand new building or the purchase of a new computer system, is perceived by some as a stressor. What is lost are familiar patterns of doing a job. The loss is coupled with the demand to do things differently.

Another potential source of stressful change is one which is unilaterally declared. The organizational structure provides a chain of command. The "commander," the boss, may too often impose or declare that a change *will* take place. A typical reaction is to fight, resist, and sometimes to sabotage the declared change.

Leader behavior

The behavior of leaders can be an important influence on the frequency, intensity, and duration of stressors. The leader's influence comes from both personal attributes and his or her position of authority and power. Leaders behave differently. Some know how to work with people, others are technical wizards, and others can blend abilities, dealing with people and technical matters equally well. The behavior of some leaders evokes stress, while some relieves stress.

Role conflict

When a person is faced with a situation in which two or more pressures are working against each other, role conflict exists. Role conflict is often discussed in terms of whether it is objective or subjective. When role conflict is objective, it means that actual contradictory requests or signals are being sent. On the other hand, role conflict is subjective when there is conflict between the requirements of the role as the person sees them and his or her needs, goals, and values. For example, a saleswoman who must sell products to do well on her performance appraisal feels conflict because she is selling to many customers who neither need nor can really afford the product.

Role ambiguity

Role ambiguity is not being certain about a job role; that is, what one is supposed to be accomplishing. The person's part in the job is just not clear. The consequences of transient ambiguity are minimal—some confusion, some frustration, but nothing very serious.

Chronic ambiguity is another issue. It means having to live in a work environment where one is usually or frequently unclear about the job, what he or she is doing, and why. Chronic role ambiguity sets off a negative stress response. The outcomes of such a response include lowered job satisfaction, depression, moodiness, lowered self-esteem, increased propensity to leave the job, alienation, and elevated blood pressure.

Work overload

It has been stated that "The greatest stress is one that keeps an individual constantly feeling impatient, constantly hurrying, and giving him the feeling that he has not done everything he feels he should have done in a single working day." These words capture what is meant by work overload. It is not only the projects that keep piling up. It is also biting off more than one can chew, not being able to say no to one more project or request.

A case of work overload is described by a computer programmer:

> *I had at least five new requests on my desk every morning when I came to work. I prided myself on helping everyone, doing as much as possible. Throughout the day, I interrupted my work to answer telephone requests for help and questions from my colleagues. This meant working late, getting home after 8:00 P.M., and eating on the run when I could. It also meant less time to spend with my family and not being able to skydive on weekends. Weekends are now catchup days; I go in to work to catch up. In the past two months, I have had insomnia, backaches, and headaches.*

Quantitative work overload exists when a person has too many different things to do or an insufficient amount of time to do the job, to act out the role. On the other hand, there is also **qualitative overload.** That is, feeling a lack of ability to do a part of the job.

Working conditions

Working conditions include all aspects of the setting in which an employee performs the job. These settings vary from the executive suite in a corporation to the operating room in a hospital or a boiler room in a public utility generator plant. The potential stressors include physical discomfort, inequities in facilities, noise, odors, air pollution, suffering general neglect, hot, cold, dark, depressing, and drafty.

For most white-collar occupations, working conditions have improved over the years. There are still, however, some poor conditions present in some white-collar and many blue-collar jobs. Stress, due to working conditions experienced by the manager of a personnel department, was expressed this way:

> *You know, everyone knows how beautiful this area is. But for nine hours a day, everyone is in the* tomb [a term used to describe the personnel department's office

area]. *There are no windows anywhere. It would make a good air-raid shelter, but it sure is depressing otherwise. We can't see a thing. It is dark and isolated..*

Inadequate group support

Social support exists when a person has a relationship with one or more other people which includes frequent interactions, positive feelings, and understanding. There are no isolation rooms or solitary confinement cells in organizations, but an employee can experience a lack of social support. Not following norms, being sent to a remote area or site to work, the breaking up of a cohesive group are all circumstances which can lead to a reduction or elimination of social support. For some, the ability to interact, to experience social support, is a necessary and attractive feature of work; for others, interaction is an obligation or a meaningless exercise. Individual differences play a role in how social support or lack of it affects behavior.

The social support offered by a group comes in many forms. Encouragement, recognition, status, communication, and understanding are all potential supportive features of group affiliation. In addition, reinforcement of needs, values, opinions, and beliefs can occur via receipt of support from groups with which one affiliates on the job. These are especially heightened in a cohesive group.

Some personal sources of stress

The stress framework in Figure 20–3 presents a set of personal and hereditary characteristics. Two especially important ones are the Type A behavior pattern and the rate-of-life changes.

Type A behavior pattern

Of all the health problems that have been associated with stress, coronary heart disease has received the most attention. No doubt this is due in large part to the epidemic nature of the disease. Coronary heart disease and related cardiovascular problems such as stroke lead the list of killer diseases in this country. It is probably not coincidental that there has also been greater interest in the relationship between behavior pattern dimensions and heart disease than is the case for any other illness.

In the 1950s, two California cardiologists, Meyer Friedman and Ray Rosenman, began the development of an approach to predict coronary disease which focused not on medical records or history but on how people interact with their environment. Out of this research grew what has come to be called the *coronary-prone behavior pattern,* or *Type A behavior pattern.* People who exhibit characteristics of this behavior pattern are classified as Type A individuals; those who do not have these characteristics are known as Type B.

In their book, *Type A Behavior and Your Heart,* Friedman and Rosenman described the coronary-prone behavior pattern, or Type A, as representing "an action-emotion complex that can be observed in any person who is aggressively involved in a chronic, incessant struggle to achieve more and more in less and less time, and if required to do so, against the opposing efforts of other things or other persons."[13]

Major facets of Type A behavior include a chronic sense of time urgency, a hard-driving and competitive orientation which probably includes some hostility, a strong dislike for being idle, and chronic impatience for people and situations which are seen as blocking efforts to get things accomplished.

It has been frequently suggested that stress and Type A behavior are synonymous, that Type A individuals are experiencing a great deal of stress, while their more relaxed easygoing Type B counterparts seldom become upset or experience stress; actually this isn't true. The underlying assumption that Type Bs are easygoing, laid-back individuals is itself wrong. Type Bs may be every bit as goal oriented as Type As, and they may be equally desirous of success and achievement. The difference is that the Type B person seeks satisfaction of those needs in a way which does not create the internal psychological and physiological havoc to which the Type A is subjected.

There is little question, however, that there is a link between Type A behavior and negative stress. Why is this true? Researchers don't know for certain, but the most commonly advanced explanation goes something like this: If you are a Type A person, by virtue of your characteristic behavior, you are increasing the likelihood of exposure to certain stressors (such as work overload) while at the same time you are decreasing your resistance to stress (through refusal or inability to relax, slow down, etc.) Thus, as a Type A, you create stress for yourself by constantly exposing yourself to stressors which your Type B counterpart avoids.

Figure 20–4 shows how to grade yourself on Type A behavior. The scoring system is given later in the chapter.

Rate-of-life changes

Researchers studied the effects of major life changes of over 5,000 patients suffering from stress-related illness.[14] As a result, they developed a variety of life change events that are associated with the onset of illness. Figure

[13] M. Friedman and R. H. Rosenman, *Type A Behavior and Your Heart* (New York: Alfred A. Knopf, 1974).

[14] T. H. Holmes and R. H. Rahe, "The Social Readjustment Rating Scale," *Journal of Psychosomatic Medicine* (1967), pp. 213–18.

Figure 20–4

Your Type A behavior

Please circle the number which you feel most closely represents your own behavior:

1.	Never late	5 4 3 2 1 0 1 2 3 4 5	Casual about appointments
2.	Not competitive	5 4 3 2 1 0 1 2 3 4 5	Very competitive
3.	Anticipates what others are going to say (nods, interrupts, finishes for them)	5 4 3 2 1 0 1 2 3 4 5	Good listener
4.	Always rushed	5 4 3 2 1 0 1 2 3 4 5	Never feels rushed (even under pressure)
5.	Can wait patiently	5 4 3 2 1 0 1 2 3 4 5	Impatient while waiting
6.	Always works hard	5 4 3 2 1 0 1 2 3 4 5	Is able to relax
7.	Takes things one at a time	5 4 3 2 1 0 1 2 3 4 5	Tries to do many things at once; thinks what he is about to do next
8.	Emphatic in speech (may pound desk)	5 4 3 2 1 0 1 2 3 4 5	Slow, deliberate talker
9.	Wants good job recognized by others	5 4 3 2 1 0 1 2 3 4 5	Cares about satisfying oneself no matter *what others* may think
10.	Fast (eating, walking, etc.)	5 4 3 2 1 0 1 2 3 4 5	Slow doing things
11.	Easygoing	5 4 3 2 1 0 1 2 3 4 5	Hard driving
12.	Hides feelings	5 4 3 2 1 0 1 2 3 4 5	Expresses feelings
13.	Many outside interests	5 4 3 2 1 0 1 2 3 4 5	Few interests
14.	Not concerned about time	5 4 3 2 1 0 1 2 3 4 5	Clock-watcher

20–5 presents the social readjustment rating scale (SRRS). It is a rough measure of the degree of stress a person is suffering at the time of testing.

The notion advanced by the researchers is that rate-of-life changes is a cause of stress. In research to validate the SRRS, it was found that 80 percent of the people with scores between 150 and 300 suffered some form

Figure 20–5

The social readjustment rating scale

Instructions: Check off each of these life events that has happened to you during the previous year. Total the associated points. A score of 150 or less means a relatively low amount of life change and a low susceptibility to stress-induced health breakdown. A score of 150 to 300 points implies about a 50% chance of a major health breakdown in the next two years. A score above 300 raises the odds to about 80%.

Life events	Mean value
1. Death of spouse	100
2. Divorce	73
3. Marital separation from mate	65
4. Detention in jail or other institution	63
5. Death of a close family member	63
6. Major personal injury or illness	53
7. Marriage	50
8. Being fired at work	47
9. Marital reconciliation with mate	45
10. Retirement from work	45
11. Major change in the health or behavior of a family member	44
12. Pregnancy	40
13. Sexual difficulties	39
14. Gaining a new family member (e.g., through birth, adoption, oldster moving in)	39
15. Major business readjustment (e.g., merger, reorganization, bankruptcy)	39
16. Major change in financial state (e.g., a lot worse off or a lot better off than usual)	38
17. Death of a close friend	37
18. Changing to a different line of work	36
19. Major change in the number of arguments with spouse (e.g., either a lot more or a lot less than usual regarding child rearing, personal habits)	35
20. Taking on a mortgage greater than $10,000 (e.g., purchasing a home, business)	31
21. Foreclosure on a mortgage or loan	30
22. Major change in responsibilities at work (e.g., promotion, demotion, lateral transfer)	29
23. Son or daughter leaving home (e.g., marriage, attending college)	29
24. In-law troubles	29
25. Outstanding personal achievement	28
26. Wife beginning or ceasing work outside the home	26
27. Beginning or ceasing formal schooling	26
28. Major change in living conditions (e.g., building a new home, remodeling, deterioration of home or neighborhood)	25
29. Revision of personal habits (dress, manners, associations, etc.)	24

Figure 20–5 (*concluded*)

Life events	Mean value
30. Troubles with the boss	23
31. Major change in working hours or conditions	20
32. Change in residence	20
33. Changing to a new school	20
34. Major change in usual type and/or amount of recreation	19
35. Major change in church activities (e.g., a lot more or a lot less than usual)	19
36. Major change in social activities (e.g., clubs, dancing, movies, visiting)	18
37. Taking on a mortgage or loan less than $10,000 (e.g., purchasing a car, TV, freezer)	17
38. Major change in sleeping habits (a lot more or a lot less sleep, or change in part of day when asleep)	16
39. Major change in number of family get-togethers (e.g., a lot more or a lot less than usual)	15
40. Major change in eating habits (a lot more or a lot less food intake, or very different meal hours or surroundings)	15
41. Vacation	13
42. Christmas	12
43. Minor violations of the law (e.g., traffic tickets, jaywalking, disturbing the peace)	11

of stress-related illness. On the other hand, these illnesses (e.g., ulcers, heart disease, headache, depression) were found to occur in less than a third of the people with scores under 150.

Managers need to be aware of a number of points about the SRRS. First, less than a quarter of the scales of stressful life changes are job related. Second, the SRRS does not account for a person's capacity for coping with stress. Despite these issues, the idea that the rate-of-life changes causes stress seems reasonable.

Coping with and managing work stress

At this point, it is obvious that stress in work organizations is inevitable. What is needed are methods to cope with and manage work stress. A vast array of methods are available. Unfortunately, there is a limited amount of research to support the use of them.

Individual coping and stress management methods

The list of individual approaches for coping and stress management is long. Only a few of the currently more popular approaches can be briefly covered.

Meditation Meditation of one variety or another is a virtually universal technique. Almost all of us take time now and then to contemplate our lives, and we all daydream occasionally. These may be considered possible forms of meditation. Prayer, listening to music, or watching the sunset are other examples. Anything that redirects our mental processes away from daily concerns may be thought of as a form of meditation. Obviously, then, many forms of meditation exist. The meditative forms that have achieved popularity in recent years are derivatives of Eastern philosophies. Foremost among these—at least in its popularity—is transcendental meditation, or TM, as its adherents refer to it.

A variety of positive outcomes have been associated with the practice of meditation (transcendental and otherwise): reduced heart rate, lowered oxygen consumption, and decreased systolic and diastolic blood pressure. Kuna reviewed the research literature on TM as a work-stress management technique. He found evidence that TM has a positive effect on work adjustment, work performance, job satisfaction, and lowering of anxiety. Kuna concluded that TM was an effective strategy for handling stress and that it fostered resistance to stress, thus serving as both a preventer and a reliever.[15]

Biofeedback Despite a great deal of public interest in biofeedback, very few people actually use biofeedback devices. In reality, there is nothing new about biofeedback—it's been around as long as humans have. Every time you take your pulse, check your breathing rate, or place your hand on your forehead to see if you have a fever—that's biofeedback. What is relatively new are the machines that monitor bodily processes and give us information about them. Conceptually, biofeedback is based on three assumptions: first, that neurophysiological functions can be monitored by electronic devices and fed back to the individual; second, that changes in physical states are accompanied by changes in emotional states and vice versa; third, that a state of relaxation is conducive to establishing voluntary control of various bodily functions.

The potential role of biofeedback as an individual stress-management technique can be seen from the kinds of bodily functions or processes that can, to some degree, be brought under voluntary control. These include brain waves, heart rates, muscle tension, body temperature, stomach acidity, and blood pressure. Most of these processes are affected by stress. The potential of biofeedback, then, is its ability to help induce a state of

[15] D. J. Kuna, "Meditation and Work," *Vocational Guidance Quarterly,* 1975, pp. 342–46.

relaxation and restore bodily functions to a nonstressed state. One advantage of biofeedback over nonfeedback techniques is that the information provided gives individuals precise data about body functions. The individual knows how high his or her blood pressure is, for example, and discovers through practice means of lowering it. When the individual is successful, the feedback provides instantaneous information to that effect. While much further research is needed into both the potential and the benefits of biofeedback, there are sufficient data to conclude that it can be of value.

Exercise Various government reports have concluded that one of the easiest, most beneficial ways to bring about a favorable change in a person's well-being is to engage in some systematic exercise activity. Many physicians believe that the single most important indicator of health is cardiovascular endurance, and that is what regular exercise can develop, particularly activities such as jogging, bicycling, and swimming. The evidence is unequivocable that proper exercise, wisely engaged in, is a positive force in physical health and well-being. But what of the mental benefits? What about stress reduction? Available evidence would support exercise as an effective stress management tool, as well as a contributor to physical health. Those who exercise report feelings of reduced tension, heightened mental energy, and an improvement in feelings of self-worth.

Organizational coping and stress management methods

There is no one best organizationally initiated method to deal with stress. As was true at the individual level, numerous approaches are available.

Health profiling An approach that has been used to prevent premature development of disease and to identify stress symptoms so corrective action can be taken is called *health profiling.* Any organization can introduce the techniques of health profiling at minimum expense. Health profiling starts with a questionnaire asking for details of the person's personal habits, family medical history, and vital statistics—blood pressure, cholesterol level, triglyceride levels. The vital statistics may have to be collected by a medical team if the results of a recent physical examination aren't available.

Information from the questionnaire and physical examination is then processed, usually by computer. This information provides individual health profiles that compare the person's characteristics with those of an average person of the same sex, age, and race. The profile predicts the individual's health prospect for the next 10 years, with particular attention to fatal disease probabilities.

In addition, the health profile information indicates how the prospects can be improved by making changes in lifestyle. For example, increasing exercise may be a way of bringing blood pressure down, or reducing the intake of fatty foods may reduce cholesterol levels. In short, a detailed health profile can provide answers to two important questions: How am I? and How am I really? The health profile technique is a feasible action step for organizations that want to prevent premature disabilities, incapacities, and even death among that most important corporate asset, employees.

Stress inoculation training Obviously, stressors in organizational settings do not always lead to disease, illness, behavioral dysfunction, or performance decrements. How a person perceives the stressors and the emotion he or she feels can drastically affect the outcome of the event. The "cognitive appraisal" one makes of the stressors can increase or limit their impact.

Stress inoculation training should focus on developing the skills of participants to cope with stressors. Participants must first learn to (1) understand stress warning signals, (2) admit that they are under- or overstressed, and (3) develop concrete action steps for coping with their specific work situation, personality, and goals.

One strategy for stress inoculation training is to develop the skills of participants to use a coping self-statement procedure. Trainees would be instructed to use a series of questions each time they perceive or feel a stress under- or overload situation. The four-stage series of questions involves preparation, confrontation, coping with feelings, and self-reinforcement. Instruction in preparing the self-statements and their use would be the core of an organizational stress inoculation training program. Examples of the stages and some coping self-statements are listed below:

Preparation for stressors:

- I need a plan to deal with the following stressors.
- What am I going to do about these stressors?
- Why are these organizational stressors causing or going to cause problems for me?

Confrontation:

- What image do I have of the stressors and my involvement with them?
- I can handle this very easily by remaining calm.
- I must relax and stay in control.

Coping:

- I must focus on the present set of stressors.
- This is not the worst thing in the world.
- Fear is natural when faced with stressors. This is a part of facing the situation as it now exists.

Self-reinforcement:

- I handled it well.
- I was able to work my way through the stressors.

- It wasn't as bad as I expected: I was prepared.
- I'm pleased with myself.

The value of stress inoculation training has potential if the participants acquire coping skills through self-analysis procedures. Managers cannot force employees to manage their stressors more effectively. However, a sound stress inoculation training program in an organization can point out the value and importance of the self-regulation of stress. Whether stress leads to decreased or increased performance largely depends upon how the employee responds to stressors. Learning to live and deal with organizational stressors requires self-appraisal, introspection, and a recognition of one's own reaction to stress.

The organization's physical environment There are a number of potential environmental stressors: light, noise, temperature, vibration, and motion. Usually, these variables are stressors when physical facilities are old or when they are part of an operation, such as manufacturing, where noise or other environmental levels are elevated because of the process.

Basically, there are only two ways to deal with physical environmental stressors, and frequently, neither is completely satisfactory. Either the environment must be altered (the noise lessened, the glare reduced, etc.), or the people in the environment must be protected from the stressors (e.g., wearing earplugs or using tinted glasses). In most problem environments, employees use protective equipment because of management and union interest and government safety requirements. Frequently, the environment has been altered to the extent that it's physically, economically, and/or technically feasible.

Short of modifying the environment or the people, management may be able to minimize negative stressors effects by judicious changes in usual operating procedures. Providing shorter but more frequent breaks, waiving customary dress requirements, changing work schedules, and providing a facility where the employee can temporarily escape the stress are examples of ways to reduce the effects of physical environment stressors.

One other aspect of the work environment may produce stress. The physical layout of the work area may either facilitate or hinder the accomplishment of work objectives and, in the latter situation particularly, create stress. For example, a work flow that is inefficient because of poor arrangement of people and/or equipment puts an unnecessary physical strain on employees. Those who are affected day in and day out can provide the best insight on needed changes. The smart manager will combine his or her own observations with the experience of those performing the job to make sure that the physical layout doesn't create any problems.

Providing employee recreational facilities A small but growing number of companies are providing a variety of facilities that employees can use to reduce stress. As an example, in 1982 U.S. firms spent over $4.0 billion on fitness and recreational programs for employees. Companies like Xerox, Rockwell International, Weyerhaeuser, and Pepsi-Cola spent tens of thousands of dollars for gyms equipped with treadmills, exercycles, and jogging tracks—and full-time staffs.[16]

Exercise facilities are not the only thing companies can provide. Some companies—for example, McDonald's Corporation at its Chicago headquarters—provide biofeedback facilities. At McDonald's, executives take relaxation breaks using biofeedback devices to lower respiration and heart rate. Equitable Life Assurance Company has a biofeedback facility available for use by employees when they feel tense. Other companies like Connecticut General Corporation and Sunny Dale Farms are encouraging (and providing time for) employees to meditate.

Organizational efforts do not have to be elaborate and involve significant amounts of capital. They may involve nothing more than arranging for employee discounts at the YMCA/YWCA or the use of a nearby school or gymnasium. What is important is that the organization is helping employees take preventive approaches to health and stress reduction, a process in which everyone gains.

Management summary

1. Stress is the consequence of the interaction between an event or situation and the individual. It can be positive or negative.
2. As individuals, we react to stress in the form of a general adaptation syndrome—alarm, resistance, and exhaustion.
3. The consequences of stress are numerous. The organization is concerned with absenteeism, turnover, and performance, each of which has been linked to stress.
4. A major finding is that stress has been identified as a contributor to poor health, especially in the area of diseases of adaptation or postponable diseases such as coronary heart disease, ulcers, and hypertension.
5. Stressors at work on the job, group, organizational, and personal levels are potentially harmful. A stressor is any external event or situation that affects a person—the leader's style, organizational structure, or group norms.
6. There are also personal sources of stress. The Type A behavior pattern and life changes fit this category.
7. Organizational and individual coping with and managing stress approaches are being experimented with by many firms and employees. To date, the research support for even the most rigorous interventions is sketchy.

[16] "Corporate Keep Well Programs: The Savings Outweigh the Costs," *Houston Chronicle*, September 9, 1981, pp. 1–2.

Review and discussion questions

1. In reviewing Figure 20–3, what stressors (A) were omitted that you feel should be included?
2. What is meant by the statement "life without stress is death"?
3. Is it possible to eliminate all types of organizational structure and leader behavior stress at work? Why?
4. Why is it important for managers to consider individual differences in coping with and managing stress?
5. Why should organizations be concerned about the costs of stress?
6. Which coping with and managing stress approaches covered appeal to you? Why?
7. Explain why it seems reasonable to conclude that stress is cumulative?
8. What would make a particular occupation stressful?
9. Is it possible, in your opinion, to alter a person's Type A tendencies? Why?
10. Does stress cause diseases of adaptation? Explain.

Suggested reading

Brief, A. P.; R. S. Schuler; and M. Van Sell. *Managing Job Stress.* Boston: Little, Brown, 1981.

Cooper, C. L., and M. J. Davidson, "The High Cost of Stress on Women Managers." *Organizational Dynamics,* Spring 1982, pp. 44–53.

Dedmon, R. E., and M. K. Kubiak. "The Medical Director's Role in Industry." *Personnel Administrator,* September 1981, pp. 59–64.

Ivancevich, J. M., M. T. Matteson, and C. Preston. "Occupational Stress, Type A Behavior and Physical Well Being." *Academy of Management Journal,* June 1982, pp. 373–91.

Lazarus, R. S. "Little Hassles Can Be Hazardous to Health." *Psychology Today,* July 1981, pp. 58–62.

Niehouse, O. L. "Burnout: A Real Threat to Human Resources Managers." *Personnel,* September–October, 1981, pp. 25–32.

Pesci, M. "Stress Management: Separating Myth from Reality." *Personnel Administrator,* January 1982, pp. 57–67.

Thoresen, C. E.; M. J. Telch; and J. R. Eagleston. "Approaches to Altering the Type A Behavior Pattern." *Psychosomatics,* June 1981, pp. 472–80.

Weigel, R., and S. Pinsky. "Managing Stress: A Model for the Human Resource Staff." *Personnel Administrator,* February 1982, pp. 56–60.

The Type A scoring system

For items 2, 5, 7, 11, 13, and 14, the right side of the *0* mark indicates Type Aness, while for items 1, 3, 4, 6, 8, 9, 10, and 12, the left side of *0* indicates Type Aness.

For items 1, 3, 4, 6, 8, 9, 10, and 12, give yourself a score of *10* if you circled a 5 on the left side, *9* for 4, *8* for 3, and so on, with *0* assigned if you circled number 5 on the right-hand side. For example, if an individual responded to item 4 as follows:

4.	Always rushed	5 4 3 ② 1 0 1 2 3 4 5	Never feels rushed

This person would assign a *7* for this item.

Calculate in the opposite way for the remaining items 2, 5, 7, 11, 13, and 14; that is, a *0* for number 5 on the left side, a *1* for number 4, and a *10* if you circled number 5 on the right-hand side.

Then, add up your score. It will be from 0 to 140. The higher the score, the more pronounced the Type A behavior pattern.

Applying what you have learned about managing work-related stress

Cases:

Control Data Corporation's Stay Well program

A widow sues for a job-stress-initiated loss

Control Data Corporation's Stay Well program*

Absenteeism, decreased productivity, high turnover, and low morale are found in most organizations. To counter these symptoms, Control Data Corporation (CDC) began a health promotion program. The program is called Stay Well and is offered as a free corporate benefit to Control Data's 57,000 U.S.-based employees and their spouses. In the second year of the program, CDC can now count 27,000 employees using Stay Well.

The program consists of an orientation session, a health screening, and a series of courses to teach skills necessary to change health-related behavior. CDC found that the cost of the program is $15–$18 a month per employee.

Those in Stay Well must undergo a health screening examination. Data are collected on each participant's blood pressure, height, weight, health history and lifestyle, and a sample of blood. These data are used to prepare a Health Risk Profile. This report compares the participant's chronological age with his or her risk age.

CDC has a very strict confidentiality policy. No one at the company has access to any individual data except the Life Extension Institute physicians hired by CDC to review profiles for abnormalities. Individuals can decide whether they would like to share information with their personal physicians.

A unique part of CDC's Stay Well program is the social support activities offered in the discussion groups. Employee groups and spouses meet regularly to discuss health-

---

* This case is adapted from Murray P. Naditch, "Wellness Program Reaps Healthy Benefits for Healthy Employer," *Risk Management,* October 1981, pp. 21–24.

related activities such as diet, nutrition, and managing stressful situations.

Not everyone is convinced that Stay Well is worth the expenditures. It is, however, an organizational program designed to improve health and to help reduce stress. There is even some hope that it will have a positive effect on absenteeism, productivity, turnover, and morale.

Questions:

1. How could a Stay Well–type program reduce work stress?
2. How would a supporter of Stay Well show that the benefits outweigh the costs of the program?
3. Why would CDC be so concerned about keeping the Stay Well information confidential?

A widow sues for a job-stress-initiated loss*

Early one winter morning, Roger Berman left for work as usual and drove into the city to his office at the corporate headquarters of a large international conglomerate. Instead of putting in his customary long day, however, he left the office abruptly during the morning. He may have driven around for some time, but eventually he went home and pulled into his garage. With the motor still running, he got out of the car, closed the garage door, and apparently sat down. His body was found there later, slumped on the floor. The autopsy report listed carbon monoxide as the official cause of death. However, in this case, there is some dispute about the cause.

Certainly, suicides are tragic, but are not that uncommon. Berman's widow has made this a challenging case for lawyers and organizations. She is suing his former employer for $6 million, claiming it caused her husband's death by failing to respond to his repeated complaints of overwork and by displaying a "callous and conscious disregard" for his health.

The case raises the question of whether an employer can, in effect, by its own action or inaction, kill with stress. At issue, besides a lot of money, is the extent to which a company may be held responsible beyond the provisions of worker's compensation laws for a mental health illness to one of its employees.

Since this is a real case, names and certain details have been changed because the case is now going to court. Here they are in a concise fashion:

- Berman went to work with the firm after graduating high school.
- He put himself through college and was regularly promoted.
- The work was so demanding when be became the manager of a large department that he asked to have his work load lightened.
- Approaching 50, and with 30 years of service, he decided to take early retirement to escape the job stress. According to the suit, his supervisors talked him into staying on. He counted on their promises, and his eligibility for early retirement ran out for this cycle. It meant that he was not eligible to retire early for five more years.
- He became very anxious and disoriented. He was referred to an outside psychiatrist by the company doctor. The psychiatrist reported that Berman was having mental health difficulties caused by the job.

* Adapted from Berkely Rice, "Can Companies Kill?" *Psychology Today,* June 1981, pp. 78, 80–85.

- Three weeks before his suicide, co-workers found Berman sitting at his desk in a dazed stupor. They could not snap him out of this state. He came out of it after a few hours.

The company is seeking to have the Berman suit dismissed. It claims that if his mental health problems or death was caused by job stress, any resulting claims should be covered by the state's workers' compensation law.

Questions:

1. Workers' compensation law covers only accidental injuries. Was Berman's death an accident under the law?
2. Can we say with certainty that Berman's stress was job related and not personal? Why?
3. Is Berman's company responsible for his and other employees' mental health? Explain.

21

Chapter twenty-one Managing future challenges and responses

Performance objectives

- **Define** what is meant by social responsibility.
- **State** why external environmental forces are considered unpredictable.
- **Describe** how business ethics affect socially responsible managerial behavior.
- **Explain** the role of government in business enterprise in the United States.
- **Discuss** why no one best way of management has been found or is expected to be found.

Management update*

The mood of citizens around the world is generally grim as they move into the 1980s. Spiraling inflation, chronic unemployment, social discontent, and major changes in personal and family values have all contributed to this gloomy attitude. In the face of that gloom, the 1980s offer hope for easing at least some of these and other problems if managers perform their jobs.

Most economists expect steady growth in the economy throughout the 1980s. The scramble for entry-level jobs is expected to ease because there will be fewer new workers seeking them. A number of occupations will grow in size during the 1980s: health care workers, professional and technical workers, data processing workers, and telecommunications specialists.

Other developments will significantly change the pace and pattern of life. Two-way television will enable you to shop, do your banking, and pay your bills without leaving home. Phonograph records played by laser beams will provide better fidelity of sound reproduction than is currently available on needle-driven records. Ovens, washers, dryers, and other appliances will be computer programmed to operate at specified times.

Electric cars will begin to capture a share of the market. Other cars will be smaller and more fuel efficient than many of those that are in use today. The "highway train," a vehicle that will travel on the interstate highways, picking up automobiles and passengers in much the same way as a ferryboat, will be tested in large growing cities such as Houston, Phoenix, San Diego, and Denver.

In the 1980s, as many as half of our meals will be eaten away from home. Electronic funds transfer—instant bank deposits and withdrawals via plastic cards—will replace cash and checks for more and more financial transactions. Personal shopping services will be offered by more stores for people who choose not to shop for themselves.

The 1980s will present managers not only with the kinds of changes mentioned above but also with more employee dissatisfaction and unrest. Employers will be more vulnerable to unrest because of inadequate opportunities for promotion; increasing inflation; more government involvement in decisions regarding the hiring, disciplining, and firing of employees; and greater employee demands for more flexible work schedules and increases in fringe benefits.

The changes in the pace, pattern, and mood all point to a turbulent decade. These changes in American society will also affect Canada, Europe, Africa, Asia, and South America. The world is truly shrinking, and decisions being made in Mexico, Saudi Arabia, Italy, and elsewhere around the world will be felt by every U.S. citizen. Such companies as General Motors, Procter & Gamble, and General Foods are aware of the changes that are occurring in the world and are becoming companies that compete on a worldwide basis. The old view of powerful American organizations operating in a limited domestic market is being replaced by a new view of becoming world companies. Even individual citizens are beginning to realize that energy, food, education, and employment problems have a worldwide impact and must be managed with that impact in mind. The decade of the 1980s will surely test the ability of managers to apply effective managerial principles and functions.

---

* This Management Update is based on "The 1980s—Problems, Promises, and Surprises," *Changing Times,* January 1979, pp. 7–12; and Bob Tamarkin, "GM Gets Ready for the World Car," *Forbes,* April 2, 1979, pp. 44–48.

The most exciting and challenging period of history is right now. Never before have societies, organizations, and people changed faster. No one can know for certain what the job of management will be like in the years ahead, but some futurists, management writers, and practicing managers are looking seriously at the future. Managers know that what they do or fail to do today can have an influence on the future.

Managers have inherited a great deal from the pioneers of management—Frederick W. Taylor, Henri Fayol, Chester Barnard, Douglas McGregor, Elton Mayo, Frank and Lillian Gilbreth. But today's manager must face new and different challenges than were faced by these pioneers, such as increasing concern about social responsibilities, increasing government involvement, and increasing numbers of women and members of minority groups in the work force. The predictions about how society and managers will meet these new 20th-century challenges are varied. Some scholars predict that civilization and its institutions are about to self-destruct. But others are confident that we have entered a new era in which people will not only be happier than ever before but will also create a more productive civilization.

Whether we are moving toward self-destruction or a new age of happiness is unknown. However, managers have to face this type of uncertainty by working harder at generating the type of performance that will permit their organizations to survive in the future. Although the future is not totally predictable, there is every reason to believe that the manager's job in the 1980s and into the foreseeable future will involve finding ways to cope with change. This chapter is an attempt to tie together what we have said about managing for performance, by setting the stage for the future. Our statements will be based on trends that are occurring today and that should continue into the 21st century.

The manager's world in the 1980s

The reality of managing people, groups, and organizations has been covered in the previous chapters. It has been emphasized that the manager's job is *not* neat, routine, easygoing, clearly understood, and easy to evaluate. On the contrary, planning, organizing, leading, and controlling functions are performed in a rather hectic, fragmented, and complicated manner.

The evidence

The evidence as reported by practicing managers and researchers indicates that:

Managers must often make decisions with incomplete information.

Communication in organizations is often unclear and misleading.

Considerations regarding individual differences get in the way of neat, orderly institutional programs.

Managers need controls, but tight controls often destroy the motivation of employees.

Innovative managerial ideas are rejected by top administrators because they are often threatening to philosophies or practices that have been in place for years.

Groups have a significant influence on individual behavior, but many managers do not understand the characteristics and processes of groups.

As noted in Chapter 2, managing is a set of roles. The manager acts out these roles—interpersonal, informational, and decisional. If all the evidence about the roles played by managers could be accumulated, and if the job of managing could be described concisely, we believe that the result would be a list of descriptions such as these:

Fragmented	Personally rewarding
Challenging	Ritual and politics
Interruptions	Enjoyable
Exciting	Tiring
Flurry of activities	Endless

These and similar adjectives describe the work of managers. Many of the comments of actual managers which have appeared throughout this book also portray the work of managers in such terms.

During the 1980s, the manager's job will probably be more closely scrutinized by researchers than it was during any other era. Through better and more thorough research, the manager's job will be made clearer to society. This should reduce the acceptance of the unfortunate myths that the work of managers is routine, neat, and orderly. The old cliché "Workers do, managers tell" will be revealed to be a silly misconception.[1] The mana-

[1] Leonard R. Sayles, *Leadership* (New York: McGraw-Hill, 1979), p. 21.

gerial work described in this book certainly requires a high level of energy, intelligence, and determination. It is managers who must convert technological, social, economic, and political changes into programs that improve the quality of citizens' lives. Managers must *do* and continue to *do* so that acceptable performance is achieved.

Competences

In order to improve the quality of people's lives, managers must possess competences. A competence is a skill or expertise that is applied to particular problems. The competences needed to manage change, implement a strategic plan, reward employees equitably, or organize a new business venture are varied. We have implied that various competences are needed to achieve performance; those which will be important in the 1980s are presented in Figure 21–1.

The competences presented in Figure 21–1 do not exhaust the list of required managerial skills. They can, however, be used as starting points in improving a manager's overall performance. Being effective also requires that managers understand the *changes* that are currently taking place in society. Resisting change or ignoring it are not viable strategies for manag-

Figure 21–1

Competencies required to manage in the 1980s

Competences	Why?
Being a problem solver	Is needed to attack the problems correctly and effectively.
Being a good listener	Is needed to learn about problems and to establish relationships with co-workers.
Managing time	Is needed to prevent becoming overloaded by work and stressed.
Communicating clearly	Is needed to establish plans, procedures, and programs and to learn about the feelings of others.
Rewarding equitably	Is needed to maintain motivation and receive the respect of subordinates.
Providing subordinates with a clear understanding of their jobs	Is needed to create an atmosphere of understanding.
Showing respect for others	Is needed to develop trust, confidence, and loyalty among co-workers.

ers. Applying the competences displayed in Figure 21–1 to such changes should make the future more rewarding to managers.

Changes in the manager's world

Significant changes have occurred in our society during the last two decades. Medical developments, technological advances, economic changes, social inventions, and political transformations have occurred rapidly. Figure 21–2 presents some of the more publicized changes. Many of these changes were not even imagined 25 years ago. Change has side effects that influence lifestyles and the quality of life. Some of the more pressing side effects of change that our nation now faces are the need for new energy sources, the depletion of crucial and natural resources, spiraling inflation, increased social activism and consumerism, rising educational

Figure 21–2

Changes in the past two decades

Medical
- Use of TV network for M.D.'s
- Use of cable TV for medical conferences
- Use of computers to diagnose psychiatric problems
- A preventive medicine orientation instead of a disease orientation

Technological:
- Astronauts landing on the moon
- Diesel passenger cars
- Use of fossil fuels
- Supersonic transportation

Economic:
- Increases in the standard of living
- The development of China
- The use of foreign capital to build new plants in the United States
- The development of third world nations, Japan, and West Germany
- Decrease in the value of the dollar on international currency exchanges

Social
- Declining birthrate
- Development of experiential communities
- Increased crowding
- Increased pressure from the third world for a greater share of material goods
- Increased welfare payments by the government

Political:
- Equal employment rights
- Signing of Middle East peace pact between Israel and Egypt
- Resignation of a vice president and a president
- Increases in the number of women winning elections
- End of U.S. involvement in Southeast Asian wars

levels, changing demographic patterns, the increasing numbers of women and members of minority groups in managerial positions and professional occupations, increased governmental involvement in business transactions, and an expansion of international business and competition.

These and other side effects have implications for managerial activities. Managers in the 1980s will have to adjust to these side effects. They will have to develop programs, policies, and actions that can succeed in an environment that is changing rapidly and often unpredictably. Managerial actions will have to take account of environmental changes so that some growth can be accomplished.

The environmental forces

An organization's external environment plays a major role in determining how successful managers will be in performing their jobs. We have described the linkage between the environment and the internal operations of organizations throughout this book. Many environmental forces are beyond the control of managers. However, being aware of important environmental forces assists managers in performing the functions of management. The environment of most organizations includes resources (natural and human), population changes, technology, social responsibilities, governmental regulations, and international competition.

Natural resources

During the last 20 years, world fuel consumption tripled, oil and gas consumption quintupled, and the use of electricity grew almost sevenfold. Clearly, such trends can't continue. Another worldwide energy crisis has begun, especially with regard to fuel for heating and travel. In the past, coal was substituted for wood and wind. However, the shift to gasoline altered the nature of travel, especially for the United States.

Managing the limited available natural resources will become a very important responsibility in the 1980s. Business, government, unions, and citizens have a stake in the efficient management of scarce resources. Inappropriate management will mean lower national productivity, inconveniences, food shortages and an overall decline in our standard of living.

We are not running out of energy. However, we are running out of cheap oil and gas. We are also running out of money to pay for energy. Some of the energy sources that have been used in place of oil and gas have created a number of problems. For example, nuclear fusion was initially considered by its developers to be a clean source of limitless power. However, the potential problems with nuclear energy were highlighted in the spring 1979 accident at Three Mile Island, Pennsylvania. Radioactive emissions created a crisis situation and a public outcry. Furthermore, the use of nuclear energy creates radioactive wastes that are difficult to dispose of safely.

Renewable energy sources—wind, water, direct sunlight—seem to offer some promise. They add no heat to the atmosphere, and they produce no radioactive materials. However, they can't meet limitless energy demands.

The highest priority in the use of natural resources in the 1980s will be given to conservation. A transition to the efficient conservation and management of energy sources is possible. However, each of the world's 150 nations has a different plan for conserving and using energy. Managerial coordination of these differing viewpoints is required. Plans and clearly understood objectives must be established. The use of the managerial functions of planning, organizing, leading, and controlling are needed in the fight to conserve energy.

Human resources

The average life expectancy was about 22 years in ancient Greece. Some individuals in that society did live to ripe old ages, but their number was small. Today, many of us reach the age of 70 and remain active contributors to organizations. Learning how to use young and old workers effectively is a continuing task of managers. In the 1980s, these human resources will be considered *the* most crucial asset of an organization.

More organizations will acknowledge that many jobs are boring and alienating. Something will have to be done to induce people to tolerate such jobs. The words *self-actualization* and *personal growth* will become more than psychological jargon among managers.

Career planning is an example of treating human resources as valuable assets. Job enrichment, training, and development are all designed to more optimally match jobs and people. To this end, organizational designs will become more flexible, working hours will be modified to meet personal needs, and technology will be modified to mesh with the talents and skills of operating employees. In addition, when middle age sets in and the challenge of the job disappears, retraining for a second career will become more popular. The era of concern about human resources has arrived, and that concern will become more pronounced during the 1980s.

Population and other demographic trends

Demographic patterns will change drastically in the 1980s. Most industrialized nations, such as the United States, Great Britain, France, Canada, West Germany, Japan, and Australia, will experience a decline in population growth as a result of decreasing birthrates.

Demographers associate increasing female participation in the work force with a decline in the number of children that families will raise. The reduced amount of time available for parenting in families if the mother works may create a demand for new school services that deal with functions usually learned at home. Schools may need to teach the skills of eating, drinking, dressing, and manners to young children.

The managerial implications of changing population patterns and parenting behaviors are becoming obvious. Population is one of the main factors affecting the demand for goods and services. Studies of population data will become a more important basis for adjustments in product development and modifications in production. For example, managers examining population data can determine that over 65 percent of the people in the United States are over 21 years of age and that approximately 36 percent of these people are over 40 years old. Since many adults have their homes, cars, and appliances, this means that other types of goods may prove more attractive to the adult population.

Managers must also consider the shifts in population patterns in locating new employees, talent, plant sites, and markets. Americans are rapidly leaving the northern and eastern metropolitan areas of New York, Philadelphia, Cleveland, and Boston and are heading for the South and West. As a result, the nation's fastest growing region is an area called the sunbelt—whose northern limits are an arc stretching from southern California to the Carolinas. America's modern-day migrants are searching for new jobs, goods, and services and for lifestyle changes. Managerial plans to meet these needs must be developed and implemented.

These demographic changes are important environmental influences on managerial plans involving staffing, career planning, product development, marketing, and training and development. Dramatic changes in the population mix, income patterns, and geographic location will continue to be concerns of managers in the 1980s.

Technology

Technology includes the knowledge, tools, equipment, and techniques that are used to convert the inputs of an organization into goods and services. In general, technology is the way things are done—the methods, procedures, and equipment that are used to achieve organizational and societal goals. The development of technology is a high-risk, costly, and uncertain activity. The world has entered an era in which many of the easy technological breakthroughs have already been achieved. Major technological improvements in the 1980s will require greater managerial and financial commitments.

Seldom is an organization able to make a technological breakthrough within management cost estimates. One of the management challenges of the 1980s is knowing when to abandon a project that is running up excessive costs. This will require careful planning, decision making, and controlling.

Recently, the managers of technological projects have had to consider a new type of costs—**social costs.** Water, air, and noise pollution have become cost items that must be considered. The government has begun to act as an aggressive monitor of disturbing side effects of technological advancements. The legal and police powers of the government are being used to impose economic and legal sanctions against the firms that are responsible for such side effects.

In some organizations, managers have been faced with huge losses because of poor planning and controlling of technology projects. Before selling most of its computer business to Honeywell, General Electric drained some $500 million into computers, nuclear power, and commercial jet engines. RCA also had to terminate its computer operations because of poor strategic planning. By contrast, IBM has managed its research efforts along a specific technology and has successfully captured the major share of the world's computer market.

The management of technological change and advancement is not easy. Organizations will have to search for the balance between too few and too many risky ventures. This search will be frustrating unless managers comprehend that technology is costly, risky, necessary, and intense all at the same time. No management team, regardless of its size or its industry affiliation, can afford to ignore the technological changes that occur in the environment.

Social responsibilities

In the 1980s, organizations will devote more attention to what are called social responsibilities. Some believe that the sole responsibility of business is to earn a profit and that in doing so, it benefits society and meets people's material needs.[2] However, this traditional and narrow view is being challenged by the newer and broader viewpoint that organizations operate only because society grants them the right to do so and that this right will continue only so long as society is satisfied with corporate results. The grantors of the right are said to include owners, employees, creditors, suppliers, consumers, and the general public.

The broader view of the role of corporations is based largely on the notion that the well-being of society, not just that of a few people, should be a goal of all organizations. The impact and scope of such a goal should encompass:

1. The satisfaction of human needs The entire range of human needs must be considered by organizations, not just economic or material needs. Thus, organizations are going to have to advocate and practice energy conservation, clean air, pure water, adequate housing, and equitable employment opportunities.

---

[2] Theodore Levitt, "The Dangers of Social Responsibility," *Harvard Business Review,* September–October 1958, pp. 44–50.

2. Using new performance measures New measures of performance will become important. Organizations will assess not only profitability, competitiveness, efficiency, and flexibility but also the overall effects of their actions on society.

3. Improved societal awareness In the 1960s and 1970s, there has been an increased awareness of product value, product and service quality, and the role of organizations in communities. This trend should continue in the 1980s on a broad range of social issues, including medical care of the aged, lifelong learning opportunities, concern for retired employees, and improving the quality of life in general and the quality of work life in particular.

Today, many organizations have become very socially responsible without having been subjected to governmental or social group pressure. A survey of the social actions and attitudes of large corporations revealed the following:

> Many organizations have created positions in the management hierarchy for employees who work solely on social responsibility issues.
>
> The most usual efforts in the social responsibility area deal with ecology and the hiring and training of minorities.
>
> Most of the organizations involved in social responsibility projects believe that their efforts have been successful.
>
> Owners of the organizations involved in active social responsibility programs support management's involvement.[3]

This survey suggests that socially responsible behavior is becoming a part of the mission and objectives of many organizations.

An example of how socially responsible activities are becoming a part of the mainstream of organizational life involves the increase of women and minorities in business. Until the 1940s, many businesses specified the desired sex and race when advertising for employees. This, of course, is illegal today and many organizations are actively recruiting women and minorities. In 1975, *Fortune* listed 379,000 black managers in American businesses, a number that had increased 50 percent from 1969.[4] Integrating more women and blacks and other minorities into organizational positions of status, power, and authority should continue in the 1980s.

Another socially responsible action that will continue in the 1980s is the hiring of more women. Projections indicate that by 1985 women will account for nearly 40 percent of the total labor force. Despite the rapid growth in the female labor force in recent years, women are still primarily

[3] Robert Parket and Henry Eilbert, "Social Responsibility: The Underlying Factors," *Business Horizons,* August 1975, p. 5.

[4] Juan Cameron, "Blacks Still Waiting for Full Membership," *Fortune,* April 1975, p. 165.

concentrated in certain industries and occupations. Most women work in the service sector, which is broadly defined to include wholesale and retail trade, finance, insurance, real estate, public administration, as well as professional, personal, entertainment, and repair services.

Since 1960, women have been entering the skilled trades at a faster rate than men. Yet, men continue to hold a disproportionate share of the highest status, best-paying blue-collar jobs. For example, in the electronics industry in the 1970s, women constituted the majority of employees, but they held only a small percentage, under 10 percent, of the skilled, high-status, best-paying crafts jobs.[5]

The managerial effort needed to change the occupational status and distribution of women should not be underestimated. Managers can concentrate on the new jobs created by the growth and replacement needs of the economy and technological changes. The structure of jobs is presented in Figure 21–3. The illustration indicates what the percentage of women in each occupation would be if, between 1969 and the 1980s, 40 percent of the new jobs in the 1980s in each category were allocated to women. The 40–60 ratio is hypothetical, and it is used for illustrative purposes only. One of the biggest changes could occur in the managers, officials, proprietors category, with an increase from 16 percent to 26 percent.

An unavoidable consequence of the effort to expand the employment opportunities open to women is that this confronts men with a new source of competition. Management will have to cope with men who are unable to obtain employment in their preferred occupations. Careful staffing and career planning steps will have to be taken by managers so that these displaced men can find employment elsewhere.

Business ethics

Practicing socially responsible behavior involves *ethics*. Ethics is the study of right and wrong. Most managers are ethical, but there are exceptions. Some managers discriminate against women, accept bribes, produce harmful products, issue false advertisements, and steal from corporate accounts. These are, in short, unethical and greedy managers just as there are ethical and socially responsible managers. It should be remembered, however, that just as some managers engage in unethical behavior, some doctors, lawyers, teachers, clergy, blue-collar employees, and persons in other occupational categories also engage in unethical behavior.

There appears to be a growing interest in minimizing unethical behavior. A major recent study of business ethics that was based on responses from 1,227 *Harvard Business Review* readers indicated public disclosure and

[5] U.S. Equal Opportunity Commission, *Employment Profiles of Minorities and Women in the SMSA's of 20 Large Cities, 1971,* Research Report no. 43 (Washington, D.C.: Government Printing Office, July 1974).

Figure 21–3

Women as a percentage of total employment in major occupations, 1969, 1974, and 1980 era

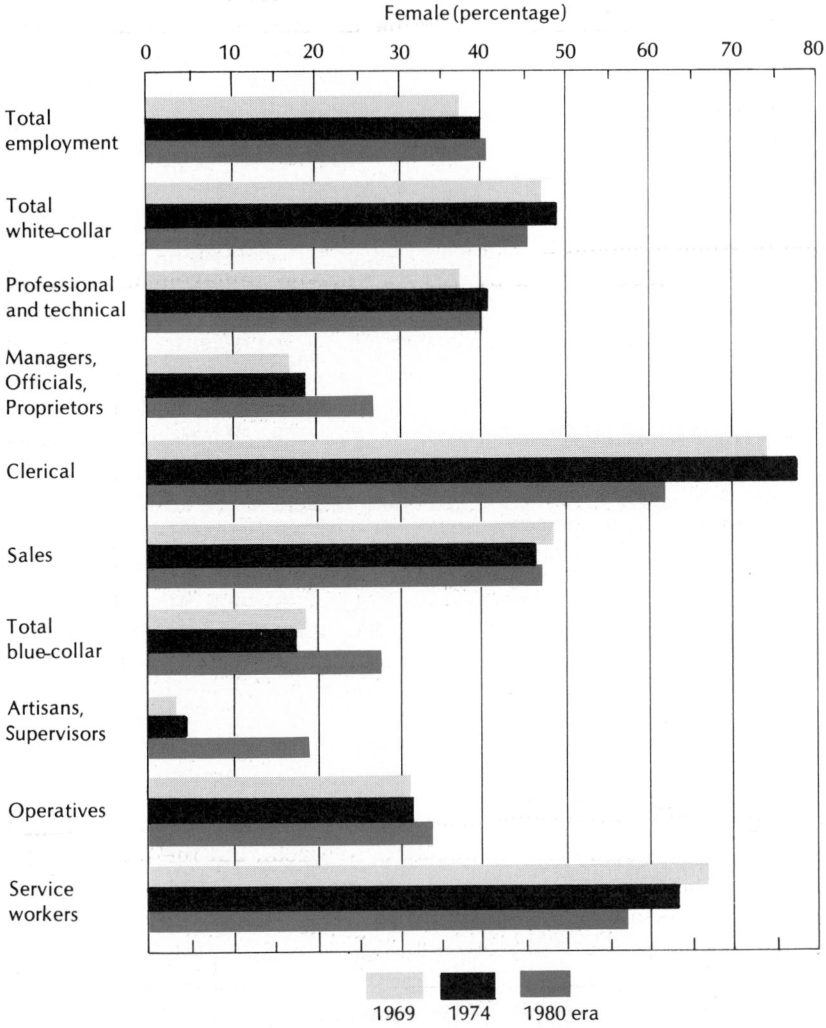

SOURCE: Francine D. Blau, "The Data on Women Workers, Past, Present, and Future," in *Women Working*, ed. Ann H. Stromberg and Shirley Harkness (Palo Alto, Calif.: Mayfield, 1978), p. 56.

public concern over unethical behavior to be the most important forces for raising ethical standards. The authors compared their findings with those of the *Harvard Business Review* study that had been conducted in 1961. Table 21–1 presents the respondent's views on the factors that raise ethical standards as compared to those that lower them.

As noted, public disclosure and increased public concern were consid-

Table 21–1

Factors influencing ethical standards

	Percentage of respondents listing factor
Factors causing higher standards:	
Public disclosure; publicity; media coverage; better communication	31%
Increased public concern; public awareness, consciousness, and scrutiny; better-informed public; societal pressures	20
Government regulation, legislation, and intervention; federal courts	10
Education of business managers; increase in manager professionalism and education	9
New social expectations for the role business is to play in society; young adults' attitudes; consumerism	5
Business's greater sense of social responsibility and greater awareness of the implications of its acts; business responsiveness; corporate policy changes; top-management emphasis on ethical action	5
Other	20
Factors causing lower standards:	
Society's standards are lower; social decay; more permissive society; materialism and hedonism have grown; loss of church and home influence; less quality, more quantity desires	34
Competition; pace of life; stress to succeed; current economic conditions; costs of doing business; more businesses compete for less	13
Political corruption; loss of confidence in government; Watergate; politics; political ethics and climate	9
People more aware of unethical acts; constant media coverage; TV; communications create atmosphere for crime	9
Greed; desire for gain; worship the dollar as measure of success; selfishness of the individual; lack of personal integrity and moral fiber	8
Pressure for profit from within the organization from superiors or from stockholders; corporate influences on managers; corporate policies	7
Other	21

SOURCE: Steven N. Brenner and Earl A. Molander, "Is the Ethics of Business Changing?" *Harvard Business Review*, January–February 1977, p. 63.

ered to be the most important factors in raising ethical standards. On the other hand, lower societal standards and competition were considered the most significant factors in lowering ethical standards.

The *Harvard Business Review* study also revealed to whom the executives felt the greatest responsibility. Table 21–2 shows these results. Clearly, the executives ranked customers as their most important responsibility. The executives were also asked what degree of responsibility they felt in each of nine areas along a scale of 1 (absolutely voluntary) to 5 (absolutely obligatory). Table 21–3 summarizes the results. Ranked the highest was being an efficient user of energy and natural resources. Assessing the potential environmental effects of technological advances was ranked second. These findings demonstrate that managers consider their social responsibilities seriously.

Table 21–2

Managerial responsibilities

Responsibility of your company to various groups	Rank
Customers	1.83
Stockholders	2.52
Employees	2.86
Local community where company operates	4.44
Society in general	4.97
Suppliers	5.10
Government	5.72

Note: The ranking is calculated on a scale of 1 (most responsibility) to 7 (least responsibility).

SOURCE: Steven N. Brenner and Earl A. Molander, "Is the Ethics of Business Changing?" *Harvard Business Review*, January–February 1977, p. 69.

The survey just described suggests that the age-old question "Does the end justify the means?" will be asked more seriously by managers in the 1980s. For example, the decision to market an unsafe but legal automobile to improve the firm's market share would be unethical, because it violates the ethical ideal of respect for life. Managers will do more analysis of how their actions will be viewed by consumers, the government, and society.

Government

The American economic system is a form of mixed capitalism. Private firms using the price system of resource allocation produce what consumers

Table 21–3

Amount of responsibility: By area

Areas of responsiblity	Degree
Being an efficient user of energy and natural resources	4.00
Assessing the potential environmental effects flowing from the company's technological advances	3.96
Maximizing long-run profits	3.78
Using every means possible to maximize job content and satisfaction for the hourly worker	3.35
Having your company's subsidiary in another country use the same occupational safety standards as your company does in the United States	3.05
Acquiescing to State Department requests that the company not establish operations in a certain country	3.01
Making implementation of corporate affirmative action plans a significant determinant of line officer promotion and salary improvement	2.91
Instituting a program for hiring the hard-core unemployed	2.28
Contributing to the local United Fund	2.17

Note: The ranking is calculated on a scale of 1 (absolutely voluntary) to 5 (absolutely obligatory).

SOURCE: Steven N. Brenner and Earl A. Molander, "Is the Ethics of Business Changing?" *Harvard Business Review,* January–February 1977, p. 70.

demand at a price which allows them to earn a satisfactory profit. However, the government is involved in what is produced for whom in our society. The government's role in the past two decades has been one of increased regulation and review of American enterprise. Through its power to enact and enforce laws, government has become a major force that influences many managerial decisions.

On balance, the role of government in the 1980s will be to support and encourage business enterprise. However, government will continue to be a watchdog of managerial decisions to see that managers act in the best interests of society. There will probably be more Ralph Naders urging greater government control of business. In addition, there will be even more regulations imposed on managers. Laws and regulations are often needed, but occasionally, they are unclear and promote the self-interest of some lobby group.

Since 1960, the U.S. Congress has passed nearly 90 major laws regulating various phases of business enterprise. Many of these laws are listed in Figure 21–4. Most of the laws focus on consumerism, minorities, safety, and the employment of women. The vast majority of managers will continue to comply with these and other new regulations. The application of effective laws and a better relationship between government and business can im-

Figure 21–4

Some significant post 1960 legislation regulating business

Civil Rights Act of 1960
Federal Hazardous Substances Labeling Act of 1960
Fair Labor Standards Amendments of 1961, 1966, and 1974
Federal Water Pollution Control Act Amendments of 1961
Oil Pollution Act of 1961 and Amendments of 1973
Air Pollution Control Act of 1962
Drug Amendments of 1962
Clean Air Act of 1963 and Amendments of 1966 and 1970
Equal Pay Act of 1963
Civil Rights Act of 1963
Automotive Products Trade Act of 1965
Federal Cigarette Labeling and Advertising Act of 1965
Water Quality Act of 1965
Clean Water Restoration Act of 1966
Fair Packaging and Labeling Act of 1966
Federal Coal Mine Safety Act Amendments of 1966
Financial Institutions Supervisory Act of 1966
Oil Pollution of the Sea Act of 1966
Age Discrimination in Employment Act of 1967
Air Quality Act of 1967
Agricultural Fair Practices Act of 1968
Consumer Credit Protection Act of 1968
Natural Gas Pipeline Safety Act of 1968
Radiation Control for Health and Safety Act of 1968
Cigarette Smoking Act of 1969
Child Protection and Toy Safety Act of 1969
Federal Coal Mine Health and Safety Act of 1969
Natural Environmental Policy Act of 1969
Tax Reform Act of 1969
Investment Company Amendments of 1969
Bank Holding Act Amendments of 1970
Bank Records and Foreign Transactions Act of 1970
Economic Stabilization Act of 1970 and Amendments of 1971 and 1973
Environmental Quality Improvement Act of 1970
Fair Credit Reporting Act of 1970
Noise Pollution and Abatement Act of 1970
Occupational Safety and Health Act of 1970
Securities Investor Protection Act of 1970
Water and Environmental Quality Improvement Act of 1970
Export Administration Finance Act of 1971
Consumer Product Safety Act of 1972
Equal Employment Opportunity Act of 1972
Federal Environmental Pesticide Control Act of 1972
Noise Control Act of 1972
Agriculture and Consumers Protection Act of 1973
Emergency Petroleum Allocation Act of 1973
Highway Safety Act of 1973
Water Resources Development Act of 1974
Crude Oil Windfall Tax Act of 1979
Energy Security Act of 1980
Depository Institution Deregulation and Monetary Control Act of 1980
Economic Recovery Tax Act of 1981

prove the quality of life within society. The development of a better business-government relationship will become an important priority for managers and government administrators.

During the 1980s, government's role in American enterprise should grow. Local, state, and federal government will continue to be involved in all of the areas covered by the legislation listed in Figure 21–4. Through more socially responsible behavior by organizations, the relationship between business and government can become more harmonious. Perhaps during the 1980s, business and government will finally realize that each has a crucial role to play if our society's quality of life is to be improved.

International competition

The American economic system is powerful, but it is not self-sufficient. The United States is becoming increasingly dependent on international trade. In fact, most industrial nations, such as Canada, West Germany, Japan, and France, need to exchange goods and services with other nations.

In order to compete internationally in the 1980s, comprehensive strategies will be needed. As noted in Chapter 19, the development and implementation of effective strategies will require managerial planning, organizing, leading and controlling. As international competition becomes more intense, the planning, organizing, leading and controlling activities of an organization become more complex. A number of factors contribute to this complexity. First, managers must be able to seize on the opportunities available in various world markets. Evaluation of market opportunities in other nations must be a continual process. Second, when an organization crosses the borders of a nation, it must do so within the laws and regulations of that nation. For example, U.S. firms selling products in Canada must comply with the requirement that packaging information be given in French and English. Japanese car manufacturers selling autos to Americans must comply with U.S. air pollution standards. Compliance with U.S. air pollution regulations is made even more difficult by the fact that different states have different standards.

Managers now realize that international competition for markets is a reality. Like other industrialized nations, the United States is becoming increasingly dependent on trade with, and goods from, other nations. International competition will receive increased attention in management circles because of its growing importance. This attention is needed because of the high risk and uncertainty that exist within international markets.

Portrait of a future manager

Environmental forces are significant and unpredictable. Few, if any, principles and functions of management apply in all situations or for all the forces described. If one message has been emphasized in this book, it is that there are no perfect solutions to management problems. To be an effective manager in the 1980s, one must understand the dimensions that make each situation unique, so that one's analysis and decision making can be adjusted accordingly. The application of all the functions of management—planning and decision making, organizing, leading, and controlling—will be contingency based.

Planning and decision making

Although systematic and careful planning and decision making are associated with better performance, there are different degrees of planning and different approaches to decision making. In some situations, rigid and well-structured plans are preferred; in other situations, flexibility and more general plans are more suitable. The same is true in decision making. Being able to adjust plans and decision processes will be needed in the 1980s more than ever before because of the frequency and the intensity of the changes that managers face. Change requires that managers be flexible enough to apply what is needed before and during the occurrence of events.

Organizing

There is no one best design or staffing procedure for all organizations. What works for Metropolitan Life Insurance may have little applicability to General Mills, Textron, or IBM. The appropriate organization design must fit the objectives, technology, environment, managerial styles, and employees. In fact, the same organization may have different design arrangements for various departments. Instead of searching for ideal designs, the manager in the 1980s will use multiple and changing designs.

Leading

Employees are the ultimate resource of any organization. Again, there is no best method of motivating and leading to fit all employees. Some employees are motivated by money, while others prefer a livable income and opportunities to advance. Managers must continually search for the leadership style and the communication pattern that works best at a particular time. Whether managers can be as flexible as the contingency approach requires is an unanswered question. Training and development may become the key for instilling the type of flexibility that is needed by managers.

Controlling

The amount and the type of control used by an organization are dependent on the degree to which control is required to accomplish goals. Weighing the costs and benefits of various control procedures will probably become a more widely used analytic procedure in the 1980s. For example, analyzing the costs and benefits of contemporary performance evaluation methods may reveal soft spots or problem areas which management will have to correct.

The manager of the 1980s will be applying the functions of planning, organizing, leading, and controlling in organizations. This is not an easy task. Many of the comments of managers that have been quoted throughout this book indicate the difficulty of applying the functions of management. To perform effectively, the manager of the 1980s must recognize the roles that managers play in organizations, the forces in the environment, and the strengths and weaknesses that he or she possesses. By having self-awareness and an understanding of the functions of management, it is possible to perform effectively. Above all, "managing for performance" is an attainable goal if one works at becoming a responsive and adaptable manager.

It seems appropriate to conclude our discussion of **Managing for Performance** with the following:

> *As nearly everyone knows, a manager has practically nothing to do except to decide what is to be done; to tell somebody to do it; to listen to reasons why it should not be done, why it should be done by someone else, or why it should be done in a different way; to follow up to see if the thing has been done; to discover that it has not; to inquire why; to listen to excuses from the person who should have done it; to follow up again to see if the thing has been done, only to discover that it has been done incorrectly; to point out how it should have been done; to conclude that as long as it has been done, it may as well be left where it is; to wonder if it is not time to get rid of a person who cannot do a thing right; to reflect that he or she probably has a family, and that certainly any successor would be just as bad, and maybe worse; to consider how much simpler and better the thing would have been done if one had done it oneself in the first place; to reflect sadly that one could have done it right in 20 minutes, and as things turned out, one had to spend two days to find out why it has taken three weeks for somebody else to do it wrong.*
>
> Anonymous

Management summary

1. The future has always been unpredictable, but trends in the environment can provide managers with clues about what events and situations will occur in the 1980s.
2. The manager's world in the 1980s will be as hectic, fragmented, and complex as it has been in the past. Thus, a contingency approach will be necessary.
3. Forces in the environment of managers are typically beyond their control. However, these forces need to be examined so that plans can be established. Specific environmental areas of interest include natural and human resources, population changes, technology, social responsibility, government regulations, and international competition.
4. Ethics is concerned with right and wrong. More concern about ethical behavior in reaching decisions will exist in the 1980s. Managers, the government, and society are demanding that ethical behavior be the rule rather than the exception.
5. The search for the one best way of managing has been futile. The manager who is flexible in applying the functions of management will be more effective in dealing with the environmental forces and with the performance of organizations.
6. Social responsibility is an accepted part of management today, and it will become even more significant in the 1980s. The importance of people and the well-being of society are now facts of organizational life. Stronger economic and legal sanctions will be used to bring irresponsible managers into line.

Review and discussion questions

1. Is the United States the only nation that is faced with the need to conserve natural resources? Explain.
2. Why must managers be concerned with social responsibilities in the 1980s?
3. Why is the topic of international competition in the marketplace becoming important in management circles?
4. Government regulations since 1960 have addressed a number of areas. Which regulation has had, in your opinion, the greatest positive impact on the quality of life?
5. How serious is the energy shortage in industrialized nations such as the United States, Canada, and Australia?

6. Why is ethics a topic of concern not only for managers but for all professionals and for nonprofessionals who make decisions that affect other people?
7. There are still some staunch advocates of the position that business organizations are intended to provide goods and services and to earn a profit. It is claimed that business is not prepared to be socially responsible because of its economic orientation. Do you agree with this position?
8. Why must management be concerned about technological advancements in society?
9. Will the application of a contingency approach make the job of management routine, neat, and easy to evaluate? Explain.
10. How can a student of management prepare for managing and for conducting the functions of management in the 1980s?

Suggested reading

Carlson, H. C. "Measuring the Quality of Work Life in General Motors." *Personnel,* November–December 1978, pp. 21–26.

Dam, A. van. "The Future of Management." *Management World,* January 1978, pp. 3–6.

Fisher, S. T. "Solid Fossil Fuels: Major Long-Term Energy Resource." *Business Horizons,* April 1979, pp. 34–40.

Fry, L. W., G. D. Keim, and R. E. Meiners. "Corporate Contributions: Altruistic or For-Profit." *Academy of Management Journal,* March 1982, pp. 94–106.

Kahn, H.; W. Brown; and L. Martel. *The Next 200 Years.* New York: William Morrow, 1976.

Kefalas, A. G. "Toward a Substainable Growth Strategy." *Business Horizons,* April 1979, pp. 34–40.

Ohmae, K. "Foresighted Management Decision Making: See the Options before Planning Strategy." *Management Review,* May 1982, pp. 46–55.

"100 Top Corporate Women." *Business Week,* June 21, 1976, pp. 56–68.

Steiner, G. *Strategic Planning.* New York: Free Press, 1979.

Glossary of terms

Activity The work necessary to complete a particular event in a PERT network. An activity consumes time, which is the paramount variable in a PERT system. In PERT networks, three time estimates are used for each activity: an optimistic time, a pessimistic time, and a most likely time.

Affective attitude The part of attitude that involves a person's emotions or feelings.

Attitude A person's tendency to feel and behave toward some object in some way.

Attribution An inference made by a person about his or her feelings or another person's feelings based on observed behavior.

Authority The legitimate right to use assigned resources to accomplish a delegated task or objective; the right to give orders and to exact obedience. The legal bases for formal authority are private property, the state, or a Supreme Being.

Behavior Any observable response given by a person.

Behavior modification An approach to motivation that uses operant conditioning. Operant behavior is learned on the basis of consequences. If a behavior causes a desired outcome (for managers), then it is reinforced (positively rewarded), and because of its consequences, it is likely to be repeated. Thus, behavior is conditioned by adjusting its consequences.

Behavioral approach to organizational design A design approach that emphasizes people and how the structure of an organization affects their behavior and performance. The advocates of a people orientation to design believe that the classical approach suppresses personal development because it is so rigid and restrictive.

Behaviorally anchored rating scales (BARS) A set of rating scales developed by raters and/or ratees that uses critical behavioral incidents as interval anchors on each scale. About six to ten scales with behavioral incidents are used to derive the evaluation.

Biofeedback A technique, usually involving the use of some kind of instrumentation, in which the user attempts to learn to control various bodily functions such as heart rate and blood pressure.

Brand-switching model Provides the manager with some idea of the behavior of consumers in terms of their loyalty to brands and their switches from one brand to another.

Bureaucracy An organizational design that relies on specialization of labor, a specific authority hierarchy, a formal set of rules and procedures, and rigid promotion and selection criteria.

Career An individually perceived sequence of attitudes and behaviors associated with work-related experiences and activities over the span of a person's life.

Career path The sequence of jobs associated with a particular initial job that leads to promotion and advancement.

Career planning The process of systematically matching an individual's career aspirations with opportunities for achieving them.

Career stages Distinct, but interrelated, steps or phases of a career, including the prework stage, the initial work stage, the stable work stage, and the retirement stage.

Carrying costs The costs incurred by carrying raw materials and finished goods in inventory. These include taxes and insurance on the goods in inventory, interest on the money invested in inventory and storage space, and the losses incurred because of inventory obsolescence.

Central tendency error The tendency to rate all ratees around an average score.

Changing external environment One in which

there are rather frequent and expected changes in the actions of competitors, market demands, technology, etc.

Classical approach to organizational design Places reliance of such management principles as unity of command, a balance between authority and responsibility, division of labor, and delegation to establish relationships between managers and subordinates.

Closed system An approach that generally ignores environmental forces and conditions.

Coercive power The power of a leader that is derived from fear. The follower perceives the leader as a person who can punish deviant behavior and actions.

Cognitive attitude The part of attitude that involves a person's perceptions, beliefs, and ideas.

Cognitive dissonance A state in which there is a discrepancy between a person's attitude and behavior.

Command group The group shown on an organization chart that reports to a single manager.

Communication The transmission of information and understanding through the use of common symbols.

Conceptual management skill The ability to coordinate and integrate ideas, concepts, and practices. Such skill is most important to top-level managers.

Concurrent control The techniques and methods which focus on the actual, ongoing activity of the organization.

Conditions of certainty A situation in which a person facing a decision has enough information to know what the outcome of each alternative will be.

Conditions of risk A situation in which a person facing a decision can estimate the likelihood (probability) of a particular outcome.

Conditions of uncertainty A situation in which the decision maker has absolutely no idea of the probabilities associated with the various alternatives being considered. In such a situation, the intuition, judgment, and personality of the decision maker can play an important role.

Consideration Acts by a leader which imply supportive concern for the followers in a group.

Contingency management An approach that considers an organization's objectives, organizational and job design, human resources, environment, and managerial skills as interacting and affecting the type of management decisions made about planning, decision making, organizing, leading, and controlling.

Controlling function All managerial activity that is undertaken to assure that actual operations go according to plan.

Cost-benefit analysis A technique for evaluating individual projects and deciding among alternatives. This technique is being adapted to the needs of public sector organizations to aid them in improving their performance.

Critical path The longest path in a PERT network, from the network beginning event to the network ending event.

Culture Culture is a very complex environmental influence which includes knowledge, beliefs, law, morals, art, customs, and any other habits and capabilities an individual acquires as a member of society. It is important to be aware that cultures are *learned,* cultures *vary,* and culture *influences behavior.*

Decentralization The pushing downward of the appropriate amount of decision-making authority. All organizations practice a certain degree of decentralization.

Decision making The process of thought and deliberation which results in a decision. Decisions, the output of the decision-making process, are means through which a manager seeks to achieve some desired state.

Decoding The mental procedure which the receiver of a message uses to decipher the message.

Defensive behavior Behavior such as aggression, withdrawal, and repression which is resorted to by an individual when blocked in attempts to satisfy needs.

Delegation The process by which authority is distributed downward in an organization.

Departmentation The process of grouping jobs together on the basis of some common characteristic, such as product, client, location, or function.

Diagnosis The use of data collected by interviews, surveys, observations, or records to learn about people or organizations.

Differentiation The degree of differences in the knowledge and emotional orientations of managers in different departments of an organization.

Direct investment entry strategy The strongest commitment to becoming an MNC is when management decides to begin producing the firm's products abroad. This strategy enables the firm to maintain full control over production, marketing, and other key functions.

Direction A method of concurrent control which refers to the manager's act of interpreting orders to a subordinate.

Discounted rate of return The rate of return that equates future cash proceeds with the initial cost of an investment.

Diseases of adaptation A type of disease that results from the imperfect attempt to cope with stressors.

Distinctive competence A factor which gives the organization an advantage over similar organizations. Distinctive competences are what the organization does well.

Downward communication Communication that flows from individuals at higher levels of an organization structure to individuals at lower levels. The most common type of downward communication is job instructions that are transmitted from the superior to the subordinate.

Dual careers Situations in which both the husband and the wife are pursuing careers.

Emergent leader A person from within the group who comes to lead or influence its members.

Encoding The converting of a communication into an understandable message by a communicator.

EOQ model The economic order quantity model, which is used to resolve problems regarding the size of orders. A manager concerned with minimizing inventory costs could utilize the model to study the relationships between carrying costs, ordering costs, and usage.

Esteem needs The awareness of the importance of others and of the regard which is accorded by others.

Event An accomplishment at a particular point in time on a PERT network. An event consumes no time.

Expectancy motivation model Views motivation as a process governing choices. In this model, a person who has a goal weighs the likelihood that various behaviors will achieve that goal and is likely to select the behavior that is expected to be most successful.

Expected time(t_e) A time estimate for each activity that is calculated by using the formula:

$$t_e = \frac{a + 4m + b}{6}$$

where a = optimistic time, m = most likely time, and b = pessimistic time.

Expected value The average return of a particular decision in the long run if the decision maker makes the same decision in the same situation over and over again. The expected value is found by taking the value of an outcome if it should occur and multiplying that value by the probability that the outcome will occur.

Expert power The power which individuals possess because followers perceive them to have special skills, special knowledge, or a special expertise.

Export entry strategy The simplest way for a firm to enter a foreign market is by exporting. This strategy involves little or no change in the basic mission, objectives, and strategies of the organization, since it continues to produce all of its products at home. The firm will usually secure an *agent* in the particular foreign market who facilitates the transactions with foreign buyers.

External change forces Forces for change outside the organization, such as the pricing strategies of competitors, the available supply of resources, and government regulations.

Final performance review The last step in the MBO process, a final meeting between the manager and the subordinate which focuses on performance over an entire period. The final performance review must accomplish two important purposes: (1) an evaluation of the objectives achieved and the relating of these accomplishments to rewards such as salary increments and promotion and (2) an evaluation of performance that is intended to aid the subordinate in self-development and to set the stage for the next period.

First-line management The lowest level of the hierarchy. A manager at this level coordinates the work of nonmanagers but reports to a manager.

Forecasting An important element of the planning function which must make these two basic determinations: (1) what level of activity can be expected during the planning period and (2) what level of resources will be available to support the projected activity. In a business organization, the critical forecast is the sales forecast.

Foreign subsidiary entry strategy As exports increase in importance to the firm, it may decide that it can justify its own foreign subsidiary. This decision usually involves joining with nationals in the foreign country to establish product and/or marketing facilities. It differs from direct investment in that some type of association is formed with a local firm or individual. This type of association usually takes the form of licensing or joint-venture arrangements. *Licensing* is granting the right to produce and/or market the firm's product in another country to an outside firm. *Joint-venture* arrangements involve foreign investors forming a group with local investors to begin a local business with each group sharing ownership.

Formal groups The established departments, units, and teams created by the managers in an organization.

Friendship group An informal group that evolves because of some common characteristic, such as age, political sentiment, or background.

General adaptation syndrome (GAS) A system of reaction to stress identified by Hans Selye that includes three stages—alarm, resistance, and exhaustion.

Generativity An individual's concern for actions and achievements that will benefit future generations.

Goal participation The amount of involvement a person has in setting task and personal development goals.

Graicunas's law A mathematical formulation of the relationship between the number of subordinates (N) and the number of potential superior-subordinate contacts (C):

$$C = N\left(\frac{2^N}{2} + N - 1\right)$$

Grapevine An informal communication network in organizations that short-circuits the formal channels.

Grid training A leadership development method proposed by Blake and Mouton which emphasizes the necessary balance between production orientation and person orientation.

Group assets The advantages derived from the increase in knowledge that is brought to bear on a problem when a group examines it.

Group cohesiveness The attraction of individual members to a group in terms of the strength of the forces that impel them to remain active in the group and to resist leaving it.

Group development The phases or sequences through which a group passes, such as mutual acceptance, decision making, motivation, and control.

Group liabilities The negative features of groups, such as the group pressure that is expected to bring dissident members into line, the takeover of a dominant member, and the reduced creativity that results from the embarrassment of members about expressing themselves.

Group norm Agreement among a group's members about how they should behave.

Group politics The use of self-serving tactics to improve a group's position relative to that of other groups.

Groupthink A phenomenon that occurs when a group believes that it is invincible, turns off criticism, attempts to bring noncomplying members into line, and feels that everyone is in agreement.

Halo effects The forming of impressions (positive or negative) about a person based on an impression formed from performance in one area.

Halo error A positive or negative aura around a ratee that influences a rater's evaluation.

Hawthorne effect The tendency of people who are being observed or involved in a research effort to react differently than they would otherwise.

Hawthorne studies Management studies conducted at the Western Electric Hawthorne plant in a suburb of Chicago. The most famous studies that have ever been conducted in the field of management.

Health profiling Collecting information and data on a person's well-being, habits, and physical condition to develop a profile of the person's health age which is compared to his or her chronological age. The profile helps a person examine his or her health prospects.

Horizontal communication Occurs when the communicator and the receiver are at the same level in the organization.

Human management skill The ability to work with, motivate, and counsel people who need help and guidance. Most important to middle-level managers.

Human resource planning Estimating the size and makeup of the future work force.

Immediate performance measures Measures of

results that are monitored over short periods of time, such as a day, a week, a month, or a year. These include measures of output, quality, time, cost, and profit. Immediate performance measures are not always easy to obtain.

Informal groups Natural groupings of people in response to some need.

Initiating structure Leadership acts which develop job tasks and responsibilities for followers.

Integration The degree to which members of various departments work together effectively.

Intelligence information Data on such elements of the organization's operating environment as clients, competitors, suppliers, creditors, and the government for use in short-run planning, and data on developments in the economic environment, such as consumer income trends and spending patterns, and in the social and cultural environment for use in long-run strategic planning.

Interest group An informal group formed to achieve some job-related, but personal, objective.

Intergroup conflict The disagreements, hostile emotions, and problems that exist among groups. These conflicts emerge because of limited resources, communication problems, differences in perceptions and attitudes, and a lack of clarity.

Intermediate performance reviews In the MBO process, periodic reviews of performance that monitor progress toward achieving the objectives that have been established and the action plans that have been developed. These reviews are an important element of control in management by objectives.

Internal change forces Forces for change that occur within the organization, such as communication problems, morale problems, and decision-making breakdowns.

Intertype competition Occurs between different types of institutions. Kellogg competes with Procter & Gamble for shelf space in supermarkets, and hospitals compete with private clinics for medical practitioners.

Intratype competition Occurs between institutions engaged in the same basic activity. Ford competes with General Motors for automobile customers. This is the form of competition that is described in economic studies.

Inventory models A type of production control model which answers two questions relating to inventory management: "How much?" and "When?" An inventory model tells the manager when goods should be reordered and what quantity should be purchased.

Investment decisions Commitments of present funds in exchange for potential future funds. Investment decisions are controlled through a capital budget.

Job analysis A process of determining what tasks make up the job and what skills, abilities, and responsibilities are required of an individual in order to successfully accomplish the job.

Job depth The relative freedom that a jobholder has in the performance of assigned duties.

Job enrichment A strategy that seeks to improve performance and satisfaction by building more responsibility, more challenge, and a greater sense of achievement into jobs.

Job scope The relative complexity of an assigned task.

Leader-member relations A factor in the Fiedler situational model of leadership which refers to the degree of confidence, trust, and respect that followers have in the leader.

Leadership In the context of management theory, the ability of a person to influence the activities of followers in an organizational setting. Management theory emphasizes that the leader must interact with his or her followers in order to be influential.

Legitimate power The power which rank gives a leader in the managerial hierarchy. For example, the department manager possesses more legitimate power than the supervisor because the department manager is ranked higher than the supervisor.

Less developed country (LDC) An LDC has a very low gross national product, very little industry or an unequal distribution of income with a very large number of poor.

Line functions Activities which contribute directly to the creation of the organization's output. In manufacturing, the line functions are production, marketing, and finance.

Macro-organizational design The design of an organization or a department.

Management The process by which people, technology, job tasks, and other resources are combined and coordinated so as to effectively achieve organizational goals.

Management development The process of educating and developing selected employees so that they have the knowledge, skills, attitudes, and understanding needed to manage in future positions.

Management functions The activities which a manager must perform as a result of position in the organization. The text identifies planning, organizing, leading, and controlling as the management functions.

Management information systems An organized, structured complex of individuals, machines, and procedures for providing management with pertinent information from both external and internal sources. Management information systems support the planning, control, and operations functions of an organization by providing uniform information that serves as the basis for decision making.

Management by objectives A planning and controlling method which comprises these major elements: (1) the superior and the subordinate meet to discuss goals and to jointly establish attainable goals for the subordinate; (2) the superior and the subordinate meet again afterward to evaluate the subordinate's performance in terms of the goals that have been set.

Managerial roles The organized sets of behavior that belong to the manager's job. The three main types of managerial roles discovered by such researchers as Mintzberg are interpersonal, informational, and decisional roles.

Matrix organizational design A design in which a project-type structure is superimposed on a functional structure.

Mechanistic system An organizational design in which there is differentiation of job tasks, rigid rules, and a reliance on top-management objectives.

Meditation An individual method of coping with stress that involves relaxing and shutting out other distractions.

Micro-organizational design The design of a job.

Midcareer plateau The point, or stage, of a career at which the individual has no opportunity for further promotion or advancement.

Middle management The middle level of an administrative hierarchy. Managers at this level coordinate the work of managers and report to a manager.

Mission A long-term vision of what an organization is trying to become. The mission is the unique aim that differentiates an organization from similar organizations. The basic questions that must be answered in order to determine an organization's mission are, "What is our business? What should it be?"

Motion study The process of analyzing work in order to determine the most efficient motions for performing tasks. Motion study, a major contribution of scientific management, was developed principally through the efforts of Frederick Taylor and Frank and Lillian Gilbreth.

Motivation The inner strivings that initiate a person's actions.

Multinational company (MNC) An MNC is a business firm doing business in two or more countries.

Need hierarchy A model that presents five levels of individual needs—physiological, safety, social, esteem, and self-actualization. According to Maslow, if a person's needs are unsatisfied, the most basic levels of needs will be more pressing than the other levels.

Negative reinforcement An increase in the frequency of a response which is brought about by removing a disliked event immediately after the response occurs.

Noise Interference with the flow of a message from a sender to a receiver.

Nonprogrammed decisions Decisions for novel and unstructured problems or for complex or extremely important problem. Nonprogrammed decisions deserve special attention of top management.

Operating management Manages the implementation of programs and projects in each area of performance, measures and evaluates results, and compares results with objectives.

Ordering cost An element in inventory control models that comprises clerical, administrative, and labor costs; a major cost component that is considered in inventory control decisions. Each time a firm orders items for inventory, some clerical and administrative work is usually required to place the order and some labor is required to put the items in inventory.

Organic system An organizational design with a behavioral orientation, participation from all employees, and communication flowing in all directions.

Organization strategies The general approaches

that are utilized by the organization to achieve its organizational objectives. These approaches include market penetration, market development, product development, and diversification strategies.

Organization structure The formally defined framework of task and authority relationships. The organization structure is analogous to the biological concept of the skeleton.

Organizational change The intentional attempt by management to improve the overall performance of individuals, groups, and the organization as a whole by altering the organization's structure, behavior, and technology.

Organizational communications Information that flows outward from the organization to the various components of its external operating environment. Whatever the type of organization, the content of this information flow is controlled by the organization (e.g., advertising in business organizations).

Organizational objectives The broad continuing aims which serve as guides for action and as the starting point for more specific and detailed operating objectives at lower levels in the organization. This book classifies organizational objectives into four categories: profitability, competitiveness, efficiency, and flexibility.

Organizational performance The extent to which an organization achieves the results that society expects of it. Organizational performance is affected in part by managerial performance.

Organizing function All managerial activity which results in the design of a formal structure of tasks and authority.

Payback period The length of time that it takes for an investment to pay for itself out of future funds.

Perception The process by which individuals organize and interpret their impressions of the environment around them.

Performance evaluation A postcontrol technique which focuses on the extent to which employees have achieved expected levels of work during a specified time period.

Personal-behavioral leadership theories A group of theories that are based primarily on the personal and behavioral characteristics of leaders. These theories focus on *what* leaders do and/or *how* leaders behave in carrying out the leadership function.

Personality The sum of an individual's traits or characteristics. These traits interact to create personality patterns.

Physiological (basic) needs Consist of needs of the human body, such as food, water, and sex.

Planning function All managerial activities which lead to the definition of objectives and to the determination of appropriate means to achieve those objectives.

Policies Guidelines for managerial action that must be adhered to at all times. Policymaking is an important management planning element for assuring that action is oriented toward objectives. The purpose of policies is to achieve consistency and direction and to protect the reputation of the organization.

Position power A factor in the Fiedler situational model of leadership which refers to the power inherent in the leadership position.

Positive reinforcement An increase in the frequency of a response which results when the response is followed by a positive reinforcer.

Postcontrol The techniques and methods which analyze historical data to correct future events.

Power The ability to influence another person's behavior.

Precontrol The techniques that are used to maintain the quality and quantity of resources.

Prescriptive management Discovering and reporting how managers should perform their functions.

Principle of management A generally accepted tenet which guides the thinking and on-the-job practices of managers.

Private sector organizations Profit-making organizations in the U.S. economy.

Profitability measures Profitability measures include the ratio of net profit to capital, to total assets, and to sales.

Programmed decisions Responses to repetitive and routine problems, which are handled by a standard procedure that has been developed by management.

Project organizational design A design in which a project manager temporarily directs a group of employees who have been brought together from various functional units until a specific job is completed.

Projection The tendency of people to attribute to others traits which they feel are negative aspects of their own personality.

Public sector organizations Federal, state, and local governmental bodies.

Punishment The introduction of something disliked or the removal of something liked following a particular response in order to decrease the frequency of that response.

Ranking methods The ranking of ratees on the basis of relevant performance dimensions.

Rate of return The ratio of the annual returns to the initial cost of the investment.

Realistic job previews (RJP) The practice of providing realistic information to new employees. The recruiter tells it like it is to avoid creating expectations that cannot be realized.

Recency of events error The tendency to make biased ratings because of the excessive influence of recent events.

Recycling The process by which one MBO cycle gives way to another. The final performance evaluation session of one MBO leads directly into the establishment of objectives for the next cycle. Divisional or departmental objectives are established, individual objective-setting sessions are conducted, and the MBO process recycles.

Referent power The power of a leader that is based on the leader's attractiveness. The leader is admired because of certain personal qualities, and the follower identifies closely with those qualities.

Reward power The power generated by the perception of followers that compliance with the wishes of leaders can lead to positive rewards (for example, promotion).

Safety needs Refers to such needs as protection from harm, ill health, and economic disaster and to the need for job security.

Scalar chain The graded chain of authority through which all organizational communications flow.

School of management A body of knowledge, concepts, and procedures that is used by managers. The authors discuss three schools of management. The *classical* school focuses on the functions of managers and on how those functions can be applied efficiently. The *behavioral* school is particularly concerned about people and how they behave and respond in organizations. The *management science* school uses mathematical procedures and scientific methods to study organizations. Each of these schools has advocates who consider its view of managing to be the most accurate and successful. The authors' preference is to show how each of the schools makes a contribution to managing for performance.

Scientific management The practices introduced by Frederick W. Taylor to accomplish the management job. Taylor advocated the use of scientific procedures to find the one best way to do a job.

Self-actualization The need to fully realize one's potential.

Sensitivity training An organizational change approach that focuses on the emotions and processes of interacting with people.

Situation analysis An attempt to understand the environment in which the organization's efforts will be expended; an important phase of the strategic planning process. Before a well-managed organization expends any effort, it conducts a situation analysis. This attempts to answer two questions for management: What should be done? What is it possible to do? The situation analysis is usually conducted in two phases: the internal analysis and the external analysis.

Situational theory of leadership An approach which advocates that leaders understand their own behavior, the behavior of their subordinates, and the situation before they utilize a particular leadership style. The application of this approach requires diagnostic skills in human behavior on the part of the leader.

Social needs Needs for social interaction and companionship.

Social readjustment rating scale A scale developed by Holmes and Rahe to determine the variety of life change events a person is facing. The higher the life change event score, the higher the probability of the onset of illness in the future.

Span of control The number of subordinates who report to a superior. The span of control is a factor that affects the shape and height of an organization structure.

Stable external environment An environment in which there is little unpredictable change.

Staff functions Activities which contribute indirectly to the creation of the organization's output. Ordinarily, staff personnel advise line personnel.

Staffing A process that includes the forecasting of personnel needs and the recruitment, selection, placement, and training and development of employees.

Stereotyping The attribution of a whole set of traits

to persons on the basis of their membership in particular groups.

Strategic management Develops the mission, objectives, and strategies of the entire organization; the top-level decision makers in the organization.

Strategic planning The activities which lead to the definition of objectives for the entire organization and to the determination of appropriate strategies for achieving those objectives.

Stress The consequence of the interaction between an event or situation and the individual as modified by individual differences.

Stress innoculation training Training that helps a person work through, cognitively, his or her situation. It is a self-analysis and coping procedure.

Stressor An event or situation that may induce stress. Examples would be role conflict, organization structure, a leader's behavior.

Strictness or leniency rater errors Ratings that are lower or higher than the average ratings usually given because of the strictness or the leniency of the rater.

Structural change A planned change of the formally prescribed task and authority relationships in an organization's design.

Supportive relations The consideration and interest displayed by a manager toward subordinates.

System 4 Likert's people-oriented organization design, which emphasized open communication, supportiveness, inputs from employees to managers, and general supervision. The opposite extreme of System 4 is System 1 organization design.

Task group A formal group put together temporarily to complete a specific job or project.

Technical management skill The skill of working with the resources and knowledge in a specific area. Such skill is most important to first-level managers.

Technological change A planned change in the machinery, equipment, or techniques that are used to accomplish organizational goals.

Theory X–Theory Y McGregor's theory that behind every management decision is a set of assumptions that a manager makes about human behavior. The Theory X manager assumes that people are lazy, dislike work, want no responsibility, and prefer to be closely directed. The Theory Y manager assumes that people seek responsibility, like to work, and are committed to doing good work if rewards are received for achievement.

Time study The process of determining the appropriate elapsed time for the completion of a task or job. This process was developed as part of Frederick W. Taylor's effort to determine a fair day's work.

Top management The top level of an administrative hierarchy. Managers at this level coordinate the work of other managers but do not report to a manager.

Trait theory Attempts to specify which personal characteristics (physical, personality, mental) are associated with leadership effectiveness. Trait theory relies on research that relates various traits to effectiveness criteria.

Transactional analysis A behavioral change approach that is designed to give individuals insight into their impact on others and their interpersonal communication style.

Turbulent external environment An environment in which changes are unexpected and unpredictable.

Two-factor theory of motivation The theory, popularized by the work of Frederick Herzberg, that the absence of some job conditions dissatisfies employees but that the presence of those conditions does not build employee motivation and that the absence of other job conditions does not dissatisfy employees but that their presence builds employee motivation. The former conditions, called *maintenance* factors, include job security, work conditions, salary, and status. The latter conditions, called *motivators,* include achievement, recognition, advancement, and responsibility.

Type A behavior pattern An action-emotion complex that can be observed in a person who is aggressively involved in a chronic struggle to achieve more and more in less and less time. Descriptors of this pattern include hard driving, competitive, and impatient.

Type B behavior pattern The opposite of a Type A. A pattern displayed by a thorough, easygoing, not overly competitive person.

Unity of command A management principle which states that each subordinate should report to only one superior.

Unity of direction The process of grouping all related activities under one superior.

Upward communication Upward communication

flows from individuals at lower levels of an organization structure to those at higher levels. Some of the most common upward communication flows are suggestion boxes, group meetings, and appeal or grievance procedures.

Value set A lasting set of convictions that are held by a person, an accompanying mode of conduct, and the importance of the convictions to the person.

Weighted checklist A rating system consisting of statements that describe various types and levels of behavior for a particular job. Each of the statements is weighted according to its importance.

Work overload There are two types of overload: *quantitative*—when a person has too many different things to do or an insufficient amount of time to do the job; *qualitative*—when a person feels a lack of ability to do a part of the job.

Name index

A

Adler, R. D., 563 n
Alexander, T., 439
Allen, F. T., 47
Allen, L. A., 72
Alpander, Guvene G., 569 n
Alton, William B., 532 n
Andrews, C. G., 471
Ansoff, H. Igor, 107 n
Aplin, John C., 238
Archer, E. R., 99
Archibald, D., 370
Argyris, Chris, 196
Arlow, P., 47
Arnold, J. D., 530
Ash, Mary Kay, 548
Auden, W. H., 577
Avery, Frederick F., 282

B

Babcock, Richard D., 532 n
Baird, J. E., Jr., 336
Baker, Eugene F., 446
Baldwin, William, 342
Baranabus, Bently, 221 n
Barker, Tom, 260
Barker, Vickie, 260
Barnard, Chester, 4, 25, 607
Barr, E. E., 263
Barrett, R. S., 229
Barton, R. F., 146
Bass, Bernard, 383 n
Bassett, G. A., 488 n
Bassord, G., 136 n
Beard, D. W., 123
Beldt, S. F., 503
Beman, Lewis, 472 n
Berelson, Bernard, 343 n
Bergerac, Michael, 306–7
Berne, Eric, 522
Billings, R., 523 n
Blackburn, R. S., 186
Blake, Robert S., 292 n, 293
Blau, Francine D., 617
Bowen, D. E., 229
Bracey, H. B., 439
Bradway, M. K., 571
Bray, D. W., 304
Breaugh, J., 523 n
Brenner, Steven N., 618–20
Brief, A. P., 600
Brinberg, H. R., 439
Briscoe, D. R., 205
Broder, D. S., 304
Brown, Bennett A., 128
Brown, Milton P., 539 n
Brown, W., 626
Bucholz, R. A., 47
Bucknall, W. L., 230
Buffa, E. S., 471
Burck, Charles G., 206, 519 n
Burns, Tom, 199 n
Bush, Gerald R., 504 n

C

Calish, I. G., 530
Cameron, Juan, 615 n
Camillus, J. C., 471
Campbell, John P., 361 n
Caplan, R. D., 587 n
Carlson, H. C., 626
Carlson, J. E., 563 n
Carter, N., 264
Cass, E. L., 25
Cathey, P., 400
Cederblom, D., 503
Chandler, Alfred D., 198
Chemers, Martin M., 299 n
Cheney, P. H., 439
Chonko, L. B., 186
Christopher, W. F., 72
Churchill, Winston, 282
Cleland, D. I., 205
Clements, W. W., 282
Cobb, A. T., 530
Conarroe, R. R., 263
Conbrough, J. A., 15 n
Cooper, C. L., 600
Cordiner, Ralph, 160
Cowan, John, 491
Cox, T., 578 n, 582 n
Cronin, R. J., 230
Crystal, G. S., 370
Cummings, Larry L., 480 n
Cummins, Robert C., 390 n

D

Dahl, David R., 256 n
Dalton, D. R., 186
Dalton, Gene W., 241 n, 246, 490 n
Dam, A. van, 626
Dassett, D. L., 146
Davidson, M. J., 600
Davis, S. M., 123, 530
Dayan, D., 336
DeCotiis, T. A., 497 n
Dedmon, R. E., 600
Delong, D., 370
Dess, G. G., 123
Dickson, G. W., 439
Donnelly, J. H., Jr., 500 n
Dreher, G. F., 230
Drucker, Peter 24–25, 108 n, 129
Dulek, R., 336
Dunlop, John T., 524 n
Dunnette, Marvin D., 361 n

E

Eagleston, J. R., 600
Ebenstein, M., 439
Eilbert, Henry, 615 n
Ellig, B., 503
Erikson, Erik H., 245 n
Etzel, Michael J., 133 n

F

Farrell, D., 400
Fayol, Henri, 15, 195, 607
Feeney, Edward J., 365

Ference, Thomas P., 251 n
Fiedler, Fred, 287 n, 299
Fielding, G. J., 186
Filley, Alan, 394 n
Fisher, S. T., 626
Fitch, H. G., 370
Flacks, N., 336
Flamion, A., 370
Fleenor, C. Patrick, 153 n
Fleishman, Edwin A., 292 n
Follett, Mary Parker, 21 n
Fox, H. W., 123
French, J. R. P., 587 n
Freud, Sigmund, 345
Friedman, Meyer, 590–91
Fry, Fred L., 365 n
Fry, L. W., 47, 626
Fuller, S. B., 278
Fuller, S. H., 187

G

Galbraith, J. K., 571
Galbraith, J. R., 205
Gallagher, G. R., 471
Gamache, R. D., 530
Gannon, M., 47
Gardner, J., 370
George, Claude S., Jr., 14 n
Gerster, Darlene K., 238
Gerth, H. H., 195 n
Ghiselli, Edwin E., 286 n, 287 n, 288 n
Gibson, J. L., 500 n
Gilbreth, Frank, 607
Gilbreth, Lillian, 607
Glueck, William F., 34 n, 112, 257
Goldfield, Randy J., 420
Grant, J. H., 471
Gray, Ed, 41 n
Greenberg, C. I., 146
Greiner, Larry E., 511 n
Guth, W. D., 95

H

Hackman, J. Richard, 358 n
Hall, Douglas T., 238 n, 240 n, 245 n, 250 n, 252 n, 258 n, 259 n
Hall, Francine, 252 n, 258 n, 259 n
Hall, Jay, 321
Handy, C., 187
Harkness, Shirley, 617
Harper, Ben, 478
Hatfield, J. D., 336
Hay, Robert, 41 n
Haynes, R. S., 370
Heier, W. D., 263
Heiner, J. Stephen, 383 n
Henderson, A. M., 195 n
Henneman, H. G., III, 497 n
Herzberg, Frederick, 352–56, 400
Herzog, E. L., 530
Hill, W. K., 439
Hofer, Charles W., 113 n
Holmes, S. L., 47
Holmes, T. H., 591 n
Horn, J., 579 n
Howard, A., 304
Hubsch, D. M., 230
Hughes, Joe K., 282
Hunsaker, J. S., 99
Hunsaker, P. L., 99
Hunt, James G., 292 n
Hunting, Allen, 337
Huseman, R. C., 336

I–J

Iacocca, Lee, 50
Ivancevich, John M., 133 n, 500 n, 503, 578 n, 582 n, 587 n, 600
Jacobson, Eugene, 383 n
Jago, Arthur, 298 n
Janis, Irving L., 392 n
Janson, Robert, 358 n
Jarvis, Charles R., 282
Jewell, D. O., 503
Johnson, G. A., 471
Johnson, George E., 278

K

Kahn, H., 626
Kantrow, A. M., 25
Kast, Fremont E., 21 n, 123
Katz, E., 336
Katz, Robert L., 32 n
Kazdin, A. E., 370
Kdandwalla, Pradip N., 37 n
Keegan, Warren J., 554 n
Keen, P. G. W., 100
Kefalas, A. G., 626
Kein, G. D., 47, 626
Kendall, L. M., 497 n
Kenny, Elizabeth J., 4, 50, 160, 416, 548
Kets de Vries, Manfred F. R., 252 n
Kiechel, Walter, III, 106, 123
Kilmann, Ralph H., 193 n
King, Donald C., 390 n
King, J. L., 100
Kissinger, Henry, 563
Klein, H. E., 123
Klimoski, R., 523 n
Knudson, Harry R., 153 n
Kogyo, Toyo, 367
Kondrasuk, J. M., 146
Koontz, Harold, 22 n
Krajewski, L., 25
Kramer, Hugh E., 559
Krauss, L., 439
Kubiak, M. K., 600
Kudla, R. J., 123
Kuna, D. J., 595 n

L

Lawler, Edward E., III, 360 n, 361 n, 362, 503
Lawrence, Paul R., 200 n, 539 n
Lazarus, R. S., 600
Leavitt, Harold J., 517 n
Lee, N., 263
Leontiades, Milton, 113 n
Levitt, Theodore, 110 n, 614 n
Lewicki, R. J., 263
Likert, Rensis, 197, 290, 510
Littlejohn, R. F., 400
Locke, E. A., 25
Longenecker, J. G., 147
Loomis, C. J., 305
Lorsch, Jay W., 34 n, 200 n
Louis, M. R., 503
Lubar, R., 471
Luck, E. J., 94 n
Luksus, E. J., 73
Lupton, Tom, 39 n
Lutchen, M. D., 187
Luthans, Fred, 22 n, 264
Lyman, D., 264

M

McAvoy, R., 531
Maccoby, M., 305
McConkie, M. L., 147
McConnell, John H., 342
McGregor, Douglas, 344, 510, 607
Mackey, C. B., 230

McLaughlin, R. A., 210
McMahon, J. T., 503
McManus, G. J., 400
McNamara, Robert, 416
Main, Jeremy, 440 n, 510 n
Maisonrouge, Jacques, 110 n
Malone, Erwin L., 360 n
Mann, Floyd C., 524
Mann, Leon, 392 n
March, J. G., 530
Margerison, C., 305
Margulies, N., 530
Markus, M. L., 205
Marolda, Anthony J., 54
Martel, L., 626
Marth, D., 305
Martin, Lorna P., 78
Martin, R. A., 147
Maslow, Abraham, 345–47, 354–56, 510
Matteson, Michael T., 578 n, 582 n, 587 n, 600
Mausner, B., 352 n
Mayo, Elton, 607
Meiners, R. E., 47, 626
Merrill, H. F., 25
Metcalf, Henry C., 21 n
Meyer, H. H., 488 n
Meyer, Herbert, 231 n
Michael, Frederick B., 576
Michel, Henry L., 236
Mills, C. W., 195 n
Mills, P. K., 205
Mintzberg, Henry, 34 n
Molander, Earl A., 618–20
Monroe, Willys H., 189
Mooney, James D., 15 n
Moravec, M., 503
Morita, Akio, 54
Morrison, A. M., 124 n, 264, 306 n
Motly, P., 336
Mouton, Jane S., 292 n, 293
Murnighan, J. K., 100
Murr, D. W., 439

N

Naditch, Murray P., 602 n
Newman, W. H., 123
Niehouse, O. L., 600
Noda, Mitz, 567 n
Nougaim, Khalil, 240 n

O

O'Connell, Jeremiah, 519 n
Odiorne, George, 130 n, 370
Ohmae, K., 100, 626
Oldham, Greg, 358 n
Oliver, B. L., 94 n
Ostland, L. E., 47
Ouchi, W., 531, 571
Owens, J., 305

P

Parket, Robert, 615 n
Parsons, Talcott, 195 n
Pati, G. C., 531
Paul, William J., 356 n
Perlmutter, Howard V., 566
Perroni, A. G., 25
Pesci, M., 600
Peters, T. J., 531
Petersen, J. C., 400
Phillips, J. R., 531
Pine, R. C., 370
Pinsky, S., 600
Pinto, Patrick R., 256 n
Pitts, R. A., 205
Placky, R. J., 305
Pondy, Louis R., 193 n, 394 n
Porter, L. W., 186, 370
Porter, Michael E., 107 n
Posner, B. Z., 205
Pounds, William F., 84 n
Poza, E. J., 205
Preston, C., 600
Price, Raymond L., 241 n, 246, 490 n
Pringle, C., 147
Purdy, Kenneth, 358 n

Q–R

Quick, J. C., 147
Rader, M. H., 336
Rahe, R. H., 591 n
Rasberry, R. W., 336
Reece, James, 34 n
Reiley, Alan C., 15 n
Reimann, B. C., 123
Rice, Berkeley, 582 n, 603 n
Rief, W. E., 136 n
Robertson, Keith B., 356 n
Robinson, L. M., 563 n
Robinson, R. B., 73
Rosenman, Ray, 590–91
Rosenzweig, James E., 21 n
Rowan, Roy, 265 n
Rowe, D. L., 439

S

Saul, G. K., 47
Sayles, Leonard R., 608
Schendel, Dan, 113 n
Schmidt, Warren H., 297 n
Schonberger, R. J., 571
Schuler, R. S., 600
Schultz, Duane, 251 n
Schwab, Donald P., 480 n, 497 n
Schwartz, H., 123
Seashore, Stanley E., 40 n, 389 n
Seelye, Alfred L., 621
Seligman, D., 264
Selye, Hans, 579 n, 580 n
Sethi, S. Prakash, 42 n, 43
Shirley, R. C., 73
Shorris, E., 47
Simon, Herbert, 80 n
Skinner, B. F., 363, 370
Slevin, Dennis P., 193 n
Smith, Henry C., 521 n
Smith, P. B., 521 n
Smith, P. C., 497 n
Smith, W. G., 100
Snyder, Neil, 34 n
Snyderman, B., 352 n
Soloman, S., 400
Spendolini, M. J., 186
Stalker, G. M., 199 n
Steers, R. M., 370
Steiner, Gary A., 343 n, 626
Stern, Frances M., 582 n
Stinson, John W., 504 n
Stogdill, Ralph, 286 n, 287 n
Stoner, James A. F., 251 n
Storrs, C., 195 n
Strickland, A. J., 469
Stromberg, Ann H., 617

T

Tagiuri, R., 95
Tamarkin, Bob, 606
Tanaka, H., 571
Tannenbaum, Robert, 297 n

Tavernier, G., 73
Taylor, Frederick W., 289 n, 607
Telch, M. J., 600
Thompson, Arthur A., Jr., 469
Thompson, H., 25
Thompson, Paul H., 241 n, 246, 490 n
Thoreson, C. E., 600
Tichy, Noel M., 359 n
Tita, M. A., 531
Todor, W. D., 186
Tolley, L., 123
Tom, P. L., 439

U–V

Urwick, Lyndall, 14 n, 15 n, 21 n
Van Sell, M., 600
Verespej, Michael A., 401
Vroom, Victor, 298 n, 354, 356

W–Z

Walker, James W., 257 n
Walton, E. J., 187
Walton, Richard E., 360 n
Warren, E. Kirby, 251 n
Waterman, R. H., 531
Watson, K. M., 305
Weber, Max, 195
Weick, Karl E., Jr., 361 n
Weigel, R., 600
Welford, A. T., 579 n
Werner, Gerald C., 192 n
Whyte, William F., 269 n
Wolf, Stewart, 579 n
Wolff, Harold G., 579 n
Woodward, Joan, 200–201
Wrege, C. D., 25
Wu, F. H., 471
Yager, Edwin G., 368 n
Zemke, Ron, 367 n, 400, 582 n
Zimmer, F. G., 25

Subject index

A

A&P, 114
AT&T, 226
Accounts receivable turnover, 465
Action commitment, 61–62
Adolescence, 245
Adulthood, 245
Advertising media-mix problems, 460
Affirmative action programs, 261–62
Aggression, 350
Alcoa, 216
American Management Association, 227
Apprenticeship, 240
Arena, 322, 324
Attitude survey, 515–16

B

Background check, 222
BARS (behaviorally-anchored rating system), 497–99
Behavior, 343, 363–66
  constructive, 347, 349
  defensive, 349–51
  goal-directed, 356
  modification; *see* Behavior modification
Behavior modification, 363–66
  criticisms of, 365–66
  operant behavior, 363
  operant conditioning, 363
  organizational applications, 365
  positive and negative reinforcement, 364
  punishment, 364
  respondent behavior, 363
Behavioral approach to management, 17–19, 23
  contributions and limitations, 18–19
  human relations, 17–18
Behaviorally-anchored rating scales (BARS), 497–99
Biofeedback, 595–96
Blindspot in communication, 322–23
Budgeting, 66–69
  complexity, 67
  financial control, 463
  moving, 68–69
  process, 67
Bureaucracy, 195
Business ethics, 616–19
Business objectives, 113
Business Week, 45 n

C

Campbell Soup Company, 57
Capital, 425
  precontrol, 452–54
Career, 238
  definition, 238–39
  dual, 258–59
  Equal Employment Opportunity Act, 260–62
  human resource planning, 258
  midcareer managers, 250–53
  pathing, 254, 256–58
  planning; *see* Career planning
  recent hirees, 247–48
  stages, 240–46
    advancement, 242–43
    establishment, 240–42
    maintenance, 243
    relation to life stages, 245–46
    retirement, 243–44
Career planning, 254
  counseling, 254–55
  job posting, 255–56
  tuition aid program, 255
Carrying costs, 449–52
Central tendency error, 495–96
Chain of command, 183
Civil Rights Act of 1964, 217–18, 221
Classical organization theory, 13, 15, 23
  contributions and limitations, 16–17
  functions of management, 16, 22
  principles of management, 15–16
Classroom training, 224
Coaching, 226
Coca-Cola, 109, 120, 562
Command group, 378
Committees, 379
Communication
  breakdown in, 326–30
    conflicting frames of reference, 326–27
    filtering, 329
    overload, 330
    semantic problems, 328–29
    source credibility, 328
    time pressures, 329–30
    value judgements, 327
  communicator, 314, 326
  decoding, 314–16
  definition, 313–14, 328
  encoding, 314–15, 326
  improvement in, 330–34
    empathy, 332
    feedback, 314, 316, 324, 331–32
    following up, 331
    grapevine, 333–34
    listening effectively, 333
    regulating information flow, 331
    simplifying language, 332–33
  interpersonal styles, 321–26
  medium, 314–15, 326
  message, 314–15, 326
  organizational, 317–20
    diagonal, 319
    downward, 317–18
    horizontal, 319
    upward, 317–18
  receiver, 314, 316, 326
Communicator, 314
Compensation as defense mechanism, 350
Competition, 44, 59–60, 62, 117
  attitudes in three different cultures, 558–59
  international, 622
Concurrent control, 424, 426–27, 447
  direction, 426–27

Concurrent control—*Cont.*
financial resources, 464–65
production scheduling, 454–60
linear programming models, 458–60
network models, 454–58
Conditions of certainty, 85
Conditions of risk, 85–88
Conditions of uncertainty, 88–90
Constructive behavior, 347, 349
Continental Can Company, 253
Contingency approach to management, 21–22
multinational companies, 569
Contingency organizational design, 197–201
environment, 199
growth strategy, 198–99
Contingency theory of leadership; *see* Situational leadership
Controlling, 12
concurrent; *see* Concurrent control
corrective action, 422
definition, 421
financial, 463–69
information, 422, 428–37
internal, 464
manager of the future, 623–24
multinational companies, 568–69
planning, 91–92
postcontrol, 424–25, 427–28, 447, 460–63, 465–66
precontrol, 423–26, 447–60, 463–64
standards, 421–22
work groups, 385
Core dimensions of jobs, 358
Corporate performance, 44–45
competitiveness, 44
efficiency, 44
flexibility, 44
internal and external environment, 45–46
profitability, 44
Counseling, 254–55
formal, 255
informal, 254–55
Country club management, 292
Culture, 557

D

Decision making, 79
control, 91–92
definition, 82
evaluation, 91–92
group, 96–98
importance of decision, 92–93
managers, 81
propensity to risk, 92, 96
values, 92, 94–96
nonprogrammed, 80–81
problem identification, 83
programmed, 80–81
reasons for studying, 79
strategies
development, 84–85
evaluating, 85–90
implementing, 91–92
selecting, 90–91
time pressures, 92–93
Defensive political behavior, 396–97
Delegation of authority, 168–69
advantages, 181–82
chain of command and authority, 183
line-staff distinction, 184–85
Demographic trends, 612–13
Demotion, 228
Departmentation, 168, 172–78
customer, 176
functional, 172–73
multiple bases, 176–77
organizational change, 518–19
product, 174–76
territorial, 173–74
Developed countries, 560
Diagonal communication, 320
Differentiation, 200
Directing, 11, 426–27
Discharge, 228
Discounted rate of return, 453
Distinctive competences of organization, 109
Diverse organizational environment, 37–38
Diversification, 120–21
Downward communication, 317–18
Downward transfers, 253
Dr Pepper Company, 282
Dual careers, 258–60

E

Eaton Company, 254
Econometric models, 64–65
Economic environment of multinational company, 560–61
Economic order quantity (EOQ) formula, 451–52
Efficiency of organization, 44, 59–60, 62
Ego integrity, 245
Emery Company, 365
Environment of organization, 107–9, 198–99
external, 37–43
Equal Employment Opportunity Commission (EEOC), 216–18, 260–62
Equitable Life Assurance Company, 599
ESCO Corporation, 318
Esteem needs, 347
work group, 383
Evaluation of information, 434
Exception principle of management, 331
Exporting, 555
Exposure in interpersonal communications, 324
External environment of management system, 37–39
diverse, 38
hostile, 38
technically complex, 38–39
turbulent, 38
Exxon, 254

F

Facade, 323–24
Fallback positions, 253
Feed-mix problems, 459
Feedback, 225
communication, 314, 316, 324, 331–32
direct and indirect, 316
job performance, 248–49
motivation, 358
organizational change, 520, 528
Finance, 66
Financial budgeting; *see* Budgeting
Financial ratios, 467–69
First-line manager, 30
decision making, 81

Flexibility of organization, 44, 59, 61–62
Fluid-blending problems, 459
Forbes, 45 n
Foreign Corrupt Practices Act, 563
Foreign subsidiary, 555–56
Formal leaders, 284
Formal work groups, 378–80
Fortune, 45 n
Friendship group, 380
Frito-Lay, 120
Frustration of needs, 347–51
Functional control information, 431
Functional manager, 31–32
Functional objectives, 112–13

G

General adaptation syndrome, 579–80
General Electric, 109, 226, 254, 446
General Foods, 57, 359–60
General Mills, 216
Generativity, 245
Geographic expansion, 198
Goodrich, B. F., Company, 78, 97, 365
Government, 619–22
  business legislation, 621
Grapevine, 333–34
Griggs v. *Duke Power Company,* 221–22
Group decision making, 96–98
Group norms, 387–89
Group pressure, 387–88
Groupthink, 392–93
Gulf Oil Company, 254

H

Halo error, 495
Hawthorne studies, 196
Health profiling, 596–97
Hershey Company, 114
Heublein Company, 253
Hill Brothers, 57
Horizontal communication, 319
Horizontal managerial specialization, 29
Hostile environment, 37–38
Human relations approach to management, 17–18
Human resources, 612
  control, 425
  performance evaluation; *see* Performance evaluation
Hunches as forecasting approach, 62–63, 65

I

IBM, 254
Impoverished management, 292
Informal leaders, 284
Informal work groups, 380–81
Information, 422
  functional control, 431
  management information system; *see* Management information system
  operational control, 431–32
  strategic control, 431
Information system; *see* Management information system
Integration in organization design, 200
Intelligence information, 432
Interest group, 380
Internal control, 464–65
International competition, 622
International Harvester, 226
Interpersonal communication, 321
  arena, 322, 324
  blindspot, 322
  direction, 427
  exposure, 324
  facade, 323–24
  feedback, 324
  management styles, 324
  unknown factors, 323–24
Interview
  semistructured, 220
  structured, 220
  unstructured, 220–21
Inventory control, 449–52
Inventory turnover, 465
Investment decisions, 425
  rate of return of capital control, 453–54

J

Japan
  leadership styles, 567–68
  multinational companies, 557, 561, 564
Job analysis, 214–16
Job description, 214–16
Job enrichment, 356–60
  core dimensions, 357–58
  diagnosis of job, 358–59
  organizational applications, 359–60
  Non-Linear Systems experiment, 360
Job previews, 249–50
Job rotation, 226
Job satisfaction, 353, 357
Job specification, 167–72, 214–16
  specialization, 170–71
Jordache Enterprises, Inc., 164, 175–76

K–L

Katharine Gibbs School, Inc., 420
Leading, 11
  communication; *see* Communication
  definition, 279, 283
  flexibility, 297–302
  function, 284–85
  Japan, 567–68
  manager of the future, 623
  managerial grid theory, 292–93
  multinational companies, 565, 567–68
  person-oriented, 284–85, 290–91, 295
  personal characteristics of leaders, 285–88, 302–3
  situational, 296–302
  subordinate-centered, 298–99
  task-oriented, 284–85, 289–90, 295
  two-dimensional theory, 291–92
Legislation affecting business, 621
Lehman Brothers, 253
Leniency rater errors, 495–96
Less developed country (LDC), 560–61
Life stages, 244–45
  relation to career, 245–46
Line, 184–85
Line-staff relationships, 519–20
Linear programming models, 458–60
Liquidity measures, 465–66

M

McDonald's, 113, 599
Maintenance factors, 353
Management
  behavioral approach, 17–19
  classical approach, 13–17
  contingency approach, 21–22

Management—*Cont.*
controversial, 8
definition, 10
exception principle, 331
influence in society, 7–8
information system, 430–37
knowledge about, 12
management science approach, 19–20
meanings, 8–9
as career, 9
as discipline, 9
as people, 8
as process, 9
multinational companies; *see* Multinational company
systems approach, 20–21
Management development, 225–27
Management information system (MIS), 144, 430, 432–37
external information flows, 432
information center, 435–36
intelligence information, 432–33
intraorganization flows, 433
organizational communications, 432–33
organizational resource, 436–37
purposes, 433–35
Management by objectives, 129–44
action plans, 136–39
benefits of, 142–43
definition, 130
information systems adaptation, 144
motivation, 132–33
objectives, 131, 134–36, 138
participation of subordinates, 132
performance evaluation, 496
performance review, 139–41
problems, 143–44
process, 133–41
timing of objectives, 131–33
Management process, 9, 22
controlling, 10, 12
leading, 10–11, 16
organizing, 10–11
planning, 10–11
Management science approach to management, 19–20, 23
contributions and limitations, 19–20
Manager, 29–32
competences required, 609–10
environmental forces, 37–43, 611–22
first-line, 30–31
functional, 31–32
future, 607–11
horizontal specialization, 29
Japan, 567–68
middle, 30–31
one manager-many subordinates system, 29–30
propensity to risk, 92, 96
roles; *see* Managerial roles
styles, 324–25, 567–68
top, 30–31
values, 92, 94–96
vertical specialization, 29–30
Managerial grid theory, 292–93
Managerial performance, 45–46
Managerial roles, 34–37, 608
decisional, 36
disturbance handler, 36
entrepreneur, 36
negotiator, 36–37
resource allocator, 36
informational, 35
disseminator, 36
monitor, 35–36
spokesperson, 36
interpersonal, 34
figurehead, 34
leadership, 34–35
liason, 35
levels of management, 37
Managerial skills
analytical, 32–33
communication, 33
conceptual, 33
decision making, 33
human, 33
level of management, 33–34
technical, 32
Market development, 120
Market penetration, 119–20
Market surveys, 63, 65
Marketing, 66
Mass production, 200–201
Matrix design, 203–4
Maturity, 245
Mazda, 367
Mechanistic organization system, 199
Meditation, 595
Midcareer crisis, 240
Midcareer plateau, 251–52
Middle managers, 31
decision making, 81
Middle-of-the-road management, 292
Minute Maid, 109, 120
Montgomery Ward, 114
Morgan Adhesives Company, 260
Motivation, 11, 343–68
behavior, 343–45, 347–51, 363–66
definition, 343
expectancy theory, 354–56
individual needs, 345–47
frustration of, 347–51
maintenance factors, 353
managerial approaches for improving, 356–68
job enrichment, 356–60
pay incentives, 360–63
performance evaluation, 483
personality, 351–52
quality circles, 366–68
survey, 348–49, 371
Theories X and Y, 344–45
two-factor theory, 352–54
work groups, 384–85
Moving budgeting, 68–69
Multinational company (MNC), 553
competition, 558–59
contingency approach, 569
culture, 557
definition, 553
direct investment, 556
economic environment, 560–61
exports, 555
foreign subsidiary, 555–56
management functions
controlling, 568–69
leading, 565, 567–68
organizing, 565–66
planning, 564
operating in United States, 555
political environment, 561–63

N

National Lumber Company, 153–57
Natural resources, 611–12
Needs, 343–51
nonsatisfaction, 347, 350–51
satisfaction, 343

Needs hierarchy, 346
Negative reinforcement, 364
Network models, 455
Non-Linear Systems experiment, 360
Nonprogrammed decision, 80–81
Norm, 387
personalization, 388–89
Northrup Corporation, Defense Systems Division, 462–63, 562

O

Offensive political behavior, 396
On-the-job training, 224
management, 226–27
Operant behavior, 363
Operant conditioning, 363
Operational control information, 431–32
Operations, 447
Operations research teams, 19
Organic organization system, 199
Organization, 11
change; *see* Organizational change
design; *see* Organizational design
manager of the future, 623
mission, 108–11
clients, 110–11, 118
distinctive competences, 109
environment, 108–9, 113–14
external focus, 110
multinational companies, 565–66
objectives, 59–62, 65–66
staffing; *see* Staffing
strategic planning, 118
structure; *see* Organizational structure
Organization chart, 167–68, 177
Organization objectives, 59–62
strategy related to, 65–66
Organization performance; *see* Corporate performance
Organizational change
behavioral, 520–23
diagnosing problems, 515–17
forces for, 512–14
environmental, 513
external and internal, 512–14
technology, 513
implementing, 528–29
limiting conditions, 525–26
management of, 511–12
monitoring, 528–29
overcoming resistance, 526–27
structural, 517–20
Organizational communications, 432–33
Organizational complexity, 57
Organizational design, 193–204
contingency, 197–201
differentiation, 200
future, 207–8
General Motors, 206–7
integration, 200
matrix, 203–4
project, 201–3
System 1, 193–96
System 4, 194, 196–97
technology, 200–201
Organizational strategies, 119–21
diversification, 120–21
market development, 120
market penetration, 119–20
product development, 120
Organizational structure
delegation of authority, 168–69, 181–85
departmentation, 168–69, 172–78
job specification, 167–72
span of control, 168–69, 178–81

P

Parsons, Brinckerhoff, Quade and Douglas, Inc., 236
Participative management, 297–98
Payback method of capital precontrol, 452–54
Payoff table, 86–88
Penney, J. C., Company, 213
Pepsi-Cola, 120
Performance audit, 365
Performance evaluation, 227, 479–501
administration, 487–90
BARS, 496–99
essay method, 494–95
graphic rating scales, 490–93
interview, 489–91
management by objectives, 499–500
process, 481
purposes, 480–84
standards, 484–87
weighted checklist, 493–94
Person-oriented leadership, 290–91
Personnel, 66
standards, 486–87
PERT (Program Evaluation and Review Technique), 455–58
Philips Industries, 317
Physiological needs, 346–47
Pitney Bowes, 317
Planning, 11, 55–71
benefits, 56
budgeting, 66–69
decision making; *see* Decision making
definition, 56
forecasting
resource, 64–65
sales, 62–64
management by objectives; *see* Management by objectives
manager of the future, 623
multinational companies, 563–64
need for, 56–59
external change, 58
organizational complexity, 57–58
relation to other management functions, 58–59
time span between decisions and results, 57
objectives, 59–62
policies, 69–71
strategic analysis; *see* Strategic analysis
strategy formulation, 65–66
Policies
criteria of effectiveness, 70–71
definition, 69
Position description, 214
Position specification, 214
Positive reinforcement, 364
Postcontrol, 424–25, 427–28, 447
financial resources, 465–66
production-operations output, 460
standard cost analysis, 460–61
statistical quality control, 461–63
Precontrol, 423–26, 447
financial resources, 463–64
production-operations, 448–60
capital, 452–54
materials, 448–52
Probabilities, 85–86

Process consultation, 520
Process production, 200–201
Procter & Gamble, 109, 120, 253
Product development, 120
Product diversification, 198
Product-market matrix, 119
Product-mix problems, 459
Production, 66, 447
Production-operations control, 447
  concurrent, 454–60
  postcontrol of outputs, 460–63
  precontrol of inputs, 448–54
Production scheduling
  linear programming, 458–60
  network models, 454–58
Production standards, 486
Professionals, 241
Profit-maximizing management, 41
Profitability, 44, 59–60, 62, 465
Program Evaluation Review Technique (PERT), 455–58
Programmed decisions, 80–81
Programs, 65
Project design, 201–3
Projection, 350
Promotion, 227–28

Q

Quality circles (QCs), 366–68
Quality control, 428, 448
  statistical, 461–63
Quality-of-life management, 41
Quantitative bases for decisions, 19
Quantitative work overload, 589

R

Rate of return on investment, 453–54
Rating errors, 495–96
Rationalization, 350
Realistic job previews (RJPs), 249–50
Recency of events error, 496
Recruitment, 213–18
  activities, 217–18
  application, 219–20
    background check, 222
    hiring decision, 222
    interviews, 220–21
    testing, 221–22
  legal issues, 216–17
  job description, 214–16
  job specification, 214–16
  selection, 221
Regression, 350
Repression, 350
Resource forecasts, 64
Respondent behavior, 363
Retirement, 240
Rockwell, 216
Role playing, 225

S

Saab-Scandia, 359
Safety needs, 347
  work groups, 382
Sales forecast, 62–64
  econometric models, 64
  hunches, 62–63
  market surveys, 63
  time series analysis, 63–64
Scientific management, 13–15
Sears Roebuck, 113
Selection tests, 221
  minorities, 221–22
Selective perception, 327
Self-actualization, 347
  work groups, 383
Semistructured interview, 220
Sensitivity training, 521
Situation analysis, 113–18
  clients, 118
  competition, 117
  cultural and social changes, 116–17
  economic conditions, 114
  organization performance, 118
  political, legal and regulatory changes, 116
  resources, 117–18
  technological changes, 114–15
Situational leadership, 296–303
  dimensions influencing leader's effectiveness, 299–302
  flexibility, 297–302
Social needs, 347
  work groups, 382
Social obligation, 42
Social readjustment rating scales (SRRS), 592–94
Social responsibility, 614–16
  management response, 42–43
  versus profitability, 40–42
Social responsiveness, 42
Solvency, 466
Source credibility, 328
Span of control, 168, 178–81
  factors affecting, 180–81
  manager-subordinate potential relationship, 178–79
  manager-subordinate required relationship, 179–80
Staff, 184–85
  line relationship, 519–20
Staffing, 211–28
  compensation, 227
  human resource planning, 212–13
  management development, 225–27
  orientation, 222–23
  performance evaluation, 227
  promotion, demotion, discharge, 227–28
  recruitment; *see* Recruitment
  training, 223
Standard cost accounting systems, 428
Standard cost analysis, 460–61
Status consensus, 398
Strategic analysis, 107; *see also* Strategic planning
Strategic consulting, 106
Strategic control information, 431
Strategic decision, 107
  definition, 107
Strategic objectives, 111–13
  functional and business, 112–13
  purpose served, 112
Strategic planning, 107
  clients, 118
  objectives, 111–13
  organizational mission, 108–11
  organizational performance, 118
  organizational strategy development; *see* Organizational strategies
  relation to functional plan, 112–13
Strategy, 65–66
  relation to objectives, 65–66
Stress
  consequences, 580–83
    absenteeism, 582
    health, 581–82
    performance, 583

Stress—*Cont.*
- coping with, 594–99
- definition, 578
- framework, 584–90
- managing, 596–99
- occupations, 584–86
- organization's physical environment, 598–99
- personal sources, 590–94
- Type A and B behavior pattern, 590–92
- work-related, 587–90

Stress inoculation training, 597–98
Stressor, 578, 581, 586
Strictness rater error, 495–96
Structured interview, 220
Substitution, 350
Survey feedback, 520
Syntex Corporation, Career Development Center, 255
System 1 organization design, 193–96
- bureaucracy, 195
- classical, 195–96
- flaws, 196–97

System 4 organization design, 194, 196–97
Systems approach to management, 20–21

T

Task group, 378
Task management, 292
Task-oriented leadership, 289–90
Task-people (T-P) leadership questionnaire, 294–96
Team building, 520
Team management, 292
Technical errors, 495
Technically complex organization environment, 37–38
Technology, 613–14
Tenneco, 216
Texas Instruments (TI), 192
Theory X of motivation, 344–45
Theory Y of motivation, 344–45
3M Company, 446
Time-series analysis, 63–65
Top management, 30–31
- decision making, 81

Training
- classroom, 224–25
- feedback, 225
- objectives, 224
- on-the-job, 224
- transfer, 225
- vestibule, 224

Trait theory, 285–88
Transactional analysis, 522–23
Transfer of learning, 225
Transportation problems, 459–60
Trusteeship management, 41
TRW, 216, 254
Tuition and system, 255
Turbulent organizational environment, 37–38
Two-dimensional leadership theory, 291–92
Two-factor theory of motivation, 352
Type A and B behavior patterns, 590–92

U

Understudy program, 226
Unit production, 200–201
Unknown factors in interpersonal communication, 323–24
Unstructured interview, 220–21
Upward communication, 318

V

Variable budgeting, 68–69
Vertical integration, 198
Vertical managerial specialization, 29
Vestibule training, 224
Virginia National Bankshares, 260–61
Volume expansion, 198

W

Weighted checklist, 493–94
Western Electric, 196
Westinghouse Electric, 226, 510
Women in work force, 615–17
Work groups
- classification, 377
  - formal, 378–80
  - informal, 380
- cohesiveness, 389–90
- definition, 377
- development of, 383–85
- economic reasons for, 381–82
- intergroup conflict, 393–95
- leader, 385–86
- location, 381
- management demands and pressure, 392–93
- norms and compliance, 387–89
- performance, 397–98
- politics, 395–97
- sociopsychological reasons for, 382–83
- status, 387, 391, 398

Work overload, 589
Wrigley Company, 113

X–Z

Xerox, 113
YMCA/YWCA, 599

This book has been set VIP in 10 and 9 point Vermilion, leaded 2 points. Part and chapter numbers are Eterna Bold. Part titles are 36 point Eterna Bold, and chapter titles are 30 point Eterna Bold. Overall type area is 38½ picas by 46 picas.

We need your feedback

In order to improve future editions of *Managing for Performance* so that the book can better serve students, we need your feedback. What did you like and dislike about our book? What would you like us to add to or subtract from the book? Comments and suggestions would be appreciated. Please take a few moments to complete the evaluation form and send it to us using this prepaid postal form.

Thank you for your help,

John M. Ivancevich
James H. Donnelly, Jr.
James L. Gibson

Please rate each chapter that you read by placing a check mark for each of the two rating categories: *knowledge* value to you personally (did you learn from the chapter?) and *interest* value of the chapter material (was the chapter material interesting?).

	Knowledge value			**Interest value**		
Chapter	Low	Average	High	Low	Average	High
1. Managers and management						
2. Forces influencing managerial and organizational performance						
3. Elements of planning						
4. Planning as decision making						
5. Planning through strategic analysis						
6. Planning through management by objectives						
7. Elements of organizing						
8. Designing the organization						
9. Staffing the organization						
10. Developing careers and human resources						
11. Elements of leading						
12. Interpersonal and organizational communications						
13. Motivation and performance						
14. Work groups and performance						
15. Elements of controlling						
16. Production-operations and financial control						
17. Human resource performance evaluation						
18. Organizational change						
19. Managing the multinational company						
20. Managing work-related stress						
21. Managing future challenges and responses						
Learning exercises						
Cases						

What did you like about *Managing for Performance*?

What did you dislike about *Managing for Performance*?

What would you add to *Managing for Performance*?

How does *Managing for Performance* compare to introductory texts used in your other courses?

It is *much worse*	It is *about the same*	It is a *little better*	It is *much better*

Fold back along this line

BUSINESS REPLY MAIL
FIRST CLASS PERMIT NO. 55, PLANO, TEXAS

No Postage Stamp Necessary If Mailed in the United States

Postage Will Be Paid By

BUSINESS PUBLICATIONS, INC.

200 CHISHOLM PLACE

SUITE 240

PLANO, TEXAS 75075

Attn: Prof. John M. Ivancevich

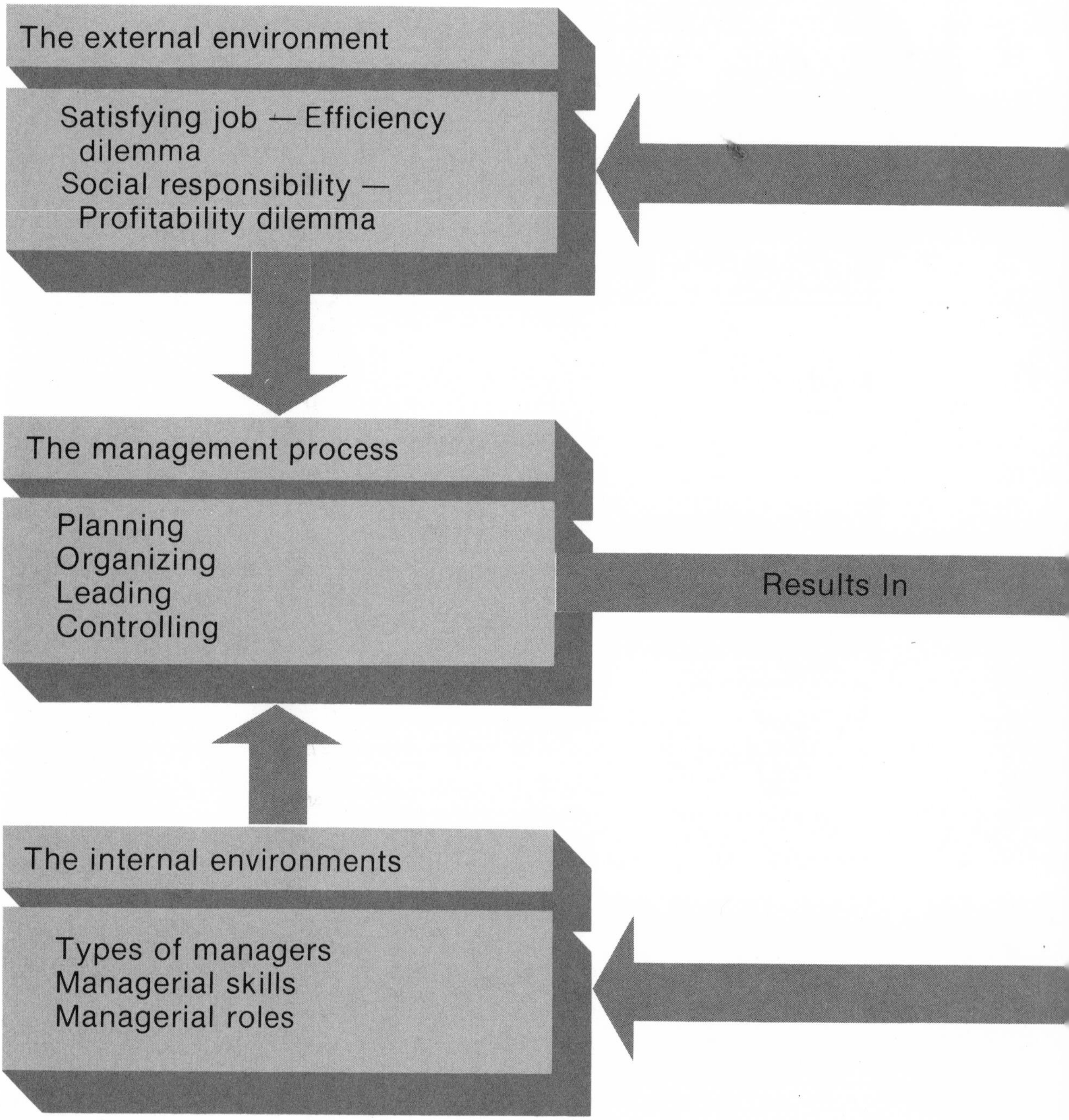
The external environment
Satisfying job — Efficiency dilemma
Social responsibility — Profitability dilemma
The management process
Planning
Organizing
Leading
Controlling
Results In
The internal environments
Types of managers
Managerial skills
Managerial roles